THE POLITICAL DIMENSION
OF RECONCILIATION

THE POLITICAL DIMENSION OF RECONCILIATION

A Theological Analysis
of Ways of Dealing with Guilt
during the Transition to Democracy
in South Africa and (East) Germany

Ralf K. Wüstenberg

Translated by
Randi H. Lundell

WILLIAM B. EERDMANS PUBLISHING COMPANY
GRAND RAPIDS, MICHIGAN / CAMBRIDGE, U.K.

Published 2009 by
Wm. B. Eerdmans Publishing Co.
2140 Oak Industrial Drive N.E., Grand Rapids, Michigan 49505 /
P.O. Box 163, Cambridge CB3 9PU U.K.

Printed in the United States of America

14 13 12 11 10 09   7 6 5 4 3 2 1

Library of Congress Cataloging-in-Publication Data

Wüstenberg, Ralf K., 1965-
    [Politische Dimension der Versöhnung. English]
    The political dimension of reconciliation: a theological analysis of ways of dealing
    with guilt during the transition to democracy in South Africa and (East) Germany /
    Ralf K. Wüstenberg; translated by Randi Lundell.
        p.   cm.
    Includes bibliographical references.
    ISBN 978-0-8028-2824-8 (pbk.: alk. paper)
    1. Reconciliation — Religious aspects — Christianity.
    2. Truth commissions — South Africa — History — 20th century.
    3. Christianity and politics — South Africa — History — 20th century.
    4. Truth commissions — Germany (East) — History — 20th century.
    5. Christianity and politics — Germany (East) — History — 20th century.
    I. Lundell, Randi H.   II. Title.

BT738.27.W8713   2009
261.8 — dc22

                                                                                          2008043911

www.eerdmans.com

To our youngest daughter,
   Fanny Elea

Contents

Contents

Abbreviations

AASF	Annales academiae scientiarum Fennicae
BArch	Bundesarchiv (National German Archive)
BenshH	Bensheimer Hefte
BGBl.	Bundesgesetzblatt (Federal Law Gazette)
BGH	Bundesgerichtshof (Federal Court)
BGHSt	Amtliche Entscheidungssammlung des Bundesgerichtshofes in Strafsachen (cited according to volume and page) / Official collection of Federal Court decisions
BGPhMA	Beiträge zur Geschichte der Philosophie und Theologie des Mittelalters (Zeitschrift)
BStU	Der Bundesbeauftragte für die Unterlagen des Staatssicherheitsdienstes der DDR ("Gauck Administration")/ Commissioner for the Stasi-files of the former GDR
BThZ	Berliner Theologische Zeitschrift
BVerfG	Bundesverfassungsgericht (Federal Constitutional Court)
BVerfGE	Amtliche Entscheidungssammlung des Bundesverfassungsgerichtes (cited according to volume and page)/Official Collection of decisions by the Federal Constitutional Court
CA	Confessio Augustana (Lutheran Confession of Faith from 1530)
DBW	Dietrich Bonhoeffer, Werke, 16 Bände, München/Gütersloh: Gütersloher Verlagshaus 1986-1998. (Dietrich Bonhoeffer Works. Translation from the German ed., 16 volumes, Minneapolis: Fortress Press 1996-.)
DDR	Deutsche Demokratische Republik (German Democratic Republic- Communist East Germany)
DtZ	Deutsch-deutsche Rechts-Zeitschrift
EGStG	Einführungsgesetz zum Strafgesetzbuch

EHS.T	Europäische Hochschulzeitschriften. Reihe 23, Theologie
EK	Enquête-Kommission(en), vom Deutschen Bundestag oder einem Landesparlament eingesetzte überfraktionelle Arbeitsgruppe (Investigation Commission of the German Parliament)
EMRK	Europäische Menschenrechtskonvention (European Human Rights Convention)
EV	Einigungsvertrag zwischen der BRD und der DDR über die DDR-Staatsauflösung / Treaty of Union (for the two German states in 1990)
EvTh	Evangelische Theologie (Journal in Theology)
FBESG	Forschungen und Berichte der Evangelischen Studiengemeinschaft
FGLP	Forschungen zu Geschichte und Lehre des Protestantismus
FSÖTh	Forschungen zur Systematischen und Ökumenischen Theologie
FZPhTh	Freiburger Zeitschrift für Philosophie und Theologie
GBL DDR	Gesetzblatt DDR (Law Gazette from former East Germany)
GrenzG	Grenzgesetz (law for the Berlin wall)
HDThG	Handbuch der Dogmen- und Theologiegeschichte
HVA	Hauptverwaltung Aufklärung des MfS (Information Office in former East-Germany/Department of Espionage)
IBF	Internationales Bonhoeffer-Forum
i.d.F.	in der Fassung von (in the edition of)
IM	Inoffizieller Mitarbeiter (des MfS) / Co-workers (of the Ministry for State Security) that secretly spied on their fellow citizens in East Germany
INDABA	Internetdatenbank Afrika, GIGA Institut für Afrikastudien Hamburg
i.V.m.	in Verbindung mit (in connection with)
JTSA	Journal of Theology for Southern Africa
KSPW	Kommission für die Erforschung des sozialen und politischen Wandels in den neuen Bundesländern
KT	Kaiser-Traktate (Book series)
KuD	Kerygma und Dogma (Journal in Theology)
KZG	Kirchliche Zeitgeschichte
LM	Lutherische Monatshefte
MdB	Mitglied des Deutschen Bundestags /Member of Parliament (MP)
MfS	Ministerium für Staatssicherheit (Ministry for State Security of the former GDR)
MPG	J.-P. Migne, Patrologiae cursus completus, series Latina
NBST	Neukirchener Beiträge zur Systematischen Theologie
PuZ	Pietismus und Neuzeit
PW	A. Pauly–G. Wissowa, Real-Enzyklopädie der Klassischen Altertumswissenschaften 1894ff.
QD	Quaestiones Disputatae
RKZ	Reformierte Kirchenzeitung (Reformed Journal in Theology)
SACC	South African Council of Churches
Sapa	South African Press Association

SED	Sozialistische Einheitspartei Deutschlands (leading party in former East-Germany)
SJZ	Süddeutsche Juristenzeitung (Law Journal)
Stasi	Staatssicherheit (Office of State Security of the former GDR)
StGB	Strafgesetzbuch (penal code)
STPS	Studien zur Theologie und Praxis der Seelsorge (Zeitschrift)
TB	Theologische Bücherei (Theological Book Series)
TBT	Theologische Bibliothek Töpelmann (Theological Book Series)
TRC	Truth and Reconciliation Commission (South Africa)
TSB	Theologische Studienbeiträge
WSAMA	Walberger Studien der Albertus-Magnus-Akademie
ZEE	Zeitschrift für Evangelische Ethik
ZRP	Zeitschrift für Rechtspolitik
ZThK	Zeitschrift für Theologie und Kirche
ZThK.B	Zeitschrift für Theologie und Kirche. Beiheft

Foreword

In the decade following the fall of the Berlin Wall in 1989, two countries —
South Africa and Germany — attracted worldwide attention around the
question: Can national societies, long riven with huge injustices and harms
to their citizens, recover from these damages without repeating them under
new regimes? In this same decade the question acquired new urgency in
fresh waves of civil war, genocide, and vengeance afflicting dozens of nations
on five continents.

What made world curiosity about Germany and South Africa so poi-
gnant was the apparent success of both countries in designing a political process for effecting "reconciliation" between previously hostile, war-inclined
groups of citizens. The word acquired quotation marks in many quarters because of its association with religion on the one hand and political idealism
on the other. What in theory and practice do religion-based ethics and the ex-
igencies of political work contribute to the coming of concrete, nonviolent
ways of effecting transitions from past civil alienation to present civil peace?

The answers of theologians and political philosophers, especially in the
West, have greatly diverged. Some on both sides have denied that there is any
realistic connection between religious and political descriptions of proper
human relations. In the proceedings of the Truth and Reconciliation Commission in South Africa, chaired by an Anglican Archbishop, critics often
raised protest at incidents of prayer, hymns, and the word "forgiveness." In
more secular Germany, as its government wrestled with the challenge of
eastern-western reunification, references to religion were rarer. But a Protestant minister chaired one of the important agencies for addressing the

crimes of the *Stasi* surveillance system of the DDR, and Germans of all religious persuasions found themselves debating differences between amnesty and forgiveness, degrees of punishment for varieties of crime, and the relation of reparations to the repair of forty years of alienation between the two Germanies.

If only in the ordinary talk of citizens of these two countries, secular and religious words, claims, and distinctions jostled each other. What might be intellectually precise ways of bringing some "order in the brawl" (H. Richard Niebuhr) of this dense mixture?

In this book Ralf Wüstenberg has written one of the most thoroughgoing answers to the question likely to appear for years to come. The product of long residences in South Africa and his own native Berlin, his book looks carefully for traces of "correspondence" between the empirical and the conceptual kinships of recent public phenomena in the two countries around the healing of large *reconciliations*. "Do the inconclusive, incomplete, open reconciliation proceedings in political reality have a fundamental connection to theological reconciliation?" (p. 281). As Wüstenberg explores the question, the result is a precise, complicated, rigorous set of analyses that will repay careful reading by anyone intrigued by the possibility that what happened in Germany and South Africa, 1990-98, has a message of hope and caution for us all.

The conversation (and conflict) between religion and politics is old, especially since the European Enlightenment, which voiced sturdy reproof of the incursion of religion into the exercise of political power. Let religion stick with asserting ideals while politicians deal with the realities of human conflict! This split between the "ideal" and the "real" has afflicted the discussion now for centuries. Tolerance for such dualisms is widespread and stubborn in the public life of many a modern country.

Occasionally, however, political philosophers themselves have yielded to a glimmering suspicion that the total split of religious faith from the practices of politics is not all that realistic. A stunning example of this suspicion is a passage in the writings of the late Hannah Arendt, survivor of the Holocaust. In *The Human Condition* she reflects that there are two pre-conditions for mending the torn fabric of a political society: its leaders must come to some new normative agreements, laws, and constitutions for their future relations, and they must overcome the lingering hostilities of their past history. The latter overcoming she tagged "forgiveness," and she credited Jesus of Nazareth with the "invention" of forgiveness as a necessary ingredient in the transformation of political alienation into political community.

Students of forgiveness in the 1990s have frequently quoted Arendt's claim as remarkable coming from a secular perspective. Indeed, having credited Jesus with this invention, she promptly made an implicit apology to her fellow philosophers by pleading that just because Jesus advanced this teaching in a religious framework is no reason to deny its realism. When Robert Frost, a secularist, wrote the line, "To be social is to be forgiving," he was advocating the same realism.

But thereby these astute writers were punching a hole in the insulation between "fact" and "value" which so suffuses the grounds of post-Enlightenment philosophy and much liberal Christian theology. The questions will not go away: Does religion occupy one of the realities in human affairs? Is a religious dimension resident, hidden or open, in even the most blatantly secular world? Is there any mutual correspondence between the realities and ideas of "reconciliation" as conceived and enacted in religious and political organizations?

Wüstenberg's book is a carefully crafted combination of "yes's" and "no's" to these questions. He has mastered the modern history of Protestant theology, and he has been a careful student of the work of Dietrich Bonhoeffer. He has sat in hearings of South Africa's Truth and Reconciliation Commission, and he has followed the legal processes by which Germany has dealt with violations of human rights in the history of the German Democratic Republic. His theological-political analyses are enriched by extensive excerpts from testimonies from victims and perpetrators in both countries. Throughout he seeks to discern in these political negotiations signs and presences of the divine that Christians believe to have been promised by one who said to his disciples, "I am with you always."

The challenge of making good on this promise over against the finite, ambiguous attempt of humans to do justice to each other is severe. Wüstenberg practices a severe intellectual discipline throughout. He is especially alert to document moments and occasions in this history where a divine Spirit "interrupts" a secular procedure in a display of "vertical" transcendence. He is equally serious about interpreting human responses to divine action in terms of temporal, historical processes leading to horizontal new human relationships with visible traces of reconciliation-begun and still-to-be-completed.

Along the way he surprises this reader with a tribute and a mining of so-called process theology, more associated with certain American theologians than continental. "God's action becomes the deed of reconciliation as it develops or 'emerges' from the historical process. . . . [I]n the penultimate a glimmer of the ultimate can be seen as the interruption of the occasion or event" (pp. 234-37). Here his debt to Bonhoeffer is clear: God loves the world by being present in it, and in this sense Christian faith is "worldly." Not always clear to me is the line which Wüstenberg draws between divine and human process, or between churchly and secular-legal concepts of reconciliation. Among the most insightful pages of the book are those that describe kinships of *ritual* in church and secular settings. Every reader will have some criticisms, of course. I think that he is wrong to confine forgiveness to an instantaneous act rather than also an act-in-process. He is somehow too Lutheran in suggesting that "restorative" justice has no place in a secular legal system. But these questions are evidence of the thought-provoking nature of this work. It crosses and criss-crosses numerous intellectual frontiers, and it calls us to become companions on the journey.

At the very end he writes an outline of "consequences" of these analyses for the life of the Christian churches. This compact straightforward summary could be the framework of a shorter book addressed to church members with little theological sophistication but with lifelong experience in political and church communities. In Christian faith, the two belong together because God creates the two to belong together. Faith perceives that a divine work of reconciliation is happening now from both sides of alienated peoples. For the building of our perception that it is *really* happening and the hope that it *really will* happen in God's human future, what could be a more important book to write?

Donald W. Shriver, Jr.
President Emeritus
Union Theological Seminary,
New York

Introduction

In picturesque Paarl, located a good hour's drive from Cape Town in the region of the Winelands, one can hear stories of the victims and perpetrators of Apartheid as reported to the Truth and Reconciliation Commission (TRC).

The city hall of this farming community is easy to find. Signs are located everywhere with the words "TRC hearing." The room that has been prepared for the event is crowded. Flowers decorate the podium. The flag of South Africa and banners with the TRC motto "Truth — The Road to Freedom" decorate the tables. The stories of those who broke the laws of Apartheid will be heard today. A candle is lit, visible to everyone in the room. After the members of the Commission have found their seats the Chairman motions for everyone assembled to rise. Tales of the victims and offenders begin to unfold.[1]

Commission: Good morning, Mr. Maxan! You are very welcome here. It is my understanding that you wish to give testimony, a very special testimony: a plea for forgiveness. This is also an area of concern for the Commission. Would you please tell us about the year 1986, when the mother of Dr. Siebert died?

Mr. Maxan: We needed weapons for our plan, which we executed to protect ourselves and to attack the enemy. The police were also ultimately armed. The underground structure of the ANC helped to procure the weapons. We were supposed to go to farm houses.

Commission: You were condemned to 10 years in the work house for the murder of Dr. Siebert's mother, among other crimes. What would you like to say to the Siebert family?

Mr. Maxan: I would like to ask once again for forgiveness. The connection to the Siebert family came through my older brother. He asked them to forgive me. Dr. Siebert honored my intention to be reconciled with him. And they have forgiven me.

Commission: With the Chairman's permission, I would like to read a statement from Dr. Siebert: "I am pleased that Philemon Maxan would like to make peace with us because I have carried the burden of rage and pain long enough. I bear no grudge against Philemon. I think this is also what my mother would have wanted. She was shot as she went to get a glass of water for Philemon. My mother would have extended this courtesy to anyone who came through her door." I think that this statement will reach deep into your heart and lighten your burden from the past. Thank you for coming here and for asking forgiveness from those whom you have harmed.

Mr. Maxan: My thanks to the Commission.

*   *   *

Under the official oversight of the representatives and of Pastor Rainer Eppelmann, an open hearing of the Investigative-Commission of the German Parliament's "Working through the History and the Consequences of the SED (Social Unity Party) Dictatorship in Germany" is in session.[2]

Today's theme is "The former Ministry of State Security." Witnesses are brought forward.

Commission: The next witness . . . has not come alone. Lothar Tautz, current administrative representative, formerly a pastor who was active in the time of the DDR, and who was involved in the work of peace and the environment, has brought with him an interior minister with whom he had contact during this time.

Lothar Tautz: I was asked as I entered what is so special about today that I have been invited to attend and I said nothing. In any case I did not say that I had brought an IM with me, just my friend Michael Altwein. I have come . . . here because I would really like to have this undifferentiated portrayal of animosity between offenders and victims dispelled. I have never felt like a victim, and I think that Michael has also never felt like an offender. . . . And in the ensuing disagreement that naturally followed when I discovered that he had worked in an unofficial capacity on my file, I still can not forget the good that we accomplished together. For this reason I see many things . . . quite differently . . . from my own experience.

Michael Altwein: I am 37 years old, currently a self-employed craftsman. I would briefly like to explain how I became an unofficial worker with the MfS. . . . During basic training with the border troops, I took part in a ¼ year long special training. The recruitment for this special training division took place during a conversation with a Stasi officer, in which I was asked whether or not I was interested in taking part in a kind of special training which wouldn't take much more effort, with the caveat that the conversation partner with whom I was speaking had already turned it down and could thus pretty much say goodbye to his studies. I agreed to do it. . . . Through friends, I gained entry into the church-based environmental group in the city of Weissenfels, and there learned to know Lothar Tautz. The Ministry for Security was interested in everything that went on with Lothar Tautz. . . . I personally viewed the environmental movement in the DDR as very necessary. In hindsight I must say that I thought that the DDR was capable of reform up to the bitter end. . . . With these statements, I certainly bring no new observations before the Commission. However, I view what I learned as the working out of my very personal history.

*   *   *

The above accounts taken from the forums of two official commissions, which were legitimately established by Parliament in a democratic fashion in order to promote the reconciliation of social breaches, is reminiscent of the central element of the Christian concept of reconciliation and its attending areas of significance: the forgiveness of guilt, the overcoming of animosity through friendship, and the re-establishment of community.[3] Do both discussions provide examples of the political dimension of reconciliation? In common parlance do words like forgiveness, guilt, animosity, friendship, also occupy common ground with politics and theology when it comes to the category of reconciliation? It appears to be an open question as to whether or not both concepts indicate the same thing as part of their essential definition, or whether in politics there is accidental agreement with a basic idea belonging to the social dimension of the Christian concept of reconciliation, namely, with the *aequivocatio a casu*.[4]

Reconciliation as a theological category has a "special place *(topos)* in the conceptual ordering of related concepts"[5] within the dogmatic. As a "topical" concept reconciliation contains "the central theological statements about the overcoming of God's anger, the acquittal of human guilt, the community of God with man and the relationship of peace between men." If one accepts the concept of reconciliation as a "topical" concept, then the following question emerges for our theme: how can reconciliation as a topical concept be theologically distinguished (at least with respect to its social dimension) if it loses its reliable dogmatic place and returns to an apparently open political connection when the "ruling place of the dogma of reconciliation within the teaching on faith" is what develops the political?[6] Does the dogmatician share then his fate with that of a natural scientist, whose research results emanate from the lab? Do theologians and the church also need a "patent" for the concept of reconciliation? Or was it already the faulty "patent" of the profane concept of reconciliation of the ancients, who allowed the concept of reconciliation to overflow from the political into the theological?

G. Sauter[7] cites the necessity of a "patent" in view of the political misuse of the Christian concept of reconciliation without, however, having attended to the evidence that has differentiated the concept within the political field. This view is based on a position that the political use of the concept of reconciliation serves exclusively strategic goals. Unexamined, however, is the question of whether the transfer of the term into the political arena will retain its legitimate core. Similar expressions of reconciliation[8] are close, although the conceptual form of the term has eliminated its theological meaning: balance, placate, compromise, finding the middle ground. Other synonyms of reconciliation are implied within the context of a deeper meaning: to end animosity, and to promote peace. In general, what is evident is that in the German language the concept of reconciliation has kept its obvious fundamentally religious etymological overtones;[9] at least the connotation of guilt remains. One speaks of the German-Polish "conciliation" or the German-French "reconciliation," but of the German-American "understanding."[10]

The political use of a religiously based concept like "reconciliation" causes problems for a post-enlightenment society: "can the religious connotation create enlightenment or is it part of an unenlightened ideological action"?[11] Stated *politically*, "every reconciliation has as its goal the creation of peace."[12] What is the relationship of this kind of statement to the peace making of Christ? When stated *sociologically*, "every reconciliation means the re-establishment of an earlier good relationship." How does this relate to the "gift of renewal of the Son-ship of God?" If it "generally, comes from the same roots . . . , which are accepted in social and political actuality," how are they connected to these "roots" analogously, *univocally, or equivocally?*[13] How can the political use of the term reconciliation be responsibly judged? Are they the "return of splendor in the world"?[14] Do we recognize in them the "fingerprints of God"?[15] Should they be connected to the "religious forum" with the instruction: this is all there is?[16] Or should we first accept the conditions of its appearance in political reality on a secondary level and communicate its implied axiom before making a theological judgment?[17]

The *problem* that will be addressed in this study concerns the political implications of reconciliation. It presents itself from two perspectives: in the question of whether the political use of the term reconciliation refers to reconciliation in the Christian-theological sense, and second, as to whether the Christian concept of reconciliation makes reference to the political use of the term. These questions imply something further in their application: are the definitions of political reconciliation and reconciliation as a theological category particularly clear, and if so, does one or the other have an exclusive hold on its meaning? Can they be separated? Are they identical at all? Do they have a similar semantic center? Does one preclude the other? Finally, does one concept proceed from the other, or are they both original?

An initial normative orientation into this catalogue of questions has immediate bearing on the state of the ensuing study: evangelical-theological research (as distinguished from religious-philosophical research) is connected with the issue that the political form of reconciliation can only be illuminated "by a theological perspective."[18] Thus, in a normative sense, a reciprocal transfer of political language into theological language is always going to be broken and only possible indirectly.[19] There is no direct transfer of the political use of the term reconciliation into the religious-theological, since it is not clear that the same concept means the same thing in the context of theology as it does in the context of politics. Theologically legitimate interests with regard to reciprocal usage are, however, not excluded from the study.

Let us suggest a schema for a first orientation to the topic:

1. Political reconciliation — theological reconciliation
   a. Illegitimate: direct transfer (the political determines the theological)
   b. Legitimate: broken transfer (conveyed) to another context (the

political is "baptized" and receives a new meaning from the
theological)
2. Theological reconciliation — political reconciliation
    a. Illegitimate: direct transfer (the theological determines the
    political)
    b. Legitimate: broken transfer (reconstruction) (the theological is
    "recognized" in the political)

The above schema has theoretical merit since it allows for no transfer of
political language into the religious such that the political language becomes
the determining element of religious language (an example would be the
"German-Christian" heresy in the "Third Reich"). However, a transfer of the
political language into the religious is legitimate in broken form. Certain political concepts are taken out of context and put into another context which gives
them a new meaning. They are "baptized" (this transfer is initially seen as
"conveyance"). The same model is under (2) as the obverse: no direct transfer
of religious language into the political, so that the religious maintains a particular function for the political (an example here is theocracy). However, theologically conceivable is a transfer of theological language into political language in broken or interrupted form, so that a relationship of correspondence
between theological reconciliation and political reconciliation within the political sphere can be seen. This schema allows for an overview of the conditions
for, as well as for critical and constructive connections between, political reconciliation and reconciliation as a theological category. A theoretically normative foundation, implied by the theological possibility of reciprocal transfer —
namely, the conveying of the political into the theological concept of reconciliation on the one hand, and the reconstruction of theological reconciliation
within the political on the other — follows in Part I (A & B). The attempt is
here to outline the relevant "points" (compare in Schema 1.b and 2.b).

The task of this study is to analyze the main elements, especially the
"regulative statements," in their political connection to reconciliation (Part
II) in order to ultimately (Part III) examine the conditions for the political
use of reconciliation *on the basis of its fundamental theological connection.*
Where is the agreement and where are the differences between the conditions for the systematic-theological use of reconciliation? The goal of this
study is to develop a contribution to the theoretical definition of the problem, taking into account the precedent for reconciliation *in* this world based
on the Biblical definition referring to God as reconciling the world to himself. The results of the possibilities of a reconstruction of Christian thinking

on reconciliation within political reality are thus connected with a concrete testing of categories that exist in common between certain axioms of political reconciliation and those of the theological doctrine of reconciliation.[20]

Three conditions emerge with the development of the problem and corresponding investigative line of questioning: (1) if reciprocity is to be researched in reference to reconciliation, it necessitates first a quantifiable method by which to analyze the political use of forms expressive of reconciliation; (2) it requires accessibility to the corresponding scope of research within the theological doctrine of reconciliation; and (3) it necessitates the analysis of theological concepts expressed in the reciprocal relationship.

*   *   *

The more current systematic-theological state of research appears deficient in several respects for our treatment of the problem. First, the conditions are not thoroughly thought out that are implied by the line of questioning of this research; i.e., which religious worldview has the political arena employed to use as models of reconciliation for the overcoming of animosity and of guilt? What are the implications of the Christian-theological language about the reconciliation of God with man for the perceptions, meaning, and formation of reconciliation in politics?

Furthermore, there is no clear theological path which helps to clarify the conditions for a perception of political reality. The necessity for such a step is eminently noticeable in the questions posed by this study. Some of the requirements for a suitable line of questioning can be listed as follows:

- There are basic personal and social orientations endemic to political activity (concepts of the worth of a person, of the order of society, of the goal of social institutions);
- These orientations have an implied religious-ideological character because they contain the basic conviction about the definition of man, the basis for and goal of reality etc.
- The goal of a definition of personal and social existence *(Dasein)* can be missed, in such a way that the required basic orientations are not realized;
- These deficits can have a personal character (for example, the denial of a basic orientation such as the worth of a person) as well as a social structure (for example, the offense against legal criteria which define a well-ordered society);

- There are transformational processes that aim at the erection of something new relative to the re-establishment of a basic orientation; for example, the recognition of personal worth, or the restoration of order in society;
- These transformational processes are multi-dimensional in nature: they have legal, political, social, and economic dimensions, but they also always have religious-ideological implications which, among other things, impact the arrangement of the individual dimensions.

Finally, the theological areas upon which the connections to conditions of political reconciliation are sought are not well verified. However, that is the other requirement to be satisfied with regard to our initial question on the relational definition between reconciliation in the political context and reconciliation in the theological context. The ensuing list of socially based arguments includes the following individual steps when they are understood theologically in the Christian context:

- faith in God, the creator, reconciler, and consummator of the world;
- a faith-based view of man that man is understood as fallible, fallen, called to reconciliation and to participation in society as part of God's particular creation;
- any talk of reconciliation must — anthropologically and theologically — be placed in relationship to talk of creation and perfection of the world;
- the model of reconciliation must be placed in relation to and its status determined by other models such as making amends for the denial of the relationship to God (e.g., salvation, justification, sin, sacrifice);
- seen from the standpoint of the Reformation, everything hinges on the distinction and definition of the relationship of *opus Dei* and *opus hominum;*
- the distinction between motifs implies a series of others: between law and Gospel, constitutive salvation and consecutive salvation, salvation and well-being; order of grace and order of creation, first and last, etc.

The question of the relationship between reconciliation in the theological sense and that of reconciliation in the political context localizes the concept of reconciliation on the map of theological-political categories as a prior condition for the development of the problem. Primarily, the question arises as to how the reconciled activity of God in Christ forms both the basis of and limitation for the reconciling activity between men. Both aspects of the issue are fundamental: (1) the fundamental question has as its goal the formulation of the horizon in which an understanding of reconciliation can be a possible goal within the reality of human political activity; (2) the limitation question unburdens the activity of political reconciliation from the promise of salvation and from an expectation of salvation, and places it on the plane of a well-ordered, living together of society.

The complexity of the relational connection between theological and political reconciliation underscores the necessity to delineate the conditions for a perception of political reconciliation and its ability to mediate within the horizon of a consistent theological theory. The lack of a working out of the problem in the theological discussion and the corresponding lack of analysis of the conditions for framing research with regard to the fundamental political connection of the concept of reconciliation provide the background for the following theoretical study.

I. Conditions for Reading the "Signs of the Times": Methodological Foundations

In this section the conditions for treating the problem will be advanced theoretically, that is, prior to an empirical analysis of the political language used to express reconciliation (Part II) and its theological implications (Part III).

In the following section (A) I will first discuss the conditions for *perceiving political reconciliation* while at the same time outlining the interdisciplinary agenda of Part II *(empirical analysis)*. In section B, the conditions for *a theological basis* for reconciliation will be discussed using an empirical analysis of the language used to express reconciliation in the political realm. This section (B) will also outline the foundations for Part III *(theological synthesis)*.

The case study method is examined first. Second, the corresponding political context for a connection between guilt and reconciliation is established on an interpersonal level as it relates to the theological doctrine of reconciliation. Finally, the question of correspondence in Part II and III is presented with its attending theological categories of analysis.

A. Conditions for Recognizing Political Reality: Adapting the Case-Study Method

1. Previous Research

In making a determination about the *political dimension* of reconciliation, the use of case studies is effective, especially for circumscribing the thematic agenda. It is worth noting that the current research on case studies being done by American political science leaves room for theological work, allowing us to investigate the political process of reconciliation along with its dogmatic implications. Recent analyses by the Center for Strategic and International Studies in Washington, D.C., clearly demonstrates how religious influence is still largely unacknowledged in the realm of political science, indicating the existence of a decisive gap which presents significant challenges for contemporary politics.

Nevertheless, preliminary theological research can be linked to case studies. For example, W. Huber[1] captured the theme of church and the public with the help of case study analysis; and prior to Huber, J. Zehner[2] investigated the basic political connection to forgiveness by means of case studies. Likewise, on the theological side of the issue of justice, ethics emerged as a theme in the case study work of J. Kreuter.[3] In the Anglo-Saxon discussion in North America, the case study research of D. Shriver is worthy of mention, and in South Africa that of J. de Gruchy.[4] While Shriver concerns himself with the politics of forgiveness, de Gruchy primarily analyzes case study diaries, including those connected with the church conflict under Apartheid South Africa and those representing the relationship between Christianity and Democracy in the former DDR. The political studies of these authors focus on previous political problem areas, such as the German-American agreement[5] or the German-Polish[6] agreement, as well as on the German-French conciliation.[7]

The current state of theological research using case studies reveals problems on the one hand, but also allows for some preliminary observations:

(a) The time frame for research using case studies should be limited. Too long a time frame hinders the use of seminal questions by which to guide the analysis of political processes.[8] In previous research using case studies, it has been found that in order for a theological discovery to be made, the process of political reconciliation needs to be viewed as a "history of reconciliation,"[9] since reconciliation develops slowly as part of the overall political process. However, the question remains as to what questions help to uncover such a process.

(b) In research on reconciliation initiatives, the scope and level of interpretation of the theological work on case studies has either been incomplete or nonexistent. In principle, a representation of the theme of reconciliation is not possible without an assumed interpretation. However, I intend to present it *analytically;*[10] that is, to examine the conditions that will ultimately lead to a systematic theological development in which the methodological problem of representation and interpretation are also considered. Finally, the conditions for the possibility of representing political language on reconciliation will be determined without allowing the theological criteria to explicitly lead the inquiry in the presentation of political processes. One conclusion of research using case studies states that "religious convictions . . . are an important foundation"[11] for reconciliation in politics; on the other hand, a "process of understanding" that is not "exclusively Christian"[12] might be helpful. This will prove to be a key point.

(c) There is also a large issue regarding the qualifications of theologically interpreted political case studies. Previous case studies have not succeeded in producing a constructive relationship between the political analysis of case studies and their theological treatment because, in part, the theological considerations are "fixed." If one wants to derive a mere theological "etiquette" of political proceedings, then one must insert a methodological "place holder" between the presentation of the case study and its interpretation. Accordingly, the presentation of case studies using analytical and guiding questions must succeed on an interdisciplinary level and also must allow for a differentiated systematic-theological analysis of the significant content.

2. Development of a Method for Theological Analysis of Case Studies

In certain instances it is possible to make connections by employing theological case study research. Indeed, no previously suitable method appears to have emerged that has helped to determine essential guiding questions in an analysis of political reality which both allows for an inquiry into the basic theological connection to reconciliation and at the same time preserves the opportunity for representing inter-subjective changes. There is no "signpost" that can help to indicate a precise — yet general — validity that incorporates the referential connection in such a way as to allow political scientists, historians, and legal experts to gain a suitable point of reference that can also be used in a theological representation.

As a theological endeavor, our project thus finds itself before a fundamental dilemma: how can the *political* dimension of reconciliation be unveiled? The restriction to case studies certainly brings with it quantitative limitations, and in terms of qualitative research there is a further problem: if I utilize case studies for the political connection to reconciliation, then I must also acknowledge the relative autonomy of other branches of scholarship. This means that the case studies must be connected to actual research (i.e., political, historical, and legal areas of research) as well as anchored in the external, existing theological discourse.

On the other hand, the theological problem of reconciliation should not be lost sight of when the theological frame of reference is abandoned for another method. A systematic theological work that takes into account the inductive approach should not, due to theological interests, advance the case study method as providing simply more evidence for an assumed thesis. Progress is made where the results of the case studies enter constructively into the theological interpretation which, in turn, happens when the political forms of expressing reconciliation are placed into question on the basis of their fundamental connection to theological reconciliation. Additionally, the research must also be able to achieve foundational results with respect to the methodology involved in the investigation.

Any method for developing a political connection to reconciliation must be developed in an interdisciplinary way. However, an interdisciplinary presentation of the problem should not exclude the theological (to which we will return in Section B), but should consciously include other scholarly avenues as well, since it is appropriate to connect the results of theological case study research with questions from other scholarly disciplines. Among others, we will see that in political, historical, and legal

5

scholarship such connections are possible and, indeed, necessary for the advancement of knowledge.

At this point it is necessary to explore the area of political science or that of the general social sciences. The questions and problems associated with the above-mentioned theological case study literature should be very concentrated and controlled because they involve basic problems of representation and interpretation, not to mention the accessibility of reliable guiding questions for the presentation of case studies. Criteria for reality that are established with the help of political science are also useful when it comes to establishing a political connection to reconciliation. Personal interests and individual actors play a decisive role in decisions about political reality; accordingly, hasty theological conclusions should be avoided. On the other hand, something can be learned from an interdisciplinary discussion, such as the questioning of global assumptions that seek to reduce political activity principally to questions of power. How does political science approach the representation of "political reality"? What categories for analysis make it available?

"Political reality" is not a homogeneous concept in the arena of political science. We have referred already to terms like "complexity" and "historicity" as benchmarks of political reality. Many political scientists speak of the "ubiquity of politics." A cursory look at the use of the term "political reality" in political science reveals that significant agreements are to be had about the possibility of legitimate boundaries for "political reality." Accordingly, the arena of political science may be described using three concepts: "political content," "political process," and "political structures." In English, they are often described using the terms "policy," "politics," and "polity." [13]

When considering "political content" (policies), "political programs" are central. Contradictions and conflicts are encountered in the area of analysis in connection to certain political programs (e.g., speed limits on highways, the length of compulsory military service, etc.). "Political processes" (politics) describe those processes whereby an attempt is made to make certain programs generally binding. In this area, decision making processes and their implementation stand at the center of concern. The area of "political structures" (polities) includes the condition of accountability, which runs along formal as well as informal lines of political activity within organizations or institutions (parties, bands, parliaments, etc.). "Political structures and their constituting norms are, on the one hand, the bedrock upon which political processes run, and on the other hand, are produced and asserted through political processes where they are, accordingly, altered." [14]

The analytical method employed by political science does not remain static along distinct lines of its own area of inquiry, but yields categories by which these areas may, in turn, be analyzed. Thus, in addition to *power* and *ideology, norm* and *communication* are also acknowledged by political science as categories of analysis.[15] W. J. Patzelt utilizes categories of analysis outlined by the three content areas of politics (policy, politics, polity):

> If one views political content as a kind of political program that arrives at certain goals one may, for example, ask: who has the *power* to realize or to prevent these goals? What *ideologies* lie at their core? What *norms* are disregarded or should be included? How are they represented and communicated? If one views political *processes* as a particular method of adjudication then one may ask, for example: who influences whom, and on the basis of what? What world views or what knowledge will provide the basis for whose activities? By means of what norms are we proceeding with what tactics? What channels of communication are used by whom in order to assert influence on the process of law making? If one views political structures in terms of a political party, then one may . . . for example ask: who has power within the party? For what problem, views, and goals does this party stand? According to what formal and informal rules do they work? How does intra-party communication take place on the one hand, and communication between party and society occur on the other?[16]

For the researcher, the analytical approach offered by political science opens up points of historical connection for the representation of case studies. Likewise, the goal of this presentation of political reality is to expose the many aspects of the treatment of its motifs so we will continue with the analyses.

If we connect the discussion of political science with the task of this investigation as formulated in the Introduction (where political forms of expressing reconciliation in terms of major entities are, for example, examined for their implicit axioms), it is then possible to support the following statement from an interdisciplinary point of view: political decisions and their attending actors are motivated by a collection of "implicit axioms" which, because they are implicit, are not obvious and as a result are not regarded as explicitly regulative statements in the language of discourse. Here, then, is precisely where our task lies; *namely, to uncover the implicit axiom that is lodged in political reality in order to better examine the inherent categories available for analysis by political science.*

The subject of "political processes" when analyzed in terms of their influence on norms and power may prove important to the development of our analysis. Behind both categories of analysis we recognize political concepts such as "ontologically normative" and "realistic" which exist in a causal relation to "analogy" and "univocal" forms of speech concerning the reconciliation of God in political reality. Meanwhile, it may prove to be enlightening for the theological world view if, along with an analysis of political reality, a large majority of categories relative to political science are utilized, instead of fixing a one-sided political position to the question of power or norms. Only when the majority of conditions for the possibility of political forms of expression have been analyzed will it be possible to formulate appropriate questions about the fundamental theological connection to a particular form of expressing reconciliation.

In terms of method, social scientists work like other scientists by using "qualitative interviews" to guide the discovery process. Indeed, interviews are valuable for constructing knowledge; they require estimates and evaluation and provide a valid way to determine the "category of the actors."[17] A hasty theological projection — or the exploitation of political processes — can be prevented by means of a method where we assemble a representation of political reality through the categories of analysis offered by political science. In this way the problem of representation and interpretation can be treated responsibly.

By exposing political processes to guiding analytical questions we are able to gain an orientation to our second major problem: namely, the issues of the connection to prior theological work on case studies as aided by the specific avenues available to political science. How may questions asked by political scientists about political reality also serve as guiding questions for our research? What areas of political science correspond to the topic under investigation? Where in the debate does the political scientist also encounter the problem of reconciliation? And, for the relevant areas of our discussion, where are these two basic questions discussed and, indeed, in what way do they have anything to do with "past politics" or that of "political history"?

With regard to the "history of the past," structures of activity are analyzed "that underlie the ordinary political constellations of power, interests, and consensus. Morality is thus just one more resource among many arguments."[18] In order to better illuminate these structures of activity, we will investigate (within the scope of this study) what lies in the "politics of the past" and in "dealings with the personal and material inheritance of a conquered system." During the course of the methodological inquiry into the politics of the past, the question about the "discourse" of justice will also be raised. This is because in dealing with the personal and material inheritance of a conquered system, only certain principally legal options are available (such as the "justified punishment of perpetrators" upon whom are imposed "limitations of civilian status"[19] through professional job disqualification, for example, as part of the restitution and reparations made to the victim). As for the notion of action, political science embraces "the category of real possibility." "It is a necessary condition of politics that the influence of society can always be seen in various ways within any area of authority."[20] P. Bock and E. Wolfrum conclude together: "at the center of research on past politics are legal, legislative, and executive decisions."[21]

The question of "political history" is more closely connected to the discussion between political and historical science. It proceeds from the principle: "history makes politics and politics makes history."[22] According to E. Wolfrum, observations should also be able to advance the cause of science so that "remembering and forgetting not only represent elementary human tasks and needs, but are given political means and shape."[23] Thus, the concept of "political history" should be developed as a "category of analysis."[24] The history of politics investigates "the public construction of images of history and identity that have bearing on, for example, ritual and discourse."[25] For E. Wolfrum, it is significant that "ritual and symbol are no mere ornament of political activity, rather they constitute elements of social reality."[26] Whoever engages in the study of political history proceeds from the assumption that "the scope of the political representation of history is far greater than that of historiography." In the "perspective of research on the history of politics, the question of the form of truth conveyed by the historical picture is not decisive, but rather the question of how, through whom, with what means, with what intent and what effect the experience of the past is thematized and is politically relevant."[27] Thus, as a concept, political history is not posited merely negatively. Of course, the history of politics cannot forget that history itself can become political, and instead of serving "reason and reconciliation, it can foster disagreement through the production of slogans."[28] On the other hand, the history of politics can also produce clarity and establish a history that is constructive for the democratic orientation of a society.

Nevertheless, there is no doubt that "close inter-connections exist between the history of politics and the politics of the past." P. Bock[29] makes the observation that "often the hallmarks of past politics are fortified and legitimized by the study of political history. However, there is a large, if not predominant, number of past political processes which, without the efforts of political history or even despite it, come to fruition. Only when the considerations of so-called 'reality politics' move to the forefront do the history of politics appear to recede. . . . Nevertheless, what remains — albeit hidden — are the interests of actors who stand at the center of the events."

3. An Analysis of the Questions Used in the Presentation of Case Studies in Part II

Supported by the above considerations, three positions for the representation of the case studies will be pursued:

(a) What are the *points of departure* or the *weak spots* in the respective areas of inquiry into reconciliation as they emerge from different contexts?
(b) What *rituals, rites, or symbolic forms of expression* encountered in political reality indicate the possibility for the reality of reconciliation?
(c) What results occur by accepted processes of political reality in dealing with guilt? Can a *balance* be drawn?

It is obvious that the first two questions are, in terms of historical research, connected to the interdisciplinary question of past politics and the history of politics. For the purposes of our problem, a "weak spot" in the current state of analysis consists in the investigation of (a) the initial historical-political conditions as well as the legal options as they are connected to the notion of "symbolization"; (b) and in the interests of research concerning the so-called history of politics. At this juncture, the history of politics will figure prominently, especially in the debate about the past which will be apparent, for example, in the "editing" of official memorial days. In this regard, we will also be able to detect the use of rites and symbols. Finally, there are three guiding questions of "balance" (c) that will emerge through the observations of theological case study research, since the case studies will be found to establish reconciliation in actual terms as something that develops through process. Thus, the political discussion with past injustices includes a *weak spot* from the outset (i.e., certain options for action are chosen, others are not) and an inherently possible *result* at the end (the chosen actions lead to particular results and evoke the question: was the chosen path successful for the reconstruction?). In order to strike a "balance" with regard to political reconstruction, we will illustrate the legal issues in Part II.A.III, and illustrate how the results can be connected methodologically to those of analytical philosophy.

Our theological interests involve using key interdisciplinary questions in an effort to gain a differentiated analysis of the conditions for political representations of reconciliation, while also taking into account the relative autonomy of the participating branches of scholarship. The categories of analysis utilized by political science may in some ways provide a suitable aid for discussing the volatile theological position regarding the basis for the movement of political activity. The assumption that political actors do not further their own interests comes up short, as does the opposite assumption; namely, that the political motives of responsible parties in politics are based solely in self-interest and are lacking in moral dictates. A careful historical political analysis of the processes makes possible the expansion of the parameters for the position of political science for the discussion at hand.

4. Choice of Case Studies

Knowledge is gained by deviation from the norm.[30] In this regard at least two case studies dealing with the development of political reconciliation should be highlighted. The three guiding questions (i.e., *initial political conditions, symbolic forms of expression,* and *balance*) are closely tied to the subject of political upheaval and transition. The position of case study research highlighted by these questions reveals that initiatives taken toward reconciliation in the period between 1945 and 1989 were squelched in theological circles by various means. As a result, transitional societies after 1989 have not been a topic for case study work.

Against the considerations of so-called historical research, it may prove meaningful to establish a historical basis for case study research by investigating references to reconciliation in the events in South Africa and Germany. The end of Apartheid directly corresponds to the fall of the Berlin wall.[31] Former President of South Africa, F. W. de Klerk,[32] pointed out the causal connection between both events in his speech of February 2, 1990, where he expressly credited the turn of events in Europe as basis for Apartheid's demise, adding that in South Africa it was now no longer necessary to protect oneself from communism to the same degree as before. D. Tutu said about the "March for Peace" on September 13, 1989, when over 35,000 people in Cape Town came together and demonstrated against Apartheid: "People marched in South Africa . . . and the Berlin wall was breached."[33]

Accordingly, an interdisciplinary research scheme precedes each of the case studies in order to anchor them in the discussions of political science, law, and history. Also included are specific branches of research, such as transitional research from cultural and social anthropology, which also proves to be informative.

B. Conditions for Interpreting Political Reconciliation: Making Constructive Use of the "Hermeneutic Circle"

An empirical analysis of political reconciliation using the expanded case study method will provide the basic condition for the development of the *theological* problem. The *political dimension* of reconciliation must first be examined in precise detail and the prominent elements of political reconciliation must also be analyzed.

In this section we will look at the conditions for a theological inquiry where we will attempt to give an empirical analysis of the reality of political reconciliation (Part II), leaving the theoretical assumptions for Part III. In light of the considerations outlined in the Introduction, we are thus confronted with a dual task: (1) to name the political forms of reconciliation that correspond to theological teaching on reconciliation; (2) and to outline a univocal theological theoretical framework that allows for the reciprocity of conceptual analysis along consistent lines.

1. Preliminary Considerations of the Hermeneutic Circle

As already stated, our inductive task is led by guiding ideas with an analytical orientation. In view of the problem of reconciliation, we now consider the question of "what is the case" and situate the formal empirical analysis of case studies (Part II) prior to the theological synthesis (Part III). "What is the case" is usually defined in terms of perspective. In theological terms, this means that the question of political references to *reconciliation* also makes the investigation a theological one within the domain of the empirical.

Whoever intends to do research on reconciliation in terms of politics must necessarily attribute to it a double meaning because (a) it is presumed that reconciliation is a central theological category (deductive perspective) and (b) because it is presumed that within the field of research this category is active (inductive perspective). Thus, (b) is predicated by (a). (In the sense of an alternative analysis it is worth mentioning, for example, that a Buddhist would not pose the question of political reality, because for him both criteria [a] and [b] are indistinguishable from each other.)[1]

The interdependence of the above-designated criteria leads to a consideration that guides the previous theological *selection process* in the domain of political science. Accordingly, the choice of the case studies may be set against the background of the gaps in political science research as well as within the conditions for theological research. Previous knowledge influences the knowledge (or foreknowledge) of previous accounts of the theological paradigm of guilt and reconciliation. This is seen in our selection of the political issue (dealings with the past) as well as in the case examples (South Africa and Germany). The question of the variety of contexts that exist for the problem of "overcoming the past" is one that is asked with particular haste and for a particular time by a "transitional society," bringing to the forefront the connection between guilt and reconciliation in the political realm. The Judeo-Christian context of both South Africa and Germany allows for a framework for recognizing the axiom associated with theological reconciliation.

For the sake of a counter-argument, one may ask whether a connection exists at all between the absence of the influence of Christian culture and a society that procrastinates about issues of its guilt-laden past, such as the Asian shame culture of Japan. In a culturally specific perspective, the context of South Africa and Germany promises interesting results because disparate theological traditions are brought into play. J. de Gruchy, for example, emphasizes this view: "The German tradition is far less optimistic about what is achievable in politics."[2] In contrast to the Anglo-Saxon tradition, the German tradition is heavily influenced by reason and views the church as part of a process that can affect social improvements for the well-being of the world (i.e., the Social Gospel movement), and has in large part taken up the theological view that Biblical hope is not to be confused with the possibilities of politics. Indeed, the TRC has, so says de Gruchy, much stronger tendencies to the first theological position than to the second. "Desmond Tutu is an Anglican as much as he is an African. Maybe more an Anglican than an African. Virtually, everybody on the Truth commission comes out of an Anglo-Saxon theological perspective rather than a Germanic one."[3]

Therefore, the issue of "culturally specific theology"[4] with regard to our problematic leads to the development of overly regulative ideas that have an influence on regulative statements and which will, during case analysis, be examined together. For example, the participants in the "Truth and Reconciliation Commission" come out of different theological conceptual frameworks than do those of the "Gauck Administration" or the "Investigative Commission." Therefore, with each case study we must be careful to factor in the implicitly superimposed axioms which, within the hierarchy of regulative statements, are to be classified in each of the above-outlined conceptions.[5] Whereas the question of the *Theology of incarnation*[6] is regulative in one case (and with it the immanence of God), in another case the issue of whether or not a theological tradition is active emphasizes an *eschatological reserve* (and with it the transcendence of God). Between these two theological positions there is a "gap" that threatens to pose some danger for our case studies. J. de Gruchy characterizes it in light of Bonhoeffer's ethic: "The danger in Anglo-Saxon theology is to say that the ultimate and penultimate are the same. The danger in German theology is to say that there is no connection between the two."

D. Bonhoeffer's criteria therefore provide a helpful orientation into the background of culturally specific variations in the context of case study research. Whereas the "ultimate" and "penultimate" are connected (Bonhoeffer speaks of a "relationship"), they are not the same.[7] Thus, ultimate things can be understood as a contingent event within political reality: they leave behind an ontic footprint, but produce no ontology. They are there, but there is no method by which to be able to identify their appearance beforehand. Ultimate things emerge from among the penultimate like "shooting stars," says Bonhoeffer metaphorically. Thus, Bonhoeffer's analysis creates the frame of reference for a systematic theological development of the problem.

In answer to the question as to what theological categories, knowledge, and criteria concerning reconciliation guide the selection of topics in Part II, Bonhoeffer's distinction between "ultimate" and "penultimate" factors prominently, as does the politicizing of the spiritual by means of the clerical element. In addition, the problem of guilt is implicit in the representation of past politics and the history of politics, but later becomes explicit in Part III, where, for example, the *coram hominibus/coram deo* — the old man–new man, worldly-spiritual, creation and redemption, sin and grace, law and Gospel, person and work, faith and action, the absolute future of God and human responsibility for the future — are presented.

2. The Question of Correspondence as a Theological Theoretical Framework

In the theological synthesis (Part III) the instances of political reconciliation will be examined using case studies (Part II) to determine the nature of political reconciliation in its corresponding relationship to spiritual reconciliation. What kind of framework should an analysis of normative texts follow? What theological concepts of analysis are required? At stake is the "search for correspondence" or the "question of relationship."

A more precise rendering of the concepts involved in the development of the political framework of reconciliation is to be gained by drawing upon a model from more recent theological theories dealing with the traditionally central problematic of basic ethical questions. Where the "last things" are approached from an anterior stance in a functional position in theology and in the church, they can be viewed as raising the question of correspondence.[8] D. Ritschl was the first to treat the question of correspondence using a rubric.[9] This model is also used by E. Jüngel.[10] Indeed, outside of theology, cultural theology is also engaged with the problem of correspondence, especially in cults where the connection between religion and politics plays a role.[11]

3. Situating the Question of Correspondence in the Realm of Political Ethics

In our work with the question of correspondence, we are not attempting to try to advance the notion that ethics are "derived from dogmatics." This idea cannot be proven due to the large number of Biblical texts which allow for the possibility of multiple conclusions on the teaching documents of the church. In addition, there are no pure deductions (K. Popper). Accordingly, we are constructing the question of correspondence on a reverse model.

Using the reverse method, the majority of possible "derivations" from disparate selections are not excluded at the outset, but are allowed. In this way, the basic premise of D. Ritschl[12] is confirmed; namely, that the question of correspondence is "the search for connections" between two "levels of questioning." For example, does the proposed activity correspond to the central tenets of the Bible and to their development in the teachings of the church? The emphasis of multiple views will prove to be different than that of political theology, in which the "search for the connection between two levels of questioning" is heavily abbreviated in the corresponding ethic.

A few remarks should be sufficient to situate the question of correspondence in the realm of "political theology."[13] (a) In the reverse method
used in the search for correspondence, the "reverse question" distinguishes
itself from a pure ethics of correspondence.[14] Its goal is not to make the
language of reconciliation into a language of social change at any price.
Rather, first and foremost the leading elements — or implicit axioms — of
political reconciliation must be articulated in order to "examine" whether
or not they correspond to the "grammar of the language of faith," as suggested by the functional critical reception of L. Wittgenstein[15] (i.e., the
question of correspondence is not characterized *a priori* ideologically, but
remains beholden to the veto rights of the source, and thus remains
"open"). (b) The resulting question forces correspondences that are discovered from the perspective of faith in a pre-linguistic area and which do not
arise from the field of politics. Since they allow the world its own relative
autonomy, the questions are forced neither into a relational ontology of
correspondence nor into a stand-alone relational ontology (i.e., question-
answer schema). Thus, the question of correspondence distinguishes itself
from an ethic of correspondence in that it seeks correspondences on the
secondary level of declarative statements and thus excludes direct one-to-
one correspondence in terms of method. In addition, the question of correspondence is different according to P. Tillich's "Method of Correlation," [16]
because it hampers the ability of political processes to stand on their own,
while accepting that the world does not need theology in order to find answers.[17] (The correspondence question is thus ultimately more open than
an ontology of correlation, because it *a priori* does not postulate an *ontic*
relationship between God and the world.) (c) The question of correspondence is thus not politically indifferent. Normative differences exist between the legitimately relative and absolute claims on this world[18] (i.e., if
there were an absolute legitimate external-Biblical claim, for example, then
war or the death penalty would be justified).

The question of correspondence is thus "open" in contrast to the relative
legitimacy of the claims of the world in which we live, despite the offer of
reconciliation which actually puts it all into question. At this point, it may be
said temporarily: the question of correspondence puts the absolutizing of
the order that it offers to people into question; people suffer, but their relative claim is "penultimate."[19] It puts into question the position that the
"penultimate" illuminates the "ultimate" and that the way of the reconciling
and justifying Word (as the actual ultimate) is realized in the penultimate
(the question, for example, is to be conceded whether a mono-thematic

working out of a system of injustice in the legal paradigm allows sufficient room for events that occur on the horizon of the reconciling Word).

In political theology the question of correspondence is therefore either abbreviated in a corresponding ethic which sees its primary claim as an ethical appeal or imperative on the basis of political activity, or the majority of possible deductions within political reality are not accounted for and force — not ethically, but ontically — the (political) world into a theological correlation for which it is not suited. If that is the case, the above-outlined points could potentially reveal that there is no point of connection at all between our research and that of political theology. For many trends in "political theology"[20] this conclusion is appropriate. However, our line of questioning does not have as its goal the making of political theology into a political religion whose function it is to exist within the religious legitimacy of a political order (as in C. Schmitt). Neither will we take the path of existential interpretation stemming from the "new political theology," whose main representative is D. Sölle.[21] Rather, we will use the points of departure from the classic blueprint of "political theology" of J. Moltmann on the Protestant side and that of J. B. Metz on the Catholic side.

Our question of correspondence will not — as much as can be thetically anticipated — lead to the construction of a new project for political theology, nor will it lead to an ethical program that will ultimately "transform politics." And instead of concerning itself with the problem of required action, it will concentrate on the theoretical perception of theological recognition. The resulting task of "taking stock" in the political arena and an examination of reconciliation theology allows for ecclesiological results (Part III.B), which actually *proceed* from what is *recognized* as spiritual existing within *political reality*. For example, how can the church strengthen this state of affairs, encourage it and equip it with new impulses? Is the church called to repentance where it recognizes that non-Christians deal with guilt as if they were equipped to deal with a basic ecclesiological relationship to guilt? On the other hand, should the church be critical where the question of the inner workings of the system leads to injustice and to the self-absolutizing of the legal domain and where there is no possibility for the notion that reconciliation might have its origin outside of the political? It is clear that bridges need to be built that have been torn down, instead of waiting until the "nasty grave" to cry out with appeals for change. Since there are so few data points that clearly indicate a path for a political theology, our reflections on politics in Part III follow upon reflections of Christian theology with respect to politics. In the broadest sense, the result-

ing theological interpretation moves within the area of a *théologie politique,*
or a "theology of politics."[22]

4. Definitions for Enabling the Question of Correspondence

Accordingly, we define the question of correspondence as an indicative
question of dogmatic agreement:

- The *condition* for developing the question of correspondence (i.e., the
  exchange of letters) is based on an analysis of prominent persons in the
  political arena. The world remains the world with its relative autonomy;
  what is expected as theologically appropriate in an analysis of correspondence in political reality are basic *public* processes.
- For the purposes of this research, the task of the question of correspondence is first to make accessible the implicit axioms that exist behind the
  politics of past dealings with guilt (empirical analysis). Secondly, questions will be raised about the fundamental theological context of reconciliation in dealing with guilt (theological synthesis).
- The question of correspondence is understood along with D. Ritschl's
  political reality as an "area of competition" or a "tangle of voices," a
  plethora of axioms from which Biblical tradition sprang to a particular
  form. They clearly show "through" and can be reasonably distinguished
  from other forms of expression with the help of categories of analysis
  used in political science (primarily categories of "power" and "ideology"). They can also be recognized according to a theologically based
  normative investigation *in* political reality that cites the fundamental
  connection of the axiom of a Christian understanding of reconciliation.
- The *conceptuality* used here follows upon the work of D. Ritschl, but
  also underscores the problem of specific modifications (i.e., means,
  changes, expansions, and limitations). The question of correspondence
  is an indicative, dogmatic question of agreement — not primarily an
  ethical question of relation. To *recognize*[23] describes findings that can be
  tested by norms (not purely "spontaneous" finding). The broadest possible *rational connection* will be drawn to central tenets of the Bible on
  reconciliation and its development through the teachings of the church
  (delineated by "the lasting important ones").
- The concept of correspondence will be asserted as something that
  "agrees in the epistemological sense."[24] There is a lot to support the the-

sis that correspondence is to be understood as an *agreement with a basic, fundamental connection to theological reconciliation.* According to a normative-theological examination, a relationship of 1:1 is assumed. However, similarity is neither implied in a mathematical nor in a theological sense. The "equation of findings" claimed in a 1:1 relationship doesn't eliminate difference. Epistemological theory retains similarity as "a special case of difference. The connection, the synthesis, which is stated by means of the same signs and is thus articulated yields the difference of the parts that exist on both sides; it does not eliminate them, but accentuates the difference even more."[25]

The question of correspondence may thus be *formulated* as follows: in dealing with personal guilt, do we *recognize* in transitional societies a basic connection to the central tenets of the Bible on *reconciliation* and its subsequent development in the teachings of the church? If yes, where and on what level does the correspondence lie? If not, where and on what basis do the differences lie?

5. The Question of Correspondence as It Is Applied to the Theological Problem of Reconciliation

It will now be demonstrated *on what relational level* agreements with theological reconciliation can be found:

- In political reality, guilt and reconciliation addresses the *relationship between people.* Under the conditions of a totalitarian system people are guilty as a collective. However, in the course of an evolving system of injustice, society experiences a change in conditions — brought about, for example, by the workings of the Truth Commission — through the perceptible process of reconciliation between people who have in common a guilt-laden past.
- Agreement with the events of political reality are looked for *in the fundamental theological connection to reconciliation,* as defined by the above-outlined question of correspondence. The discussion of fundamental theological connection can now be adequately articulated. To what extent is the process of reconciliation implied in the work of the Truth Commission? How should it be established? It is important here to identify what was meant by the avoidance of direct correspondence in the course of the events.[26] Correspondences between events in the in-

terpersonal domain of the political realm are not seen in terms of direct agreement with the processes *between God and man,* which instruct us via theological teachings on reconciliation. However, the events between God and man do have an effect on those *between men.* To formulate this in transcendental theological terms: *the condition for the possibility of reconciliation between man and man is the condition of reconciliation between God and man.* The corresponding relational step to the interpersonal events of political reality is the step that is taken "in Christ" based on a new relationship that Paul expresses in the words: "Whosoever is in Christ, is a new creation; the old is gone, see, the new has come" (II Cor. 5:17). Our question of correspondence thus emerges from the recognition of this *becoming new* as the reconciliation between man and the old world. To what extent, then, are we able to recognize the interpersonal *relatio* of political reality as an eschatological relationship?

- In a totalitarian system people are not unconditionally guilty as a collective. In theological terms, one may say that in the interpersonal arena the condition for the possibility of guilt is predicated on the confession of being a sinner before God. We are not saying that guilt and sin are identical — or that sin is removed from the sphere of reality in the basic, public problem of dimensions of guilt (moral, legal, etc.). Rather, we are proposing that the transcendental formulation for a theoretical designation of the framing conditions for a *theological* view of guilt and reconciliation can be *admitted into* the *political realm.* The congregation of God that is destroyed by human guilt and the reconciled God-man relationship provide the condition for the possibility of recognition of guilt and reconciliation in the world. In other words: I must know something about the reconciliation of God with man (as a condition of the possibility of interpersonal reconciliation) in order to be able to recognize (interpersonal) reconciliation in the political arena as that of the overcoming of guilt through forgiveness. Accordingly, let us update the levels of correspondence in the chart on page 22.

The levels of correspondence illustrated in the schematic structure (p. 22) provide a visual representation of the issues involved in the question of correspondence. An *a priori* network of connection between man and man in the political and eschatological reality can be established in terms of theological content, but not as a condition for normative examination. Rather the basic connection from word to reality — from spiritual to political reconciliation — is the goal; political and eschatological reality are not

	Political Reality	**Theological Perspective**
Correspondence Level	Guilt and reconciliation between men	Guilt and reconciliation between men
	Political reconciliation	**Spiritual reconciliation**
Transcendental theological conditions	The condition for the possibility of interpersonal guilt is the sin of men before God.	The condition for the possibility of interpersonal reconciliation is the reconciliation of God with men.

applied as already ontologically determined (as in the Aristotelian-Thomist theory of correspondence).

The poles for our question of correspondence are thus contained in contrasting Biblical metaphors like old and new, dark and light, death and life. In terms of Biblical evidence, reconciliation is constitutively bound up with the crucifixion of Christ. Pre-Pauline tradition, which proceeds from a concept of the confession of sin (as in Rom. 3:25; II Cor. 5:19), is later radicalized by Paul. It is theoretically recalled that it is not the sins themselves that are the issue, but through Baptism into the death of the Crucified One, the sinner dies with Christ (Rom. 6:3f.) and the sinlessness of Christ is attributed to the sinner in the place of the sin (II Cor. 5:14). The sinful self is no more and is abolished (Rom. 6:6; 8:3f.). Christ dies in the place of the godless who, through his powerful death, are made righteous (Rom. 5:8f.). The death of the Son in place of the godless person (II Cor. 5:14) makes a reconciled person out of one who is otherwise the enemy of God (Rom. 5:10); it creates a new person who is now at peace with God (Rom. 5:1f.). The reconciled person is now a *new creation* (II Cor. 5:17), and not merely a debtor to whom *sin is no longer attributed* (II Cor. 5:19).

In terms of the counter-argument, it is easy to see that from Biblical evidence the concept of forgiveness is easier to convert into political terms than is the Pauline concept of reconciliation. The reason for this is forgiveness does not have an explicit soteriological connection. For example, in the Lord's Prayer (Matt. 6:12; Luke 11:4), interpersonal forgiveness is supported without reference to the Cross. There are also other Biblical citations where the concept of forgiveness is not formulated in the same exclusively soteriological way as is the concept of forgiveness.

For the development of our problem, the soteriological character of the

concept of reconciliation concerns the establishment of norms for identifying the difference between the political manifestations of reconciliation and
reconciliation as a soteriological category — which, by relying heavily on
Paul, we can now propose with some qualifications. Where reconciliation is
concerned, the obstacles for a reciprocal transfer between theological and
political language are particularly numerous and direct correspondences are
thus excluded. In political reality there is much talk of "reconciliation" when
dealing with guilt, but there is greater distance between the soteriological
content of the concept of reconciliation and political reality than there is
with the concept of forgiveness. The framing conditions for an investigation
of the political connection to reconciliation are taken from other Biblical
sources than are those dealing with forgiveness. In addition, the theological
weight of scholarship on reconciliation illustrates a deep normative difference for our question of correspondence.

6. The "Reconciled Being" as a Normative Point of Reference for the Question of Correspondence

As already indicated, Paul proceeds outwardly from forgiveness. Sin is not covered over (Rom. 4:6), merely suffered (Rom. 3:25), nor is it not allowed (II Cor.
5:19), but the basis of sin — the sinner himself — is destroyed through Christ's
representative death so that, by the Holy Spirit, the awakened person is a new
person "in Christ" who now lives for God. This *newly created person* in Christ
provides the place of correspondence for a normative examination (Part III)
of individual processing of guilt in transitional societies (Part II). The relational level of our question of correspondence is therefore built on the acceptance of "occasions" by which we may recognize this "new," reconciled person
in the midst of political reality — in the midst of the "old world." We therefore
formulate our question of correspondence as follows: do we *recognize* in personal dealings with *guilt* in transitional societies a basic connection to the central tenets of the Bible on reconciliation and their gradual development in the
teachings of the church? What is the relationship to the second part of our
question on the systematic unfolding of the theoretical theological (Part III)
against the background of the defined level of correspondence, namely to the
"basic connection of the central tenets of the Bible on reconciliation and their
gradual development in the teachings of the church"?

In the first place, the formal connection established by the connective
"and" in the formulation of a question ("central tenets of the Bible *and* their

gradual development in the teachings of the church") is not to be viewed as the reason for possible interpretative misunderstandings *(scriptura et traditio)*. Rather, it will be seen in accordance with the points outlined in the introduction that, from the abundance of the Biblical texts, several deductions are possible when relying on the teaching doctrines of the church.

With regard to a point of entry into the theological discussion on reconciliation, Part II.A.I.3 demonstrates that: (a) a written Evangelical-theological investigation does not suffice simply by using direct Biblical derivatives for the concept of reconciliation; (b) that various levels of development in the thinking on reconciliation within theological history are given weight; (c) that relevant models of reconciliation as types are introduced that emphasize various historically central tenets of the Bible on reconciliation;[27] and (d) that these models neither radically harmonize with each other nor are profiled against each other. At the end of this section, in Part III.A.I.4, normative ideas from the Christian understanding of reconciliation are retained, which will form the basis for further considerations.

We must also consider the question of the interpersonal arena which is raised as part of the fundamental theological connection to reconciliation; namely, the model of theological reconciliation in its normative form with a view to the καινὴ κτίσις. An exegetical view of the concept of reconciliation offers different key terms for a dogmatic classification of the levels of reconciliation that are treated in the question of correspondence: (1) where it has to do with the Christian-anthropological New Creation, our discussion of reconciliation will take place in the dogmatic context of the doctrinal elements of soteriology and eschatology;[28] (2) the theology of the Trinity is anchored in the corresponding level of pneumatology[29]; and (3) sacramental theology is located in Baptism and the Last Supper.[30]

By assigning type to general models of reconciliation in Part III we will highlight the conditions for the possibility of interpersonal reconciliation: namely, reconciliation as an event between God and man that describes the eschatological exchange of existence of the enemies (i.e., man) of God so that in the course of the exchange, the now justified sinner steps forward into the center as the main "event." Again, the theme here is the reconciliation between God and man as the condition for reconciliation between man and man.

Finally, we need to consider with each of the case studies what can be categorized under the rubric of *political analysis* (Part II) in terms of the interpersonal problem of guilt and reconciliation. Interpersonal guilt and reconciliation can not be directly placed in a fundamental connection to the teachings of the church on reconciliation, because in the church it essentially has to do with the reconciliation between God and man (reconciliation as the ultimate "last [thing]"). Accordingly, the three guiding questions for the case study analysis in Part II are: (1) the initial conditions for reconciliation in South Africa and in Germany; (2) the symbolic forms of expression of political reconciliation, (3) and the balance that is struck in political dealings with guilt. All three demand a normative examination of the theological concepts for analysis (Part III) which — as will be shown — are taken from the areas of (1) legal ethics, (2) new metaphors and research on symbols, (3) and process theology. These are connected to theological reconciliation in as much as they provide important contributions to sub-areas of theological understanding of interpersonal reconciliation (i.e., reconciliation as the "last" thing).

Theological connections to reconciliation are connected in terms of systematics under the category "the last and next to last things (penultimate and ultimate)" (Bonhoeffer). Here the basic assumption changes in a "relation" of the "last things (ultimate)" (as the justifying and reconciling Word of God) with the "next to last things (penultimate)," which in our case is the treatment of guilt within the political system. We therefore can expand our schema as in the chart on page 26.

7. The Question of Correspondence in the *Analogia Relationis*

When the question of correspondence has been defined in terms of method under the above-stipulated conditions as the recognition of agreement between an action that can be carried out now (i.e., the political and legal handling of *guilt* of persons according to system changes) and the central tenets of the Bible on *reconciliation* and their development in the doctrines of the church, the problem of applicable analogies inevitably arises. Analogies are constantly visible in many places of the analysis in the cross-linkages between theological statements as well as at the point of intersection of the reason for the connection. However, an open question remains concerning which concepts of analysis may be helpful for a reconstruction of Christian thought on reconciliation in the political realm.

Our question of correspondence concerns itself with the *structural possibility of correspondence* of interpersonal reconciliation in political reality and the reconciliation of God in Christ which makes men a "new creature," but not an *analogous Being*. As has been stated previously, political and eschatological reality that applies to us is not mediated ontologically. Correspondences that are sought in a theological connection to reconciliation can

	Political Reality	**Theological Perspective**
Next to last (penultimate)	Political Analysis: Guilt and reconciliation between men I. Political conditions for proceeding II. Symbolic forms III. Balance of political reconciliation	Theological-normative correspondence area: Guilt and reconciliation between men I. Legal ethics II. Theories of metaphor III. Process theology
	Political Reconciliation	**Spiritual Reconciliation**
Last (ultimate)	The condition for the possibility of interpersonal guilt is the sin of men before God.	The condition for the possibility of interpersonal reconciliation is the reconciliation of God with men. Models of reconciliation

not *a prior* presuppose an analogy of being. Thus, there is the issue of the question of correspondence that resides in the theory of truth of the *analogia entis.*

The following statements with regard to the question of correspondence will not proceed in a direct ontological manner from these presuppositions, due to the evidence for a substantive difference between political reconciliation and reconciliation as a soteriological category in view of the Pauline concept of reconciliation.

Accordingly, we must clarify the definition for the treatment of our problem; namely, how the question of correspondence is to be connected with any other analogous form of *analogia entis* in order to be able to arrive at a suitable concept that can serve above and beyond the formal-methodological approach as a constructively functional theological category of analysis. It seems that from two vantage points the *analogia relationis*[31] is an adequate form of analogy because (1) the poles of the question of correspondence are yet to be determined; and (2) the *analogia relationis* (circumstances of the *analogia fidei*) is value-laden: namely, they exist "in relation." These two points of reference make up the structural possibility for a corresponding interpersonal "Being-In-Relationship" *by itself* from one of

"Being-In-Relationship" to God, which presumes the precise opposite of *analogia;* namely, the *entis.*

This thetically generated formulation develops in the following way: the *analogia relationis* is an adequate form of expression in terms of method because it "fits" the formal scheme: in each instance it is compared to "relation." According to Karl Barth, through the relationship of God to Jesus there is an analogous relationship between God's Being-in-Himself and his relationship to man.[32] The connection of the *analogia relationis* can therefore be described as "God — God is analogous to God — Jesus is analogous to God — man. Thus, the analogy for this analogous relationship is one of the relationship constituted by the love of God."[33] For our treatment of the question of correspondence, the third *analogia relationis* is decisive, which K. Barth articulates in the area between the Being-In-Relationship to God and the Being-in-Man as you and I, similar to what creation theology discusses in the relationship between man and wife. In the God-Creature-Relationship the relationship between people can be expressed as: just as God is "in relationship" so also the person created by God is "in relationship,"[34] and "as God is for man, so man is for man."[35]

The above chain of analogy can be expanded: God — God is analogous to God — Jesus is analogous to God — man is analogous to man — man. The univocal core is contained in the relationship, since the first relationship is mediated through the final *ontic* and *noetic.* However, the last relationship is established in the first Christological, indeed, Trinitarian theological relationship.

The *analogia relationis* man-man, which comprises the content of the connection that will be treated in this study, forms the basis for our problem where the analogies of the *analogia relationis* intersect the poles of the question of correspondence. The second part of the statement "as God (is) for man, so is *man for man*" forms the normative pole of correspondence by which to test the interpersonal forms of expressing reconciliation in political reality. The *analogia relationis* man-man corresponds to the Pauline καινὴ κτίσις ("new creature"), which is the condition for the reconciliation of God-man. The other pole of the question of correspondence — the relationship of man-man in political reality — is *not* drawn into the above scheme of analogy, but rather is first examined on the basis of the reasons for that connection in a three-part theological *analogia relationis.* Is there a correspondence between the empirically analyzed relationship — that *between men* in the past political forums of the TRC or the EK — to that *between men,* which has its origin in the relationship constituted by God's love? We also find here an *analogia relationis*.[36] Thus, the problem that is to be treated incorporates the *analogia relationis* as a two-dimensional expansion and not as an extension of a one-dimensional scheme of chain of analogies.

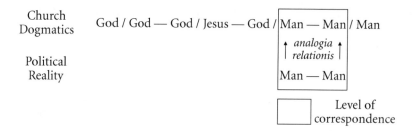

The above scheme is of course not suitable where "thinking in two spheres" (Bonhoeffer) is simply reproduced. Rather, it has to do (and in many ways contrary to K. Barth's ethic) with the relative autonomy of the political; it holds that political reality, despite *de-ontologically* based hope, is open to a new politically decisive reconciliation and develops (as already mentioned) from this gap the systematic position as a dogmatic-theologically productive inquiry brought about by recognition.

After we have classified the *analogia relationis* in a formal methodological stage with regard to the question of correspondence, we will begin the material development of our second thesis, which states that the *analogia relationis* is an appropriate, theologically normative form of statement for the treatment of our problem. At the center of this stage are theoretical considerations about the connection to the levels of relationships between man-man *(analogia relationis)* in view of the problem of reconciliation, as well as questions of correspondence and demarcation (K. Barth) concerning other forms of analogy — above all the *analogia fidei* on the one hand and the *analogia entis* on the other.

We have already indicated that the intersection between the analogies of the *analogia relationis* and the poles of the question of correspondence forms the *analogia relationis* of man-man: "As God is for man, so is man for man." However, what is there to say about this level of relation that will serve us as a normative pole by which to investigate the forms of appearance of interpersonal reconciliation in the political realm? First, according to K. Barth, the relation between man and man "is not dependent on the connection between God and man"; rather it is "mediated by it."[37] In this way K. Barth expresses the notion of creation as the external basis for the Covenant; namely, "that inherent in the structure of creation are the conditions for a realization of the *analogia relationis*."[38] These "conditions," this external basis of creation, are made possible through God's loving "yes" to man — in His will for the Covenant as the internal basis of creation. In his "yes" God creates the external basis for his Self-revelation in Jesus Christ. The "Being-In-Relationship" of man contains the creation-theological structural conditions of correspondence to the "Being-In-Relation" of God, without presupposing an analogous Being.[39]

What then is an analogy of relation? Where does the correspondence between the "Being-In-Relation" of God and man lie? Is it love that is the point of intersection between the analogies of the *analogia relationis* God-God and God-Jesus? With these questions we arrive at the starting position for our research: namely, "the analogy between the inner-divine, i.e. God-man relationship on the one hand, and the interpersonal relationship on the other (is) also that of a relationship to the constituting love of God."[40] The statement "as God is for man, so man is for man," is set against the background of "Barth's designation of humanity as a determination of man by God" and is to be understood as "the beneficence of God toward man . . . not only (as) the original model, but also (as) that which constitutes interpersonal relationships."[41] Thus, the analogy between the relational levels of the inner-divine (i.e., God-man and interpersonal) does not consist in characteristics that can be attributed to both God and man, as if "Being in its essence (were comparable) to other Beings in their Being." Rather, the *analogia relationis* according to Barth is seen as "that of the pre-eminence of the Creator, the call of the Creator Being in its Essence: God in correspondence to the "yes" that He Himself promises."[42] Thus, the analogy is not in general a concept of Being that forms the basis for the *analogia relationis,* but rather is "a position of God over against man by which the corresponding human condition is constituted through this divine relationship."[43]

K. Barth says of the analogy of correspondence that "loving behavior" is the connection between the *analogia relationis* and the *analogia fidei:* "Within the *analogia fidei* Barth describes this behavior with the concept of 'readiness' (God for man and man for God). Within the framework of the *analogia relationis* Barth chooses the concept of 'relation' (God to Himself, to Jesus, to man and of man to God, to Jesus and to other men)."[44]

From the above statement we arrive at a starting point of reference that indicates the suitability of the Barthian concept of analysis for the treatment of our problem of reconciliation:

- In the doctrine of the *analogia relationis* there is talk of in and with creation as an established analogy.[45] Since this concerns the inner connection of creation and covenant, the framing conditions are thus shaped for our discussion of reconciliation within political reality. "Reconciliation," says O. Weber aptly, is "the grasp of the Creator for his creation."[46]
- According to Barth, the primary analogy for creation is "relation." In the ensuing examination of the levels of relationships existing within political reality, as well as in the theological doctrine of reconciliation, the focus is on dealing with guilt and reconciliation "in relation" (between man and man and God and man). This means that the creation-theological axiom is applied in a fitting manner to the reconciliation-theological axiom.
- The connection to reconciliation emerges where the conditions of the *analogia relationis* are reflected. J. Track writes: "An *analogia relationis* is to be found where the person allows himself to be taken in by God's corresponding mercy."[47] Isn't this "allowing oneself to be taken in" (passive!) the same thing as the "allowing oneself to be reconciled" of II Corinthians 5?

8. Is Reconciliation a Relational Category in Paul?

The above points of reference for an analysis of the *analogia relationis* as a theological concept take on new urgency in the context of reconciliation where our deliberations on content are brought into direct contact with the results of theological exegesis. The historical derivation of the concept of reconciliation from the language of diplomacy allows us to raise a question that is of concern to our systematic theological inquiry; namely, whether or not the theological-relational aspect in the Pauline concept of reconciliation is modeled on a political one.

For the purposes of our research, which will build upon the results of C. Breytenbach, the examination of meaning described by the *di-* and *katalas sein* in the "*Corpus Hellenisticum* is the area from which the interpersonal and above all the inter-(city) state relations derive" and which describes "the conditions of animosity in war."[48] Now the question of the possibility of reciprocal *transferability of political language into theological language* can be raised on the basis of Biblical findings. A direct transfer of political (language) into theological and (vice versa) from theological into political is ruled out, but what can we learn from more current exegetical research about "indirect" transfers, or "broken" transfers?

Let's first take the question of the transfer of the language of political reconciliation into theological language. Following the work of C. Breytenbach, we will show how Paul is the first to use an implicit axiom in theological language. The Apostle demonstrates the transfer of the political concept of reconciliation into a theological concept of analysis, which in turn expresses something about the soteriological relationship of peace between God and man, as well as revealing something about the apostleship of Paul himself.[49] Thus, through critical transformation, the concept acquires theological meaning.

The transfer of the concept is given an entirely new meaning by Paul as he draws it logically through the content connected with the death of Jesus, something that is evident from the comparison with the concept of forgiveness: "Forgiveness means not only, that God doesn't think about man's sins anymore, but that He will re-create man anew. This explains, without the use of analogy (in the sense of the *analogia entis*), that God (Subject) reconciles the world (Object) to Himself; namely, that He has not only intended to end animosity, but also the existence of the enemy (sic!) and will create everyone anew who, like Paul, allows themselves to be reconciled."[50] The Pauline "Baptismal Act" of the secular concept of forgiveness means a discontinuity — an internal break — in the use of the word. Although Paul receives the concept of reconciliation from the political sphere, when it is used theologically it is not controlled by the political (as if one could advance forgiveness on its theological meaning above the political). Rather, Paul's concept of forgiveness makes use of an implied axiom that defies analogy and is for the first time to be found in theological language; *namely the idea that God is the subject of reconciliation and that he, Paul, is the conveyer of this message.* In this critical theological systematic point, which excludes an *analogia entis* in the process of translation, we follow upon the work of C. Breytenbach.

In order to establish a possible connection to the *analogia relationis* guided by Breytenbach's exegesis of Paul, we finally may submit the following for consideration: *is the relational aspect of the political concept of reconciliation capable of being translated into a theological one?* Stated another way: despite the inner break in the concept of reconciliation, does the relational aspect still remain intact as a structural possibility that is apparent in the Pauline translation? Is reconciliation to be defined at all outside of the category of relation? Does "relation" appear as *the* ontological constant in the transfer as the stated "precondition" (K. Barth), or as the *ontic* footprint, which we — according to normative testing in the frame of the *analogia relationis* — are able to appropriate? There is a lot to be said for pursuing these questions and, in terms of Biblical evidence, to assume that reconciliation is a relational category.

Paul has fragmented the political concept of reconciliation, translated it into theological terms, and connected it with central soteriological statements. This brings us to our *second* question regarding the transfer back of the theological concept of reconciliation into a political concept.

It is undisputed that once it was transferred into the theological, to a great degree the concept of reconciliation lost its political-social dimension in Paul.[51] Consequently, it has become an apolitical, universally univocal theological concept for describing the soteriological saving activity of God in Jesus Christ. From this exegetical insight a further argument for the inadequacy of direct correspondences is to be gained; but this time in the transfer of the theological concept of reconciliation onto the political. The concept is defined strictly soteriologically. Once it is determined theologically, reconciliation precludes analogy in view of its analogy of Being, but it is capable of analogy in the sense of the *analogia relationis*. Since political reconciliation receives its similarity only from a theological understanding, the current results of exegetical research which are raised in terms of the political dimension of reconciliation need not worry us; they rather strengthen us in our project.

A retro-fitting of theological language into the political can take place only "indirectly," and in "broken" fashion. Through the recognition of the "places of fracture" of Christian thought on reconciliation into the political, the task of systemic reconstruction emerges after theological-normative testing. Biblical evidence[52] strengthens the acceptance of the possibility of a reconstruction, in so far as it is acknowledged that the reconciliation of God-man "breaks through" on the level of the interpersonal. "In Christ" the person is a "new creature." On the other hand, the question of correspondence can be placed only on *this* level (old man-new man), that is, on the path to recognition in the sense that there are direct transfers of forms of expression of interpersonal reconciliation in political reality that are excluded by the reconciliation of God-man. The level of correspondence is inter- (and intra-) personal (existence of man in political reality — existence of man in eschatological reality), where the condition for the possibility of reconciliation between God and man in the death of Christ is a condition which itself, however, can not be directly transferred. For Paul, the reciprocity in the question of transferability of the concept of reconciliation is already politically and theologically attached to clear conditions. This means that for the treatment of our problem a connection between theological thought on reconciliation and political reality (which without question also for Paul is the case)[53] can only be meaningfully asked in terms of recognition.

This investigation moves now epistemologically to the question of correspondence and includes the Pauline-based non-exchangeability of the indicative and the imperative (i.e., we have already defined the question of correspondence as a dogmatic-*indicative* question of agreement). Second, reconciliation-theological is indirectly (re)constructed; that is, the question of correspondence is placed on the level of Christian anthropology: the "new creature" of Paul's description stands as a normative pole between political reconciliation (the horizontal level) on the one hand, and Christological reconciliation (the vertical level) on the other hand. Here, the political forms of expression of reconciliation are examined on the basis of their forms of expression, which have their condition in the reconciliation between God and man. Finally, the question of correspondence is based on the expansion of the *analogia relationis* in K. Barth, developed under the rubric of "relationship."

The question of correspondence leads from an appeal to current exegetical research to a second course of argumentation (according to the systematic theological observations of K. Barth), namely, to the question of the adequacy of the *analogia relationis* as a theological category of analysis for the treatment of our problem. A reconstruction is meaningful in view of the problem of reconciliation in Paul as it relates to the category of *analogia relationis*. Our question of correspondence in terms of the fundamental theological connection of reconciliation as it appears in political forms of expression having to do with the treatment of guilt in transitional societies thus examines the relationship between men (such as that between victim and abuser) from a theologically normative stance on the basis of the *analogia relationis* of man-man, which has its condition in the *analogia relationis* of God-Jesus, i.e., God-God. Thus, it has to do with the recognition of the καινὴ κτίσις ("new creature") in political reality.

Finally, the plan outlined in the Introduction states that in the treatment of political references to reconciliation, the *analogia relationis* is the theological form of statement where the strength of the univocal and analogy come together in the possibility of reconciliation. We will univocally speak of reconciliation in its soteriological form; at the same time we will take into consideration the structural possibilities (not an analogous Being) that reconciliation does not remain apart, but can be *recognized* in the political.[54] For these possibilities creation-theological assumptions are forged, such as the "relationship" between "man-man."

Finally, one more thing is to be emphasized: the question of correspondence gains theological clarity through a normative line of questioning. For faith, the implicit axiom of political forms of expression of reconciliation must be examined on the basis of Christian ideas of reconciliation — any direct transfer is excluded. Only from the vantage point of faith can there be certainty for an application of the "signs of the times" (Part II) and the knowledge by which to define it (Part III).

Under the above-outlined conditions, the correspondence model promises to offer a methodologically thorough treatment of our problem for the interplay between an analysis of political reality on the one hand, and a reflection on the impulses that drive Christian tradition on the other.

II. Recognizing the "Signs of the Times":
An Empirical Analysis

A. Dealing with Guilt in the Wake of Apartheid: South Africa 1990-1999

Empirical research on South African case studies is capable of being incorporated into the history of research when viewed in an interdisciplinary context. The country of South Africa is connected to the global experience of transitional processes, particularly through the work of the so-called "Truth Commission," and is active in the global project of "Justice in Transition."[1] Before presenting the following three sections of research on case studies I would like to make the following preliminary observations, all of which are derived from the history of research:

I. The *initial political conditions for dealing with guilt in South Africa* (I) are analyzed with respect to the results of research on political transitions.[2] In terms of methodology, specific options for political response provide the analytical framework for an investigation of the initial political conditions for treating the issue of guilt in South Africa in the wake of apartheid.

II. *In order to determine the historical political perspective of the symbolic forms of expression used for processing systemic injustice* (II), I use the results of the international literature on the "Truth Commission" as a general guide,[3] as well as that of the TRC specifically.[4] In terms of content, selections from the hearings of the South African "Truth and Reconciliation Commission" (= TRC) are documented and analyzed with regard to their symbolic forms.

In an attempt to understand the written accounts of the minutes of the hearings between the members of the commission and the witnesses that were brought before them, we must reflect upon a culturally specific problem: how can events be interpreted that take place in a cultural context that is foreign to the author? In methodological terms, the problem of the development of an empirical textual analysis that is concurrent with a theological analysis impacts the texts in additional ways. The method offered by empirical social science research is one of the "participating observer," which has proven successful in the area of cultural anthropology. An "exact study of another culture (is) only possible through participation in its life," because "the researcher cannot inform himself through documents," but must be "in the field."[5]

What follows first from this approach to the treatment of our problem is the need to make observations that go beyond mere analysis of documents, since the research is comprised of available recorded transcriptions of manuscripts from the hearings, and to be able to actually take part in the hearings and to record observations.[6, 7] Additional concerns for the procedure includes: (a) in order to attempt a systematic investigation, transcripts are taken primarily from hearings in which I was personally present and able to observe, or from those in which others were present. The type and manner in which something was said and, in general, the atmosphere of the hearing are also given weight; (b) in the adapted transcriptions there are words and phrases that are associated with a very different kind of symbolism. Thus, in order to convey the complexity of the "African traditional religion," the adapted transcripts are thoroughly reviewed by Africans and, accordingly, the cultural background is included as the context for many of the statements. In many respects the TRC itself is a "participating observer"; it is "neither victim, nor perpetrator, but charged with the task of understanding."[8] In using the term *participating observer* regarding the events of the TRC, I basically concur with the sociologist H. Adam.[9]

Within the context of South Africa the development of the concept of political reconciliation requires the use of the "qualitative interview," in addition to that of *textual analysis* and of the *participating observer.*[10] The interviews derive from the period in South Africa between September 12, 1996, and February 4, 1999, and include selected parties of the TRC,[11] of the non-ruling party (NGO),[12] from the South African Church Body (SACC),[13] in addition to observations by politicians,[14] sociologists,[15] philosophers,[16] African scholars,[17] as well as scholars of Islam.[18] To construct the *textual analysis* sources had to be supplemented by books and essays from available literature and from other unpublished documents. Important sources were found in the archives of the TRC in Cape Town and in the private archives of Wolfram Kistner of Johannesburg. In both archives, significant documents were found that were indispensable for the investigation of the case studies.

As a basis for historical research, the TRC's five-volume Final Report is used in an attempt to *balance the political processing of system-wide injustice in South Africa* (III).[19] Overall, March 1999 is taken as the *terminus ad quem* of the case study research. (The parliamentary debates of the TRC Final Report in February 1999 in Cape Town are included. The range of literature that has emerged since 1999 has, with some exceptions, been left untouched.)

In the following work with case studies, the *interview* method and that of the *participating observer* used in the field of social science will be apparent in the systematic analysis and interpretations of texts. In general, the interrelationship of both methods appears to be adequate for treating the problem.[20] By employing both methods, the political forms of reconciliation in dealing with guilt after apartheid can be empirically analyzed before proceeding on (in Part III) to an investigation of the attending theological norms.

I. Initial Political Conditions Surrounding the Issue of Guilt in South Africa

The course was set at the beginning of the 1990s for the process of reconciliation in South Africa. A journalist and trusted friend of President Mandela's wrote in retrospect of the period between the release of Nelson Mandela in February 1990 and his swearing in as the first President of a democratic South Africa on May 10, 1994, that it "will be entered in the annals of history, and the many interrelated events that threaten to derail the negotiation process are thereby annulled."[21] This section of the book will concern itself with these events; not by way of a historical reconstruction, but rather as an analytical representation of how it is possible to determine the "regulative statements" (D. Ritschl) behind the process of reconciliation. What initial conditions led to the fact that reconciliation became a central theme in the political language of South Africa? What ideas did the political actors have in mind during the period when, by acts of violence, twelve thousand people died? And how were past political options for action weighed out against each other in the course of the political discussions during South Africa's transition to democracy?

In connecting the results of the comprehensive and internationally led research from the fields of law and political science on political transitions, we find that there are five courses of action open to a country that is dealing with a guilt-laden past.[22] These options form the systematic framework of analysis by which to determine the initial conditions for dealing with guilt at the end of apartheid:

- Prosecution of serious human rights violations.
- The opposite: do nothing, either in the form of general amnesty or simply "leaving it in peace."
- Exposure of past injustices, for example, through a "Truth Commission."
- Compensation to the victims (for example, returning their land, material remuneration, legal restitution, moral restitution, etc.).
- Professional "disqualification" (for example, cleaning out of public service departments, especially the police and military, of implicated coworkers).

Ultimately, the option that a country chooses depends in large measure on the nature of the system of transition. Three types of system change are outlined in the international literature: "overthrow, reform, compromise." "Being overthrown is the fate of a regime that has refused to reform: opposition forces become stronger and finally topple the old order. When reform is undertaken, the old government plays the critical role in the shift to democracy as, initially at least, the opposition is weak. In countries where change is the result of compromise, the existing regime and opposition cannot make the transition to democracy without each other. Such was the case in South Africa."[23]

The later vice chairman of the TRC describes the initial situation in South Africa simply: "It was impossible for the state to put down the growing resistance and it was equally impossible for those who resisted to overthrow the state by force. It was a classic stalemate."[24] As of February 11, 1990, the words of Nelson Mandela to P. W. Botha in a memo proved to be politically astute: "Reconciliation can only be achieved when both parties are willing to come to a compromise."[25]

1. Punishment for Perpetrators of Political Crimes

When it comes to the prosecution of serious human rights violations after system change, we must consider the following, among others:[26]

- Truth and justice demand prosecution. The new government has the moral duty to punish those who have perpetrated human rights violations; they owe this to the victims and their families.
- Prosecution is necessary to demonstrate the superiority of democratic norms and values; in this way trust in justice is re-established.

- After a recent transition to democracy, criminal law can only work as a deterrent when past human rights violations are punished. With regard to general prevention measures, the entire population must be shown that human rights violations will not be tolerated.
- Prosecution of the perpetrators is necessary so that, in general, human rights violations are seen as a criminal act. (Responsible citizens usually say that they haven't done anything wrong, but have "defended the state" and "fought terrorism." Freedom fighters likewise say that they have not committed any "crimes," but have fought against the system.)

In the discussions on South Africa, the arguments for pursuit of criminals have found little resonance. This is due to various factors, three of which I am able to extract: the character of the system change, legal conditions, and the political will of the actors.

Prosecution is incompatible with the nature of system change in South Africa. Instead, it has provided a negotiated transition without victors. "Neither side in the struggle (the state nor the liberation movement) had defeated the other and hence nobody was in a position to enforce so-called victor's justice."[27] There should also be no "victor's justice": "the triumphalist approach of victor's justice, with its inevitable selectiveness and political opportunism, was rejected in favor of ideals of nation building and reconciliation between the oppressors and the oppressed."[28] However, from the legal standpoint, the example of the "Nuremberg Trials" was also rejected: only a fraction of the perpetrators were brought to trial; the German people were not actually involved in the process; and in the end the attention of the process was on the perpetrators and not on the victims. "The lesson of Nuremberg is that there should be no other trials following the model of the Nuremberg trials."[29]

Criminal pursuit of human rights violations binds the legal entities together. Therefore, in order to strengthen a *trust in justice,* events must be handled justly by the state. If one proceeds from the premise *that justice demands prosecution,* where does the case of South Africa fit? At first it is not clear whether or not the process would lead to accusations, given the burden of proof on the side of the state.[30] One can only imagine the toll it would take on the process: "any systemic attempt to investigate and prosecute many hundreds and thousands of cases on an individual basis will require massive resources and will bog down the courts for many years to come."[31] Other punishments would not even come before the courts if one considers that "the legal system of the apartheid state prevents punishment despite human rights violations."[32] Finally, we need to think of the victims. They could be cross-examined, but that would only cause their trauma to be repeated instead of contributing to healing, and the victims could potentially be abandoned by the state for a second time. B. Naudé comments on the above problem in summary: "and if we wait for the day when all justice has been meted out legally, it will be too late for reconciliation."[33]

In summary, the criminal punishment of human rights violations has neither the political will of both parties nor of its respective main proponents, F. de Klerk and N. Mandela. With regard to both parties, R. Goldstone, a judge in South Africa, observes curtly: "No political party in South Africa is calling for mass trials of those who were guilty of the crimes of apartheid."[34] Furthermore, both official parties — the NP and the ANC — were involved in human rights violations which made it difficult at the outset to bring the involved parties closer to agreement on the fact that the *committed actions were criminal acts* (compare the above argument). The ANC also never concerned itself with punishing politically motivated crimes. Rather, it attempted to morally legitimatize the resistance to the violation of human rights: "the Apartheid regime deployed its massive resources with deliberate and systematic violence. By contrast, the anti-apartheid resistance committed sporadic lapses, due to its material deprivation and refugee status."[35]

Additionally, in terms of numbers, the dead and wounded in the fight for freedom can not be compared to the number of those who died defending apartheid. There is also the problem of evaluating human rights violations: namely, can the violations that were committed by the apartheid regime be compared to those of the armed resistance? The political debate focuses on the phrase "even-handedness," whereby the human rights violations of the past should be judged "in an even-handed manner."[36] However, in this regard, both viewpoints are put in the same double bind: (1) If one considers future human rights violations illegal according to South African law ("domestic law"), such as torture or disappearance perpetrated by the government, or murder and homicide perpetrated by the armed resistance; (2) then one will not be able to put an end to the human rights violations of the apartheid system itself — such as enforced re-settlement, etc. — which is illegal in terms of "international law."[37]

The issue for the main actors is simple: F. de Klerk wanted to retain power. N. Mandela recalls: "Despite his seemingly progressive actions, Mr. de Klerk was by no means a great emancipator. He was a . . . careful pragmatist. He did not make any of his reforms with the intention of putting himself out of power. He made them precisely for the opposite reason: to ensure power for the Afrikaner[38] in a new dispensation."[39] Mandela, for his part, will not promote the punishment of crimes because he wants to direct the view strictly forward to the future. "I would not mince words about the horrors of apartheid, but I said, over and over, that we should forget the past and concentrate on building a better future for all."[40] But where Mandela does look back, he does not condone punishment.[41] Rather, his hate is directed against the system: "I wanted South Africa to see that I loved even my enemies while I hated the system that turned us against one another."[42] And one cannot pursue a system using criminal means as one would pursue a criminal; one can only expose a system's injustices (Option 3).

By using the term "system," we run into a specific problem within the context of South Africa; namely, apartheid was not the *cause* of human rights violations, it was *itself* a "crime against humanity."[43] At this very basic level, South Africa can not relate to the experience of other countries in dealing with the past. To be sure, in Uruguay, Chile and Argentina horrible violations of human rights took place, but there was no apartheid. The authors of the book "Reconciliation through Truth" write pointedly: "Apartheid was evil."[44] "Apartheid (which means 'apartness') was fundamentally built on the idea of irreconcilability of peoples."[45] Thus, no "bridge to reconciliation" could be built upon the ideology of apartheid.[46] Here it quite simply has to do with right and wrong. "In the political context, reconciliation is a shared and painful ethical voyage from wrong to right."[47] This view, however, is not that of either President de Klerk and the NP nor of the other white parties during the transition negotiations, including the Freedom Front (FF) and the Democratic Party (DP). "None of the predominantly white parties (FF, NP and DP) . . . have addressed the fundamental question whether the history and policy of apartheid has to be regarded as a violation of human rights and as such a crime against humanity."[48] That being the case, in October 1995 de Klerk warns his future government "to randomly alter or undo what we have done in the spirit of reconciliation and the maintaining of security and stability in South Africa."[49]

It is important to note that the initial arguments were weighed against each other. The case against punishment was made during the transitional phases for the sake of the "common good," using phrases like "national unity" and "nation building." South Africa wanted to overcome the thinking that says reconciliation is only possible after punishment. On the other hand, requirements still had to be outlined to make the desired reconciliation possible.

2. Amnesty for Human Rights Violations

The following arguments[50] speak against punishing the perpetrators; thus, in favor of general amnesty or simply of "leaving it in peace" (Option 2):

- Amnesty is necessary in order for the young democracy to be placed on a solid foundation. The consolidation of democracy takes priority over the punishment of individuals.
- Democracy must be built on reconciliation in order to overcome the divisions of the past.
- In most cases the governing party, as well as the opposition party, were entwined in human rights violations. Thus, a general amnesty offers a better basis for transition to democracy than does punishment of either side.
- Amnesty, or the "leaving in peace" of the past, can prevent an emerging democracy from sudden decline. On the other hand, punishment can provoke a coup.
- The former governing parties are only ready to give up their power if amnesty is secured for them.

The negotiations between the ANC and the government began at the beginning of 1990 with the question of amnesty for ANC political prisoners and ended with the Amnesty Clause of the Interim Government at the end of 1993. In order for the parties to be able to come to the negotiation table, rules had to be established, which ultimately led to the release of political prisoners and made possible the return of exiled ANC members. In his historic speech of February 2, 1990, President de Klerk announced the release of Mandela and a small circle of other political prisoners (compare Hansard 1990). Through the law exempting legal punishment, or the so-called Indemnity Act, the ANC countered with a demand for guaranteed exemption from punishment for exiles. The government, however, went even further. In view of the continuing show of force, de Klerk submitted a bill called the Further Indemnity Act[51] to Parliament in October, 1992. He based this decision on the fact that the current amnesty laws did not do enough to include those who had merely followed orders. In contrast to the earlier agreement which was made in support of the Norgaard-Principles, the Further Indemnity Act takes into consideration political motivation as the sole criteria for exemption from punishment. The context and the type of deed were not to play a role.

Nevertheless, the ANC threatened not to recognize the amnesty laws outlined in the Further Indemnity Acts. In an open letter to de Klerk, human rights organizations wrote saying: "We believe that no decision can be made to forgive crimes before the truth of those crimes is known."[52] Of course, the ratification of the Further Indemnity Acts could not be halted; but the ensuing discussion threw a specific term into the political debate: namely, *truth*. South Africa would, of course, accept an amnesty ruling in view of the crimes of apartheid; but it would not "leave the past in peace." Among other things, the debate focused on the year 1992 when there was concern that the young democracy would be jeopardized by a confrontation with the past, as well as with the opposing view that "The confession and renunciation of past violence by past violence can strengthen democracy immeasurably."[53] The resulting debate took place in the fall of 1993 in the political negotiations of Kempton Park (Johannesburg) which led to the passage of a new constitution for South Africa (Interim Constitution) on November 18, 1993, and made possible the first secret and free elections of April 27, 1994.

The South African constitutional judge, A. Sachs, recalls the political positions that were represented in the discussion: general amnesty on the National Party (NP) side connected to the argument that "The cooperation of the Defense Force and of the South African Police was necessary during the election. How could they be expected to co-operate, if they did not have the assurance that the new government would not prosecute them?"[54] On the other side the rejection of amnesty with the reasoning that "an amnesty would take account . . . of the needs and the pain of the victims."[55]

The result of the negotiation of Kempton Park was a political compromise which appears in the Postscript[56] of the Interim Constitution under the title *National Unity and Reconciliation*, saying: "This constitution provides a historic bridge between the past of a deeply divided society . . . and a future founded on the recognition of human rights. The pursuit of national unity, the well-being of all South African citizens and peace require reconciliation between the people of South Africa and the reconstruction of society. . . . There is a need for understanding but not for vengeance, a need for reparation but not for retaliation; a need for *ubuntu*[57] but not for victimization. In order to advance such reconciliation and reconstruction, amnesty shall be granted in respect of acts, omissions and offences associated with political objectives and committed in the course of the conflicts of the past. To this end, Parliament under this Constitution shall adopt a law determining a firm cut-off date, and providing for the mechanisms, criteria and procedures, including tribunals, if any, through which such amnesty shall be dealt with at any time after the law has been passed."[58] In short, the problem of amnesty is connected with the overriding necessity for "National Unity and Reconciliation."[59] With the phrase "amnesty shall be granted" the course is set for amnesty; however not for general amnesty or it would neutralize the process of reconciliation.

To be asserted: the course was determined well before the vote on amnesty *and* the truth findings. However, no matter how the amnesty law is worded, room must be made in the transitional phase for the amnesty question to be decided by a freely elected parliament. Nevertheless, *de lege lata* is the current state of the existing amnesty regulations.

3. The Exposing of Past Injustices through the Activity of the Truth Commission

The following arguments support "exposure" of past injustices (Option 3):

- Large segments of the population are not aware of the dimension of past crimes. Public exposure of past injustices is therefore necessary in order to avoid society's misconceptions of history which can potentially (among other things) glorify the authoritarian past and thus hinder the spread of a democratic orientation.
- Individuals and groups (parties, churches, etc.) in society carry guilt about crimes that were perpetrated by a totalitarian system. Comprehensive exposure and clarification of crimes can therefore help aid the transfer of responsibility to society at large.
- For a young democracy it is essential that responsibility be assigned to the past government for its activities. Otherwise, proceedings against former officials may be misconstrued as acts of individual caprice and will be omitted from public scrutiny. In addition, neglecting to assign responsibility could lead to a closing of ranks within the police, and military power structures and, generally, within the public service sector.

Option 3 is frequently used by countries whose system transition is characterized as that of a *political compromise*. Historical examples are El Salvador, Namibia, Nicaragua, and Uruguay.[60] Option 3 arguments are primarily connected to those in favor of Option 1: namely, if prosecution is not enforceable at least "the truth" about the crimes should come to light. "Truth is what you offer when you can't offer justice," comments the observer.[61] Justice must not necessarily be suspended in favor of truth, as the above-cited comment suggests. Instead of retribution — where justice is only first re-established when those who have committed human rights violations have been punished — a different result is introduced into the arena of international research on transitional processes. Thus, the approach of many young democracies that have had to deal with their past is the following: the knowledge of the truth about a crime is just as important as justice. "Such an approach holds that knowledge of the truth is the most important part of a process of healing."[62] Exposure is thus a third option between prosecution on the one hand and the forgetting of the past, on the other.

In view of system change in South Africa, specific arguments for Option 3 are highlighted: the key terms are *apartheid* and *"African traditional justice system."*[63] With this option all of the power is concentrated in overcoming the consequences of *apartheid* and the emphasis is on "nation building." (One could say that the expression "Nation Building" becomes in the course of the discussion an opposing concept to "apartheid.") However, in order to "build" a new nation South Africa must know its history which necessitates a "common memory." This "common memory" among other things may be able to accomplish the following: "it will provide a basis for a collective acknowledgement of the illegitimacy of apartheid; it will facilitate the building of a culture of public ethics for the first time in South Africa and it will make room for genuine reconciliation; it will enable privileged South Africans to face up to collective understanding and, therefore, responsibility for the past in which only they had voting rights; finally it will allow for a necessary process of historical catharsis as the previously excluded speak at last for themselves, and the privileged caste joins the South African family for the first time."[64] Main features of the "African traditional justice system" reflect the phrase: "there is a need for *ubuntu*." The necessity for *ubuntu* lies in acceptance that "no one is a person without other people."[65] The Zulu word (which in German is only partially communicated by "humanity" [*Menschlichkeit*]) expresses respect for the other person. "When I destroy the humanity of another," says Tutu, "then I ultimately destroy my own."[66] The need for "humanity" does not wish the destruction of the offenders, but desires their reintegration into society. "Reconciliation is in Africa a collective concept. The community should be re-established."[67] However, when I set out to destroy another person I can no longer be reconciled with them. In the context of South Africa justice does not mean "vengeful justice" or "blood for blood." C. Villa-Vicencio says: "If justice, however, means that people who were once perpetrators are now able to participate in the building of a new society, then a constructive justice can emerge from vengeful justice. Justice and reconciliation are then synonymous."[68] Where the prosecution of serious human rights violations is not politically enforceable, then the course is set for exposure. R. Goldstone says incisively: "There is a far more efficient and satisfactory way of accounting for the past and that is to expose it."[69] The initial situation is characterized as such: "Many people had an intuition that human right's violations were there, but always wished that it was never true."[70]

Certainly the question of the correct strategy by which to overcome the past was not an item for political debate about the democratic future of South Africa (CODESA). Nevertheless, the course was set for processing the past in a transitional phase, which is obvious from its connections to the amnesty debate. As we saw under Option 2, a general amnesty in South Africa was not feasible because it would have meant amnesia; for if amnesty is to be granted, then at least the truth should come to light. At the height of the amnesty debate in 1992 the idea was first conceived of establishing a Truth Commission in South Africa. The processing of the past in connection with the forming of a "commission" appears also to have its pragmatic reasons: a commission is able to provide a context — or a forum — for reconciliation upon which a "common memory" could be maintained, while at the same time keeping the tension "between the politics of compromise and the radical notion of justice."[71] Politics thus creates parameters.

According to the *results* of the discussion in Option 3, I agree with the statement of the Executive Secretary of the IDASA: "South Africa has decided to say no to amnesia and yes to remembrance; to say no to full-scale prosecution and yes to forgiveness."[72] As a regulative idea I therefore submit that reconciliation is not possible without truth.

4. Reparations to the Victims

The following arguments support reparations:

- An official recognition of the victims' suffering contributes to a re-establishment of their worth. Accordingly, previously pursued persons are able to gain some self-respect in the new society.
- Reparations to the victims are vital so that, from their perspective, the injustice does not continue. Such treatment of the victims reinforces the legitimacy of a young democracy.

- A democracy is dependent upon the support of all kinds of populations, even those of the victims. Rehabilitation with its goal of inclusiveness in the new order advances the stability of a fledgling democracy.
- Without rehabilitation of the victims there can be no subsequent reconciliation with the functionaries of the old order, which ultimately results in endangerment of the social rewards of transition to a democracy.
- International agreements make the question of reparations for the young democracy a pressing one.[73]

How should the suffering of victims of Apartheid be "compensated" for? If one thinks of "the three and one half million blacks in South Africa who were driven from their land," "how should justice be re-established?" B. Naudé sees it realistically: "Humanly speaking it is impossible" and argues "If we make justice a condition of reconciliation, then will reconciliation in our sinful world is impossible."[74] From the beginning it is clear that any attempt to do justice to the term reparation is impossible. Quite simply, reparations in the sense of complete material compensation are impossible in South Africa in view of the sheer dimensions of the incurred injustices. Reparations would not only by far exceed the capabilities of the country, they would have to be considered in the context of Option 4: the course is set in the transitional phase whereby the legislation of apartheid can not be retrospectively declared illegal (compare the models for Option 1 and 2).[75]

How can reparations take place under these conditions? In the debate, the arguments in favor of reparations are connected to those closely related to the exposure of past injustices. Thus, in Option 3: if justice can not be exercised in the sense of criminal law then at least the truth about the crimes must officially come to light. The argument is that if justice can not be expected in the sense of full material reparations, then at least the suffering of the victims must officially come to light. Accordingly, the basic need of the victims to have their suffering acknowledged will be officially recognized. "Most of the black people are walking around with things that are really disturbing them and they couldn't come to terms with what happened to them in their lives."[76] The definition of "truth" in terms of Option 3 is thus extended on the basis of specific criteria: it does not have to do with mere *factual truth*, but also with *truth as acknowledgement*; it has to do no longer with the reduction of *factual truth* on the basis of legal application, but also with a *healing truth*. The South African discussion connects both aspects of truth in its own experience as well as in the international experience of the Truth Commission. R. Goldstone writes about the omissions of an investigative commission that he himself had chaired[77]: "My commission has never told South Africans anything they did not really know. It was not so much knowledge that was being sought but acknowledgement from an official source."[78] With these remarks, Goldstone raises a decisive point for a future Truth Commission. Through his work he recognized the significance of the victim's perspective: "An official exposure of what caused their hurt and suffering is the only way to enable them to begin their healing."[79] History itself shows these experiences in dealing with the victims for South Africa are very important.

A. du Toit, one of the architects of the South African TRC, reveals that torture was used as a political tool during the era of Apartheid. "It had to do (above all) for the perpetrators to demonstrate to their victims that 'You can scream all you want, but nobody will hear you! And when you tell your story, nobody will believe you. Because in our land torture doesn't exist!'"[80] "That," says du Toit, "is the core of an authoritarian and undemocratic regime." In contrast, it is extremely important that when the victims are for the first time able to publicly tell their stories they encounter an attitude of appreciation: "We are really listening and taking your word as experience and you don't have to prove it. We accept that these things happened."[81] With the decision that *truth is acknowledgement,* the worth of the victims is again reinstated and in the process a contribution is made to the democratization of society.

As outlined above in the key term *ubuntu,* the question of reparations also arises: the view of justice in the sense of implementation of rights (be it through prosecution or material compensation) addresses only marginally the need for justice for many victims of apartheid. R. Goldstone brings the problem of rights and justice to the point: "fundamental to all forms of justice is official acknowledgement of what happened, whether by criminal process or by truth commission."[82] The victims must be at the center, otherwise the discussions about penal law or amnesty, lawsuits or truth commissions only arrive at a "highly stylized debate of the white middle class," which has nothing to do with the needs of the people on the "grass root level."[83] A litigious western style of thinking is therefore set against the background of a political history of oppression and of African culture and is something foreign to many South Africans who suffered under apartheid.

To be asserted: within the political transition process the path is set for moral reparations. Victims should be compensated so that their stories of suffering are officially acknowledged. The idea that reconciliation has something to do with acknowledgement is regulative.

5. Professional "Disqualification" of Complicit Co-Workers

The following arguments are in favor of sanctions beyond prosecution, as in the emptying of public offices of implicated co-workers:

- Democracy respects the law. It must be made clear that no one is above the law; not even those in high office or the military.
- A democratic process is not reliably possible without a change of the elite.
- Should the police or the military succeed by political influence to become free of prosecution, a country is still not a democracy and must fight on for the establishment of a democratic structure.
- The exclusion of charged people from public office is necessary, including police and military, in order for the loyalty of the executive branch vis-à-vis the new government to secure and usher in the process of reform.

South Africa can learn from neighboring Namibia that a comprehensive concept of political reconciliation after system change includes all populations and classes. The former Prime Minister Hage Geingob said about the beginning of his government: "the government's reconciliation effort is based on bringing together estranged communities, estranged politically, militarily or socially, into one non-antagonistic whole, all working towards a common goal of making a better Namibia."[84] This concept of reconciliation was also the engine for the South African transitional process. The nature of system change, which was similar in Namibia to that of a political compromise, is to maintain the continuity of the police and the military. From that standpoint it is understandable that Option 5 was discussed in South Africa at the beginning of the 1990s, above all in connection with Option 2 (amnesty). Contrary to the position of police and military who want amnesty for all crimes, there are the interests of exposing crimes which, above all, are represented by segments of the population containing the victims of the most serious human rights violations. Thus, Option 5 is also discussed in connection with Option 3 (exposure). If the military isn't prosecuted, at least the truth about their involvement in human rights violations needs to come to light.

If Option 1 (prosecution) fails, then Option 5 (professional disqualification of implicated co-workers of the apartheid regime) should still be maintained. However South Africa must consider two basic hazards in dealing with sanctions outside of criminal law, which includes the military and the security police: if the transfer government is too lenient then the democratic beginning can be jeopardized, but if it is too harsh, it won't command loyalty. In the worst case scenario, a coup can loom on the horizon. Thus, the politics of President F. de Klerk aimed for balance. The Further Indemnity Act served also to integrate loyal employees of the office of security police. The hard-liners in the police and military, who did not want to cooperate with the process of democratization, were isolated. The government and the ANC acted to integrate soldiers from the armed resistance into the South African armed forces. Certainly the military and the police lost political influence in the course of the transfer process, which also thus indicates that they could not enact a general amnesty. But their influence did not disappear entirely, which is reflected in the proceedings of Kempton Park where G. Werle remarked in summary: "And despite the revolutionary substance the transitional constitution forces an external continuity in the law, police, and military."[85]

To be asserted: prior to the vote the path was set against job disqualification of implicated co-workers of the apartheid regime, including the police and the military. For democratization to work, the functionaries of the old order must be held responsible. The idea is regulative that reconciliation includes the integration of all professions.

6. Analysis of "Regulative Clauses" Behind the Initial Political Conditions for Reconciliation in South Africa

The following analysis of regulative statements is made with the goal of preparing the groundwork for the Question of Correspondence in Part III. Conditions for political reconciliation need to be established first in order to test the subsequent "regulative statements" on their fundamental connection to theological reconciliation.[86] One may term "regulative statements" as the "steering mechanism for thinking and speaking with which a person or a group is tested and which provides for orderly activity."[87] The preceding empirical analysis of the initial conditions immediately yields "regulative ideas" about reconciliation, which were guiding in the political debate. They emerged "behind" the debate as, for example, the way in which the arguments articulated the different political options that were positioned opposite each other in the South African debate. Regulative ideas were operative, such as:

- Reconciliation is not possible without truth.
- Reconciliation has something to do with acknowledgement.
- Reconciliation means an all-inclusive invitation to integrate into society.

Systematically establishing "regulative clauses" involves the attempt to communicate the underlying "implicit axioms" (for example, the political debate). In an "implicit axiom," formulated statements are not the key issue; one must go back to an analysis of the statements that exist behind the debate. With regard to our problem this means that "regulative statements" are not synonymous with quotations taken from participants in the reconciliation process in South Africa; rather these quotations are guided by certain "implied axioms." Many of the collected statements about reconciliation suggest the "implicit axiom" of process theory. An analysis of "regulative statements" aims at the unfolding a "commonality of the usage of language"[88] (in our case the *political*). The aggregate of political expressions concerning reconciliation can be understood by looking back to the empirically analyzed statement that says the gap between overcoming the past (apartheid) and the building of a nation (nation building) has priority among political decision makers.[89]

The political form of reconciliation assumes a specific function in the process of "nation building": "reconciliation should bring together into dialogue the different groups in South Africa which otherwise stand as opponents in war."[90] The regulative statements that exist behind the political debate of the country can be stated as follows:

- Through "nation building," reconciliation overcomes the gap created by apartheid.

One could say that this statement (i.e., nation building) leads either directly or indirectly into the political debate as a whole.[91] Beneath this level, other activities have been viewed in the political discourse as instrumental by representatives of human rights organizations, the ANC, and the church. Which statements are regulative behind these political powers? With regard to reconciliation I suggest:

- Reconciliation cannot be brought about by apartheid, rather only between people, who have guilt towards each other as the result of past politics.

- Reconciliation can choose not to levy punishment on the perpetrators, but it can not punish the truth about the incurred injustices.
- Reconciliation demands a "common memory"; with a common memory different opposing views can co-exist that otherwise exist across a divide.
- Reconciliation demands another type of justice as retributive justice.
- Reconciliation excludes revenge.
- Reconciliation is society-building; *ubuntu* makes possible the position for reconciliation.
- Reconciliation presupposes the readiness to work with a new South Africa.

Among the above-mentioned political powers, above all in the ANC, there are some voices which, along with others, partially oppose the implicit axioms, especially those that are ready to support the complex issue of "reconciliation and justice":

- Basic rights are not to be sacrificed in favor of national unity.
- Reconciliation excludes the right of the individual to bring their tormentors to justice.

F. de Klerk and K. Asmal indicate how the understanding of reconciliation within South Africa can be directed by mutually exclusive axioms. We cited above de Klerk's opinion: "to randomly alter or undo what we have done in the spirit of reconciliation and the maintaining of security and stability in South Africa." Which "implied axiom" is recognizable here? Behind his statement is hidden the "regulative statement" still at work from the days of apartheid:

- Reconciliation means the toleration of the division of former days.

K. Asmal grew up in a small South Africa town where it was expected that he should make room on the street for any white person that he encountered. From the above-cited sentence we have: "reconciliation is a shared and painful ethical voyage from wrong to right." This sentence contains the implied axiom:

- Reconciliation assumes that apartheid is recognized as a "crime against humanity."

II. Symbolic Forms Used in the Political
Assessment of Systemic Injustice

The preceding discussion of the options for action is descriptive of the paths used by past politics in the political context of South Africa. These institutions are the visible results of past political discussions that figure in political reality.

At the close of the South African debates in 1995, the TRC was formed. Before we update the symbolic forms of expression as well as the political-historical consequences resulting from the work of the South African Truth Commission, we must first distinguish the different options for action that were made available by the functioning of the commission in the past political discussion of South Africa between 1990 and 1994. Then we will explain how the TRC not only contributed to the exposure of apartheid injustices (Option 3); but by its suggestions for reparations during the hearings how it also contributed to reparations for the victims (Option 4); and how it was able under legally regulated conditions to confer amnesty on perpetrators (Option 2), thereby suspending only temporarily the general validity of criminal law (Option 1).

1. Foundations of the Truth and Reconciliation Commission (TRC)

By virtue of the initial political conditions for reconciliation, the area for a legal settlement through the TRC is limited:

- The option for criminal punishment of the perpetrators and a general amnesty is eliminated.
- The question of amnesty is connected to the discovery of the truth.
- Past human rights violations must be viewed as non-partisan.
- Victims must be rehabilitated.

Further discussion of the parameters of a truth commission for South Africa involved what the scope of the period of activity should be; how the investigation period would be determined; what criteria would be used to choose the members of the commission; and how to achieve a balance between the legal task of dealing with perpetrators and that of a primarily therapeutic stance toward the victims.

On July 19, 1995 the Parliament passed the Promotion of National Unity and Reconciliation Act,[92] which was to form the legal foundation for the TRC:

- The period of activity of the perpetrators handled by the TRC will consist of 18 months (with the option of a 6-month extension)
- The period of investigation by the TRC will be from March 1, 1960, to a yet to be determined cut-off date.[93]
- The number of members of the commission will be between 11 and 17 persons, who will be appointed by the president according to a determined selection method.[94]

In order to do justice to the content of the proceedings resulting from the course that was set for its work, the TRC was divided into three different "committees":

- The Human Rights Violations Committee[95] was primarily concerned with past human rights violations and functioned primarily for the victims. The victims were able to tell their stories publicly, which also contributed to their ability to come to terms with the past. Thus, the task of moral rehabilitation (Option 4) encountered the need for exposure (Option 3), but also the need for impartiality.[96]
- The Amnesty Committee[97] will discuss the question of amnesty for offenders belonging to parties still in conflict. The desire for amnesty is connected to exposure (Option 3). The statements of offenders are — as are those of the victims — important sources for findings of truth. Again, non-partisanship is fundamental.
- The Committee on Reparation and Rehabilitation[98] is occupied with the question of reparations to the victims who suffered human rights violations and will make recommendations for possible compensation (Option 4).

The job of the TRC encompassed, among other things:

- "establishing as complete a picture as possible of the causes, nature and extent of the gross violations of human rights." Act No. 34 (1995), Ch. 2. Sec. 3 (1) (a)
- "facilitating the granting of amnesty." Act No. 34 (1995), Ch. 2. Sec. 3 (1) (b)
- "establishing and making known the fate or whereabouts of victims." Act No. 34 (1995), Ch. 2. Sec. 3 (1) (c)

- "compiling a report . . . which contains recommendations." Act No. 34 (1995), Ch. 2. Sec. 3 (1) (d)

The commission worked independently and in the absence of any advice, had its own budget, staff, and organizational composition. It was able to summon witnesses, to interrogate, and to swear in. In addition, it had the right to search and seizure, as well as to make decisions about material and state employee positions. However, the TRC was not a court: it could not judge anyone, but it could make decisions regarding amnesty applications and conduct its own internal investigation. Thus, the oversight of the amnesty committee went beyond that of other committees.[99] Once a decision was made by the amnesty committee, no further legal determinations were allowed with respect to criminal prosecution or civil rights liability.

The South African Truth Commission has made legal history with respect to the material connection between process and amnesty. Through the National Unity and Reconciliation Act amnesty legislation was passed which for the first time allowed the offenders to cooperate in the amnesty process. If amnesty is at all an act of mercy, then the offender should at least be able to contribute to his own amnesty. Individual amnesty is consequently tied to conditions: the whole truth must be told.[100] In addition, the deed must have a core political motive; the reasonableness of the remedy must be allowable; and the amnesty claim had to be submitted within a certain time frame, namely up to May 10, 1997.

The prescribed time limit in which the amnesty claims had to be lodged gave the process an internal dynamic since the prospect of exemption from punishment was granted only within a specific time frame. Where offenders failed to lodge a request for amnesty or where their claim was rejected by the TRC, prosecution posed a real threat for them at the end of the commission's work. The TRC thus also contributed to the precedent whereby the implementation of punishment as recompense for serious human rights violations are accepted only within a limited time period (Option 1). W. Kistner[101] upholds the constructive connection of options for action mandated by the TRC: "Indeed, one must distinguish between that which is short-term and that which is long-term in the service of justice. In the short term, one is inclined to say that the offender must be punished. In the long term it is very important that what has happened comes to light." And against the background of the political initial requirements of South Africa, L. du Plooy said: "I don't think the TRC is the best option, but it is the best option we have at the moment."[102]

2. Documentation of Selected Testimonies of the TRC and of the "Participating Observer"

C. Villa-Vicencio observes: "The TRC Act can do no more than lay the foundation for reconciliation to happen. The completion of this process lies in the hand of every peace loving individual."[103] However, the individuals appear as a collective because the testimonies of the TRC create a *forum* for reconciliation.

From October 14 to 16, 1996, the stories of victims of the apartheid era were heard in the City Hall of Paarl, a farm community near Cape Town.[104] Close to the entrance of the hall the white *Taal* Monument towers on the mountainside above the buildings and against the blue sky. *Taal* is Afrikaans and means "language." The monument is a symbol of the Afrikaans language which originated from the Dutch.[105] In the stronghold of white Afrikaners enough statements concerning human rights violations can be gathered to warrant TRC testimony.[106] From among these "statements," certain individuals are chosen to make public statements based upon certain criteria.[107]

At the entrance of the city hall the police search the audience for weapons. The room, which has been decorated for the event, is well attended. The members of the commission have taken their places at tables which are covered with white tablecloths and arranged in semi-circles on the stage of the city hall. The victims who will be telling their stories today sit together with their families a bit apart from the commission and from the others gathered in the hall. The victims sit on the stage and take their places at a table that is placed so that they have eye contact both with the commission and with the audience. A pastor makes the "opening statement":[108]

Rev. Maart: Good morning, I welcome you, the commissioners of the Truth and Reconciliation Commission, on behalf of the Paarl community. We are grateful to you for the important work that you are doing and for all that you are doing to promote the cause of peace and reconciliation within this country. We believe this process is absolutely necessary for the healing of our land. . . . The legacy which we inherited as a town is one that caused much pain and suffering, which both communities suffered. . . . People were afraid of a knock on the door. It could mean death or arrest; many of us were arbitrarily incarcerated under the emergency laws of 1985. . . . It was the arbitrary tear gassing of people — just ask the people of Mbekweni[109] about tear gassing, they will tell you. A lady was busy working in the kitchen preparing supper and somebody arbitrarily threw a tear gas canister into the house. Old people died as (a) result, children's lives have been wrecked — some of them for life. I want to ask this morning who were the persons in the blue bakkie which drove through Mbekweni shooting randomly at people, innocent people sitting on a — on a stop. Who was it? Who caused the death of so many people, torturing them? Who are responsible for Philemon Maxam's desperate act, to go and fill on a farm, a white farmer and a servant in order to get arms? . . . We in the valley are hopeful of our future, there are signs of change. . . . That South Africa will as of now be a symbol . . . of national reconciliation and racial harmony. Of co-existence between black and white. . . . This is our dream of the dawning of a new millennium.

Today in Paarl eight stories are heard. Among them is the story of Conraad van Rooyen:

Dr. Orr: Good morning Mr. van Rooyen, you got up early this morning to drive all the way from Saldanha and we say thank you very much to you. Before we listen to your story would you please stand to take the oath.

Dr. Orr: Thank you, I will ask Glenda Wildschut to lead you through your evidence.

Ms. Wildschut: Good morning, Mr. Van Rooyen, how are you this morning? Is everything well? Thank you that you have come here today; thank you that you've agreed to share your story with us. You are from Saldanha and your story is about a shooting incident in Saldanha in 1987. Would you please tell us a little bit more about yourself, where you work, what do you do, and then proceed with your story.

Mr. Van Rooyen: I am Conraad van Rooyen, I live in Saldanha. At present, after the shooting incident, I work as a construction worker. I — I am a trained welder. After this incident I can't work continuously any more because three or four times a month I have to go to see the doctor. And this causes that employers are not very interested in me and therefore I do construction work which I can do for short periods at a time. . . .

Ms. Wildschut: Please go ahead — please go ahead with your story.

Mr. Van Rooyen: A few of us — a few friends were spending the day together at the beach. We stayed there the whole day. . . . While we were there . . . we heard sounds like (fire)crackers in the Diazville Township. We decided round about half past 6 that evening that we'd had enough and we were going home, . . . but unfortunately I had to pass a house where a policeman and his wife were living. His name was Johannes Stroebel. . . .

When I crossed the park . . . people were scattering in various directions. I did not know what was going on and I decided just to go ahead. . . . I started running because I became frightened because at that specific day children were wounded in Saldanha. I started running. . . . This policeman followed me and he shot . . . into my back. I ran into somebody's yard. I jumped over the fence to try and get to my own house. I was wearing a black sweater and that got caught in the fence and at that stage he got the chance to grab me and pull me back. He swore at me and he took the butt of the shot gun and he started hitting my head. When I fell . . . he kept on hitting my head. Fortunately, I must have lost consciousness because the bystanders said he took me by my sweater and dragged me across the road to his house. My family . . . went to fetch my wife. I was in his yard at that stage — he kept on kicking me and hitting me with the butt of the shot gun. That's what the people said because I had lost consciousness. When — in my yard he told my wife and children that if they came any nearer . . . he would shoot them dead, so they remained at a safe distance. That evening a police van came — they put me into that police van. I was unconscious and the bystanders said they kept on assaulting me in this police van. And they then took me to the Charge Office, there I partly regained my consciousness and I remembered that they dragged me to the cells. That night when I regained my full consciousness I felt very cold and all — the whole cell was flooded with water. And I sat huddled in a little corner, most of the time I was half conscious and I spent the night like that. The next morning I heard the rattling of keys; one Constable, Stroebel's wife, said: "Open this cell that I can see what this pig looks like. This pig who threw stones at my house." And she said: "Why did you throw stones at my house?" And I asked: "Was it me, I couldn't remember that I've done that." And she said: "Close the door and let this pig just die." A little while afterwards I shouted through the window that I wanted to see the officer in charge, now he was Captain or Lieutenant Kitchener. I asked to see him because I was urinating and vomiting blood and I would like to go and see a doctor. Could he send somebody to take me to the doctor. For the whole day he showed no interest and I was suffering extreme pain for that whole Monday. The next morning the police opened the cell and I asked them to please take me to see a doctor because I was going to die and he then said: "Bring him out." And I was standing there — I was crawling rather from the cell and I asked please — please take me to a doctor because I'm going to die. Then he decided take him, put him in the police van and take him to the doctor. They drove at a high speed to the doctor; it was 11 km to the hospital. I sat there for a whole hour at the hospital and I asked them — they could ask the police who had accompanied me please to take me to the doctor immediately because I am suffering extreme pain. When the doctor eventually examined me he said that I should have gone to Tygerberg Hospital on the Sunday already because I was bleeding internally. I can't remember how I came to Tygerberg Hospital but on that Wednesday morning they operated (on) me — on my stomach. Afterwards I stayed in hospital under police protection for three to four weeks. I've asked my attorney — I approached an attorney — why — there was police guidance in this hospital and my attorney had said — instituted a charge and the charge was that I was involved in stone throwing. When this court — when I appeared in court I was acquitted. This is what my story is about. . . .

Ms. Wildschut: Do you know which injuries you sustained or why you were operated on?

Mr. van Rooyen: According to the doctor I had internal injuries like my pancreas was injured, my intestines were damaged. And they had to remove that.

Ms. Wildschut: You know that our Investigating Unit has started investigating this whole matter and I will read a small bit of the report they've compiled so far: The book in the Police Station in which they write all the events of the day — this book (indistinct) shot by Constable Stroebel with shot gun and that he fired bird shot at you. But the entry makes a claim that the victim was not injured as a result of the shooting. (Unrest in the hall.) I — I'm — I think that most of us in this audience will struggle to understand the logic that you are shot but you are not injured as a result of the shooting. I do not have any more questions to ask you, I'll hand over to the Chairperson. I'm sure my colleagues might have questions to pose. . . .

Adv. Potgieter: You mentioned your family. Are you married? How many children do you have? What are they doing?

Mr. van Rooyen: I have four daughters and one son. Presently three of them are working. My son still attends school. At that time one daughter was at university, but after I was injured I could not afford it to keep her at university any more and she had to leave. The State gave me disability — they declared me and assisted me. I received a pension at that stage.

Adv. Potgieter: Do you receive it at the moment?

Mr. van Rooyen: Not any more.

Adv. Potgieter: And then a very last question. You say that you would like to work but at the moment you can only do piecemeal work because you have to go to the doctor regularly. Why do you have to go to the doctor regularly?

Mr. van Rooyen: Three or four times per month I have to go to Hospital because I have said I am a trained welder and if I work very hard I can't work the whole day through because I start to vomit. The doctor prescribed a tablet — Pentolax — a very small like the head of a match and . . . fourteen of those tablets cost R177-00 and that is the only medication which still helps today. This — if I take one in the morning, it helps me through the day otherwise I vomit all the food I take in. Once a month a specialist comes to Saldanha, Dr. Luyt, and he says — he said I need another operation to be completely healed. This operation will cost about R9,000-00.[110] I said to him in that case I will have to die because I do not have that kind of money. At the moment as you've said I am — do piecemeal construction work for periods of three weeks or four weeks, but three to four times per month I have to go and see the doctor.

Adv. Potgieter: Thank you very much. . . . Mr Van Rooyen, just one aspect, this policeman Stroebel he was a Constable in 1987 when he shot you and assaulted you in public and his wife was also a Police Officer?

Mr. van Rooyen: She was also a Constable.

Adv. Potgieter: So husband and wife were both Constables in 1987?

Mr. van Rooyen: They were both promoted — the wife is a Lieutenant at the moment and both of them are inspectors at the moment.

Adv. Potgieter: So both husband and wife have been promoted?

Mr. van Rooyen: After this incident they were promoted to Inspectors.

Adv. Potgieter: Are they still at the police in Saldanha?

Mr. van Rooyen: No, they are in Vredenburg at the moment. They are involved with the Vredenburg-Saldanha Police.

Adv. Potgieter: How do you feel about that? They were promoted and you are sitting with all the pain?

Mr. van Rooyen (calmly): I have friends at the moment who have progressed in life. They could build houses, they could buy motorcars. I could have been at that level as well but because of all these things which had happened to me I could not do the same things as my friends. And this policeman Stroebel was promoted all the time, he has — he owns a big house. I could have had that as well if it was not for this incident. I could have given my children a better life and a better education if it were not for all these things.

Ms. Gobodo: Thank you, I just want to say that we cannot begin to fathom the impact of the injuries that were inflicted upon yourself. On your person, on yourself as a man, on yourself as a potential earner and to say that it is very difficult for us to understand, to know fully what it means for you to suddenly be found — find out that you cannot be gainfully employed. But now you have been reduced to piece jobs — work that you can do only for two weeks. That kind of uncertainty as a result of injuries that were inflicted upon you for no apparent reason at all. . . . You suffered the abuse — the gross violations in Saldanha because you were excluded from the realm of humanity. Those policemen did what they did to you partly because they were policemen, but mostly because there was the race factor as well. Some of it — a lot of it has got to do with racism and you experienced it and you suffered the consequences of it and the consequences reflect also in the economic situation that you find yourself in now. . . . Thank you for coming this morning and for sharing with us your pain. We will do our best again to assist you in whatever way we can in sorting out some of the issues that you have raised in your statement. Thank you.

Mr. van Rooyen: Thank you very much. I appreciated that you could listen to my story.

Observations:[111]

- The stories tell of capricious acts according to the laws of the TRC, which are classified as serious human rights violations (which are illegal according to the laws of apartheid). The inhumanity is expressed here by the statement, "Just let this pig die."
- The statements show the difficulties of reparations (Option 4): pension and medical care are necessary. The case is passed along to the Reparations Committee of the TRC. Additionally, this story connects to the problem of the lack of cleanup in public offices (Option 5). According to African thinking, reparations can not come through a third party. Njeza makes this point: in order for the healing process to succeed, peace must be made with those who have thrown the victim's life off course. For Conrad van Rooyen, the TRC hearings may at least have initiated the healing process.[112]
- This case demonstrates an astonishing measure of calm. Despite the incurred injustice, van Rooyen expresses no feelings of revenge and exhibits no expression of rage even though he knows that his torturer was

promoted. Rather, he expresses a great deal of sadness: "It could have been me." In the context of African tradition and according to Kwenda, it is unlucky if the course of a life is interrupted. Only with a straight life course is one able to become an *Ahne* (ancestor). Therefore, healing must proceed. In any case, the straight course of the person's life will be reinstated through the hearings. The process helps to "channel" the sadness and to dignify the suffering, says Njeza.

- The level of reconciliation achieved, according to the classification[113] of the TRC, is on the level of one's own story ("Coming to terms with painful past"). In this case the TRC contributes to reconciliation in a very limited fashion; "the reconciliation of victims with their own pain is a deeply personal, complex and unpredictable process."[114] Reconciliation as the personal encounter with the past is the main event in the hearings of the human rights committee; it does not intend to bring together offenders and victims. The TRC contributes, however, by listening to the stories and through that listening, dignifying them. The "articulation" of what has happened plays a decisive role in African thinking. Most rituals begin with a story.[115] In every instance of demonstrated injustice other feelings are brought to the fore. The story of van Rooyen illustrates the job of the TRC: "The road to reconciliation . . . means both material reconstruction and the restoration of dignity."[116]

After Conraad van Rooyen is led out by his attendant, Philemon Maxan is asked to make his request.[117]

Ms. Gobodo: Good morning Mr. Maxam. . . . We welcome you — we welcome you this morning as you are going to give your testimony. A testimony that is different from the usual, a testimony of forgiveness, this is what this commission is about. We thank you for coming forward so that even those people that are still in the dark can see the necessity of coming forward to ask for forgiveness. Did you grow up in Mbekweni or did you grow up elsewhere?

Mr. Maxam: I was born in Mbekweni and I grew up in Mbekweni.

Ms. Gobodo: In 1985 and 1986 there was an organization here in the township. . . .

Mr. Maxam: As we should remember the violence in the townships warranted us to protect ourselves and the community as people who have been shot and killed and the police will just hang around the townships. . . .

Ms. Gobodo: Could you please tell the Commission about 1986, the incident in 1986 where Dr. Ivan Siebert's mother died.

Mr. Maxam: We will remember that . . . we needed arms. Because even the Government was armed within the townships. And [through] the underground structures of the African National Congress there were opportunities for us to acquire these firearms. It is in 1986 that I got involved in the shootings. We had to acquire our arms, as we had to protect ourselves. . . .

Ms. Gobodo: So what is it exactly that you want to say to the Siebert family?

Mr. Maxam: I . . . ask for forgiveness from the Siebert family and all those people that were badly affected. Even those who are still in prison, I ask for forgiveness from the parents of those imprisoned children.

Ms. Gobodo: Have you tried to get in touch with the Siebert family . . . ?

Mr. Maxam: The connection was between the ANC branch in Mbekweni; my elder brother went to the Siebert family, to ask for forgiveness. They appreciate the fact that I actually came out to ask for forgiveness, they have forgiven me.

Ms. Gobodo: Would you like to shake hands with the Siebert family to ensure forgiveness?

Mr. Maxam: I trust and believe that it is more real for one to shake hands with the forgiver rather than hear it on the radio or television.

Ms. Gobodo: So your request to the Commission is to bring you and the Siebert family together so as to ask for forgiveness in person.

Mr. Maxam: I would be very glad.

Ms. Gobodo: I am going to ask you a last question: what is your advice to us in connection with the Mbekweni community?

Mr. Maxam: So that previous sins are not committed again.

Ms. Gobodo: What is your advice to the Commission to ensure reconciliation between the two sides?

Mr. Maxam: As I've always said, besides the fact that I am here in the Commission, I think it is important that what is in the dark, what was performed in the previous resume, should be put in the light now. People should come forward, especially people from Mbekweni. Mbekweni is a peaceful community; you can walk even in the middle of the night and nothing will happen to you. Therefore it is becoming, it is only becoming for people to come forward and confess. I wish the people of Mbekweni absolute peace, even the people I have not mentioned here.

Ms. Gobodo: Thank you. I want to read a document here from Ivan Siebert with the permission of the Chairperson. "I am very happy that

Maxam wants to make peace, because I, too, felt the burden of the anger laying heavily on me over the years. I called his brother, Pat, last year to my office, and told him that I wanted to make peace with his family. I have no grudge against him (that is Philemon). I think that my mother would have wanted it this way. She would have done that act of kindness to anybody coming to her door. She was a type of person who wouldn't hold a grudge. So I am glad that Philemon is doing this for her and for me." I think that statement will go a long way in your heart, to relieve you, to relieve your burden. I hope that now you are in peace.

Mr. Maxam: I want to ask for forgiveness yet again. I want to ask my parents to forgive me, when they heard the news that I had murdered, they were obviously not happy about it, they were grieved, all these years they have been so grieved. My father died. . . . I ask for forgiveness from my home, even my children.

Adv. Potgieter: I just want to see if we can't be of assistance to you as well. The sentence that you are serving at this stage, does it relate to your activities in implementing the M-plan[118] in Mbekweni?

Mr. Maxam: Yes, Sir, it is so.

Adv. Potgieter: And were you convicted of — of how many offenses?

Mr. Maxam: Two offenses of murder and an offense of having broken into a shop. I was sentenced to ten years and two sentences of death. But because of my attorney, Ms. Jone, in 1992, March 23, according to the petition from Mbekweni with 68 signatures they then turned my sentence around to 25 years only. . . . During my prison term even before this sentence of 25 years, I realized that it is still very dark in our communities because there are people that I've left behind.

Adv. Potgieter: How long . . . must you still serve?

Mr. Maxam: It will be until 2004-2007 should I be serving effectively. . . .

Adv. Potgetier: . . . what I wanted to bring to your attention or to ask you is whether you are aware of the amnesty provisions which relates to this Commission and whether you have in fact applied?

Mr. Maxam: . . . I have been advised to apply for amnesty to the Truth Commission. I will — I can only follow the procedures if I receive guidance.

Adv. Potgieter: I just wanted to make sure that you are aware of that possibility. . . . It would be a pity if a person in your position, application from you is not considered or is not brought to the Commission at least for consideration. So I thank you very much for that information.

Ms. Gobodo: Thank you, you may go.

Observations:[119]

- African background: Reconciliation is not considered as transmitted, but rather as entirely objective. Njeda indicates that physical contact is important: "To shake hands" is for Maxam "more real" than to see reconciliation on the television.
- It occurs to me that Maxam is seeking re-entry into his community. He wants to "make peace with his community." The hearings play an important role in this. "Yes, I believe many have experienced the TRC as cleansing," says Kwenda in a speech: "They can now return entirely different into the community." The guilt, caused through the offence, is cleansed. "It is a way of cleansing the soul, cleansing the conscience, cleansing the mind."[120] Kwenda also alludes to the fact that a ritual is considered binding once it is completed. The community can no longer make reference to the "offense."
- Interestingly enough, Maxam uses "Christian" terminology of "sin" and "confession" when talking about the TRC. Kwenda indicates: Sin as an ontological concept does not exist in the African conceptuality. Instead, "sin" is spoken of in terms of "doing wrong." It occurred to me: Maxam reflects on his "wrong-doing" using the concepts of "dark" or "light" ("I realized that it is still very dark in our communities because there are people that I've left behind"). According to Kwenda, the relationship of dark to light is a very important one in African thought.[121] The meaning is that everything will come to light! An African saying is: One cannot wrap up an animal with horns (that is: the horns will always stick out of the wrapper).
- The repeated reference to the community of Mbekweni appears to have still another meaning: here reconciliation cuts across several levels; the individual and society are inseparable — reconciliation occurs between victims and offenders. But the deed also concerns the individual family as well as the community. Forgiveness must be requested. Thus, forgiveness is obviously not just an individual matter. The Commissioner understands this: "Forgiveness is what the Commission is about."
- The first level of reconciliation is between people ("Reconciliation between victim and perpetrator").[122] It is interesting here that the son of the victim, Dr. Siebert, seeks reconciliation. The assumption is clear that only *together* can the past be overcome in such a way that does not burden the future. The second level of reconciliation is between levels of offenders and the community (Mbekweni), "Reconciliation at a community level";[123] reconciliation with family members is also sought.

In the twenty-hour newscast the photos of the day appear again displaying the TRC-Banners, the tables with white cloths and flowers in the city hall of Paarl. The next day's headlines in the daily news read: "Killer sorry — and victim's son bears no grudge." The case of Philemon Maxam is taken up again by the Amnesty Committee of the TRC in July 1997, three-quarters of a year later.[124] Classified as a "gross human rights violation," it *must* be heard in public. The chairperson opens the amnesty hearings with the statement of proceedings:

Chairperson: This is a session of the Amnesty Committee comprised of myself, Judge Wilson on my right and Ms. Khampepe on my left, and we are ready to commence proceedings this morning in connection with the applications of Mr. Maxam, Mr. Ndinisa, and Mr. Tisana. Please come forward and place yourselves on record.

After the swearing-in, the attorney for the applicant has the first chance to cross-examine. Advocate Lourens attempts to underscore the political background of the Maxam murders.

Adv. Lourens: . . . It is correct that the term of imprisonment that you are serving now is the result of an incident that occurred on 15 April 1986?

Mr. Maxam: Yes, it is.

Adv. Lourens: You spoke about the fight against the government and that violence had to be met with violence.

Mr. Maxam: A lot of things happened especially December, late 1985. We were burying people all the time. . . . There were police vans patrolling the place. They did not do anything about this. . . . The situation at Mbekweni was terrible. Even the people who were delivering furniture at Mbekweni could not go in. . . . Our people were being destroyed. We decided that we needed weapons. I said . . . that the ANC was saying that it supported us buying our own weapons to protect our own communities against the enemy or we could get arms from farms, white people's farms, because they kept a lot of weapons. . . .

Adv. Lourens: So, do I understand you correctly that at this stage when the situation, as you described, was terrible, there seemed to be civil war in Mbekweni, you decided that it was time to retaliate and do something about it? Is that correct?

Mr. Maxam: Yes, that is so.

As the lawyer tries to expand the discussion about the political circumstances, the chairperson interrupts and steers the proceedings to the event; namely, the circumstances of the amnesty appeal. Philemon Maxam eventually comes to speak about the farm.

Mr. Maxam: We went to the farm believing that we would get weapons. When you were at Mbekweni you could see, you can see the farm. . . . When we got to the house we did not go to the door. I saw someone in the house. The rest of the youth went around to the door. I asked for water from the lady that I saw from inside so that she could open her window. I was then going to request for her to open the door after she had opened the window. We had not gone to fight any particular person in the house. All we wanted was weapons. . . . As she was giving us the water and I had the glass in my hand, then I asked her to open the door. I could talk to her face to face as she had opened the window. There were others standing around me as well. I said to her we were armed, but even though I am armed I have not come to shoot anybody, but to defend myself, because what we wanted were weapons. During that exchange of words I think Madoda Tisana[125] grabbed the lady. He grabbed the lady because she was refusing to open the door. This lady screamed. As I was just next to Madoda I took out my gun as she was screaming and I shot inside. As I was shooting I was pointing towards her even though I did not realize that when Madoda let go of her, I thought that she had fallen down. The other had broken the kitchen door down. . . . I heard someone saying that we must beware. When they screamed out we got out running. I had not realized that I had shot this lady already. I shot at her again, because I did not want her to be able to identify us if the police came or the neighbors. The gardener was outside.

Adv. Lourens: When you had planned now to go to the farm house, to Vlakkeland, did you, was it part of your plan that you would kill people who were possibly standing in your way of obtaining firearms?

Mr. Maxam: It was not part of our plan to shoot anybody. . . .

After the members of the Commission and the attorney for the prosecution have heard the statements of Maxam, the case for amnesty is examined. Was the robbery of the farm politically motivated or a criminal act? Did the applicants act solely from personal motivations?

Judge Wilson: What about all the other things that were taken from the house? You told us you were the one who went into the house and searched.

Mr. Maxam: Truly, I did not take anything personally. . . .

Judge Wilson: I ask you again, what happened to the other things that were taken out of the house by these young people who had gone there with you whom you had planned to go to this house with?

Mr. Maxam: This is a good question. They will know. The people who took them will know what they did with them.

Judge Wilson: Were you ever told . . . that things were stolen including a video recorder, jewelry of considerable value, a large quantity of clothing and R220,000 in cash? Do you say you were not aware . . . that any of these things had been stolen . . . ?

Mr. Maxam: Sir, please do not make me appear like a liar. This happened very fast and we had to escape. We all just ran in different directions. If anybody stole anything from there, they must answer for themselves. . . .

Judge Wilson: So you are asking us to accept the fact that when you went and searched the house, as you told us in some detail a short time ago, that you led the others in to search the bedrooms and the other cupboards, you did not notice that they were taking things like a video recorder, large quantities of clothing, jewelry, money? You are asking us to believe that, are you?

Mr. Maxam: I want the Committee to know that I, as Philemon Kabila Maxam, did not take anything else except what I am talking about. I will not come here and swear and deceive the Committee. . . .

Another member of the Commission, Sisi Khampepe, leads the examination of the political motive for the deed.

Ms. Khampepe: So, in short, your response is that you never had an opportunity to discuss among yourselves what had been stolen in the house in question? You never had that opportunity?

Mr. Maxam: I did not have this opportunity.

Ms. Khampepe: Were you in charge of the operation which involved the intention of stealing arms from the house in question?

Mr. Maxam: Yes, that is so.

For the Chairman of the Amnesty Committee the question remains open, whether or not the murder of the woman was politically motivated. From the cross-examination:

Judge Wilson: You asked for a glass of water so that she opened the window and she handed out the water to you. Is that not so?

Mr. Maxam: Yes, that is so.

Judge Wilson: So she was an arm's length away from you and would have a very good view of you. If you were too frightened of being arrested why did you not hold back, why did you not let someone else do this, because now you had to kill her?

Mr. Maxam: To answer the question, I was the person who asked for water and we were there with the intention to look for weapons, all of us. I had to be the one to ask her to open the door for us so that we can search the house. . . .

Chairperson: I want you to understand and think carefully. You knew that she would have a good view of your face when you went there and stood at the window and asked her for water. You knew that, that she would have a good look at your face.

Mr. Maxam: Yes, that is correct, she could see me.

Chairperson: . . . You killed her because you were afraid she was going to identify you. That is also correct?

Mr. Maxam: Yes, that is correct. She was going to identify us to the police.

For the amnesty decision it is crucial whether the applicant assumes responsibility for the deed. His attorney therefore asks him:

Adv. Lourens: Mr. Maxam, do you take responsibility for the shooting?

Mr. Maxam: Yes, I do take responsibility for the shooting.

The attorney for the victim, Mr. Swart, is moved in another place in the hearing to bring the political motive of the applicant into question.

Mr. Swart: Now, the domestic worker and the gardener were surely part of the oppressed rather than of the regime. They were not your political opponents and yet you killed them.

Mr. Maxam: Yes, that was my statement. It was very difficult for us to do this, because these people were also oppressed. We wanted them to be liberated also, but this incident happened to them. That is why I made amnesty to the Commission and I asked for forgiveness to the members of the family, and Mrs. Siebert's son . . . forgave me and the community in Mbekweni also forgave me. . . . I am not here to the Commission to ask for forgiveness, because I feel guilty.

An additional criterion for a decision in favor of amnesty is the believability of the applicant. Whether or not Maxam is telling the truth is determined by means of previous documents from the proceedings. The opposing council, Mr. Swart, tries to entangle the applicant in contradictions. He has made other statements in past proceedings than those he now makes before the TRC. I would like to single out one example that was dealt with in detail during the hearings. Mr. Swart cites from the proceedings documents.

Mr. Swart: It goes on further to say, "He noticed the gardener who had been tied up with wire and heard someone shout that the gardener should also be shot otherwise he would implicate them. The appellant thereupon shot him and the gang made its getaway."

Mr. Maxam: That somebody shouted and said I must shoot, because we are going to be identified by the gardener, that is not true. Crosby Ndinisa said I must not shoot. Nobody said I must shoot. It was just a way to protect myself from the court itself. Nobody said I must shoot. I thought that I must shoot myself so that nobody could identify me. That is the truth.

Mr. Swart: Was the gardener tied up with wire?

Mr. Maxam: Not as I saw him as he was lying there.

Mr. Swart: How did you protect yourself by telling the court or making a statement to say that he was tied up when you shot him?

Mr. Maxam: At the time I heard, even from the police, that he had been tied up with the wire. I thought I should take it as the police heard it. I am personally not certain whether he was tied up with wire. Nobody said I must shoot either. I just shot. I was given no such order. . . .

Mr. Swart: Was it not the policy of your organization only to shoot people in self-defense?

Mr. Maxam: It is self-defense, it is protection, you are protecting yourself when you are shooting somebody so that they are not able to identify you. . . .

Judge Wilson: You said it happens a lot "in our organization." I am asking you what is the organization.

Mr. Maxam: I am talking about the African National Congress. . . .

Mr. Swart: Mr. Maxam, must we accept that you would have shot any person you found on the premises, because they could have identified you?

Mr. Maxam: That is so. . . . Truly, we went there to look for weapons and if we found anyone else in that place we would have killed them, whether we found weapons or not; even if it was not the two people who were there.

The hearings end abruptly. The Chairperson of the Amnesty Committee is allowed to pronounce judgment over Maxam and both of the co-applicants: "We accept that the Applicants regarded it as necessary that they should follow . . . instruction and obtain firearms so that they could achieve what they regarded as their legitimate political objectives. . . . We are satisfied there was no personal gain. . . . We turn now to the murders. It is clear from the evidence that there had been no prior discussion as to the killing of any person during this operation. There was *no* suggestion in the evidence that this was regarded as a *political objective* within their express or implied authority. . . . There was no need to kill these people in the furtherance of any instructions from the A.N.C. or elsewhere. The killing was justified by the Applicant (Philemon Maxam) on the ground that he did not want the deceased to identify him. This is not, in our view, an act which falls within the provisions of Section 20 (1) (b) or 20 (2) of the Promotion of National Unity and Reconciliation Act no. 34 of 1995. We are further of the view that the killing of these two innocent people was so *disproportionate to the aims* sought to be achieved, that is to obtain arms with which to defend themselves, that it is not an act associated with a political objective for which amnesty should be granted. Our decision is accordingly: (1) All three applicants are granted amnesty in respect of the housebreaking at Vlakkeland Farm on the 15th of April 1986. (2) The First Applicant's application (Maxam's) in respect of the *murders* . . . on the 15th April 1986 *is refused.* . . ."

Observations:

- Formally, the transcripts are longer and there is no comparable ritualized structure to the proceedings as there are in the Human Rights Committee. The atmosphere is one of a court proceeding. In this case, another element is added: the offenders are represented by legal counsel, as are the victims. There is also a private meeting between the relatives of the victims and the offenders.
- The level of reconciliation is not verifiable. Reconciliation between the offenders and families of the victims takes place prior to the amnesty negotiations. Obviously, the TRC's Amnesty Committee is *not* a forum for reconciliation. Reconciliation on the interpersonal and "commu-

nity" levels had already taken place. ("He [Dr. Siebert] forgave me and the community in Mbekweni also forgave me.")

- Maxam feels that by the forgiveness of those he hurt he will be freed of guilt ("I am not here to the Commission to ask for forgiveness, because I feel guilty"). For him the *legal* proceeding of the amnesty process itself does not appear to be connected to the question of personal guilt and forgiveness. Kwenda comments at this point: "Yes, that's entirely correct!" "In the African way of thinking, the legal process plays itself out within the community."
- The decision of the Amnesty Committee underscores *legally* that revealing the truth is not the only criteria for amnesty. *Morally* it is clear that reconciliation can occasionally be stronger than amnesty. Njeda elaborates stating that forgiveness cannot be legally negotiated because it involves both parties: "The third party is not necessary. The amnesty committee could not contribute anything new to the process of reconciliation that has happened."
- Linguistically, mention is made in connection with the deed, "organization," or "it happened in those days." ("Those people were shot so that they would not be able to identify us. This would happen a lot at the time, even within the organization.")

The case of Maxam appears to highlight the much-voiced criticism of the Amnesty Committee, as representing the atmosphere of division within the TRC; namely, whether the Human Rights Committee may be similar to a confessional and the Amnesty Committee closer to a court of law. Despite this internal division, the criticism that the TRC was not able to bring together victims and offenders must be revised as exemplified by the case of the Kapstadt Police Chief J. Benzien.[126] A. Krog states: "The amnesty hearing of police captain Jeffrey Benzien seizes the heart of truth and reconciliation — the victim face to face with the perpetrator — and tears it out into the light."[127]

Sitting across from his victims, the infamous torturer makes his statement and names the victims by name.

Mr. Benzien: I apologize to the people whom I assaulted during interrogation, namely Peter Jacobs, Ashley Forbes, Anwar Dramat, Tony Yengeni, Gary Kruse. . . . Director Gary Kruse[128] contacted me last week and we talked about reconciliation. In the position which I am sitting here today, the persons whose names I have now mentioned, have come to me and have shaken my hand. . . . It has strengthened me in this difficult position in which I find myself.

During the amnesty proceedings the victims are allowed to ask their former torturer questions.[129]

Mr. Forbes: Can I ask . . . if you perhaps remember the 16th of April when I was arrested?

Mr. Benzien: I concede yes.

Judge Wilson: Of what year, 16th of April?

Mr. Forbes: 1986. Can I also ask that when I was arrested, do you remember saying to me that you are able to treat me like an animal or like a human being and that how you treated me, depended on whether I cooperated or not?

Mr. Benzien: I can't remember it correctly, Sir, but I will concede, I may have said it.

Mr. Forbes: Do you remember that when the wet bag method[130] was used, that people are also undressed? That I was undressed and . . . the wet bag was pulled over my head and suffocated?

Mr. Benzien: I cannot remember it specifically, but I am willing to concede it. If you can remember that aspect, I may concede, yes.

Mr. Forbes: . . . Most of these things, they stand out vividly in my mind. . . . Can I then also just ask if you remember that while I was lying on the ground, that somebody inserted a metal rod into my anus and shocked me?

Mr. Benzien: No, Sir. As heinous as it may sound, I used an electric generator on one person and then did not use it; it was on Peter Jacobs, not on you.

Mr. Forbes: This is something that I do remember.

Mr. Benzien: I am sitting in the position, Sir, where I cannot remember that, but if I can remember I am not trying to squirm away from my responsibility.

Mr. Forbes: Can I then also ask that if you remember why the date is significant, that always on the 16th it would be the day that the assaults would happen? . . .

Mr. Benzien: . . . Mr. Forbes, in the spirit of honesty and reconciliation, I am sure you are making a mistake about the 16th of every month was the day that I would assault you.

Mr. Forbes: Mr. Benzien, maybe I will take you through the next time that I was assaulted and I will just see if there are aspects of that torture that you may remember. For example, on the second occasion do you remember that I was wrapped in the carpet?

Mr. Benzien: That was the Monday, the Monday night.

Mr. Forbes: Do you remember for example that my clothes were removed and that the wet bag method was again used on me?

Mr. Benzien: I would concede it could have happened.

Mr. Forbes: Do you remember saying that you are going to break my nose and then putting both your thumbs into my nostrils and pulling it until the blood came out of my nose?

Mr. Benzien: I know you had a nose bleed. . . .

Mr. Forbes: Do you remember choking me and then knocking my head against the wall until I . . . lost consciousness?

Mr. Benzien: No Sir, I am not aware of Mr. Forbes losing consciousness at all.

Adv. de Jager: What about the knocking of the head against the wall?

Mr. Benzien: Sir, I doubt if I hit his head against the wall, because all this could have led to marks.

Mr. Forbes: Mr. Benzien, after about three months in interrogation, I tried to commit suicide, just before the 16th, I think it was of July. . . .

Chairperson: Were you aware of the fact that he tried to commit suicide?

Mr. Benzien: I was so informed, Mr. Chairman. What actually led to that, I cannot say; except that I concede the method of detention was a draconian law instituted by the then Nationalist Government, Sir.

Mr. Forbes: Mr. Benzien, if you could just focus on the suicide (attempt) for a moment and I think, at this point I am still just a little not satisfied in terms of your explanation to actually try and help the Commission and us. . . .

Mr. Benzien: Unfortunately, Sir, I cannot. . . .

Adv. de Jager: Were you the only policeman seeing him at that time, assaulting him and torturing him or were other police also involved?

Mr. Benzien: No, there were other people that would visit him, like the Duty Officers, the Inspector of Detainees, District Surgeons. During working hours, because we had this good rapport, he was telling me things about Umkhonto Sizwe,[131] how the whole setup worked and what have you. And that was in sometime, he would get paper, he would go write, he would come back and we would work on this.

Adv. de Jager: Was he distressed because of giving you information about his colleagues after being assaulted and knowing that he is sort of betraying his comrades?

Mr. Benzien: Your Honour, it is a long time ago. . . .

Another of his victims, Peter Jacobs, who was the first to survive Benzien's "wet-bag-method," would like to know the answer to the main question of "why?"

Mr. Jacobs: I was your first survivor of this torture method of yours, you would concede that, you say?

Mr. Benzien: Yes.

Mr. Jacobs: Yet, you appeared very effective at what you were doing. How come, given that you have had no experience before that, supposedly, how come you were able to do it that effectively?

Mr. Benzien: I can't answer that, how effectively it was.

Mr. Jacobs: Are you a natural talent of this, I mean do you think? Because it is the first time, you admitted yesterday?

Mr. Benzien: I wouldn't know if I have got a natural talent for it;, it is not a very nice talent to have.

Mr. Jacobs: Okay. . . . If it is not a very nice talent to have, you went on, if you say from nine o'clock till two o'clock, which is quite a few hours, you went on for a long time with something you are not very comfortable with? How do you explain that?

Mr. Benzien: Mr. Jacobs, the method employed by me is something that I have to live with and no matter how I try to interpret what I did, I still find it deplorable. I find it exceptionally difficult, sitting here in front of the news to everybody. I concede that no matter how bad I feel about it, what was done to you and your colleagues must have been worse. Believe me, I am not gloating or trying to prove that I am somebody who I am not.

Tony Yengeni, who prompted Benzien to demonstrate the method of torture asked his former torturer:

Mr. Yengeni: What kind of man uses a method like this . . . to other human beings . . . listening to those moans . . . and taking each of those people near to their deaths — what kind of man are you . . . , what happens to you as a human being?

Mr. Benzien: Mr. Yengeni, not only you have asked me that question. I, Jeff Benzien, have asked myself that question to such an extent that I voluntarily approached psychiatrists. . . . If you ask me what type of person is it that can do that, I ask myself the same question.

At the beginning of the amnesty proceedings, the believability of the applicants is a decisive criterion. As cited, Peter Jacobs accused Benzien of not divulging everything. The TRC requested a psychological opinion, which may help to explain the contradictions between the recollections of the victims and that of the perpetrators. The psychologist writes about Benzien: "It is my professional opinion that he suffers from post-traumatic stress disorder as a direct result of the work he did in the security branch, in example the methods he used in the interrogation of people in order to obtain information from them. . . . He cannot recall important features or details about the events. . . . Mr. Benzien suffered from . . . a major depressive episode caused by the events he experienced. . . . He expressed remorse and self-loathing and wished he was never appointed to the task." Further, the opinion stated: "In my professional opinion Mr. Benzien does not suffer from a personality disorder which includes anti-social personality disorder also known as psychopathic." From the discussion of the Commission with the psychologist:

Adv. de Jager: I think it's relevant that we know what his condition was when he testified here before us. . . .

Ms. Kotze: His condition whilst testifying for you was that he was extremely tense, most of the symptoms described in the report were present in a serious degree.

Benzien received amnesty in March, 1999.

Observations:[132]

- Apart from the legal process, moments appear in the course of the hearings that go beyond the process of examination outlined in the amnesty application. It offers both victims and offenders the opportunity to view the past in a light that transcends the past. They no longer sit across from each other as enemies, but as traumatized individuals who wish to come to terms with the past for the sake of their future.
- Level of reconciliation "between offender and victim." Here the TRC becomes the *forum* for reconciliation. Reconciliation now appears possible due to a visible change in the offender. Benzien shows empathy toward his victims ("no matter how bad I feel about it, what was done to you and your colleagues, must have been worse"). The condition for the possibility of change is clearly a *meeting with the victims*.

- Reconciliation appears first in retrospect, where it is viewed as possible in a fully changed historical context. Now Benzien can put his deeds and, as it appears, his character into question ("If you ask me what type of person is it that can do that, I ask myself the same question"). B. Hamber makes it clear that this insight is only possible *in a new context*, since prior to this time and in the political context of the 1980s, it would only have made the offender more defensive.
- The various experiences of both victims and offenders are articulated: Professional style with Benzien ("I doubt if I hit his head against the wall, because all this could have led to marks"). Victims rehearse traumatic memories ("most of these things, they stand out vividly in my mind").
- Forbes wants Benzien to remember the torture. Hamber guesses the reason for it is because Forbes wants to understand his own fate: "Why did he torture me so terribly?" "Why did he simply not just kill me?"
- Offenders and victims appear traumatized. The offender *is able* merely to give opinions about the trauma (which is expressed in the form of suppression of the deed), but he does not remember. The victim is traumatized and *is forced to* continually remember, to the point where his faith in humanity has been shaken.

3. Inclusion of Symbolic Forms and Rituals for Recovery

Reconciliation is not "orchestrated" by the TRC. On the other hand it should — so says the law — "demand" reconciliation. Tom Winslow observes critically: "One of the supreme ironies of the TRC is that reconciliation is a signature theme of the commission's work, but there is no apparatus in its structure to help achieve it."[133] What Winslow sees as a weakness can also be seen as a strength: didn't the legislator act wisely by not prescribing the process for reconciliation and thus allowing the inner dynamic to find its own level in the process of reconciliation? The hearings point to a level that obviously goes well beyond the limits of the legal system. However, the question of exposure remains: what *symbolic forms and rituals* serve to develop the process of reconciliation within the South African context?

Dumisa Ntsebeza, one of the seventeen Commissioners of the TRC, answered this question with a reference to the South African Transition Condition of 1993. The work of the TRC has consisted in nothing other than the *symbolizing* of the moral concept of the Postamble, where it states: "There is a need for understanding but not for vengeance, a need for reparation but not for retaliation, a need for *ubuntu* but not for victimization." Ntsebeza concludes: "The TRC has been a symbol of hope."[134]

In the following section we suggest a broad symbolic understanding as the basis, not only as it exists in the South African TRC literature,[135] but also as it is encountered in the conversations with Africans.[136] In general, T. Sundermeier has said it well: "In African thinking, the symbol does not bring two realities together, as may be presumed from the use of the concept in the Greek tradition . . . , but rather makes the segment of reality so accessible, that the details in the relationship to the whole are not lost."[137] "Dreams, foreshadowing, and ghosts . . . are not something in the hereafter that come to us in this life, but are always immanent as active agents." This thinking "only symbolically comprehends (reality), because there is no other communication." In summary: "In traditional African thought, which also influences the workings of the TRC, the phrase *unio analogica* serves as a formal principle for overcoming the world. Reality is represented as symbol."

From the vague way in which D. Ntsebeza speaks about the symbol of hope, we may be able to conclude that there are other symbols that also contribute to the development of the historical and political dimensions of rebuilding in South Africa. Robben Island is occasionally mentioned in the literature. This island of captivity in which Nelson Mandela spent the most time is now a museum and is described as a "sacred symbol for a new polity."[138] In this sense a place like Robben Island can become a "place of healing" but it must be purified according to African ideas. "Robben Island could be made a ritual site."[139] In March 1997 a ritual cleansing was completed. "There was a cleansing process of the Island," recalls a pastor who took part.[140]

There are also other places that have become symbols of reconciliation. Among them are the discussion forums of the non-government organizations (NGOs) which have become meeting places between offenders and victims of apartheid in Johannesburg or Cape Town, such as the Trauma-Center in Cape Town or the Centre for the Study of Violence and Reconciliation in Johannesburg. In other places, courses are offered in churches where the victims can try to come to grips with their own experiences.

The TRC can not ensure that it is the *only* forum for reconciliation in South Africa, but it is a *politically initiated* forum. James Cochrane remarks that a "political forum" has the task of initiating other forums. "Something done on the political level has to be recapitulated analogically at every other level in society (business, church etc.)."[141] Cochrane observes: "Many people in South Africa misunderstood the TRC as *the* forum for reconciliation." The TRC is only a "signal," acting as an "impulse" to be understood on a political level, which sets in motion other processes. To understand the work of the commission in this way does not diminish its significance. W. Kistner advocates the view: "Here in South Africa, it was necessary to provide a forum on a national level in order to make possible living together as a people."[142] The intention is not that reconciliation on a national level seeks its own path and doesn't need a forum. In contrast to J. Cochrane, for whom the TRC represented the reality of life of many South Africans precisely because it is a political instrument, C. Villa-Vicencio argues with regard to the African understanding of symbol: "The TRC was a symbolic intervention in the journey towards reconciliation. A highly visible intervention. That's what symbolism is. It is there, it is alive; you can see it, you can feel it."[143]

To speak of a *forum* for reconciliation within the framework of the TRC process is also meaningful for western conceptuality. I cite in this regard J. Zehner, who defined "forum" as follows: "existing in the *midst of public life,* available to *all sides,* but clearly defined and ultimately still a *self-contained domain.*"[144]

- The activities of the TRC took place in the presence of the media; "in the midst of public life." In certain respects, the TRC exposed the reality of apartheid for South Africans. "I turned off the radio because I felt so ashamed," is what one Boer is reported to have said to Commissioner G. Wildschut.[145]
- The TRC was "accessible to all sides." Anyone could attend the hearings and submissions were welcome from all areas of society.
- The TRC was bound to its mandate and to that extent it limited the circumstances of the investigations as well as the time period. It thus represented a "clearly delineated" and "self-contained domain."

As a *forum,* the TRC could not determine the process of reconciliation, either in space or in time. Reconciliation took place through the process of the TRC, as documented, as well as on various relational levels (personal, interpersonal, community, and social) as also on the level of various forms of behavior. In the case of Philemon Maxan, the process of reconciliation preceded the hearings and was sealed by it. In the case of the policeman Jeffrey Benzien, the reconciliation process preceded the hearing, was deepened during it, but not entirely completed. Finally, the TRC did not serve as the forum for Conraad van Rooyen's reconciliation, at least not on the interpersonal level.

What symbolic forms and rituals can aid reconciliation in the TRC political forum? I intend to distinguish five mutually interdependent and defining symbolic forms of expression and ritual. The reality of reconciliation is developed through (a) the composition and cultural inheritance of the TRC, (b) its ritualistic process, (c) the importance of narrative, (d) its national and (e) its religious symbolism.

(a) The Composition of the TRC

The actuality of reconciliation is developed through the composition and cultural inheritance of the TRC. W. Kistner thinks that "the TRC itself is a symbolic form: that these people, who were so different, found commonality — there is the commissioner Chris de Jager, a conservative African, then the high church Desmond Tutu, then also Moslems and Hindus were asked to sit on the Commission. The tensions, which the TRC had experienced,[146] but also the common ground, which one must always seek, all came together in one year-long spectacle: all of it consisted in a symbolic character that is otherwise characteristic of great events."[147] In this regard, the TRC is a "microcosm of the new South Africa; it has survived incredible tensions, which resulted from the time of incredible conflict."[148] The TRC symbolically anticipates which areas of society should prevail; it develops the basis for democratic ways of thinking. In this sense, says the TRC Commissioner Malan: "the TRC is but a small bit of the future of this country."[149] The commission also invites a "ritual context"[150] in which the past can be viewed with clarity. For the TRC it is more than the law that makes things possible: "There was a framework in which the TRC operated, but it was more than a legal framework; it was a ritual."[151] Even the historical process of appointing commissioners has symbolic meaning. The theologian Fani du Toit maintains of the process that led the TRC: "it was a legitimate and democratic process through consensus. This is itself a reconciling symbol."[152] Finally, the mandate of the TRC fostered the promotion of national unity and reconciliation in a general sense: namely, it should be fulfilled "in the spirit of understanding that *transcends* the conflicts of the past." What does this mean? The African cultural social-scientist Zakes Mda says: "true reconciliation will only come when we are big enough to confront what happened yesterday, without bitterness."[153]

(b) The TRC's Ritualistic Approach

The reality of reconciliation is developed through the ritual process of the
TRC. The testimony of Conraad van Rooyen exemplifies the symbols evident during the hearings:

- The hearings were conducted in the *city hall* located in the African
  stronghold of Paarl. It is charmingly decorated with white tablecloths
  covering the desks. What is symbolized? The choice for the setting indicates that the victims were not only at the center of media attention, but
  also the city of Paarl itself. The message is: "Let us play host to you!"
  "Today you are the center of attention!" "You may for three days take
  your place in the Hall, which previously was off limits to you!"
- At the entrance to the hall the listeners were searched by the *police;* then
  they were shown the way into the Hall. What is the symbolic meaning
  here? Police are now engaged in safeguarding the cause of the victims.
  They had to search those present in the audience for weapons. Now they
  do not symbolize oppression, but rather support: "We are now on your
  side!" "We will help see to it that you will be able to tell your stories in
  safety!"
- The tables of the commission are situated on a *podium* so that the audience has to look up to see the victims. The tables are placed in the shape
  of a horseshoe. Whoever is speaking has someone sitting next to them
  for assistance. What is symbolized here? The podium forces the glance
  upwards: "Look at the victims!" The horseshoe shape points out that
  "We sit together, not in confrontation, but because we want to share!"
  And the assistant at the side of the victim indicates: "You are not alone!"
  "Someone will accompany you during the hearing!"
- Headphones are supplied for the audience in the auditorium. Anyone
  can listen in their own language and the stories are translated simultaneously. What is symbolized here? The translation chamber, the mi-
  crophones, and the headphones point to the democratic principle of
  equality. Next to Afrikaans and English, other African languages are
  recognized as equal. "Tell your story in your language!" "They will be
  understood by everyone!"

In addition to the symbolic meaning of the individual elements, the TRC
hearings in their entirety are interpreted as ritual in the literature.[154] Accordingly, four elements of ritual are distinguishable:[155]

(1) "Acknowledging the sacred space."[156] In the ritual an isolated, "sacred" space is made for the victims by the assembly of commissioners, which, according to A. Krog, looked like a procession with all of the lit candles. Then there follows a moment of silence in which the victims of apartheid are remembered. The entrance of the victims is announced next with the command for all to rise. Finally, the opening of the session includes Bible songs and prayer (when D. Tutu presided). In the case of Conraad van Rooyen the pastor gives the "opening statement." What is the significance of the above-described opening ritual? The social-anthropologist F. Ross sees it aptly: "The ritual has a particular capacity to resolve conflict by creating spaces through which negotiation can occur."[157]

(2) "Initiation into being one of the few who have been chosen."[158] There follow next the swearing-in of the listeners and a personal greeting from the commission, along with appreciative remarks. In our case, these include statements like "Good morning, Mr. van Rooyen, you got up early this morning to drive all the way from Saldanha . . ." or "Mr. Maxam, we welcome you this morning as you are going to give . . . a testimony that is different from the usual, a testimony of forgiveness, this is what the commission is about." Before the invitation to share their individual stories with the Commission, the victims are given the opportunity to relate something personal: "Mr. van Rooyen, would you please tell us a little bit more about yourself"; "Mr. Maxan, . . . did you grow up in Mbekweni or did you grow up elsewhere?" A. Krog has observed: "This kind of approach always immediately brings the hearing into a very intimate and personal zone."[159] A well-designed personal question addressed to the victim allows them to forget for a moment the large prepared manuscript and gives the "narrative" a chance to flow. "This can break the ice like nothing else."[160]

(3) "Letting go of the bad." Now comes the story. During this ritual many tears are shed in the hearings. "Weeping is a part of the catharsis."[161] But when — as in our cases — no tears are shed, the hearings can also serve as an African "cleansing ritual."[162] That is what we saw in the account of van Rooyen, but also in the story of Maxam the perpetrator. Obviously, in order to reach this goal as much leeway as possible is afforded the applicant to tell their story in their own way. In the case of Conraad van Rooyen it was read.[163] The story was long; Maxan told it freely. It can also be ordinary — see Krog — that is, as in the case of Maxan with regard to the redundancy or elaborating upon details. However, what was

instructive for the TRC was, in contrast to the amnesty hearings, the perception that the "oral history" (more exactly, the "private narrative"[164]) in hearings on human rights violations takes precedent over the "objective" search for truth.[165]

(4) "Becoming part of the blessed greater community." This is how A. Krog characterizes the final ritual that comes after the telling of the story. It is completed in three phases, according to which first the Commissioner himself inquires after their condition: "How do you feel now?" and then the question: "What do you want from the Commission?" Finally, the victim is thanked for his appearance and the story is given a context. Tutu especially has this ability: "He always manages to transcend the particularity of a story: he fits it into a broader, higher scheme of things. He assesses the victim's mood and pain quite instinctively and then explains to her the deeper meaning of the story."[166] The testimony of Conraad van Rooyen should exemplify how the ritual works. The question, "How do you feel about that?" which Conraad van Rooyen is asked, referred to the promotion of police officials. The answer, especially the serenity with which he answers, is obviously directly connected to the ritual of the hearing: the rite of telling channels the rage and the helplessness and helps to dignify the sadness of a broken life. What Conraad van Rooyen wants from the TRC is obvious: the means to buy supplies and medicine, education for his children, and a pension. The contextualizing of the story by the female Commissioner Gobodo alludes to the political conflict of the past, but it also shows why this happened to van Rooyen: "because you were excluded from the realm of your fellow humanity." Now however, in the final ritual, the victim is symbolically accepted into the community where human dignity is upheld. The fact that this ritualized "snapshot" occurs by means of a state-appointed commission is a symbol in itself. "The official acknowledgement by representatives of the state makes it very symbolic."[167] The explanation is offered: "Part of the importance of the . . . hearings was precisely the public . . . acknowledgement of experiences that have been officially denied in the past."[168]

The above-mentioned rites can be observed exclusively in the TRC hearings of the Human Rights Violations Committee. The contrast to the Amnesty Committee is evident in the type and manner of questioning of Philemon Maxam and also of Jeffrey Benzien. In addition, the entire ritual framework is missing from this committee. B. Bozzoli has researched the symbolic form of the TRC and observes in view of the Human Rights Violations Committee: "The questioning commissioner would adopt a gentle, respectful tone, quite unlike the tone used in the courtroom. Thus those called in a legalistic sense 'witnesses' behaved unlike witnesses in a court."[169] In summary this means: "The commission has chosen to use the method of ritual rather than that of law to carry out its purpose."[170] Although the TRC was criticized for many things, there was one thing that is was not criticized for; namely, whether or not it provided an alternative to the hearings. In many respects, the statement appears to have merit: "Rites are practices that are ends in themselves."[171] The Danish social anthropologist L. Buur says: "the hearing as a way of playing out questions of guilt and injustice gives meaning in itself."[172] F. Ross maintains about the TRC in general: "It . . . gives visible . . . shape to the past, providing . . . a ritual context within which the past can be examined."[173]

A ritual can take the place of a legal proceeding, as we saw in the case of Maxam. In the sense of the African Traditional Religion: "whatever was wrong is corrected through appropriate rituals."[174] By virtue of a ritual the person gains new status.[175] Maxam is accepted back into his community (black community) again; he is "re-socialized." (It appears from the hearing that this was more important for Maxam than the requested amnesty.) One may conclude on the social level that the significance of ritual for black offenders before the Human Rights Violations Committee corresponds to the legal rehabilitation of white offenders before the Amnesty Committee.[176]

(c) The National Symbolism of the TRC

The reality of reconciliation becomes accessible through the national symbol of the TRC. The individual stories of the affected victims of the apartheid era are not to be separated from the "psyche of the nation." The psychologist B. Hamber assumes that "Nations have psyches which experience traumas similar to individuals."[177] From this Hamber says that the national process of overcoming the past is irrevocably intertwined with its personal aspects. Also B. Bozzoli observes: "peoples' lives and stories came to carry meanings beyond the personal"[178] which was the intent: "Their stories were meant to be transposed from the private to the public sphere."

(d) The Importance of Story

Through the element of the oral history the private narratives contribute to what is described in the literature as belonging to a "common memory." The historian B. Harris sees a connection: "narration does more than represent particular events being remembered. They connect the individual understanding and memory of the event with other personal experiences."[179] Harris continues: "Unlike written narratives, however, narrated memories are not stable. They are constantly open to mediation, alternation and distortion."[180]

Other victims who have met a similar fate feel represented by Conraad van Rooyen's story of victimization. Moreover, the story contributes to the *common memory*, to the "never again!" The stories of offenders, such as those of Jeffrey Benzien, also enter into the collective consciousness of the nation. A member of the Commission, Dumisa Ntsebeza, recalls: "Even a Benzien was able to say, 'I asked myself continually what sort of a person I am.' And that does not come easily to the lips of a person who for years and years was brought up to believe that he belongs to a super race and what he was fighting for was sanctified by the Bible."[181] Ntsebeza continues: "Benzien came to symbolize to a lot of people that there is hope."

When D. Ntsebeza speaks about the TRC as "a symbol of hope" at the beginning of the process of reconstruction, there is an obvious African understanding of symbol at its core. For Africans, reality is only accessible through symbols. "Once the public hearings hit the scene, then people began to say, 'there is hope in this country.'"[182] The view of the hearings on reconciliation in the TRC forum opened the door to hope for a changed, new South Africa. And in this hope there lies symbolic power which is evidenced on a national level through the individual, personal stories of victims before the forum of TRC.

To what extent the TRC has actually become a "national ritual" can be determined in several ways. A. Krog, who introduces this question, also raises another consideration; namely, he suggests that the TRC is *the* national symbol for those present in the hearings. "Reporting (on) the Truth Commission has become a ritual in which the nation participates via television both because of its regularity and because of its visual symbols."[183] The nation not only participates passively in the work of the TRC, but also actively: individuals can — according to the suggestion of the TRC Commissioner Mary Burton — express their personal sorrow over apartheid in a "Petition for Reconciliation." There are among the entries short letters containing gripping statements of white South Africans who, in the course of the hearings, were so shaken that they consequently confessed their own misdeeds. Finally, the TRC hearings proceedings were equipped with a national symbol, to the extent that the witnesses were given to understand that they *stand before the nation and at the same time are in a new South Africa.* South Africa's new flag was visible in the background at every hearing. Tutu says, "the nation acknowledges that awful experience and, in a way, the nation is saying sorry."[184] On the other hand, there is the question of whether, as a "national ritual," the TRC was dependent on the actual participants for this ritual. In contrast, A. Krog suggests that the TRC did not become a national ritual[185] at all, because one must participate in a ritual. According to Krog, such involvement also includes the readiness by the offenders to make restitution and, in general, to remember. Thus, the conditions outlined here require a forward process toward "nation building" — something that a nation can only accomplish through a common ritual. *National rites* thus become an indicator of *nation building.*

(e) The TRC's Religious Symbolism

The reality of reconciliation is developed through the religious symbolism of the TRC. The sociologist and the TRC critic H. Adam remarks: "I found it remarkable that in an officially secular society the religious symbols and in particular the Anglican Christian symbols dominated and we considered them to be the state symbols."[186] Adam, a native German with primary residence in Canada and a temporary teaching post in Capetown, was criticized in South Africa for his basic liberal position, because it ostensibly did not reflect the social reality of South Africans. "The whole idea of reconciliation and establishing a TRC (and not trials!)," so says the systematic theologian D. Smit, "one could relate to cultural convictions, to religious convictions and definitely to Christian convictions."[187] The TRC thus brings the above-outlined convictions together; they are part of a "cultural communication process in society."

Co-existing religious, traditional, cultural, and Christian ideas which are, in part, mediated by each other, are documented in the transcripts. Philemon Maxan uses Christian concepts like "sin" when testifying before the Commission; and the thought world of the African Traditional Religion is reflected elsewhere in his statements. The problem takes on another dimension when one of the white perpetrators, like Jeffrey Benzien, claims that the entire Christian tradition (Dutch Reformed) was involved. "The churches were always involved," maintains W. Kistner. "Most of the offenders, who committed the most heinous of crimes, were practicing Christians. In part they intended to do a service for the kingdom of God by protecting the community from the threat of communism."[188] In the example of the church accounts, we saw that churches were very closely interwoven with the social process in South Africa as that of "offender" and "victim."

It is immediately clear if one looks at what is involved in the *hearings,* that the proceedings of the TRC are not capable of being categorized using western liberal categories and areas. "The themes, which during the hearings of the Truth and Reconciliation Commission in very concrete and immediate way came to light, are the central themes of every Sunday church service . . . : sin, remorse, recognition of guilt, atonement, and new beginning."[189] However, the process of the hearings, which we have interpreted in the above sense of the African rituals, can be understood in a Christian sense: "The hearings developed their own liturgy," says John de Gruchy, and he continues: the recollections "on the past are survived and healed through penance, forgiveness and a commitment to atonement. The ritual is painful . . . , but it is full of mercy, justice and hope."[190] Also Charles Villa-Vicencio recalls the connection of the Christian church with the TRC. "We hear it in the benediction: 'Go now into the world. The grace of our Lord Jesus Christ, the love of God, and the fellowship of the Holy Spirit be with you all!' 'Go!'" This is the notion that we get in the Eucharist and ideally, it is what the TRC is about: to invite people to come, to reflect, to inwardly digest, to go into the world and to put right something that was wrong. Villa-Vicencio draws parallels to this idea: "I see the TRC as symbolism, as theatre, as ritual, as liturgy."[191]

The religious overtones of the hearings are inherently embedded in the TRC. C. Villa-Vicencio, who oversees the research department of the TRC, takes an extreme position. On the other side is the TRC Commissioner W. Malan. For him the TRC is cluttered with religious symbolism. "The Bible was used not as a canon, but as a cannon," he writes in his "Minority Position."[192] "The danger of applying religious frames to phenomena in general should not be underestimated." Over against the excessive expectations placed on the Commission, which was also fed by religious motives, Malan warns that the TRC is able to fulfill its mandate only incrementally. He says: "The post-amble is in a sense eschatological in its essence." Meanwhile, most of the TRC Commissioners have neither doubted nor stood in the way of the religious interpretation of symbolism of the TRC nor have they doubted that the Christian religion plays the role that Malan has described. The lawyer D. Ntsebeza, speaking of the position of his TRC colleague W. Malan, suggests: "South Africa is predominantly a religious country. And the work of the TRC is obviously shaped by the expectations of the people of South Africa. At all the gatherings that we went to people were singing hymns although it was not a service. And there was never the suggestion that the TRC should not allow that. I can understand Malan taking that view, but I can't see what else he is bringing to the table. What is his suggestion? I am influenced by a Christian understanding of reconciliation but I never thought of pressure. I was not going to say to the Archbhishop, 'Look, please don't open the hearings with a prayer!' I disagree that religion by itself played a critical role determining the visions of reconciliation."[193]

It was actually the head of the Truth Commission who made a "spiritual commission" from the TRC because he knew of the power of religious and cultural tradition: "Desmond Tutu draws on the power of these traditions."[194] It also appears that Tutu, who always wore his Anglican Archbishop's robe during the hearings, essentially "baptized" this tradition and ritual. The TRC Chairperson does not stop with the remark: "There is an appeal to some sort of transcendental reality in the hearings."[195] For D. Tutu the "reality" of reconciliation is Jesus Christ. Christ breaks into political reality — he "becomes flesh." Where B. Naudé says: "God has a hand in the game" or when W. Kistner speaks of the "tracks of the risen Christ,"[196] Tutu uses the vocabulary of "holy." Captivated by the apology that one offender brings before the TRC (similar to the case of Philemon Maxam) he says: "I think we need to keep quiet because we are in the presence of something very special and very holy."[197] Of the readiness to forgive of so many blacks in front of the TRC, Tutu remarks in another place: "So many of them are ready to forgive, which sometimes makes you feel as though you should take your shoes off because you are stepping on holy ground."[198]

4. Analysis of "Regulative Statements" Behind the Symbolic Forms of Political Reconstruction in South Africa

The analysis of "regulative sentences" is once more aligned with the goal to prepare the ground for the question of correspondence. The conditions for the possibility of political reconciliation should first be determined in order later to examine the "regulative statements" for their basic connection to theology.

Statements concerning the formal conditions for the possibility of reconciliation are:

- Reconciliation requires a forum for encounter.
- Offenders and victims need each other for reconciliation (as is impressively the case of Maxan and Benzien).
- The personal encounter with the offenders can facilitate the victims' personal "coming to terms with the painful past."
- The offenders become conscious of what they have done through the encounter with the victims.[199]
- Reconciliation with one's personal fate is not possible without a personal encounter (as in the case of Conraad van Rooyen).
- Reconciliation on a national level is possible through the encounter with personal "narratives": namely, that is our story and it should never again happen.

Statements about material conditions of the possibility of reconciliation:

- Reconciliation assumes a petition for pardon and its acceptance.
- The petition for pardon is connected with the following concerns:
  - with the admission of guilt (as in the case of Philemon Maxan)
  - with the contemplation over the deed and the challenge to one's own personal life (as in the case of Jeff Benzien)
  - with the regret of the deed (as in the case of Philemon Maxan)
  - with the acknowledgement of the suffering (as in the case of Conraad van Rooyen)
  - with the explanation of the historical context (as in the case of Frederick de Klerk)
- The acceptance of pardon can mean materially:
  - to forgive, that is, to seek community again, such as
  - in which an offender is again incorporated as a full member into the community (compare Maxan and the community of Mbekweni)
  - in which offenders and victims extend their hands to each other (compare Maxan and Dr. Siebert; Mr. Benzien and Mr. Forbes)
  - to co-exist, which means to tolerate community, as in the willingness of the victim to continue to live in the same town as the offender. (The person does not seek community, but does not kill anyone either; compare Conraad van Rooyen and Constable Stroebel; Mr. Benzien and Mr. Yengeni.)

The idea is regulative in the statement:

- Reconciliation assumes the request for pardon and its acceptance
  - that the individual elements are connected to the extent that the condition for the goal leading the reconciliation process is the being present of both fundamental elements in combination with various forms: namely, *(1) apology* in the form of suffering and the *request for pardon;* and (2) *acceptance* of the apology in the form of *forgiveness* and the readiness to seek *community* (compare the case of Maxan). In this way, the succession of the basic elements remains open-ended. In the case of Maxan, the following regulative ideas appear to be dominant:
- Reconciliation does not necessarily involve reparations.
- Reconciliation also helps the victim.

III. Taking Stock of Systemic Injustice: The Political Nuances

1. General Balance

If one considers the many honors that were granted by the entire world to Desmond Tutu and other members of the commission for their contribution to reconciliation in South Africa, one could say of the success of the commission along with W. Kistner: "In each case has the TRC has brought in something of the world agenda."[200] The South African commission had to contend with a considerable attempt at balance: 140 hearings were conducted across the country; 21,400 victims made written application; 27,000 were registered; 7,124 offenders of egregious human rights violations lodged amnesty claims. The commission brought to the world agenda a way to prepare for political compromises when dealing with the issue of social reconciliation. The presentation of prizes indicates that the process of reconciliation as depicted by the African national symbolism has also become a symbol for the political dimension of reconciliation worldwide. "The whole world is looking at us," observed Desmond Tutu.[201]

The question of balance is complex in the process in South Africa. It is, philosophically speaking, a "mixed question."[202] In order to respond to it, at least three other problems must be considered: (1) disparate ideas of reconciliation direct the South African process of proceedings; (2) there is the question in which framework at all the results are to be evaluated; (3) it appears to be open, whether the results first at the *end* or already *in the course* of a process are formulated. Do we expect an absolute, relative, open or process-oriented formulation of results?

If at first the question of results is raised in the framework of evaluation, then I am confident that there is no acceptable "framework" for an assessment of the TRC process in current research.[203] And if, in the framework of the case study method, theological reconciliation is eliminated as normative reference point, then we must rely on an analytical approach to the work of the TRC itself. In order to examine the conditions for the possibility of reconciliation in the political reality of South Africa, the Final Report is an indispensable resource. In contrast to the Interim Report,[204] the Final Report includes a chapter on an evaluation of the reconciliation process[205] and serves, in the language of the discipline, as a "reference point."[206]

In the following pages, the basis is laid for research on the Final Report and the results of the proceedings are assessed within the framework of the mandate of the TRC. What were the goals of the TRC and to what extent have they been achieved? In the chapter on the Concepts of the Final Report, the goal of the TRC is highlighted: "The overarching task assigned to the Commission by Parliament was the promotion of national unity and reconciliation."[207] The formula for "promotion" is interpreted: "Reconciliation is both a goal and a process." Reconciliation in this overarching sense — as a synonym for "national unity" — is to be understood as "process." National reconciliation should be advanced by the work of the Commission, but cannot be fully achieved. It remains a goal. Those presiding recall: "the TRC is expected to *promote,* not to *achieve* reconciliation."[208]

The TRC report states: "The experience of the Commission illustrated the particular difficulty of understanding the meaning of unity and reconciliation at a national level."[209] In an in-depth discussion, W. Verwoerd, former research department of the TRC and the person responsible for the above-cited assessment, says more clearly: "The notion of reconciliation in the Act and the Interim Constitution is not clear."[210] In addition, commissioner G. Wildschut maintains that the concept of reconciliation itself was not the cause for the debate within the TRC; that was not its mandate.[211] It thus raises the question: how should the TRC fulfill its mandate, namely to *promote national unity and reconciliation,* if it is not clear what "national reconciliation" means?

Consideration of the content of the proceedings yields methodologically, that apart from an allusion to its mandate, no decisive frame for an evaluation yet exists. On the other hand, the way to investigating the result is circumscribed: it has to do with reconciliation on a *national level.* Secondly, it is assumed that such reconciliation is accomplished through a *process.* In this chapter it is examined according to relative, but not according to absolute results. Results are expected in *the course of the process.*

If one wants to approach the meaning of "national reconciliation" in terms of content, one must look prior to the *National Unity and Reconciliation Act* to the conditions that led up to the law. Our analysis of the initial proceedings (I) led to the conclusion that reconciliation exists in a causal connection to *nation building.* In order to build a *nation,* "national reconciliation" is important. This explains the almost interchangeable use of "national unity" and "reconciliation." It concerns the mutual understanding of two nations that were separated during three years of colonialism and stood opposed to each other in war over forty years of apartheid. In a conference of the TRC, the sentiment can be heard: "Reconciliation is a national issue. There were two worlds in South Africa, and they were at war."[212] In order to do justice to the national use of reconciliation *(thin reconciliation),* C. Villa-Vicencio speaks of "co-existence." It must first once be guaranteed that the black and the white part of South Africa can peacefully co-exist. "We have to learn that we don't kill each other."[213] The goal, however, was the creation of a multi-cultural "rainbow-nation" in which racial distinctions not only are accepted, but are celebrated.[214] In this regard, reconciliation is a "national project" (Tutu).[215] "Inasmuch as reconciliation touches every aspect of our lives, it is our nation's lifeline" (Mandela).[216] National reconciliation thus serves the goal of "nation building."

Representatives of the public debate understand that "national reconciliation" is to be understood as tied to the concept "the re-building of society" or "the overcoming of animosity."[217] "To be reconciled means to look at themselves as one nation, as one people although there are different cultures and languages."[218]

How did the Law to Promote National Unity and Reconciliation in the work of the TRC become an institution which *in itself* was a "practical consequence of a negotiated bridge"?[219] What balance can be drawn? The Final Report decisively sees that during the activity of the Commission the theme "national unity and reconciliation" was not on the agenda. The media brought no analysis to the complex issue of "national reconciliation," but rather reported overly sensational statements by individual victims before the TRC. It also had to do less with what the political philosopher S. Dwyer calls the "macro-level" of reconciliation than with the "micro-level,"[220] which comprises the interpersonal realm together with its complex network of relationships: "relationships of individuals with themselves; relationship between victims; relationship between survivors and perpetrators; relationship within families; between neighbors and within and between communities; relationships between different generations; between racial and ethnic groups, between workers and management and, above all, between the beneficiaries of apartheid and those who have been disadvantaged by it."[221]

The Final Report concludes on the one hand: "it was not part of the Commission's mandate to effect reconciliation between victims, the community and perpetrators."[222] On the other hand, it explicitly acknowledges these events: "there were a number of significant instances where the Commission directly facilitated the beginning of this complex process." Here the Final Report speaks again — in view of the "macro-level" of reconciliation — of a reconciliation *process* and mentions many examples of it in its chapter "Reconciliation." This corroborates the above observations where, for example, in part the TRC reconciliation process was introduced on an individual level (as with Benzien and his victims). However, we also saw that the reconciliation proceedings of the TRC can take place beforehand (as in the case of Maxan and the Siebert family). In each case it is a paradox that the TRC is encouraged to promote reconciliation on a *national level*, but that it concentrated in its proceedings on the process of reconciliation *between individuals*. The Final Report also makes reference to the problem that on each of the levels various ideas of reconciliation are in play. The experiences of the TRC have disclosed a dangerous mix between two versions of reconciliation; namely, "between a religious, indeed Christian, understanding of reconciliation, more typically applied to interpersonal relationships, and the more limited, political notion of reconciliation applicable to a democratic society."[223]

How do the "macro" and "micro-levels" fit together in the reconciliation process? What connection exists between the coming together on the national level for the purpose of reconciliation and that of coming together on a personal or interpersonal level? Here again the Final Report provides a decisive clue without, however, further complicating the problem. It intends to bridge a relationship between the personal and the national process of healing: "People came to the Commission to tell their stories in an attempt to facilitate not only their own individual healing process, but also a healing process for the entire nation."[224] The individual process of healing, the idea of "coming to terms with the painful past" is indissolubly linked with the fate of the nation. In order for growth to occur on a national level in the future one must look back to the individual stories of apartheid. In this regard, the following observation is significant: "reconciliation has both forward and backward looking dimensions."[225]

The example of South Africa shows that it is possible for a nation to come together in the stories of individual victims: "reconciliation needs to be built from the bottom up."[226] The individual level encompasses the national level of reconciliation as well as the obverse: the national level was given a forum by the TRC for healing on an individual level — for "coming to terms with the painful past." However, both levels were mediated *symbolically* through the work of the TRC. The whole is *exposed* on the basis of individual stories. The forum for reconciliation provided by the TRC is a window to the past and at the same time a bridge to the future.

If we ask about the results of the reconciliation process in South Africa, then the question (in view of the above observations concerning the "mixed question") with respect to the complexity of "national reconciliation" must be asked: if by reconciliation we understand the *promotion* of "national unity and reconciliation" then what is the chance of reaching a *relative* result in the framework of the political reconciliation *process?* As an intermediary point between the results of this chapter, I would like to suggest that *national unity and reconciliation are promoted through the work of the TRC, but are not reached.*

Reconciliation has become reality in the form of political "coexistence."[227] "We sit together in Parliament, discussing, arguing and creating political frameworks."[228] The Final Report, however, says clearly: "Within its short lifespan and limited mandate and resources, it was obviously impossible for the Commission to reconcile the nation."[229] In the sense of coexistence the concept of reconciliation was nevertheless watered down. W. Kistner says sharply in view of "national reconciliation": "When politicians reach a compromise, they also speak of reconciliation. But that doesn't mean healing."[230]

The process of "nation building" is not finished. In politics "two nations" is still made reference to mainly by politicians who think of the social dimension of "nation building."[231] Another school of thought claims that South Africa has become *one* nation. As an example, sporting events are conducted so that other countries are encouraged to see South Africa as one nation.[232] However, according to my observation, consensus exists on the following level: people tolerate each other, but ethnic differences are neither celebrated nor are they seen as enriching. However, that remains the goal.

The fact that the individual and national levels of reconciliation are connected is not a point of argument for South African critics of the TRC. However, their criticism involves the concept of reconciliation used by the TRC and its connection to other concepts, primarily that of justice and truth. W. Verwoerd[233] distinguishes three basic criticisms of the reconciliation process in the use of the concepts of truth, reconciliation, and justice: "truth based criticism," "reconciliation based criticism," and "justice based criticism."

Further evaluation of the TRC process needs to be done employing the framework of these basic criteria.

2. Critical Questions

(a) Truth as Condition *sine qua non* of Social Reconciliation?

The TRC banners in the hall where the hearings took place are inscribed with the words: "Reconciliation through Truth." In many places one can find posters bearing the Biblical injunction: "The truth will set you free." W. Kistner states critically that at the beginning of the work of the commission concepts like "truth" were used as absolutes. The boundaries were blurred that were set for a commission like the TRC in its work. "As a result, rather high expectations were raised in the public which could be fulfilled only partially."[234] On the other hand, the commission was given the charge to investigate the truth beyond mere *fact*. It was concerned with more than the answer to the question: *who did what to whom?* C. Villa-Vicencio[235] refers correctly to the mandate of the TRC by which it was charged to hold investigations in many different areas.

The search for truth follows evidence contained in the statements of victims, those from the perpetrators, as well as the results of the so called Investigation Unit. The search for truth thus has a dual target: it aims at uncovering the facts *and* at healing those who were affected. This double mandate — which I call the task of "exposing" and "healing" — is the catalyst for "Truth-based criticism." How can one seek the historical truth and at the same time achieve healing for the individuals concerned? How do the historical truth and the portrayed truth relate to each other (i.e., the problem of the "objective" writing of history[236])? Can there be a "historical" truth without posing the question of "moral" truth (problem of non-partisanship)?

Before we turn to the problem of the relationship between the forms of truth (cc), we should first ask: what results have been achieved in the search for *factual* (aa) and the *healing truth* (bb)?

(aa) On the "Factual Truth"

The job of the TRC was to complete a Final Report on the activity and findings of the commission based on "factual and objective information."[237] The report presented its "findings" in Volumes II-IV and in a summary Volume V.[238] A key finding of the TRC states: "The state — in the form of the South African Government, the civil service and its security forces — was, in the period 1960-94 the primary perpetrator of gross human rights violations in South Africa."[239]

There is a consensus that the Truth Commission has brought much to light that would have remained in the dark without such a Commission.[240] In the literature as well as in the discussions, the task of the TRC regarding the "factual truth" is evaluated so that it is possible to say: a *lie* about the atrocities of apartheid is no longer possible at the close of the Commissions work. There is consensus in the South African discussion that the commission as a "truth" commission has, in the framework of its mandate, made a contribution to reduce the "number of lies, which are held by society."[241]

The partial question is contained in the sense of the "mixed question": if the idea of uncovering the facts is connected to reconciliation, how far has the reconciliation process come? The TRC fulfilled its mandate with respect to the *factual truth* in which it reconstructed the *most possible full account* of the events during the investigation period and with it laid the groundwork for social reconciliation.

(bb) On the "Healing Truth"

The search for facts feeds on the determinations of the Investigation Unit, which preceded the hearings. But primarily through the statements of the victims, perpetrators, institutions, political parties, etc. the entire picture demanded by the mandate was sketched out. When victims speak, they carry in their "personal narrative" the "apartheid narrative." "Each story of suffering provided a penetrating window into the past."[242] The public acknowledgment of the suffering through the revealing of information and naming the names of victims in the Final Report[243] can also lead to healing of the spiritual wounds. This acceptance is also supported by surveys of victims, who appeared before the TRC.[244]

Meanwhile, warn observers, we must keep the victims of apartheid from romanticizing the expected effects of healing through the mere process of the hearings. Of course, a genuine healing process can be triggered, but the story of suffering must be gone through again until it is coaxed out as a "story" and can be understood. Only when those affected stop fleeing from their memories can the healing process begin. Therefore, it is important that the victim who has lost faith in humanity due to permanent harm to his own human rights comes to understand that what happened to him took place within a particular political context. Such an understanding — connected with the re-discovery of his own dignity — is a longer process that cannot be completed within the scope of the hearings of the Commission. We only need to think of the case of Conraad van Rooyen! A recommendation of the psychologist is thus to place at his disposal the means for recovery that are warranted for a long-term participant in apartheid.

The process of healing can also be initiated for the victims by the statements of the perpetrators. Offenders who apply for amnesty must tell "the whole truth" which has led in more than 50 cases to the discovery of the remains of anti-apartheid activists.[245] Tutu comments: "I doubt that this information would have ever seen the light of day without the TRC processes."[246] For the families it is a great relief to at least have certainty after such a long time. "Their families are happy because at least they have been able to give a decent burial to the remains of their loved ones." On a personal level, it is in many cases a reconciliation with one's own fate to be able to say good-bye to the past: "the Commission's disclosure of truth helped people to reach closure."[247] Furthermore, the victims were rehabilitated by virtue of the fact that illegal records were expunged in the process. In the debate of Parliament over the TRC report it was suggested to continue the process of exhumation, because many cases still remained open and a coordination effort needed to be initiated by the Office of the President.[248]

In the sense of the "mixed question" we may ask: if reconciliation is connected with the idea of healing through the telling of the truth or through the burial of the remains of the relatives, how far has the process of reconciliation come? Reconciliation on a personal level — in the sense of "coming to terms with the past" — is mainly able to arrive at closure in cases where the human remains can be buried. In other cases — especially in light of the stories — the healing process has just begun.

(cc) On the Interdependence of "Factual" and "Narrative Truth"

The above observations emphasize the view the "truth is not a homogenous concept in the TRC."[249] In the execution of its duties, the commission has understood various forms of truth — "exposed" and "healing" truth, forensic and lived truth, factual truth and narrative truth — as complementary for the formation of a complete historical picture. Its mandate was not to formulate a historical picture of the apartheid era, but rather to ask "why and how history happened."[250] Accordingly, we must not judge it by the criteria of formal historical writing. "We recognize," says President Mandela about the Final Report, "that it is not a definite or comprehensive history."[251] The problem of objectivity is obviously not settled; it appears again in the form of "non-partisanship." The question therefore arises: "Is the report a . . . fair overview of everything that happened in our country during the years of apartheid? Or is the report . . . a one-sided caricature of reality . . . ?"[252]

The TRC has been criticized that it has variously construed its basic tenet "amnesty for truth." It provides a non-transparent area of maneuvering for "which" or "how much" truth must be revealed in order to obtain immunity. For example, doesn't the exposure of the truth always lead to amnesty for everyone for the sake of non-partisanship? Has a man like Jeffrey Benzien given a "completely" full account according to what the TRC law means regarding "full disclosure"? Many of his victims doubt it. When he received amnesty in March 1999, there were protests. "It didn't feel like there was a closure at all. We know this character and I think Benzien haunts many people up to this day," said the wife of a torture victim.[253] The TRC was given a sharp reprimand. "They are playing politics with our people's trauma." Indeed, if we recall the large gaps in the memory of the amnesty applicants, the criticism appears understandable. On the other hand, the opinion of the psychologist explains the missing elements of memory. In the many-sided debate of the Amnesty Committee, it says: "As a matter of course, it was customary for the police to deny that they had tortured their victims." The testimony of Benzien is in agreement with the practice of the time and was cross-referenced with that of other police accounts. "In order to extract information from suspects, unconventional methods of interrogation were used. It was accepted by all in the police force that the end justified the means." The conclusions of the amnesty committee reflect the agenda of non-partisanship: "the offences for which the applicant seeks amnesty were committed during and arose out of the conflicts of the past between the State and Liberation Movement."

From the point of view of the victims, the decisions of the Amnesty Committee demonstrate not too little, but too much objectivity. Its decisions are directed by legal precedents. The legal distinction between morality and justice is upheld by the TRC, but the question remains: how does the political charge for non-partisanship agree with moral claims of reform?

This question points to the gap with which the TRC has struggled since its inception in both of its committees (i.e., Human Rights Violations Committee and Amnesty Committee) and which comprised the main source of criticism in the political debates, as documented in the parliamentary debates of the Final Report, 1999. It highlights how the TRC became a projection screen for unrealized expectations.[254] Indeed, one report says that the TRC did not fulfill its mandate. Meanwhile, the disappointment appears to side against political compromise which, however, preceded the TRC mandate.

Another report says that the TRC went too far in its even-handedness with respect to crimes committed during the apartheid era. The proponents of the ANC applaud the fact that the TRC uncovered the human rights violations committed by the apartheid regime. One report also cites "serious reservations." For example, Thabo Mbeki says: "One of the central matters at issue was, and remains, the erroneous determination of various actions of our liberation movement as gross violations of human rights."[255] There is no greater human rights violation than apartheid itself. D. Ntsebeza thinks the language used by Mbeki is "outrageous." "It sounds like the violence of the ANC is excusable violence and therefore there can be no finding that the ANC is guilty of gross human rights violations."[256] The TRC Commissioner, who earlier himself represented relatives of victims of the resistance (freedom fighters), who were killed in the exile camps of the ANC without the benefit of any legal process, says decisively: "For whatever reason those people got killed we (the TRC) take the view that these excesses were not proper." In the parliamentary debates there were also moderate voices on the side of the ANC. One delegate said: "The TRC report is nothing else but the culmination of what exactly happened in our country. It is the truth. It is bitter to some of us, and yet acceptable to many of us."[257] Another opinion is that the TRC didn't go far enough with its objectivity and represented a one-sided view of the ANC. The opposition leader complains: "It was a mistake to appoint a commission dominated by members and sympathizers of only one political party."[258] One delegate of the Inkatha Freedom Party (IFP) is clearer in reference to the process of truth finding by the commission: "Its final report is a clumsily crafted anecdotal mythology through which it has sought to give credibility to yesterday's liberation propaganda." A representative of the Freedom Front (FF) went the furthest by saying that reconciliation could not be reached while offenders on one side were demonized while those on the other side were declared righteous. "We in the FF never ask our people to accept this report." However, the opposition held different opinions. A delegate of the TRC process says of the exercise in pluralism: "The TRC is a mirror in which we must not only read our history but also see ourselves from different angles."

What then is "true"? Did the report go too far or not far enough? Was the process of non-partisanship in the truth findings worth it? The parliamentary debates offer many opinions, but few clues to an evaluation of the report. The essence of the truth-finding process of the commission is clearly that the TRC tried to fulfill its mandate. But exactly that is what appears to be criticized. Is the fact that the report is attacked by all political camps, an indication that the TRC has fulfilled its mandate perhaps too well? The criticism of the report is understandable against the background of political compromise. The TRC mandate raises at the same time the historical-political issue of whether it can arrive at a historical truth without at the same time raising the question of morality. Can the report contain an evaluation of apartheid? Shouldn't it point decisively to central questions, such as those that ask whether apartheid is not practically achievable, or whether it is morally reprehensible, or even illegal in a popular sense?

At any rate, these questions outline the movement in play in the initial (political) context at the beginning of the 1990's. Under the influence of the work of the TRC and its Final Report, the view that apartheid ended because it was simply not manageable any more from a practical standpoint largely disappeared from the political discussions. Rather, it points to the view in the parliamentary debate that apartheid was immoral and unjust. "I am glad," says a delegate of the ANC, "to note that . . . the so-called New National Party now subscribes to the view that the government that the NP headed for 46 years was immoral."[259] More must be written about this partial truth, says another ANC politician. "To say apartheid was unjust does not say anything. It was unjust, because it was criminal. Once one accepts that, one is moving." *The* truth, which *leads to reconciliation,* is connected to the view: "apartheid was evil." And a cabinet minister continues: "If we are to be reconciled, the truth must be known."

It is evident that the job of the Final Report was to uncover the historical truth about the crimes of the apartheid era on both sides, but also to provide the criteria by which to evaluate the stories.[260] These provoke a critical discussion with the past instead of quoting partial truths about apartheid to connect to an official report. Reconciliation *through truth* does not aim at the attention of the story, but for *change* in *the face* of the story. Wherever the truth is confronted, there will be resistance. The attempt at political even-handedness does not mean moral apathy. "Even-handedness . . . does not mean . . . that moral judgment was suspended or that the Commission made no distinction between violations committed by those defending apartheid and those committed to its eradication."[261]

The Final Report is also very clear in its choice of words. It speaks, for example, against repeated false citations in the press of a "just war," which led one side of the conflict. In the sense of the theory of just war[262] it distinguishes between the *jus in bello* and the *jus ad bellum*. The TRC has gone very far and has intentionally taken into consideration the fact that all conflicting parties felt they were fighting for a just cause. "The Commission accepted that many people had clearly believed that they were fighting against communism and anarchy and not, in the first place, for apartheid."[263] At the same time, however, it must be argued in the sense of international law that the deeds on the side of the apartheid regime ultimately took place in defense of a system that was condemned by the international community for its "crimes against humanity." Thus, in the sense of the *jus ad bellum* one may deduce: "those who fought against the system of apartheid were clearly fighting for a just cause."[264] However, that does not mean in terms of the *jus in bello* that all of the deeds that were committed to end apartheid were necessarily legal, moral, or acceptable.[265] In the course of the report, it is mentioned in connection with the Freedom Movement entirely in the sense of "just cause."[266]

Unfortunately, the Final Report was not taken to heart publicly by many members of parliament. If it were, D. Ntsebeza is not able to explain many of the comments contained in the parliamentary debates. In the sense of the "mixed question" we therefore must ask: if social reconciliation is based on the non-partisan disclosure of the truth, then how far has the process of reconciliation in South Africa come? The Final Report documents that it was not only non-partisan in its uncovering of human rights violations on both sides of the conflict, but its contribution to the process of reconciliation is also to be seen in the power of the formula *reconciliation through truth* for uncovering the truth of the horrors of apartheid so that the public had to respond. Here it is not simply about "knowing enough." The regulative idea is: truth helps to reconcile only when it motivates change. Thus, the Final Report does not precipitously promote the view of its writers that apartheid is a *crime against humanity*. Rather it anticipates this view in a social sense in the knowledge that reconciliation is a long-term *process* whose successful end is only achievable by the total rejection of all parties that subscribed to the ideology of apartheid.

(b) Reconciliation as a Category in Political Handling of Guilt?

"The matter of reconciliation is far more difficult than the issues of truth," say the members of the commission.[267] That is immediately clear if we but contemporize what it has to do with the context of South Africa. "If by reconciliation we understand the complete absence of animosity between different races, ethnic groups, classes and political parties in the South African society, reconciliation will not come the day after tomorrow or next year, it may take generations to come."[268]

At least the TRC had a specific research context in its search for truth; namely, to find an answer to the question, "how should the goal of the 'national unity and reconciliation' be reached?" A. Boraine maintains: "Some said that truth was fine, but not reconciliation. They were wrong. The TRC has broken the deathly silence about the grotesque consequences of the apartheid system."[269] We saw that the stories of truth in many cases led to personal reconciliation. However, the "truth" did not lead in every case to reconciliation, especially not on the interpersonal level, which is documented by the amnesty hearings. A study of the Centre for the Study of Violence and Reconciliation (CSVR) has summarized the voices of victims on reconciliation and has come to the conclusion that victims can only forgive offenders when the offenders are "honest" and sincerely regret their actions.[270] TRC investigations came to the same conclusion: "If people who have committed crimes come forward in all honesty and sincerity then it will be a good thing," one voice is cited as saying.[271] The mere depiction of the truth, the account of "full disclosure" as required by the TRC rules for application does not by itself build a bridge to reconciliation between offenders and victims, nor does it empower victims to forgive their offenders. On the contrary, by virtue of its amnesty legislation the impression was reinforced that the TRC pronounced forgiveness to the victims. What is amnesty if not forced forgiveness? "What really makes me angry about the TRC and Tutu is that they are putting pressure on us to forgive," criticized an injured party about the work of the Commission. "For most black South Africans the TRC is about us having to forgive people I know don't make subtle distinctions between reconciliation and forgiveness."[272] It is also widely stated that the demand to forgive came from religious corners. Within the Commission, W. Malan criticized that the attention received by the work of the TRC was primarily that of individuals involved in reconciling with each other "in a direct religious experience paradigm."[273] C. Niehaus thinks that meanwhile it is practically impossible to transfer the political agenda for social reconciliation to a personal level: "You have to reconcile!" is something that Niehaus also deems "unchristian."[274]

The criticism over the missing connection between truth and reconciliation in South Africa must be taken very seriously. Meanwhile, the projection onto the TRC (in my opinion) makes several mistakes in judgment.[275]

Mistake 1: Identifying amnesty with forgiveness. Where forgiveness was regarded as forced by the TRC process, it had to do with the application of the concept of the national reconciliation concept on an interpersonal level. A quotation illustrates the problem: "I am disturbed about Amnesty," says the father of a Freedom Fighter and says in the next sentence, "I don't know how I can *forgive* my son's killers."[276] However, for the TRC, amnesty is not equal to forgiveness.[277]

A "model case"[278] for the clear distinction between forgiveness and amnesty in which the legal differences between moral and legal are operative is the case of Maxan before the Amnesty Committee. Even though the family member had forgiven him for the murder of his mother, Philemon Maxan was not granted amnesty! *The amnesty committee made its decisions on the basis of legal justice, not on the basis of the readiness to forgive by an aggrieved party.*

According to the TRC law, a victim's readiness to forgive can not be forced, nor can the forgiveness of an offender protect him from prosecution. On the other hand, an offender is not expected to show regret, nor does the demonstration of regret lead to freedom from prosecution. In the discussion it is largely discounted that on a national level there exists a very broad, but "thin" understanding of reconciliation in terms of a national cohesiveness or "growing together." It should be achieved through amnesty for offenders on the one hand, and through the acknowledgement of the suffering of the victims on the other hand. Here, reconciliation is *not* synonymous with "healing" in the interpersonal or personal arena.[279] First there has to be the establishment of *co-existence.* "We don't kill each other. We agree to live in the same country."[280] C. Villa-Vicencio comments: "That's the lowest level." However, *reconciliation* means much more by virtue of its intent: "It involves a commitment to one another to work together, to solve common problems. It involves relationships." *Forgiveness* is still something different. It is a hurdle, over which the above-described form of reconciliation must leap. "It is the highest form of finding one another. And we found that that is a deeply, deeply personal thing." This is because forgiveness is a personal decision that is made in the context of an admission of guilt. The TRC has only been able to lay a foundation for the co-existence of the various individuals or groups.

The distinction between the above three notions of reconciliation adds to the problem when attempting to choose appropriate concepts for the yet to be developed criteria for prioritization. Thus, it may be argued that the TRC does not exert pressure on victims because *forgiveness* is an individual issue. It is validated on another level as part of the political process of amnesty which is achieved for the sake of the agenda of peaceful co-existence. The conclusions of the Final Report are to be understood thusly: "Reconciliation does not necessarily involve forgiveness. It does involve a minimum willingness to co-exist and work for a peaceful handling of continuing differences."[281]

With regard to our "mixed question," the question is to be asked: if reconciliation is to be understood as "peaceful co-existence," how far has the process come? The answer can only be: the TRC has made an important contribution to the stabilization of society. "Peaceful coexistence" has in view of the question of ethnic affiliation become reality.

Mistake 2: Forgiveness aims not at the deed, but at the perpetrator. In the case of the policeman Jeffrey Benzien we observed that forgiveness is publicly possible when one of the outlined changes occur in the offender. "If you ask me what type of person is it that can do that, I ask myself the same question," said Benzein to one of his torture victims. Change means seeing the horror of one's inhumanity in the encounter with the victim.

The loss of humanity is inherent in the language of Apartheid.[282] "Language, discourse and rhetoric *does* things. It constructs reality. It moves certain people against other people."[283] The use of torture, so says Benzien, was part of the "total strategy"; it had to do with "eliminating" the enemy. In this connection Benzien's testimony breaks up: "No, there were other people that would *visit* (torture) him, like the Duty Officers, the Inspector of Detainees, District surgeons. During *working hours* (torture hours). . . . Torture is portrayed as ordinary, regular "work"! D. Foster, who has researched the motives of offenders for the TRC, writes: "The social system changes people."[284] Foster continues: "violence is not a matter of individual psychology alone. It is the combination of personal biographies interwoven with institutional forms (organizations, military structures, hierarchical arrangements of power) and an escalation of events in historical terms that provide the assemblages or configurations that produce awful deeds."[285]

How far should we go to understand the offender? At what point will the victim be degraded? The TRC Report maintains the controlling criteria that an understanding of the perpetrator may not be confused with the desire to excuse.[286] It should not lead to making the perpetrator a victim of his own circumstances. "First, it is important to recognize that perpetrators may in part be victims. Second, recognition of the grey areas should not be regarded as absolving perpetrators of responsibility for their deeds."[287] In this connection, it is helpful to recall the charge of the TRC: "to promote national unity and reconciliation which *transcends* the conflicts and divisions of the past." The law allows room to make a distinction between the offender and the deed. "While acts of gross violations of human rights may be regarded as demonic, it is counter productive to regard persons who perpetrated those acts as necessarily demonic."[288]

In the view of the TRC, it is possible to reinstate the humanity of the perpetrator. "Reconciliation meant that perpetrators of gross human rights violations must be given the opportunity to become human again."[289] Reconciliation thus aims at the perpetrator and not at the deed; namely, the person should be separated from the political context in which the act was perpetrated. "We believed it was the right thing to do!" The victims are invited to try to see the person behind the deed; in our case to see the *man* Jeffrey Benzien behind the "Wet-bag" torturer. However, is it possible for the victims of torture of the notorious police captain to see the humanity of their tormentor? For many it is not, as evidenced by the reactions of the amnesty applicants,[290] but there are exceptions. A. Krog knows enough at the end of the hearings stage to remark: "As everybody is leaving, Benzien grabs the hand of Ashley Forbes tightly in both his own."

How does the "story of reconciliation" move forward? W. Verwoerd, who later was able to speak with A. Forbes, cites these words of Forbes: "That picture of Benzien showed what the TRC can achieve. It brought to light in a vivid manner what both Benzien and I went through — and helped heal us both. I forgive him and feel sorry for him. Now I can get on with the rest of my life."[291] Forbes does not forgive the deed — what was done to him cannot be forgiven. Rather, he forgives the doer and can even say, "I feel sorry for him." This statement further proves the real advantage that is gained by forgiveness from the victim: "I can get on with the rest of my life." This citation by the involved parties says something about the concept of forgiveness of the TRC. It shows in an exemplary way what the TRC report means when it says: "a healthy democracy does not require everyone to agree or become friends."[292] The fact that Forbes has forgiven Benzien does not mean that they have become friends, but it helped him — the victim — to put closure on his past. Furthermore, it was his free decision to forgive. *Reconciliation* in its political meaning of "peaceful coexistence" does not force *forgiveness* on the interpersonal relation level. These concepts must be distinguished in the context of South Africa. The TRC can, however, contribute to "understanding"; it can invite victims to say "yes" to the *possibility* of forgiveness.[293] Forgiveness, like reconciliation, does not lend itself to "arranging" or "organizing,"[294] but from our examples it shows that for the "rediscovery of humanity" — as it is stated in the language of the Final Report — a meeting between the perpetrator and the victim is important. In this regard, C. Villa-Vicencio speaks of *metanoia,* which is possible in a meeting with the victim. Against the background of such considerations, one of the claims of the Johannesburg residents of the Centre for the Study of Violence and Reconciliation, says that creating structures for the purpose of advancing reconciliation helps to make it possible. Structurally, for example, "survivor-offender mediation networks" are being considered.[295]

In the context of our "mixed question," if reconciliation means the "reestablishment of humanity" for the perpetrators, how far has the TRC process come? The TRC creates conditions for the possibility of making a distinction between the deed and the perpetrator.

Mistake 3: Reconciliation is undervalued for its religious potential. By trying to balance the means and the ends, the notion that reconciliation has had its time[296] is advanced further to the "true" reconciliation (one speaks of "true" or "thick reconciliation" in order to distinguish it from the "thin reconciliation concept" with its connotation of "political compromise" or "peaceful coexistence"). The TRC critic Mamdani freely cites theologians when it comes to the correct understanding of reconciliation. So does F. Chikane, General Secretary of the SAAC until 1994, when he says: "For me, the deeper and more critical meaning of the word 'reconciliation' . . . involves people being accountable for their actions and showing a commitment to right their wrongs. Ideally, South Africa needs voluntary disclosure — and I use this phrase in place of the theological term 'confession.'"[297] In the religious understanding of the concept of reconciliation there is a hidden power that can work openly in the political context of the TRC. In the theological dimension of the concept of reconciliation there is first clarification as to why reconciliation can at all be employed as a category in political handling of guilt. It is therefore significant that the TRC "brought to the forefront" the concept of reconciliation at a particular time in the history of South Africa.[298]

W. Kistner[299] distinguishes historical concepts of different phases in the South African "struggle for reconciliation." In the 1950s, reconciliation was employed as a Christian concept of struggle for the first President of the ANC, Albert Luthuli: the way to political freedom leads from the Cross. Struggle is synonymous with "passive resistance." Models for South Africa are Gandhi and Martin Luther King. In the 1960s and 1970s under Mandela, the concept is first mentioned in connection with armed resistance. The senseless shedding of blood, like the massacre at Sharpville, shows that passive resistance does not lead to change in the system. The ANC included the armed resistance in its strategy to break down the apartheid system. (To that end it also serves the basic theological model, which was based in part on a comparison with the church resistance against National Socialism.[300]) In the 1980s,[301] reconciliation was used by the apartheid regime to praise reforms which then were being implemented in an attempt to neutralize the resistance. The authors of the Kairos Documents saw, however, that there can be no reconciliation with apartheid, just as there can be no reconciliation with evil. Reconciliation can only occur in the realm of *justice,* which means under a change in balance of power; above all in the abolishment of apartheid and in free elections. This "expensive" concept of reconciliation prevailed and the way was free for Mandela, who introduced the concept into his politics. The staff of "justice" has continued to adhere to the concept of reconciliation: just as in the 1980s with regard to political justice, so now, at the end of the TRC, it has adhered to economic justice. Kistner did not conceal the fact that in the beginning of the movement toward democracy in 1994, the question of economic reform was cautiously approached. In the foreground stood reconciliation as "nation building" as peaceful coexistence. Only through Mbeki can there be a complete change.

In the perspective of W. Kistner, reconciliation has never had the connotation of "weak compromise." Rather, it was a battle cry — a challenge with the goal of change. If the phrase "no reconciliation without justice" rang out in the middle of the 1980s, so at the end of the 1990s the phrase rang out, "no reconciliation without economic justice."[302] And it is from the concept of reconciliation that focuses on change that the TRC process gained its internal dynamic.

In the end, is it *not* the religious concept that is problematic and "has had its time," but rather a pragmatic one — one could even say a strategically illegitimate concept of reconciliation — that impacts the balance of power? In the sense of our "mixed question," if under reconciliation political and social change is meant, how far has the process come? Change in view of the legal political reality in the new South Africa (and redeemed as the "expensive" concept of reconciliation by virtue of the Kairos Document), and in view of social justice has only just been *introduced.*

Mistake 4: Reconciliation can only be expected from the TRC. There is criticism from many corners that entire areas of reconciliation are left out in the perspective of reconciliation of the TRC. Thus, for example, reconciliation between communities has not been the focus of the TRC. Certainly, at the center of the debate the individual and national levels of reconciliation were promoted along ethnic lines, and also along the lines of "white" and "black," but reconciliation within and between black communities ("black on black violence") and also white communities (if one considers the reintegration of white offenders in their community) remains untouched. In general, it must be asked at the level of community: what is the state of reconciliation between white and black communities? "Does racial reconciliation between blacks and whites require that individual blacks and whites seek reconciliation with each other?"[303] A study by the Centre for the Study of Violence and Reconciliation (Johannesburg), which took place after an intensive inquiry in a township on the East Section (Gauteng), indicates that reconciliation within and between communities has a great deal of meaning. On the level of reconciliation between communities, reconciliation therefore means: "Reconciliation as promoting inter-cultural understanding."[304] On the level of reconciliation within the community: "Reconciliation as building community." The TRC has accepted the constructive criticism that it has been more successful on the national level than on the community level[305] and has integrated the cited study in its Final Report in the chapter "The Way Forward."[306]

(c) Justice for Human Rights Violations?

According to general agreement, which still looms large on the question of whether or not the TRC has brought about the truth, it is already more clear what is involved in the question of reconciliation. Still less clear, however, is whether or not the TRC has produced justice. From an analysis of the political conditions for beginning (I) the theme is evident that a basic problem was inherent in the construction of the TRC. At the beginning it was said that individual amnesty is the next best solution to punishment. However, in the course of the TRC process, the voices increased claiming that punishment was the second best solution.

The narrow line upon which the TRC has defined its work is captured by the basic question: "When does the pursuit of justice turn to revenge?" And on the other side: "When does reconciliation turn into an embrace of evil?"[307] While the second question warns of too broad a concept of reconciliation which must inevitably arrive at untenable moral compromise, the first question is built on the perception that reconciliation cannot be too narrowly defined: reconciliation excludes revenge.[308] The dimensions of justice in the South African discussion are defined between these two guideposts.

The question of whether or not the TRC has brought about justice belongs as a "mixed question" along with two other questions: justice for whom and what form of justice?

For whom has the TRC brought justice? Foremost, it is the victims who criticize the TRC process for lack of justice because it was their rights that were most clearly denied. For them the TRC not only failed to bring their former tormentors to justice and to administer punishment, but through the amnesty laws of the TRC victims of the most heavy human rights violations were, on the basis of civil law, denied the right to exact compensation from their tormentors in the event that their tormentors may have received amnesty. Thus, basic rights were curtailed and the rights of the individual were sacrificed in favor of national reconciliation.

What form of justice is hidden behind the question: has the TRC brought about justice? The main points of the critical statements about the TRC relate both pre- and post-TRC to the lack of retributive elements when dealing with the offenders. There was a range of opinions, including the one that held the Truth Commission lacked decisiveness and was too easy on offenders.

Three views are prominent in the debate about whether or not the TRC has brought justice: the first agrees that justice was sacrificed in favor of truth and reconciliation. This argument says that amnesty is important for ascertaining the truth (i.e., truth finding has positive consequences; for example, it paints a complete historical picture) and that positive results will lead to reconciliation. The advocates of this position could only affix a very weak moral justification to the violation of basic rights; namely that the amnesty legislation would eventually lead to democracy. The compromise made here by the TRC was a purely politically pragmatic one established without moral principles: namely, there is no justice for the individual.

Other voices do not give up so easily on the question of justice for the TRC process. They feel that the advocates of the view described above proceed from a very limited understanding of justice; namely, justice is put on the same plane with the idea of retributive justice. However, if one proceeds from this premise, the question must be asked whether elements of retributive thinking were not included in the TRC process if, for example, one considers that the offenders were punished at the end of the TRC process when they did not receive amnesty. Isn't the public shame which follows from the meticulous depiction of the deed also a form of punishment? The idea of justice is thus broadened and demonstrates how many facets of the concept can be brought into agreement with the TRC. Unfortunately, the assumption that justice is best realized in a retributive sense through prosecution remains firm.

A third position is represented by the opinion that the TRC could be brought not only partially, but fully, into accord with the demands of justice. Methodologically, the idea of an ideal of retributive justice is leverage in aid of its own argument *ad absurdum*. It needs to be asked, how the *lex talionis* connects with the process of transformation with respect to the most egregious of human rights violations: is justice something that can be produced so that torturers can themselves be tortured? The problem of proportionality has been revealed as one of the major weaknesses of the theory of retribution. Can the moral message that should ultimately be conveyed by punishment, only be mediated? It still is the case that the jail cell is a symbol of justice. Must one first segregate the perpetrator in order to be able to rehabilitate him? Hasn't the TRC broken new ground with its message — *"what you have done is wrong!"* — making possible the active participation in building a new society by exposing the truth and by reparations, rather than through punishment? The Final Report of the Commission confirms the answers to these questions. And behind the answers lies the assumption that the TRC does not sacrifice justice, but rather it sacrifices certain means which had been commonly accepted as leading to justice.

On the basis of the Final Report, the final idea of justice contained in it should be upheld. However, the question of *what form of justice is rendered* can not be answered, but only outlined. However, the "mixed question" remains; namely, what the TRC conceptualizes as "process" when it comes to the reestablishment of justice. The question therefore must be asked: how much "restorative justice" can the TRC generate? For the victims "restorative justice" as outlined in the Final Report means, among other things, the acknowledgement of the suffering of the victims; the reestablishment of their dignity and worth before a public forum; but also "reparations" as compensation for the curtailment of potential civil complaints.

The only point emphasized by the various politics of reparations of the TRC is that next to material compensation, symbolic reparations are planned. Here it has to do, for example, with the administrative task of filing death certificates. In addition, exhumations need to be done; burials and funerals made possible. In many cases family members have simply asked for money for gravestones for their loved ones. Symbolic reparations should involve the renaming of streets or of public buildings, as well as the erection of memorials as is the case, for example, of Robben Island.

For the TRS, reparations involve a comprehensive process in view of the encompassing dimensions (symbolic and material) as well as the time frame that is involved. The dimensions of the symbolic and material compensation are not played out against each other." Glenda Wildschut observes that from practical experience many victims perceive material compensation as important. But money cannot make things right. "To receive a check of R60,000 is cold comfort for the loss of a child." In this case would renaming a school after a child, who was once an alleged freedom fighter, adequately "compensate" the parents?

Reconciliation can only succeed as a total social effort. The members of the reparations committee hope that it will succeed in involving the private sector and especially society at large in the politics of reparation. Overall, one must see that the TRC can not close the gaps between the suffering of the victim and possible reparations.

Whether the reconciliation process will succeed in the end very much depends on the broader social effects of the TRC. The spark must be ignited. The basis of a human rights culture is set, but there are still high fences and empty streets in the "ontology of power."[309]

3. An Analysis of "Regulative Statements" behind the Political Balance of Dealing with System Injustice in South Africa

The analysis of "regulative statements" maintains the goal of laying the groundwork for the question of correspondence. The conditions for the possibility of political reconciliation should be established first, in order later to verify the "regulative statements" on the basis of their basic relationship to theological reconciliation.[310]

A key axiom of this section is "process." One of the general "regulative statements" indicates that:

- Reconciliation is a process. Results are formulated in *process*. However, which implied axiom motivates the discussion of the *process* of reconciliation? In the following chart, the guideposts of the process are marked ($\rightarrow$), thus outlining individual goals for each offender, especially the victims, as well as goals for the *nation* (national reconciliation process).

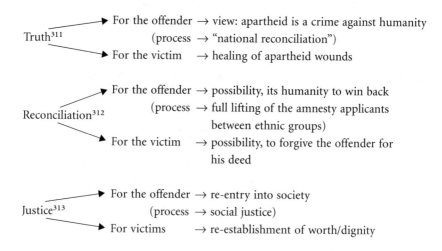

Truth[311]
- For the offender → view: apartheid is a crime against humanity
  (process → "national reconciliation")
- For the victim → healing of apartheid wounds

Reconciliation[312]
- For the offender → possibility, its humanity to win back
  (process → full lifting of the amnesty applicants between ethnic groups)
- For the victim → possibility, to forgive the offender for his deed

Justice[313]
- For the offender → re-entry into society
  (process → social justice)
- For victims → re-establishment of worth/dignity

The implied understanding of process is equivocal. In the statement "reconciliation is a process" at least two ideas of "process" are at work: next to a teleological there is a de-ontological one.

For a *teleological understanding,* the process of rebuilding is imbedded in a total connection of the requirements that are appropriate and of its goal of lying outside of a defined time frame. (That applies also for the in the graphic to the right indicated goals.)

One is *politically* guided by the idea that:

- In politics we can only expect something limited. Reconciliation is a political enterprise; its realization remains a goal.[314]

Or one is guided by a *legal* agenda:

- The conclusion of the process can only be measured by virtue of its mandate.[315]

There is a similar position in which the implicit guiding axioms can occur next to each other:

- Reconciliation presumes "full disclosure of all relevant circumstances" (legally, for example Ntsebeza).
- Reconciliation assumes the taking over of responsibility (political and psychological, for example K. Christie, for the psychology, for example B. B. Hamber).

In a de-ontological understanding, reconciliation is contained absolutely *in the* expectation of the *process* of working it out. It is conclusive in its beginning as well as in its approach to the end. (The goal, which is indicated by the graphic on the right *must* be reached in the course of the process.) This view is fortified by "regulative statements" such as:

- Reconciliation can be reached in the TRC process.
- Politics can bring about reconciliation.

Under the rubric of a de-ontological understanding of process, the critics of the TRC say that, among other things (on principle) they expected the TRC to be able to bring about reconciliation and on balance, the process has failed. Since in this model everything appears to be connected to this view, is indicative of a quasi-religious absolutizing of the TRC process.[316]

Intermediary Theological Observations
(Theological Interlude)

These intermediary observations are not intended to serve as a summary, nor should they be construed as a theological interpretation of the preceding analyses. Rather, this section is meant to serve as a bridge between the theoretical foundation established in Part I and the ensuing theological synthesis contained in Part III.

First, these observations attempt, in their depiction of political reality, to retain the various relational connections to the terminology that surrounds the concept of reconciliation which also serve to make up the categories for the case studies in the German context. Second, in anticipation of Part III, theological questions are formulated that emerge from a representation of the political forms of appearance of reconciliation. Finally, it is necessary to look back at Part I in order to make a comparison with the second case study in terms of its ability to reflect progress made in the area of theological knowledge.

1. A systematic rendering of the theological doctrine on reconciliation is not defined *a priori* on the basis of its connection to politics. Rather, the concept remains "open" in terms of its political connotations. The political forms for expressing reconciliation encountered in the analysis of South Africa's dealing with the past are multifaceted. In South Africa, reconciliation exists primarily on two levels: the individual level and the national level. One may also speak in terms of a "micro-level" and a "macro-level" of reconciliation. The "individual" level of reconciliation further branches out into three areas: personal reconciliation, interpersonal reconciliation (offender-victim), and communal reconciliation (offender and community; "commu-

nity," that is, between communities). The personal dimension of reconciliation can also be divided further into two areas: for the victims, "personal reconciliation" means "coming to terms with the painful past" (restoring dignity); and for the offenders it means "restoration of their humanity" (restoring humanity). The regulative idea is that both the dignity of the victim and the humanity of the offender be restored through the "process of reconciliation."

2. The identified political forms for expressing reconciliation are limited in Part II to a normative examination of the theological categories of reconciliation and of the gaps between these categories. Thus, on the one hand, it is appropriate here to ask a critical question: if reconciliation is an individual theological category, how can the political idea of "national" reconciliation take shape as a category for the community? On the other hand, there appear to be active distinctions that lie behind the designated terms for reconciliation which, upon closer examination, appear to have something in common with the theological doctrine of reconciliation (such as the distinction between the deed and doer of the deed) where the condition for interpersonal reconciliation is the "change" that takes place in both participants through the reconciliation process. The offender regrets his action as a result of an extended confrontation with the truth, but also through a confrontation with the truth in the confines of the TRC. The victim changes his perspective and begins to see the person behind the deed: his dignity and humanity. As a result, community is again made possible ("restoration of justice"). Theologically, processes such as this should be examined to find out whether the regret of the offender corresponds structurally to the regret of the sinner in confession *(passiva contritio)*. What are the prevailing conditions for this process? Is there a basic connection between the desire of the victim to differentiate between the deed and the doer of the deed and the theological motive for reconciliation that exists between the sin and the sinner? Is there correspondence in the process of political reconciliation similar to the type of "change" implicit in what the Biblical tradition understands as "transformation" *(metanoia)*? After the collapse of a political system, to what extent is the political effort to restore community between the offenders and the victims the result of overcoming — through Christ — guilt-based alienation? All of these questions need to be examined on the basis of explicit categories of thought concerning reconciliation and the gaps existing between these categories.

In terms of making a formal determination of possible categories between spiritual and political reconciliation, the evidence of individual case

studies will be examined for their basic theological connection to reconciliation in each specific area of correspondence. In this regard, references will be
made to legal-ethical, symbolic-theoretical, and process-theological discussions.

The empirical analysis of the initial political conditions for dealing with
guilt in South Africa (I) will be examined primarily in the area of legal ethics
for its connection to theological norms. Accordingly, parallel sections of the
theological synthesis are treated in Part III.A.II.3.a. Among the questions to
be discussed are: Is punishment justifiable (Option 1)? Are amnesty and forgiveness synonymous (Option 2)? Is "reconciliation through truth" to be
viewed as a method or as "preparing the way" (Bonhoeffer) (Option 3)?
Does the concept of "restorative justice" assume a positive view of humanity,
even though morality and the law are indistinguishable and the concept of
sin is apparently missing (Option 4)? Does the political concept of reconciliation, which allows the integration of everything, relinquish the eschatological *proviso* (Option 5)? The condition for a theological examination of these
questions is a theological approach to the law (compare Part III.A.II.2.c).
Similarly, the questions relating to the chapter on balance in the South African case studies can not be developed without a theological approach to the
concept of process. From the area of process theology, the following questions are treated in Part III.A.II.3.b, among others: to what extent does reconciliation appear as a soteriological category in the general terms of "process"? Under what conditions does the regulative statement "reconciliation
is a process" appear in a fundamentally theological connection to reconciliation? Does reconciliation flow from a process or does it interrupt the process? Do we recognize *kairoi* in political reality? Are we witnessing the presence of the free grace of God at certain points in time when all of a sudden
the victim is ready to see a person behind the perpetrator? What elements
comprise the process of interpersonal reconciliation in the forum of the
TRC, and to what extent are they either similar to or different from the path
of spiritual reconciliation? Finally, the analyzed symbolic forms of expression for working out of guilt in South Africa (II) are put through a theologically normative examination of the theological correspondence to reconciliation in terms of contemporary metaphors, symbols, and research on ritual.
In addition to individual metaphors like "victim" — which has theological
"overtones" from the "tension" of its double meaning (i.e., that of past politics and of the Christological) — the function of the symbols conveying the
theoretical perspective is forced into a fundamental relationship to "worship
service as ritual" during an examination of the rituals involved in the TRC

hearings. *Condicio sine qua non* for the working out of this problem is the theological approach to symbol, metaphor, and ritual.

3. Knowledge is acquired by observing what deviates from the norm. With this basic presupposition, we will first formally establish the necessity of employing at least two case studies to treat the problem. We recognize in the development of the first case study what will be actively represented as "norm" in subsequent case studies: the analyzed forms of appearance of reconciliation in the case examples of South Africa (national reconciliation etc.) yields specific results that guide the presentation of past political proceedings in Germany after the fall of the wall. Accordingly, deviations in dealing with guilt are taken seriously and knowledge is thus gained by observing deviations from the norm with respect to *political* reconciliation.

For an analysis of historical documents, it is possible to distinguish different aspects leading to the acquisition of knowledge through the use of the comparative method. If we assume this constructive differentiation for the development of our problem, the following connection emerges: the *heuristic* view encompasses a broader horizon of questioning that includes an analysis of the proceedings in South Africa and allows the political dimension of reconciliation in Germany to be viewed in another light. For example, whatever is discovered on the level of reconciliation consequently elicits the question: doesn't this or any other level not also impact us, where previously, though not explicitly, there was talk of reconciliation? From an *analytical* standpoint, this comparison will be applied in terms of the *pure* definition of deviation from the norm. The determination of a yet-to-be-realized distinctiveness illuminated by virtue of the comparative method forces the question regarding conditions, thus leading to the possibility of political discussions on the topic of reconciliation; discussions that ultimately yield a *paradigmatic* rendering of the alternatives. As a result, the "German way" for working out systemic injustice sheds its previous connotation.

While a comparison of the *paradigmatic* and *heuristic* aspects yields contemporaneous results for "comparative politics," the comparison itself forces an *analytical stance* above and beyond the case study's internal deviation from *political* reconciliation and into the area of theological inquiry. Thus, the explicit conditions for the possibility of overcoming guilt through reconciliation are able to emerge from within political reality. Our case studies therefore contain a two-fold objective: 1) first, within the framework of case study presentations we evoke the question *"why"* with respect to the various ways of dealing with systemic injustice in South Africa and Germany. In this way, political-sociological knowledge is acquired by way of an *empirical analysis* (Part II), taken primarily from the deviation of political norms in both South Africa and Germany.

Accordingly, the *theological synthesis* (Part III) asks in theologically normative terms about the basic theological relationship to reconciliation as one of several possible conditions for this serious deviation in empirical analysis. The third section, which presents a comparison of the theological perspective *(tertium comparationis)*, provides the conditions for a basic theological relationship to political reconciliation as a condition for the possibility for the deviation from the norm.

In addition to a certain generalizing of consequences, which is achieved from across a broad spectrum of evidence, a comparison yields — upon closer analysis — a similarity to the second case study with regard to the working out of the political aspects of reconciliation.

B. Dealing with Guilt after the Fall of the Berlin Wall 1989-1999

Contrary to the case studies in South Africa, the following *historical research* is not tied exclusively to global transitional research and thus prevents the formation of a conceptual bridge by which to conduct an analysis of the context of "transitional justice." In Germany, the internal perspective in dealing with the past was decisive. Even foreign observers knew it to be a unique case: "In Germany, the historical developments after 1989 were constantly compared to those of 1945," observed the English historian T. G. Ash.[1] P. Steinbach says: "No other state in our century is connected to the evolution, expansion, and dissolution of two anti-civil societies and their political orders of this century in quite the same way as was Germany."[2] Therefore, it is possible to make the observation that "the experience of two German dictators comprises a negative starting point for liberal democracy."[3]

Our case study research presupposes the results of analytical-comparative research (i.e., comparison of dictators).[4] Meanwhile, the fixation on the national socialist dictator conceals dangers. R. Reissig, in his research on social transitions, writes critically in hindsight: "The selected paradigmatic framework in which the questions were treated already presumes a predisposition with regard to the answers."[5] Therefore, it is important to go beyond the confines of the internal perspective and to place the East German transformation process within the larger context of research on international transition processes.[6] P. Hayner, who has compared truth commissions on the international scene, suggests: "As a rule, one has much to gain by looking beyond one's own borders."[7]

First, in terms of historical research, what follows from the previous considerations is that they are tied to results of distinct branches of research on dictatorial regimes and transitional processes. Second, both discussions are juxtaposed against the same background;[8] namely, that it was previously "not successful" to "connect Germany with international research on transitions (to democracy)."[9]

Contrary to South Africa, where, to cite K. Jaspers,[10] under the auspices of the TRC, not only the "criminal," but also the "political," "moral," and hence the "metaphysical dimension of guilt" were treated, the German process appears less homogenous.[11] The multiple situations regarding the appropriate medium for coming to terms with the past therefore impacts the methodology.

The initial political conditions for dealing with guilt in Germany (I) are again analyzed individually within the framework of past political options for action from the standpoint of international research on transitions. In order to mediate the *symbolic forms of expression of systemic injustice* (II) from the historical political perspective, it is necessary to go into detail in the work of the Investigative Commission (IC) in its "Working of the History and Consequences of the SED Dictatorship in Germany" (1992-1994) and the subsequent "Overcoming of the Consequences of SED Dictatorship in the Process of German Unity" (1995-1998). In terms of historical research, the results of a "comparison of dictatorships"[12] are assumed by the work of the Commission itself. Additionally, we must consider that the international research on transitions has classified the role of an "Investigative Commission" as that of a "Truth Commission."[13] In terms of evidence, selected hearings of the IC are again documented and analyzed on the basis of their symbolic forms.[14] In order to achieve a balanced discussion regarding the historical basis for a political working out of systemic injustice in Germany (III) the Final Reports of both the ICs (1994 and 1998) are enlisted. And, against the background of the claim that the IC had no legal authority in contrast to the TRC, the results of criminal proceedings against DDR injustices are also included.[15]

I. Initial Political Conditions for Dealing with Guilt in Germany

During one of his visits to Berlin in 1998, the TRC commissioner D. Ntsebeza said: "The German people now have the huge task of building a new and unified nation, of reconciling perpetrators and victims."[16] How does Germany cope with this charge? And how is its path determined based on its unique initial conditions?

In terms of the rubric of international system change, the German transition process is best positioned within the category of government "overthrow," which includes the initiation of reforms that the SED Regime "had opposed to the very end":[17] "being overthrown is the fate of a regime that has refused reform: opposition forces become stronger and finally topple the old order."[18] However, under the category of "overthrow," only the first phase of the transitional process can be identified; namely that of "peaceful revolution."[19] By the end of 1989 it was already clear that a stable process of democratization within the DDR was not feasible and a call for reunification was made.[20] Traits of a "political compromise" are also evident; however these forces are increasingly in play between East and West Germany and not between the former powers of the DDR and its citizenry. This asymmetry is also reinforced by the fact that the "process of the German unification was not the convergence of two democratic states and systems," but "the assimilation of the one — unsuccessful — state into the other successful state."[21]

In comparison to South Africa, indicators leading to the question of dealing with the past in Germany quickly emerge. For example, it is possible to determine the time frame for the investigation period for this section as occurring in the 329 days between the 9th of November, 1989 (fall of the Berlin wall) and the 3rd of October 1990 (creation of state unity). Further indicators can be found in the ratification of the *Unification Agreement*:

- punishment of SED regime criminals
- rules for the Stasi files
- reparations for the victims, and
- examination once accepted back into public office.

Additionally, we will analyze what part is played by the principal options for action among the list of options at the disposal of a country that is in the process of political transition.

1. The Punishment of Offenders after the Overthrow of a Government (System)

While there are strong arguments that speak in favor of Option 1 after system change[22] — such as *truth and justice demand punishment* or *human rights violations should be punished* — the issue of the *moral obligation of the* new government was rejected in the South African political debates, but plays a decisive role in the German debates.

The revolution of 1989 took place peacefully.[23] There was no "night of long daggers," "in which the desire for justice and the cumulative desire for retaliation would have been given a chance to unleash itself against party officials and ministers, the police, and those complicit with the Stasi."[24] The opportunity for "revolutionary justice"[25] faded away. Accordingly, the appropriately termed "peaceful" revolution had its price: "The authentic establishment of peace within society has still not been achieved. . . . The need for atonement continues to languish and has turned to the constitutional state and to the judicial system. The constitutional state now has to try to accomplish what the revolution was not able to accomplish."[26] "We wanted justice and got a constitutional state," are the often cited words of Bärbel Bohley.[27] However, here we encounter the basic problem in any attempt to develop a system of justice from the DDR's past and one that will occupy us in the following case studies. Does a constitutional state stop being a constitutional state when it starts to fulfill the expectations of justice connected with political transition?

Included in the acts of violence along the East-West German border where almost 100 people were killed between 1971 and 1989,[28] damage was done to body, life, and freedom (the three "personal goods").[29] Within the German context of Option 1, the legal language that emerges with respect to the alleged "protection of the wall" is especially informative[30] and is clearly discernible along the entire span of the judicial reconstruction.

On November 3rd, 1992, the German Federal Supreme Court considered the following case[31] for review: during the early morning hours of December 1, 1984, two members of the border patrol fired shots at a 20-year-old East Berliner, "who attempted to climb over the wall at the (East) Berlin city of Pankow into the district of Wedding."[32] The escapee was met with "shots from an automatic infantry gun," "as he attempted to climb a ladder that had been leaned against the wall." The gun was put on "repetitive fire." During the five seconds in which the escapee tried to climb the ladder, one border guard unloaded 27 cartridges. The other guard, "who had previously given the order to stop and had fired warning shots, fired from a guard tower at a distance of 150 meters." A shot "penetrated (the victim's) back, just as he was putting his hand on the top of the wall." The victim was taken to the hospital after a period of two hours had elapsed, where he subsequently died. "The delay was the result of secrecy rules and regulations that were not known to the accused."

The grounds for the decision in this case yield a benchmark for the issue of prosecuting serious human rights violations in a reunified Germany. The German Federal Supreme Court first considered the legal position. According to DDR border law,[33] "the order to shoot" was "justified in order to prevent the immediate execution or continuation of a criminal act, which would result in a felony."[34] "Unlawful crossing of the border" was a crime according to DDR law.[35] The border guards were ordered to "prevent" anyone from escaping. The soldiers had been trained to "follow the plan": "Warn the escapee — try to reach the escapee on foot — fire a warning shot — aim a single shot; if necessary, shoot several times in the leg — keep firing if necessary and shoot until the flight is stopped." The adage was: "Better a dead escapee than a successful escape."[36]

The basis for the decision conforms to a specific interpretation by the Investigative Committee: the DDR law should only be observed when it does not lead to a serious breach of human rights. Accordingly, murder is a punishable offense. The core issue places the decision by the (German) Federal Supreme Court into a larger context in the international debate on political transitions. "Despite much mention of human rights," criticized the Federal Supreme Court, "it lacks the very immediate and powerful impact of the basic idea that the protection of universally valid human rights is something that the legal reconstruction of a dictatorial regime should be engaged in and authorize."[37]

The example of the so-called "wall protection policy" very effectively underscores attempts that were made to avenge serious human rights violations. In the debate surrounding the decisions on protecting the wall, the arguments in favor of punishment for *serious human rights violations* (Option 1) are visible. At the same time, the prosecution of those who guarded the wall clearly indicates the basic problems encountered in the process of judicial reconstruction:

- The following argument is firmly entrenched in the German discussion: *the punishment of serious human rights violations is necessary in order to demonstrate the superiority of democratic norms and values.* However, the injustices of the DDR are *not* only characterized by serious human rights violations (compare this to apartheid). The major portion of DDR injustices fall within an area that is off-limits to the law;[38] namely, remaining unpunished are the "the forty years of servitude, the incapacitation of the majority of the population, the indoctrination from childhood"; in short the multilayered aspects of "loss of opportunities in life."[39] Here we can expect no legal ruling that could be regarded as having representative symbolic power for society. For the Constitutional State, the priority is the re-establishment of the failed judicial order; for the victims the priority is restitution. One may justifiably ask, what use it is to the mother of a victim of a shooting at the wall when the offender gets off with only a suspended sentence?[40]

- The other argument for Option 1 — *to ensure general prevention, the entire population must be shown that human rights violations will no longer be tolerated* — carries only partial weight in the German debate. In view of the decision to defend the wall, the question must be asked: how can a suspended sentence serve as a deterrent? And for whom? Isn't the problem so thoroughly thought out that it can't happen again?[41] Or is it not as settled as we would like to think, as long as there are dictators who give the command to shoot in other parts of the world?[42] In general, is prevention even possible by means of the law? In any case, the fact that it could ever come to the point of committing such violations of human rights is now firmly entrenched in the human consciousness.

- By way of clarification, the argument that *truth and justice demand punishment* does carry weight. "As in the NS proceedings, so also the practice to shoot in protecting the wall comprises *nolens volens* an important chapter of political enlightenment and education."[43] The litigation process works against "any diminishment of the violent crime committed on the border."[44] However, other voices argue that the truth that has come out about the punishments levied for protecting the wall does not go far enough. These deeds comprise only a portion of the damage. "Such deeds, as bad as they are, comprise only an expendable part of totalitarianism, which one should counter not only on the basis of this facet alone, but also in general terms."[45] G. Werle arrives at the problem of distinguishing between morality and justice when he points out that justice via punishment is sooner restored for the victims on a symbolic level.[46] A constitutional state can not assume responsibility for recompense to the victims. Sensitivity to the victim, as important as it is, is not a criterion for measuring punishment. The crux of the matter is still: "The victims demand punishment."[47]

The *result* is accordingly: the course is set for the punishment of *serious* human rights violations. In the process of protecting the wall it is clearly evident that serious human rights violations must be prosecuted. The assumption is regulative: punishment cannot be ignored in the process of reconciliation.

Since the relevant arguments for Option 1 have been outlined, the analytical question can now be raised in comparison to South Africa: how are the opposing arguments to be evaluated? The answer appears to be possible not only in terms of the differences in the kinds of system change, even if the political non-enforceability of punishment in the system change of South Africa is retained as a solid argument. According to the evidence, two additional viewpoints should therefore be considered: (1) if one asks from the perspective of cultural differences whether apartheid solved the injustices encountered by certain segments of the population involved in ongoing conflict, then one thing is clear: *not in legal terms,* but rather through ritual, etc. Accordingly, how is conflict resolved in Germany? (2) It appears to be a very critical factor as to what point in time a society decides to become concerned with its past. What kind of value is attributed to a constitutional state at the point in time of system change? In the case of South Africa, the constitutional state was primarily understood in terms of its ability to rebuild the country. Does that also mean embracing a general amnesty for serious human rights violations? After 1989, Germany was able to uncover the vestiges of a forty-year-old stable constitutional state in the form of the previous German Federal Republic. Thus, the situation in Germany after 1945 appears to be more similar to that of South Africa after 1990 where, in hindsight, one may find indications that it was easier to receive amnesty in the 1950s.

2. Amnesty for Human Rights Violations

The nature of system change in East Germany ("overthrow" of the government), and also the larger scope of developments en route to unity did not make the political necessity for a *general amnesty or "truce"* (Option 2) immediate. In the context of the above, it is obvious why the arguments[48] for Option 2 did not prevail in the German discussions. Namely, there was no threat of a coup; the young democracy was not going to be threatened if it prosecuted serious human rights violations. The former rulers did not have to be enticed by an amnesty law to relinquish their power. Additionally, the argument for transition — namely, that amnesty is necessary *in order to erect a young democracy on a solid basis* — did not carry in the debates. The reason for this is obvious: after the fall of the wall the former rulers posed no threat to democracy (comparable with international processes). In addition, the asymmetry which was later to mark the process of German unity contributed to integration of the young democracy of East Germany into the stable West Germany; thus — employing strict terms of government unity — an unstable, "young" democracy in terms of the research on global transitions no longer existed. Finally, the argument that a reconstruction of the judicial branch through innumerable processes over countless years was slow and expensive was ultimately rejected. The argument that a constitutional state has ceased to exist "when the overwhelming number of cases is a justifiable reason for allowing amnesty"[49] is countered by the one that says that in Germany a "perpetual motion of proceedings"[50] is to be feared. In sum, the German process lacked the political urgency that forces the usual amnesty regulations into a transitional phase.

Wherever amnesty is granted after political upheaval, the motive is *exclusively that of political necessity.* We also saw this in the case studies of South Africa and have interpreted the situation in connection with the discussions on Latin American countries. Certainly, there is also plentiful historical evidence for these causal connections. H. Quaritsch, in one of the many cited examples in the legal literature regarding amnesty granted during civil war conflicts from the Peloponnesian War right up until the French Revolution, concludes that amnesty is not the "result of human love, forgiveness, and forgetting or an inner change to powerlessness."[51] "Rather, amnesty is compelled by the circumstances or at least suggested by them. Such coercive circumstances were lacking in 1989/90. Thus, a general amnesty in favor of the supporters and actors of the SED regime was and is not to be expected."

A "celebratory amnesty," which is not forced by the character of system change, but is granted "for example, during a state festival,"[52] was expected by very few people. On September 5, 1990, the delegate H. Daubler-Gmelin stated in Parliament: "The wall has fallen, the barbed wire in Germany is gone, and the iron curtain through Europe has been rent. We think that everyone, not only Stasi co-conspirators, should be granted amnesty and we present this challenge: let's have a general amnesty for the sake of German unity which then entirely eliminates all accompanying judgments and discriminations."[53] (The protocol registers applause from the SPD, also from the Green Party and parts of the FDP.) B. Hirsch identifies the basic problem in the debate. To be sure, he dislikes the term "celebratory amnesty." But the problem also has to do with the question "whether or not we should utilize this unique historic occasion . . . to heal the wounds that we have inflicted upon ourselves."[54] When one speaks of "healing of wounds," one may notice a reliance on the argument of global transitional research that is aimed at overcoming the results of past conflicts: *democracy must be built on reconciliation in order to overcome the divisions of the past.*

Particularly the second constitutive part of the above argument plays a decisive role for Germany's overcoming the "divisions of the past" which, in the context of German unity, means to overcome the East-West conflict in which the DDR and the old German Republic, with its geographically convenient position, played a decisive role for espionage in the "cold war."[55] For the sake of reconciliation of the Germans, should the resulting espionage offenses against the German Republic (which in the letter of the law belong to the past because in comparable form they are non-repeatable) be disturbed again or should they be granted amnesty? Is it not here morally legitimate to just "let bygones be bygones"?

The problem highlighted by these two questions has many aspects; namely, it depends on the evaluation of the espionage activity. While those promoting amnesty for espionage argue that every country in the world maintains intelligence services and that espionage is espionage, their opponents ask: is it possible to separate the espionage department within the MfS (the HVA)[56] from the other powers of the Stasi? Isn't the reconnaissance abroad of the DDR biased toward "typical DDR injustices"? Doesn't espionage also (as "co-criminals") immediately assume serious human rights violations that one should not "leave in peace"?

The argument that is embedded in the questions steers the political discussion both before and after the establishment of state unity and the rise to power of the EV. Provisionally, one may say that before March 10, 1990, the first line of argument prevailed. Behind the regulations for the disbandment of the MfS[57] is the notion that one intelligence service is the same as any other intelligence service. However, after the completion of unification in Germany, the discussion became more complex. Accordingly, the rise to power of the EV meant only a temporary respite. For the EV, the discussion of the problem of espionage was finally concluded neither by a "leaving in peace" nor by an amnesty ruling. When considering amnesty rulings, a constitutional state does itself harm. Where amnesty cannot be politically enforced through the character of system change it is consequently eliminated as a political option. Immunity laws are thus, almost without exception,[58] considered under the category of serious human rights violations.

The *result* is therefore that doing nothing by "leaving things in peace" is excluded as an option in the face of serious human rights violations, as is that of a general amnesty.[59] The regulative idea is that the punishment of the offenders takes priority over their integration back into society.

3. The Exposure of Past Injustices by the "Truth Commission"

Contrary to South Africa, the exposure of incurred offenses does not serve as a means of avoiding prosecution. In the German debate a constructive connection was already made: even lawsuits could make a contribution to the explanation of past injustice, as proven by the wall protection process. The judicial process retained a very exemplary character: "no history book refers to an evaluation of criminal proceedings."[60]

After 1989, the German discussion appears to be defined by a constructive "communal" use of the judicial process in its historical-political dealings with the past. At the very least, criminal prosecution and exposure do not appear to be opposed to each other in an alternative "either-or." K. Tanner formulates the core of the situation: "This clarification reflects less of an interest in punishment than the fact that many representatives of the national movement in the old DDR still maintain the demand for criminal prosecution."[61] To this extent, the basic tenet holds true: "the Truth Commission does not exclude . . . criminal prosecution."[62]

This basic line of demarcation is already noticeable at the time of the fall of the wall and branches out into two areas for discussion in the decisions made by the People's (DDR) Parliament (which was later to include the EV): (1) In one area it leads to the resolution of the Central Round Table of January 7, 1990, which disbanded the state security apparatus that was under civil control, putting a halt to the destruction of documents as well as to the People's Parliament law of August 24, 1990; the latter having led to the Stasi-document act of December 20, 1991, regulating the legal framework for the members of the Federal commission concerning the documents of the former Federal Security Office of the DDR (BStU, according to their former Chief/Head also called "Gauck-Administration"), making it possible for affected parties to gain access to their records. (2) In the other area, it reaches into the relevant debates for an open tribunal which led to constitutional control and the establishment of the Investigative Commission's account of the history and consequences of the SED dictatorship in Germany on March 20, 1992.

In order to communicate the conditions for political reconciliation, we need to explore the connection of how arguments from the international debate on transitions in Option 3 are weighed. At the center of the developments is the previously mentioned law of the People's Parliament of August 24, 1990, which arranged for the "political, historical, and judicial order of rule of law."[63] "This triad shows," comments J. Gauck before the People's

Parliament, "that an integrated account of history is required, not merely a legal one."[64] The latter was not only a signal for the question of how to deal with the Stasi documents (a), but also for the problem of which public form an accounting for the DDR past should take (b).

(a) "Stasi Documents"

With the dissolution of the MfS, the destruction of documents was indeed halted, but the problem of custody was not solved; and along with custody, the question of inspection also had to be explained. Speculative accounts of factual or alleged unofficial assistants (IM) of the MfS were circulated by the media, which were based on illegitimate methods and, in part, even purchased Stasi documents. "In the alleged interest of openness," the documents could be used as "a political weapon and the means for an increasing number of articles."[65] With it a basic element of the constitutional state was also lost, because the denunciations were now used to prove guilt.

The problem of access to documents has to be solved; there was no legal security. To whom did the documents belong? Who was allowed to see them? How could the information be protected from theft by unauthorized persons? It is within this area of questioning that the transition to Gauck's "Constitutional State" concerning the evidence left behind by the Stasi begins to take on significance.

The soon to be disbanded State Security Service Document Law had to relinquish the task of trying to coordinate "the interest of the victims with the interests of criminal prosecution."[66] As a "principle of the "Gauck Administration" it was suggested that the State Security Service Document Law "1) allow citizens access to the information stored by MfS as well as give an explanation of the influence it has had on his life; 2) protect the right to privacy of civilians by controlling foreign use of this information; 3) provide for the historical, political, and legal renovation of the MfS, and 4) provide for public and non-public setting for disclosing the necessary information."[67]

In terms of the law, the scope of the problem of political reconciliation takes the following direction: reconciliation is made possible only through truth. Only when I know what has happened am I able to say good-bye to the past. "Reconciliation through truth" is, in terms of the work of the "Gauck Administration," limited to the personal dimension of reconciliation.

The level of reconciliation, the conditions for which were created by the State Security Service Document Law framework, appears to be comparable with the South African idea of "coming to terms with the painful past." Interestingly enough, the moment of "exposure of the fate of missing persons or those killed" also plays a role. The law allows close relatives to view the documents.[68] A basic decision was made by the State Security Service Document Law: in the center stands the individual and his actions (reconciliation level: individual). The goal of the law is to help clarify "the degree of influence of the state security office on his personal fate."[69] The law is so conceived that the victims of the Stasi stand in the middle; over against their tormentors they have the advantage of information by which, by means of documentation gathered from a wealth of sources, they are able to reconstruct the main events of the past.[70]

A contribution to the exposure of injustices by the DDR, which in terms of the individual stories are now part of the public record, was not to have symbolic power for the social process of democratization by the construction of the Gauck Administration, nor was any symbolic power expected to emerge through the workings of the administration. *The Gauck Administration was not a Truth Commission.* The significant arguments from research on global transitions, which speaks in favor of the exposure of crimes by means of a Truth Commission, were also not part of the debate concerning the Gauck Administration.[71] However, they aimed at "public exposure" as well as "assumption of responsibility."[72]

(b) Public Exposure

In the course of the year 1991, a social situation emerged in Germany which made the activity of the Parliament in view of a parliamentary disagreement with the DDR past necessary and even compelling: the Stasi disclosures created a climate of mutually groundless suspicion.

There was an interest in the accounts that were limited to dubious press reports and yet lacked an analysis of the historical process. In terms of the Stasi debate, a social counter-balance needed to be created. "Instead of a media controlled account with the offenders" the inclusion of the "reports of the oral statements of victims" is demanded.[73]

In addition to the disclosures made by the Stasi, the entire political situation — not only because it was marked by occurring economic disappointments — compelled a comprehensive debate with the spiritual legacy of the DDR. East Germany was featured in the headlines as right-wing radical youths torched the homes of asylum seekers. A culminating point of this development was marked by the situation in Rostock: photos of burning blocks of homes and fleeing asylum seekers appeared around the world. Finally, in order to single out a further strand of the discussion, it came to a crisis point a year before the above-discussed BGH (Federal Supreme Court) decision, when the criminal reconstruction process was threatened by public disdain. In the legal discussion (as, for example, in connection with the proceedings against *politbureau* member Harry Tisch) it was unanimous that an offender could not be punished retroactively. Among the general population, it was widely known that severe punishment for the responsibility of the dictatorship could not be expected and where punishment was possible, there also remained the assumption within legal quarters that social liberation through the legal process was highly questionable. "Punishing the offender who perpetrated harm to the victim speaks not only in favor of compensation, but rather adds on top of the offense to the victim a further offense: namely, the punishment itself becomes an offense to the offender."[74] Here also was the basic problem that moral guilt is not legally enforceable. "Disappointment grew in the circles of the former civilian movement."[75] Thus: what is not legally enforceable, must at least be articulated in another forum.

In this regard, some decisive historical points are brought into play that speak in favor of appointing a Truth Commission in the sense of action Option 3: *without the uncovering of past injustice, historical conceptions are perpetuated within society that tend to glorify the authority of the past and consequently hinder the spread of a democratic orientation*. In addition, the assignment of responsibility plays an important role in the international discussion: *for a young democracy it is essential that the responsibility of the past regime and its henchmen be assigned*. Finally, the historical point (in time) of *reconciliation on the interpersonal level is established*, which is very relevant in the case of the South African TRC.

The establishment by the German parliament of an Investigative-Commission (IC) to initiate a discussion about early German history leads, on the one hand, along the path of moral components in parliament: moral and political decisions about system overthrow can only be rejected by parliament. On the other hand, the events depicted in the year 1991 also added to the desire for a comprehensive exposure of the structures erected by the (DDR) power apparatus. Therefore, at least in spirit, the fall of the wall could be discussed with respect to the exposure of the facts without focusing on assigning responsibility to individuals.

Since it was given a two-fold assignment, the genesis of the Investigative

Commission combined the notion of historical exposure with the request for a discussion about morality; its task was "to compile contributions for political-historical analysis and political-moral assessment."[76] In the title of the first Investigative Commission (= EK), the basic directions for the entire project went under the rubric of "the development of the history and consequences of the SED dictatorship in Germany." Thus, right from the beginning, the EK allows for a depiction of the social situation in its conceptual formulation: "to this day, the legacy of the SED dictatorship still impacts the task of people who are looking for others (affected by the SED dictatorship) in Germany. The experiences of injustice and persecution, humiliation and incapacitation are still alive. Many people still seek an explanation and wrestle to find an orientation in dealing with their own and an alien responsibility and guilt."[77] The task of the commission is the "attempt to expose the injured sense of justice through the disclosure of the injustice and the naming of those responsible," and also, at the same time, to contribute to the reconciliation of society. Reconciliation appears in the connection between "society" and the act of "finding each other." In light of the TRC, one could say that the Investigative Commission was to contribute to what is called "national reconciliation."[78]

The result is conclusive: in both the "Gauck Administration" and the Investigative Commission conditions were created for a "private" and a "public" form of accounting for the DDR injustices. The idea is therefore regulative that reconciliation is only possible through truth.

4. Reparations for the Victims

The question of rehabilitation and restitution gained weight immediately after the fall of the wall; it stood in the midst of the public discussion next to the exposure of bureaucratic power and the corruption of SED functionaries, but was quashed in the Stasi debates after December 1989. While the Modrow government provided only for the criminal rehabilitation of victims of the DDR regime,[79] the first free voting People's Parliament drafted a rehabilitation law under the pressure of the West which, in addition to legal punishment, also provided for legal rehabilitation of victims. However, it also stated that in the administration of the DDR Constitution, the otherwise guaranteed human rights would have to put up with some disadvantages. A lack of majority killed the Bill because it did not include the provision stating that the value of the compensation should be equal to the replacement value of the damages.[80] In the proceedings of the Federal Government and the DDR People's Parliament of June 15, 1990, the question of dispossession was ruled in favor of compensation.[81] The basic statements of the many-faceted DDR rehabilitation law, above all in the question of compensation for both moral and legal rehabilitation of the victims of DDR injustices, were subsumed under the unified People's Parliament in both the so-called "illegal adjustment laws."[82]

Behind the term "compensation" there lies a basic legal tenet: compensation is a fundamental job of the law. The lawyer Rudolf Wassermann comments: "It is convincing when it corresponds exactly to the injustice."[83] In a real sense, compensation should *make good again any* suffered injustice so that the original situation is restored.

Restitution processes "have great symbolic character within the space of political transition."[84] In a comprehensive sense, compensation correlates to atonement. In this regard, one may argue: Option 4 belongs to the formula of *compensation* with the argument that *the compensation to the victim is fundamental so that, from the victim's perspective, the injustice does not continue.* Why has this formula been so controversial in connection with DDR injustices? From the complexity of the discussion, I am able to single out the relevant historical point that it has something to do with the unequal handling of victims of communist and fascist dictatorships.

After the beginning of the mentioned Proceedings between the BRD and the DDR, it says that the dispossessed should be allowed the "basic capability of having their former possessions returned to either them or their heirs." "However, the wording of the explanation in the laws is disappointing to the victims of the SED regime." Now, "provision was made for the dispossessed to have the property returned that had not been compensated for prior to the founding of the DDR."[85] The basic restrictive tendency of the law contained the language: "only discrete injustices should be compensated."[86] Thus, dispossession during the time of the Soviet Regime remained excluded from laws of possession. One wanted to take into account the sensibilities of the people of the former DDR.[87] Therefore, although one imbalance (East-West) was corrected, others were erected in their place so that the injustice nevertheless remains. In view of this tension, the question arises to what extent it is at all possible for politics to make amends. Wolfgang Schäuble admits: "In history, one can not delete war, separation, injustice, dictatorship."[88] The question for him is "how can the injustices . . . during these 45 years be overcome and repaired in such a way that the present and the future are not harmed too much, and new injustices are not created from the old ones?"

Let's proceed in the following to the issue of moral rehabilitation. We immediately encounter the question, when the *material compensation is not equal* to the corresponding injustice that was incurred, how should then material compensation for injustice be handled in dealings with others? For example, how should the many years of imprisonment — which is also connected with psychological and, in some cases, physical torture — be made good again? It is obvious: compensation in terms of jail time isn't sufficient in such cases.[89] In addition, what about when the area of injustice is elusive and the punishment really doesn't make sense? How can victims of the "perfidious measures of corrosion" by the MfS whose "consequences are still being felt today"[90] be made good again? How can a life of missed opportunities through the exclusion from college entrance exams and university study, or through hindered professional careers because of alleged "political unreliability," be made good again retrospectively? Or how can the daily repression experienced by DDR citizens be adequately repaid?

One example can be cited from the everyday life in a public event involving the Gauck Administration; under the title "Persecution and Its Results" a mother tells the story of repeated humiliations. "During the DDR period my children were beaten up in school practically daily for two years. Once, my son had to go to the hospital as a result of injuries suffered in school; and there was no teacher to accompany him because children of the enemies of the state did not deserve that."[91]

There is a large area of injustice in which a legal ruling is impossible and political parties have tried to bring this problem to parliamentary committees. In the blueprint of the Green Party/90 there is the passage: "the experiences with the administration of both SED injustice compensation laws have shown that many affected people place particular worth on moral rehabilitation without any links to material claims."[92] *Behind this statement is the concept that the reparation of dignity does not occur through material compensation, but as a symbolic act.* In addition, from the perspective of many German victims, reparation does not primarily mean material settlements, but rather the society's acknowledgement of the damage. For the victims of legal injustice, the naming of the deed is also an act of public rehabilitation. The civil rights leader Ulrike Poppe says in regard to the 250,000 judgments of life imprisonment on political grounds: "Lost years can not be given back. Material damages can help to ameliorate the physical and psychological consequences of imprisonment; but still more important is the moral rehabilitation, the recognition of suffering and the dignity of the victims."[93] In the above statement, the argument from international research on transitions says that *official recognition of the suffering of the victims contributes to the re-establishment of dignity.*

During the process of South African transition, moral rehabilitation was connected directly to the establishment of a Truth Commission; in this way, the lawgiver created the framing conditions. In Germany, one could argue, the function of the BStU[94] was to create, in conjunction with the Investigative Commission, a public forum specifically designed to hear the testimony of victims of the SED dictatorship and statements by witnesses at the trials. The symbolic worth that was intended for German society in general by the implementation of such atypical projects is, by comparison to South Africa, very small. Nevertheless, "there was and is a series of efforts to provide a forum for the victims," wrote U. Poppe, who conducted for the NGO-Area: "Educational establishments, memorials, initiatives, institutes, foundations and the media try with events and exhibitions to channel the stories of the victims into society's field of vision."[95]

As a result, I would like to suggest the following in terms of the German process: paths were not created for ratified legislation on criminal punishment, career, and legal rehabilitation, because conditions were not created by the state to address the moral dimensions of reparations. The regulative idea here is that reparations have to be determined both legally and materially.

5. The Disqualification of Charged Co-Workers from Professional Positions

In the German process, three phases of political discussions about the past can be outlined with respect to "sanctions outside of punishment" (Option 5): the transition phase within East Germany; the phase during which the unification of Germany took place; and the phase that involved the legal rulings of the Unification Agreement (EV).

(a) Transition Phase

The first phase after the fall of the wall in the DDR is classic with regard to transitional processes. As in South Africa and due to a shortage of personnel, there was no change in the ruling elite, even in the courts. It is questionable whether Modrow was serious about disqualifying affected staff. The Stasi theme verifies that, after the wall came down, the government only undertook reforms under pressure of Round Table Reforms. De Maizière acted "from calculated *real politik*. Up until 1990, it was not clear if unification would succeed and speculation continued well into 1992. Until that time the DDR regime and its apparatus had to remain intact."[96] Without lawyers and the police force, but also without the military, such a thing would be difficult to imagine. Finally, the elections of March 18 would also not have been possible without loyal supporters. Still, in April 1990, de Maizière says of the situation in the (new) federal government, "that he could not disband the National People's Army (NVA) because the dismissed officers and their subordinates would be a security risk for him and his regime."[97] On the other hand, there was the need for action. How should, for example, rehabilitation be convincingly achieved if the judges in the criminal court system reversed their former decisions? *Thus, a democratic process can not be convincingly established without a change of ruling elite, according to one of the arguments of Option 5.*

(b) Unification Phase

The change of ruling elite who were in charge was first made possible by the anticipation of Germany unity. In the phase of the negotiations of the treaty on unification, the argument for inner stability played only a very minor role; no other concessions were needed. During the time when there could have been upheaval among the ruling elite, it was the unspoken consensus both in the parliament and in the federal government that it would not be handled in a similar manner as it was after 1945 where there was a "cleansing" in large sectors of public office.[98] Schäuble wanted to "hang tight" in order not to compromise the opportunity for unification.[99] Next to this tactical argument there was also the assertion that the basic decision for long-term continuity of "all Germans" to found a new state should be made "with honor and not in a panicky rush."[100] An "honorable way to unity" (Lothar de Maizière) should be made possible. Additionally, there was the desire to counteract the tendency "of the media to mercilessly attack all of those, and their families, who belonged to the old government with its oppressive apparatus."[101] Egon Bahr expressed the character of the time in a simple sentence: "The chance for each individual, in so far as he is free of any evidence of personal guilt, is not the same thing as the requirement to be a spokesperson or banner carrier."[102]

(c) Legal Rulings Phase

The EV created the legal basis and identified the foundational elements for the process of investigation: an orderly termination (from employment) can take place later on if "the workers, due to lack of training qualifications or personal inclination, do not meet the requirements."[103] Particular reasons for termination emerge in other places. They are implemented "if the worker 1) has made an infraction against the basic tenets of humanity or the law, especially those guaranteeing human rights as outlined in the *International Pact on Civil and Political Rights* of December 19, 1966, or has breached the basic elements contained in the *General Declaration of Human Rights* of December 10, 1948; or 2) has worked for the previous Ministry of State Security in the interest of national security, making it improbable that they adhered to the professional code."[104] The last statement referring to both reasons for dismissal "is so outlined as to require a constant need for on-going individual test cases."[105] The guidelines of humane treatment are thus clarified: "Through the reference to the norms of international law it should be clear that here it has to do with decisions by practices that are in accord with generally recognized norms" (ibid.).

The following can be asserted: sanctions existed outside of the criminal code. Although complicity with the Stasi as such is not punishable, neither can it be the basis for dismissal from public service. (Where Option 1 does not apply, Option 5 comes into play.) Information was provided by the Gauck administration and decisions that affected their officials. The regulative idea behind the Investigative Committee can also be formulated: the burden of personal guilt can be sanctioned by job disqualification. Reconciliation does not mean peace at any price.

6. Analysis of the "Regulative Statements" behind the Initial Political Conditions for Dealing with Guilt in Germany

The analysis of "regulative statements" again aligns with the goal of preparing the groundwork for the question of correspondence. The condition for the possibility of political reconciliation should first be determined in order ultimately to test the "regulative statements" with respect to their basic connection to theological reconciliation.[106]

In the following paragraphs we discuss past political options for action and the ensuing regulative ideas that emerge with respect to political reconciliation:

- Reconciliation can not exclude punishment.
- Punishment of the offender must occur before he/she can be integrated back into society.
- Reconciliation has something to do with exposing the truth.
- Reparations can be expressed both legally and materially.
- Reconciliation does not mean a new beginning at any price.

In these regulative statements, the conditions for political reconciliation are ties to the debates:

- Reconciliation places sanctions on the burden of personal guilt at the beginning, be it through punishment or through termination of the work relationship.
- Reconciliation assumes a form of reparation at the outset.
- Reconciliation assumes knowledge of the truth.

In individual (cases) the statements lead into sub-sections[107] and can thus lead to a partially self-contradictory implied axiom. Statements supporting prosecution:

- Human rights violators must be punished.
- Prosecution makes an internal investigation of the events possible.
- Reconciliation is not possible after a disregard for human rights.
- Guilt is too great and must be expiated.
- The damage to human rights in life makes reconciliation impossible.

Statements supporting Truth:

- Truth heals.
- Reconciliation places the explanation of the fate of missing persons at the outset.
- Not forgetting, but remembering frees a person.
- Reconciliation assumes a questioning of the activities of the guilty.

Sentences supporting exemption from punishment:

- Amnesty has nothing to do with reconciliation.
- Amnesty means that forgiveness can take place.
- Forgiveness is expected and reasonable.
- Amnesty is the active contribution to reconciliation.
- One must make a new beginning possible for offenders.
- Guilt belongs to the past.

Statements supporting reparations:

- Compensation for injustice has to be comparable to the damage done.
- Justice demands the same thing in return.
- In politics, compensation can only have limited success.
- Justice is possible only within the framework of the rule of law.

II. Symbolic Forms of Expression in a
Political Appraisal of Systemic Injustice

In comparison to South Africa, the various options for action in Germany which are at the disposal of any country in the process of transferring to a democracy, did not lead to the establishment of an individual governing institution. Rather, at the end of the discussion on past politics there were several institutions left standing:

- The public defender's office II at the regional court in Berlin, together with the other public defender's offices, authorized criminals for prosecution by the DDR regime (Option 1);
- Both of the "Investigative Commissions" (EK) were founded as parliamentary bodies whose task consisted in the "political-historical analysis and political-moral evaluation of the SED dictatorship" (Option 3) and were charged with making a contribution to the rehabilitation of victims through public hearings and legal means (Option 4);
- Members of parliament were designated to oversee the personal documents of the state security office of the former DDR ("Gauck Administration"), who not only played a role in the exposure of the personal fate (Option 3), but also acted as signalmen for rehabilitation proceedings (Option 4); as well as those who were a decisive instrument for the enforcement of sanctions outside of the penal code (Option 5).

The analytical, multi-faceted nature of the "institutionalized overcoming of the past" hides a methodological problem that describes the perimeter of as well as the extension for the following section; namely, not *all* institutions can be investigated on the basis of their symbolic forms of expression. (Finally, the legal branch of accounting for the past is also equipped with its decisions on wall protection, but above all, the so-called "polit-buro" with its large historical-political potential.) I limit myself however — also because of the comparison with the South African TRC — primarily to an analysis of the Investigative Commission and on a secondary level, to the "Gauck Administration." An extension is included because the intra-personal dimensions of reconciliation factor more prominently in the mediated conflicts between victims and offenders.

1. Fundamentals of the Investigative Commissions' (EK) Reconstruction of the SED Dictatorship

In contrast to South Africa, reconstruction via a "Truth Commission" continued for two and a half years. During the session of the 13th German Parliament, a second Investigative Commission was appointed: *Results of the SED Dictatorship in the process of German unity (1995-1998)*. "This Commission should also contribute," says Rainer Eppelmann on his appointment, "to the strengthening of the democratic self-consciousness, of an open sense of justice, to the anti-authoritarian consensus in Germany, and (should) work against all tendencies that want to justify a dictatorship."[108] The lengthy debates of the year 1994/95 on financial matters, amnesty, and the statute of limitations proved the necessity to get on with the work that was begun; they yielded "approaches to the repression of historical accounts that are the stuff of legends."

Eppelmann demanded on March 12, 1992, during the parliamentary debate concerning appointments: "Let us then restore justice: help and support, heal and explain, grasp, understand, reconcile."[109] Willy Brandt spoke on this date of "the possibility of much unveiling and exposure"; of the "working out of the SED inheritance" as a wholly German task, and a "contribution 'to any reconciliation that assumes truthfulness.'"[110] "Accordingly, two political-moral points of emphasis were fixed for the work of the Commission, which was agreed upon by the party factions," says a member of the Commission; antithetically stating that what should determine the Commission's future work is "not the 'inability to grieve' but rather the ability to ask; not defense from guilt, but the question of responsibility and not the marginalization of the offenders."[111] The task of the March 1992 Investigative Commission was thus two-fold: to "contribute to the political-historical analysis and to work for a political-moral assessment."[112]

In the implementation of its task, two crucial points of intersection were addressed. On the one hand, the Investigative Commission had to move between "science" and "politics." To the degree that it tied historical clarification to moral value, the Truth Commission accepted a typical task; namely to portray the history of politics in a positive light. The "saying" was: "Do everything in order to forget, to expel it, and to transform it . . . with all of your might!"[113] On the other hand, it took its task on before the entire nation: "to reconstruct the history and the consequences of the SED dictatorship in Germany."

In contrast to South Africa, the question of "reconciliation between victims and offenders" does not coincide with "national reconciliation" and "nation building." In the German process, the trajectories lead in a different direction. On the one hand, the Commission had to deal with the victims and offenders of the SED dictatorship as part of the "East German inheritance"; on the other hand, the SED dictatorship is *itself* the result of the separation of Germany and with it of the national trauma that was caused by National Socialism. It also has to do with the ordering and overcoming of alienation of both parts of Germany, without considering one as offender and the other as victim.

The Investigative Commission was resolved in its work to consider all viewpoints simultaneously. The expert Ilko-Sascha Kowalczuk speaks of the "dilemma" that existed for the TC to have to consider "external German security, economic and internal political conditions and constraints, while at the same time considering perspectives of the victims, their non-readiness to adapt and finally also not to neglect the 'ordinary' citizen."[114]

One may say principally in view of the problem of reconciliation that in Germany, similar to the situation of the South African TRC, reconciliation was not institutionally orchestrated. However, it was the task of the Investigative Commission to make "a contribution to reconciliation in the society."[115] Once again the balance is maintained between two theoretical ideas; namely (1) "that rebuilding is primarily a social task,"[116] and as such neither may be "regulated" or "organized," but that it (2) requires "the state's support" in order to be successful. Law givers acted — as in the case of South Africa — wisely here, in that they limited things, created framing conditions and forums which made possible a multi-layered discussion of the past. One could even say: the Investigative Commission became a *forum for reconciliation.*

The South African Commission lives by virtue of the symbolic power which it was able to bring to bear on its forum. Guilt and reconciliation were equally represented in the individual stories. Also, in the literature of the Investigative Commission one finds the reference to that fact that "rebuilding should seek the connection between individual experience and the social consequences of the collective experience."[117] On the other hand, we do not see independence: it has to do not only with a "connection," but also with the fact that the truth about past repression develops principally from the possibility of sympathy over the fate of the individual. Thus, the individual experience conceals symbolic power for the social process.

Rainer Eppelmann originally promoted such ideas in the Commission. "We must differentiate ourselves!" was his appeal. "In order to understand the daily life under a dictatorship, we need the living picture of the individual: What gave them strength? What gave them courage? Who stood the test of friendship? Where did adjustments have to be made? Where were opposition and resistance possible?"[118] Eppelmann at first had the idea of driving a bus through East Germany to collect people's stories. The "Eppelmann Model" (Peter Maser) was integrated into the workings of the EK so that a series of public hearings were created. Also, the theme of everyday life in the DDR was included.[119] However, the stories were less impressive for the work of the Investigative Commission than was the scientific-historical profile.[120] A historian remarked: "the many and often contradictory ways of life and arrangements in the 'contaminated state' of the SED dictatorship, in which large groups of people were interwoven in the DDR, is still a very broad area for research."[121] Another reaction was harsher: "four decades . . . of biographies" were omitted from analysis in the transition process.[122] The paths in favor of economic rebuilding had yet another consequence which was connected with the anticipated success of a "Truth Commission": "the scholarly . . . evaluation, however, relegates to the background the actual meaning of the Commission as a political historical instrument of the first united German Parliament. . . . The appointment of the Commission assumes that by forming a common historical picture in which the partitioning of Germany is understood as a common national fate, it (i.e., the Commission) may help contribute to the overcoming of that fate."[123]

Before we document the following from the hearings of the EK, four points need to be established as the boundary and possibility for considering the EK within the category of "Truth Commission":

1. The EK can not be similar to the TRC Forum of Reconciliation because it does not meet the formal criteria of a "forum." As stated, the main criterion for a forum is that it be "in the midst of public life."[124] Although from the side of the EK, pains were taken to communicate the events in society (through publications), the "general public (has taken) little interest" in its work.[125]

2. The Parliamentary Council cannot serve as an interpersonal forum for reconciliation, because it does not bring offenders and victims together. The basis for this lies in its structure: statements made by witnesses from the upper echelon of the SED before the Commission could be used against them in criminal proceedings. Thus, the offenders received the invitation to testify prior to the start of the Commission, not afterward. In contrast to the examination committee, one can not be subpoenaed beforehand.[126] "Thus, in our society it was an important element of necessary catharsis that the opportunity to publicly confront those responsible with their actions is left to the legal system."[127] An expert of the EK goes on: "still today, the hardest thing for many former DDR citizens is that they could not deal with . . . what triggered such severe damage on the people in the DDR."[128]

3. The Parliamentary Council can, however, serve as a forum for *personal* reconciliation of victims. They can tell their stories. Of a total of 134 meetings of both Commissions, 68 were made public. The designation of "hearing" was also in vogue in formal parlance (similar to the parliamentary concept of "session"). The numbers varied "between several hundred people with generally very interesting political themes and a few dozen with special themes."[129]

4. The EK can serve as a *national* forum of reconciliation to the extent that "the center of the political system, the German Parliament" governs and declares itself in charge of "appointing special institutions appropriate for the political reconstruction of an epoch of German history."[130] In its task, the "Parliament has established a sovereign sign" that has "no parallel in other countries, with the exception, perhaps, of the Truth Commission of South Africa."[131] The particular proximity to parliament, however, also contains a danger. The EK is more than a commission established by parliament — it is a parliamentary council. The resulting problem of possible political party obligations is thus weighed on various levels.

From the above, the result is that the analysis of the symbolic forms of expression for political reconciliation can only be restricted to evidence used by the EK. The kind of hearings that play out the *interpersonal dimension* of reconciliation in the South African TRC context are rare in the hearings protocols of the EK.[132] However, isolated elements of the *personal dimension of reconciliation* can be determined, which — depending upon the media presence — also take on a social dynamic.

2. Documents of Samples from Select Hearings of the EK

A small section of news in the Berliner newspaper tells of the "first public hearing of the Investigative Commission (Investigative Committee) in Berlin."[133] The two-day hearing from November 30 to December 1, which took place in the Berlin parliament, went under the theme: "The SED dictatorship: political, spiritual, and psycho-social oppression experienced in everyday life."[134] The discussion by the leaders introduced the witnesses and asked them to tell their stories.[135]

Eberhard Wendel: . . . These are experiences that I can only relate in arid words, and I would like to say to you, ladies and gentlemen, that it is still somewhat strange when a person such as myself, as an ex-prisoner, still has to go through this. . . . Whoever, as I have, has spent many years in imprisonment and had their left kidney destroyed in interrogation; that person still lives in mortal terror. That person is in mortal terror when he thinks that the state security office might be observing him. . . . He always shakes when he is in the presence of power. For example, when the party secretary looked at me — who knew exactly who I was — either directly or from aside, I felt immediate fear. And if one tries to rebuild his only social life — his family — it is even more difficult, because then it not only involves just yourself; for there were also Hitler puppets in the (DDR) communist dictatorship, so that one had to be concerned about one's wife and children. . . . The worst thing for this land of 16 million people who were not lucky enough to be in an American, British or French zone, was that they were (then) forced, after twelve years of Nazi dictatorship, to have to live under 40 more years of dictatorship. That means a total of 52 years of uninterrupted dictators was imprinted onto the lives of two generations of people in this country. . . . (The protocol indicates applause.)

Discussion leader Markus Meckel: Many thanks, Mr. Wendel. In your remarks you said that you have suffered much, which is very moving. Now Ms.

Ruehrdanz, I would like now to ask you to tell about yourself and your experience.

Siedrid Rührdanz: . . . My experience is a very human one. . . . I will briefly outline it. In January 1961, when my son was born, he showed signs from the beginning of a medical problem; he was a sickly child. . . . Torsten could not be adequately treated here so I brought him to the Westland Clinic. He was able to receive help there very quickly. He gradually began to recover, but only on the condition that he be allowed to receive medical assistance and medication that was only available in the West. . . . Torsten came home July, 1961. I was able to obtain medication and medical help with the approval of the Health Minister of the DDR. Then came the Wall, and the whole story changed (on August 13, 1961). The result: a relapse of my son's condition. Because no one here could help him, he was brought to a West Berlin clinic on September 8, 1961. This began our separation; as I have said, "the wall went right through my heart." I was separated from my son; I couldn't visit him. . . . At that time I began to argue with the authorities. . . . I finally succeeded in obtaining a pass to attend the emergency Baptism of my son in the hospital. . . . I came back, and fought again for another pass. There were so many difficulties that we decided to leave the DDR because we wanted to be together. It was difficult. I tried to make connections for obtaining the passes, but the first attempt to obtain passes failed and the second attempt failed because of an escape through a tunnel. Since this attempt also went bad, I expected to be arrested and was arrested in 1963. I will have to stick to my text for the sake of my story, otherwise I will break down. On February 1963 I was forced into a car in the open street of Staats-Schergen. . . . The interrogation, which lasted five months in all, was often gruesome and brutal. At the beginning I was interrogated for 22 hours straight. At some time during the process, somebody mentioned that my husband was also there. As I later found out, he was being held in the jail on Magdalene Street. After a two-hour break, I was transported in a closed "Green Minna" to the jail in Hohenschoenhausen. There I endured fourteen days of continual interrogations; sometimes also at night. At night, the cell light was always on. Every three minutes someone looked at me through a peep hole. I suffered terribly from sleep deprivation. The so-called "lights out" lasted only from 10 pm to 5 am. The remaining time I sat on a small wooden stool without a back in front of a small wooden table. I was strictly forbidden to lean back or to support my head. At the least, I might receive permission to read after finishing the interrogations, if at all. Any slight resistance to the interrogator was punished. As a result, I once received three days of no mattress and had to sleep on bare wooden slats. The result was fist-sized blisters on my back. . . . If one did not follow instructions, one was threatened with chains or the rubber cell. There were two in the cellar area in Hohenschoenhausen. I observed how someone had to endure it in there for three weeks. I will never forget his screams as long as I live. These people could really destroy a person. When I was ordered to clean out the rubber cell, I had to clear away blood and feces. (Protocol indicates: speaker sobs, fights back tears.) Now I have lost my train of thought. . . . During the interrogations something really terrible happened when my interrogator said to me: "you can leave this jail as a free person . . . or you can receive a very long jail sentence." The result was that they put a pass in front of me — presumably a pass to see my son — that I could use to visit my son in the hospital, who was at that time seriously undernourished because he was so sick. . . . They then said to me that I could go. When I asked them what the catch was they demanded that I meet with the sociology students who had been helpful to me in obtaining a pass for my previously planned escape. "And we will do everything else," said the Stasi. Since this was just another scenario that I couldn't agree to, I naturally said no. The result was four more years in prison. I didn't want to be guilty of leading others into danger. . . . Finally, after nineteen months we were set free. . . . After that another eight months passed, until we could take our child in our arms. By then he was almost five years old and addressed us with the formal "thou." . . . After the Fall of the Wall . . . I continued to fight. Now, two years after the Fall (of the Wall) my petition has been granted; twenty-nine years after the fact. For me, it is similar to the previous speaker, in that I believe I would have finally blocked out everything. . . . But it is all there again and must be spoken about. These atrocities must be reported. . . . Now I have to contend with my rehabilitation and perhaps to expect some recompense; but for me it has to do with the internal rebuilding and that is not finished. That is my story. (Applause.)

Discussion leader Markus Meckel: Many thanks, Ms. Rührdanz, for your powerful story. You have mentioned that your son Torsten is here among us. It is wonderful that you are all able to be here. (Applause.) . . . We see a great variation in individual fates depending upon the times. It was a characteristic of the DDR to make sure that one knew nothing about the others so that the area of experience was often divided just as it was by the high wall. Therefore it is so important that we today are able to speak about it and to be heard. Many sincere thanks to those who have spoken up today.[136]

Observations:[137]

- It is impossible not to notice how powerful the stories are in these hearings, just as in the TRC hearings. Even in the stories that do not illuminate a single concept, the endured injustice is palpable ("the power of the narrative"). Thus they are not only told extemporaneously, but in part are read from a script prepared by the victim.
- From the analysis of the text of the report there are indications of tensions due to the time constraints under which the Commission operated for the hearing of the individual fates and the clear need of the family members to be able to tell their stories. "Whoever could not curb their recollections quickly received a parliamentary admonition to keep it short," observed an attending journalist.[138]
- The stories reflect gratitude for the opportunity to finally be able to tell them. ("I can't express enough joy that I have finally been given the opportunity . . . to relate my previous experience." Or the public outcry of Mr. Vogt: "One should tell all of it!").
- The question of *why?* stands front and center of many of the stories, and with this question there is no trace of hatred. Revenge is not sought, but rather a discussion with the offender. In addition, witnesses express their wish to finally have their stories believed by officials.

In the final debate of the EK on July 17, 1994 Keller said in Parliament:[139]

I think that this . . . Investigative Committee should be an example . . . of how discussions with each other should be conducted. (The protocol records applause from the PDS and the SPD and a delegate of the FDP.) All of us, although we are witnesses, although we are included in this story, carry the responsibility to judge the story as it was, and as we would like it to be. And with this I come to the complex problem of the victim. I find it fitting that the Investigative Committee has decided to listen during the many hearings to the victims' accounts of human rights violations and lack of justice. I myself must say: these hearings have been the bitterest time of my life, not primarily because I did not know everything, but because I understood how everything was done in the name of socialism, and how my ideals and my ideas, my hopes and wishes, were misused. I see it as a member of the Investigative Committee of the PDS/Left as my moral duty and responsibility, to apologize to the victims of the SED dictatorship. (The protocol registers applause by all sides.)

Observations:

- Reconciliation means change. This clearly does not come "suddenly," but through a process. Change is obviously a process that constantly means dealing with the accounts of the victims.
- The applause of all sides indicates that the apology was openly acknowledged by the assembly.

3. Documentation of the Dialogue between Offenders and Victims of the SED Regime

From the number of constructive examples for dealing with the media regarding the past of the DDR, I have chosen a discussion that took place on the invitation of a daily newspaper.[140] It involves a disagreement between the former Minister of Culture of the DDR, Dietmar Keller, and the writer Erich Loest, who after the demise of the party in 1956, spent seven years in jail in Bautzen. The discussion was preceded by an open letter from Loest in which he blamed the former official who had censured and plagued him. Keller defended himself in the series of articles. Now, for the first time, Loest and Keller sit at a table across from each other. I have excerpted sections from the discussion which was allowed to "run its course" without editing, and which made the newspaper famous and was cited as "an example" of "a further attempt to work out the DDR past."

Loest: . . . They were integrated into the Stasi system. I have here an especially odious document — an action plan — in which it says, for example: "Concerning the Loest children comprehensive measures are to be employed whose results should be used as further starting points to bring about the development of private conflict situations." And another piece further along says: "Regular information for the First Secretary of the district leadership of the SED, Member Horst Schuhmann." The Party, the SED, experienced everything immediately; nothing was left out. (Keller was at that time Secretary of the District leadership of Leipzig.)

Keller shakes his head.

Loest: But it could not have been otherwise. They certainly had no compunction about cooperating with the Stasi. The Ministry for State Security was a part of this state. . . . They have said that two thousand artists would have cooperated with them, but only Loest feels wounded by it. I would have regretted it all, if they hadn't been parliamentary delegates and if they had not insisted that they had hurt no one. . . . I didn't want to be governed by them. Thus the whole matter.

Keller: I am not doing this, because it makes me look good. I do it, because it's my job to say to you: as harsh as your article was for me and hurt me, it did not change my opinion of you as a writer. The more I know — and my knowledge has, like yours, grown considerably in the past months (i.e., with the opening of the Stasi archive) — the greater my esteem for you has grown, and for what you have undergone, especially with regard to this terrible process after 1956 (Party Ousting). . . . Every journey of an artist . . . every exhibition had to be approved. It was the case, however, that naturally the Stasi were managed by the Party. And who was the "Party"? The Stasi were led by the SED Politburo. They had their own internal pecking order. . . . I avoided the Stasi whenever I could. In that regard there was an event that struck me as crazy: my telephone was tapped, after I became District Secretary. . . . No one knew any longer exactly with whom one was speaking. It was a well-known fact that the state security (forces) were operating everywhere. . . . Yes, out of necessity I worked knowingly with the state security forces in my capacity as District Secretary. That was something that every upper school director, every district attorney, and every mayor had to do. . . . I was . . . responsible for the culture and the documents that I received from Gauck; they have completely surprised me because I now know that in my civil service role someone was around me who was an informal co-conspirator. It is also very possible that a lot took place in conversations of which I was not aware.

Editorial staff: Mr. Keller, in the foreword to your book, *Minister on Call*, we read what also in a PDS brochure was written about the parliamentary vote: they had not hindered or excluded anyone from voting. Is this statement correct?

Keller: From my current perspective this statement is relatively false. Even when I subjectively am honestly convinced not to have knowingly harmed anyone, I naturally have harmed people through my activities in the party apparatus. Also, even if I personally was perhaps inclined to do some damage control and even if in many respects I took a different view than others engaged in cultural politics.

(Loest nods.)

Loest: My nod is to indicate that I find this shift interesting.

Editors: Mr. Loest, you mean to say that roles like those which Mr. Keller had, were actually mere "either/or" roles in the system. . . .

Loest: I don't care if one hundred percent or zero percent of the system was in play. I was in the SED for ten years and had one function or another during that time. With this there were many transitions. Now they can be talked about. We were not allowed to look at Stasi documents. . . . I do not want to know that a person was an IM, but rather, I want to know how did they get there, how long did it last, why did he himself not come clean and admit that he was an IM?

Observations on the text:

- In the stories of the individual biographies of "offenders" and "victims" structural connections are visible. The interpersonal dimension of reconciliation can have a healing function for the nation on a symbolic level when the successful coming together of two biographies is communicated publicly.
- Interpersonal meaning: offenders and victims need to come to a mutual understanding. Where people are brought together, change is possible, which is clearly healing on both sides. The former officials are confronted with the consequences of their politics — consequences that they had earned — and also the victim's perspectives are broadened in that the dimension of guilt becomes more complex. Nevertheless, for the "victim" it is very important that a "transformation" occurs. Change is a precondition for forgiveness.
- A constructive discussion also needs to be moderated by a third party as part of an insulating framework; namely, as a "forum of reconciliation" so that in the course of an "analysis of the reality of the elements of pain and suffering" (J. Gauck) neither side can be omitted or left uncontrolled.

4. Inclusion of the Symbolic Forms of Expression
and Rituals in the German Renovation Process

Similarly to the TRC, reconciliation was not orchestrated by the Investigative Committee. On the other hand, the Committee was supposed to make "a contribution to reconciliation in society."[141] Again, there is no clear methodology to indicate how this goal should be achieved. Rather, parameters were created: "Through the experiences in the Investigative Committee, the maxim 'No reconciliation without truth' gained credence. The victims of the previous unjust regime have a right to truth. Only when the truth is laid bare and responsibility is assumed by the offenders can also talk of reconciliation commence."[142] (This idea was given as a reason for the work of the Commission on documents of the state security service. The German process appears to be more positive in contrast to the South African, in so far as criteria were developed which can be counted as a contribution to reconciliation.)

As moral criterion for social reconciliation, the Final Report of the EK (IC) refers to the level of guilt. On the one hand, there was not allowed "in the process of growing together . . . in Germany any general or lasting exclusion of anyone . . . who had contributed according to their function as active subordinates within the dictatorial system. In addition, they are requested to cooperate in the formation of a unified Germany."[143] On the other hand, there was opposition to comprehensive integration with regard to the political use of reconciliation. "Persons who through their guilty demeanor or who had compromised their place in the power apparatus are not suited for a leadership position in a democratic state or in a democratic party. This basic rule should not be confused with a lack of readiness for reconciliation."[144] At first blush, for the "Gauck Administration" it means: "Also the possibility for monitoring the Stasi document law (State Security Service Document Law) should not be understood as social defamation."[145]

What symbolic forms and rituals helped to develop the recovery process in Germany? In the context of South Africa we distinguished four conditional symbolic forms and rituals. The reality of political reconciliation was developed from the following: (a) through the coming together (composition) and legacy of the TRC, (b) its ritualistic approach, (c) its national and (d) its religious symbolism. In the following we make use of the agreed upon criteria and discuss, under assumption of the findings from the previous paragraphs, both deviations from and correlations to the South African process.[146]

(a) Composition of the EK

The reality of reconciliation is conceived through the composition and legacy of the institutions. This statement applied only conditionally in the German process. In the question of composition, the EK certainly has other functions than, for example, as parliamentary inquiry committees; they can work with experts (that is non-partisan respectively not tied to factions)[147] and conduct public hearings. The composition of the EK is, however, not the result of a lengthy, multi-level process of voting, but is determined in the bylaws of operation of the Parliament. (The membership is decided from among the factions according to a formula.) So, for example, it can't accept advice from the general populace. The larger parties positioned dominant former representatives of the EK.[148] A certain symbolic value could be seen in the appointment of a theologian to the head of the council. In the involvement of the PDS in the EK one can find references to the fact that political reconciliation is possible where the mutually diverse experiences and viewpoints of the past are juxtaposed (such as, impressively, the apology of the PDS delegates). However, this moment has involved no social dynamic. The EK was an undertaking that was "practically at the exclusion of the public."[149] Also, the formulation of the job of the EK is relegated to the members of the parliamentary council. It was preceded by a long discussion between scholars, foreign specialists, members of the human rights movement as well as members of both the old and the new system. In summary, one may say that the composition and legacy of the EK was a "top down" enterprise: and in this respect the EK was different than the TRC as a Commission. For the East German population the formation of a "Truth Commission" was not an immediate object lesson in Democracy; rather the rules of play of parliamentary Democracy were presupposed.[150] Also, it could be asked of the EK, to what extent the members of the Commission of the East German population represented the German[151] silent majority.[152]

In contrast, the "Gauck Administration" emerged from a basically democratic process — namely, at the "grass roots" level — and was then legitimized by the entire German Parliament and eventually conformed in terms of organization to a form of governance (doubtless its form of government, in view of the legal data, has certain advantages). However, in its internal composition there is little recognizable symbolism. The Gauck Administration has — admittedly for pragmatic reasons — incorporated former "offenders" in their work: former Stasi assistants show the way through the labyrinth of the secret service MfS.[153] At the apex of the hierarchy there is even a theologian. Many assistants come from the area of civil rights.

(b) The EK's Ritualistic Approach

The reality of reconciliation is developed through the ritualistic processes. The documented hearings before the EK as well as the process of access to records in the "Gauck Administration" allow for a form of ritual.[154] First, in the Investigative Committee: against the background of the South African model we find symbolic elements in the course of the formal two-day hearings at the Reichstag.

Individual observations:[155]

- The hearings took place in the Reichstag. My question as to whether or not the setting was consciously chosen was answered by the words of a member of the EK: "The choice of the Reichstag played, according to my recollection, a representative role throughout. In order to honor the victims, the Parliamentary President took part in this event at the very end with very personal words that had nothing to do with his prepared remarks, and which made a very strong impression on the family members."[156] At the future location of the Supreme Court the victim(s) were heard. One hears the message: "Today you stand in the midst of what oppressed you under the SED regime!"
- Just as with the TRC, the witnesses told their stories from a podium. The audience had to "look up" to them since the podium forced the gaze upward. Also the tables were arranged in a semi-circle. Once again, the message here was: "We sit together to share together, not in confrontation!"
- In terms of language, the EK spoke of "witnesses," not of victims. (The State Security Service Document Law consistently uses the term "affected person.") In South Africa we encounter in the discussion the connotation that was connected with the concept of "victim": that of a passive, helpless being. Is there hidden in the talk of "witnesses" an intentional elevation of the concept of victim?

In the course of the hearings, not all rituals used in the TRC hearings were in evidence. The celebratory entrance of the Commission is omitted, also the white tablecloths, the candles, and the prayer. A "healing place," a separate area for the victims, was not designated. The actual story is not embedded in a before and after speech. Also the "sending forth" at the end of the hearing is omitted.

A marked difference to the TRC hearings is that — as with all hearings of the EK — the reports precede the actual stories. The assumption appears to be: one must first give something in order to hear the story ("oral history," "personal narrative"). Don't stories speak for themselves? Don't they serve a factual purpose in the hearing process? These are questions that result from the diverse acceptance of the proceedings in South Africa and clearly indicate a cultural gap.

Formally, correspondences are encountered in the TRC ritual: the members of the Commission rise as the victims enter and the witnesses have a definite time frame in which to tell their stories. Many of the family members expressed satisfaction that the stories were finally told. However, whether one can freely speak in the African sense of a "cleansing ritual," is questionable. Other traces of the events of the TRC are noticeable where, for example, Markus Meckel takes up the story of Mrs. Rührdanz with obvious sympathy and segues to the next story. Did one knowingly permit the theologian among the Commission's membership to moderate at the victim's podium? Once more Peter Maser: "The emotional tension escalated with every statement. It was a good thing that among the members of the Commission there were also experienced clergy, otherwise the situation could have potentially been totally derailed piece by piece."[157] Perhaps it can be said that the hearings of the EK generated some isolated symbolic significance: namely, what was intended by the SED government is projected in the victims' stories. In addition, the number of visitors and media coverage were above average during the two-day hearings in comparison to other EK sessions. Nine regional and national newspapers reported on it.[158] If one notices what and how events were related, it is evident that almost all of the newspapers reported their stories in narrative form. The stories of Mrs. Rührdanz appeared in almost all of the print media.[159] Things were not written *about* her, but rather her story was related. Does the media realize the power of narrative? "The ability to tell stories creates insight and loosens the blockade of oppression," writes the editor of the (Berlin) *Daily Mirror (Tagesspiegel)* and observes: "A look back, either in anger or resignation, facilitates current biographical narratives which, in a curious way, appear by chance and at the same time strike us as unique."[160] So it was that the "representatives of the media who only wanted to look in on the hearings, stayed longer than planned" (P. Maser). Commissioner Dirk Hansen demanded after his two-day hearings that "for the continuing work of the Commission there will be direct questioning of the witnesses — victims as well as offenders."[161] The Investigative Commission/Investigative Committee should "more than before, seek to contact those who suffered under and survived everyday life in the SED dictatorship and still, in many respects, overcame it."

The Gauck Administration: T. G. Ash cites his impressions with the insight in the single Stasi dossier: "It brings back with vividness many things that you had forgotten, or remembered in a different way. There, described minute by minute with the cold clinical eye of the secret policeman, is a day in your life 20 years ago."[162] The actual insight into the files, of which Ash speaks, is embedded in a "ritualized process."

1. After a long waiting period, the applicant is informed by the authorities that his file now is ready for inspection. The affected party, after he has turned in his passport, is ushered through the doorway to the authorities by an employee. The talks take place in a closed room. Details of the file are highlighted, and the number of third parties are pointed out, having already been stipulated by the State Security Service Document Law. According to my sources, the affected parties listen only half-heartedly while they wait with suspense for the chance to view their own file. Sometimes there is a loud exclamation: "Yes, those are Stasi methods; to take away your passport!" Others complain that the assistants already know what's in the files. Shame and insecurity mount: "How could this happen?" The assistants try to calm the affected parties by, for example, explaining that these precautions were taken in the interest of the applicant.

2. After the talks, the affected parties are escorted into one of the reading rooms designated for the inspection of files. The atmosphere of this room is eerily sterile and reminds one of a classroom. About fifteen tables are arranged with a minimal distance between tables. In the front sits a proctor. Bright neon lights fall on the yellowed paper of the files. "The time of my humiliation was again brought very near to me," said an affected party.[163] I was told that in the inspection, emotions were released and tears fell uncontrollably.[164]

3. After the inspection of the files, the affected parties were taken to a debriefing room. During this discussion I was told that the affected parties were very candid. The impression was that there was a mutual relationship of trust. "At least now I can talk to someone" was the general sentiment. "They understand me! They know my file!" Many statements were made like: "In normal, everyday life such things would not be understood." In many instances, affected parties sought reconciliation. During the debriefing they were told that they could request a so-called assumed name decoding,

in order to clear their name. There were also cases where, for example, the telephone number of a psychologist was given or a referral to a trauma clinic was administered to the affected parties.

The effectiveness of what I would like to describe as ritual[165] in the preliminary inspection of files and debriefing process can be gleaned from statements of co-workers. Sometimes, days later, telephone calls take place in which the affected parties have expressed their gratitude for being given the opportunity to view their files. In sum, it would apply as a firm rule: "The applicants come upset but leave relieved." I would like to suggest that we are dealing with statements that are similar to those found in the South African context of "healing ritual" on the personal level of reconciliation during the inspection of files. The inspection of files was an essential step, as one affected person summarized it, "to be able to close a chapter (in my life)."[166] In many cases the healing process also took place on an interpersonal level which can take its bureaucratic point of departure in the "request to decode an assumed name." Thus, as it was told to me, an affected person found out in his file how a distant relative had spied on him. The applicant said: "Next week we are having a family reunion. Then I will find out what was going on!"[167]

(c) The EK's National Symbolism

The reality of reconciliation is completed through national symbolism. In South Africa there were disagreements about whether a Truth Commission could become a "national ritual" (A. Krog). In the German process it is appropriate to ask whether a "national symbol" can be recognized in the summary debates on both EK commissions which were held on a date that was symbolic for the entire nation: June 17, 1994.[168] To what degree then does one nation develop the reality of inner unity and reconciliation from former West and East Germany through such proceedings? Joachim Gauck already urged in 1995: "The case of the Wall not only has meaning for the freedom of the East Germans, it also conveys a western style dialogue, which is established on overcoming the limitations of the mind-set of imprisonment."[169]

The question is, whether the proceedings are applicable at all for interpersonal reconciliation, which in the forum of the EK, but also with respect to the right of inspection in the "Gauck Government," is connected to the idea of national reconciliation. What symbols have been claimed on the national level, for example: "We must mutually tell about each other, otherwise we will have no peace in our land?"[170] At least, the stories were heard before a parliamentary assembly. Meanwhile, the earlier "IM debate" appeared to be a "national ritual": "The discussions over the Stasi files . . . form from the beginning a key piece in the parliamentary debate on rebuilding from the DDR past."[171]

Now we return to the core problem of the German process: the reality of reconciliation did not develop from the inspection of files as well as from specific victim hearings to a national ritual; rather a climate of irreconcilability developed. What interested the nation in the long run were the spectacular personal accounts. In the "common memory" of the "historical consciousness of the nation" (C. Klessmann) the picture of East Germany as a clandestine state was solidified against any historical truth.[172] Whether the Investigative Committee could achieve a paradigm shift whose goal was to conceptualize the events in the East — and also in West Germany — as a product of the German partition,[173] still remains to be seen. The "anti-totalitarian consensus" as an "immaterial value" (D. Hansen) is suited especially for "nation building" if one nation understands it as a consortium of values.[174] The EK would then be considered a social precursor or "microcosm" as Tutu said of the TRC; namely, the EK projects in miniature, what still must be accomplished on a larger scale. For that to happen, however, the EK, like the TRC, would have to change the social consciousness. D. Hansen sees realistically: "An Investigative Committee can not change the entire German consciousness."[175] In summary, it appears questionable whether the EK has reached the total German consciousness at all. Large portions of the public knew "nothing or only little of the EK."[176] The headlines, so says Hansen critically, were dominated, among other things, by the simultaneous reports of the daily "Stolpe investigative committee."[177]

(d) The EK's Religious Symbolism

The reality of reconciliation unfolds through religious symbolism. In so far as both institutions are superior to theologians, it is possible to attribute religious symbolism to the "Gauck Administration" and the EK. When asked whether he could introduce himself in a similar way to Tutu who wore his cassock to the hearings, Eppelmann responds: "the other members of the Investigative Committee would not have understood it: 'You are here as delegate and not as a pastor!' It also seemed strange to me. I never wore the cassock outside of the church, and would have perhaps put it on if the Stasi had tried to take me from my house. Tutu is obviously a different kind of person, who also lives in another realm."[178] Of the request, as to what degree being a theologian played a role in his political office as chairman of the EK, Eppelmann says that he never consciously acted as pastor. "But the person always is there who tries to live as a Christian, even when he is not recognized as a pastor. Being a pastor is not the decisive thing, but rather the biographical attempt to emulate Jesus of Nazareth." Here distinctions are made that are important for a "theological synthesis." Methodologically, we must first put in check the notion that for the affected parties no direct retrospective to religious symbolism is permitted in the "institutionalized overcoming of guilt." What remains noticeable is that religiously grounded concepts and pairings permeate the political process: regret-guilt, new beginning, truth-reconciliation. "Not theologians," so says the political scientist Petra Bock, "spoke of the oppositional pairing of 'Remembrance-Punishment' which amounted to a social and political exclusion, or 'forgetting–not forgiving,' which should amount to integration."[179] The question to be answered is whether with the alleged correspondence concept pairing also allows the confirmation of commonalities in the categories between theological and non-theological language.

Apart from the individual concepts, it must be asked whether over the ritualized course of an EK hearing and similar to the TRC hearings, references to the ritual of worship and with it connected symbolism of reconciliation occur. In the Benediction, for example, Villa-Vicencio saw a "real agreement" between the worship service as ritual and that of a TRC hearing. However, it is the case that the ritual of the EK is not only "liturgically" more impoverished, also it is missing the actors. Where no offender appears before the Commission, one is unsuccessful in looking for political reverberations of liturgical elements such as "forgiveness of sins" or a "new beginning."

5. An Analysis of "Regulative Statements" behind the Symbolic Forms Expressing Political Reconstruction after System Injustice in Germany

An analysis of the "regulative statements" again has the goal of preparing the groundwork for the question of correspondence. The conditions of possible political reconciliation should at first be determined, in order to ultimately investigate the "regulative statements" for their connection to theological reconciliation.[180]

General statements, which were in part effective in the initial political discussion of requirements:

- Reconciliation has something to do with change.
- Reconciliation is only possible with the truth.
- Reconciliation means to truly break with the past.
- Reconciliation can not be organized.
- Reconciliation requires frameworks.

Statements on the conditions of personal reconciliation with one's experience:

- Reconciliation assumes the public recognition of the individual's experience.
- Reconciliation requires a protected space.
- Reconciliation needs a healing ritual.
- Reconciliation has something to do with change; it means for the victims:
  - I can break with the past.
  - I can develop new perspectives on reconciliation.
- Reconciliation is only possible with the truth. It means for the victims:
  - Externally: my story is true and not a lie.
  - Internally: I can accept my fate (I must not repress the truth).

Statements of interpersonal reconciliation, which in part are not logically consistent:

- Reconciliation has something to do with change and presumes interpersonally:
  - Change of the offender; insight into his guilt.
  - Change on the side of the victim; readiness to forgive.
- Interpersonal reconciliation has something to do with closure and a new beginning.
- Interpersonal reconciliation completes itself as a process.
- Interpersonal reconciliation belongs in the area of the private.
- The deed and the offender are not the same. (The condition for reconciliation is the difference.)
- The deed and the offender are the same. "You are as bad as your deed."

Assumptions for reconciliation on a national level ("national reconciliation"):

- There is no (possible) national reconciliation between West and East. (Reconciliation presumes a relationship of guilt.)
- National reconciliation is important (reconciliation means understanding, "growing together" of East and West).
- Reconciliation has something to do with change; that means for the one the condition: the consciousness of the Germans must change on *both* sides; for the other: only the East Germans must change.
- Reconciliation in truth means here: to tell the stories as they were and not as we would have liked them to be.
- National reconciliation as growing together of East and West Germany is a process.

III. Taking Stock of System Injustice: Political Nuances

1. General Counter-Balancing Arguments

If one takes to heart the words of former South African president Thabo Mbeki, then one will be able to speak of the success of the German unification process. In Parliament he stated that the German process of "national reconciliation" is exemplary:

> As the honorable membership is aware, the two post-war German states were united into one country in 1990. After 45 years of division into two states with competing social systems, the German leaders and people understood that, truly to become one country and one people, they too, like ourselves, would have to address the central questions of national unity and reconciliation. This was despite the fact that here we speak of a people who share the same language, color and culture. The seriousness with which the German people treated that process of the promotion of German national unity and reconciliation is reflected, among other things, by the extraordinary volume of resources which the richer, developed West Germany transferred to the poorer and relatively underdeveloped East Germany.... Further to illustrate the enormity of this effort, these transfers amount to 75 times the size of the national budget which this House is currently debating.[181]

In effect, the numbers are impressive. There is a transfer of benefit for the rebuilding of the East projected at about 900 billion US dollars, which is unsettling for a country like South Korea, who could use the same amount.[182] The first Annual Report on the State of German Unity[183] makes a bid for the improvement of the East German infrastructure: up until 1996, 5,000 kilometers of rails as well as 11,000 kilometers of new highways were respectively converted and renovated and 5 million telephone lines and 4.2 million apartments in total either built or renovated.

It is obvious, why Mbeki cites the German efforts as exemplary: the material side came up short in the South African process. A solidarity tax according to the German model had to be rescinded after a short time. The transfer of resources was not made a "priority of national solidarity." In South Africa it appears that one had an intuition about where the priorities lay in the German process: was "nation building" a transfer of resources from West to East? In South Africa the impetus for nation building was, as shown, "national reconciliation." Both parts of the nation were ordered to make concessions to the other — but also to change — in order to become one nation. How did that work in Germany?

The aim of the Federal Chancellery was the establishment of German unity.[184] "My goal remains — if the historical hour allows — the unity of this nation,"[185] said Helmut Kohl before the ruins of the Dresden Frauenkirche on the 19th of December, 1989, before thousands of excited DDR citizens and a "sea of black-red-gold flags."[186] In order to reach the goal of unity, Kohl laid out his double strategy: on the one hand and with regard to the allies, he remarks that the self-determination of Germany persisted in favor of national unity; on the other hand, with a calming effect on his European neighbors he points out that the "house of Germany" is built under the European roof.[187] In the analysis of the content, there is emotional ambiguity. "What should we do," recalls Kohl in the situation of Dresden, "when suddenly the masses begin singing the German national anthem and then the first lines of the stanza 'Deutschland, Deutschland über alles'?"[188] One appears happy, but is also irritated when the emotions are stimulated by the revival of the idea of one nation. The idea of "national unity" was formally brought forward on October 3, 1990. However, was the contracted "unity" really the unity of a nation?

"Nation-building" appears to this point in time to require at most the material approximation of the life-long relationship. In the sense of our "mixed questions" we first ask:

If there was new and efficient realization of the judicial role in the unification process, to what degree was it realized?

The result falls unanimously under the research on transitions: "System change is successfully concluded." [189] "Unification was an asymmetrical process, in which the West German institutions of the former DDR were integrated quickly and relatively efficiently."[190] In transition research, this is regarded today as the "privilege of the East German case of transition." "The quick institutional organized consolidation of East Germany, the targeted high measure of rule of law, the German welfare gain of the East Germans and the swift modernization of the infrastructure in the new regions were essentially made possible through this transfer of benefits."[191]

(a) Modification of the Goal: "Establishment
of Internal Unity in Germany"

In the course of transition, the fulfillment of "individual happiness" ran up against limitations.[192] The remaining economic miracle and the rapidly growing number of unemployed in the new regions made it clear that German unity, in addition to external politics, the adjustments of the law, and the economy, still included other political areas.[193] After unification, in the foreground loomed the "internal" as well as the "historical political aspects of unification."[194] Thus, the original goals were relativized, which included, above all, the economic aspects of unity. Indeed, the reformulation of the basic legal article 72 is striking. In the 1994 version it speaks of the establishment of "equal living conditions" (Article 72, Paragraph 2 GG). The objectives of institutional equalization were expanded. The citizens of the earlier DDR needed to be brought to "a level of reciprocity with the democratic institutions of the federal government."[195] The objectives were modified and new goals were set. From foreseeable observations like "Germany is one, but not united" (Rita Süssmuth)[196] or "despite a common language and common history we move further away from each other in the past 40 years" (Johannes Rau),[197] the objectives were subsequently modified. The establishment of "inner unity" became the "target of the unification process."[198]

Whatever "inner unity" means, is not only defined in various ways, but the concept belongs to a process,[199] which allows us to anticipate some preliminary formulations: "The process-wise definition opens limitless research opportunities":[200] "For some it has to do with the 'cultural and mental westernization' of the East Germans. For others it demands mediation of the mental joining together of both parts as a condition of unity. Other indicators highlight the problem of the various political orientations and views of social marketability, many withdraw on the many-sided stereotypes as an essential block to growing together; others stress the connection of national identity and inner unity. And some attribute various understandings of democracy as a deficit to inner unity or examine the similarities and differences in the political culture *ad nauseum*."[201] In all, the research included statements from "all walks of life and levels of human existence, politics, society, and psyche" (ibid.).

As Veen shows, talk of "inner unity" is closely tied with the idea of "nation," that is of "national identity." In the literature, the concepts are also related to each other on many levels. A certain idea of "identity" has an impact on the understanding of nation; a decisive opinion about the necessity of "inner unity" corresponds mainly with a certain view of "national identity." For critics, the idea of "inner unity" comes dangerously close to the "history of national unity." "Inner unity" polemically speaking "is a construct of an identity taken from the mothball closet of Carl Schmitt, whereby political unity should be internally homogenous and equal."[202] Advocates point to the other side of the argument where the term for identity, stemming from the Latin word *idem*, means "the same," but not "equal." Identity does not mean conformity; rather, something unique is not meant, but something delimited.[203] As we can see, in this controversy the problem is already visible. "The popular definition (of nation) still persists," which is to define a German "according to 'ethnic origin.'"[204] It is very difficult, in view of National Socialism, to speak of the German nation without baggage. "A look back into history leaves no doubt," says Eberhard Schulz in an excursus into the rich history of the years 1806, 1871, and 1919, "that we Germans with respect to our nation have always had orientation difficulties."[205] The problem is that, "in contrast to many other lands in Europe, in Germany democracy and the nation were long ago separated."[206] But that has fundamentally changed, which makes the Englishman Timothy Garton Ash speak of German courage. While previously other countries could have learned a lot from Germany (not only about democracy), today "the West German model of democracy (is) very relevant."[207]

In light of the developments in West Germany after 1949 and the experiences of peaceful revolution of 1989, one may think that in the re-unified Germany the attempt would be to combine "freedom, democracy, and constitutional state with nation, patriotism, and fatherland."[208] Such a combination of "emotional feeling and a legal relationship" which is manageable in the tradition of November 9, 1989 "without national undertones"[209] can be evidenced in the constitutional patriotism of Dolf Sternberger.[210] So why has the entire German national consciousness not developed along these lines? Marry Fulbrook attributes the reason for this to both the East and West: "Instead of propagating the concept of a self-conscious dynamic, uni-fied society, much energy is expended in historical-political arguments. Thus, it is not only the case of the IM's, but primarily the fights about the West Germans. 'What was your relationship with the DDR?' appears today to be the important German-German question: . . . In this regard, other questions arise: for example, what is your opinion about the open wound caused by the separation of the two Germanys and, in relation to the consti-tutional state, what is your opinion about freedom and unity?"[211]

The above reasons offer information why in reunified Germany there was lack of motivation to combine "freedom, democracy and constitutional state with nation, patriotism and fatherland."[212] In the Handbook on Ger-many Unity, we find one of the counter-balances to the year 1999: until then, German unity could "never develop an identity-forging impulse."[213]

For further research it would be interesting to explore two basic ideas among the ruling opinions in the discussion on nation and identity:

The first notion — also noticeable behind the preceding paragraph — assumes what was called "thick unity" in South Africa: "inner freedom" has an identity-forging element, without decaying into the excesses of myth.[214] "Unity doesn't mean homogeneity."[215] Arguments against an "excessive use of the concept inner unity" are "well founded and justified."[216] On the other side, a national feeling of togetherness, as it existed after the fall of the wall, contributes decisively to the "socio-psychological success of the unification process."[217] With the key phrase "feeling of unification" at least a partial as-pect of the national concept is communicated.

> *If under "internal unity" the successful connection of the legal and emo-tional relationship is understood in the national consciousness, then how far has the process come?*

The counter-argument says: the project of "German unity" has, in this ques-tion, come up short "of its possibilities."[218]

The second basic idea is this. Next to the idea of "thick unity," the no-tions of "unity," "identity," and "nation" are encountered again in the public debate, similar to what in South Africa was understood under "thin unity": a homogeneous community is not what characterizes the "liberal democracy of the basic law," rather "the equality of the unequal," or even "the pluralistic society."[219] Veen takes from "inner unity" (as a broader form of constitu-tional patriotism) the goal for the project of "inner unity." Namely, it must remain true to "the legitimate basis of the constitutional state."[220] From this we have: "the criteria of inner unity may not reach substantially any further, it may not demand any more commonalities than the basic consensus of the basic law" (ibid.). It has to do with a "minimal consensus, not a maximum consensus." In this sense, Stephan Hilsberg also estimates that the theme of "inner unity" does not have anything to do with "harmony," but rather with the "affirmation of the now united country with its public institutions, its achievements, and its history."[221]

> *If by "inner unity" the total German affirmation of the basic consensus of the basic law, "bolstered by the social market economy and the integration of the West, is understood as national identification and basic empathy," then how far has the process of German unity come?*

The counter-balance to the argument emerges with a positive result: we already have the "inner unity" in terms of "what it can legitimately mean. We live already in the condition of inner unity, and that means increased diversity."[222]

(b) The Task of the Investigative Committee and Political Goals

Here it should be mentioned to what extent the scope of the EK corresponds to political aims. The problem grows from the comparable question posed by the proceedings of South Africa, where the TRC seamlessly inserted the goal of "nation building" into the entire political arena.

"Political aims" of the Investigative Committee between the years 1992 and 1994 were "to de-legitimatize the SED dictatorship through explanation of the norms and benchmarks of liberal democracy; to allow the victims compensation; to foster a democratic consciousness and 'anti-totalitarian' consensus; to awaken in the West Germans a deeper understanding for the DDR reality and decades-long oppression; and thus, to a certain degree, through education on all sides to contribute to mutual understanding and reconciliation."[223] This project is still preserved in the subsequent commissions with some modifications.

An expert in the EK/IC has compiled the three goals of the Commission since 1995: "1. A demand for anti-totalitarian consensus in the federal government; 2. the memorializing of victims of the dictatorship and any person whom the DDR attempted to shoot; . . . 3. to contribute to the development of historical views of the DDR, free of myth and damage."[224] In short: "the Investigative Committee should help people with their various biographies to better find each other in the conciliation process. Also, it should contribute to reconciliation in the society and to establishing a desire for transparency, openness, the historical truth, and mutual understanding."[225]

The phrase "reconciliation through truth" from the first Commission remains clearly current.[226] However, along with the conceptual formulation of the EK, namely to contribute "to social reconciliation," the concepts of nation, internal unity and identity are still missing. This is because the focus is on the individuals who — through their stories — should be able "(to) find" (themselves) again in the "unification process." Accordingly, it is clear that it was only a very narrow goal of the EK to bring about "national reconciliation." Here, once again, the area of intra-personal reconciliation steps to the foreground. Both dimensions — the individual and the nation — appear connected in a different way than with the South African commission. In South Africa, the national understanding was about the individual stories, but at the same time the nation took part in the fate of the individual ("the nation is saying it's sorry"! [Tutu]). However, in Germany it was the opposite: the individual remained alone with his story; he was advised to "find himself again" in society via his story. In Germany, the feeling was that the story should not be dragged out into society. Thus, one could say that the macro and micro levels of reconciliation in South Africa and in Germany are inversely proportional. The assumption in the German process is that reconciliation is an individual process, while in South Africa the national dimension of reconciliation was emphasized.

Now we can return to our objectives. The goals followed by the EK are directly connected to the total political objectives stated after the 3rd of October, 1990; namely the "establishment of internal freedom." For the Investigative Committee it was clear that the "non-politicized" concept of nation, which the West has kept in the sense of a cultural nation after the fall of the wall, was not viable.[227] Meanwhile, the EK completed its Final Report with no major binding together of the concepts "reconciliation," "inner unity," and "nation" which otherwise was suggested by its task. Thus, in contrast to South Africa, reconciliation had become the motivation for "nation building."

The report, however, does reach some conclusions in connection to "internal unity." From the results of the Final Report we can deduce a concept of internal unity, which was used as its basis. Here it has to do with a liberal understanding of unity in the sense of "thin unity." The result of the EK/IC is thus:

The democratic state and the internal unity of Germany are not harmed by the mental distinctions between East and West. National unity does need not need to mean comprehensive socio-cultural agreement of its citizens. Thus, a political-ethical consensus is reached, as in the general agreement of the law expressed in a basic bill of rights, as well as a certain mutually "elemental sympathy" of people for each other in unified Germany.[228]

Interestingly, the Final Report follows almost verbatim the analysis of Hans-Joachim Veen, who also refereed the Commission.[229] Meanwhile, the formulated result is a consequence of another objective and analysis of the idea of internal unity, which we could gather from the task of the EK. If one makes "reconciliation through truth" the criterion for internal unity, then one is not able to view the unity as quickly achievable, which is suggested by the subsequent formulations of the Final Report. And according to my observations, there is a gap remaining between firm talk of "reconciliation" as a concept and by comparison, the vague presumption of an "elemental sympathy," over against which the process appears to have been evaluated. The gap consists necessarily between the mandate and the arrived-at result, if a "thin" understanding of "unity" is set aside. A member of the Commission has said as a counter argument: "the actual request for a Commission to promote German unity did not bear fruit."[230]

As a result, the EK/IC attempted to put a positive face on the themes and complex objectives of "internal unity." The German populace reached a "consensus guaranteeing the stability of a different kind of development which in increasing measure is going to be defined in terms of the adjustment to life relationships, opportunities, and values. The feeling of East German 'alienation' had, for the most part, lost momentum where the individual finds and accepts his place in the new society and feels intrinsically valued and acknowledged."[231]

2. Critical Analysis

In the following section, the process will be more closely evaluated alongside the conceptual connections between "truth," "reconciliation," and "justice." The relevant debates show that again these three key concepts are where the conflict is focused.

(a) Truth as *condicio sine qua non* of Social Reconciliation?

For successful "growing together" and for the "healing of the nation" the quest for truth contributes to both the system and the people. In this regard, how far has the process come?

The system and the individual's story are combined together into one. The East Germans, for example, have an abbreviated picture of the truth about the DDR with regard to the mechanism for repression "which they have assumed on a humbling and personal level and understood it as part of the internal German fight for acknowledgement."[232] Such a view is encountered in the rhetoric of West German politics without the resulting symbolism becoming public. "The truth is still," says, for example, Rudolf Seiters, "that the DDR was an unjust state that forced consensus and spied on its people. . . . What it accomplished economically and ecologically was a crime."[233] And who in this statement is the "DDR"? Seiters clearly means the system. But is the implied distinction in East Germany a successful one? Many former DDR citizens may feel challenged by such statements in their previously self-conscious acceptance of "right living in a false system" (W. Thierse). The mixing of the system and individual life stories, which yields from the real-life historical experience of those exclusively in the system of suppressed "truth," has not had any healing effect on a national level.

Among other things, the system and the individual's story are artificially separated. While prosecution of criminals in the government both revealed and at the same time contributed to a gain in knowledge of the structures of the SED dictatorship, when it came to individual experience, as we have seen, the most important thing was the inspection of the files. However, there was no connection between either of these strands of rebuilding (i.e., the system or individual).

In comparison to South Africa, a positive counter-argument can be seen with regard to the truth-finding process regarding criminal acts. If we restrict ourselves entirely to statements before the TRC, given the quantity of archived material, it is possible to presume that in Germany the responsibility can be located right up to the political leadership of the DDR.[234] The Final Report of the EK/IC says in its summary of 1998: "Through the judicial reconstruction of the government concerning the criminal activity of the SED regime, including the mid-point demarcation of the individual guilt of the offenders and the enforcement of the state's commitment to punish, significant historical knowledge was gained."[235]

Next to the introduction of the rehabilitation process, for many victims it was not only a matter of the inspection of files of the Gauck Administration on the basis of legally applicable truth of fact, but also on the basis of healing truth.[236] "I want to know where I stand," was for many the reason to bring an application to inspect their files. For over half of the surveyed applicants,[237] it was important to have been given the opportunity to examine the alleged suspicions against them. "The re-establishment of continuity for the survivors is based in their interest to be connected with the victims by knowing what went on."[238] Richard Schröder writes later that the inspection of files had a double effect: "the disappointment over a friend who betrayed me and my disillusionment in view of a groundless suspicion" (ibid.). Some victims "received amends, release, relief, joy" through the inspection of the files; most of those questioned admitted "that they personally could now close this chapter of their lives."[239] The encounter with the written form of the truth from the Stasi files had, for many victims, a healing character: "To the extent that the victims could read in black and white what happened to them, was for them confirmation: I have truly suffered, and thus and thus happened to me."[240] If one evaluates the authorities with respect to the partial aspect of "informing" on a personal level then one can find a positive balance: "up until 1999 almost 1.4 million (people) were at one time or other involved in giving information, inspecting, or publishing of records for the one-time state security office in the DDR."[241] Quantitatively, this number far exceeds the actual performance of the TRC. There could — at least in a very short time span — be a good 21,000 registered victims of apartheid crimes, who later were to have any claim to reparations from the government.

As an intermediary result we assert: the system and the individual stories are either separated or mixed together in the German rebuilding. The "truth" about the "normal" life in the DDR emerges neither through legal means nor through Stasi files. What if the EK were to make possible a differentiated public debate, which could separate the system of the DDR from the life of the people in the dictatorship?

If the task of the EK/IC was to demand "total social reconstruction," how far has the work of the EK/IC come?

Again, everything depends on the understanding of the word "demand." The EK/IC has certainly not achieved a social catharsis. On the other hand, a judgment has already been made on the work of the first Commission that it has "thoroughly fulfilled" its job of making a "contribution to the political-historical analysis and political-moral evaluation of the SED dictator-ship."[242] Thus, in both Commissions the (critical) analysis appears to out-weigh the evaluation. The analysis is useful in the sense of historical and political reconstruction, says Wolfgang Ullmann, but brings little "to social reconstruction." [243] The impression that the preponderance of evidence hides the core issues is not obvious in the second EK/IC. The results of the first Commission are seen as ineffective: they "are so detailed, that they can hardly be appreciated by a large segment of the populace or not at all."[244] From a historical perspective, it is politically decisive "that an understand-able, generally accessible picture of the past is drawn, which can be under-stood and accepted by most people."[245] It was also the intention of the EK/IC to demonstrate "the openness in examples and differentiated historical-political rebuilding of the DDR past to display/demonstrate."[246] It was suc-cessful in demonstrating reconstruction as "an open, discursive process and to practice coaching people in quasi-pluralism before the eyes and ears of the public."[247] To initiate building as the total social task is not successful, counters Wolfgang Ullmann.[248] One may study how extensive social re-building functions from the case of South Africa. Meanwhile, the mandate of the EK/IC exists, as shown, only to demand a total rebuilding of society. "We have never reached 80 million people or set in motion some of the most powerful figures," guesses Eppelmann, who then qualifies this guess: "of those with whom we had dealings — a couple of thousand — very certainly. That will have an eventual effect, for example, in school textbooks. Here one can not expect minute success."[249] If one uses the vocabulary to "promote" to describe the beginning of the process, then is one able to say: the EK/IC has fulfilled its mandate. If however to "promote" is decided at the end of the process so that the results are visible immediately at the close of the work of the Commission, then the result appears to be minimal, since the truth that is told at the end has no ability to develop the power of social change. Also here the EK/IC appears to act as a representative for the social opinion.

If the task of the EK/IC was to solidify "anti-totalitarian consensus," how far has the work of the commission come?

An anti-totalitarian consensus means "the refusal of any form of totalitarian ideology, program, parties and movements." Behind it stands the credo of democratic politics after 1945: "Never again war on German soil, never again dictatorship on German soil!" In keeping with its charge, the resulting Com-mission should "cement" this consensus. However, social anchoring of a basic anti-totalitarian consensus is difficult to measure. Should it be linked to voting? To the outcry of the extreme right? To the reflection of East Germans about their life in the DDR? There is an abundance of research on all these areas.[250] I would like to limit myself to one indicator: the second Investigative Committee was to "cement" a contribution to the anti-totalitarian consensus in society. Such a contribution is, in my opinion, achieved sooner through the testimony of contemporary witnesses, as well as through the practical action recommendations for action, especially in the area of memorials.[251] A "fatal historicizing" was thus avoided; and "any explanation of the historical truth, which merely reconstructs it and which, in the interest of scientific objectivity, forbids any comparisons at the outset as well as any assignment of value."[252]

The basic criticism after the inappropriate mixing of system and the individual's life story is one that can not be generally supported, but is still hard to deny. Doubtless both Investigative Committees of the German parliament have contributed to a differentiation, if one compares the picture of the DDR at the high point of the Stasi debate with that of ten years after the fall of the wall. However, the Commission's task appeared to be that of defusing "all tendencies to minimize and justify dictators"[253] in the long run. Along the way, it was to "shape the overcoming of the past so that it can make a contribution to the overcoming of the present" (P. Steinbach), which would serve as a milestone for political knowledge and the culture of remembrance.

In quantitative terms and in answer to the question "what truth has emerged from the Truth Commission?" one may say: the majority of institutions (legal system, Investigative Commission/IC and "Gauck Administration") brought a "majority" of the truth to the forefront, if one uses South Africa as a point of comparison. In the sense of the relevant historical-political task of communication, one may ask: does the exposed truth also have an effect on social change? One opinion maintains that for many historians interesting facts were uncovered. Others contend that it brought "less" on facts and "more" on communication and society. Doubtless, through the specific character of system change in Germany, the dictatorship of the SED is much better able to be researched than the system of apartheid, which was not even able to be the subject of research by the TRC. While in Germany the emphasis of the research was on the system of repression, in South Africa one had experienced much in terms of how a repressive system affects the life of its people. And that has the ability to develop social power. In view of the entire process, Wolfgang Ullmann[254] criticizes that after 1989 a variety of forms of rebuilding emerged: from the legal, to the historical-political, right up to the archives of private individuals. However, what was missing was the rebuilding of society. (For future transition research a comparison with the proceedings in South Africa is likely to yield unexpected results: the anti-totalitarian consensus is clearly easier to anchor socially when a Commission determines the effects of a system, than when it takes the system as a subject for analysis.")

(b) Is Reconciliation a (Viable) Category for the Political Coming-to-Terms with Guilt?

F. Schorlemmer responds in 1999: "A coming-to-terms with this costly word 'reconciliation' is meanwhile extremely inconsistent."[255] The former minister of justice of Saxony, Steffen Heitmann, maintains a rash leniency for the offenders who are responsible for the sickness of the East Germans: "for the social process of integration that we need in Germany the concept of reconciliation is not viable."[256] The last state Privy Council declared critically: "On 9 November, 1989 the people on both sides of the wall thought more in terms of comparability and reconciliation than about assigning respective guilt."[257] Against statements such as this one, it is immediately clear why Heitmann (and his name stands for others) does not consider reconciliation an acceptable category for political dealings with guilt. The concept has a certain connotation for him; essentially that of "comparison" without the denotation of "guilt" and without "truth." One could also speak of a strategically illegitimate use of the term reconciliation.

Indeed, Heitmann underscores that another morally legitimate understanding of reconciliation has suffered in the political debate. As we saw, the entire work of the first Investigative Committee, to cite only one branch out of the "institutionalizing overcoming of the past," depended on the foundation of "reconciliation through truth." In the subsequent Commissions these premises were again explicitly embedded in their charge.[258] In the debates surrounding his appointment a representative explained: "I am very much in favor of the victim and the offender being able to one day shake hands. However, the presumption for that is the establishment of guilt. Whatever point in time the reconciliation takes place, above all the opinion of the victim is gathered first, and then secondly the opinion of the offender."[259]

At first, "reconciliation through truth" was applied as a principle within the Commission, which led to a change in perception. Eppelmann states

auto-biographically: "Although since childhood I have been a politically engaged person and lived in the DDR until the end, I am now certain of a lot
more. I notice that, for example, in dealing with former members of the
Block Party there were also members of the SED. Today I regard them very
differently and perhaps with a bit more fairness, than I did in 1989. However,
my judgment of the share of the responsibility that should be claimed by the
top officials is more severe than before."[260]

"Reconciliation through truth" can mean at least two things: the critical
reception of information on a social level and the determination of guilt on
an individual level. However, both ideas have the connotation of change.
Consequently, the EK/IC had to take a middle position in the "fight about
reconciliation."[261] Certainly, the political concept of reconciliation is limited
and qualified, in that a general amnesty on the one hand and the general social exclusion of the offender on the other hand are ruled out. But the point
of argument remains: what meaning is attributed to justice? Do reconciliation and justice mutually exclude each other? Do they necessarily belong together? In the publicly held debates, two basic positions are discernable:

On the one hand, the push for reconciliation does not eliminate the
law.[262] "Reconciliation is an eschatological component that does not remove
the element of justice."[263] Truth means not merely "wanting to know what
happened," but includes a "clarification of legal relationships." The mere
naming of guilt is not enough. Justice must be applied to the full extent,
which means to rehabilitate the victims and punish the offenders. In these
arguments one should guard against "ideology and strategies for reconciliation" which, along with theological arguments, de-personalize a critical account of the past or, in the name of a social reconciliation, put the entire
project (i.e., a critical account of the past) into question.[264]

For others reconciliation may replace "jurisprudence." Consequences of
this will be drawn from the experience of legal reconstruction. It has been
shown that "jurisprudence does not replace reconciliation."[265] However, reconciliation can replace jurisprudence insofar as it focuses the view toward "a
common future, loosening it from the shackles of the past. One therefore
ceases constant calculations and endless remonstrances." Reconciliation replaces jurisprudence where it fulfills certain conditions; and certainly "first
and foremost the courage on behalf of those to whom injustice was done."
Reconciliation "demands acceptance by a heart filled with shame of an invitation to reconcile from those to whom the injustice was done. The hinge to
the door of reconciliation is the truth."

While the first position is that of the victims, the second is argued by representatives for the offenders. Accordingly, the victims have to take the first step. Spokespersons of the first position have in mind the personal reconciliation of the victims with the perpetrated injustice, while the latter position is considered from the interpersonal position as belonging within a larger social dimension of reconciliation. Both positions still continually enliven the political debates. Sharp contrasts exist between positions in the actual political debates. An example is the "grace" debate of Egon Krenz. For the one applied: "Egon Krenz must shoulder his punishment!"[266] The others are directed from the conception that "reconciliation cannot replace justice."[267] "Whoever, like Krenz, held a leadership position in the DDR for such a long time, must also assume that he will be brought to justice for it."[268] For representatives of the second position the conviction of the offender suffices; "individual guilt is demonstrated so that now mercy can be shown."[269]

However, representatives of the EK take a third position. Regarding the "mercy debate" for former politburo members, R. Eppelmann says:

> Theologically . . . a new beginning is not possible if the person doesn't first "beat their breasts." I would, for example, have difficulties speaking about a new beginning when it comes to Krenz. I would have to ask: "Are you ready, to start fresh?" . . . I have the impression that for Schabowski, but also for Kleiber mercy and showing of mercy would be something that they would be interested in speaking with others about and would like to think about. For Krenz, as he has stated publicly, it would be an insult. He will have justice; but he has absolutely no feelings of guilt. In any case, that was the impression he gave me. If I were to say to them: "I forgive you!" he would spit at me as if to say: "What kind of a bad opinion do you have of me anyway?"[270]

If reconciliation involves confronting the past, how far has the process then come?

The idea of "reconciliation without the truth" has not prevailed in the political debate in Germany. Former German Chancellor Gerhard Schröder balanced in his address on the state of German unity, November 11, 1999: "Only the legal account of injustice done to the individual and the political-historical working out of the history of both German states as the common project of post-war history can forge a legal peace and make social reconciliation possible."[271] The "cheap" concept of reconciliation, which Heitmann considers politically untenable, has been rejected.

Levels of political reconciliation: In the following pages, the German process will be discussed utilizing the South African process and the levels of reconciliation that were analyzed in that process. The differentiation of levels of reconciliation (i.e., personal, interpersonal, etc.) makes possible the formation of a simple grid whereby the various aspects of accounting for the past (legal, etc.) can be observed without having to subject them to a rigid system. In terms of content, differences and similarities emerge in the question of dealings with guilt, which promises results for a comparison of analyses.

IV. The Personal Dimension of Reconciliation
("Coming to Terms with the Painful Past")

The reconciliation of the individual with his experience includes, at least in the German process, three aspects: the "ability to tell," "to acknowledge the truth," and to be able to "integrate back into society."

If reconciliation can be achieved through the opportunity of telling one's own story, how far has the process come?

In comparison to South Africa, fewer affected parties were given the possibility to tell their stories within the framework of a "Truth Commission." For those who were given the opportunity, the "ability to tell" meant, according to the appraisal of Commission members, a contribution to reconciliation with their own experience.

If reconciliation is made possible through the opportunity to tell the truth, how far has the process come?

Here there appears to be a positive balance: the experience of truth has, primarily in view of the files of the secret police (Stasi), contributed to the process of individual reconciliation. The ritualized framework of the process surrounding the inspection of files, especially the preliminary talks, has also helped offenders to introduce the truth to what is portrayed about them. The survey maintains the value of an IM: "it is a very positive indication that I never met a neutral person, which was very remarkable."[272]

If reconciliation means re-integration back into society, how far has the process come?

Also there appears to be a justifiable positive balance: reconciliation has been reached in this dimension. For a person to find their place again in the new social order can also be part of the economic improvements made in connection with the change of the elite in power. Ulrike Poppe refers to the fact that many citizens of the DDR lived on the edge of minimal existence and were only able to stay afloat (economically) with help. After the fall of the wall, people have been able to develop their potential and to engage in politics. Many have had success in such ventures. This contributes to "reconciling oneself with the times in which one (previously) had lived with difficulty."[273] (Also, Markus Meckel says people have had to learn to define their place in society.[274])

1. The Interpersonal Dimension of Reconciliation

The Gauck Administration: in many instances individual concern with the past flows into the area of interpersonal exchange. For example, after the inspection of files a discussion took place either in a family circle or was sought with an IM;[275] or it was decided, for example, to advise the person to visit a doctor[276] in order to advise the course of a possible rehabilitation; or an offender-victim restorative mediation was requested.

> *If reconciliation includes the interpersonal dimension, how far has the healing process come?*

In contrast to the South African TRC, which created the framing conditions for the meeting between offenders and victims, the interpersonal dimension of reconciliation in the three examined areas (legal system, Gauck Administration, and EK/IC) was *not* advanced. Whether Rudolf Wassermann says: "Reconciliation can take place only person to person"[277] or whether Markus Meckel on that indicates: "Reconciliation is not the task of the state"[278] — one encounters on balance what the two Investigative Commissions concluded in their Final Report: "a dialogue or even a reconciliation between victims and offenders can not be forced by the state, but would have to be a matter of individual action in any event."[279]

The missing frameworks for the meeting between offenders and victims have, in part, been counterproductive for mutual acceptance. Some of these viewpoints follow, to name a few:

- The constitutional guaranteed protection of offenders in criminal procedures *(in dubio pro reo)* is often unbearable from the perspective of the victims: "The constitutional state favors the offenders" over against the victims.[280]
- The advantage of the knowledge that the victims gain through inspection of the files can burden the atmosphere of the occasion for talks with the offenders. This is objectively overreaching, can not be substantiated and is not believable.[281]

2. The Communal Dimension of Reconciliation

Reconciliation of the individual with his/her community acquired meaning in documented South African case studies, such as that of Philemon Maxan. Among other things, he sought reconciliation in his "black community." We have not seen this level of reconciliation in the framework of the "institutionalized overcoming of the past."

To be conjectured is that a comparable "community" idea in Germany was not achieved. Meanwhile it may be considered, whether the basic social structure of small groups, for example in East German villages, was achieved.[282] It is questionable, whether unmasked IMs had been avoided by the village community or whether possibilities of reconciliation with the community resulted, and if so, what this looked like.

3. Reconciliation on a National Level

The results of the above observations on "nation building" (III.1) should accordingly be set within the broader context of the debate in counter arguments for the process of German unity.

> If the task of the EK was to contribute to "reconciliation in society," how far has the process of German unity come?

The fact that the literature does not lay out the question is seen in an assessment of the narrative interviews.[283] Commission members who were asked the question gave various answers. "On the construction site of reconciliation" both Investigative Committees were "a pair of day laborers." To that extent "a contribution was made" says Eppelmann. For Peter Maser "the process of German unity was not essentially furthered by the EK." Markus Meckel counters with the opinion that the EK has "fulfilled its mandate." The various estimations I attribute to the differing views on the term "contribution"; namely, in response to the question how far the process has come. A "contribution" in the sense of "making co-existence possible" has been fulfilled. The liberal constitutional government expects nothing more than this. Meckel believes that a "contribution" has been fulfilled in the sense of a common appreciation of history, because he is thinking of the conversion of the recommendation into action: it has to do with the construction of a common "culture of remembrance." The memorial concept of the EK/IC has generally been politically realized.

If one places the definition of "contribution" within a broader context, the deficits of the previous process as well as the perspectives for the growing together of East and West are formulated more clearly than they were in the framework of the EK/IC. The broadest formulation in the public debate on the political balance of the German unification process is given by Richard Schröder. German unity is complete, he says, when two conditions are fulfilled: "When we dispense with the East-West distinctions as we have with the North-South distinctions, and when we have become so accustomed to each other that we can relate a common history, even over the past fifty years."[284] In light of this goal the criticism surfaces even more sharply: "A common view of a history of separation," writes Jürgen Kocka in the year of the publication of the Final Report of the EK, "still evades us."[285] A common historical picture hides the knowledge of the danger of totalitarianism, says Lothar Fritze. "Admittedly," Fritze continues, "we know this mainly from experience."[286] With these observations, the strands of the debate merge. Whether Hans-Jürgen Misselwitz of the Brandenburg central office for political education exhorts to "listen to the divided East and West," in order to communicate a "common, but also different historical picture about the time between 1945 and 1990";[287] whether Richard Schröder laments the need for "more personal contacts and encounters"[288] between West and East Germany; or whether Wolfgang Thierse remonstrates in view of "a common historical consciousness": "What we need is a greater readiness to tell of the personal experiences and of the individual biographical developments, and to make these available thus for public discussion between generations of West and East Germans."[289] The common perception appears to be: history is something one learns through stories, and "national reconciliation" must be based on a common historical viewpoint. With this assumption the striving for balance proceeds haltingly. On the 3rd of October, 1990, for Germany, the post-war period came to an end.[290] Joachim Gauck remarks on the 9th of November, 1999, at the ceremony at the Parliament: "The people of this nation have given each other a gift. Hopefully, when we meet here again in ten years, we can knowingly and joyfully accept this gift."[291]

4. Interdependence of the Levels of Political Reconciliation

The levels of reconciliation, as the processes have taught us in both countries, can not be duplicated; it would be a mistake, however, to deny any interdependence at all. There are also other examples in German politics in which the personal dimension of reconciliation receives national attention. To the extent that an individual acts, he or she acts representatively for others. Their actions can create a freeing effect for the nation. A well-known example: Willy Brandt kneeling before the memorial of the Warsaw ghetto in December, 1970 or Richard von Weizaecker's speech of May 8, 1985. Such events are, according to Donald Shriver, "powerful examples of the relevance of public contrition; a verbally public embodiment of the process by (which) nations can firmly plant their feet on the ground of reconciliation."[292] In view of our time frame for research, one may seek in vain for examples by which individual politicians, especially from the circle of the Politbüro, have placed themselves in a comparable symbolic act on the side of the victims of the SED dictatorship. However, an attempt can be seen in the apology of Dietmar Keller. Also, there should also have been considerations to honor those who suffered under the oppression of Communism in East Germany.[293]

V. Justice and Reconciliation

"We wanted justice and got a constitutional state." (Bärbel Bohley)

"What is justice?" asks Richard von Weizsäcker: "As lawyers, do we (even) know? Is it any different or easier for us than it is for theologians, philosophers or social scientists, for whom only approximations are possible? The Federal Supreme Court does not seem to know the answer. It states what in concrete instances may not be regarded as just any more."[294]

False and improper justice must be guarded against by justice (true justice must avoid it). This is emphasized as the basic decision to shoot in protection of the wall?[295] Both positions with respect to the idea of justice —

"justice and the securing of the law" — have been "impressively relinquished in support of justice."[296] Is the relationship between law and justice thus not so improper in the attempt to work it out by constitutional means? The answer depends on the point of view of the observer. Here, as in the case of South Africa, it must be asked: for whom has the process brought justice and what form of justice? From the perspective of the victims, the constitutional state does not go far enough in dealing with system injustice. (It seeks justice in the acknowledgement of pain, in reparations, and in punishment of the offender.) For those responsible for the old order, the constitutional state goes too far, if only in connecting responsibility to punishment of criminals (i.e., justice as punishment is "winner's justice"). The constitutional state reacts "not only to the pain endured by the victim"; it also responds "to breaking of the law, and indeed freeing (the victims) from the effects in which the victim as victim turns against his oppressor."[297] For both offenders and victims this fact remains relatively difficult to communicate. The offender does not recognize that laws were broken, and the victims expect that the constitutional state completely honors their loss. The Final Report of the EK balances in 1998: "A law that is just in all individual cases in the complicated social field of tension between victims and offenders is not conceivable."[298]

In the following section, various aspects of the "mixed question" will be considered: for whom has the process brought justice and what form of justice? I will first deal with the victims and will pose the balance question: to what extent could justice take the form of reparations? To what extent could it take the form of acknowledgement of suffering? On another level, should it involve "justice as punishment"? Is this a way for the victims to receive reparations? And what effect has the criminal process had on the offenders?

1. Justice as Reparations[299]

In the foreword to the "Handbook on Criminal Rehabilitation and Restitution"[300] the connection between reparation and inner unity is explicitly made: "The internal reunification of Germany has proven to be a more difficult process that will certainly continue for years to come: the division based on biases, misconceptions, and politically conditioned alienation will only gradually recede. A condition for this is reparations for the decades of injustices caused by the SBZ/DDR." In a regulative sense, there is the idea that without reparations there is no internal reunification.

Attorney General Christoph Schaefgen[301] indicates a differentiation of the victim's perspective: it has to do with the difference between legal rehabilitation and the judicial valuation of the process. Schaefgen explains the difference using examples from legal practice. Justice must be re-established through reparation of the breach of law, which applies especially to those who suffered under the injustices of the DDR. Victims' groups point to the non-abandonment of that which was unjust in the DDR state — where the lofty goals of socialism presumed to be able to interfere with the law — as measured against the current standard of human rights protections. In legal circles this aphorism was shared: "The mere fact of stating that one has suffered an injustice can be offered as a minimal claim for justice."[302]

"More important than rehabilitation," says Schaefgen further, "was the ranking of criminal law." With regard to the example of the Delikt Group's perversion of justice, he explains:

> If someone, because of a trifle, was sentenced to a longer jail term, it was simple rehabilitation to lift the unjust judgment. In a rehabilitation decision it is proof that this decision was contrary to the constitutional state and thus today has no application and must be lifted. The premise is: "If this had been in a constitutional state — and not in the unjust state of the DDR — then you would have not been sentenced." It also stands that: you were unjustly sentenced under the government of the DDR.

Schaefgen comments: "That is something many people disagree with!" In praxis, he depicts the bitter experiences of victims: the criminal justice system must continually apologize and say, "I am sorry. . . . I cannot hold the judge who made this decision responsible." Then the affected party says: "It seems to me as if today I have been sentenced all over again." In these cases rehabilitation plays a minor role. For their welfare it is important to be able to say to their tormentor through the sentence handed down by the law: "That was the law breaker, not me!" If the offender goes free, then the old judgment remains intact. "And that knocks many people off their feet," Schaefgen explains, because for the affected parties it does not have to do with "long jail sentences, but rather that a judgment is made." Behind that is clearly the idea: "Conviction includes the official recognition of past injustice as well as the suffering of the victim."[303]

If reconciliation means the re-establishment of justice by means of rehabilitation, then how far has the process come?

The Final Report of both Investigative Committees finds a "cautiously positive" balance between regard for the power of criminal law and for the legal obligation for professional rehabilitation.[304] "In the vast majority of cases, the process had a generalized freeing effect for the victims."[305] However, the balance, especially in view of criminal law on rehabilitation, is "not at all conclusive." Previously, only a third of the estimated total number of political detainees had submitted applications for rehabilitation. Up to 1998, a total of 133,000 applications were processed.[306] Finally, the writers of the Final Report still inserted one more criterion for assessment: whether or not the "final goal of rehabilitation" is reached, "namely the satisfaction of expectations of the claims of the victims," and the re-establishment of their "individual worth," "always depends on individual . . . lived experience of the person, which can never be generalized and which the law giver, despite all attempts, can never fully set to right."[307] The majority of suffered injustices are absolutely not justifiable. It should now be asked, which non-justifiable forms of reparation exist within the "institutionalized overcoming of the past"? Which forms of re-establishment of justice was the EK to make possible?

2. Justice as Acknowledgment

Outside of the justice initiatives, the re-establishment of the dignity of the victims is also assumed. For the chairmen of the EK, "to re-establish justice" means to "help and support, heal and explain, grasp, understand, conciliate."[308]

> If the mandate of the EK/IC was to remember the "victims of injustice and coercion" and to reestablish "the dignity of those affected by injustice and suffering,"[309] how far has the process come?

Assistants of both Investigative Committees draw a positive balance: the public hearings of the EK/IC contributed to establishing the "social acceptance of victims."[310] If the Stasi debate is defined by the discussion around the offenders, then a corrective has been reached. Concerning the documentation of parliamentary hearings, Peter Maser says: "In its entirety, this hearing would be very strained for the organizations representing the victims, but it also would be considered as an appropriate honoring of victims and their fates."[311] It is important "that the experiences of people are upheld. At least in hindsight, for them justice must be served."[312] It is also assumed that the forum offered by the Commission was an immediate contribution to the moral reparation of those affected. Furthermore, the memorial concept[313] was to contribute to a "social recognition" and "moral rehabilitation" of SED victims, in which, for example, the "name and fate" of individual places of suffering are listed. "The memorials have given an account through the placement of memorial books, individual memorial areas, and memorial plaques." The Final Report continues: "The individual naming of the victims with their fate also sharpens the focus on the historical dimension of the crimes."[314]

3. Justice as Punishment

Retributive justice was requested by some representatives in the South African debate in dealing with the offenders. Justice is ideally achieved through the punishment of the guilty. Using such arguments, people reacted to the amnesty law. In the German example it can be demonstrated that the critics of South Africa overestimated the possibility of developing criminal law to the degree of enforcing retributive justice after a system change. There are two reasons for this: there are sufficient legal decisions indicating that modern criminal law follows different objectives than the implementation of retributive justice.[315] A sense of fairness is not congruent with the task of constitutional criminal law. Rather, "punishment is legitimized in its application for the future."[316] Secondly, the German process employed the use of criminal law (as it still is administered) in only a few cases of "punishment." Despite the legal criminal code, prison has not become a symbol of justice in Germany.

If reconciliation for the sake of justice includes the avenging of severe human rights violations, then to what result has the rebuilding process come?

Egregious human rights violations have been avenged. This fundamental idea from the legal literature was validated in the Final Report of the Investigative Committee.[317] In connection to the decision of the Federal Supreme Court (where the retroactive prohibition of the basic law does not prevent the prosecution of severe human rights violations) Gerhard Welre and others demanded a retraction of the corresponding International Law *proviso*,[318] which was explicitly designed as a political recommendation for action by the EK/IC: "Indicated is a cancellation of the proviso of Article 7 par. 2 of the Convention for the protection of human rights and basic freedoms (EMRK), which the Federal Republic of Germany had attached to the ratification of the

European human rights convention in the year 1951 with a view to cancellation of the prohibition. Thus, in the process of overcoming SED injustices, a position could be reached on the documentation of justice as it develops."[319]

Let's go back to our comparison with the TRC process. In the South African process, the request for "justice as punishment" leads to the idea of conciliation between offender and victim. The connotations were "recompense," "sin," etc. This means "justice as punishment" is, in the sense of a theory of punishment, closest to the notion of "negative special prevention"; namely, the wrongdoer goes to jail and the victim receives recompense. As we have seen, this goal of punishment in the assessment of the DDR injustice was followed least. Including homicides, almost 90 percent of prison cases were placed on parole.[320] Thus, we see that the use of criminal punishment in dealing with the DDR injustice does not mean the implementation of the South African request for "justice as punishment."

There were not only cases of probationary punishment. The Politburo members Krenz, Schabowski, and Kleiber had to serve jail sentences for their legal decisions in manslaughter cases.[321] Is "justice through punishment" realized here?

Egon Krenz says in his memoir "The Process and the Judgment": "I was judged for my role in the DDR."[322] For him it is clear: "The state attorney general stands in the service of politics. And he has to sentence to jail the last of the state officials of the DDR chosen by the People's Parliament."[323] The entire proceeding was "unfair," as were the dealings with the DDR in general: "The East has the accused, the West has the judges. The story of the DDR was vilified and that of the old BRD was glorified."[324] Krenz admits: "Naturally, I am not free of guilt, which affected my political life." Every death at the wall was one death too many. "The problem was only," Krenz goes on to say, "that until 1990 we lived in a world that was armed to the teeth. On German land two competing social systems stood opposed to each other on German soil. . . . Between them the rule of morality did not apply."[325] Those responsible would have had to have been handled in light "of historical circumstances and realities."

We know the basic tone of the chairmen presiding over the final Privy Council in the case of South Africa. In addition, the last head of government of the apartheid regime argued with words to that effect that he (personally) was not guilty, because guilt was the result of "historical conflict." Egon Krenz also denies personal responsibility. The newspapers commented on the judgment under the title, "It was not me!"[326] "There is the insistence, never to assign responsibility." "The totalitarian dictator doesn't deny the crime, just the responsibility."

The criticism of a "winner's justice" is false both historically and in terms of content. Unified Germany has continued the criminal prosecution of government officials. As we have seen at the beginning, immediately after the fall of the wall the process began and had to wait until re-unification for a cautious counter-balance. In terms of content, it has been noted that the process against Krenz and the other Politburo members was incorrectly described as a "Polit Puro process." The SED Politburo did not sit on "prisoner's row" like a group of "criminals," "an organization was not judged as was the case in the Nürnberg trials of major war crimes against the group of political leaders of the NSDAP (Nazis). In this process it had to do with individual responsibility and the individual guilt of the three remaining prisoners who, as members of the Politburo, were responsible for the death of four unarmed escapees who, between December 1984 and February 1989, tried to climb the barbed wire along the DDR across from West Berlin and were shot by the DDR border patrol."[327] (The context for the proceedings also involved 4,263 deaths on the inner-German border, which were administered by the counsel for the prosecution.)

In the legal decisions, the role of Egon Krenz in October 1989 was mitigated. Krenz, Kleiber and Schabowski were to be punished as "indirect offenders" and not just as "accessories." (This explains the difference in jail time from the sentences that were handed down for the wall shootings.) They backed the decisions of the Politburo, among those sanctioning the use of firearms where death was to be considered the price of doing business. The presiding judge of the 5th criminal court of the BGH explained: "One can not just blame the border soldiers for homicide, but also those who gave the order."[328] While Krenz commented on the statement that the German Republic has "violated human rights" in the process, both Schabowski and Kleiber accepted their sentences. In the sense of pro-active prevention it would be appropriate to ask whether the process of individualizing the guilt of offenders like Schabowski provided the occasion to deal with their concern for gaps in the system. General prosecutor Schaefgen thinks it's possible that Gunter Schabowski's attitude put "things in another light than (was) previously (the case)"[329] and that this view was admitted into the decision. (Schabowski received three years, Krenz six and a half in jail; Schabowski was paroled after a year's imprisonment, and Krenz is still serving his sentence.)

If reconciliation means to reestablish justice for the victim by punishing the offender, then how far has the process come?

Members of the victim's families said that after the decisions of the BGH their "trust in the legal system slowly returned."[330] Barbel Bohley states, however, "that the decisions came too late." Yet, for many victims it signifies "making amends." Stephan Hilsberg thinks the sentence "was too mild, if one takes into consideration the pain of the affected parties." In the last vote, it became apparent that a compromise with guilt can not be made in the sense of an absolute theory of punishment. Accordingly, the Final Report validates our question in a relative sense: "The Investigative Committee has taken a stand for legal reconstruction, one that it overwhelmingly fulfilled. It validates the capabilities of the legal state, even if the expectations of victims for legal reparation could not be satisfied in all areas."[331]

4. Justice as "Restorative"?

Up until now, were three viewpoints: (1) justice as reparation, specifically with regard to (2) acknowledgement (of suffering) for the victims, as well as justice in terms of (3) punishment for the offender. However, what is the status of the re-establishment of justice for both the offender and the victim, a model which goes well beyond the idea of justice as reparation for the victims through the punishment of the offenders? To what extend could "restorative justice," as it is called in the South African context, be achieved?

The concept of "restorative justice" exceeds the limits for the punishment of criminals. This is clearly acknowledged in the German debates: "punishment of criminals can not atone for either history or politics."[332] "Restorative justice" includes moral, political, as well as legal dimensions and to that extent exceeds the limitations of the possibilities open to a constitutional government. This is because the constitutional state is only responsive in terms of criminal punishment. It can guarantee formal justice and determine individual guilt by means of strictly regulated process. To again use the example of the process in the "wall shootings," we may observe the members of the SED Politburo: "Material justice, namely decisions that everyone regards as just, is something the constitutional state can not guarantee, because not every one regards the same thing as just."[333] However, the formal constitutional state pushes the envelope where legal peace comes into play: "What a majority considers as manifestly unjust can not be accepted as a decision."[334]

We saw that "restorative justice" exceeds the possibilities of criminal law. It has thus conveyed sanctions outside of the criminal justice system that seem to be appropriate ways to re-establish justice in society. One reacts to the injured sense of justice of the victims. "For victims it is an ethical and aesthetic impertinence to once again discover the offenders in the field of education, in the police force, and in the church; going about their business in non-confinement and in public areas. . . . Disgust and loathing are authentic emotions, the repression of which no one has any business demanding of the victims."[335] Next to the desire for legal retribution toward the elite, a second area has been schematized with regard to individual guilt: "Those who serve in the areas of public service, scholarship, and teaching and in the political arena must be expected to have personal integrity worthy of the status of their office, in addition to professional qualifications and job skills."[336] The Final Report of the EK, which also offers a counter-weight, maintains: "Those in the former system . . . continually maintained that discrimination did not occur in the course of public service."[337]

If one asks about the social and political dynamic that developed through the public handling of personal guilt, it appears that the contribution to a social differentiation is questionable. In the public perception, different procedures do not play a role, as was depicted in connection with the commission of Brandenburg. Rather, here we see the separation of offender and victim. Meanwhile, the voices that criticize this polarization say, "we need to get to a point where we no longer distinguish between victim and offender," as Richard von Weizsäcker suggests.[338] Friedrich Schorlemmer says: "a one dimensional victim-offender polarization is theologically, humanely, and 'legally' highly problematic."[339] In the question of "restorative justice" a differentiated perception of both groups — victims as well as the offenders — is important. Victims still retain the notion of having had "back luck," having "been on the wrong side," or somehow of having "been guilty of their own fate."[340] "Restorative justice," which we saw in the case of South Africa, thus expresses true social sympathy for the fate of those people who suffered under the SED dictatorship. In the social political "fight about reconciliation"[341] there has also been a differentiation among the groups that assumed minimal responsibility in the DDR. "Former SED members, who meanwhile took responsibility for their past on the one hand, and on the other hand credibly acknowledge the benefits of democracy and a constitutional state, need the encouragement and security of knowing that their abilities and their engagement in a free society are valued and sought after."[342] Whoever takes such a position quickly becomes suspect of making the same concessions for former co-workers of the MfS.

This indicates how strained the debate was. Thus, a modified idea of justice appears to be regulative.

"Restorative justice" does not advocate ignoring steps in the re-establishment of justice on either side of the debate. "Reconciliation is the (re-)establishment of a dissolved relationship, in the course of which both sides must not allow the burden of the past to influence the present or the future."[343] Political papers immediately appeared guided by the idea of "restorative justice." Thus, in the design of the party it says:

"The chance for reconciliation and conciliation is necessarily tied to assumptions that can not be over looked. It is also not the job of politics to create these assumptions. This process presumes the acknowledgment and acceptance of guilt, as well as the rejection of revenge. Conciliation can not be demanded or orchestrated; it should also not become a feather in the cap of proliferation or a vote of war for the parties. Reconciliation is a long-term, social process, that exacts a lot of time, courage and honesty, and which includes much sadness on the part of everyone affected. The desire for reconciliation should not be abused by rendering injustice harmless."[344]

> *If reconciliation means the restoring of justice for the victims and the offenders, then how far has the process in Germany come?*

This question can only be answered in relative terms. The re-establishment of justice for both groups "is not successful, when neither 100% of offenders nor 100% of victims declare: that's correct, that's how it really was. Now the world is once again in order."[345] However, elements of "restorative justice" appear fulfilled by the practice of the legal renovation:

- Integration of the offenders is made possible by the fact that homicidal acts are avenged with probationary punishment. (This concerns mainly the border patrol.)
- Acknowledgement and acceptance of guilt and regret, which is reached through the process of the confrontation with the past, is worked out during the sentence.
- In public service thorough individual checks are made which, in the case of minor charges, make possible a new beginning in society.[346] In private business there has been no such scrutiny.
- The Investigative Committee's "working out of history and consequences of the SED dictatorship in Germany" has provided a very differentiated concept of reconciliation to the political profile, whereby it can not concede reconciliation at any price. "Persons who have compromised themselves through their own culpable behavior . . . are not suit-

able for leadership positions in a democratic state. This basic statement should not be confused with a hesitation for reconciliation."[347]

Along with the concept of "restorative justice" it is necessary for offenders to expose their authenticity and for the victims to be able to speak about what they have experienced. In the South Africa process the establishment of the Amnesty Committee made it possible to hold on to the principle of the constitutional state on the one hand and, on the other hand, to gather the offenders and victims before a public forum. Offenders like Jeffrey Benzien were exposed by the authentic stories of their victims, even though the victim's readiness to forgive did not lead directly to amnesty. In the German process, no such provision was made for a "direct encounter between victim and offender."[348]

We may conclude that a strategic use of reconciliation concerning the past and within the historical political discussion in Germany could not be enforced. The following ideas are regulative:

- For the sake of reconciliation there can be no continuity of previously ruling elite.
- For the sake of reconciliation there can be no new beginning without paying respect to those who were killed at the wall.

On the other hand, the possibilities for a morally legitimate and intentionally beneficial reconciliation for the sake of internal peace appear not to be exhausted. Politics has framed the requirements for making reconciliation possible. For the further social working process, much can be learned from the approach of goal setting and the hope connected with the South African concept of "restorative justice."[349]

Does a constitutional state cease to be a constitutional state when it begins to fulfill the expectations of justice connected with political transition? The Final Report of the Second Investigative Commission responds to this question with: "Justice is assumed in the constitutional process."[350] In response to Bohley's criticism that says "people wanted justice, but they got the constitutional state," R. Schröder answers: "1. The constitutional state should be satisfied that it prevented a dictator. 2. We should be proud that we can say to the offender: we will treat you differently than you treated us."[351]

5. Analysis of the "Regulative Statements" Behind the Political Counter-Arguments for the Working Out of System Injustice in Germany

The analysis of "regulative statements" again follows the goal to prepare the ground for the question of correspondence. The conditions for the possibility of political reconciliation should first be articulated in order to examine the "regulative statements" for their basic connection to theological reconciliation.[352]

We have already seen the "regulative statements" on political reconciliation which are, to some extent, contradictory:[353]

- Reconciliation concerns the nation.
- National reconciliation doesn't exist.
- Reconciliation is a process.
- Reconciliation can be had without the truth.
- Reconciliation is possible only with the truth.
- Reconciliation replaces justice.
- Reconciliation does not eliminate justice.
- Reconciliation has something to do with force.
- Reconciliation makes possible a new beginning.
- Social reconciliation presumes sanctions, be it criminal punishment or job disqualification.

For a systematic analysis of the regulative statements, the area of "reconciliation and nation" needs to be addressed first:

- Behind the statement "national reconciliation is important" a condition is discernable; namely, any talk of reconciliation presumes a connection to guilt.
- Behind the statement "there is no national reconciliation" is the idea that reconciliation presumes a context of mutual guilt. "The basis of the opinion is that there is no connection to guilt here and thus talks of reconciliation on a national level are meaningless: West and East have merely existed apart from each other."
- Both statements understand what is meant by "national reconciliation" or "inner freedom" as described by a "process." Behind the statement "reconciliation is a process" there is a teleological understanding of process (the process of "internal unity" is a closed one according to the idea of "thin unity"; however, according to "thick unity" it is an open process).

Other statements that express the conditions or the lack of conditions of reconciliation in connection with justice or truth need to be distinguished according to the three levels of reconciliation.

The statement "reconciliation presumes the truth" is active behind all levels of reconciliation: whether it has to do with closure regarding the individual's past, or in terms of the reconciliation between two people, or in reconciliation with society: *I must know what happened.*

On the intra-personal level, several ideas are operative behind the statement "reconciliation assumes the truth," among others:

- Truth has an intrinsic ability to heal and puts me right again.
- Truth must also help me to justice.

On the interpersonal level, several ideas are operative behind the statement "reconciliation presumes the truth," among others:

- Truth reconciles to the extent that the truth is demanded from the offender as a one-time event.
- That truth splits if, in order for reconciliation to occur, the truth about guilt is constantly demanded from the offender.

On the national level, operative ideas behind "reconciliation presumes the truth" are, among others:

- Truth in the sense of historical information reconciles, to the degree that it gives an accurate account of the system as well as of the kind of life lived under the authoritarian regime.
- Truth makes possible the distinction between a system and a people.
- The truth that was suppressed in the totalitarian system can at least be understood as a symbolic condemnation of the system, even for those who lived under it.

The sentence "reconciliation makes a new beginning possible" is active behind all levels of reconciliation. Thus, the political discussions link different conditions to the statements.

On an intra-personal level, behind the statement "reconciliation makes a new beginning possible," there are different conditions, among others:

- No conditions ("water under the bridge," "forgive and forget").

- Truth as a condition for a personal new beginning (for example through the examination of files).
- Justice as a condition for a personal new beginning (for example in the form of the recognition of suffering or reparations).

Behind the statement "reconciliation makes a new beginning possible," on an interpersonal level there are the following conditions:

- No conditions, to the extent that reconciliation as a new beginning is offered at any price; otherwise it will be said: "I don't assume any guilt; it was the historical circumstances."
- Change as condition for interpersonal reconciliation (reparations as a morally required sign).
- Reconciliation logically assumes change (reparation is not an obligation; it "flows" freely from a change in disposition).
- Overcoming of individual guilt and a new assessment of past deeds as a condition for interpersonal reconciliation.
- Forgiveness as recognition of the change in the offender and his readiness for a new beginning.

Behind the statement "reconciliation makes a new beginning possible," on a national level there are the following conditions:

- No conditions ("let us look forward!" or "let's have closure!").
- Sanctions: the victim can start over again in society if they make a "new" beginning possible. That means to make up for injustice and to "set (things) to rights" by tracking criminals, changing the elite chain of command, and thus, officially acknowledging the victim's truth.
- Readiness to forgive: with society the offenders can have a new beginning, if they make a "new" beginning possible by not allowing the offender to be burdened by constant reminders of his injustices; by not marginalizing him from society (for example, putting him in jail); by allowing him to earn a living by keeping professional areas open to him for employment; by accepting his desire to change and his new view of the past; and by encountering him with a readiness to forgive.

III. Interpreting the "Signs of the Times": A Theological Commentary (Theological Synthesis)

The graduated progression of Part II and III is an epistemological construction that, in general, interweaves perception and meaning with personal accounts.[1] As a rule, perception must be interpreted. A formal distinction between a perception of the signs of the times and its meaning therefore necessitates some preliminary considerations.

At least in two aspects, every perception is already guided by meaning and (on the one hand) it is always perceived selectively. Thus, for example, the eye of the painter of a landscape sees it in a different way than does a cartographer. Perspective is selected out from the whole. It would therefore be inadequate to ask the question whether one of the perceptions is less selective than the other. The problem that certain things are not seen cannot be resolved. There is always a guiding interpretation, be it an aesthetic or a functional one. However, a particular meaning can still exercise influence over perception. "Without a doubt, we all perceive 'more than we see' in a situation and hear 'more than we hear' in listening to a sermon."[2] This problem does not have to do with selection that is determined by *a priori* decisions; namely, by an interpretation that precedes perception. Instead of a shortage of perceptions there is a surplus, since in the course of perception more is perceived to be there than actually exists. This surplus of perception is affected by the interpretative framework of perception, which is also determined by values.

What conveys philosophical reflections as interdependent of perception and interpretation for a theological reception of political-ethical reality? To what degree does it lead beyond what has already been discussed? Let us begin with the second question: the problem of selective perception illustrates from a different vantage point that what is otherwise guided by the interests of knowledge does not (in the end) lead beyond what has already been stated: namely, that a faith judgment is a criterion for selection in the perception of political reality. However, as we have seen in the beginning of our empirical analysis, this is theoretically problematic.[3] Our concern now is with the issue of theological reflection that takes place after an empirical analysis of political forms of reconciliation. In this regard the second articulated problem area is relevant; for, according to the portrayal of political reality, the question is: does an interpretation of the "signs of the times" also have something to do with the fact that more of a theological interpretation is placed on political forms of reconciliation than are really there; namely, signs of the presence of God's grace?

In using philosophical theory to reveal the interdependence between perception and interpretation in our analysis, caution should be exercised in positing a one-sided favorable answer to the question of whether or not perceived political reality includes some form of theological reconciliation. Rather, the philosophical discussion creates a very conscious problem for what is "more than visible," which is always present in the moment of perception. "However, an interpretation of the signs of the times belongs to the central task of believing Christians."[4] How can we approach this task under the given conditions? The answer, which will be elaborated upon in the following section, will reveal how the final systematic interpretation manages to become the *theological synthesis of the preceding empirical analysis.*

This synthesis proceeds accordingly with a glance back at Part II. The focus of the empirical analysis was to use inter-disciplinary means to investigate reconciliation as a category of political reality on an inter-subjective plane in which reconciliation emerges in the political arena after system change. Our theological "view" became apparent when any of the connections within the realm of political science interpretation — namely of past or present politics — were highlighted in cases where reconciliation was politically relevant; that is, where it comprised one of the many possibilities of dealing with guilt.[5] The presentation remained open to the extent that our guiding interests have not been intended to provide a binding interpretation for all that concerns the processes of the political past. Diversification with regard to political reconciliation and its disparate implied axiomatic first had to be considered as *perception.* Indeed, we forwarded these perceptions in the course of our *theological* investigation. We will now proceed with the explication of what is "more than visible," which results from an interpretation of perceived events. However, the differences between political analysis and theological interpretation will not be bridged via dissimulation. Where faith brings its orientation to an interpretation of the "signs of the times," an indifferent juxtaposition of political reconciliation and reconciliation as a soteriological category is also rejected, as is an authoritative identification. A theological synthesis is not dependent on the Christianizing of the world or on the secularization of the church.

We can formulate briefly that in this investigation perception and interpretation are connected to each other methodologically in such a way that the inductive perception of political reconciliation *precedes* a judgment by faith. This (faith) judgment is elaborated upon in Part III in "deductive steps" so that, with a glance back at Part II, we may conduct the normative theological investigation. One may say that in Part III the entire inductive process is "deductively interrupted" in several stages and that the theological highlights emerge retrospectively in Part II. What has been already implicitly perceived as a judgment of faith will now be theologically explicated. It would therefore be inaccurate to say that the inductive path has now been "left behind" and that we may now move forward deductively as if only the development of the theological remained to be completed. On the contrary, an interpretation of the information should take place, and indeed, a theological interpretation.

On the level of basic theology, which is guided by God's decision to reconcile the world to Himself, there is a certain continuity from Part II to Part III that may be described as a relationship of the implicit to the explicit. The discussion of reconciliation in Part II is reiterated in order — using an informational metaphor — to compare it with the "encoded data" that will be "unpacked" in Part III.

Discontinuity is evident on the level of the following theologically normative investigation. The *ontic* track — which will be taken up during the process of "unpacking of the data" — can only be evaluated responsibly from the standpoint of faith. From this perspective it remains open whether or not the normative examination of the "unpacked data" is identical with that of the "encoded" data. The categories of interpretation are not inherent in the presentation; they stem from existing reconciled reality and must be examined on the basis of the categories in common with political reconciliation.[6] Accordingly, Part III says something different and new in contrast to Part II. To use philosophical logic, it concludes synthetically and not analytically like Part II. To this end, the following will serve as the theological synthesis of the previous empirical analysis.

The formal and informal distinction of both the empirical analysis and a theological synthesis is appropriate for the development of our problem. In the stepwise graduated process of Part II and III, the theoretical interdependence between perception and interpretation is not overlooked, and where, within the overall analysis of the political connection to reconciliation, such a gradation is employed it is primarily for pragmatic reasons.

A. Reconstructing the Doctrine of Reconciliation in the Political Arena

The ensuing theological synthesis is an attempt at a systematic reconstruction of the Christian idea of reconciliation within political reality. The question of correspondence regarding a fundamental connection to theological reconciliation as it appears in political forms of reconciliation will be presented in three sections. First, in a formal segment (I) it will be examined whether or not there are categories that exist between the empirically analyzed forms of political reconciliation and those of the Christian idea of reconciliation. Finally, two material segments will follow focusing on the theologically normative examination of categories associated with the individual case studies. In the logical segment (II) the theological synthesis of the chapter "Setting the Direction" (Part II.A.I and B.I) will be presented and a "Balance" (Part II.A.III and B.III) will be presented with the corresponding field of legal ethics and of process theology. In the symbolic passage (III) we will examine the case studies for existing symbolic forms with a critical look back at the chapter on symbol (Part II.A.3 and B.3), as well as for rituals of past political reconciliation as they correspond to theories on metaphor and the current research on "worship as ritual."

I. The Question of Correspondence —
A Preliminary Formal Rendering

1. The Theological Task

The task of this chapter is to formally assign categories that may potentially exist between the analyzed forms of political reconciliation and axioms of the theological doctrine of reconciliation. The condition for the development of the problem is the creation of a material foundation, and therefore the question of correspondence will be prepared in two deductive steps (sections 2-3): (1) the theological foundation of reconciliation will be developed and normative guiding ideas concerning the Christian concept of reconciliation will be developed (section 4); and (2) finally, the political forms of reconciliation will be examined for potential categories, especially with regard to evidence of a break with the Christian idea of reconciliation (section 5). Are there indications that suggest that the common use of the term "reconciliation" proceeds from a common fundamental category with respect to its usage in past politics and in theological teaching on reconciliation?

2. Orientation to Theological History (First Deductive Step)

A preliminary look at the problem of reconciliation from the point of view of a history of theology reveals how varied the accents are placed. Anselm's problem *cur deus homo* was quickly eliminated from the Doctrine on God in the ethics (Abelard),[7] a view that was decisively expounded upon by M. Kähler[8] who subsequently concluded that God's reconciliation with man does not have to do with ethics, but with a new creation. In Christ, "God has placed himself in a new relationship to humanity."[9] In connection to M. Luther, M. Kähler interprets reconciliation christologically: namely, Christ humbles himself. It has to do with "empathy with the suffering of the sinner to the fullest extent."[10] For M. Luther reconciliation means that Jesus Christ takes our place entirely and completely, even to the point of our final inner struggle with God's abandonment (doubt). We may *feel* that our sins are taken away,[11] but the "happy exchange"[12] also means that "sin" and "grace" cannot somehow be quantified. The person acts in accord with reconciliation; he cannot contribute to it. He cannot fight sin, but he must "be swallowed up and drowned" in Christ.[13] In response to an ethicized understanding of guilt, M. Kähler says that "guilt is . . . not merely the knowledge of guilt."[14] Alternatively, F. Schleiermacher and A. Ritschl contend that reconciliation can only be experienced within the congregational setting and that it always includes an ethic. "The Redeemer assumes the believers into the fellowship of his unclouded blessedness and this is his reconciling activity."[15] Reconciliation is understood as "inclusive"; as "the burying of the sins of man in general forgiveness."[16] Everything results from the "intent" of the "hidden motive,"[17] an idea that can be at least traced back to P. Abelard.[18] Even though his teaching on reconciliation was later called "ethicism,"[19] A. Ritschl was always clear on this point: Christ's "task is singular in type. . . . Therefore, no one can directly imitate him."[20] In contrast to F. Schleiermacher and A. Ritschl, G. W. F. Hegel had viewed it earlier as not being mediated through the "believing congregation" (for Hegel it has to do with "reconciliation of the mind with knowledge"[21]), a position that was later also taken by K. Barth. He assigns new priority to Jesus' prophetic task of dedicating reconciliation: as God reconciles the world to Himself in Christ, He is Himself the word of reconciliation. "The subject of the doctrine of reconciliation is the knowledge of Jesus Christ."[22] For K. Barth, reconciliation means "bridging the divide" "to man." This act of bridging is done "exclusively by God" (ibid., 87). Whoever would like to know something about reconciliation must look at Jesus Christ, in whom reconciling God and reconciled man are one and the same. In short, the project is "the doctrine of reconciliation as Christology" (ibid., 140). W. Pannenberg[23] criticizes both K. Barth and M. Kähler, stating that they lose sight of man's moment of acceptance of the act of God's reconciliation (compare 460) and goes on to say that ultimately reconciliation must "also take place on the side of man" (496). The idea of representation, especially in Barth's teaching on reconciliation, allows no "room" "for the human, creaturely, individual nature of the one represented" (461). However, W. Pannenberg tries to create this space by distinguishing "representative sins" from "reconciliation."[24] He also sees a correspondence: "reconciliation explicates and clarifies the necessity of the dedication and acquisition of the sins that are at the basis of Jesus' death" (474). In criticism of Hegel's philosophy of religion, he argues for the on-going, incomplete nature of the process of reconciliation throughout history. "The reconciliation of the world through Jesus Christ has indeed been proven by the faith of the congregation, but it is still not identifiable as the final result of world history" (490). According to W. Pannenberg, reconciliation has its completion in the spirit. It "lifts people beyond their actual finality so that they can take part in faith in those things that are outside of them; namely, in Jesus Christ and through His death in God's final event of reconciliation" (498).

The above highlighted positions from the history of theology create an awareness of the difficulty involved in proceeding with a development of the question of correspondence with respect to a fundamental connection to theological reconciliation of political forms of reconciliation and the problems involved in determining a generally useful standpoint regarding the theological doctrine of reconciliation. Instead of a unified idea of reconciliation, the outline underscores some basic problems concerning theological reconciliation: does reconciliation complete itself "exclusively" (as for Anselm, Luther, Barth) or "inclusively" (as for Abelard, Hegel, Ritschl)? How does "Christ as "the true man" affect God's relationship to humanity?"[25] Has the Son of God completed everything, or does He take those whom He represents into His death and resurrection? "How should we think of the fact that God assumes the guilt of man for Himself instead of leaving it all to man?"[26] Does reconciliation complete itself both "exclusively" and "inclusively" (Pannenberg)? And, furthermore, is the work of reconciliation in the believing congregation mediated in terms of the consciousness of the believer (Schleiermacher, Ritschl) or is it mediated through the "word" of Christ as the resurrected one (Kähler)? Does reconciliation remain limited to benefiting the release "of the change of attitude"[27] (Schleiermacher) or does Christ, both God and man, "define" it over and above the interests of the individual (Barth)? Can the doctrine of reconciliation be something other than Christology (Anselm) if it does not intend to be an ethic (Abelard), but a new creation (Kähler)? These and other related questions, some concerning the doctrine of sin and justification, representation and sin, spiritual reality,[28] and gaining salvation, as well as the relationship of redemption to reconciliation are brought out in the process and are guided to responsible decisions in the following pages using "deductive steps."

3. Assigning Type to Theological Models of Reconciliation (Second Deductive Step)

In a second step, the historical theological reflections of the issue of the reconciliation problem will be treated in more depth. In the context of our first orientation (in which we were not able to locate a single generalized idea of reconciliation regarding the development of a basic connection to theological reconciliation), the problem now arises as to how to adequately address a theologically normative categorization of the question of correspondence in terms of the numerous versions of theological reconciliation.

A proven possibility for this is offered by assigning type to the ideas. Its strength "consists in criteria for a systematic order by which to convey the concepts of reconciliation."[29]

Within the scope of the history of the research, the Swedish theologian G. Aulén,[30] who was a considerable influence on the "Lunder School," developed the first great typology of Christian thought on reconciliation. This typology is further developed in the current German[31] and American[32] discussions (among other things, it goes beyond Aulén's three-part typology, which catalogues the "historical process" as part of reconciliation thinking of the twentieth century).

Our typology, however, follows the connection to the current state of research as well as contrasts with it. Indeed, in hindsight, we could use Aulén's typology to arrange our description of the theological position of Anselm historically with the Latin type; M. Luther with the classical type; and finally F. Schleiermacher and A. Ritschl with the idealist type. But it would quickly become apparent that some of the above-mentioned "types" are difficult to categorize (like Calvin, Hegel, or Pannenberg). The resulting division of larger models of reconciliation according to types connects formally to the current state of the research,[33] but contradicts the basic tendency of all previous typologies. The guiding interests of the above typology of reconciliation obviously lie in stressing the "classical" type over against the others. Meanwhile, it will be seen that classical ideas of reconciliation also occur in various forms in other models. Thus, we will not cultivate a singularly "classical" type to which Luther, Kähler, or Barth could be exclusively attributed.

Furthermore, it appears advantageous to broaden Aulén's typology with respect to the ancient church, since the cosmic dimension of reconciliation can not otherwise be taken into account.[34] However, it does play a meaningful role with Origen, as will be seen in the final section.

(a) The Cosmic Model[35]

"The ancient church has developed next to nothing in the way of a doctrine of reconciliation. It understands Christ less as a reconciler with God, than as a savior from the demonic powers of this world."[36] This statement allows for a confirmation of a theory of redemption which was espoused by representatives such as Origen and, among others Augustine and the Cappadocian, Gregory von Nyssa.

Origen uses the analogy of ransom money, which to some extent perpetuates Irenaeus's[37] idea of spiritualization. Ransom money, which is mentioned in Mark 10:45, is paid to the devil (and not to God). Christ buys off the sinner; He offers his soul to the devil as ransom. However, since the devil cannot contain the sinless soul of Christ, he loses both: the person and the ransom. The devil is thus outfoxed, ultimately to his own gain; for in the end he is also redeemed.

The theory of redemption, which is also represented by Origen is, however, anchored in his entire dogmatic[38] and appears difficult to understand, especially where it is not situated within the broader context of his anthropology and cosmology. For Origen, the work of the reconciling Christ consists in the step-wise purification of the *entire cosmos* from human sin. The core thesis of *De Principiis* (I.6.1) states: "At any rate we believe, that God's goodness *(bonitas dei)* through his Christ *(per Christum suum)* will lead the entire creation *(universam creaturam)* to a single end *(in unum finem)* in which all enemies will be overthrown," and certainly to the "salvation of the downtrodden *(salutem subjectorum)*."

To update Origen's model of salvation in broad terms: the *logos* is God the Father (acc. to John 1); and according to the model of the *logos*, which (after Gen 1:26-27) is in the "image of God," God created "rational beings" *(logica)* right at the beginning, even before the existence of this material world. All *logica* (angels, people, demons) were, in their original state, bodiless spirits (*logoi* or *noes*) that were immediately subordinate to the Holy Spirit and were devoted to the Father's countenance. The *logica* were of the same nature; their differences first appeared after the fall (of Adam). The Son and Holy Ghost could not sin, but by contrast the subordinate *logica* were not perfect. According to Origen's speculations, God had the choice of either allowing no free will at all or of taking their fall into sin into account and ultimately decided for the latter. Thus, it was always God's plan that the fallen *logica*, through their free will and His guidance, should again adhere to the good. Of course, along the way there would be many setbacks and large lapses in time; for the return to conformity with God's original plan of salvation is a long, laborious process. The fall (of sin) is like the cooling of love, which is explained as a weariness of God's countenance. The *logica* thus fell to various levels: many became angels, others people, others became demons (the latter were led by the devil who became the first fallen *logicon*). In the fall the material world was created, which is nevertheless the expression of the immediate intention of the Creator himself. God wanted, at least externally, to arrange the diverse strivings of the *logica* in the creation of the universe (in the three levels in which the *logica* were broken down according to worthiness after the fall). Thus, the *logica* begin to live in time. For humans, they either stand the test or they sin. The universe becomes a place of punishment:[39] the goal of instruction and renewal is to return to the Creator. Origen is of the view that in the end good finally prevails from two reasons. First, the rational core of the soul is indestructible. In it the light of the glory of God has left behind its imprint (symbolism of light!). Second, and similar to the view of God at the beginning of creation, there is a progression from "letting off steam" to weariness and, finally, reversal. A restoration of all things *(apokatastasis panton)* must inevitably take place. However, so that this does not mean an eternal waiting period for eternity, *logos* emerges in the purification process and ultimately takes on a special meaning in the incarnation and the re-ascension. The becoming man of Jesus offers a pedagogical model for the free, obedient human will created entirely by God. Jesus' teaching is carried on in the preaching of the church; it is broadened in triumphal procession over the earth and people are improved morally. Through the education and support of Divine Providence this same freedom, which leads to the case of the *logica*, is finally attributed to that of the constant oversight of the triune God. The created universe will pass away and a unity of the final state with that of the original will again be restored.

Regarding the critical assessment of the idea that reconciliation is a cosmically conclusive event effected by God, we come back to the cosmic model in the course of our examination to the question of correspondence (section 5a). First, three characteristics of the model should be outlined:

1. Origen holds to the hope[40] of universal reconciliation; the idea of reconciliation excludes "without a doubt *(sine dubio)* any special limitation" *(De princ.* IV.4.4). "The work of reconciliation is incomplete until all spiritual beings are brought to salvation and God is all in all."[41] The prevailing reconciling work of Christ does not play out in the inner person, but is conceived cosmically.[42]

2. The hope of universal reconciliation connects with an overall movement that encompasses the original and final situations. Creation strains back to its origin in God. Although Origen does not think linearly, but cyclically, the process of improvement does not include all of the fallen at the same time[43] (according to the newer research on Origen, a circular flow [*sine fine*] is not what is intended, but rather the [future] eschatology of the last word).[44] For Origen, reconciliation is a

historical process of healing that also comes to an end. He sees it modeled, for example, in Israel's flight from Egypt.[45]

3. The reconciliation process, according to Origen's basic line of thinking,
   proceeds in a step-wise manner "because it is God's way not to use force,
   but to preserve freedom."[46] Freedom is thus neither to be understood as
   mythical nor deterministic, but arises out of the historicity of the message of reconciliation.[47] Reconciliation includes the hope of (moral)
   change here and now.[48] Accordingly, Origen's "universal hope" does not
   mean a "passive belief in the chance of natural fate."[49] "Freedom is the
   inalienable possession of the rational being who stops being responsible
   when he stops being free."

Despite many of the apostasy teachings that were later attributed to him,[50]
the ideas of the ancient church continue to play a principal role in Origen:
embodied in the concept of salvation is immortality imparted by God's ever-
lasting life. The embodiment of evil is death.[51] Reconciliation thus is
thought of as the saving and awakening response of the life of the divine to
the human world of death. Salvation is thus not primarily forgiveness, but
liberation.

(b) The Legal Model

"With Anselm of Canterbury, a new chapter in the history of the doctrine of
reconciliation not only begins with Anselm of Canterbury, but he is the first
to develop a strict correlative."[52] Whereas the theology of the east appears
defined by the ideal that the saving activity of God ultimately aims at the de-
ification of man, western theology turns its attention to the event of reconciliation. In simple terms one could say: it has to do with the question of
what happened between God and Jesus Christ and how this event is to be
understood.

Let us bring ourselves up to date with the basic tenets of the *cur deus
homo*. Anselm[53] argues in the form of a dialogue that Christian teaching on
salvation is purely rational *(sola ratione)*.[54] For him, there is a problem with
regard to understanding. "The question, upon which the entire work centers" (I.1) circles on the possibility of being able to consider simultaneously
God's majesty, his lowliness and weakness, as well as his visible powerlessness in the person of Jesus of Nazareth. How does the majesty and lordship
of God fit together with the passion of the crucified one? What does becom-

ing man say about the being of God? In short: why did God become man? According to Anselm, man is meant for blessedness *(beatitudo)*. To live justly before God means to give back to God what is due Him. "If angels and humans had given back to God what they should have, they would never have sinned."[55] What is due God? According to Anselm we are guilty of (not) recognizing God for who He is: the Lord of all Creation. We should submit ourselves to His will.[56] Sin thus means for Anselm that the rational creature does not serve the will of God and thus deprives Him the honor owed Him. Sin is directed against God himself; it denies His lordship and is a violation of the first commandment. Through sin "all of human nature is corrupt *(tota humana natura corrupta)* and at the same time totally spoiled by sin *(fermentata)*" (I.23). To what extent can sin affect the honor of God? Anselm writes: "It is impossible for God to lose His honor."[57] With regard to His person, God can not be dishonored. The consequence of sin is not an insulted God, but the destruction of the world order. God's intention for man — to bring him to blessedness *(beatitudo)* — is thwarted. God is thus dishonored with respect to his work: *"nonne abstulit deo, quidquid de humana natura facere proposuerat?"*[58] God and man, creator and creation are caught in an irresolvable relationship, which may be seen as a legal contract[59] initiated by man. Thus, man ultimately dishonors himself as God's partner. He does not honor God (which means to follow the first commandment), but condemns both himself and his own future in the community of God. Anselm discusses possible reactions of God to sin. Using the Augustinian distinction between power and justice, he rejects the idea of removing the devil by an act of force. In general, he opposes the basic tenet of redemption theory that the devil has power over man (I.7).[60] Rather, God's justice demands a reaction to sin itself. Thus, ameliorating or ignoring sin as an option for action is rejected. And God's mercy allows sin to remain; even to the extent of the destruction of the world order and the beauty of creation. God is therefore indifferent to justice and injustice. When God wants to make man ready again for community with Him, He must purify man — even free him from sin, since a person can not be led from injustice into justice by forgiveness alone.[61] "I see that another mercy *(aliam misericordiam)* must be sought" (I.24). This relates to the history of action of the formulaic phrase *"aut satisfactio aut poena"* (I.13, 15, 19). Punishment would mean to leave the sinner to himself; to accept foreclosure on the contract with man and to give him over to death as lost because of his sin.[62] But this goes contrary to the divine plan of salvation that says "yes" to man's blessedness. God keeps his covenant. Community with God thus cannot be re-established "without satisfaction, namely, without the freely willed acquittal of guilt."[63] For how could the person who is otherwise imprisoned by sin remove guilt *"secundum mensuram peccati"* (I.20)? On the one hand, the person must remove the guilt, and on the other hand, only God can offer satisfaction. The subject of the work of reconciliation therefore must of necessity be God who became man in Jesus Christ (II.6 & 7). God became man, but without sin and therefore only He could give himself freely unto death (i.e., death is the result of sin). The death of Jesus was necessary to purify man, because it necessitated something that the enormity of human sin itself could not itself overcome.[64] The necessity *(necessitate)* consists in the person.[65] The death of Jesus Christ is the sufficient basis for the salvation of humankind. In faith[66] the person receives interest in the earnings of the God-man (*fructus et retributio suae mortis* [II.19]), in order to conform to his example of perfect justice (*imitatores* [II.19]); through emulation the person achieves the blessedness that was previously allocated as his. Why did God become man? God wanted it so, because He keeps his covenant with man.

It is not possible here to discuss the history of the consequences or the many-voiced criticisms of this model.[67] Rather, two viewpoints from the teaching on reconciliation of Anselm of Canterbury should be highlighted that are helpful for the subsequent development of our problem:

1. The relationship between God and man is conceived along a spectrum. Reconciliation is about a justly ordered relationship, which the person on his part does not keep. The breach is thus not spanned and Christ must set the relationship right again. "Clearly, the mercy of God is not conceived of here as dispensing legal justice, but as fulfilling it in every detail."[68] "Cheap grace" is excluded; the simple phrase "forgive and forget" can not re-establish a relationship with God. Man has not only sinned, but is caught up in sin. "And only now is it discernable what it has cost God to reconcile with man."[69]

2. *Aut poena aut satisfactio* provides no alternative for legal options for action. Got does not wager with regard to human fate. The alternative of "death or blessedness"[70] is always decided in favor of blessedness.[71] Rather, it provides the option for demonstrating the appropriateness of the satisfaction that makes a new beginning with the person possible and reestablishes God's community. Here God argues for His justice. "Accordingly, the idea of God reconciling with Himself is in a corresponding relationship to the idea of God reconciling with the world."[72]

(c) The Humanistic Model[73]

Only a generation after Anselm of Canterbury, an entirely different concept than satisfaction was placed at the center of the model for reconciliation: love.[74] Whether Peter Abelard actually can be seen as an "antipode" to Anselm is debatable.[75] However, it is not debatable that in his version of reconciliation, which he essentially developed in interpretation of Romans,[76] he makes the case for a counter concept to *cur deus homo*.[77] If Anselm conveys the law-fulfilling effect of Jesus in *status exinanitionis* as satisfaction in the event of the cross (and experienced here as its own actual meaning), Abelard conveys the human appearance of Christ during his life on earth as the love of God, which for its part awakens human love and separates it from sin. Reconciliation is thus the activity of the overabundant love of God in the person of Jesus Christ. In short, one could formulate: Anselm's Christology of the deed is replaced by Abelard's Christology of the person.

"However awful and unjust it appears," says Abelard with reference to Romans 3:24, "that someone's innocent blood had to be demanded as ransom, or that an innocent had to be killed; not to mention that God considered the death of his Son for such a task so that through Him the entire world should be reconciled (to God)!" it was necessary. For Abelard, it is no small necessity that God had to redeem humanity through the incarnation and death of Christ on the cross.[78] As an argument in favor of this he says: "Ever since the forgiveness of sins, on whose behalf man was punished, there is no longer any reason that man should be punished any further (on account of sin)." Christ has already forgiven sins before His death. The cross means that God has bound "us even more closely to himself through love." "Our salvation thus comes from the highest form of love which not only frees us from the bondage of sin, but purchases for us the true freedom of children of God. . . ." For Abelard, faith has an ethical quality because this "love is expanded in us." This is because "God in Christ unites himself with our nature and through his suffering has purchased for us His highest love . . . , we are thus bound to Him as to our neighbor for His sake by an indissoluble bond." The love of God opens for the believer — and only for the believer[79] — the possibility of interpersonal forgiveness.

This type of reconciliation with both of its related main aspects — a humanistic God and a moral human viewpoint — has been favored by the history of ideas due to Enlightenment thought and later on by the liberal theology of the Renaissance. Because of its characteristics, the imprint of the *humanistic model* can be found in modern form without having to individually unpack the historical lines of development.[80]

The direction of Abelard's idea of reconciliation during the period of the Enlightenment corresponds to a basic anthropological approach. Reconciliation is a "subjective" event; it completes itself in man. In Anselm's doctrine of reconciliation the "allowance for human action" was missing.[81] An "objective" understanding of reconciliation as an event external to man was no longer conceivable under the changing direction of the history of ideas. The "talk of God's wrath as pacified by the blood and sacrifice of Christ" was seen as "an accommodation to the 'idea' of a Jewish theology of sacrifice and its practices."[82] "Furthermore, one turned his argument from the principal non-substitution of the individual against the Biblical teaching grounded in the *satisfactio vicarii.*"[83] G. Wenz says: "The teaching of the dedication of salvation was, for modern theology, to undergo one of the most important upheavals of the entire pre-modern reconciliation teaching . . . separating it from its roots to a basic regrouping."[84]

So, for example, the Socinians teach that "each person has to achieve for himself the fulfillment of the law by way of his own actions and deeds."[85] Guilt and satisfaction, forgiveness and restitution are mutually exclusive. Thus, the fact that the sinner is already forgiven and neither his sins nor the accounting of the sin is credited to the person has theological consequences. K. Heim characterizes it in the phrase: "The God of the Enlightenment takes guilt lightly."[86] Christ is the theological rationalist's first "true man." The divinity of Jesus is contested. "In Socinianism, salvation is ultimately a thing of good will; the person's own redemption is basically up to him to effect. Christ serves only as a teaching example."[87] The modification in contrast to Abelard clearly moves into the realm of Christology. For the Socinians, Christ is not actually the revelation of the love of God, but a "form of manifestation of divine teaching,"[88] with which God's love is linked.[89]

In addition to G. Aulén, in a classical manner, K. Heim abstracts the historical development of the characteristics of the humanistic model of the Enlightenment, distinguishing them from the nineteenth century, and once again underscoring the opposition to the legal model of reconciliation. "For the humanist, ethical teaching on reconciliation, which was introduced with the Enlightenment and is continued with strong modifications by Ritschl, is not a legal act, but a moral process within the person through which man's tarnished relationship to God is set right."[90]

The title "Justification and Reconciliation" follows the intent of A. Ritschl in a notation that "the acceptance of a change in God from wrath

to mercy through Christ is eliminated."[91] The material evidence by which
A. Ritschl judges the course of history is defined as "the distinction between
an ethical and legal version of reconciliation."[92] In his comparison between
Anselm and Abelard, A. Ritschl stays away from legal categories of the
church's doctrine on reconciliation and sides with Abelard.[93] The ethical imprint of the idea of reconciliation thought is connected with the basic theme
of its agenda; namely, the dominance of the moral spirit over the natural
world.[94] The reality that has begun with the Gospel proves "that because of
God one has a higher value as a spiritual entity than does the entire natural
world."[95] According to A. Ritschl, reconciliation can not be conceived of in
legal categories. God can not be thought of in terms of objective ideas.
Rather, reconciliation refers to the pre-eminence of divine love over against
any power of wrath. With the annunciation of Christ who is victorious
through his death, God reveals himself in unconditional love and in the
readiness to forgive. The person is reconciled to God when he comes to an
awareness of this consummating, justifying event.

Newer typologies[96] fall into subjective categories of twentieth-century
ideas of reconciliation. The modification of the dominant humanistic model
of the nineteenth century primarily results from the fact that reconciliation
no longer is seen as "an inner stance of man"; rather, it is given "meaning
primarily in its social-political dimension."[97] (In the context of this classification, many of the concepts of reconciliation that are classified with the imprint of the humanistic model in the twentieth century are discussed in the
Introduction.)[98] As a whole, the observed movement from a motif of change
in the consciousness of the individual to a program of social-political reconciliation retains the distance that is encountered in the humanistic model of
reconciliation since Abelard.

For the purposes of this study, I would like to suggest that the basic humanistic models conveying the theme of reconciliation are still with us today, albeit in different forms. Abelard's "very large question" has lasting
meaning: "What is salvation through the death of Christ?"[99] How can we
conceive of the "arrival" of reconciliation? What does it mean for the person
and his forgiveness? Is there interdependence between the love of God and
love of one's neighbor? The central problem lies in the basic Christological
decisions that precede the concept of reconciliation and the anthropological
consequences that come into play as a result. Representatives of the humanistic model of reconciliation emphasize that reconciliation invites consequences; its representation is not suited to moral laxity. At the same time,
however, the assumption that on principle the person would not be able to

stand before God (as is decisively asserted by the Enlightenment) can only
be advanced using a relative concept of sin. "Thus, the problem of reconciliation," sees G. Aulén very clearly, "has lost its edge and deep gravity."[100]
B. Seiger [101] summarizes the ambivalence of what is classified as the humanistic model where he says that the "main characteristics" of the model serve,
on the one hand, as a "reference to reconciliation thinking and hope for
progress based in ethical behavior"; on the other hand they serve to retard
"the understanding of reconciliation as the creation of God's community
through the suffering for our sins of Christ."

(d) The Historical-Process Model[102]

In this model, another dimension of reconciliation is rediscovered and at
the same time is expanded in a manner that is otherwise underrepresented
in the Aulén typology. Following Aulén, proceeding along the lines of the
legal and the humanistic model, where the implication is that reconciliation is exclusively a God-God problem in terms of God's relationship to
man,[103] another added dimension emerges; namely, the universality of
God. In the center of the idea of reconciliation there now stand the spatial
relation of God-World, World-Man, Man-Man and, characteristically, the
historical process. Through this addition, the model receives a new emphasis over against the cosmic model as well as Aulén's model, reflecting the
change in the history of ideas over the 1920s and 1930s. For Aulén, the issue
of reconciliation still needs to be answered on an individual basis. "Reconciliation takes place through God's action in Christ or through a change in
the consciousness of man. The notion that in the process of reconciliation a
divine or human subject can not be individually identified and thus is of no
recognizable interest, is also foreign to Aulen's model."[104] The historical-
process model is founded on an epistemological basis as it has evolved in
connection to A. N. Whitehead's process philosophy, and above all, in
C. Hartshorne's theology.[105]

"Process" thinking[106] is the condition for the possibility of accepting
reconciliation in process theology. "Reality is a process of becoming, not a
static universe of objects."[107] Thus, it consists of an inner connection between the event of reconciliation in Christ and the ongoing development of
mankind. Divine activity has set in motion a change in man that affects historical change in a comprehensive sense. "Every event in history is God's activity and being inserting itself into history. In this sense, every event is an

incarnation" (ibid.). In principle, this incarnation can not be separated from the becoming man of Jesus, because each time it emerges from a "whole new subjectivity" which was made possible through Christ's obedience. That is the result of the life and death of Jesus: "all events, including human actions, are given their initial design by God; they are each a revelation of His character" (art. cit., 535). A distinction between *revelatio specialis* and *generalis* is thus meaningless. "There is only unique revelation: direct, intentional, and conscious acts of God. But every event has this quality" (ibid.). The absent connection of transcendence has consequences, among others, in eschatology. "The future is never known, always free and open. Until it decides itself, it has no reality and cannot be predicted — even by God. Consequently, revelation could be inerrant" (ibid.). D. L. Wheeler is able to trace the "internal type of atonement," which for him is the historical-process model of reconciliation, back to the ancient church. He draws a line from Irenaeus and Origen (167f.) to Schleiermacher (169f.) through Teilhard de Chardin (176f.) and on to process theology (181f.), the latter playing a much more marginal role in support of the model.

In the context of our typology, we can observe similarities between the historical development of the naming of witnesses and a historical process type of reconciliation in Origen[108] and also in F. Schleiermacher. As was seen in the representation of the humanistic model above, Schleiermacher's idea of reconciliation does not completely belong to the "subjective type," as Aulén would like us to think. D. L. Wheeler confirms this observation where he, along with F. Schleiermacher, observes a connection between subjective and objective reconciliation and moreover sees a connection to the basic tenets of the historical-process model of reconciliation. In regard to the teaching of faith (62-63) Wheeler says: "it seems to me that Schleiermacher, although accused of subjectivism, actually presents us with a combination of 'objective' and 'subjective' elements in his doctrine of the divine-human relationship, thereby providing a model that can be of great service today. God's redeeming act in Christ is not simply a 'strange body' thrust into human history from without; it is the perfection of our created natures. And at the same time it is not simply the realization of an ideal as merely exemplary. . . . It is a new and unique power and capacity emerging by the grace of God at this place in human history."[109]

The historical-process model of reconciliation according to D. L. Wheeler[110] will first be characterized according to its basic tenets and then[111] deepened with respect to the theological reception of process philosophy in J. Cobb:

- In the relation of creation to reconciliation, reconciliation does not contribute anything fundamentally new in terms of creation thought. Rather, the life and death of Jesus is creation as it is realized in God's creative will. "Christ as individual is the consummation of God's creative purposes" (182).
- Regarding the impact of Christology, the assumption of the idea of progress in reconciliation is guiding, which, in contrast to the humanistic model, is not just focused on the individual. Christ is in a universal way the "exemplar of divine-human unity."[112] The idea is that Christ embodies himself "expansively" and "progressively" in the world and as a common, communal body. Divinity and humanity are no longer distinguished from each other in historical "events" in the reconciling activity of God.
- To try to separate God and history would thus be a contradictory undertaking for a model of reconciliation. God is never an external subject. "The process itself in all its wonder and its inexplicable there-ness is grace" (165). Something new emerges as a result of the dynamic that is inherent in the process. An event can thus only be proven to be divine retrospectively in view of previous events *(a posteriori)*. The aspect of transcendence is missing an understanding of revelation. The "sudden intervention" of God is not characteristic of an act of reconciliation, as it is for the historical meaning of theological revelation.[113] Rather, God's action becomes the deed of reconciliation as it develops or "emerges" from the historical process.[114]

We may now deepen the historical process concept of reconciliation using a central idea from J. Cobb's process theology;[115] namely, the concept of "creative transformation." "Creative transformation" is for Cobb "not simply the history of Christ and the course of world history, but rather where creative transformation succeeds, it brings with it the history of Christ into the history of man; indeed, it brings Christ Himself."[116] The process of "creative transformation" has to do with the "universalizing of the Christ event," of "an all process . . . initializing, all fixing, resolving, and relativizing event" (193). Thus, "every individual and any group can grow beyond itself and transcend itself without having to step into some other expanding and all contemporary field of power" (194). Indeed, it has to do with "the power field of the event of the love of God . . . that Christ engendered."[117] "Creative transformation" according to Cobb is "the re-discovery of a power field" (194).

The previous formulation of a "re-discovery," together with the Christian basis for Whitehead's theistic philosophy (upon which we cannot elaborate here), invites a systematic-theological interpretation of our case studies. I use the term "function" to focus the development of the question of correspondence which is still to be determined and which would facilitate a final conclusion. Here the inquiry into the historical-process model will need to be included: how can the assumed continuing incarnation be clearly distinguished from that of an ideology of growth? What "sense of direction"[118] does process theology contribute to the process if everything is still "open"? What about "destiny"? Can the distinction between Creator and creation still be maintained? Where does sin factor in the historical-process model of reconciliation? Can God still be thought of on a personal level if human and divine activity are inseparable and related to each other in an evolutionary dynamic? D. L. Wheeler summarizes the list of criticisms at the end of his presentation: "What does one do, from a process perspective, with questions of the power and persistence of evil, the *parousia* and final judgment, vicarious suffering, sacrifice, propitiation, repentance, the grace of creation, the grace of redemption, and the costliness of redemption?"[119]

In the final analysis, the regulative idea to be stressed behind the historical-process model is that reconciliation is not, from the point of view of process theology, an action that recedes "to the sphere of apparent hidden-ness in the world of the congregation"; rather it "asks about the universality of God. It asks about a God, who defines human existence, here, today."[120] In contrast to the legal model, incarnation thought is not "torn asunder"; in contrast to the humanistic model it is radicalized, and indeed, to the extent that it refers to the universality of the cosmic model. It has to do with the understanding of "God's saving work carried out within humanity" for a theological understanding of the "real relationship to our historical self-formation."[121]

(e) The "Classical" Type of Reconciliation

One could say that a representation of the type of model for theological reconciliation that has its beginnings with G. Aulén is incomplete where the "classic type" of reconciliation is tacitly passed over.

G. Aulén designates the "classical" idea of reconciliation as that found in the New Testament, the ancient church, and in Luther. Characteristic of the classical type is Christ as victor. "The basic element of the classical type can be formulated briefly: God reconciles the world through the victory of Christ over the powers of evil and death."[122] Aulén sees humanity handed over to "the enemy powers of corruption like death, the devil, law, and wrath"[123] and threatened by the law of death because of sin. "As long as these powers rule the world there is animosity between God and the world. When they are conquered the animosity stops: God and world are reconciled" (506). In "Christ's fight" in the "drama of reconciliation" either man's rescue or man's corruption is decided. Thus, in his characterization of the classical type of reconciliation, Aulén assigns value to the fact that God acts in the incarnate Christ. "God never stops being the subject of reconciliation. The sacrifice is offered to Him, but He is fundamentally the sacrifice. There is reconciliation, but only because it is God who reconciles Himself with the world" (509). The conquering Christ is the "path to reconciliation." He "does not move from below to above; He is also not partially below and partially above, but rather entirely and completely a way from above to below — from God to man" (510).

The newer four-part typology[124] follows closely G. Aulén's designation of the singularity of the "classical" next to the other types of reconciliation, as if the other reconciliation models did not adopt anything that could be considered "truly" "classical." Don't the other models also develop the idea of reconciliation in the New Testament? This question will be discussed in addition to two others: namely, whether Aulén's characterization of the "classical type" actually takes into account all facets of Christian thought on reconciliation, and secondly, whether the arrangement of elements of the "classical type" according to M. Luther is included.

One must, however, agree with G. Aulén and his work on the typology of the idea of reconciliation that the "classical type," if not unique, assumes a particular function. D. L. Wheeler reveals the corrective function of the "classical type" with regard to both the historical-process model and the humanistic model: "The external type affirms that atonement is at once something realized within history, something particular and genuinely new (not simply an ideal that is indifferent to the place and time of its realization), and yet at the same time it is something from 'beyond' history, and not simply a product of history."[125] In this way the dominant role of the classical aspects of reconciliation can be ranked accordingly; namely, the "classical" is not profiled next to the other types, but acts as a corrective behind the other models, each one being analyzed in terms of their agreement with basic "classical" tenets.

An analysis of the larger reconciliation models in the previous paragraphs makes it difficult to agree with G. Aulén's reduction (model) where he suggests that the "classical type" uniquely represents the "true" idea of reconciliation. More likely, it shows how basic classical tenets emerge in both the cosmic and the legal model. Therefore, in principle it should be asked whether a "classical model" should be allowed to develop exclusively along with other models and if so, whether the categories "below," "above," "subject," "object" provide an adequate description of what is described as "classical." Are the implied assumptions of Aulén's typology "classical"? In other words, is reconciliation to be understood exclusively as a problem of the "God-man" relationship, thus marginalizing the political and social dimension of reconciliation? To pose the question means to say "no." Instead, repeated evidence of the historical-process model offers a basic outline suggesting the problems involved in Aulén's typology for a development of the question of correspondence.

The attempt to develop our own "classical model" would not be appropriate. First, the multiplicity of characteristics of the "classical" idea of reconciliation (our conclusion from the previous section concerning type) would not correlate to the development of a single model. The many-layered aspect of the idea of reconciliation in its systematic-theological context in the history of theology is adequate for making a connection to the disparate Biblical concepts of reconciliation. Second, the many layers of the idea of reconciliation convey the material frame of reference for the theologically normative questions of correspondence within political reality. The political forms of reconciliation should be examined on the basis of their correspondence to and difference from a fundamental connection to theological reconciliation. Third, this investigation is conducted in a political reality where the political connection to reconciliation may be "accepted." It is the individual facets of reconciliation lying behind the implied axioms that will be examined with respect to their basic connection to "facets" of the Christian concept of reconciliation.

4. Normative Ideas Belonging to the Christian Concept of Reconciliation

The following statements on reconciliation can be suggested as preliminary results that carry regulative (normative) meaning for the question of correspondence. What has been stated up until now has made minimal demands on the coordination of an index of norms which is, so to speak, a *condicio sine qua non* of the Christian concept of reconciliation:

- Reconciliation assigns the destruction of God's community to man.
- God's reconciliation says: in Christ our connection to God is reestablished.
- Reconciliation "in Christ" restores community with God; the guilt between God and man has been annulled. God begins anew with his world "in Christ."
- Reconciliation with God is not attributable to any human work or effort; neither is human effort a requirement for, or a result of, reconciliation.
- Reconciliation is not sought for the sin, but for the sinner; a death sentence has been pronounced over the sin.
- The death of Jesus was necessary for the purification of man. The creation of God's community is inconceivable theologically without the atonement of Christ.
- Reconciliation with God means that Christ makes man ready again for community with God and his neighbor. (What kind of relationship does the restoration of community with God have with restoration of community with one's neighbor? Does one precede the other — or result from the other — or are both healed at the same time?)
- Reconciliation means the salvation of the world as well as the new creation of the world.
- Reconciliation includes hope for change.
- God's reconciliation is an event external to man that encounters him in political reality.
- The representation of Christ does not exclude the human, physical autonomy and responsibility of man.[126] In the person of Jesus, the love of God is connected to the love of one's neighbor. The reconciliation of Christ calls for emulation.
- God's reconciliation has left its imprint behind on creation.
- Christ is as reconciler is "on the move" in the world. The power field of the love of God can be seen in political reality.
- Reconciliation is not a closed event, but rather an incomplete, open process that is dependent upon God. Where there is reconciliation, it changes existence in the here and now, making possible reversal and placing things in correct alignment.

5. A Formal Examination of the Possibility of
Categories for Political Reconciliation

After the basic connection to theological reconciliation has been developed in two steps and normative principles pertaining to the Christian concept of reconciliation have been highlighted, the question of correspondence can then be developed in an initial stage. The political forms of reconciliation should first be formally examined for indications of breaks with the Christian idea of reconciliation. In a second stage (II), the question of existing categories can be arranged according to content: does the common use of the term "reconciliation" used in past politics and that of the theological doctrine of reconciliation have a common origin in some other category?

(a) The Cosmic Model and Its Capability for Correspondence

In the cosmic reconciliation model, the themes "freeing of the world," "participation in divinity," but also "alienation from the world" were regulative. Do categories of political reconciliation exist? Does the cosmic model correspond with political forms of reconciliation as seen in the case studies?

In the broadest sense, the insistence of the newer research on the translation of *apokatastasis* as redemption of all (instead of "reconciliation of all") is helpful for our project: "reconciliation of all is different from the redemption of all . . . because it is clearly freedom terminology (compare freeing or liberating, making free from a superior power)."[127] This observation with regard to terminology also pertains to the cosmic model: the term "reconciliation" would, in hindsight, be easy to exchange with that of "redemption." Furthermore, the philosophical conditions for the preference of the redemption paradigm in the cosmic model need to be clarified. In terms of his ontology, is Origen closer to redemption than he is to reconciliation theology? Where do ontology and Christology converge in the cosmic model? And what is their relationship to the ontological conditions for our question of correspondence?

First, in formal terms, the cosmic model proves capable of correspondence for a normative examination of political forms of reconciliation to the extent that redemption is thought of as a total cosmic event. The redemptive work of Christ concerns all of creation. Reconciliation is a spatial, universal category. A superficial commonality with the cosmic model emerges in Part II: in the category of universality divine reconciliation reaches into all of political reality. It streams unhampered into the public political forum, including that of past politics. The eschatological conception of the redemption of all brings "the boundless and unconditional love of God impressively into play."[128] However, the question still remains as to whether or not an actual category exists that accommodates a common ontology for political reconciliation and the reconciliation of all. The coupled ontology of the concept of the redemption of all is distinguishable from those that are at the basis of our question of correspondence to theological reconciliation. A common category might exist between the cosmic model and Part II under the conditions of the ontology of Plato's middle period. However, it is not available and here lies the difference or break between the categories. An ontological concept of redemption does not allow time or space for suffering. The dimension of reconciliation in the category of *analogia relationis* has thus been left out. "The pain over the lost life of the victim" as it is justly seen, is "not to be connected with the eschatological concept of the redemption of all life."[129] The acceptance of this dimension in the problem of reconciliation, as well as that of non-reconciliation and animosity, but also in the successful process of reconciliation and friendship, is what our case studies are about. A theological model of reconciliation that ontologically places the acceptance of the problem of reconciliation in the paradigm of redemption proves to be unsuitable for making connections to the question of correspondence.

Regarding the discovery of breaks or gaps in categories there still remains to be seen whether a category can be discerned between the cosmic reconciliation model and political reconciliation within the category of time. Here also the ontological distinction is decisive. There is a double meaning: on the one hand, the eschatological perspective of Origen's cosmic model remains speculative. Indeed, for Origen the good finally triumphs; yet how this process can be understood christologically (i.e., how ontology and Christology come together) appears open. Jesus merely offers a pedagogical model of "emulation in the world." The redemption of all touches on the "penultimate" primarily as education with the support of divine providence. The cosmic model thus remains essentially in the area of the ethically moral. The hope of change in the here and now is based primarily in free will (and allowed by the divine work of redemption). Clearly, "for Origen freedom is more important than redemption."[130] In this statement, however, the deep ontological difference between Plato's middle period and reformation theology again emerges.

On the other hand, as we have seen, Origen sets limits on the ontological force of philosophical determinism by stressing the autonomy, creative power, and spontaneity of man, as well as his responsibility as a rational creature over against a passive faith in reconciliation as an a-personal, predetermined event. With regard to our problem, Origen identifies a decisive problem without fully explaining it: how can we conceive of God's all-redemptive activity in relation to the soteriological powerlessness of man? In the more current research, the position is advanced that Origen does not recognize the powerlessness of man although he feels that man actually holds "the key correlate to all redemption."[131]

Is the cosmic model capable of correspondence in view of the political forms of reconciliation from the case studies? The answer is briefly: more likely no, than yes. Of course, there are points in common. We have already discussed using formal categories that redemption concerns the entire cosmos. Yet, how the "penultimate" extends into the category of space and time remains a bit murky. The cosmic model proves itself to be inadequate to the material development of the question of correspondence. The element of uncertainty of the universal quantifier in the term "redemption of all" must be held to account. Precisely the "all" in the phrase "reconciliation of all" is not to be overestimated for the transfer to our problem; rather the category of universality is connected to the previously discussed conditions which do not have their starting point in a philosophical ontology, but in the event of the cross. In terms of content, the area of correspondence, which is the *condicio sine qua non* of the normative examination of theological reconciliation, remains unoccupied. More precisely: between the concept of divine redemption on the one hand and the human concept of freedom on the other there is an empty soteriological place to be had upon examination of correspondence with the cosmic model.

(b) The Legal Model and Its Capability for Correspondence

The question of categories between the legal mode and the analyzed political forms of reconciliation in Part II runs into the problem that Anselm (as was Origen) is essentially concerned with God's relationship to man. The question concerning the restoration of community with God, as well as that of between men, is not discussed.

G. Wenz observes a "relationship of correspondence" in Anselm's notion of "the reconciliation of God with Himself in the idea of the reconciliation of God with the world." How can these observations be based in material terms? In making the transfer to our problem, the framework is limited by which we are able to seek answers to this question because the relationship of correspondence is not examined in terms of a direct correlation. We saw that Anselm's legal considerations in his concept of reconciliation are not to be understood in the sense of legal options for action. God does not weigh things out: the *beatitudo* is always an "option" for people. In his tract, Anselm supplies the reason for this question. Here we first receive a clue that a common category does not exist in the area of punishment between political and theological reconciliation. An approach to the questions of correspondence using the legal model results in, among other regulative ideas, a *cur deus homo*:

- Justice as reestablishment of community with God.
- Reconciliation as restoring the relationship between God and man through the one-time atonement of Christ.
- Reconciliation as expensive grace that applies to the sinner and not to the sin.

These three interrelated statements are, according to the inner logic of the legal model, related to the relationship of God to man. For our line of questioning, a connection emerges to the active categories of the regulative statements: the restoration of community, the restoring of relationships, and the distinction between the sin and the sinner. These categories will be examined formally for their ability to establish correspondences. Does the restoration of community between God and man include that of between men? Does the restoration of the relationship between God and man at the same time restore the relationship between man and man? If so, then are both communal relationships to be created anew as the "exact original"? Does human guilt, which empirically can only be qualified in moral terms, refer to sin? In view of the relationship to God, to what extent does the distinction between sin and sinner refer to the interpersonal distinction between the deed and the doer of the deed?

For both of the previous questions, let us fall back on our work on the case studies of South Africa. In reviewing the documentation of the hearings, one may ask whether phrases like "just let this pig die"[132] illustrate that "all of human nature is tainted by sin." In the victims' accounts, we see expressions of inhumanity that evoke the moral theological question whether contempt for the creative will of God is evident. For the victim, the jailer takes the place of God. He is "Lord" and determines life and death. Do we see here again that sin rears up against God? Do the excesses of the apartheid bailiff make a connection between *ontic* sin and moral guilt? Does it become visible that sin is a precondition for possible guilt? We will address these questions in the following section.

In political reality, the burden of guilt does not correspond to the degree of reparations sought by the victims. In most cases they do not seek revenge, but simply want to know why they were victims. In many cases they are even able to differentiate between what was done to them and the person of the perpetrator (impressively in the documented case of torture victims of Jeffrey Benzien, the policeman).

Let us summarize the observations that require further development — also with respect to the other questions mentioned above:

- Where reparations in the sense of *lex talionis* are not demanded there are indications referring to a reality in which the sin committed is acknowledged, thus putting an end to the cult of victim (and this reality is embodied in part by people who are not Christians!).
- Where the restoration of community is sought instead of retributive justice, the question arises regarding the interpersonal dimension of "restorative justice"[133] as it corresponds to the notion of theological reconciliation: the "community with God . . . will and should be restored."[134] To what extent does the political refer to an attempt to restore eschatological hope which, in Christ's atoning for guilt has happened "once and for all" (καινὴ κτίσις)? To what extent is the regulative idea reflected that a "true making of amends is not possible through politics," while on the other hand it is reserved for the "eschatological"?
- Where the victim tries to see the person behind their tormentor and not the deed (i.e., in other words, to forgive the perpetrator) the question from a theological perspective is one of a basic eschatological connection: if the "new person" lives as a result of the distinction between sin and sinner, then does the "new person" also appear on an interpersonal level in political reality where a distinction is made between the deed and the doer of the deed? Can we recognize signs of "expensive grace" in the midst of past political disagreement?

There is much evidence in the research to suggest that a category can be established to support both the theological doctrine of reconciliation as effectively guiding the distinction between the sin and the sinner and the implied axiom of making a distinction between the deed and the doer in political reality.

(c) The Humanistic Model and Its Capability for Correspondence

In contrast to the cosmic model and the legal model, the humanistic model of reconciliation, upon examination, appears not to contain the problem of accentuating the understanding of reconciliation as primarily God's relationship to man; in fact, this emphasis appears to be missing. The contrast to Anselm is not apparent in its ethic, but in its concept of God. Whereas for the humanist type of reconciliation God and the world are placed in an unproblematic relationship to each other, according to the legal model God is "not the occasion of our experience in the world. And the experience of the world as such, while in reference to . . . God, is not the experience of divine self-revelation."[135] In the Socinian version of the humanistic model the image of God is very clearly humanized and the concept of sin is strongly relativized: representation is superficial, whereas redemption is produced on its own. The contrasts between the view of humanity and that of God could not be greater than in these models.

In this context, it is no wonder that the humanistic model proves itself to have an obvious capability for correspondence to political and social reality. It extends into the aspect of time. Only in passing does it mention the model of the nineteenth century, such as that of A. Ritschl and his professional ethics!

In our representation of the humanistic model, theological problems emerge that necessarily intersect with the outlined ability for correspondence. The ability of the model to connect with political and social arenas, especially in its Socinian aspects, appears to be possible only at the price of Christology. Is the basis for the rejection of content in the model of theological reconciliation the misinterpretation of the point of departure for reconciliation for the humanistic model of reconciliation? To ask the question means to negate it in connection with two other considerations.

1. The fact that Abelard's initial question does not contribute either in its conception or in the later aspects of the humanistic model to the theological norming of this project does not constitute an argument for whether or not the question itself is unsubstantiated or false. Rather, it appears conducive to the handling of our problem. Abelard asks: "What is the redemption through the death of Christ?" The correlation to our initial research question is obvious. To the extent that we factor in the structural possibility of a "new man" in political reality, our question is: how does it extend "in Christ" to actual reconciliation in the dealing

with guilt as a result of political turmoil? What connections exist? What contribution does the connection between "the ultimate and penultimate" (D. Bonhoeffer) have to make here? Abelard looks for a connection beyond equivocation in the concept of love: he sees interdependence between the love of God and the love of man. Thus, he succumbs to the usual humanistic model which tries to resolve the constructive tension between the "ultimate and penultimate" in favor of the moral-ethical. For the believer, says Abelard, the love of God opens up the possibility for love of the neighbor and for interpersonal forgiveness. We are "with him as with our neighbor" "bound in an indissoluble bond of love" because "God in Christ has bound himself to our nature." How is this "bond" to be qualified? Does God's love extend to the "penultimate" in the love of the neighbor? In reference to our problem, can "the love of God" be seen in the readiness of the victim to forgive system injustice? The humanistic model certainly provides answers to these questions as discussed above, but none that would be considered normative for advancing our undertaking.

2. The humanistic model conveys *e contrario* an example for theological interpretation. The rejection of effective similarities that lies behind the humanistic model (i.e., all that is humanistic is also theological) is a condition for a theologically normative examination of the forms of reconciliation in political reality. (In an uncritical connection to the humanistic model one may be inclined to qualify the summary of regulative statements as theological which, according to the *analogia entis,* can be included as a formal principle of the theological recognition of God's abundant love.) Only where reconciliation is seen as an event *extra nos* do we gain theological insight and observe the ambivalence of the political forms of reconciliation. To clarify with an example: a basic assumption behind the humanistic model is of the hope and belief in the progress of ethical behavior. In the *analogia entis* there is a close correlation to the regulative statements of the case studies, as for example "reconciliation has something to do with change." If one follows the theology of the humanistic model, one could establish a category between political and theological reconciliation. However, where the humanistic model is not employed in a theologically normative sense, no category emerges in common. For the development of the problem it thus follows that the question of correspondence concerning the basic, underlying connection to theological reconciliation can not be developed using the framework of the humanistic model for unpacking regulative statements like

"reconciliation as change." However, without developing of the question of correspondence one cannot move away from equivocations. In addition, political reality in all of its ambivalence would not otherwise be capable of being evaluated critically. Along the spectrum of questions of correspondence, the category of "change" in the statement "reconciliation has something to do with change" is not examined for its underlying connection to reconciliation as is the Biblical category of "turning." Can the empirically observed "change" of many perpetrators in our case examples be included in the theater of moral improvement or in the aspect of Biblical turning?

We do not have the answers to the above questions. Rather, we were directed in the examination of the capability for correspondence of the humanistic model to the many sides of the problem that emerged in the theological debate with regard to the political connection.

(d) The Historical-Process Model and Its Capability for Correspondence

In contrast to the humanistic model, the notion of reconciliation in the historical-process model experiences an aspect of broadening: Christ is the universal example for the unity of God and man — He embodies it both expansively and progressively in the world. It consists in an inner connection between Christ's reconciliation and the future development of mankind. The kingship of God emerges from the cosmic historical process.

The use of the term "process" was also used with respect to political reconciliation. "Reconciliation is a process" was a central regulative statement. Is there an underlying basic category for a common use of the term? The process theological concept of reconciliation is a temporal category for the historical-process model. Reconciliation exists only in time; it arises from the timeliness of political reality (and not only achieves the timeliness of the political or begins to exist in time). As outlined above, one must factor in the "new" as a result of the dynamic that is integral to the historical process. It is clear that wherever theological criticism is levied concerning the ability for correspondence, the question is already answered to the extent that it is not placed in the framework of the historical-process model.[136] Political reality is always reachable by Christ. Reconciliation is a long process that extends over a long period of time. How then is the assumed capability for correspondence to be verified in view of our analysis of the political case studies?

Reconciliation takes place in the attempt to work it out in South Africa and Germany on varying levels: as reconciliation with one's own fate, as reconciliation between the offender and the victim, and as national growing together. Within this systematic division, the element of time is constitutive. Thus, for example, reconciliation with the offender is not possible the day after the deed. From the outset reconciliation requires historical distance as well as a change in context, as was especially clear in the examples of dealing with apartheid's past. Let us recall the cases of the victims tortured by the policeman, Jeffrey Benzien. Ashley Forbes was not suddenly able to see the person behind the torture; it required a process that finally led to this result. The result, however, is forgiveness. It appears to mark an end point to the reconciliation process. Thus, one could say that (reconciliation is) a process that proceeds successfully, but also comes to an end.[137] In terms of process theology, the act of forgiveness would be what is "new" as a result of the dynamic that is integral to the historical process itself: in this context one could then speak of "an event of the power field of the love of God" (Cobb).

A condition for reconciliation in past politics, in addition to the intentional creation of a space (it requires a forum for reconciliation where the offenders and victims can meet and where the victims can relate their stories), is to allow for developments to occur over time. The opening up of the time dimension is required where reconciliation involves the "acknowledgement of suffering"[138] (as in the case of Conraad van Rooyen), something that begins with the "reflection on the deed and the confronting of the person" (as in the case of Jeffrey Benzien), or is forged by gestures, such as a handshake between offenders and victims (as with Benzien and Forbes). In general, an understanding of process appears to guide an evaluation of what is at stake; namely truth, reconciliation, and justice (compare Part II.A.III/B.III).

Whether encountering the truth leads to insight on the part of the offender (i.e., "apartheid was a crime against humanity") or whether, for the victim, the depiction of the truth contributes to the healing of the wounds of apartheid, the overriding assumption is that both are only imaginable as a process in time whose goal is "national reconciliation." Whether reconciliation includes the possibility of becoming human again for the perpetrator and leads to forgiveness of the person (behind the deed) for the victim — the assumption is that both are only imaginable as a process in time with the goal of the complete removal of animosity between ethnic groups. Whether or not in the end justice for the perpetrator makes possible his re-entry into society and reestablishes the worth of victims, the assumption is that both are time-bound processes with the goal of the complete restoration of justice ("restorative justice").

Accordingly, we can agree that the category of time provides common ground between political and theological reconciliation in the context of theological interpretation using the historical-process model. *Kairoi* appears in political reality. Yet, how this is related to *kairos* — namely how and whether the category of community can be confirmed materially — can not be responsibly determined at this point. The reason for this is the issues involved in qualifying the category of process as an appropriate concept of analysis for the question of correspondence. On the other hand, the achieved position could leave out regulative statements from the underlying connection to theological reconciliation, constituting a break in categories. A yet to be treated core problem is to identify what is left out in the historical-process model in the idea of process and what appears at the same time in place of the idea of revelation, exclusive of the *extra nos*. The relationship of correspondence of the teleological concept of the process of political reconciliation to that of eschatological reconciliation requires further clarification, as does, with help of the category of present time and the presence of grace, the issue of how reconciliation can be captured in political reality.

(e) Interim Theological and Methodological Reflections

The examination of the typology of the reconciliation model for its ability to correspond with the political forms of reconciliation yields ambivalent results and leads us to interim considerations.

Unforeseen hurdles need to be overcome in order to develop a formal treatment of the question of correspondence according to an underlying connection to theological reconciliation for political reconciliation. In order to come away from the typology of reconciliation model and to inquire about a category of political forms of reconciliation, hurdles from two opposing positions need to be overcome: (1) the missing social ethical aspect of reconciliation; and (2) the aspect of the lack of transcendence. While model (a) and (b) interpret reconciliation essentially as an individual act of redemption, leaving its correlation to political reality largely untouched, the models (c) and (d) are not clear in showing how reconciliation in its social dimension as providing for community still appears in a basic connection to the restoration of community with God through the free grace of Jesus Christ. In short, could one say: in the first case, the concept of reconciliation lacks any social dimension, and in the second case the social ethic is abbreviated, or "ethically exploited" (G. Sauter). In the context of the varying results of the process, it clearly has to do with an abbreviation of this assessment because it identifies a basic problem that can not be left untreated in an examination of the political dimension of reconciliation: to what extent does our theological concept of reconciliation still provide an orientation for external theological discourse? Does it have anything at all to say about our political reality? Or does it touch on the "penultimate" only as teaching on redemption, in that it absolutizes the "ultimate"? Has it reduced Christianity to a "religion of redemption," in which the "question of meaning is (merely) posed and the answer to the suffering and problem of death in the here and now is avoided"?[139] Must theology and the church, in view of what goes on in the world, indulge in critical self-reproach and speak of reconciliation in Docetic terms, as they withdraw from intra-church discourse?

Our theological interests bring us to this question, because for us two criteria converge regarding the value of a theological doctrine of reconciliation. The first criterion is a Christological one and leads to the question: what doctrine of reconciliation is more appropriate for expressing the event of Christ and the reconciling gratitude of the free grace of God? The second criterion, which at the same time provides a regulative title for the case analysis, asks: in view of our task, what theological doctrine of reconciliation is best to use in interpreting the process of historical reconciliation between people in their political dimension in a situation of collapse? In addition, the opposing side of the question above is that an examination of the political dimension of reconciliation must therefore principally remain open so that both criteria are not excluded. The development of our problem leads thus to an *aporia*.

In the course of our interim theological reflection, two assessments should be highlighted with respect to the problem:

1. It is correct that none of the four models fulfill both of our criteria, which otherwise would lead us to use at least one as an exclusive model of reconciliation for the working out of our problem.
2. It is false that both criteria necessarily lead to an *aporia* in the search for categories in connection to the basic model for a doctrine of reconciliation.

The second criterion has already been extensively treated. Clearly, in very different ways the model has the capability for correspondence where we pushed it to the level of categories and the attending question of common categories. To consider reconciliation under the yet-to-be-clarified conditions of universal space and time is a *condicio sine qua non* for our question of correspondence in Part II. These categories could, in a normative theological examination, potentially fulfill the second of our above named criteria. Of all the models, the first criterion which expresses the Christ event as an act of divine reconciliation is most closely fulfilled by the model of legal reconciliation.

As we proceed, the problem to be mastered is how an investigation of the correspondence model can be combined with a material analysis of categories. They prevent a thorough systematization. Moreover, the regulative ideas of "reconciliation as change" or the categorical differentiation between the "deed and the doer of the deed" motivates a systematic-theological examination of commonalities for the theological category of "turning" or, in view of deed and doer, of the distinction between the sin and the sinner.

D. Bonhoeffer's lectures on ethics allow for a critical inquiry into the results of the cosmic and historical-process model because, and in view of the functional classification of morality and justice, they serve as a substitute for the humanist model which, as we saw, is closer to the issue of mixing (especially where the separation of morality and justice is conveyed) instead of constructive differentiation. The distinction between the "ultimate and penultimate" has merit in view of our second criterion; merit for the interpretation of our case studies because it allows the reality of God to be thought of in space and time in political reality and, accordingly, the connection between model (a) and (d) comes to a standstill.

Of all of the models of reconciliation, it is most likely the process-historical model that will prove capable of handling the further development of the question of correspondence. In critical reference to the normative difference between the "ultimate and penultimate," the "relationship" (D. Bonhoeffer) between political reconciliation and reconciliation as a soteriological category should be mentioned since the methodological and theological can only be conceived with both of the above-named criteria simultaneously. The capability for developing the process-historical model will be examined in a way in which the story is not defined by a dialectical law of reconciliation. Rather, the Christological in the idea of reconciliation should also include a protest against what is left unreconciled in historical reality (and not just the claim that history itself carries the movement of the law that equips reconciliation with absolute spirit). A "dialectic of reconciliation" will emerge as having the capability for correspondence (1) which accepts the known unresolved aspects in historical reality and carries the eschatological condition of judgment; and (2) which precludes an understanding of reconciliation as an entelechy of the historical process itself. Instead, we must always reckon with one abiding reconciliation that can never be captured historically. Thus, in view of the meaning of reconciliation, an attempt to locate it within political reality is also a clue to its fragmentary character and incompleteness, especially with regard to the potential danger of it being misused — even theologically.

II. The Question of Correspondence — A Second Logical Rendering

1. The Theological Task

The question of correspondence according to an underlying connection to theological reconciliation in the handling of political guilt during system change in South Africa and Germany enters a theological discussion. I call this discussion "logical," because logic generally has to do with "concepts, judgments, decisions," and its task is "to discover and formulate all of the rules for conclusions, if one wants to arrive at relevant results and conclusions."[140] In this rendering, the formally defined categories between political reconciliation and reconciliation as a theological category are laid out in terms of their content. The development of a necessary theological category for analysis confronts us with the following problem: if the question of correspondence with respect to the political idea of reconciliation is to be approached deductively from a theological stance, then its connection to the historical-process model must first yield a systematically sustainable concept of reconciliation. Such a "model," which would be adequately guarded from dissent, can not be developed within the framework of this study. A closed reconciliation model that "fits" our problem is a theological *desideratum* upon which, however, the following can perhaps help to measure the character of the preliminary studies. Thus, we see that instead of a closed theological reconciliation model, two important categories of analyses are available for further development; namely, process and justice.

2. "Process" and "Justice": Analytical Concepts of
Theological Reconciliation (Third Deductive Step)

The deductive theological process opened with the distinction between "ultimate and penultimate" (D. Bonhoeffer). This distinction provides the potential for a viable framework which, in turn, is offered by a theological interpretation of the basic political and legal-ethical questions involved in the case studies. Accordingly, Bonhoeffer's categories provide a strong basis for interpretation with respect to process theology, as well as the legal ethical point of view.

(a) The Theological Reconciliation Approach
to a Concept of Progress

Bonhoeffer's distinction overcomes the theological fixation on "thinking in two spheres." The differentiation between "the ultimate and penultimate" opens up a perspective on reconciliation as an event in space and time. In critical correction of the historical-process model, the contours of the process come into view which are united with the above-named first criterion and will be shown to have (second criterion) the capability for correspondence with the regulative statements of our case analyses ("reconciliation is a process").

According to Bonhoeffer, political reality is penultimate only because of the ultimate. Thus, the distinction between penultimate and ultimate is already a judgment of faith. "What is the penultimate?" Bonhoeffer[141] describes as penultimate everything that "concerns the last things — namely, the justification of the sinner by grace alone — which, on the basis of the ultimate, are designated as penultimate." "The ultimate is thus not a condition in itself, rather a judgment of the ultimate over what has preceded it." In view of the category of time this means that the penultimate "is not the present, but rather always something that has happened." It becomes the penultimate. Here we observe movement: the penultimate is addressed by the ultimate and accordingly the penultimate "precedes the ultimate." It is not the case that the justifying word addresses the penultimate in order to explain itself before the ultimate. Rather, we have evidence that justification is not a one-time act, but rather describes an event in which process and actual elements are mutually interdependent. Thus, the thinking is overcome that reconciliation expresses itself in penultimate categories. In place of "order" the idea of a (dynamic) "process" appears. For Bonhoeffer the former contains the result that the penultimate "must be granted" for the sake of the ultimate, since the justifying word reaches us only in the penultimate. One can only be guilty in time. Likewise, one can only be justified "of what is already (happened) under the indictment of time." The last things (ultimate) are not only "qualitatively" "ultimate" as we above saw, but they are also "the last word in time." This word is always preceded by the penultimate: "an activity, suffering, . . . hoping, thus the entirely great span of time whose end it comprises." The word "last" in time means a "break" with the next to last or the penultimate. "It provides a time for acceptance, waiting, preparation for God, and there is a final, last time." Wherever the ultimate "judges and breaks" with the penultimate we have "the time of grace." Bonhoeffer emphasizes that "not all time is the time of grace" but "now, precisely now . . . is the 'day of salvation' (II Cor. 6:2). The time of grace is ultimate in the sense that it is never possible for me to count on a further, more acceptable work of God than the Word that I now encounter."

Placed within the context of our problem this means in qualitative terms that nothing more can be expected than the last word, nor can we count on a future time of grace (i.e., "incarnations" in the language of process theology). An evolutionary (determinative) process idea is also excluded, such as a vague optimism for the future. Both take into account a qualitative and time-bound "more." Where the justifying and reconciling word impacts the penultimate, it changes it totally and irrevocably. Thus, Bonhoeffer say that the ultimate is not the "apex" of the penultimate, but constitutes a complete break with it. And yet he does not reduce it to actuality. Rather, the idea of process appears in the interdependence of the penultimate and ultimate. In accepting his thinking on the repeated break between the penultimate and the ultimate, Bonhoeffer raises the critical question "whether man can live alone from the ultimate, and whether faith can, so to speak, be prolonged."[142] Rather, it appears more likely that faith "is only actual as the last in a span of time of many time spans in life." Faith is not "realized on a daily, hourly basis." Rather it must "always be endured in the time span of the penultimate . . . for the sake of the ultimate."[143] By looking at his manuscript on ethics we find answers to our question of how, with the aid of the category of time, to explain the absence of grace in political reality.

The above outline of Bonhoeffer's thought contains indications for a theological analysis of the process of political reconciliation. It contributes by articulating a central question: is forgiveness an act that is distinct from the process of reconciliation? Where and how can we pinpoint the insertion of the ultimate? In order to proceed further with these questions, the manuscript on ethics needs to be set within the context of process theology. Although Bonhoeffer does not specifically make the concept of process a condition for consideration, there are nevertheless indications of connections to process thought. A basic underlying criticism of process theology has been generated once more by this examination and the lengthy critical constructive analysis must limit the selection of aspects to be treated in our problem. In any case, the concept of process should be appropriated as a theological category of analysis for the development of our case studies.

Bonhoeffer's line of reasoning sets basic axioms of the historical-process model in a critical light. An inner *(ontic)* connection between Christ's reconciliation and man's further development is theologically inaccurate: Christ does not emerge from a chronology of immanent political processes, but rather causes the break in the "penultimate" with the "ultimate." Where the promise of history guides the axiom of understanding, the difference between promise and history is in danger of being flattened. Bonhoeffer can be read in reference to the Lutheran tradition concerning this distinction; for him the earthly historical "salvation is only partially actual" and at the same time remains threatened "by its opposite."[144] We therefore will maintain a critical view of the "open" concept of process. According to earthly historical conditions it appears "open, because the struggle between God and the powers of evil around man and the world will finally end." Accordingly, the outlined "openness" is a different category from Bonhoeffer's idea of "holding open" the penultimate, because for process theology the eschatological character (i.e., in the dimension of Christian hope) is missing. However, faith alone knows why it remains open. Openness means here to hold itself "open" for "the coming of the kingship of God."[145] It is included in an eschatological knowledge of "the immanent coming of the kingdom which is to a great degree hindered by opposing powers that can and will be replaced."[146]

In the meantime, Bonhoeffer would likely agree with John Cobb "that process lies at the basis of all reality."[147] He would certainly also say that at the base of all reality lies the process of the penultimate which will continue so that the justifying and reconciling word can continue to break in. For Bonhoeffer, the "process of transfer from occasion to occasion is accomplished in time,"[148] is a penultimate process. However, the "break" of the penultimate can not be considered in process theology, because process theology reckons with a succession of events — comparable to a film which is comprised of succession of individual shots (i.e., "only what the structure of an occasion exhibits is 'real'").[149] For the constructive connection of

Bonhoeffer's differentiation between the ultimate and penultimate and the idea of process we must take the position of process theology into consideration. In the transfer from one occasion to another something new and unfamiliar emerges; however, this newness is recognized as an immanent process in view of the preceding occasion (and not in view of an interruption of the process). What happens, however, when "occasions" that initiate new knowledge are not, in the process, tied to an immanent occasion, but to its interruption and thus to something "ultimate"? Can a "cause" then become a "moment of revelation"[150] released by recognition? Do occasions themselves provide a "moment of the holy spirit" (P. Lehmann), because suddenly it is clear that "so, this is God! So we must see things from the perspective of God"? The recognition of restorative "occasions" would then not be part of the process, but rather its interruption.

The decisive message in Bonhoeffer's adopted process theology is that in the penultimate a glimmer of the ultimate can be seen as the interruption of the occasion or event. The concept of process is thus theologically qualified as different from "times of grace" or moments of revelation. Thus, it does not gradually lose theological meaning of the penultimate, but keeps it for the sake of the ultimate: we experience justification and reconciliation (the "last things") for things of which we are guilty in the context of time.

Theology allows for a validation of the concept of process. While it is known that God does not "grow out of" the process, but rather means its interruption, it is still theologically legitimate to create (entirely in the sense of process theology), in view of the preceding, "occasions" that contain a basic hope for the future. This hope is one that is grounded in the liberating experience of the interruption of the processes which are viewed as historically immanent lawfulness. Hope is here the active form of the power of God in the reality of earthly relationships. Such hope is, for the person who has experienced it, immanently recalled "in the tracks of time."

In order to clarify that God is a true God who keeps His covenant using a Biblical example, we can recall the experience of remembering Israel's historical flight from Egypt. The command "remember!" is interwoven like a banner throughout Deuteronomy. The content of the remembrance is servitude in Egypt and liberation by God. This unifying theme, which holds together the different laws of Deuteronomy, shows a "tendency that leads past all casuistry and gives spiritual meaning behind the individual laws," as the "pressure of the subjective present" and "inwardness" (G. von Rad).[151] The example for the development of our case studies is immediately clear, because instances of political freedom appear in a basic theological connection. The Biblical injunction to remember God who liberated his people, whose saving justice creates right, and who endures oppression (Ps. 146:7), provides a paradigm of interpretation for many theologians who had political responsibility in the revolutions of South Africa and Germany.

The idea of process in the statement "God emerges from His world" must be defined so that the "world" remains ontologically on the side of creation; meanwhile God is in a different category as Creator of the world. He emerges as "alien" in the world but, as such, is still true to His creation and is Himself, as Creator, the occasion for the petition. To speak of the "Father in heaven" "means nothing less than to ask God if He would emerge from what is for us the realm of the relatively undefined to the available realm of the world; as, for example, from out of what we today call a dark future to what according to His will is His reigning new creation."[152] The new creation as a central hallmark of reconciliation (II Cor. 5:17) is thus the "movement of the world through God," "a movement of heaven and earth, which means forgiveness and becoming new"[153] — and which is humbly longed for in prayer. From here entry into the central theological classification of the talk of the process of reconciliation is possible: it has (in Trinitarian theological terms) a place in the pneumatology.

Mention of the "creative transformation" of "the power field of God's love" undergoes (in the sense of our first criterion) the necessary theological clarification. "Creative transformation" takes into account that "in the history of mankind the history of Christ, indeed, Christ himself" is advantageous and can be enlisted as a theological category of analysis for the interpretation of our case studies, at least in the sense of a critical corrective. "Creative transformation" must have its place in the doctrine of the Holy Spirit, otherwise it remains loaded down with statements about a process of growth in which Christology and pneumatology are not kept separate from each other. According to Cobb, the workings of the Holy Spirit are not up for discussion when Cobb formulates: "man, in the completed act of creative love . . . is creatively transformed. Thus, Christ gives reciprocal as well as creative human love."[154] Statements like this run into the danger of being interpreted on the horizon of the humanistic model. The fact that it has to do with the "creative transformation" of "freedom from anxiety in the world" — not with an "increase in possibilities," but with "the enduring and overcoming of the abandonment of God through the life and death of Jesus Christ" — threatens to detour us.

Bonhoeffer is undisputed where he reckons with the consequences of the interruption of the penultimate through the ultimate, justifying and reconciling Word. Nevertheless, his conception to that effect arrives at an *aporia,* in the sense that this moment of interruption can not be stated in active theological categories. What can we say about the interruption of the penultimate by the ultimate? How is the coming of the kingdom of God to be conceptualized? These questions yield various trajectories, to the extent that an overarching connection can be established between the idea of "interruption" of the penultimate, creative transformation, and the workings of the Holy Spirit.

Although a basic pneumatology is lacking in process theology, Bonhoeffer's ideas are nevertheless anchored in Trinitarian theology. In the constructive coupling of basic axioms of process theology to pneumatology, we can make connections to the current state of the discussion as to how to appropriately address the kingdom of God: namely, it remains "immanent."[155] On the one hand, the "new creative event" "under the conditions of this world is notoriously non-conclusive, and on the other hand it is annulled, confused, suspect, argued over, fought about, and derided." In this regard, the idea of seeing the Holy Spirit "as (the) universally active power of the presence of God" is helpful since creatures certainly move and act "in the field of its glory," but "not at all always in conformity with its orientation."[156] This important distinction is anchored pneumatalogically in the difference between teleology and eschatology: there are the few illuminating moments in which the goal of creation conforms with the goal of its Creator and, indeed, breaking with the former and not in connection to it. For Bonhoeffer, openness means in this context to allow oneself to be "interrupted" by the "streaming power" field (of God); to leave oneself "open," yes, even to "believe." Pneumatologically speaking, where the reference is to the "power field of God" the metaphor should not be interpreted uncritically in process theology as a one-sided "power of weakness." Also, in view of the concept of reconciliation, the implication for the Spirit-effecting "power field of God" is always both (if not at the same time): namely, it is both the suffering nature of God and God's initiating potential for protest against suffering. The effect of the spirit of God is thus not to be interpreted from only one side as reconciling, which would make protest impossible. Rather, the Spirit constitutes a "many sided . . . field of power."[157] "The formula 'spirit of God' . . . implies the dynamic of going before and bringing forth."[158] God allows Himself to be recognized in that He interrupts the penultimate (for example the disastrous push-pull connection of political reconciliation) and produces hope (which can include new actions). Whether God's spirit was "at work" or whether we have anything to do with it in an action of conformity that is aligned with the field power, is something that we can again recognize as an "occasion." The question to be asked, however, is whether such "occasions" — for example that of "freely willing self-redemption"[159] in political reality — are valid. We may recall Nelson Mandela's dealings with his former political enemies or, as seen in the hearings, Dr. Siebert's letter in which he explains that he "would like to make peace" with Philemon Maxan who had murdered his mother! Are the moments of forgiveness and testimonials of "self-redemption" somehow a recompense to the extent that they are a free-will rejection of the meaning "coin for coin"?[160]

G. Sauter succinctly formulates the connection to our discussion: "to be reconciled is not a situation, but it is also not a process. It is at one and the same time a space, a power field, in which requests and prayers are invited to remain."[161] Where reconciliation is spoken of as a "process" the political and theological use of reconciliation is linguistically transferable to the extent that it belongs to the penultimate process necessary for the Christian (in the sense of preserving it for the "ultimate"). Meanwhile, political reconciliation remains distinctly apart from intentional theological categories; for the political manner of reconciliation describes "the entire long process, started with the first knowledge of the injustice and going beyond the abolishment of injustice to the ritual of conciliation and the emergence of normal relationships."[162] Rather, reconciliation as a qualitative and timely "ultimate" emerges as the interruption of such a process in political reality: the word of reconciliation allows something fundamentally new to emerge that neither grew from the past nor necessarily resulted from it. The (political) result is not given theological credence in the formulation of "the emergence of normal relationships." Reconciliation in the theological sense is something "ultimate" about which qualitatively nothing more can be said or thought. However, included or assumed in this concept of reconciliation is always the "complete overcoming of injustice." Thus, a continuity of political and theological talk about reconciliation occurs in the sense of "preservation" and a discontinuity in the sense of "completion." Finally, *ontic* traces are, however, "continually" visible in the interruption of the penultimate by the justifying and reconciling Word in the political reality that is left behind; something that we can accept in the course of a theological synthesis of the empirical analysis. The recognition of the occasion (or moment) of release should be described as a transcendent sign.

For the purposes of our analysis, the defined concept of process is distinguished in terms of category from ideas that are identified with political processes, namely:

- the open, indifferent, neutral future (as in philosophical currents),
- as actualization of human identity (as in humanistic-secular ideas),
- as a future that is qualified through pure process immanent hallmarks (as in basic trajectories of process theology).

(b) Theological Reconciliation as a Point of Entry for a Concept of Justice

In Bonhoeffer's ethics, the theological teaching of the path to differentiation is retained. On the other hand, the "relationships" between the ultimate and penultimate are elevated (even when ethically emphasized in the question of correspondence). In the acceptance of "relationships" Bonhoeffer certainly utilizes the doctrine of the Two Kingdoms, but the history of ideas of the doctrine of the Two Kingdoms contains a cloudy historical point. The question is whether or not in using it he opens up the possibility for a counter argument to the basic idea of the so-called doctrine of the Lordship of the Kingdom of Christ. In Bonhoeffer's use of the term "relationships" one can find points in common with the Reformed tradition. On the one hand, Bonhoeffer's ethic contains indications of the resistance of *current* Lutheran tendencies, such as the challenge to solidify the differences and to isolate things that belong together in the doctrine of the Two Kingdoms in order to strengthen the idea that "the Gospel apart from the law is not viable for the (current) state of society and political life."[163] On the other hand, Bonhoeffer maintains the view of the earthly kingdom "as the area of cooperation between Christians and non-Christians on the basis of reason."[164] Bonhoeffer is not to be identified as interpreting the doctrine of the Lordship of Christ in such a way that the state could be said to serve as a direct "extension" of the Kingdom of Christ, "as something similar, an expression of, or an analogy to what the church believes and proclaims as the kingdom of God."

In the context of the political theory of the "doctrine of the Two Kingdoms" and "teaching on the Lordship of Christ," our question of correspondence aligns with Bonhoeffer. We first must reckon with a fundamental openness in the political dealings with guilt and then inquire about the recognition of theological basis for reconciliation within the relatively autonomous conditions of political reality. Our search for signs of transcendence embedded in the eschatological tension created by the activity of salvation of the triune God in the created and fallen world is appropriate: God has reconciled the world to Himself in Christ (II Cor. 5:19) and overcome hell (I Cor. 15:25); at the same time Christianity still has to wait for the new heaven and the new earth (2 Peter 3:13). In the development of the question of correspondence we can formulate that, on the one hand, the world does not fully correspond with the judgment of Christ and often even contradicts Him, while on the other hand it inquires about correlations.

Elements from the reformed tradition[165] are instructive for our problem such as, for example, the interpretation of the idea of the kingdom of God. With regard to the situation of political transition in South Africa John de Gruchy says: "The vision of democratic transformation resembles in many ways the eschatological vision of the coming of the kingdom of God. We know that the reign of God is not something which we can bring into being through social action, and we also know that the reign of God is always something ultimate, something beyond our achievement. At the same time, the reign of God can be anticipated in concrete ways here and now."[166] Michael Welker systematically complicates the element of "at the same time." "The activity of the Spirit and the activity of the Word have something in common with the coming Kingdom of God since they do not arrive like a train or a bus so that we can say, 'now it is here, or now it is not here.'" Rather, "the kingdom of God is already active among us and yet at the same time is still to come. It is an expanse from beyond; an expanse that meets us from the future and it is at the same time among us as the living present. It is externally visible . . . in that justice and mercy bear fruit. And it remains at the same time hidden in the listening; in the remembering and the expectations. The Kingdom of God is thus no illusion, but it is the form in which God rules in actuality in servitude to man."[167]

Next to the outlined differences, the constructive connection between the doctrine of the Two Kingdoms and the Lordship of Christ is to be noted. To a certain degree, Bonhoeffer anticipated the shape of the later discussion when he left himself open to interpretation regarding both models: the difference between the ultimate and penultimate is not so narrow that Christian existence can not be split into two realms in which one outwardly lacks noticeable unity, nor does it appear to have tendencies to worldliness (as in the individual laws of the realm of politics).

The mode of the doctrine of the Two Kingdoms and the teaching on the Lordship of Christ correlate to the concept of theological justice.[168] Stated more simply: while in the (Lutheran) tradition justice is "distinguished" as relatively independent, there are indications of a "classification" behind the basis for theological justice in the (Reformed) tradition. Thus, the former approach is in danger of uncoupling justice from morality so that the space of justice is relinquished in favor of legalism and there is an uncritical blending of the relative and absolute autonomy of justice, even as a divinely created order is accepted.[169] The latter approach hides the danger of combining justice and morality, while theological differences are scrapped and the history of ideas of the western tradition of justice, which ultimately led to a secularization of its religious roots, remains unheeded. Against the background of the danger of a separation of morality and justice, it must be made clear that there are unalterable values at the core of the issue — such as the worth of people which is to be upheld unconditionally — even if these values can not be ultimately defined. They impact the corridors of state power which, by exceeding the autonomous boundaries of the legal sphere, extends to the theological perspective. It should also be emphasized that the danger of mixing morality and justice is that the realization of human rights is not identical with the realization of the righteousness of God, which is received in faith. "Thus the proclamation of the Gospel frees the law for its own timeliness and worldliness."[170]

This basic position does not appear in the outlined polarized debate on legal ethics. However it does mark the extremes that are informative for a Protestant legal ethic.[171] The Lutheran type is encountered in the current discussion as a modified legal ethic from the theological perspective,[172] while the Reformed type is differentiated on several levels as theological foundation for the law.[173]

To the extent that our examination connects to "legal ethics from a theological perspective," punishment is seen as something purely "worldly," as a "necessary structure."[174] "A mythical sacred meaning of earthly punishment has become baseless," after Jesus "gave Himself for the entire person in the place of their sins and has once and for all canceled the cycle of guilt and sin."[175] Accordingly, there is no negation of the relative justice of the state's handling of punishment. According to Romans 13:4, "authority is God's servant to bring punishment on the wrongdoer. Nevertheless, the punishment that is given to state authority from God's hands and that will be completed can no longer be understood as sinful. It must have a worldly goal and thus be related to the legal harmony of the human community. An identification of divine punishment with human punishment is no longer possible."[176] Eschatological and teleological goal setting distance themselves from the question of punishment: the goal of punishment of criminals is categorically different from God's goal of reconciliation in Jesus Christ.

In summarizing the ethical discussion for the development of our problem it should not be overlooked that the theological model is a theoretical development of ethics. The position of the question of theological entry into justice identifies the framing conditions for the question of correspondence: while the legal ethic of the theological perspective proceeds from the basic assumption that not all politics necessarily have to have a theological dimension, the Christological foundation of justice is guided by the opposite axiom: namely, that analogously all politics has a theological, even a spiritual dimension. The difference determines the context for the theological appraisal of our case studies. A clear boundary of the task is marked where the systematic application of justice is not made directly dependent upon conclusive theological foundations, but is limited in its theological perspective to a critical evaluation of its own legitimacy. For the relevant legal-ethical parts of this examination need not always be "Christological," nor are the presented discussions on criminal justice to be settled with finality. Rather, political activity remains indivisible "from the transcendent expectation for salvation of the world of faith and the power of a freedom upon which no one can lay a hand."[177]

3. An Examination of Evidence of Commonalities between Spiritual and Political Reconciliation

After conducting a more in-depth deductive analysis of the theological categories, a further synthetic step will be made in an attempt to analyze the political aspects (of political reconciliation) with respect to theological norms. The concepts of "justice" and "process" will be treated first in the question of correspondence. These concepts allow for a possible theological synthesis of the political forms of reconciliation that were presented in the case study Chapter II.A.I/III and B.I/III.

(a) What Were the Past Political Options for Action in Their Basic Connection to a Theological Ethic of Justice?

The political discussion concerning options for action was defined by an uncontested logic. For example, in South Africa, amnesty was granted for the sake of "nation building," but in Germany it was rejected because it would not have advanced "internal harmony." Amnesty has a basic connection to "internal harmony" when it comes to "national reconciliation." Linguis-

tically, the use of the term reconciliation with respect to the term nation occurs more frequently in German in phrases like "inner unity," and "growing
together," to name a few.

The answers to our question of correspondence concerning a fundamental connection to theological reconciliation in political forms of expression
will be investigated in the following by examining the evidence for commonalities: namely, do the common terms for "reconciliation" in past politics and
the theological doctrine of reconciliation also draw from common underlying categories? We will follow this guiding question first with respect to legal
ethics as we take a look at the common areas — as well as the gaps — in the
active categories existing behind regulative ideas for legal action on the one
hand, and basic ideas existing behind a theological ethic of justice on the
other. The theological-normative task ahead is, namely, to examine the synthetic options for action (Options 1-5) for a "spiritual" form of reconciliation.

Prosecution and amnesty, the empirically analyzed options for action
(Options 1 and 2), are legal categories that carry independent meaning
within the judicial system. In transitional societies they also gain a political
dimension to the degree that they comprise the principal options for action
for dealing with past injustices by the state. They are the principal options
for action, because both options are not open in the same way to every society undergoing change. Previous political analysis correctly holds to the category of "power": amnesties for past offences are enforced wherever political
power makes it possible. The same thing is true for the (rare) case of prosecution. The differentiated analyses of the proceedings in Germany and
South Africa should therefore not be condensed or abbreviated; the points
of intersection that are crucial to the theological perspective need to be considered. Our thesis is: the prosecution of serious human rights violations is
not determinative, nor is amnesty to be confused with the theological category of forgiveness.

The fact that the state's handling of punishment is not directly derived
from the theological has already been discussed. In addition, the fact that
criminal law serves to protect is, in theological terms, an "earthly matter."
"Reformation theology, which departs from the idea that justice proceeds
from God's law alone, would never find itself connected to a criminal law
based on revenge."[178] Meanwhile, new light can be shed on criminal law because it undergoes strict limitations from the theological perspective: the in-
fliction of (worldly) punishment can only mean a judgment on the deed, not
on the person. In the worldly court system it has to do with "external," quantifiable guilt and not with the "inner" person. It views the person by exter-

nals and not from an individual perspective. Thus, in terms of the law, remorse (in a theologically univocal sense) can not be exacted. Here lies a critical function of the doctrine of the Two Kingdoms: it allows only for a regulated use of the law. The value of a human being remains inaccessible to criminal law (which is why considering capital punishment as legally ethical is theologically objectionable). The difference between morality and law — a key idea in a free, democratic constitutional state — can be recognized where the worth of the offender remains intact, even though he has "trampled heavily" on the worth of his victim. Dealings with the perpetrator of serious human rights violations in both South Africa and in Germany confirm this basic element of system change.

Regulative statements — such as "reconciliation can eliminate the need to punish the offender," or the opposite, "reconciliation cannot ignore punishment" — prevent a theological synthesis. Reconciliation is viewed here on the "macro level" and is placed entirely in a basic political relationship of "national" reconciliation. However, what promotes social interaction and what hinders it? The driving force is the common good. In the context of disparate initial conditions in South Africa and in Germany, politicians have arrived at correspondingly varying conclusions. These, however, do not need to be theologically conclusive.

Is it possible to theologically reconstruct a "spiritual" position that goes beyond the conservative view in connection to Option 1? Theological benchmarks can be found with respect to the question of human rights. In Germany (as in South Africa) the value of punishment for past human rights violations was never seriously contested. The discussion centered more closely on the question of the ability to punish. The notion of protecting human rights was regulative and was connected to the discussion of the value placed on punishing human rights violations in the criminal code: namely, "the perpetrator must be punished," "prosecution precedes integration," and "infractions of justice toward humanity demand prosecution."

The core idea of protecting human rights, whose basic principle is that of human worth, is a fundamentally open one. On the one hand, this makes possible a point of departure for theological discussion and on the other hand, caution is advised in view of the obvious pairing of the protection of human rights with legal prosecution. (Primarily the latter, because in principle an implementation of human right protections can not be ruled out. In the political debate, whoever demands the prosecution of past human rights violations need not necessarily be compelled by the idea of human worth. In addition, the protection of human rights can be idealized.)

When "fundamental openness" is mentioned, especially in the theological debate, it infers universal application and a Christian position on the foundation of human rights. I use the model of correlation and difference in the theological interpretation of human rights, whose core idea is, on the one hand, to pose questions about correlations between the current form of human rights and the basic content of the Christian faith, and on the other hand, to take seriously the secular character of human rights regarding attempts to derive them theologically. The following section will be limited to basic positions and problems that are relevant to the treatment of our examples:

- The unconditional value of human rights depends (theologically) on making the distinction between the person and his deeds. The essence of human worth lies in the fact that it does not depend on conditions or on any final accounting of itself, "but transcends all. The fact that people may believe they are worthless does not mean there is any earthly reason to declare them as worthless."[179]
- The fundamentally open formulation of human rights is important for the sake of its universal application. Meanwhile, this indicates a basic problem for theological concern with human rights. "A look back into the history of all human knowledge of the law shows that it is opposed to falling back on natural law. An exclusively Christian foundation contradicts the fact that the concept of human rights itself is only taken seriously when everyone, independent of their religious and political convictions, is guaranteed (their human rights)."[180]

Amnesty is not to be equated with the theological category of forgiveness. Our case studies indicate that the "forms of reconciliation" within past politics "are not to be thought of as taking the form of confession of guilt and of forgiveness."[181] If one asks who the subject of this form of reconciliation is, one distances oneself increasingly from individual, personal ideas. The subject of the goal of "inner unity" or "national reconciliation" is nations, skin color, and geography. The "healing process" connected with these goals is expressed in a-personal categories and invites the critical comment that time "'heals' only by the fading of memory and not through forgiveness and makes much bearable what burdens the individual memory, as well as the collective memory."[182] An a-personal healing process (i.e., without forgiveness and without the admission of guilt) is something that Dietrich Bonhoeffer describes as the "cicatrisation (scar tissue) of guilt."[183] Here the ultimate does not interrupt the penultimate, which would otherwise be the case in acts of personal forgiveness. The "worldly" healing process leads to cicatrisation and remains an uninterrupted and entirely penultimate one. Precisely this understanding corresponds to the legal options for action of "amnesty" in terms of the "leaving in peace" past human rights violations. We cited H. Quaritsch above who, in his conclusion to a historical legal analysis, came to the conclusion that amnesty has never been the "result of human love, forgiveness or other internal change toward vulnerability." Rather, it was forced by circumstances or at least something close to that.[184]

Viewed from the standpoint of theology, what happens here is that guilt "is certainly not justified," but it is also "not let go of or forgiven," but "remains in place."[185] Personal categories (from the area of morality) like forgiveness, remorse, acceptance of guilt, or remembrance — all of which are theologically open to interpretation — do not suffice where (also from the area of law) amnesty for perpetrated human rights violations stands as a political option for action at the very end of past political discourse. For the offender this means that they are not forgiven; their guilt cannot be worked off or, at best, forgotten. For the victims it means that nothing about them is remembered; their wounds cannot heal, let alone scar over. And for the new society it ultimately means that the difference between victims and offenders is flattened; "somehow" "everyone" was fooled.

These observations lead to various results in a theological synthesis. First, the "spiritual" and the "worldly" must be carefully distinguished from each other.[186] Secondly, this difference (on the ground of reason) can lead to an autonomous assessment of the political: there are initial conditions in transitional societies, in which for the political sake of peace, amnesty includes "the world." (In South Africa this was the case in the transition process.)[187] Third, "worldly" reconciliation (amnesty or "inner historical" forgiveness) can also result in the sense of *conservatio mundi*. When guilt becomes scar tissue, continues Bonhoeffer, it is the result of the "force of power from an arbitrary order that has crafted peace from war."[188] Fourth, the "worldly" categorization of the process of reconstruction finally frees the state from having an eschatological expectation for healing placed on it. "Scarring" as a gradual healing process (for example to cover up injustice, and to treat it constitutionally — a highly incomplete measure) is also in this scenario the more likely expectation.[189]

This section is intended to argue that amnesty as a political option for action is suitable as a reasonable measure. However, no category of forgiveness emerges. In fact, it is the opposite: categories are adjusted where the categorical differences between (political) amnesty and (Christian) forgiveness are not adequately recognized.[190] Amnesty in terms of the faith question can be clarified precisely on the basis of whether or not it will ultimately be justifiable. However, where theologians are in favor of amnesty for political violations, they must be also prepared to specify political reasons for it!

From the legal ethical perspective, a general amnesty is particularly worthy of criticism: it contains no room for the occasion of working out of guilt, but aims at forgetting. Theological perspectives for the working out of guilt are open to remembering guilt through the admission of guilt in the personal encounter between the offenders and victims and in the breaking free of the guilt connection through forgiveness. These systematic viewpoints match the conditions of "paving the way" (Bonhoeffer), which we have mentioned several times as taking place during the proceedings (i.e., a closed area, a moderator, etc.).

It is the theological task of this section to examine the political options for action with respect to their basic, underlying connection to theological reconciliation. As a result, we suggest that within the past political debate on prosecution or amnesty for serious human rights violations we have come across no occasion indicating divine reconciliation or that could be based upon a normative examination of theological reconciliation. The political idea of national reconciliation, which is achieved without overcoming the guilt relationship through forgiveness, does not correspond to spiritual reconciliation which, in turn, is concerned with the healing of personal relationships. They can, however, be understood as an expression of God's preservation of the world. Neither of the meanings of reconciliation is theologically transferable to the other, but each has its own individual application.

Between the (legal) options of prosecution and amnesty there is no theologically deducible connection to spiritual reconciliation. In legal ethical terms, "reconciliation can not be commanded by means of punishment or achieved by means of external power."[191] This statement has strict application to the difference between the legal and moral categories. In contrast to prosecution and amnesty, reconciliation is "a process that involves openness to search for the whole truth and the readiness to admit one's own deeds."[192] In the legal category, the "search for truth" and "acknowledgement" are morally different.

The distinction that I am attempting to make does not appear to contradict the empirical analysis in the Option for Action 2 (explanation of past injustices). Included in the Options for Actions 3-5 are categories (truth, making restitution, new beginnings) which, in addition to the legal course of action, are open to moral or symbolic explanation. Legal and moral categories are relatively open to interpretation; however, they remain distinct from each other. Here it will be seen how theology stands in correspondence to and as distinctly apart from these interpretations. Do commonalities exist between the categories of truth used in the political statements, reparations, and new beginnings of past politics and the spiritual meaning of these categories in the (Christian) doctrine of reconciliation? Are categories so constructed that the expressed forms of political reconciliation appear in a basic connection to theological reconciliation?

The legal Options for Actions 1 and 2 were closed to a "spiritual" approach. However, another light is shed on an option where the legal system is open to moral categories. With regard to the past political debate, the key section interfaces with Option 3.

The connection of law and ethics is meaningful in view of the South African amnesty law in which punishment is rejected only after receiving the cooperation of the offender so that the appropriate level of the punishment can be determined. Here amnesty is not just a legal endorsement by the state; on the contrary: the endorsement is made public with the naming of names. The culpability of the deed must be determined (not merely whether it deserves punishment) before punishment is rejected as an option. As for exemption from punishment, we assert that "punishment is dispensable, but the truth is not." In order to be able to inquire about the basic theological connection of this statement, the dimensions of truth in which the forum of the TRC operated need to be elaborated upon; namely, the legal, the moral and, as is later to be seen, the symbolic.

The legal dimension of truth lies in the material premise of freedom from punishment. Telling the truth here means as much as making a confession and is coupled with the legal concept of guilt. It involves an examination of responsibility and punishment (using appropriate guidelines for punishment) and is less concerned with what leads to discernment and humility. Relevant facts must be placed out in the open in order for punishable actions to be ascertained and for amnesty to be conferred. The research on legal truth is afforded limited boundaries. The principle of material truth has its limitations in the "protection of the person of the accused."[193] Thus, theologically speaking, the law only takes an interest in the "external" person. When inquiring about the truth in legal terms, it has to do with "the very limited framework of the debt owed the accuser."[194] Kraus goes on: "Whoever demands 'more' and 'other' truth, or 'better' research on truth must place the entire process . . . under scrutiny." In a constructive sense, this is what a Truth Commission attempts to do. The South African TRC made it possible to build some bridges. A space was provided in which (of one's free will) the one-dimensional aspect of the search for legal truth could be bridged. The aspect of free will grows from the view of "ethical-social guilt,"[195] but is not decisive for the outcome of the amnesty process. It remains limited to the legal concept of truth and guilt.

As an intermediate result it can be asserted that the legal dimension of truth, beyond a desire for amnesty, opens up the chance to work out the personal guilt of the offender and, secondly, can prepare the way for victims or those who remain behind to come to terms with their fate.

The moral dimension of truth lies in making remorse possible for the offender and making forgiveness possible for the victim. The public confessions of human rights violations have legal significance on a personal level for both victims and offenders[196] that can extend to the moral realm. Law and morality remain different and apart from each other, as indeed is seen in the appearances before the TRC requesting amnesty, where each advances the development of the situation, but everything else remains "open." Here the "truth statements" before the TRC receive a further dimension that reaches beyond the personal level. The truth concept of the TRC is capable of establishing (on an intra-personal level) a connection between the desire for amnesty on the part of the offenders and the relentlessly probing "why questions" of the victims. What is promising in this event is that a protected place is provided in which the offenders and victims can work out their guilt. For example, victims such as Ashley Forbes willingly sought to speak with Jeffrey Benzien before the TRC, especially if the discussions were "open." The victims may be able to forgive, but they don't have to. And the offenders are free to provide insight into their personal moral guilt. Nevertheless, justice and morality also remain distinct on the intra-personal level. The connection between the legal and socio-ethical view of guilt takes place only in the moral "I" of the offender. No decision, not even that of the TRC, can compel connections between the legal and moral dimensions of truth. Therefore, in the statutes of the TRC there is also no provision in which the offenders must feel remorse when confronted with a description of the truth. However, it allows the victims legally to cross-examine the offenders and to confront them to some extent (morally) with the consequences of their actions. As an intermediate result of the theological synthesis, three points should be advanced:

- In view of the intra-personal process, there is nothing that necessarily leads from the legal to a moral insight into guilt; to sin and remorse on the part of the offender; and ultimately to forgiveness on the part of the victims. On the one hand, the legal ethical position is decisive that the theological concept of sin is to be clearly distinguished from a legal or moral concept of guilt. On the other hand, we consider in the overview of our theological analysis of the concept of process signs of transcendence those that are not worldly or temporal at the end of the process and that may not mean simultaneous successful closure.

- With regard to the offender, it should be emphasized that remorse as a theological category is felt by the "inner person"; it is a process *coram deo,* which means something quite different than "remorse." Final *judgments about remorse remain with God, even if worthy actions and explanations are coram hominibus,* pointing to signs of transcendence in the reality of spiritual reconciliation. However, these hide a historical overflow of promise that corresponds to the difference between any legal and moral truth of the "inner person," which comes to light when "all lies, notions, and deals are done away with."[197]
- With regard to the victim, the personal dimension of reconciliation should be emphasized. "That a person has been the victim of a crime and can forgive the offender without knowing him or about what was involved in the deed, is . . . very unlikely."[198] To be able to see the person behind the deed requires a meeting and dialogue between offenders and their victims. An interpersonal "space is created" to accommodate the perspective of the other. Thus, the guilt that exists between people has to be acknowledged and forgiven.

In terms of our theological-normative task of examining the synthetic options for action with regard to their connection to spiritual reconciliation, we firmly assert as a result in view of Option 3: legal truth-seeking can be placed on the moral interpersonal level in the process of working out of guilt between victims and offenders, the interruption of which can be regarded as signs of transcendence of spiritual forgiveness and of remorse. Examples of moments (occasions) of release are also indicated on the personal level.

Reparations for the victims are an option for action offered in system change. Restorative actions carry the benefit of inner peace in transitional societies. The movement of morality and justice toward reparation — different from prosecution or amnesty — brings them especially near to each other. Does political reconciliation in the form of reparations appear in a basic connection to theological reconciliation?

From the theological perspective, legal attempts at reparations are to be viewed critically. The "ultimate and penultimate" are confused where "making amends" must first be "convincing" "as they correlate to the injustice."[199] Theologically, a mistake is made here. The goal of justice (as a human order) can not be put on the same level with the goal of promise, according to which everything is made good again (restored) when God perfects His creation. Representatives of a legal ethic thus maintain that from the theological perspective "the idea of complete justice is an eschatological idea."[200] Only where reparations (in the reciprocal sense) are conceived of as something "ultimate," can they safeguard political efforts from being overestimated. Moreover, we saw that where justice makes true amends possible (e.g., through the return of belongings), other injustices arise. A theological design that acknowledges the categorical difference between "the ultimate and the penultimate" is free of eschatological expectations for salvation in the legal realm.

Reparations as a political option for action are in danger of being absolutized. "The idea of making amends goes sour when it thinks that it can re-establish the conditions that existed before the deed occurred."[201] Clearly, one could say here that justice can not be in the business of providing solutions. If that were the case, justice would then be made the "occasion of a legal statement"[202] in a theological sense. In terms of dogmatics, justice is not a "means of grace," but it can serve to preserve (i.e., without making a theological judgment).[203] Here the difference between the worldly and the spiritual is clear, which in our cases also has significance for the area of pastoral care in dealing with the expectations for justice in system change.

The openness of the category of "reparations" in the context of morality and justice is meanwhile to be examined for normative theological correlations. As a normative statement of spiritual reconciliation we can say that reconciliation "in Christ" makes community with God possible again; the guilt between God and man has been set right.

Do the political dealings with the victims through reparations have a fundamental basis in the restoration of the relationship between God and man? Let us update this question with the implicit axiom that we enlisted for the empirical case studies in the following:

The regulative idea was that political "reparations have something to do with acknowledgement." With this so-called "moral" making of amends we see a good example of "reconciling one's fate" and the "coming to terms with the painful past," as it appears in the final report of the TRC. Making amends should be connected to the individual story; the person should be able to heal his memories. In "intra-personal reconciliation" making amends is "not to be expected between adversaries, but within the reality that suffered damage; in the "fate." Here we also hear a longing for justice, for which, however, "concessions" must be made. These descriptions of the process of "self-reconciliation" often correspond to — contrary to retributive justice — the concept of "restorative justice."[204] Justice should not be re-established in a partial sense (for example in the comparison with the offender in the sense of *lex talionis*); an exact legal accounting is rejected. However, this rejection is not to be confused with unwillingness or quiet suffering. Rather, it contains eschatological qualities. The perception of seeking to reconcile with one's fate correlates to "conformity to God's view of things."[205] "Because He keeps Himself hidden and is 'above things,' He turns the position of weakness into one of strength." Thus, the circle of power and counter-power through the distinction between deed and doer is broken. With respect to the TRC hearings one can ask: isn't the readiness to share one's fate already an expression of love for the enemy? As a rule, one only shares one's story with those one loves. Questions and statements like these obviously interrupt a rational pattern of explanation. Such persistence with appropriate deliberation gives the self-reconciling person the advantage over against hate of the enemy, because otherwise "the respective offender is given an unjust power over the identity and the life (of the victim)." In the sense of theological synthesis, the basic openness to making amends is significant. Political processes can also be interpreted spiritually. However, at the center of this interpretation there must be respect for human life and worth.

Concerning the theological task to examine the synthetic options for action for their connection to spiritual reconciliation, we firmly assert as a result in view of Option 4: making amends is basically an open category. Material compensation and legal rehabilitation are appropriate. In the course of moral reconciliation *(coram mundo)* individual signs of transcendence can be observed. However, although personal reconciliation *(coram mundo)* in terms of a spiritual process has a particular meaning: they are *(coram deo)* transferable for the purposes of interpretation. The acceptance of one's own fate proves the acceptance of man through God and there has its actual foundation. The restoration of the God relationship is the condition for the possibility of coming to terms with one's own individual story. To this extent, a "new person" can be found in the person who is healing.

The use of "sanctions outside of criminal law," as was seen in our example of professional disqualification, clearly depends on the nature of the system change. While in South Africa the regulative idea prevailed that national reconciliation contained the lack of conditions for offenders to make a new professional start, in unified Germany it was the opposite: for the sake of a new social order the elite of the old order could not credibly work alongside others in the building of a democratic society. Rather, they were disqualified by virtue of their prior participation in a dictatorial regime. The idea was regulative that personal guilt is sanctioned by professional disqualification. Reconciliation is not to be exchanged for the unconditional reemployment of complicit co-workers.

The differentiated analysis of past politics allows us to make some summarizing statements at this point. In South Africa amnesty was the means for social integration so that the decision for Option 2 (amnesty) also meant a simultaneous decision against Option 5. In Germany, on the other hand, the prosecution of human rights violations (Option 1) was supplemented by the possibility of professional job disqualification (Option 5) so that criminals who could not be pursued legally (as for example Stasi co-workers) at least were given a basis for dismissal from public service. It has already been discussed in theological terms which social groups were mainly affected by these processes. While in South Africa the concerns of the former powerful elite were the focus (with the result of amnesty and generous rules for continuing in professional service), by contrast in Germany the focus of attention was on those who were previously oppressed. Whereas the former focused on the offender, the latter focused on the perspective of the victim. "For victims it is an ethical and aesthetic impertinence to have to discover the offender again in education, in the police force, in the churches, in non-confinement, and in other public areas as somehow having changed."[206]

To what extent does political reconciliation appear in relationship to professional disqualification in a basic connection to theological reconciliation?

We will concentrate on one category in the political discussion that reveals the central content of theological reconciliation teaching; namely, that of a new beginning. As we have asserted in the conclusion to the second deductive step (section 1.4), reconciliation means God "in Christ" begins again with the world anew. Reconciliation is not limited to the redemption of the world; it promises at the same time a new creation in the world and anchors the eschatological hope of change as one of interruption and disturbance of the old (compare esp. II Cor. 5:17). God holds this new beginning for us ready in Christ. Are politically administered new beginnings in a relationship corresponding to spiritual new beginnings? Is there an overarching category that includes both?

These questions suggest direct theological correspondences. Is it not the case that the South African process is more appropriate to the Gospel because there the offender was very publicly "forgiven," making possible an unconditional "new beginning" in society? On the contrary, is the German process ethically underdeveloped because it overtly "tracks" guilt and does not unconditionally forgive? These resulting questions provide an uncritical theological framework with respect to political reality and the attempt to find conceptual equivalents (in the sense of *aequivocatio a casu*).

Equivalents can be found by looking at the differences in categories. Thus, for example, the difference between the spiritual new beginning and the denial of continuing professional employment of Option 5 should be highlighted. The former involves the inner person and the latter the external person. Whoever begins anew spiritually, does this as *simul iustus et peccator* on a daily basis; worldly existence is marked by this process. New beginnings that involve a change of heart are not to be confused with political new beginnings in terms of professional job continuity.

The above named questions are linked to others by a specific concept of reconciliation. The active idea of reconciliation behind it corresponds to the humanistic model. Thus, the term "unconditional" is used problematically. The legal model of reconciliation, however, shows that God does not forgive unconditionally, but the condition for reconciliation is the interruption of the relationship of guilt between man and God which led to the death of Jesus. Reconciliation is "dear." Accordingly, the tracking or counting of reasons for guilt is not a legitimate way to look at guilt when it comes to forgiveness, whose condition for reconciliation in Christ is its acceptance in faith.

Direct correspondences combine the "worldly" and the "spiritual"; they are relativized not only through the spiritual, but in the final analysis they do not allow the worldly to be the worldly. It should not be overlooked from a theological perspective that personal guilt has social repercussions. The fact that a new beginning is possible and legitimate where it theologically distinguishes between persons and their deeds, and the Stasi-collaborators who for the sake of belief in a new political beginning with their prior deeds must be identified and therefore cannot be employed again, is just as important for society as it is for the individual.

In addition to the distinction between a "spiritual" and a "political" new beginning, there are also, from the theological perspective, connections to be had. Direct correspondences are avoided, where is it shown that the one (the spiritual process) is recognizable in the other (the political process) as having its basis in God's reconciling activity in the world.

Nevertheless, criminal law makes possible a new beginning where it stays away from the implementation of the punishment. Internment did not become a symbol of justice in Germany. Reflections on legal ethics from a theological perspective are problematic because the denial of freedom is an offense to human dignity and worth. The fact that most of those who were involved in shootings at the wall had to "do penance" during their internment still does not prove that the German process contained a spiritual quality. Neither is progression from the legal category beyond the moral to a spiritual new beginning possible; although the latter can be seen in the former, especially when the former reinforces the latter. The process remains an uninterrupted and penultimate one. From the theological perspective, the legal ethical view does not provide a conclusive foundation either in terms of the punishment or the renunciation of punishment. The theological synthesis is thus moderate in its deliberations: on the basis of reason, the German process is more convincing because it required a change in the ruling elite and in its implementation of penal law more than did the South African process.

The category associated with the new beginning brought about by the legal proceedings of Option 5 is not theologically transferable, in terms of either correspondence or difference. There is a difference to the extent that a new beginning is possible in political reality based upon univocal expressions of spiritual new beginnings: namely, that offenders may not be prosecuted by criminal law nor professionally disqualified is able to emerge as the *conditio sine qua non* of peace and justice (as in South Africa). Correlations to the levels of dealing with guilt can be seen in tandem with spiritual reconciliation: guilt is taken seriously; its development in the moral "I" of the offender has the result of change on the part of the offender.

RESULT 1

In this section we considered the question of to what extent the regulative ideas in the framework of the empirically analyzed options for action of past politics corresponded to basic elements of theological legal ethics and to what extent they appeared in a basic relationship to the Christian idea of reconciliation. It was the theological task to synthetically examine the five options for action on the basis of "spiritual" reconciliation. As a result, it should be firmly asserted that dealing with guilt during political upheaval by means of action Options 1 and 2 (prosecution or amnesty, especially "leaving in peace" and not doing anything) is not based on theological reconciliation. Punishment and amnesty remain entirely "penultimate" and are not transferable to spiritual reconciliation. There is no common category underlying political and spiritual reconciliation. The categories of truth, however, behave differently with regard to reparations and a new beginning, which are connected to Options for Actions 3-5. Their openness as conceptual categories paves the way for the theological reconstruction of reconciliation in political reality. Wherever politics searches for truth, and wherever we encounter reparations and new beginnings with respect to guilty deeds in totalitarian regimes, the question of correspondence yields results for a recognition of the basic relationship of central theological statements on reconciliation with respect to political dealings with guilt. The category of past politics adapts when it comes into contact with the category of faith. Believers know about the actuality of the proceedings behind the use of political-legal analysis categories 3-5. They know that truth in an actual sense means freedom:[207] reparations result in the reestablishment of God's community through Christ and a new beginning precisely because of His action for us. Only in light of spiritual reconciliation does political reconciliation have its "actuality"; namely, the promise of the "ultimate" and with it spiritual reconciliation.

To emphasize the ontological difference between political and spiritual reconciliation, one could conceivably view the transfer of the concept of political reconciliation (as making amends or new beginning) to spiritual reconciliation as an "act of baptism." This would mean that the concept of reparations (making amends), or a new beginning as it connects to the process of political reconciliation in the moment of recognition, loses its original meaning and even "dies," taking on a new meaning under the same name. Elements of the occasion (moment) for reconciliation are thus set in relief. The judgment of faith recognizes normative guiding ideas of the Christian concept of reconciliation as existing in the implicit axiom of past politics. In part, the reconstruction of Christian reconciliation thinking appears to approach what could be considered the process of spiritual reconciliation "translating" itself into political reality.

Signs of transcendence of spiritual reconciliation can be seen in the process of the working out of a guilt-laden past in the political arena. In the designated categories above, the content of political reconciliation is "non-transferable" to theological reconciliation under ontological conditions: there is no way in which to "reconstruct" reciprocity with the political.

In this context (of non-transferability), there clearly emerges what both the church and theology realistically would expect of political processes; namely, a fundamental openness. The proceedings observed in political reality may have a theological dimension, but they are not all suitable for a

An Overview[208]

"Penultimate" (political reconciliation)		"Ultimate" (spiritual reconciliation)
Legal Categories *Moral Categories*		*Theological Categories*
Punishment (Option 1)	≠ (not reconstructed as transferable)	(punishment is not ultimately valid)
Amnesty (Option 2)	≠ (not reconstructed as transferable)	(freedom from punishment is not forgiveness)
	↔ Truth (Option 3)	↔ (at the time spiritually reconstructed) Christ as the truth that makes free
	↔ Making amends (Option 4)	↔ (at the time spiritually non-transferable) Christ restores our connection to the Father
	↔ New Beginning (Option 5)	↔ (at the time nontransferable) God holds ready for us in Christ a new beginning

mono-causal theology. Justice does not produce (effective) reconciliation, but it can lead to it and can guide the processes to an acceptance of guilt, as seen in cases where the TRC was able to motivate offenders like Jeffrey Benzien to make statements before the commission. Furthermore, what is encountered in the interpersonal or "inner" dimension of the process remains "open," and must necessarily remain open. Here a legitimate theological criterion applies: justice must conserve the basic worth of humanity. From the theological perspective it is desirable that the law aids in avoiding political "self-absolutizing" in transitional societies and instead remains open to an interpersonal relationship of a "higher quality," thus allowing occasions for the recognition of spiritual reconciliation in intra- and interpersonal processes. The rules of the TRC, the appointment of the EK, but also those of the 1991 State Security Service Document Law are examples of where the South African Truth Commission clearly showed how a morally and legally differentiated process can provide an open space for an event which, external to human possibilities, has its basic content in the "paving the way" for the "ultimate" by the "penultimate," and thereby, from a methodological standpoint, does not force reconciliation.

(b) The Process of Political Reconciliation
and Spiritual Reconciliation

In the chapter that discussed counter arguments regarding political reconciliation (compare Part II.A.III/B.III), we firmly asserted the regulative idea that "reconciliation is a process." The question now, however, is how political reconciliation bears up under the theological process of reconciliation (see under 2.a). The question of correspondence suggests: does political talk of "reconciliation as process" have a basic connection to theological reconciliation as its own concept of process?

This particular question of correspondence will be developed in two stages. First, we will examine the basic connection of the idea of "national" reconciliation as a process in order to consequently examine the empirically analyzed "interpersonal" reconciliation process for its basic theological connection to spiritual reconciliation. To what extent does the reconciliation process correlate to and diverge from Biblical reconciliation?

The South African goal of "nation building," as well as the goal of "inner unity" (after a change of heart), was achieved according to a "process." Let us recall the title of the EK: "Overcoming the Consequences of the SED Dictatorship in the Process of German Unity." In addition, the Final Report of the South African TRC mentions national reconciliation as both a "goal and a process." Appropriate to the political self-understanding of this "process," we evaluated results with regard to the development of the proceedings in both countries in the context of their stated goals (aa), (bb), etc. and focused on key points from analytical philosophy (the "mixed question"): the framing conditions of the chapter on balancing, or counter-arguments (Part II.A.III.1/B.III.1) were defined by mandates (tasks and goals) on the one hand, and final reports (results) on the other. The formulated results were those of process. The political self-understanding of process reckons with a succession of events in (sharply) defined goals. In this predominantly teleological understanding of process, the goals applied were evaluated at the end as either reached — or not reached. In part, the expectations of the unconditional fulfillment of the goals were established in process (deontological understanding). In the theological synthesis we saw the political reconciliation process from an eschatological perspective. The relative goals with regard to ends which were inherent in the proceedings are, in terms of validity, no longer viewed from the standpoint of human activity, but are interpreted from the perspective of God's promise for history, which is fulfilled through God's activity. Are the relative goals of political processes ultimately constituted by the fulfillment of God's promise for the future?

The understanding of process that has been developed in these pages does not reckon with a process (progress, etc.) of salvation in the historical-political realm, but with one that is interrupted through the (in terms of time and of quality) final, justifying and reconciling word of God. Thus, "time" remains a "partial place" as a category between political and spiritual reconciliation, since only the person who in time has been charged and found guilty (as well as by God) is able to be justified and reconciled: justification and reconciliation are completed in the interruption of the connection of guilt which means the "breaking in" of the ultimate (times of mercy) into the penultimate as an interruption and intervention. A person (justification) or a relationship (reconciliation) is thus essentially changed and is fundamentally new. Signs of transcendence in such events are not discernable in the empirically analyzed material of "national reconciliation" with respect to "the growing together of East-West." Rather, the process of "German unity" and of "nation building" still remains uninterrupted.

The word "reconciliation" is emphasized in the political process of South Africa: here we encounter explicit talk of "national" reconciliation. The requirements for terminology are theological only in so far as a "connection of guilt" exists between blacks and whites. A reconciliation process which could (on a national level) provide for the admission of guilt of whites and the forgiveness of blacks is missing. In any event, individual elements of it can be seen in the process. However, for a theological synthesis the question of subject is determinative (similar to the problem of amnesty). The nation as a subject of "national reconciliation" is an a-personal category. A nation can not (theologically viewed) feel "remorse" nor can it "change" or "forgive." Guilt and reconciliation can only be thought of as occurring between people; they are personal categories having to do with guilt and reconciliation between white people and black people, not between blacks and whites as national entities.

However, it must be considered that the South African process of transition is fundamentally open in its political self-understanding; in any case "reconciliation" is not used theologically univocally. If one uses the term reconciliation in an exclusively Christian sense (with its connotation of guilt and sin), one has to choose the English word for "atonement." However, there is no discussion of "national atonement." In South Africa it had to do with inner peace — of peaceful co-existence — which does not include forced dealing with guilt or forgiveness. Political reconciliation in view of "nation" thus means something quite different than spiritual reconciliation. In this context, the German "process of growing together of East and West" completely avoids the vocabulary of "reconciliation," which appears to be theologically appropriate. One could view it as an indirect indication that reconciliation in the German prefers the connotation of English "atonement." (The weaker English word "reconciliation" is obviously not connected with the German word for reconciliation.) There is a connection to content in the language itself: the missing connection of guilt between former East and West Germany is not just ascribed to the a-personal category of "national" reconciliation. There are several omitted examples in the German case studies which (in comparison to South Africa) could have been used to show how East Germans and West Germans (as people!) would have been guilty toward each other, which would have led to a level playing field and making amends.

As a result it can be asserted that political reconciliation as the growing together of a nation does not appear to have a basic connection to theological reconciliation. The regulative statement "national reconciliation is a process" that is active behind the political reality of both transitional societies, is not transferable in spiritual terms. As in the theological synthesis of past political options for action, punishment with regard to amnesty for serious human rights violations does not theologically devalue the final establishment of a political attempt at national unity and reconciliation. On the basis of reason, this attempt can be seen and understood as an expression of the loving desire of God to preserve His creation.

In this section, we will examine the observed interpersonal reconciliation proceedings of the political forums of the TRC and the EK for their basic connection to the Biblical reconciliation process. To what extent does the political reconciliation process correspond to and diverge from the Biblical? Answers to these questions are found through an analysis of the interdependence of the observed elements (telling the truth, forgiveness, new beginning, making amends) in contrast to Biblical reconciliation. These analytical steps are different from the previous ones to the degree that the elements do not provide any opportunity for synthesis, but are examined for their reciprocity (political as well as biblical): to what extent are the conditions for reconciliation based on telling the truth, remorse, forgiveness, making amends, and a new beginning? Here we are reminded of the regulative statements that were analyzed for elements of the political path to reconciliation.

What is the Biblical path to reconciliation? What elements does it include? In order to be able to examine interpersonal reconciliation in political reality-referencing norms, these questions must first be discussed using an interim deductive step. This leads us behind the principles of systematic theology's observations on process (from 2a) back to the individual Biblical elements of its witness regarding reconciliation. An analysis of the pertinent Biblical references has, in view of our problem, already been done. We will now consider the actual state of research in which C. Breytenbach has emphasized central elements of the reconciliation process in the Pauline corpus[209] as well as those from the Synoptic Gospels, especially with regard to the path to reconciliation in Matthew in the work of Joachim Zehner.[210] Donald Shriver[211] has developed the elements of Biblical reconciliation in particular reference to the Joseph story. In addition to these significant studies, which provide a paradigm for the development of our problem, there is the weight of systematic-theological literature which allows stories of Biblical reconciliation to be interpreted within the context of political processes.[212] The actual state of research reveals a gap indicating the lack of a constructive connection between the various individual results of the larger studies. In what systematic connection does the Pauline path to reconciliation stand to Synoptic stories of reconciliation or to those of the Pentateuch? Are there, for example, elements that are structurally the same or similar that serve to advance a normative examination of the observed interpersonal path to reconciliation in the politics of the past?

Let us first proceed to the studies mentioned above. C. Breytenbach's view of the Pauline adaptation of the concept of reconciliation from the language of diplomacy now becomes important with regard to process. Breytenbach speaks of the process of reconciliation as including specific elements: "(a) the invitation to reconciliation by one of the opposing parties, (b) the acceptance of the invitation by the other side, (c) the new relation of friendship that replaces the old one of animosity. Accordingly, Paul situates (a) the deed of reconciliation in God (II Cor. 5:19a; Romans 5:10); (b) allowing of oneself to be reconciled (II Cor. 5:20) with respect to the acceptance of reconciliation (Romans 5:11); and (c) the new relation of peace between the reconciled parties (Romans 5:10) as the three aspects of the reconciling event."[213]

According to Breytenbach, the three-pronged path to reconciliation positions the political and theological in a structurally logical relationship (and does not cancel the elements of God's reconciliation over a process in time): between the invitation to reconciliation, its acceptance, and the new relation of friendship, no time elapses in the analogous relationship of God to man.

Here we first obtain an indication that the (spiritual) path to reconciliation is not the same as the (political) path to reconciliation. J. Zehner says that divine and human forgiveness are decidedly different where, on the one hand, he speaks of forgiveness between men as a "process of forgiveness," "because many years pass between the first meeting . . . and the readiness to forgive."[214] On the other hand, through confession the person experiences "the entire and immediate absolution of forgiveness because it is God's forgiveness. Here there is no process of forgiveness; no time frame which is sometimes necessary for man and can be meaningful in interpersonal forgiveness on the path to reconciliation."[215]

Zehner formulates the "path of reconciliation" from his analysis of Matthew 18:10ff. The goal of the Biblical passage is not to chastise the church, but reconciliation. Through forgiveness, brothers or sisters will be won again for the congregation. Zehner states in terms of terminology that the "path of reconciliation" is a better concept for interpersonal forgiveness than confession or repentance because it names the goal right away and has the character of process; "the way of forgiveness is a better expression."[216] The path of reconciliation includes the "reprimanding of the sinner and the revealing of guilt." A "process" or "path" is made. The three-pronged path to reconciliation includes the elements for the process of forgiveness: (a) remorse, guilt, (b) recognition of sin, absolution, (c) and an Evangelical understanding of making amends (reparations). The "three stations" are suggested as "accepting the forgiveness of God through the understanding of the Christian week and church year," where on Saturday the traditional confessional element of "remorse" leads to Sunday's "acknowledgement" and "absolution"; the following week days, understood in the Evangelical sense, are designated for "making amends."

Similar to J. Zehner, D. Shriver[217] makes a distinction between divine and political forgiveness. "For God, forgiveness may be a single, mighty act, but for man — and even if there are only two (people) — the classical components of forgiveness require time."[218] Again as in Zehner there is a teleological process that guides the understanding of "reconciliation" — "as the final, longed for condition (sic!)."[219] Teleology and eschatology appear to mean the same thing for Shriver.[220] Forgiveness is "procedural" in terms of individual elements and designated components. The "steps on the path to reconciliation" are: "1) the opening and the naming of the injustice, 2) refraining from revenge 'coin for coin,' 3) the development of empathy with the offender; 4) and the attempt at a new community." These four elements encompass the "process of forgiveness." The element of "forgiveness" in rec-

Overview

Elements of the path to reconciliation in Paul (in the interpretation of Breytenbach)	Elements of the path to reconciliation in Matthew (in the interpretation of Zehner)	Elements of the Biblical and political path to reconciliation (in the understanding of Shriver)
a) Invitation to reconciliation		
Political: through one of the two contesting parties	Political/legal: readiness to meet each other	Political: 1) Acceptance of a moral judgment; 2) thankful acknowledgement of the rejection of revenge; 3) empathy for the injuries incurred
b) Acceptance of the invitation		
Political: through the other side	Political/legal: discussion of the deed, recognition of the consequences	Political: 1) naming of the injustice/ recollection of the horror; 2) rejection of revenge: 3) empathy
c) New Relationship		
Political: friendship that replaces the old animosity	Political/legal: work at compromise	Political: 4) the attempt at renewed community through striving for a new relationship to the enemy
Theological: new relation of peace of the reconciled	Theological: Evangelical understanding of making amends	Theological: see former column (new relationship of peace between the reconciled)

onciliation also subdivides into four parts. Shriver's view is strictly aligned with the perspective of the victim (in the interpersonal reconciliation process). He includes the offender only in passing: "in the end, forgiveness still has a twin called remorse. Without remorse there can be no true forgiveness" (the mention of a "twin" is important for the question of interdependence of the individual elements on the path of reconciliation; the metaphor indicates the same origin for a relationship to remorse and no chronology for the institution of confession). Shriver's analysis of the concept of forgiveness is based on Biblical and basic theological ideas. A clearly recognizable element from the Joseph story[221] is the "naming of guilt" (element 1), but also the main theological difference between the sin and the sinner (behind the elements of forgiveness 2 and 3). Similar to Breytenbach, element c, the "new relation," appears in Shriver as an aspect of forgiveness 4, which now makes possible a new beginning and the "renewed community."

It is interesting that all three designs, although directed by different Biblical motives, represent specific fundamental connections between theological and political reconciliation. A harmonizing of the three models is rejected, even if structural parallels can be seen in the developed paths of reconciliation that correlate to the political level (see overview). Rather, the independence of the models should be acknowledged to the extent that they have their own specific "political context" and pose "their" own questions of correspondence. For the development of our problem, the work on reconciliation by Breytenbach and Shriver is particularly fruitful. However, let us first ask about the basic theological relationship to reconciliation of the outlined criterion. The models have parallel elements to the path of reconciliation taken from Biblical evidence (in whose fundamental connection the political proceedings are placed). The classical elements of repentance emerge; namely remorse and forgiveness (absolution), which lead to a new beginning in relationship to God (and to man, since reparations are a sign of "active remorse").

The elements that were developed from the Biblical findings (Overview) will be enlisted in the following theologically normative examination in which the interpersonal reconciliation processes, observed on the forum of the TRC and also the EK, will be examined. However, our analysis of process (2a) makes it necessary in advance to use conceptual precision as well as to manipulate the content. Obviously, in the context of our category of process there are gaps in the process understanding of forgiveness with respect to Zehner and Shriver. These gaps concern key theological contents of the political analysis; namely the fundamental relationship of spiritual reconciliation. For Zehner as well as Shriver, the logical elements of reconciliation (above all the element of forgiveness) are released over a period of time whose end point is then termed "reconciliation." Both models appear to be directed in an Aristotelian-teleological understanding of process. If both models were to be shaped constructively, then they can only be so through the critical transformation of two basic problems: first, the concept of process must be more precise; and second, the relationship between the concepts of forgiveness and reconciliation ought to be weighted differently.

266

According to our deliberations, eschatology and teleology (2a/b) are distinctly different categories. Spiritual reconciliation does not occur at the end of the process as its *telos*. Rather, it interrupts the process and declares it as something penultimate. Reconciliation does not complete time, but judges it. The Word arrives in time as something that fractures time — and something new emerges. The Evangelical concept of process justification and reconciliation can not be conceived of using an Aristotelian-Thomist category of time. Redemptive events of the penultimate are not expandable in terms of time, even if they necessarily require the time-bound, penultimate in order to achieve actuality. Only in time can we speak of guilt and reconciliation; and so, only in terms of the breaking through of the process connection by faith in the justifying and reconciling word of God.

What does this knowledge mean for the path to reconciliation? First, it means that theologically as well as linguistically "process" is to be distinguished from "path." The political process of reconciliation is open and indeterminate. The spiritual path to reconciliation is defined by hope. It counts on the promise that is hidden in the elements of remorse and forgiveness and says nothing, however, about their respective process in time with regard to inner development. Before the questions of subjective-anthropological or objective-Christological foundations can be formulated we must clarify that a "process" is never a spiritual process according to Evangelical understanding, but is a "way" that names "spiritual" elements or stations that designate the end or turning point for reconciliation (like remorse and absolution). Strictly speaking, there is no such thing as process of spiritual reconciliation: "spiritual" and "process" are mutually exclusive. However, the path to reconciliation can identify "stations" without having to configure the time frame for the "travel plan" that designates the arrival time for the stations of spiritual "interruption."

How are these interruptions in the political reconciliation process discernable? The answers lies (deviating from Shriver and Zehner) in that they are discernable in the elements of spiritual reconciliation themselves: forgiveness interrupts the process of political reconciliation which seeks the overcoming of guilt. Forgiveness itself is the act, the "process" that interrupts sin.[222] Something new emerges: a "relationship of peace" is possible. Thus, forgiveness marks a central element in the path to spiritual reconciliation. "Through a single act of forgiveness the never-ending chain of evil can be averted."[223] The guiding difference between divine and human (forgiveness) thus does not lie in the concept of forgiveness, as Zehner and Shriver would have it, but in the concept of process. Forgiveness is always spiritual. Where "spiritual" and "process" exclude each other, it makes no sense theologically to speak of a "process of forgiveness."

One could say that with forgiveness God leaves behind his "finger prints"[224] on political reality. Where forgiveness actually is understood and not burdened by an understanding of process means that, at the same time, there is an unburdening of the weight of the concept of forgiveness. Now the entire path of reconciliation does not need to be placed under the category of forgiveness. The path of reconciliation is accordingly neither a pure "process of forgiveness" (Zehner) nor must the concept of forgiveness carry the burden of all elements of the path of reconciliation (of the "naming of guilt" until to the "new peace relation," Shriver). Rather, forgiveness is an element — albeit a central spiritual element — on the path to reconciliation.

Where forgiveness is released from the concept of process, constructive elements affiliated with the path to reconciliation in Shriver and Zehner can be observed. Now the single elements of forgiveness (which, for example, Shriver names) must not be thought of in a historical succession as a "redemption process"; rather they mark elements of the "spiritual preparing the way" (Bonhoeffer). They do not describe "forgiveness as a spiritual act," but as a station of the penultimate: wherever guilt is remembered and given a name, there the way for forgiveness is prepared. However, the recollection of guilt with regard to giving it a name is not forgiveness. Where revenge "coin for coin" is rejected, the way to forgiveness is prepared; yet, "refraining from revenge" is still not forgiveness. Where the victims take the trouble to empathize with their offenders "the way is prepared" for forgiveness; but forgiveness as a spiritual act is still an event. Where the attempt is made to renew community there forgiveness has begun; but this is also not a description of forgiveness.

Spiritual reconciliation does not describe "the entire long process,"[225] "begun by the first knowledge of the injustice, to the abolishment of the injustice, and to the ritual of conciliation" (as in an ontological concept of process); nor does it mean "only the rite of conciliation" (re: Shriver and Zehner). The spiritual path to reconciliation cites "stations" or elements which must be present if, in theological terms, traces of spiritual reconciliation are to be recognized in political reality. The *condicio sine qua non* of spiritual reconciliation is remorse and forgiveness (absolution), which leads to a new beginning in relation to God (and man).

The order of the reciprocal conditions of the individual elements must therefore be settled. It must also be examined whether a reconstruction of theological reconciliation with respect to the interdependence of individual elements within past political dealings with guilt is possible. Do interpersonal reconciliation processes, as we have observed them in the political forums of the TRC in South Africa and the EK in Germany, appear in a fundamental connection to the spiritual path of reconciliation?

In a first step, let us recall the observed elements of the process of political reconciliation. On the interpersonal reconciliation level, the following were regulative in TRC process:

- On the side of the offender: apology in the form of remorse and in the request for forgiveness.
- On the side of the victim: acceptance of the apology as forgiveness and the readiness for new community.

These basic elements correlate to the political path of reconciliation according to Breytenbach (offer of reconciliation, acceptance, peaceful relations). However, do they also stand (as in Paul) in a fundamental theological connection? Formally, it must be maintained that elements of the spiritual path of reconciliation are encountered in political reality. Let us recall, concerning the "invitation to reconciliation," the request for forgiveness by Philemon Maxan, the apologies of Jeffrey Benzein, and those of the former DDR minister of culture Dietmar Keller before the EK. Let us also recall the "acceptance of reconciliation" and the "rejection of revenge" (Shriver) by Conraad van Rooyens, which reoccur as structural statements by victims of the SED (such as Herr Brümmer or Frau Rührdanz). And let us consider the "new relation of friendship" in the example of the desire for renewed community between Maxan and Dr. Siebert.

Accordingly, the chart on pages 270-71 provides a summary of the specific elements of the process of political reconciliation:

The analyzed elements of the process of political reconciliation will be considered from a theologically normative position in the following. In terms of the above overview, the contents of the gaps move from left to right: from "invitation to reconciliation" to the "acceptance" of "new peace relation of the reconciled." As outlined above, these distinctions do not describe an *ordo salutis;* rather, they are arranged as individual statements with respect to the question of correspondence in order to be able to situate its fundamental connection to remorse and forgiveness (absolution). Is the process of political reconciliation something that can be reconstructed as corresponding to the spiritual; namely, that remorse leads to forgiveness?

1. The "invitation to reconciliation" encountered in political reality is

Acts of Remorse ↓		Acts of Forgiveness ↓
"Invitation to Reconciliation" on the side of the offender: as a process that includes: asking for forgiveness/remorse/apology/change/"acceptance of moral judgment" (Shriver); on the side of the victim: "the naming of the injustice" (Shriver)	"Acceptance of Reconciliation" on the side of the victim: as a process that includes: "Rejection of revenge/empathy with the offender" (Shriver) On the side of the offender: "empathy for the injured" (Shriver)	"New Relations" as a process that includes: "Attempt at a renewed community through striving for a new relationship with the enemy" (Shriver)/making amends

TRC Hearings

Maxan: ". . . ask for forgiveness"	Dr. Siebert: ". . . hold no grudge against him" (empathy with the offender)	New relations between Maxan and the Siebert family (interpersonal) and new relations between Maxan and his community (communal level of reconciliation) (reparations are missing)
(Naming of the injustice)	Van Rooyen: ". . . It could also have been me at that level" (Rejection of revenge/no empathy on the part of the offender/no forgiveness)	(No new relation with the enemy, but co-existence)
Benzien: ". . . I apologize" (apologies)	Forbes (empathy on the part of the offender/ — forgiveness). Other victims of Benzien only: rejection of revenge	(A new relationship as well as making amends — on the side of Benzien — is missing)
". . . I, Jeff B., have asked my self that question to such an extent that I voluntarily approached psychiatrists. . . . If you ask what type of person is it that can do that, I ask myself the same question." (Remorse?)	Benzien: ". . . I concede that no matter how bad I feel . . . what was done to you, must have been worse . . ." (empathy for the injuries)	

EK Hearings

Sigrid Rührdanz: "The horrible deeds must be told" (naming of the injustice)	Brümmer: "I have no hate toward the people who flailed me. I would gladly have a dispute with them." (Rejection of revenge/no empathy in the offender because there is no meeting/no forgiveness, but co-existence). Rührdanz: "To me it had to do with recovery, and that is not acknowledged."	(new relation missing) (making amends on the part of the state through rehabilitation and reparation)
Keller: ". . . we all carry . . . the responsibility to see the story as it was and not as we would like to see it" (apology)	Yes, in so far as the statements of the participants (in the sense of taking part in observations) allow.	(missing)
	Keller: ". . . the hearings were the bitterest hour of my life. . ." (empathy for the injured)	(missing)

Print Media — Disputes

Loest: ". . . regarding Loest there are comprehensive measurable explanations to be made" (naming of the injustice)	Keller: "The more I know. . .the higher is my esteem for you and what you have lived through." (empathy for the injuries)	(missing)
Keller: ". . . I have naturally offended through my activities in the party apparatus" (apology/remorse)	Loest: "My nod indicates that I find this change significant" (empathy of the offender)	(missing)

multifaceted; the elements are not defined (inherently) individually (univocally). Thus, the expression of the "remorse" or the "apology" reaches through political players (in the reception of the hearer) at various "depths" and appears (correspondingly) to be "accepted or not accepted." Normatively it can be stated that (a) forgiveness does not describe a process, (b) is a personal category, (c) assumes a connection to guilt, as well as d) the distinction between deed and the person. In order to be able to discuss it as differentiated from the other examples, we ask in what (univocal) theological sense remorse *(contritio)* is mentioned. I will limit myself to the basic features of reformation theology.[226] According to the Confessions of Augustine,[227] confession consists of remorse and faith *(fides)*. *Contritio* means, "the terror that follows upon the knowledge once the sins have been made known." The other part of confession is "the faith which is received and given by the announcement of the Gospel *(ex absolutione)* that for Christ's sake one's sins are forgiven and so is comforted and freed from terror *(liberat)*." The two parts are structurally based in Luther's[228] ideas in the 95 Theses: remorse over sin and forgiveness from God alone,[229] and faith that drives the behavior of confession in which the entire life of the person is now transferred to a reliance on the grace of God alone.[230] In his *sermo de poenitentia* (1518),[231] Luther does not discuss remorse, but rather faith that allows us to take part in the mercy and forgiveness of God through the person of Christ. Forgiveness is not attained because of one's worthiness, but because of faith. Confession achieves a different end which does not rely on the ability to remorse, but on the word of Christ.[232] Indeed, Luther retained formally the three parts of confession *(contritio cordis, confessio oris, satifactio operis)*,[233] but essentially nullifies their meaning: where faith is lacking there is no need for remorse, confession, or absolution.[234] Article XII of the Augburg Confessions corresponds to the outline of Luther's understanding of atonement: atonement is not a particular action, but it is (as are remorse and faith) given to the Christian life in the Word of God, according to the law and the Gospel.[235] Reformation theology understands atonement as a work of God, and indeed as His alien, foreign work *(opus alienum)* that drives people to his *opus proprium*. Remorse is then a *"passiva contritio"*; not a work of men, but the revealing of sin through the Gospel.[236] Accordingly, there is a systematic connection between the Reformation understanding of atonement and our analysis of the category of process: namely, there is a corresponding relationship of "law" and "Gospel," and "remorse" and "faith," that can be correlated to "process" and "interruption." "Remorse" describes the deep, final turning point of a process which, when interrupted, is judged by and then freed through the Gospel (*liberat!* Confessions XII). Remorse is the way in which God leads man to himself. And because man always exists in sin, he must always be led anew to the Gospel; namely, to live in atonement (in this connection it is clear why Bonhoeffer speaks of atonement's "preparing the way").[237]

The normative intermediate step allows the progression of the theological synthesis. From our case study research, the dialogue on the interpersonal level of reconciliation between Benzien-Forbes, Maxan–Dr. Siebert, and Keller-Loest should be examined where the first (reconciliation) plays a key role. Concerning the theological discussion of amnesty, we asked whether any of Benzien's statements during his amnesty hearings before the TRC touched on a theological understanding of remorse. This question should now be considered with more precision. Thus, we ask in a first step about understandings of remorse that should be excluded. That is, no doubt, the *attritio.* Remorse as a result of fear of punishment is not advocated. According to the statutes of the TRC, amnesty was not connected to remorse. In any event, Benzien's amnesty proposal at best was not compromised by loopholes. A discussion of missing memories can be absent in Evangelical considerations, because they correspond to an understanding of confession where all individual deeds *(omnium delictorum)* must be fully listed.[238] Furthermore, the appearance before the TRC does not correspond to a confession. The Reformation emphasizes the private character of confession in the church.[239] Although certain ideas of remorse can be left out, we proceed to a constructive interpretation on the horizon of the Reformation understanding of remorse with regard to several of the key dialogues:

Mr. Jacobs: I was the first survivor of your torture method, you would concede that, you say?

Mr. Benzien: Yes.

Mr. Jacobs: Yet, you appeared to be very effective at what you were doing. . . .

Mr. Benzien: I can't answer how effective it was.

Mr. Jacobs: Are you a natural talent at this, I mean, do you think? . . .

Mr. Benzien: I wouldn't know if I have a natural talent for it; it is not a very nice talent to have.

Mr. Jacobs: Okay. . . . If it is not a very nice talent to have, you went on, if you say from nine o'clock till two o'clock, which is quite a few hours, you went on for long with something you are not very comfortable with? How do you explain that?

Mr. Benzien: Mr. Jacobs, the method employed by me is something that I have to live with and no matter how I try to interpret what I did, I still find it deplorable. I find it exceptionally difficult to relate, sitting here in front of everybody. I concede that no matter how bad I feel about it, what was done to you and your colleagues, must have been worse. Believe me, I am not gloating or trying to prove that I am somebody who I am not.

273

Mr. Yengeni: What kind of man uses a method like this . . . to other human beings . . . ?

Mr. Benzien: I, Jeff Benzien, have asked myself that question to such an extent that I voluntarily approached psychiatrists. . . . If you ask me what type of person is it that can do that, I must ask myself the same question.

The theologically conspicuous passages in Benzien's responses are "it is not a nice talent to have" or "I find it exceptionally difficult to relate, sitting here in front of everybody." While the first statement revolves around a new interpretation of the deed, the last one openly expresses "shame." The problem of the "public" is already responded to. Shame forces something else: the "inner person" steps forward. The change not only affects the deed, but also the people. An innermost change reveals itself; the "conscience is terrified with horror." In the last sentence, Benzien questions himself: "I must ask myself the same question." It becomes clear that *contritio* not only addresses individual offences, but grounds itself in remorse in the knowledge of the sin that is brought by the law which says that everything about man stands under the curse of sin. Benzien "awakens" from the nightmare of apartheid, which is now recognized theologically as a sin against God. To this extent, it is an awakening from animosity against God. Repentance is an "awakening," as Karl Barth aptly says: "The sleep from which people are awakened from the oral to the written, is their journey on a path of turning: a path upon which they know themselves to be changed and also must remain changed."[240]

Benzien's "awakening" did not happen because of fear, necessity, or intimidation; it arose from an inner, free willingness ushered in by the naming of the relevant circumstances in fulfillment of the criterion for amnesty (legal level). "Truth" receives yet another level in the personal encounter with the victims, indicating a moral dimension: the victims place the person behind the action "in question." The offenders are hounded by suspicion. In this "hounded by vigilance" the spiritual function of the "atonement sermon" can be recognized (theological level). Now it no longer has to do in a moral paradigm with the "recognizable benchmark of moral behavior."[241] Now the person will, through the law and beyond, be led to the deepest point of (confusion), putting the old "I" into question. Shriver's criterion for forgiveness, "naming of the injustice," is the theological component of the "invitation to reconciliation." It has to do with the call to repentance which precedes the change. In "naming of the injustice" (according to Yengeni and

Forbes) the call to "turning" of the Gospel and the prophets can be recognized. The example of Benzien shows that reconciliation (in the aspect of remorse) places confrontation with the truth (as the naming of the injustice) at the forefront. To this degree, the truth (in the form of confessional sermon) prepares the way for reconciliation. Thus, the political formula "reconciliation through truth" can be "translated" to the spiritual (level).

Of all of the empirical analyzed examples of dialogue, that between Benzien and his victims is theologically the strongest, because in his statements we encounter signs of transcendence in political reality.

2. "Acceptance of Reconciliation." "When we have taken this first difficult step of repentance," writes Miroslav Volf, "we have traveled a good distance on the road to reconciliation. The next step is forgiveness." [242] Volf meanwhile disagrees with Shriver's time-bound process solution for reconciliation.[243] For Volf, there are graduated logical steps on the path of reconciliation, but they do not reveal their historical consequences. Our examples likewise show that the acts of "remorse" and "forgiveness" exist quite apart from each other. Between the remorse felt by Benzien and the forgiveness of Ashley Forbes there is a "distance" that is bridged by the hearings. When the act of forgiveness occurs, it remains hidden. Yet, it occurs: "I have forgiven him," as we have cited Forbes above as saying. Between the act of forgiveness, time elapses — as do processes — in the penultimate: whether the offender shows "empathy for the injuries incurred" preceding the actual act of remorse, or whether the victim displays the "rejection of revenge" with regard to "sympathy with the enemy" in the actual act of forgiveness. Shriver's categories name penultimate moments that logically precede the ultimate in time; however, they are not spiritual. Shriver makes the point in one place very impressively: "Forgiveness begins with the victims giving up thoughts of revenge and the offenders renouncing their protests of innocence."[244] The invitation to reconciliation can thus commence either from the side of the victim or that of the offender (see Overview).

How are both elements connected in our examples of the case studies: does remorse determine forgiveness? Or does the readiness to forgive on the part of the victim require the knowledge of guilt of the offender? Interestingly enough, our examples with respect to these questions are not obvious; they indicate, however, that both elements must be present. The example of Benzien-Forbes shows that they mutually affect each other: the invitation to reconciliation as the questioning of the person (not only the deed) and the acceptance of reconciliation as the distinction between the deed and the person. Where the offender questions himself and the victim is ready to accept the person (behind the deed) a way is prepared for forgiveness. It is especially impressive that forgiveness is a personal event. Where forgiveness is lacking, the offender languishes together with his deeds and is consigned with them to death. In forgiveness, however, the eternal breaks into our temporal existence. The pressure to connect the offender and his deed is interrupted. To this degree, forgiveness is a freeing event of release; it shows once more that the person is more than the sum of their deeds.

Both elements of the political path of reconciliation — the placing into question of the person and their acceptance — correspond to the work of God in remorse and absolution. They are to be understood in fundamental connection to the treatment of guilt, which God in Christ has made possible for us; namely, through reconciliation.

The "invitation to reconciliation" is not accepted in all political cases. While Dr. Siebert — similar to Forbes — *expressis verbis* certifies that he had forgiven, univocal statements in the dialogue between Loest-Keller are difficult (to find): Loest finds the change in the former DDR Minister of Culture very "respectful," but an act of forgiveness is not perceptible. (Keller's "sympathy with the injuries" of Loest also does not correlate with those that would be understood theologically as remorse.) This example shows that Shriver's category of "avoidance of revenge" and "sympathy in the offender" indeed can prepare the way for forgiveness, but they ultimately do not compel forgiveness from a methodological standpoint. We therefore have evidence that the process of reconciliation remains "open ended" in political reality.

In summary, three conditions emerge for the "acceptance of reconciliation" on the political scene:

1. *Remorse on the part of the offender.* Our introductory hypothesis, whereby the acceptance of reconciliation depends on the "depth of remorse," proves to be reliable on the basis of our reflections on confession: "depth" here means that the person questions himself. The addressed person appears to "sense" the "inner change." We receive a clue to the theological definition of remorse where, in the example of the former DDR minister, an apology (through the applause of the members of Parliament) is acknowledged.

2. *The readiness to forgive on the part of the victim.* The example of Rooyen, but also Brümmer and Rührdanz indicate that the "invitation to reconciliation" is not credible where it does not involve a personal encounter with the offender. "Where nobody asks for forgiveness, they can not receive forgiveness."[245] Indeed, we encounter in the above examples elements of the process of reconciliation such as the "avoidance of revenge" or the "naming

of the injustice" (theologically translated: "confessional sermon"). But "it is not enough," as Rainer Eppelmann says of the interpersonal character of forgiveness, "if only one party says: I am ready! The other must also follow suit."[246] For example, Mr. Brümmer says before the EK: "I harbor no hatred against the people (sic), who have harmed me. I would gladly have a talk with them." Still, where the personal encounter with the victims is missing, so also the "naming of the injustice" on the part of the victim is also missing; a process of "sympathy with the injuries" of the victims cannot take place, which is preceded by remorse. Accordingly, the guilt remains unresolved on the part of the offender (as neither forgotten nor forgiven). The interpersonal process of reconciliation for the victim is then limited to the intrapersonal level.

The conditions for the "acceptance of reconciliation" indicated correlations between the process of political reconciliation and Biblical reconciliation. The political invitation to reconciliation appears in fundamental connection to the Pauline, where it is argued: "Christ, the Word of reconciliation, places himself between the offender and the victim and bridges the divide that exists between them. Only thus is forgiveness possible, which does not attempt either to justify the past or to deny it. This Word also indicates the boundary of healing between the silence that is unacceptable for the victim . . . and the unending self-recriminations that cannot heal and that hold the victim captive."[247]

In addition to correspondence, the following observations regarding differences come to light: there is a wide gap between the "invitation to reconciliation" and its acceptance in the interpersonal process, as we saw in the example of Benzien-Forbes. The space between remorse and forgiveness means a "risk" for the political process of reconciliation. On the political scene — even if they simulate closed spaces — an offender can also not be sure of expressed "remorse" of "absolution." On the other hand, the forum of forgiveness in the church must *(debeat)* be given to those who repent *(cum conventuntur)* and absolution *(absolutionem impartiri)* as well.[248] Forgiveness and remorse work closely together, because sin can only be first seen in light of forgiveness.[249] The Reformation understanding of a forced interdependence between remorse and absolution (in so far as both are an original work of God) is lacking in the political realm. Rather, the *reservatio*,[250] at least in the sense that it is reserved for the victim to forgive, is encountered.

The Kantian notion that only the victims have the right to forgive[251] receives new meaning in the idea of representation. Now it means the end of the myth of sin and with it to accept Christ as *the* sacrificial victim and to demand no other victim's sacrifice. Thus, the right of the victim not to forgive loses its integrity from the theological perspective, for ambivalence about forgiving is not tenable for the Christian.

According to the Reformation understanding of repentance there is nothing automatic about absolution. A "method," as shown, is also excluded. The condition for absolution is faith: *fides*. The path of reconciliation with God is that of a "wager": a giving of oneself over to another in the hope of something good. The difference between the process of political reconciliation and spiritual reconciliation thus does not describe some kind of total uncertainty of the outcome on the one hand, or a false security *(securitas)* on the other. Against this background, one could ask whether correspondences exist between the level of "wager" of the offenders who "question themselves" in the interpersonal reconciliation process and hope for forgiveness, and the believers who "rely on God and thus risk a wager — in the hope of (ever new) assurance."[252] (The analogy would then be hope.) Certainly there is a theological correlation in view of the desire for pardon. Pardons from political reality that reject self-justification and are placed on the (merciful) judgment of another, asking for a pardon which they wholly expect to receive, are transferable into the context of the theological. Villa-Vicencio writes: "To apologize is to declare voluntarily that one has no excuse, defense, justification or explanation for an action (or inaction)."[253] (This particular situation of people in relation to their neighbor correlates structurally to their situation before God. The manner in which these correlations can be expressed, which would supply an appropriately analogous model, will be discussed at the end of this chapter.)

Let us update the counter argument for the dimensions of the "acceptance of reconciliation" that we encountered in the forum of the TRC: the legal dimensions of the proceedings allowed for the cross examination of offenders by victims in the course of their application for amnesty. The law also gave the Commission the right to counter-examine statements by the offenders in order to be able to accept their decision for amnesty; namely, the testing of "full disclosure." The question of moral judgment remained untouched in the legal process. However, the process of questioning and placing into question a dynamic process may not be legally meaningful, but is interpersonally meaningful. The examples of the hearings of Benzien went according to the pattern of a moral dimension of process. The meeting made it possible for the offender to be confronted with the consequences of his deeds; in Shriver's category the "sympathy with the injuries" of the victim can lead to "empathy with the offender." "Empathy" is the key category not only in Shriver, but also in African self-understanding of the TRC. "The feeling of empathy is important in a restorative justice approach."[254] "Restorative justice is a process whereby all parties with a stake in a particular offence come together to resolve collectively how to deal with the aftermath of the offence and its implications for the future."[255] The category of empathy defines a moral process. One might say that the theological dimension of the reconciliation process consists in the correspondence of the mutual-sided empathy of people to the empathy of God with man; finally, "the Jesus of the Gospels as the embodiment of the empathy of God . . . , is experienced materially in peace and reconciliation."[256] These conclusions are not self-evident. They must be produced synthetically-theologically. Their confirmation requires the clarification of the relationship of correspondence in the category of empathy. Empathy is not a (morally) normative concept for the theological category of reconciliation. Reconciliation can't be prescribed; it reckons with the incalculable intersection of remorse and forgiveness that is portrayed in Biblical stories of reconciliation. Reconciliation interrupts human possibilities and does not come at the end of the (moral) process; in fact, it even reckons with the failure of the moral process. Whether in Shriver's moral categories or in the concept of "restorative justice," the temporary nature and the integration into the penultimate must emerge for the theological perspective. Where empathy is elevated to a normative concept or to something "penultimate," then (in theologically normative terms) there is a category break with spiritual reconciliation, such as the category of God's empathy. The two-sided, free view of change that marks Biblical reconciliation is the way of *theologia gloriae*. In view of "preparing the way," "reconciliation through truth" does not underscore the (moral) accusatory dimension of truth, but the theologically freeing one. The fact that "the truth is only in its original element when it frees — that is the Gospel in its original form (John 8:32)."[257] The freeing power of truth to which the Gospel of John testifies is admirably translated by Miroslav Volf as interpersonal reconciliation: "The truth will make you free, said Jesus. Free for what? — free to make journeys from the self to the other and back again, and to see our common history from their perspective as well as our own, rather than closing ourselves off . . . ; free to live a truthful life and hence be a self-effecting witness to truth rather than fabricating our own 'truths' and imposing them on others; free to embrace others in truth rather than engage in open or clandestine acts of deceitful violence against them."[258] Under these conditions, the reciprocal empathy

279

between offender and victim appears in the same manner in which they will be empirically analyzed upon political forums in its fundamental connection to God's empathy as it is embodied in Jesus Christ.

3. *"The new relationship of peace of the reconciled."* For diplomatic political reconciliation processes, which according to Breytenbach are based on the Pauline concept of reconciliation,[259] "a new relation of friendship, which replaces the old animosity" occurs upon the acceptance of the invitation to reconciliation. This correlates to the "new relationship of peace of the reconciled (Romans 5:10)" as a result of the "acceptance of reconciliation (Romans 5:11)" in terms of "allowing oneself to reconcile (II Cor. 5:20)." If one considers this correlation, three things emerge for the purposes of our inquiry: first, the political and theological have the same original logic of reconciliation. Second, (as a result) reconciliation in either the political or the theological is completed where all three aspects of the reconciliation event are fulfilled. Third, (in regard to the last aspect) the acceptance of reconciliation is connected with a new relationship in both the political and the theological.

If we examine our case study examples by means of these criteria we become aware of the fragmentary process of political reconciliation. The legal gap in the tabulated overview remains without a description in most of the examples. That being the case, the invitation to reconciliation was not submitted (as in the Stasi debate) or, where it was submitted, no body was located (as with van Rooyen or the cases before the EK). Benzien's process is theologically challenging: although we interpret his statements as remorse (and Forbes forgave him), the old animosity was not replaced with friendship; rather they both live on in "co-existence." From the theological perspective this observation marks a request for the "acceptance of reconciliation." For, according to the inner logic of the Pauline concept of reconciliation, theologically (and politically) a new relationship is created in the acceptance of the reconciliation. However, does this mean that with forgiveness the "acceptance of reconciliation" does still not take place?

Forgiveness, as we saw, interrupts the guilt connection, but does not remove it. The person is (in Pauline terms) not dead to sin; his sins are "merely" not counted against him. Reconciliation is more than forgiveness. It creates the basis for a new community. The process remains fragmentary not just because the element of "new relation" is missing; rather, it is missing because of the failure to "accept reconciliation." Failure to accept reconciliation does not mean moral regression; rather, the process is still (theologically) appropriate. The case of Benzien remains a model one despite the lack of "success of reconciliation," which "must" be seen in the "new relationship," since the case of Benzien does not only exhibit the gravity of the guilt connection (i.e., the problem of the acknowledgement of guilt and of subsequent forgiveness), but also the fragmentary nature of the entire process. The question of correspondence is again raised: do the inconclusive, incomplete, open, reconciliation proceedings in political reality have a fundamental connection to theological reconciliation? Or, are political and spiritual reconciliation opposed to each other like incompleteness and completeness? Answers to these questions are to be found in connection to theological reflections on Paul: "Because reconciliation, as well as the universal reconciled state of God, and also the human individual's acceptance of reconciliation, encompasses the universal reconciliation of the world with God as an incomplete action" (II Cor. 5:19a). Thus, reconciliation remains fragmentary, despite (forgiven) interruptions in the "penultimate." The incompleteness that we accept in the political reconciliation proceedings correlates to the incompleteness of the reconciliation of God with the world. Open or interrupted proceedings are not external to the underlying connection to theological reconciliation despite their incompleteness. They are rather part of the *status quo.*[260]

Let us finally turn to the remaining question: does a "new relationship of peace between the reconciled" occur within reparations to the victims? J. Zehner made clear that the path to reconciliation leads to reparations.[261] He thus takes up the invitation to a discussion of economics by D. Sattler in the discussion of "the human satisfaction."[262] Accordingly, as shown, Zehner's work on the theological understanding of legal proceedings regarding offender-victim-compensation indicates that reparations by the offender to the victim can take the place of punishment. The subject of reparations concerning human rights violations was the state, as seen in the examples of our case studies, and as presented in the theological synthesis of Option 4. When we examine the dialogue of the hearings for interpersonal reparations, we find a negative result: even on the basis of free will reparations do not play a role either after the forgiveness or before. Thus, the question of correspondence asks: does the process of reconciliation still exist in a basic theological connection when interpersonal reparations are lacking?

The theologically normative examination again yields results for the understanding of repentance: where *fides* and contrition are both identified as the constitutive parts of repentance, there is a connection to the statement on good works in the Augustinian Confessions XII that says they should subsequently follow *(sequi debent)* as the fruit of repentance *(deinde).*[263] If one conceives of reparations as a good work, then according to the Augustinian Confessions it would not be an essential part of repentance, but the "fruit" *(fructus)* of repentance. Here the *deinde* indicates the temporal, not final connection with the spiritual event. The fact that — as in CA VI — faith and works are connected with a "should" *(debeat)*, is not to be over es- timated linguistically, and plays a role in the further development of Melanchthon's theology.[264] In terms of content, Luther should again be mentioned where he says that the righteousness of faith means to give God honor, which means wanting to receive everything from His mercy (in Christ) so that the question does not even arise about what the person can do in relation to God. Here Christ can (represent) the person, not only at the beginning, but also for one's entire life long. Any *satisfactio* with God is ex- cluded. Indeed, repentance becomes a continuous lifelong conversion (as the movement from the law to the Gospel, of remorse to faith, or of process to uninterrupted freedom) through the dying of the old man and the becom- ing blessed by the representative atonement of Christ. According to the Ser- mon on the Sacrament of Repentance (WA 2, 713-24) suffice it to say, the best satisfaction is never to sin and to do good to one's neighbor. For Luther the idea that faith should bring forth no works at all is completely excluded, be- cause they follow with inner necessity from faith and do not need to be de- manded by means of an imperative.[265] What is important for our purpose is Luther's consideration that Christ has joined in God's work in service of the neighbor in that He is united in faith with God's work. This notion is re- ferred to in another place in an analogy to the incarnation: as Christ became man (although he as God had owned everything) so also faith becomes (al- though it has everything, namely the almighty and merciful God) "incar- nate" in love for one's neighbor.[266]

Proceeding from the normative intermediate step, two considerations are important for our line of questioning: first, the *satisfactio* (in terms of God) is excluded; second, good works (of men) flow from the acceptance of reconciliation, without which they would otherwise have to be required. In view of the "new relationship" one can formulate that where the relationship between man and God has again been made right the relationship between man and man can also be made right. Zehner summarizes the Evangelical understanding in the sentence: "Making amends is only a sign of remorse and serves to ameliorate the consequences."[267] In relation to remorse (as the process of the inner person), the idea of reparations as "an external sign of an inner behavior"[268] is valid. These descriptions are encountered in new economic discussions with those who see reparations not as "compensation, but as a symbolic function."[269]

It appears pressing to conceptually evaluate the constructive considerations of "human" reparations. Talk of sin should be relinquished on the interpersonal level of (so also E. Seidler 1995, 10f.) reparations (so also J. Zehner 1998, 214f.), especially with regard to satisfaction (so also D. Sattler 1992, 389 — despite critical self-reflection). Here it appears necessary again to go back to the theologically univocal conceptualizations and to limit the use of this terminus exclusively on the basis of the soteriological. Reparations appears — under the watchful eye of the theological synthesis to Option 4, which expressed reservations — to be an appropriate concept to describe a process that can only have Christological meaning.

Does our process of political reconciliation still appear to have a fundamental theological connection even when interpersonal reparations are nonexistent? According to the theological considerations, the question can be affirmed to the extent that the striving of humans to compensate for guilt can never be the *condicio sine qua non* of forgiveness. However, D. Sattler[270] refers to the "church's celebration of reconciliation . . . in which not simply everything will be good again." Sattler[271] recommends thus "concrete forms of human *satisfactio*" "for lifting of the sorrowful consequences of a deed." It demands "a strict correlation to the type of sin committed to indicate the type of 'making amends' for incurred injuries," stating: only thus can "the sacramentally celebrated reconciliation . . . be experienced and lived." This narrowing of the framework is not Evangelical and does nothing to contribute to the theological understanding of our case examples. "Reparations" are not referred to as the precondition for experienced and lived reconciliation (which would still be expected afterwards). The apology to the son of the murdered mother was a public request for forgiveness made publicly. Whether or not it includes reparations, the act of forgiveness remains a very unique one. How should reparations look in the case of Maxan? How should it look in the other cases of serious human rights violations? (It affirms that Sattler's — like Zehner's — theological considerations are connected to legal examples of light to medium criminal counts.) Thus, theologically, we are compelled to consider that serious guilt and its overcoming through reparations is not to be demanded in areas external to the church!

Looking back on the stations of interpersonal path of reconciliation in political forums, our examination also disproves the South African view that the TRC process can be understood within the framework of the Catholic institution of repentance.[272] In any case, (accordingly) powerful equivocations are suggested by the scheme of *contritio, confessio, absolutio,* and *satisfactio.* However, then the appearance before the TRC of contrition must correlate to truth telling and to the *confessio oris* and "full disclosure," and amnesty must correlate to absolution. Where a Catholic understanding of the concept of repentance is assumed, legally and theologically it means something different. What result is achieved by a theological synthesis from an Evangelical perspective?

RESULT 2

The question of correspondence according to a fundamental connection to theological reconciliation in political forms of reconciliation will be looked at in this section on the analysis of observed interpersonal reconciliation processes from the forums of the TRC and EK. The question is this: can the spiritual path of reconciliation be reconstructed within the political reconciliation process?

As a general result of the theological synthesis it can be asserted that spiritual reconciliation — which includes the invitation to reconciliation, its acceptance and the new relationship of peace relation of reconciliation — can be seen in the examined political forums in attempts to work through guilt. There are, as the analyzed examples show, categories in common.[273] However, since all elements of the path of reconciliation are constitutive to reconciliation, reconciliation remains fragmentary in political reality. In order thus to be able to enumerate the individual results of the theological reconstruction of reconciliation, it is easier to identify the statements exhibiting theological reconciliation that exist in the political arena.

First, there is the problem of how the inner connection in the spiritual path to reconciliation and the process of political reconciliation process stand with respect to each other: does spiritual reconciliation condition the political in the idea that the offender and victim "need to reconcile with God, in order to be reconciled with each other"?[274] Does interpersonal reconciliation with God have to precede the other in regard to the view that before man steps before God, he must first be reconciled with his brother?[275] Do spiritual and political reconciliation have the same origin, in so far as they emit from "God's reconciliation . . . , which includes the necessity of the interpersonal and indeed not as a second, consequential necessity, but as one that is included from the beginning?"[276] Do God's mercy and human political activity work together so that acts of political reconciliation are "integrated" and "bound together" in the "all-effecting activity of God"?[277] Does the person respond to the spiritual in political reconciliation?[278] Or is it Christ, the third power,[279] who steps between the "guilt and the injury" and

284

"brings together again those who were parted through guilt"?[280] The theological synthesis clearly indicates a similar origin in which human reconciliation is "included" in the divine.

God's invitation to reconciliation in Christ correlates with His "open" relation to man; reconciliation, Christ's work, applies to the world. God testifies in Christ to his "being for man."[281] God's being-in-relation to creation in Jesus Christ correlates to the being-in-relation of reconciled man with other men and creatures. Processes between men indicate the bond that Christ means when he testifies to "God being for man." Thus, the idea that Christ stands between the offender and victim (Beintker et al.) is not to be understood substantively, but rather in terms of a correlation of the relationships.[282] It is not that people do not have something divine in themselves or between them, but recalling Bonhoeffer: "The similarity, the analogy of man to God, is not an *analogia entis,* but an *analogia relationis.* This means: (1) the relation is not one of man's own ability, or possibility or structure of his own, but it is a gift, an accorded relationship, *justitia passiva!* And in this relationship, freedom is accorded. From this follows (2) that this *analogia* may not be understood as if man has this similarity somewhere in his own person, at his disposal, but *analogia* similarity is very strictly to be understood that what is similar has its ability from an original, which for us also points to the original and only in this way is "similar."[283]

The statement exhibiting the possibility of reconciliation theology in the political arena opens itself to the category of the *analogia relationis.* Within the relationship of reconciliation between men in political reality, theological reconciliation in terms of the (καινὴ κτίσις) can be reconstructed to which the person is called "in" Christ:

- The interpersonal invitation to reconciliation in which the offender submits to the victim (or the reverse), experiences its similarity only from the invitation to reconciliation that God makes to man in Christ.
- The request for pardon, in which the offender submits to the victim, knowing that he can not contribute to the pardon, experiences its similarity only in the relationship of God to man through the law and the Gospel.
- The (victim-offender) relationship, in which for example Forbes differentiates the person of Benzien from his deeds, experiences its similarity only from the relationship of the justifying God in Christ *(opus proprium).*
- The (offender-victim) relationship, in which Forbes accuses Benzien

285

and calls him into question, experiences its similarity only from the relationship of God, who convicts men in the law leading to the deepest point of doubting the old "I" *(opus alienum).*

III. Question of Correspondence — Third Symbolic Passage

1. The Theological Task

The question of correspondence regarding a fundamental connection to theological reconciliation in the working out of guilt in the political arena after system change in South Africa and Germany will now be treated from the symbolic perspective. Since the fact that a change of perspective with regard to the preceding logical section is assumed, the symbolic content of our past political observations will then receive an independent meaning. I will use the recent philosophical and theological research on metaphor in outlining the difference between logical arguments and symbolic understanding for insights gained from the discussions on the one hand, and the stories, statements, and images used to either make a claim or to communicate, on the other.[284]

Metaphors serve not only to produce images, but they say "something new about reality"[285] and they have a function in a theological reconstructive function. "Whereas the older theological hermeneutic was essentially interested in the reality-illuminating function of metaphor, the current research on metaphor study is focused on its ability to create reality."[286] The traditional metaphor lives by virtue of the fact "that there are non-metaphorical words."[287] The innovative metaphor, on the other hand, receives its theoretical meaning in that "true metaphors (are) non-transferable" and opens up — even creates — by their "'theoretically creative logic of discovery' . . . new horizons of interpretation."[288] The main direction of the metaphor theory of the twentieth century can be described by the acceptance of non-transferability.

For our theological task, we have evidence from the research that the logic of reconciliation in God's activity and being does not correlate to the conceptual clarity of theological arguments; rather, it is accepted (1) that a particular logic steers them and (2) that they transgress conceptual images, imagination, and symbols in the Bible. In theory, truth emerges from both points of view, as has already been stated in the theoretical section, with respect to the question of correspondence, as they extend further than the model of coherence. However, here it has to do not only with the question of conceptual consistency and the (identity of) logical agreement of the working out of political guilt in a basic connection to theological reconciliation, but it also has to do with the question of agreement (correspondences) with regard to the referential function of symbol and ritual.

The empirically analyzed ritualized processes in the hearings before the TRC appear especially to hide a potential for theological reconciliation that indicates "non transferability into ordinary language."[289] Our task will consist in examining the ritual of reconciliation — which can not be mediated in the medium of language — for its basic connection to theological reconciliation. Thus, the task of symbolic interpretation of the hearing events is different from that of the preceding section on logic (II.3.b) in that now the processes are not researched according to individual elements, as for example are the steps in reconciliation, but according to the stories of the TRC; namely, dialogues, but also non-verbal processes such as the ritualized processes of the entire observed proceedings. It also does not have to do with the verbal interpretation of the processes, but with the symbolic. The political reconciliation process indicates that something theological can be found in this entire ritualized process. The constructive gap is in the distinction "between verbal and metaphorical interpretations of the message."[290]

In the symbolizing sections of Part II (A.II.3 and B.II.3) we are forced to acknowledge a plurality in reference between the symbolic and ritual. Thus, we found in the course of the empirical analysis that, theologically viewed, ritual and symbol are basically open; be it the African symbol of reality of the general ritual or the symbolic ideas of the so-called history of politics. The overarching task of this section will, however, consist in inquiring about the basic, underlying connection to theological reconciliation of the empirically mediated reality of reconciliation through symbol and ritual.

In order to be able to accomplish this task, we must first consider the boundaries from a theological perspective: what distinguishes a picture from letters, the symbol from the metaphor, the word from an argument, and how are the pairs arranged in relation to each other? These questions can thus not be treated creatively, because they are situated in a paradigm of defined statements and, as such, are inadequate to the task. However, basic orientations for the formulation of our task appear to be necessary. Pictures and arguments obviously lie the furthest apart; between them can be found symbol and character, although closely related with a similar origin. "Over against the indexed character, the picture can objectively represent something that really does not exist (for example, centaurs); on the other hand, however, they are similar and the same. The final characteristic is the occasion that distinguishes the picture from the symbolic character."[291] The particular closeness of metaphor and symbol consists heuristically in that the metaphor "mediates a symbol that otherwise cannot be articulated."[292] The difference can be seen in that "with symbol, in distinction to metaphor, in many cases it not only involves language, but also the actions connected with it."[293]

Thus, we receive clarification from the above statement for our task with regard to the diversity of the research: namely, it has to do with both metaphor and symbol. Thus, a metaphorical view of words like "sacrifice" touches on the main point of the analysis in its historical political and reconciliation theological horizon. It refers to the empirically analyzed ritual processes of the TRC hearings, but also the symbolic reality of dealing with the deeds of the Stasi in a symbolically reconciled reality that can be potentially examined for its fundamental connection to the ritual of the worship service. Are the received experiences of redemption and forgiveness adequately transformed in the process?

The task of this chapter (after inquiring about the fundamental connection to theological reconciliation in the political arena as mediated through symbol and ritual) as it relates to the newer theological discussion brings us methodologically into the area of semiotics where "the development of methods to analyze religious processes in non-church rituals" is a rare thing. M. Buntfuss says at the end of his research: "The inner dogmatic as well as the overarching category of the discipline can also serve to go beyond a desire for order and achieve theological knowledge. The liveliness of the theological language and the theological knowledge feeds off such an enterprise and also hinders it to the extent that its own terminology can become entrenched in rigid categories, which also cuts it off from a fruitful exchange with other scholarly languages."[294] Thus, our interdisciplinary overarching work does not lose its theological identity in view of semiotics. Our task, achieved as a theological synthesis of empirically analyzed reality, has progressed from a theological-deductive perspective.

The resulting deductive step (2) from current discussions on metaphor and symbol should thus be able to prepare the ground for a theological development of an analysis of categories of reality and make possible the subsequent (3) theological synthesis of the case study sections (Part II.A.II.3/B.II.4).

2. Analytical Concepts from Current Research
on Symbol and Metaphor (Fourth Deductive Step)

Based on the Truth Commission hearings and related research on symbolic forms pertaining to the political reconstruction process in Part II, the question now to be addressed is one of categorization: namely, what category is the most appropriate for making the connection between the "penultimate and ultimate," and between spiritual and political reconciliation, with respect to symbolic forms?

In conjunction with this deductive step, the previously introduced concept of "signs of transcendence" will be developed in its symbolic dimension for use in analysis. "Remembering," "storytelling," and "solidarity" will also be developed as analytical concepts, which for our purposes will include a theological route to the symbolical representation of the reality of reconciliation in the case studies, by which we subsequently expect to gain entrance to the "connections" between the penultimate and the ultimate from a symbolic theoretical perspective.

(a) Signs of Transcendence

The recognition of spiritual reconciliation that exists in the midst of political processes that are geared toward reconciliation as containing moments ("occasions") of release has been generally described as containing signs of transcendence. To what extent can the discussion of signs of transcendence be connected with more current metaphors and research on symbols and the evidence more closely defined in terms of a theological synthesis from the perspective of a theory of symbol? A definition follows where we argue (1) that signs of transcendence have a referential function, that (2) they are universal, and (3) that they are fundamentally "open."

(1) Conceptually, signs of transcendence can also be described as symbols of transcendence to the extent that the recognition of "moments of release" may also include activities. If one goes further with regard to symbol theory, one may apply the thinking of E. Cassirer in the case of our signs of transcendence; namely, that the image is not identical with the thing (as in myth). The symbol is a representative sign that does not somehow melt into the represented content, nor does it make an independent determination of the content's meaning. Symbolic representa-

tion is to be understood as a transcendent sign that is not immediately contemporaneous, but acts as a mode of reference. With this mind, we may arrive at a provisional explanation of the symbolic function of "signs of transcendence." The theological intercepts the theoretical in the functional reference between symbol and ritual.

(2) The transcendent sign of reconciliation has a certain ubiquity. The universality of the invitation to reconciliation — which is Christologically based in eliminating the difference between the profane and the sacred, to call upon a motif used in the letter to the Hebrews — correlates with the ubiquity of the transcendent signs of reconciliation in political reality. Everything can serve as "a symbol or similarity for the claim of the kingdom of Jesus here and now." There is a condition, however: "Where religious symbols refer to Jesus Christ they are relativized and, in their unique brokenness, take part in His truth."[295]

(3) The claim of universal truth for ubiquitous signs of transcendence will be examined with respect to what can be theologically normed on the forum of faith. The believer has an interpretative framework which allows symbols to break into political reality and there to develop a theological form. "Is there anything else besides theological criterion that makes it possible . . . to go beyond symbols and to break through with an all-encompassing manifestation of salvation; namely, Jesus Christ?"[296] Theological interpretation as that which surpasses and interrupts symbolic forms in political reality can not appropriately eliminate any general claim that symbol and ritual have on people. Thus, we can differentiate signs of transcendence in the world from the use of sacramental signs in the church.

Next to the necessary distinction concerning the mode of interpretation, there is a connection between signs of transcendence and sacramental signs with respect to theological meaning. In the same way that Melanchthon's definition of *signa sacramentalis* as a "sign of God's mercy" is valid on the condition of its sacramental character,[297] so also our signs of transcendence are valid: they have to do with the faith's recognition of the "signs of the mercy of God" in political reality.

The fact that we are speaking of signs of transcendence and not of sacramental signs means that there is a theological distinction to be made with respect to the sacramental concept. Furthermore, the choice of terms should be able to express the relative openness of the political process.

(b) Remembering, Storytelling, Solidarity

In a well-known statement on historical research, J. B. Metz states programmatically that

> from the beginning, Christianity . . . was not primarily a community of interpretation and argumentation, but one of remembrance and story telling: the recounting of stories of the cross and of the resurrection of Jesus. The *logos* of the cross and of the resurrection has an indispensable story structure. The exchange of the experience of faith, as of every original experience of the new and the never-having-been, does not take the form of an (didactic) argument, but rather of story. Faith in the redemption of history and in the "new man" is shared in view of the history of human suffering through stories that tell of being freed from danger.[298]

Framed in the theological antithesis of story and (didactic) argument, we encounter three key terms in the above-cited quotation, which will be advanced later on as "categories of political theology":[299] "remembering," "storytelling," and "solidarity." We will focus on these categories and at the same time clarify their individual definitions as to how they will be used as basic theological concepts in the case studies and to what modifications they will therefore be subjected.

(1) Remembering

The thesis of faith as remembrance is related to the content of faith *(fides quae creditur)*. The content of faith is defined by J. B. Metz[300] as *memoria passionis, mortis et resurrectionis* of Jesus Christ. These "defined recollections" have a mobilizing power and motivate imitation. Dogmas represent the expressions of these recollections as the "simultaneous collective remembrance transmitted through a formula," with the church acting as the "open conduit of Christian recollection." *Memoria* has a long conceptual history that reaches from the Platonic *anamnesis* to Augustine, and beyond to the "dangerous recollection" of critical social theory: remembrance places the present into question, awakens hope, delimits horizons, and calls into action. "Here a dangerous recollection is meant which confronts the present and puts it into question, because it recollects a non-abiding future."[301] In contrast to the existential theological concept where faith resides in a decision and primarily has to do with an act of faith *(fides qua creditur)*, Metz places faith "in the form of eschatological recollection" and the content of the remembrance at the forefront. The content of remembering *(memoria)* hides a critical, releasing, and freeing potential. "Faith as *memoria* answers the question of the mediation between the 'already' and the 'not yet' of the eschatological redemption granted in Jesus."[302]

The thesis of *memoria,* which in outline form has been placed within the category of political theology, has been carefully reviewed in more current theological publications on reconciliation. An immediately relevant connection between the remembrance of the suffering of Christ and that of people is made by M. Volf, with explicit reference to J. B. Metz: "As we remember Christ's suffering, we are reminded to remember the sufferings of his brothers and sisters for whom he died. In the memory of Christ's suffering, the memory of all the pain inflicted and suffered is sanctified."[303]

Volf refers to *anamnesis* in the Last Supper ("do this in remembrance of me") with respect to the meaning of suffering in the category *memoria.* "The Lord's Supper is the ritual time in which we remember the broken body and the spilled blood of our Saviour. As we partake in it, we remember that night in which the 'Lord of glory' was betrayed, humiliated, subjected to a mock trial, and brutally murdered; we recall why Jesus Christ was crucified and what the consequences were. There can be no Christian faith without *that* memory."[304] In the category of *memoria,* one may conclude for our line of questioning that there is a formal community of categories that exist between sacramental signs and transcendent signs. However, the extent to which transcendent signs refer in a material sense to the recollected suffering of Christ in the sacramental signs of the Last Supper (under exclusion of the *analogia entis!*) must be considered in the following theological synthesis (3).

If we view our task assisted by the category of terms belonging to *memoria* as that of addressing how the church's recollection of the sacrifice of Christ connects to the remembrance of the victims of totalitarian regimes, then according to Metz the analytical concept underlying its use, despite basic agreement, reflects significant modifications to the development of the problem. *Memoria* is, among other things, both an abbreviated concept and an extended one when applied in a theology of politics.

Recollection Is a Personal Category   The reception of a thesis of *memoria* in political theology abbreviates the problem that is discernable, among others, in the question of the process of recollection. The *memoria* thesis proceeds unilaterally from the fact that the believer is also the subject of the recollection. Thus, the interdependent character of the recollection does not convey a theological meaning that results directly from the reciprocity between God's recollection as the allocation of His great mercy and grace and man's request to God should he be moved to remember how the individual or the community turn to God with the request "remember (me/us)!", because God also calls his people continually to repentance through the injunction "remember!" There is a gap between divine and human recollection. The subject of the "motivating power" mentioned above is not human thought. Rather, "God's memory . . . is an active and creating event" that constitutes a real change in the actual situation through God's active intervention. Thus, divine and human thinking do not degenerate into a duality. Rather, the ultimate is established in the penultimate and, indeed, in symbolic form. Proceeding from the Biblical observation that God keeps His covenant which He renews by virtue of His promise, O. Meyer says: "In the reconstruction of what God does, man also has to remember the past deeds of God; His past laws as well as those demonstrated in the past, and thus also those of the present and the possibilities of the yet to be created future."[305] The main condition of remembrance of Israel — the freeing from slavery in Egypt — is recounted in the Passover as it is in the most important festival days, the Sabbath (Deut. 5:15) where creation and the goal of creation are universally remembered (Gen. 2:3; Heb. 4:3ff.). The recollections of the church are not distinguished in terms of the meaning of *memoria*, but rather in the occasion for the recollection: it is not about a particular historical liberating event, but about the liberator himself. Jesus is "our Paschal lamb" (I Cor. 5:7), the sacrifice for our freedom from slavery, sin, and death. The occasion of *memoria* is thus a person and accordingly, remembrance is a personal category.

Remembrance and Eschatological Forgetting   The term *memoria* extends the political theological where it uses statements about eschatological liberation from the past. Wherever recollection or remembrance appears as a fundamental theological category it always remains in the framework of the basic eschatological dimension of the Gospel, relying on the making present of God himself. From the theological perspective remembering is quite simply "rescuing the past," "a past that exists in the present of God." Thus, the past is an "oral history . . . brought to expression by God Himself."[306] The connection to the present and the open horizon of the term *memoria* in a theology of politics is unclear in this context. How can remembering open up a change in perspective that is oriented toward the future, if it can't yield an eschatological forgetting? The Old Testament's "do not forget!" and the hidden eschatological joy of the New Testament that encourages forgetting, appear unreflective in their connection to political theology and seem to reinforce a dualism.

The inner connection between remembering and forgetting is meanwhile contained in the deliberations on content that are already considered in post-exilic literature. Essential elements of expectation of the relationship of a New Covenant between God and his people as expressed in the subsequent formulation of the New Creation are such that "the past can finally wither away; that it is always about forgetting as much as it is about overcoming the dangers of the past, which are mediated into a future that ultimately brings a good ending."[307] The last chapter of the book of Isaiah says that with the surpassing quality of the new heaven and the new earth we can forget the old conditions with confidence: "For the past troubles will be forgotten" (Isa. 65:16). Here, forgetting clearly means not to eliminate the past, but rather: "The former things will not be remembered" (Isa. 65:17). The past is actually gone and done away with. This is the logical condition necessary so that something new can actually come to be: a world without problems and tears, without dying children, without exploitation, and with the assurance that God hears us (compare Isa. 65:19f.). The condition for the possibility of something new is God himself: He creates, makes and does, and continually, as stated in Isaiah 65: God mediates between the old and the new. For man the new appears as break, as interruption of the old, because he is still entirely immersed in the old situation. In this fundamental connection, the logic of Paul appears to have its place where he says to "forget what lies behind," a statement that both marks the break and is bound up with the longing "to win Christ" (Phil. 3:7ff.). The difference (not the condition!) between the testaments is in the remembering; namely, now (in the sense of the eschatological νύν) it is a person who makes forgetting possible. "In Christ" is the old gone and everything is made new (II Cor. 5:17).

As analytical concepts, remembering and forgetting are only useful in political processes where they can be qualified theologically as univocal or we run into the danger of equivocations. With this in mind, three things need to be clarified: first, political memory can not be superimposed onto the theological dimension of remembering (i.e., the danger of *analogia entis* appears latently accessible in the political theological concept of *memoria*). Remembering alone does not bring redemption,[308] since it has to do with the content of remembering as well as with the synthetic process of association made in the recollection. Second, it cannot *a priori* be excluded that correspondences may exist on the level of implied axioms between political forms of remembering of human suffering, such as, on the one hand, the Truth Commission and the forms of the sufferings of Christ remembered by the church on the other hand. Third, the term *memoria* threatens to overstrain political theology as an absolute concept of Christian faith where it includes the eschatological joy of being able to forget.

The content of remembering is normative: it is the *memoria passionis, mortis et resurrectionis* of Jesus Christ. This remembering enables the synthetic ability to bring historical and eschatological recollections into connection with each other and to achieve the healing of forgetting. Under these conditions "grace (is) the eschatological boundary of forgetting and the goal of all public recollection. It breaks through in emblematic ways, wherever guilt is relieved and where reconciliation between offenders and victims or their descendents is made possible."[309] In eschatological forgetting, the recollection is that of the injury that has been overcome. Truly, here it is possible for everything to become new. In its specific metaphor, according to which reconciliation is visually depicted as an "embrace," M. Volf writes: "As a fruit of both the suffering of Christ and the glory of God's new world, eschatological forgetting finally removes the memory of injury as the last obstacle to an unhindered embrace."[310]

It is significant when the interdependence of remembering and forgetting correspond to basic theological distinctions. Just as no forgetting is possible without remembering, so also no Gospel is possible without the law (in the sense of *usus elenchticus)* or — as we have seen above — no forgiveness is possible without regret (reformation qualified as *contritio passiva).*

(2) Storytelling

According to Metz,[311] as a community of remembering the church is also a community of story telling. What is remembered must be told: the remembering generates the story. For theology it follows that a discursive and hermeneutic theology must also be supplemented by the addition of a "theology of narrative."[312] It depends on "the remembering and telling potential of Christianity not to hide or to deny itself out of sheer anxiety from insecurity, but to protect itself and to find a new way to mobilize itself against the spell of a presumed post-narrative time."[313]

For Metz the narrative function of theology is therefore of great importance, because the story is performative: it both shares in the experience and awakens the experience. There is a constructive connection between telling and revelation, which will be taken up in more depth in the following pages. This connection results in the symbolic dimension: namely, telling can be a sign all by itself. For our differentiation between transcendent signs and sacramental signs, it is significant that narrative theology can refer both to the structure of story in the Judeo-Christian Bible and to the Gospel; to the Jewish as well as the Christian tradition. "For Martin Buber, the author of *Stories of the Hasidim,* and as for Gershom Scholem, the story is a *signum efficax* or an active sign: a category in Catholic theology that was limited to the area of sacramental theology. In the Christian tradition, Augustine, Bonaventura, Pascal, Kierkegaard, Newman, and Bonhoeffer have all done theology in such a way as to allow for the literary genus of story. The *Memorial* of Pascal is a particularly authentic piece of narrative theology: it distinguishes between the 'God of Abraham, Isaac and Jacob' whose deeds could be related, and the 'God of the philosophers' about whom one merely discussed and argued."[314]

The preceding, brief characterization and historical embedding of the main features of story as a category of political theology should next be placed in connection to the more current literature with respect to some of the major questions of narrative theology. Accordingly, using the guiding principles as an entry point into the theological meaning of "story" we hope to better include or "unlock" the theological aspects through an improved conceptual analysis of the narrative passages included in the case study chapters.

Let us now first go to the controversial discussion of the qualifications for a "narrative" theology, in order to finally debate the question of to which category the story belongs. It is clear that we are not able to give the time or space here to a thorough discussion of the almost three centuries of debate on the re-discovery of the category of story for theology. As far as I am able to tell, such an undertaking is a *desiderata*[315] and would not contribute much to the furthering of our goal; namely, to negotiate the story as an analytical concept for the development of our empirical case studies. On the other hand, the story can not be adopted as a basic concept of political theology of the 1970s from the point of view of historical research without giving consideration to more current discussions. Accordingly, in my critical evaluation of the category of story I will use two exemplary essay collections that provide a cross-section of the state of the discussion at the end of the 1980s as well as in the 1990s and into 2000.[316]

The criticism that was expressed in the 1980s was less about the acceptance of story as a basis of faith than it was about the formation of a theory of and program for narrative theology. Critics argued that conceptual formulations like "narrative theology" do not do justice to theology and asked whether such a project did not rather cause more confusion for actual theological ideas, problems, and tasks.[317] As a result, they contended that it would be difficult to reach a theological agreement if everything was reduced to narrative. In addition, if theology essentially proceeds from narrative and consequently, if story forms the basis of faith, then it had to be made clear to representatives of "narrative theology" that "theology is regulative, not narrative."[318] Finally, its main premise was questioned; namely, whether or not the limits of argumentative theology do not at the same time delimit the boundary of theology itself: "a boundary that is not to be overcome by a broader, narrative theology, but a boundary that . . . indicates that theology is a very after-the-fact business."[319]

The (above) criticism eliminates the essential systematic theological difference between faith and theology and appropriately discounts the theoretical claim and the regulative function suggested by the concept of "narrative theology." Perhaps one can simply say: the *fundamental* language of faith is not that of argument, but of story. On the other hand, the *explicit* (i.e., regulative and theoretical) language of faith as theology is not one of story, but of argumentation. The meaning of story as a basis for faith should be stressed. The theological knowledge that faith must be shared finds expression in the semiotic insight: "whatever one can not speak about theoretically, one can tell about."[320] First, there are central contents of the Christian faith such as "God's activity and lordship; Jesus' teaching and passion; and the present and future of God and Jesus, that are only comprehended through narrative."[321] Second, the "community of faith and story of the church (is) dependent upon individual self-understanding . . . of the confessions and dogmas, the recognition of which may not first emerge or solidify in the recitation of the text. Rather, condensed stories must continually flow from these texts where they are innovatively and contextually transformed." Third, "stories (are) basic for faith because only thus can the story of God and Jesus be connected with our own." These are transmitted as "open-ended stories, in which believers take part."

In the current discussion, an analysis of the problem of the theological category of story shifts entirely to this level. It does not limit itself to the conceptual formation of a "narrative theology," but looks for theological statements about the relationship between "revelation and history";[322] reflected here is the process of story telling as the basis for faith and not the level of theoretical formation and regulative function of a "narrative theology."

Meanwhile, what can be evaluated is that which can be said to be theologically fundamental according to what appears in the Bible as revelation and God's proclamation.[323] Here we can now see the constructive connection of story: "stories can help to communicate God's revelation in that they reveal who God is. Stories can make us open to an encounter with God."[324] In this connection, the current discussion, which is central for our problem, focuses on whether we "only encounter God's revelation in the reading of the Bible." "How do Biblical stories relate to what we call 'history' or to our own story?" The question is thus central to our problem because — now on the level of the narrative — we again encounter the problem of recognition and its "basic element of revelation" (D. Ritschl). To what extent do we recognize in the stories of victims the theological story of the suffering of Christ as victim? Do the stories told before the forums of the TRC or the EK "break into" the Biblical stories of the suffering of Jesus? Does one encounter again the remembered content of the Christian faith? What are the conditions for recognition of a revealed theological perspective?

We have defined *recognition* in Part I as an analytical concept according to D. Ritschl, and have incorporated it into the previous section on theological synthesis. The development of the concept of revelation in the current literature regarding theological categories of story contributes in a particular way to the clarification of the problem concerning recognition and revelation, and thus contributes an answer to the question of how the "basic element of revelation," which otherwise is "revealed" in the process of recognition, might be categorized in terms of a "theology of narrative." G. Sauter and J. Barton [325] suggest, as an alternative understanding of revelation, the "informing of supernatural knowledge,"[326] implying a concept of personal revelation, since "revelation is first and foremost God's encounter with those with whom He wants to communicate. This communication can happen in various ways and in various areas." With Sauter and Barton we see that "the theological concept of 'revelation' raises our attentiveness as to how we expect a basic encounter with God to occur; and indeed not merely with respect to individual stories, but also in terms of a continuing life relationship. 'Revelation' is not just a state of knowing by which these encounters may be known in a concrete way. Revelation has to be *related* and *imparted* further."

Like Sauter and Barton, revelation is for us the condition that yields the possibility of theological recognition. In connection to the task of this research — which hinges on a theological analysis of the political connection to reconciliation — the theological context (between prior faith judgments and subsequent normative examination) that in this chapter provides the background for the previously analyzed stories of victims of totalitarian systems, is thus described by J. Barton: "Our theological research, wherever it may end, begins with the facts of the Christian tradition and with the things that Christians have always regarded as 'revealed.' These facts are indivisible from those connected to what the Bible communicates to us in the form of story; the story of the life, death, and resurrection of Jesus of Nazareth. We do not begin with research on the basic possibility of knowing God, but with the confidence that something has been told to us — something that we could not have told to ourselves."[327] If we follow this premise, then our question is to what extent the stories of victims of political injustice can be recognized as similar to those contained in the Biblical stories.

To what extent do Biblical stories assume a normative character with regard to other stories taken from political reality? How "do *stories* function, when they communicate to us the revelation of God?" J. Barton[328] explains with a comparison to Greek tragedy: "To the extent that they draw the reader into the story, narrative texts uncover human possibilities (and human limitations, which are otherwise not discovered). Obvious examples of such stories are the Joseph stories (Genesis 37–50) and the succession to the throne (2 Samuel 5–20; 1. Reg. 1–2)." A characterization of Biblical story telling is its inability to be reduced to an ethical principle. "Naturally, principles can be exemplified in the stories; for example, in the Joseph stories envy is evil, forgiveness requires courage, and resentment is unworthy of mature people. The story can not thus be substituted by a representation of principles." Rather, these (principles) are uncovered mainly and exclusively "through the inter-play of characters and situations." The non-reducible nature of the story into theological argument is expressed by Barton in a simple sentence: "We learn when we read Biblical stories, but it is not easy to tell what we learn." The principle of the non-reducibility of the story in logical categories brings the narrative into structural proximity with the complexity of symbolic communication. "Even if symbolic communication takes place purely verbally, in elevated, written, linguistic form, it can not be reduced to precise statements, but conveys the 'unregistered' (P. Ricoeur) that exists between the signs."[329] According to Barton, the Biblical story uncovers "realities that could not be unveiled in other ways (even after the unveiling) or could ever occur again without the story itself becoming superfluous."[330]

Finally, Barton defines the process of revelation within the category of story: "Revelation occurs when God speaks to us, breaks through our expectations and dispenses with our judgments about what is truly unveiled and what is not." With Barton we also survey not only the danger of the one-sided claim of "similarity (or even equivalence) of divine revelation and human unveiling through narrative texts." Yet, we follow the view that it is "essential" to see where a similarity lies.[331] In both cases are we challenged by something that lies externally to us; something that we ourselves have neither made nor discovered, but which has opened our spirit to welcome in an alien truth. This is the core of what we mean when we bring revelation into connection with story: God reveals himself when He imparts to us new things that make us entirely changed and new.

Such "things" are not limited to Biblical stories; thus the written signs relate to the theologically normative function *(norma normans)* against similar experiences and life stories in political reality. Occasions for recognizing the "things" that make us new and change us can theologically and legitimately lie hidden in stories that are not told in the Bible and which, for example, play out on past political forums. This is "because the Bible tells of the revelation of God in the humility of common, everyday life" and thus Biblical stories draw their material from "similar experiences and life stories. From the start they have, so to speak, created a space and provided a language for the experiences and stories of the genre of ordinary, everyday dealings with people."[332]

(3) Solidarity

According to Metz, remembering and story telling are practical for solidarity: "together remembering, story, and solidarity comprise the categories of a practical fundamental theology."[333] The category is defined as solidarity with those who have died and with the victims; with the human "stories of suffering."[334] In light of Biblical redemption, the story is "not only 'solidarity at the front,' with the arrival of relatives, but is also 'solidarity at the back,' in the deathly silence and forgetting. . . . It does not take the victor's view of successfully overcoming, but that of the conquered and the victims in the open world theater of our history. In this respect it is close to the category of literature, even the tragedy, which keeps watch against the impulse of our notion of historical progress by telling the anti-history of suffering that has gone unpunished."[335]

According to J. Moltmann, solidarity takes place in the interdependence of political theology and political ethics. "Political ethics determines my path."[336] It has to do with an "ethics of hope that fuses together 'resistance' and 'anticipation'": "1. In the fight for economic justice against the exploitation of people by people; 2. In the fight for human rights and freedom against the political oppression of people by people; 3. In the fight for human solidarity against the cultural, real, and sexist alienation of people by people; 4. In the fight for ecological peace with nature against the industrial destruction of nature by man; 5. In the fight for certainty against apathy in personal life."[337]

Solidarity is primarily, in reference to J. B. Metz, a category of political ethics; while remembering and story telling are practical aids to solidarity. For our problem, a direct transfer of solidarity as a category appears to be impossible — despite agreement with respect to content — or is at least limited from the standpoint of the many considerations involved. In the section on Theological Synthesis we have already seen that our problem is not the application of theological views to political processes, but rather with the opposite; namely, the reconstruction of the axiom of theological reconciliation in the area of empirically analyzed past politics. Whoever would consider first accepting the implicit axiom of political processes and then begin to test for their basic connection to theological reconciliation would need a uniquely theological conceptual analysis. It is questionable if a concept like solidarity can achieve this, or whether it doesn't rather have a unique conceptual core that lies beyond theological discourse. At the very least, it appears to be ideologically contingent, in which the drawing of boundaries for a non-theological use of a concept — which Metz as presented above, has demonstrated — is not always done consciously. Furthermore, we must consider whether or not solidarity is a core category for Metz or whether it is a cipher that represents a central theological theme for the actual; namely, the remembering of the suffering of the victims against a "secondary Darwinian notion," or one that illustrates an "objective cynicism concerning suffering."[338] Thus, the theme of suffering and victimization offers a theological point of reference for our case studies to the extent that the redemptive story of Jesus "frees one from focusing on the suffering and (disappointed) hopes of the past."[339]

The first question to ask is to what degree the theme must be predicated on the category of solidarity. Much speaks in favor of eliminating "solidarity" as an analytical concept for the development of our problem and substituting the more precise "participation in the Being of God in the world," which D. Bonhoeffer developed in his "Outline for a Book."[340] To be determined is whether or not the term "participation" is appropriate for fundamentally relating political theology to political ethics, and furthermore to validate the earlier discussion of suffering and sacrifice in their political and theological dimension without equivocating.

In contrast to the usual reception of D. Bonhoeffer's political ethics, his speech on "participation in the life of Jesus" was not primarily based on an imperative challenge to action, but indicatively defines the essence of Christian faith. "Jesus is there for others," and "faith is participation in the life of Jesus." Accordingly, the Christian life is "being (there) for the other."[341] "Participation" is a key concept, since the use of "participating in the life of Jesus" defines the essence of faith as well as the condition of "being there for the other." Both the indicative and the imperative come together so that a political ethic for the lives of others is based solely in the indicative participation in the life of Jesus.

The conspicuous ontological implications in the phrase "being for" once again exclude the *analogia entis.* "God is not a supreme Being, but one that, in Christ, is a Being for the other."[342] The "encounter with Jesus Christ" hides the "experience, that here an exchange of human existence takes place."[343] For the development of our problem, the refusal to employ substantive metaphysical thought results in a differentiation of category between political forms of suffering and the suffering of God. For Bonhoeffer this means that "faith as participation in the life of Jesus" is primarily "participation in the suffering of God in earthly life" (LPP 395) or, as he says elsewhere, "in this life to share in God's suffering" (LPP 402). The connection between human and divine suffering according to the previous statements does not mean that the same word ontologically denotes a similarity (between human and divine suffering). Rather, Bonhoeffer's category of "participation" creates the condition for rejecting equivocations. Where suffering is to be defined as an analytical theological concept for our case studies, clarification is necessary despite basic agreement with Metz's outline because it involves an already problematic conceptuality. Equivocations are suggested where, juxtaposed with the word suffering, the *theologia crucis* is ontologically connected to forms of suffering in political reality.

From our vantage point, there is a contrast in the productive function of dogmatic theology — in the transfer of a theoretical category of metaphor — which still maintains the element of "tension" (Ricoeur) in the use of the church's theological language on suffering (and in this connection also that of "Cross" and "sacrifice") on the one hand, and that of the political on the other: only when we consider the difference are we able to ask about the connection between the two (thus, not as simple to implement as a law). In regard to this question there is a marked difference between Moltmann and

Metz. I will align my comments with Moltmann rather than Metz, who underscores the difference between the soteriological and human suffering in various places and thus, in the final analysis, appears to be too one-dimensional. For example, where J. B. Metz speaks of one's "own ability to suffer" thus allowing one to be "capable" of sympathy with "the sufferings of others and thereby to approximate the mystery of suffering,"[344] Moltmann[345] points out that to take up the "Cross" (Mark 8:34) is "not a symbol for pain. To take up the Cross means, in actual terms, to accept a death sentence." The natural acceptance of suffering and pain does not lead to a direct, unbroken path to a spiritual death from whence new life springs. "Whoever follows the Son of Man, there his proud 'I' is sentenced to death. He receives the freedom of new life from the Son of Man. He has, so to speak, already died."

The category of "participation in the suffering of Christ in the world" ultimately underscores the soteriological difference between the sufferings of Christ and the Christians. "No one can or should carry the Cross of Christ. Everyone should carry his own cross. No one can or should take on the sins of the world and suffer the distortion that characterizes the reconciliation of the world. This task can only be accomplished by Jesus Christ. That was the measure of his suffering. The burden of the world is His. It is not expected of anyone else to take on the burden of the world and to repeat Golgotha. The Son of Man alone has fulfilled this necessity. Thus, his suffering can be called the suffering of reconciliation. The subsequent suffering is a *freeing suffering* on the basis of that once-and-for-all suffering of sin."[346]

3. Symbolic Completion of Spiritual Reconciliation in the Political? Theological Synthesis of Symbolic Forms in Political Dealings with Guilt

For the development of our problem, modifications in the analysis of political theology should make a contribution to theological implications that are embedded in empirically analyzed symbolic forms of reconciliation within political reality. In a formal sense, we will establish the principal referential function of the symbol and limit our understanding of signs of transcendence to real symbols on the one hand, and to strict representative symbols on the other; however, what remains open for discussion is the clarification of the content with respect to the referential function of symbol. In order to establish a material distinction and formal limitation of the theological synthesis, we will arrange this section in connection to current research on the dual function of metaphor and symbol from the perspective of a theory of referentiality.

First, we will examine (a) the form of symbolic reference that emerges from the outlined theoretical perspective. Next, the "external occasion connection" is viewed on a lower level than is the "articulated whole," both in terms of the "inner classification" of the symbol and the process of becoming symbol.[347] The theme is the form of symbol formation; namely, the particular characteristic of creating forms. With this line of inquiry we expect to find a passage into observed rituals that connect with the hearings of the TRC and the EK, as well as with the access to records in the "Gauck Administration." Theoretically, we inquire into the "conditioned laws of (its) emergence," of the "texture" and "structure" of symbol.[348] Finally, the connection to the conditions for ritual in the church will be investigated: to what extent does the "conditioned capacity for law" correlate to what is active in the liturgical worship service? Are structural elements discernable in basic liturgical forms? If so, to what extent do observed rituals of reconciliation in political reality refer to the soteriological reality of reconciliation that is symbolized in the worship service?

In a second step (b), we examine the form of symbolic referentiality as it emerges from the theoretical perspective. In this perspective, the particular form and function of reference is not defined through the internal configuration of the symbolic form as a "whole," but by its external reference to the subject. For example, such a form of reference to the subject is already shown in (1), the "representation" through which a subject is presented in its form. Thus, as a rule, the entire symbolic process does not fall within the field of vision of analysis; rather, individual words are examined on the basis of their reference to the subject. The choice of the theoretical perspective of reference in its connection to the referential function of symbol lies at the basis of the theological discussion which, for example, allows the one-word-metaphor "victim" to denote something specific and, viewed in terms of dogmatics, creates a productive "tension" through its double — that is, political and theological — usage.

Both perspectives distinguish between weak and strong references. From the theoretical perspective we have the *mimetic* form of symbolization in which the individual characteristics of represented things, such as the historical features of a person, reveal their nature; the *analogous* form of representation, in which the similarity to the thing is included in the medium of the represented symbol, but is not entirely relinquished; and the *pure symbolic* representative form, in which only the internal structure of the symbol defines the process of the expression, but where there is not any similarity between the circles of the world of the subject and the world of the symbol. In a systematic arrangement of the definition of signs of transcendence this means that while *mimetic* symbolization is very close to the real symbol, the *pure* symbolic form of presentation appears in principle to be closer to what was described above as *representative* symbol. Accordingly, the theological foundation of signs of transcendence in political reality will — in more precise terms — be made within the framework of the *analogous* form of representation. In addition, the theological synthesis relies on the assumption that "synthetic judgments" will always present "the unity in the difference."

The difference in the articulated theoretical perspective (between the *analogous* forms of representation and the *pure* symbolic form) clearly correlates to the theoretically referenced (perspective) in terms of what exists between representations in the form of strong and of weak metaphors. The former creates reality, the latter illuminates it. This distinction has theological significance, because in one case a "basic element of revelation" (Ritschl) is to be expected and in the other case it is not. (Here revelation precedes *a priori*.) We will therefore norm reference reality-creating signs and symbols according to the definition of signs of transcendence. The issue concerns the recognition of signs of the grace of God in their symbolic performance in political reality as they are released in moments, or occasions.

(a) Are There Rituals for Political Reconciliation
with a Basic Connection to Liturgical Worship?
Theological Synthesis from the Theoretical Perspective

The connection to worship has already been established in the South African hearings. Despite the fact that W. Kistner observes that "the central themes of any Sunday worship service," such as sin, regret, and confession of guilt, reappear in the hearings; or that J. de Gruchy thinks "the ritual" is "painful," but "full of grace, justice, and hope"; or, finally, where C. Villa-Vicencio draws parallels to the Eucharist ("I see the TRC as symbolism, ritual; as liturgy") — the *event* of the connection may be postulated, but the basic connection itself is not examined from a theologically normative position.

Similarity exists where the reciprocity created by the recognition of the connection to religious liturgy in the area of political results is utilized for the purpose of political ethics. While D. Smit[349] thoughtfully formulates: "A public, and virtually liturgical process can, in terms of symbol, play an extremely important role in the national psyche; something that is analogous to the Christian service," T. Kneifel makes clear in the Afterword to the German edition of the TRC Final Report[350] that "a successful process of reconciliation requires both symbol and a collective liturgy in order to effect a catharsis in society. These 'political liturgies' require — analogous to the religious liturgy of confession — symbolic moments: a) a collective searching of conscience, b) believable confessions of both individual and collective guilt, c) the request for forgiveness, d) the ritual of a visible gesture of forgiveness and its articulation through the victim or the victim's symbolic representative, e) a symbolic sign of the will, on the part of the offenders, to make amends to the victims, and f) a closing celebration."

The theological components refer emphatically to the meaning of the connection or relationship and designate, as with T. Kneifel, comparable elements that exist between political and religious liturgy; on the other hand, the urgency of a systematic theological analysis of the observations is evident. As qualified as the claim appears to be, it is lacking a normative examination of the postulate. Thus, it could conceivably be the case that the reciprocity between political and religious liturgy does not exist in a (subsequent) claim of church insight over against the political, but rather the opposite: ritual processes from the worship service performance itself provide a possible ground for the healing power that would be required for the working out of injustices due to past political policies and activities (like the help in channeling guilt, rage, and helplessness).

The guiding question emerges from the theoretical perspective concerning the "conditioned laws of the construction," on the "nature" and "structure" of the ritual. Let us recall the empirical analysis of ritualistic elements in the TRC hearings, as well as those in the EK and the proceedings of the "Gauck Administration" and inquire about their correspondence to "worship as ritual."[351] To what extent do empirically analyzed rituals in political reality appear in a basic connection to what is symbolically expressed in the worship service?

It was clear to theological observers in South Africa, but also in Germany, that in the hearings of the TRC, as well as in the EK, more is hidden than is revealed by the legal framing conditions. The "symbolic added value"[352] develops in the ritual. We distinguished above (in connection to A. Krog) four basic features that comprised the hearing ritual of the TRC: a creation of a sacred, separate space (by the entry of the commissioners, lighting of the candles, moment of silence for reflection on the victims of apartheid, and the entry of the victims in conjunction with the rising of those in the auditorium); the initiation ritual (one now belongs to those who were allowed to tell their story); the cleansing ritual (through the releasing of evil acts in the telling of their story) and a closing ritual, in which the story is embedded into the larger connection of the history of oppression and officially acknowledged as being "true." The hearings before the EK were, as shown, not accompanied by the same ritualized ceremony, even if individual elements — such as standing as the victims enter or the ability to release evil in the act of telling — are recognized. The healing dimension of the ritual appears especially to emerge in the process allowing access to records. "The complainants come agitated and leave satisfied," as we cited a co-worker of the Gauck Administration as saying. The course of hearings, access to records, and the closing discussion as analyzed above in cross-reference to the proceedings in South Africa correlates to basic components of the TRC ritual, and above all, to a purification ritual. "A chapter is closed," says one of the affected parties.

Elements of ritual encountered in political reality are fundamentally open. Their meaning emerges not primarily nor only from a Christian connotation. "Everything ritualistic has an ambivalent character."[353] Before we examine the observed ritual for its basic connection to the ritual practice of the Christian faith, we will align with W. Jetter and will first analyze the political forms of ritual culture anthropologically; namely, as a "religious mode of expression."[354] Accordingly, every ritual works "expressively and is thus at least implicitly always accompanied by a wish for linguistic meaning. It wants to be understood, even when it can not be replaced with a verbal explanation."[355] W. Jetter cites different benchmarks[356] for religious rituals, which pertain to nearly all of our empirical observations of the hearings in South Africa and Germany.

- Rituals are islands of trust and order so that those living in secrecy and fear can "have it done and over" (93). The ritual grants a "space for respite" (94f.). "Life requires protection and space that should shield one from constant threat" (97). (The secrecy and fear that require a space of respite are, in view of our research, the situation in the stories of serious human rights violations.)
- The ritual is an "aid for behavior" (95). The "inner always requires external protection." (As in the religious ritual of W. Jetter, it "is dangerous" to get close to God, and in similar manner it appears "dangerous" in the past political ritual to tell one's story without the external protection of the ritual.)

- The ritual is a "mediator of tradition" (96f.), because "ritual keeps the old and makes it ready for the future." In other words: "wherever there is ritual, something has already been ritualized" (96). (In returning to our problem, there is the question of what type of ritual is represented by the past political forums that "were already there." Does this have to do with a "comprehensive" notion of ritualized religious practice?)
- Ritual "creates a boundary for a community of like-minded people" through induction and communication rituals, says W. Jetter: "Because ritual interprets values and goals and demonstrates the historical consciousness of a community, it tends to separate its participants from those who do not share the same orientation. That results in both internal and external limitations. Represented is something akin to the classical notion of *'notae ecclesiae'*: the boundary markings are there as the integrative symbols of a positive religion" (99).
- Ritual defines sense, trust, and hope. "Don't all religions represent something that permeates all of life with meaning, trust, and hope? It should help people deal with the unexplained, the mysterious, and the puzzle of evil, and help them to better cope with the impenetrability of death" (101). (For the religious connotation, this also refers to the ritual implementation of the TRC, the EK and the Gauck Administration. It is a helpful aid for "being done with" the unexplained, the mysterious, and the puzzle of evil. Furthermore, it should be determined to what extent the specifically Christian ritual is again seen to penetrate life in the implementation of ritual in past political policies and activities.)
- Further hallmarks of religious ritual are "repetition" (103f.), "representation" (105f.), and "certification" (107f.). A cult has repetition, which can also make the ritual "as strong as it is tiresome." Everything that is desired must continually be desired, written about, or danced about. Thus, the actual discomfort of what is intolerable becomes tolerable. The "non-formed receives a form. In addition, through repetition it is practicable, learnable through mimicry, comprehensible in an unreflective way: everything institutional expresses itself this way" (104). (The hallmarks of repetition as well as the qualification of the characteristics again center on political ritual. Of interest would be the interdependence of institutionalization and ritual which accompanies the "institutionalized overcoming of the past" — either through the forming of a ruling commission, an investigative commission, or some other kind of administration. In all of these institutions the unformed, namely, the encounter with the past through storytelling, gains form through ritual.

In addition, the negative side of ritual becomes apparent: the ritualized hearings of the TRC are stronger than those of the EK, which is characterized as "tiresome.")

As a result of the first passage we may assert that there are clearly points in common between religious ritual practices and the analyzed rituals of past politics. In the empirically observed rituals, which accompanied the events of the TRC, but also were present in the EK and the Gauck Administration, religious hallmarks can be recognized; indeed, they appear to be in a basic religious connection as the political reconstruction of ritualized religious practice. Thus, the basic openness of a religious pluralism is maintained. The aggregate of hallmarks of ritual as the religious expression of relationships can be seen in "traditional African religion" as well as in the faith of Israel. Accordingly, the analyzed rituals of past politics will be examined for a specifically Christian explanation; namely, for hallmarks of "worship as ritual."[357]

In a second rendering, where the basic theological connection to forms of ritualized expression will be examined within past political forums so that the "worship service as ritual" can become the normative benchmark for our analysis, the internal theological discussion of justice and the limits of ritual in worship will, however, not be ignored. On the other hand, the basic problem connected to whether "the church service in its ritualized performance is basically in a position to measurably determine the subject of faith,"[358] cannot be adequately treated here. However, it still appears necessary for the sake of this research. The problem connected with "worship as ritual" has, in my opinion, been discussed at length.[359] W. Jetter and the more current literature[360] understand ritual in the church as "dangerously essential"; the danger lies in replacing a legal ritual with "mere, goal-defined routine actions."[361] Finally, worship cannot be categorized as ritual because it always involves an "overflow of meaning."[362] Rituals are indispensable to the Christian faith, in so far as a "theologically responsible treatment of ritual" can be of "practical assistance . . . without binding it to the (hope) of salvation."[363] The Christian representation of faith needs the aid of ritualized self-presentation so that the "representative presentation (of) action and of meaning, as well as that of personal participation" can be expressed. Thus, both of the fundamental Christian rituals of Baptism and the Lord's Supper are "indispensable for the transmission of faith for every Christian."[364]

Under certain conditions the talk of "worship as ritual" is meaningful and may help to affirm our initial question as to whether or not the worship service with its ritual is in a position to appropriately formulate the subject of faith. The outlining of the conditions corresponds to the goal of preparing the ground for a normative examination of the symbolic forms of expression used in political dealings with guilt:

- In so far as ritual has the power to unlock "the implied meaning," then worship "as a regulated course of activity (can) as a whole be seen as ritual."[365]
- The worship service "places a ritualized form of dealing with God in a place where the congregation is constituted through acknowledgment (of God); where it is given a future and is renewed through present activity of salvation."[366]
- In contrast to other religious rituals, Christian worship lacks the "taking of an oath to a mysterious power" where one is captivated in space and time by a super-god and requires shielding from their arbitrariness. However, the other meaning of religious ritual is conditioned by "the commitment in which one doesn't influence the divinity, but abandons one's will to its influence and allows oneself to be taken into its power,"[367] even in the Christian worship service.
- The "overwhelming" sense that is hidden in the ritual of worship cannot be interpreted as aiming at a concept or type of teaching, but has its meaning "in its clear referential character."[368] A ritual is "silent knowledge."[369] The "unity of experience and form"[370] expresses itself in the "action and the completion of the action."[371] "Interpretation" in the ritual of worship is thus "always an interaction that consists in active participation."

After we have determined the above conditions, we will inquire about the content: is there anything of ritual in the Christian worship service? Where is ritual suggested? The specific meaning of the Sunday worship service is taken from the "week-long Easter vigil":[372] it's about the symbolic remembrance of the passage through death into life of Christ; the "taking part in the life of Jesus" (becoming man, the cross, and resurrection) as we will formulate in reference to our conceptual analysis. "Here we encounter in common the path that Jesus took: through suffering and death into renewed life given by the Father."[373] The "legitimacy" (E. Cassirer) that lies at the basis of ritual can be formulated as symbolizing the passage from old to new, as in the passage through death into life. After the celebration of the Last Supper and at the end of the worship service there is the "accepted and renewed person."[374] To the extent that the symbolic reference to the worship service is a person (i.e., in Jesus Christ the person has become a new creature), the passage is from old to new. However, the passage from old to new in other religions is a central, universal and unassailable symbolic representation from the Christological perspective. The way out of guilt leads through death. Everything converges so that the person recognizes how he is known in Christ (compare Gal. 4:9).

After the clarification of the conditions and content of the Christian worship service, we can turn to the theological synthesis of the symbolic forms of expression used in dealing with guilt on the political scene. E. Hauschild asserts that ordinary rituals — here from the area of the political reconstruction of an unjust system — act as guides and complete the passage from the everyday to the transcendent: "They exist in the corridor between the everyday and the transcendent."[375] According to the classification, the rituals of the TRC, the EK, and the "Gauck Administration" all fall under a type of ritual of world view ("rituals of the everyday"[376]), that are set in relation to the central Christian religious ritual (worship, Lord's Supper). The types of ritual belonging to the politics of the past and their correlation to and differences from the area of Christian ritual are being examined here. Thus, the question of correspondence is: to what extent do empirically analyzed ritualistic practices of political reality appear in a basic connection to the analyzed "legitimacy" of the ritual of worship as depicted in the passage from old to new? Do we recognize elements of Christian religious "original activity" in political performance? In addition to an analysis of worship as a whole, can any of its elements be viewed under the auspices of ritual communication? Do individual rituals from the political process also appear in worship? What meaning do they have there? In this regard, to what extent can new light be shed on the basis for "political liturgy"?

In returning to the previously outlined conditions for the possibility of understanding worship in terms of ritual, it is obvious that the theological aspect is enclosed within narrow political boundaries: "God" does not *(expressis verbis)* factor in the rituals of the past politics; politics is not formally a ritual practice of worshipping God. These observations serve as another warning for theological caution with respect to the question of direct correspondences. D. Smit writes in view of the South African TRC: "there are no direct links between Christian convictions and behavior and that of public life in a modern democracy."[377] The theological meaning is meanwhile aligned with the interest of including indirect connections to theological reconciliation; namely, with the reconstruction of central components of "worship as ritual" within political rituals and their symbols.

The observation that God does not appear as the subject of political ritual — as it is not the occasion for adoration — but that it is still governed by doxological language, is relativized when we ask the question about symbol in worship. We assert with K. F. Daiber[378] that the worship service "is a symbolic expression for the fact that renewal is only possible where God is, where people can rely on the activity of God, and where they know that they are accepted by Him and can take part with thanksgiving in His work of salvation." We will examine to what extent the anticipated renewal of man that is expressed in worship reappears in certain individual ritualistic elements in the Truth Commission. R. Volp[379] writes with respect to the recognition of individual "original actions": "Every time people eat and drink, expressing the basic characteristic of the Last Supper of Jesus with his disciples, this is portrayed." If one follows this model, then for our problem the question is of the basic relationship to the origin of the "rising of the congregation," the "remembrance," the "observing of silence," etc. How did these emerge in worship? What meaning do they convey? Do basic relationships exist between the actions of worship and politics? Are the ritual forms of past politics based in the worship service?

Let us take a closer look at these questions by first examining the individual components of past political rituals for their basic connection to theology. To what extent do the empirically analyzed four components of the TRC ritual correspond to the components of worship: opening, invocation, proclamation and confession, last supper, and blessing? To what extent are they different? In a second step, we ask about the corresponding meaning of the structure of the worship ritual and the ritualized practice of the hearings in general. Does the symbolism of the TRC ritual, analogous to the worship service, create a new reality? Is God's new activity with regard to man expressed here?

The first part of ritual: Provision is made for a secluded, protected space through the entry of members of the Commission, the lighting of candles, the moment of silence for the remembrance of the victims of apartheid, and the entrance of the victims in conjunction with the rising of the auditorium. (Many components reappear in the German reconstruction process. Additionally, the hearings of the EK took place in a protected place; likewise the reading room provided by the "Gauck Administration." Nevertheless, the space was not the means of symbolic implementation for those left behind and protected.) Among the conditions for ritual that we will be using (i.e., "an activity that is repeated and therefore expresses an action that takes on symbolic meaning"[380]) there emerges the question for the development of our problem: what meaning is expressed by past political ritual? What basic relationships to the worship service are evident? The meaning of the ritualized entrance, which we highlighted above in case studies as making provision for a "sacred" enclosed space, has a basic connection to the "celebration space" of worship. Those gathered for worship "meet in a space that emphasizes a place of celebration, which from its conception points to the symbolic meaning of worship."[381] The worship space becomes a worship space through revelation and invocation. These structural components are connected to individual elements such as the hymns, Kyrie, Gloria, the greeting, and the Collect prayer. "The worship service contains the symbols of the coming of God. This is especially clear in the Kyrie, which is modeled after the announcement of the king's entrance."[382] It would be inadequate to try to bring the ritual process of political forums into direct correlation with the worship service. Such an assumption would entail that anyone taking part in the TRC ritual would have to take into consideration that he/she must reckon with the coming of God in Jesus Christ. In the meantime, an indirect correlation to the worship ritual does exist to the degree that the performance of the entrance ritual symbolically creates a "space" in which a powerful change in reality that transcends the possibilities of the human must be acknowledged. The entrance ritual of the TRC is a symbolic expression for the renewal that is possible when people acknowledge the activity of a "higher power." However, in contrast to the Christian worship service, the definition of the subject remains absent.

The second part of ritual: In the institutional ritual of the TRC, one is fully integrated into the community of those who may contribute to the historical consciousness of the nation (common memory). (Connections to Germany: preliminary talks prior to accessing files; one belongs now to those who can see their own files.) Initiation rituals are basically "activities that convey acceptance into a group and identification with it."[383] In worship, the initiation ritual encounters the framework of the causal action: "Baptism is the initiation ritual through which the congregation reproduces itself as a social entity. It is molded into a social unit that is theologically qualified by the body of Christ. It releases people from their previous life and places them as members of the people of God on a path that is different from the goals and ways of other people. As the baptized, they communicate in a new relationship to the world. They effect what they describe and refer beyond themselves."[384] Indeed, one could argue that a structural element of ritual returns externally into politics and that the Christian religious meaning of the initiation ritual leaves behind an *ontic* trace in the past political form. However, a correlation appears to be possible only when powerful equivalents are involved, since the initiation rite of baptism means something quite different than that of the TRC ritual.

The third part of ritual: The purification rite of the TRC as the releasing of evil through the act of storytelling (also the case for the documented stories of the EK as well as for confrontation through viewing of Stasi files). According to the empirically analyzed process of working through guilt, in the center of political ritual is the confrontation with the truth of those who suffered system injustice and how that injustice is reflected in the victim's story depicting acts of injustice perpetrated by the government. Preceding this are the rituals of introduction: namely, the advance discussions with respect to the access to files. Afterward, there is the final ritual; namely, the closing discussion. In this ritualized framework the narrative of the victim (as well as of personal insight into the files) is told within a specific space, and in telling their stories, the victims "reveal" themselves. In the reading room provided by the Gauck Administration, the affected parties are confronted with past memories. "My time of humiliation was again very near to me," as we have cited one of the affected persons as saying.

Let us now ask the question from the articulated theoretical perspective about the similarity in structure of these proceedings to the worship service. We find in the worship service that in response to calling upon God the Introit, Kyrie, Gloria, and Collect Prayer provide an "answer through the proclaimed word."[385] In each instance of self-revelation through story in the ritual of past politics we encounter the ritual of the worship service; or at least something that is structurally parallel to it in the element of the sermon and confession (Epistle lesson, Gospel lesson, Confession of faith, Sermon, Absolution, Thanksgiving, Intercession).

Obviously, it is not appropriate to seek direct correlations. However, indirect links can be found using the theological categories of memory *(memoria)* and narrative. As D. Smit writes: "Christian worship is rooted in remembering. . . . In every worship service the Christian community remembers. We remember the Good News, the Gospel. We remember the story of Christ's life, suffering, death and resurrection."[386] From the perspective of the "sermon," new light can be shed on the political process to the extent that the stories can be valued quite differently; they do more than potentially contribute to the "common memory" of a nation. From the theological perspective, the question is to what extent they refer to the suffering of God himself and make a constitutive contribution to *memoria passionis, mortis et resurrectionis Jesu Christi.* In any event, these interpretations mean spreading the word, because the sermon fits the category of over-coming the ambivalence of history. The stories themselves can be expressed as "signs," but as signs of transcendence (but not sacramental signs like the Last Supper, nor otherwise *nota ecclesiae*[387]). The question of to what extent the stories of the victims of the TRC or the EK reflect the Biblical stories of the suffering of Jesus, will be taken up in the theoretical perspective (b).

The fourth part of ritual: The final ritual, consisting in the embedding of the story within the context of apartheid injustice, its acknowledgement by the Commission, and the exit of the witnesses, has a strong presence in the fo-rum of the TRC. (It appears in a weaker form in the EK hearings and its main features correlate, as seen in the case study analysis of the Gauck Administra-tion, to the ritualized debriefing discussion that follows a review of the Stasi files.) In terms of theological structure, a comparison can be made with com-ponents in the worship service to individual elements that emerge, such as the "acknowledgment of the story" and the "exiting of the witnesses." It is ap-propriate to ask whether or not the official recognition of the story has any kind of indirect connection to the recitation of the Creed during worship. The victim's story is acknowledged in the act of acknowledgment by the Commission. Of course, this does not happen formally, nor do other formal symbols express it (i.e., such as the audience rising), but it is clearly a repro-duction of a central worship ritual process; namely, the idea that one has a re-lationship to what is remembered and in a form that one can recognize.

In the worship service the Lord's Supper follows after the sermon and the creed and in the Last Supper the dialogue of worship comes to a close. This symbolizes the union between God and man in the symbol of the Cross. D. Smit draws parallels to the TRC ritual with the worship service and says: "We must remember and confess in order to be reconciled with God."[388] Smit sees an inner connection between reconciliation with God and reconciliation with one's neighbor: the ritual enactment in connection with the Last Supper indicates a connection between reconciliation with God and the neighbor. For our agenda this connection is expressed symboli-cally in a gesture: the "shaking of hands in the passing of the peace or in to-gether receiving the Lord's Supper."[389] In this interpretative framework new light is shed on gestures in political reality, such as that between Forbes and Benzien in the framework of the TRC final ritual: the shaking of hands can be a sign of transcendence.

The blessing appears at the end of the worship service. The final blessing is the expression of what has taken place in worship: the renewal of the per-son and the congregation through the encounter with God. At the end of the

TRC ritual there is the "release of the witnesses." Similarly, we observe in connection with the ritual the access to the files. Thus, the empirical case analysis refers as a whole to the character of renewal, which is also the case in the performance of past political rituals.[390] The structural proximity between the elements of worship of the blessing and the TRC ritual of "letting go" is explained by C. Villa-Vicencio: "We hear in the benediction: 'Go now into the world. The grace of our Lord Jesus Christ, the love of God and the fellowship of the Holy Spirit be with you all!' 'Go!' . . . Ideally this is what the TRC is about. To invite people to come, to reflect, to inwardly digest, to go into the world."[391]

In a table format, the examined structural components can subsequently be placed opposite each other in their basic forms:

Political Ritual (TRC)	*Worship Ritual (acc. to K. F. Daiber)*
1. Entrance ritual (makes the "sacred" space through entry of the Commission, etc.)	1. Opening
2. Initiation ritual	2. Calling (Baptism)
3. Telling of the story and acknowledgement of the story (gesture: "shaking hands")	3. Sermon and confession
4. Exit of witnesses	4. Lord's Supper
	5. Benediction (blessing)

After an examination of the individual components, let us review the ritual practice as a whole. To a certain degree, there is correspondence between the rituals of past politics and the worship service as ritual. However, the correlation lies in the efficacy of each; both convey a sense of the renewal and acceptance of the person. The basic legitimacy of the worship ritual corresponds to the ritual of past politics to the degree that in their implementation they both provide for the passage from "old" person to the "new" one. However, the acceptance of a correlation does not imply a statement about the quality of the renewal, nor does it say anything about *who* the subject of the renewal and acceptance is. The concept in past politics and in worship is not the same — even if we use the same terminology to describe it. Indeed, aside from formal linkages there are basic differences in content. While "from a phenomenological perspective, worship is a process in the course of which the distance between God and man is overcome,"[392] the ritual process of political reconstruction contains implicit transcendent aspects. In other words, participation in past political rituals does not replace worship. However, from the theological perspective the symbolic performance of the worship ritual can be recognized in past political rituals.

RESULT 3

From the theoretical perspective, we conclude that *the correlation between the ritual of a TRC hearing and the "worship service as a ritual" is of a "purely symbolic" type.* A reconstruction of Christian reconciliation thinking in political reality is possible, but the connection is a weak one where only the inner structure of the symbolism defines the terms of reference for political expression. Similarities need not exist: the symbols of the TRC and the EK do not force an interpretation in connection to the worship service, even if they are open to one. (There are also no similarities in the sense of an analogous form or of mimetic symbolization, whereby the essence of the worship service could be reflected in political ritual.)

(b) The "Victim" as Metaphor in the Politics of the Past and in Theological Reconciliation. Theological Synthesis in a Theoretically Referenced Perspective

After concluding from the theoretical perspective that there is a weak connection between the rituals of the TRC hearings and the worship service, we shall now (cross) reference the particular function of forms: not by arranging the symbolic forms as a whole, but by investigating them from a theoretically referenced perspective. Our theological interest focuses on the development of the "tension" that results from placing the meaning of a one-word-metaphor like "victim" in additional contexts; namely, in both a political and theological context.

In the discussions of past politics, those who had been pursued by a totalitarian regime as it came to an end were, as a rule, described as "victims" of capricious state government. In the German discussion it is noteworthy that other terms were also used. In relation to the EK, the use of "contemporary witnesses" was popular and the Stasi documentation laws consistently used the terminology of "affected persons" (although in legal parlance, the use of the term victim is common throughout). In the Final Report of South Africa, the use of "victim" is the rule, even if other descriptions are also chosen; such as, for example, "survivor." The deviations in terminology can, among other things, be explained against the background of metaphor. For the critics, the use of "victim" for the description of those persecuted under a totalitarian regime is in the double sense a weak metaphor: it is translatable and therefore has a "weak" connotation. Victims stand for "bad luck"; they "are obstructions" on the path to forgetting; and everything that has to do with the victim is somehow "painful."[393] In these connotations we observe a criticism of a political culture that reduces history to winners and losers. Whoever refers to victims in the "cult of victory" has already made a judgment about those so labeled. That does not apply where the choice is made to speak in terms of "contemporary witnesses" or "survivors." Obviously, such cultic language needs to be overcome wherever the talk of "victims" is the norm.

Finally, we will argue from a theological perspective that a contribution to an overcoming of cultic practices is not accomplished through the avoidance of certain vocabulary, but through the rediscovery of the "tension" which is conveyed by the Christian metaphor of victim in critical reference to political usage. E. Neubert gives cause for reflection in the debate on the German reconstruction: "In the Christian tradition the concept of victim is a wholly positive one. The Christian way of life and form of living is to be that of a 'gift and sacrifice' in the wake of Christ, understood as 'God's fragrant offering' (Eph. 5:2). The concept of victim does not mean passive acquiescence, but marks a certain act of renunciation by means of creative asceticism. This tradition does not espouse renunciation for the sake of renunciation, but views it as part of fulfillment in life. In this regard, the role of victim is not a disagreeable fate, but rather is seen as an achievement and an enactment of a fulfilled life."[394] In accord with E. Neubert, we view the transfer to the political as creating the danger "that the positive conception of victim means to walk a thin tightrope between the different chasms of its misuse. There is always the danger of making victims into heroes." The cult of the victor as described above corresponds to just such a problematic cult of the victim.

A theological examination of past political language about victims has normative repercussions for the Christological concept of victim. "In its center is the radical Christian criticism of all victimhood. The belief that God has once and for all taken upon himself the sins of the world in Christ means that, for man, the fear of the consequences of their mistakes and the anxiety about their salvation is taken out of their hands."[395]

The legal reconciliation model provides an explanation for the rejection of the idea of representative victims: God can only see a victim in a sinless person in order to be adequately reconciled. The absence of purity in human nature is championed by God himself. "Representation places on an individual level what has been instrumental in the Judaeo sacrificial metaphor of punishment, victim, and sin."[396] From Anselm and those that came after him, we have the idea that Jesus offers himself in place of the person's sin and thus the person is not the victim or sacrifice before God. "In the relation to God, the Cross of Christ is not the place of sacrifice, but the place of reconciliation which once and for all thwarts the cult of sin and of sacrifice."[397] Whoever thus "still seeks to be a sacrificial lamb to atone for his guilt has not understood that according to God's will, the time for sacrifice is long gone."[398]

As the reconciler Jesus Christ is representative in a double sense. First, He represents the people before God, in that he becomes victim; here the one and true God allows Himself to be struck without striking back, and draws all power to himself in order to break the hold of power. Secondly, he represents God to the people through giving of Himself; as true man He makes himself into pure, powerless entity, which takes away from the *circulus vitiosus* any justification for producing more victims.

If one follows this view, the normative result to our question is that only the theological reference to victim in its representative function is appropriate. To speak of the sacrifice of Christ still only has meaning *coram hominibus;* namely, in place of the cult of victim. The Christological qualification of the concept of victim also determines the framework for the use of metaphorical language.

The representative function of the reconciler has been discussed from the argumentative perspective; the church's "language of reconciliation"[399] can be expressed through "certain metaphorical and at the same time symbolic signs and language in connection to Jesus Christ . . . as the lamb, who takes away the sins of the world." In the church's "language of salvation" of Christ as the lamb of God "salvation is expressed as the transfer of a burden." C. Gestrich describes the task of the metaphor as "a verbal representation in the midst of representation." The burden should "be carried where it is less damaging so that the net of representation that holds us together doesn't tear." (The metaphor of "Jesus as the lamb of God" was appropriate in its function as portraying the manner in which Jesus represents man before God: He allows himself to be slain without fighting back, so he is like a lamb. The question remains whether this metaphor still describes the "tension" of a metaphor that describes a man as lamb, or whether it has evolved into a traditional metaphor. McFaue rightly criticizes: "Theology should never hold only to tradition for that would mean to give up the tension that is the essence of metaphor."[400] The innovative aspect of our question emerges precisely in this connection; namely, the metaphorical "tension" is not sought in the internal church discourse, but proceeds from the concept of victim and is to be found in the overall tension between political and religious language.)

Referring back to the basic theological connection and after considering the above, the designation of "victim" for those pursued under a totalitarian system has meaningful implications under certain conditions. These will be considered in the following order:

- Meaningful connotations mean those that can be comprehended and which do not submit to any direct meaning, to the degree that there is no acknowledged Christian sense for producing victims. Rather, it is precisely the meaninglessness of the sacrifice that generates the question "why."
- A meaningful connotation can not, in view of the developments in our case studies, have any direct correlation to the Christological concept of victim. Wherever a direct explanation can be transferred from the theological into political, the result is — in addition to other problems — the lack of a basic openness and, in the political arena, Christians are implicated without fail.
- The development of indirect connections is appropriate for our case studies. Under these conditions questions can be asked, such as, whether the observed function of a political forum like the TRC exists in a correlation to the invitation to renewal and acceptance, as the worship service has for Christians. According to our empirical analysis, it satisfies the sense of relief that victims of state capriciousness have sought by means of the Truth Commission. In this regard, the TRC in its symbolic enactment (i.e., its linguistic and visual forms of expression) appears as an "institution of unburdening" for the therapeutic processing of sad and destructive experiences. Where this unburdening succeeds, the production of new victims is avoided and the *circulus vitiosus* of power is broken. In short, will the symbolic representation of Christ be validated?
- The representation of Christ is both valid and certified in worship. The "place of reconciliation" that provides the context for the above is the Last Supper. It symbolized as representing "the unity between God and man in the symbol of the crucifixion of Jesus" (Daiber). "The *amnesis,* that is the idea of the redemptive action of Christ, does not mean a call-

ing forth of the presence of Christ, but is a remembrance prior to any recollection or cultic contemporizing of the eternally present gift of salvation of the sacrifice of Christ, which benefits us due to His eternal presence."[401]

- From the combination of both previous points, a question arises with regard to the consequences of the proceedings involved in a political forum. Is the experience of renewal and acceptance that is felt by the victim in the forum of the TRC a symbolic reproduction of the personal aspect of faith in Jesus Christ, which is otherwise expressed in the enactment of Christian worship? Under what conditions can a political forum be interpreted from a theological perspective as a "place of reconciliation"?

The answer to these questions may be contemporized by the symbolic interaction of the hearings and may be asked initially with regard to the structure of communication that takes place during a TRC hearing. The victims of state capriciousness tell their stories before the forum of the TRC, but also in front of the EK in a personal encounter. In South Africa, as in Germany, the audience, the commission members and members of the press comprise the other partner.

Communication on the Forum of the TRC and EK
Person of the victim — Commission Members
                 Audience for the hearings
                 Representatives of the press

The Commission members, listeners and press representatives come under the framework of "symbolic communication"[402] with respect to a specific representative function: the commission members represent the "state," and their function lies in the state's acknowledgement of the injustice, removing any denial of human rights violations by the previous regime.[403] The audience in the hearings represents current "society." Its function consists in the social recognition of the suffered injustice. In this regard, the representatives of the press symbolize the "public." Their function is that of mediator; they contribute by depositing the stories into the "common memory." Additionally, all other victims are represented in the person of the victim, either by the media who observe and record the stories or by those who are present at the hearings. Let us elaborate on the above with the following model:

Representation		Representation
	The victim — Commission members	"the state"
"other victims	Listeners	"the new society"
of the old regime"	Press	"the public"

The fact that the victims are ready to take the step of telling their stories before the Truth Commission is obviously highly symbolic: "Speaking together with one another implies . . . an element of reconciliation that can be identified as *apriori:* the non-reconciled obviously do not talk to each other. Whoever speaks together is already enclosed in a spirit of reconciliation."[404]

The previous observations are made primarily on the level of philosophical symbol. A theological entry point emerges with the observed reciprocity of symbolic communication. As a result, we will argue that a reciprocal relationship in the symbolic interaction of past political forums exists well beyond any mutual dependency; namely, the interdependence between telling and listening symbolizes the theological reconciliation process of the "happy exchange."

Let us proceed inductively from political reconciliation: it is completed in the symbolic process of the hearings as an interpersonal act between the teller of the story and his/her listeners. The interdependence of telling and listening creates references in political reality which, from the theological perspective, allow for the development and transfer of political language into the theological, albeit in broken form.

Let us first deal with the process of story telling. The complexity of a story is a "benchmark of symbolic communication."[405] This is true not only for Biblical stories, as seen earlier, but also for the stories told before the Truth Commission. The stories do not allow themselves to be reduced to "exact statements," but evoke "the 'unregistered' that exists between the lines" (W. Jetter). What allows a theological view to emerge "between the lines" in the victims' stories? Which connections exist? To what extent do we see Jesus Christ in the stories of victims' suffering? First, the statement from narrative theology can be applied here; namely, that one indeed learns from stories, but it is not easy to quantify precisely what one learns. A TRC observer expresses this thought in one simple sentence: "the implicit message of the narrative is one of reconciliation."[406] The stories contain a "dangerous recollection" (J. B. Metz) that pursues the present. However, and key to further considerations, is the negative condition of theological recognition; namely that political remembrance cannot be forced seamlessly — without breaks — onto the theological dimension of remembrance. The political reality of the suffering of people under dictatorships and the theological perspective on the suffering of Christ can not be immediately communicated ontologically through the use of the same word "suffering." The positive connection — or the "permeability" of the political into the theological idea of suffering as well as its opposite — is produced only by the theological perspective; namely, where the reconciliation history of Jesus sets one free to pay attention to the suffering and the disappointed hopes of the past. From this perspective, in the process of remembering, synthetic connections are possible with the *memoria passionis, mortis et resurrectionis* of Christ. Then, indirectly, Jesus Christ enters into the victims' stories. The experience of remembering has its actual theological climax *not* in the act of remembering something morally abhorrent. The stories evoke something other than a nightmarish depression in the face of the morally incomprehensible: they contain hope. It is the hope that God does not abandon the world, but adds his imprint to it based in the hope of a transformation that is effected by Him alone and enters into the world today, here and now. These *hic et nunc* are the moments or occasions of the hearings in which the audience, as representative of society, participates in the stories of the victims during the hearings. Through participation in the stories of suffering, their view of the victim is changed. Here we see evidence of political healing on a spiritual dimension: the relationship of God-given individual worth is restored.

If one looks at the classification for symbolic representation, there is much evidence to suggest a "pure symbolic presentation" of spiritual reconciliation. The above-referenced theological stance over the victims' stories is, according to the above classification, "weak." The lofty development of a soteriological reality is not compelling in the political process. No similarity exists between the meaning of the victims' stories and the reconciliation story of Jesus. The similarity exists only in the structure of the symbolism; that is, in the process of telling. Let us expand the above sketch with the model outlined on page 324.

Proceeding further along the lines of theological symbol, the extent to which the victims' stories relate back to the reconciliation story of Jesus requires a deeper examination of the interdependent communication structures of forums that deal with past politics. The issue is no longer what the victims' stories are able to say from a theological perspective, but what function the process of telling has for the individual victim and to what extent this function is conditioned by the reaction of the hearers to the story.

According to these guiding questions, the hearings' process can thus be characterized as follows: the victims of serious human rights violations are

Theological reference *("purely symbolic")*	"dangerous remembering" that puts the present in question. Reference to reconciliation history.
Political Function	Truth about the past in a system that violates human rights.

Victims tell their stories

↓

Commission, auditorium, listens

Political Function	Official recognition of the story and contribution to the common memory of the nation
Theological reference *("purely symbolic")*	Participation in the suffering of Christ and contribution to the *memoria passionis, mortis et resurrectionis Christi*

relieved of their burden; that is, of their helplessness and their pain. The victims find their voice; telling the story brings relief. The silence is broken in the forum of the TRC and the EK. If no one believed them before, their stories are now heard and acknowledged. If they didn't believe in their own worth before,[407] now the victims are reassured that they are worthwhile. The suffering was not for nothing; it was heard. Thus, the past can be "restored."

In terms of content, the stories tell of violations of human worth. These are stories of dehumanization and we must ask how the TRC and the EK contribute to the reestablishment of the worth of the victims. The answer is to be found in the observed symbolic interaction. Who is the subject of the event? The reestablishment of human worth is difficult to grasp on a purely intrapersonal level. A fate is to be acknowledged, but who does the acknowledging? Who effects the contribution to the reestablishment of worth? First, there are the events that occur between those gathered in the hall of the TRC and the EK: the victims' stories do not fade away, but are listened to. In the process of listening and hearing, the story is again arrested and it completes itself symbolically as an "exchange." Suffering is relinquished. Through the participation of the listeners, the suffering of the victims is removed and a new perspective on life is gained. From the perspective of reconciliation, the victim can again see himself as he is seen by God; namely, as a person of worth. Now the process does not deal with a victim, but with the participation in a TRC hearing. Those present in the hearing represent a new society that upholds the worth of people. They provide an echo for the story and thereby contribute to reestablish worth: they set things right.

Symbolic processes are impressive indicators of interdependence, as can be seen in the case of South Africa, as well as in the German commissions. Everyone rises as the victims enter. This occasion is a symbolic presentation of fact that the worth of the person is sacred and must be respected, despite the fact that they may have been trodden underfoot. Symbolic "gestures can have a visibly healing power . . . for the survivors of political atrocities."[408]

The evidence of a "happy exchange" is also evident in the symbolic processes of political reality. In a representative manner, society gives something back that the previous social order had taken away. Exchanged are the experienced injustices and the devaluation of human worth in the symbolic process of setting things right, which contributes to morally rectify the prior devaluation. Yet, we must ask whether or not in this "past political exchange" between listeners and story tellers we can recognize, from an anthropological Christian point of view, the "happy exchange" in the actual change that occurs in the victims.

Let us contemporize the development of our question with a short definition of what Luther described as the "happy exchange":[409] "God's reconciling work binds Jesus Christ to our destiny. What was intended for us is taken up by him — sin — so that through Him we receive what we ourselves could never achieve: God's righteousness."[410] Proceeding from this definition, one could one ask whether the "happy exchange" in terms of content contains what is already contained in the profane Greek word for reconciliation καταλλαγή,[411] which has its word root in the original "(to) change," "exchange," or "change money." The image of "exchanging money" symbolizes both the similarity and the difference of the exchange. In any case, this complicates the added value and the element of contrast of receiving in the present what should be expressed theologically, since the unique theological sense cannot be conveyed by semantics. At this juncture, it is not a question of how the political concept appears in theological language and how, in the process, it changed once it came into contact with the relationship to God; rather, proceeding from this change, we must ask about its acknowledgment in the political sphere. Accordingly, it does not have to do with reception, but with reconstruction: to what extent is the theological form of reconciliation in the "happy exchange" recognizable in an "exchange of the political past"?

Man's enmity toward God is exchanged in the "happy exchange," in favor of the new relationship of joy. "The καταλλαγή is the expression of turning away from a relationship of enmity between God and man, which is brought about through the 'new Adam' (Romans 5:12 ff.) in Jesus Christ."[412] The reconciliation of God with man completes itself on the "path of personal representation."[413] As shown, it involves two aspects: "In place of our despair, Jesus Christ steps in for man before God. This true man completes the action in his own suffering. He identifies himself through His passion with the action of all. In the role of sacrificial lamb, Jesus stands before God in the place of man: this true God allowing himself to be slain without defending himself."[414]

In this context we inquire as to the extent to which the processes in political reality provide "occasions" for theological recognition:

- The participation by listeners in the victims' suffering makes possible a change of perspective. Is this participation by listeners an indication that Christ as true man carries out the action of all in his own suffering? Are we dealing with a symbolic reproduction of that action here?
- The effectiveness of the change in perspective of a past political "exchange" appears to create no new victims. Thus, a victim cult is overcome.[415] The *circulus vitiosus* for those who take part in the TRC ritual is interrupted. Is the process of validating the representation of the "happy exchange or fight"[416] symbolically depicted as reproduction; namely, that "all non-virtue and sin" are "swallowed up and drowned" "in Christ"?
- The current view with regard to the victims' change in perspective means in many cases "closure,"[417] or an interruption of the old order of things.[418] The conversion to a reconciliation perspective which, among others, is described as a "symbolic break with the past,"[419] replaces the threatening perspective of repayment. To what extent does this "closure" or "break" constitute a symbolic reproduction of what in the Christian faith is meant by the acceptance of the judgment of death; namely, in freedom to receive new life from the Son of Man?

Let us now take the time to tabulate the individual components in the political process with those of the "happy exchange"; that is, to compare them to each other and in the process define their symbolic reproductions (see p. 327).

The interdependence between telling and hearing symbolizes the Christian exchange of existence in the "happy exchange." Proceedings of past po-

Political process	Symbolic production (theological synthesis)	Theological process
Process between persons (relation of person-person)	Reproduction of the process of Christ-man on the relational level of man-man	Process between persons (relation Christ-God, Christ-man)
Seek for unburdening/ letting go/relief from sorrow in process of telling	The end of the victim cult is symbolically reproduced, in so far as the process of unburdening creates no new victims	"Give your troubles to Christ." Jesus steps in as the sacrificial lamb of God for man.
Hearers represent the new society; symbolic promise and reestablishment of the worth of people	Listeners take representative part in the suffering of the victims and symbolize (reproductively) participation in the world of the suffering of God	Christ steps in for us as true man before God and identifies himself in his passion with the actions of all sinners
Victims can "close" a chapter	Symbolic reproduction of the death of the old person	To take up one's cross as the old person dies; that proud "I" is dead. ("Not I that lives, but Christ lives in me.")
Victim's life can have a "new beginning"	Symbolic reproduction of what is represented by καινὴ κτίσις.	"If anyone is in Christ, he is a new creation." (II Cor. 5:17a)

litical forums, leading through reconciliation to a change in the victim's perspective, symbolically portray the theological reconciliation process as a passage through death into new life. This formula remains very general to the extent that the central theological question is open as to what type of "symbolic reproduction" is constituted. How is the symbolization to be classified? Is it a "purely symbolic" type; if so, is it analogous or mimetic?

There is much evidence to suggest that the symbolization in the examined cases is neither of a mimetic nor of a pure symbolic type. They are "less" than mimetic representation. Political and theological processes do not correlate to actual symbolic means, where the (mimetic) historical characteristics of a person reveal their essence. On the other hand, we are able to say

327

something "more" about the possibility of the pure symbolic form of presentation; the similarity imposes itself beyond the inner structure of the symbolism. In the analogous form of representation the similarity is transformed in the medium of the always present symbolism, but not relinquished.

In a theologically normative sense, we are dealing with the symbolic reproduction of the "happy exchange" in political reality according to a general classification of an "analogous" form of representation. Our use of analogy is specifically referenced with respect to a theoretical basis. Accordingly, our question of correspondence deals principally with the structural possibility of a correlation of the forms of expression between interpersonal reconciliation in political reality and the reconciliation of God in Christ, who created the "new" person who is not, however, an analogous being. Eschatological and political reality does not encounter us as already ontologically mediated. The *analogia relationis* emerges again as an appropriate category of analysis, first, because it considers normatively the structural possibility of correspondence of the interpersonal "being in relationship" alone and of the "being in relationship" to God, and secondly, because it formally examines the poles of the question of correspondence and the analogy of the *analogia relationis* for specific benchmarks: thus, they stand "in relationship."[420]

Still to be investigated is whether the theoretical foundation contributes to the results of the theological synthesis. Formally to be determined is what specifically is involved with the benchmarks in the form of "relationships": in the "happy exchange" with the relational steps of "Jesus analogous God/ 'man analogous to man,'"[421] and in an "exchange of political reality" with the relational steps of "man analogous to man" (as in the relation between the victims and their listeners). The question to be asked is, according to the theoretical evidence, whether a further *analogia relationis* can be found between the relational steps of "man analogous to man" in both political and eschatological reality, so that political reconciliation appears in a basic connection to reconciliation as a soteriological category. Does the empirically analyzed relationship between people of past political forums of the TRC and the EK correlate to an *analogia relationis* which has its origin in the relationship constituting love of God? The answer is yes, and indeed, "in relationship" as symbolic reproduction. Wherever the new person "in Christ" is allowed to participate in the sufferings of God in the world (relationship of man-man in eschatological reality), it is symbolically reproduced through the listeners in their relationship to the victims (relation man-man in political reality).

"Symbolic reproduction" is thus theologically reconstructed as fundamental change. Those who are involved are symbolically placed in another place in which eschatological reality is modeled as the unity of God with man, as reproduced symbolically in the Last Supper. "When God reconciles, He incorporates 'in Christ.' He does not place himself merely in a . . . new relation to people, but he changes them and accepts them, in that they are taken to another, totally new place."[422] Under these conditions, the Christian idea of reconciliation can be reconstructed in the process of "political forums"; namely as a symbolic reproduction of a process in which the Last Supper creates a real "space" of reconciliation for the Christian faith.

B. Consequences for the Life and Witness of the Church

In regard to our perception of the "signs of the time" and its meaning there are, among others, references to the church: do perceived signs of the grace of God in political reality require acknowledgment by the church? What contribution is open to the church to move the impulse forward? To what extent do politically perceived signs of transcendence call into criticism the activity of the church and give it cause for critical self-reflection? Can it be a means of comfort if we can accept that signs of God's grace also exist outside the walls of the church? What criticism must the church introduce into the political discussion when dealing with human guilt?

I. The Church Is a Place of Thanksgiving

1. If the reality of God's grace can be seen in a political process, then this is a reason for the church to give thanks.
2. The church is a community that can make explicit what others only implicitly perceive is possible. It is the community that is lifted up and is called and equipped to give thanks for the reality of divine reconciliation.
3. In order to be thankful, the church must not assume the signs of reconciliation. It is not necessary to name the sacramental signs, as if it had to do with derivative processes that have their actual reality within the church only.

II. The Church Also Has a Political Role

1. The church is led by the hope that people "in Christ" are changed; they are altered and capable of change.
2. The task of the church during political upheaval lies in overcoming the barrier between the larger vision and the small steps toward achieving it. Its space is open to all people in order to contribute to reconciliation. The establishment of offender-victim-dialogue circles is a hopeful example, because here the framework of the church is taken into consideration as something that can make possible encounters between people and give air to victim's stories.
3. As "liturgist" the church reinforces the political reconciliation process where it makes room for sadness, grief, and healing. In public memorials, to which the Christian community can contribute as a "liturgist of the state," the knowledge of the damage and the loss of the victims can be expressed publicly.
4. Reconciliation is possible in the framework of the Last Supper, which is not otherwise possible outside of the church. It is very different when a victim of DDR injustice meets a previous offender at the Last Supper during a Sunday worship service than when he/she meets them on a podium to discuss SED injustices.
5. The church must consciously learn to take the place of forgiveness seriously in the worship service.

III. The Church Reveals Itself in Its Treatment of the Victims

1. The church should not equate teaching on the justification of the sinner with the political integration of the offender.
2. For the sake of its own self-understanding, the church should embrace family members of the victims. Dealing with the victims demonstrates the legitimacy of the church of Jesus Christ. Do the victims of acts of violence feel welcome at worship and does their suffering receive meaningful consideration?
3. By participating in self-criticism, the church has played its part in acknowledging how society tolerates system injustice and is able to be a model for dealing with guilt in society at large.

IV. Christ Is the Hope of the Church

1. The church impacts political reality so that it will not be deserted by God.
2. The church also acknowledges the signs of grace of God in the political reconciliation process.
3. Reconciliation is an incomplete, open event of the future. Christ is present in it and with us — in the church and in the world.
4. The church's message testifies to the presence of God and proclaims the "word of reconciliation." If the church does not proclaim it, who will?
5. The church's message should be more confident in the service of reconciliation and should embolden the congregation to share the word of reconciliation. In contrast to the political arena, the unique responsibility of the spiritual office is clear.

V. The Church Provides a Critical Contrast to Politics

1. The church is there to remind the political realm that in dealing with human guilt spaces need to be maintained for occasions in which human possibilities surpass the capabilities of the legal process.
2. The change in perspective brought about by reconciliation leads beyond the admission of guilt and the gift of forgiveness. The church must remind politics of the normative character of reconciliation.
3. The church has the social responsibility to focus the attention on the opposition between the legitimate use of the word of reconciliation and its strategic misuse.
4. The concept of reconciliation hides the potential for political debate. Reconciliation is something different than the perspective of "working (something) out"; it opens up the future so that guilt can be relinquished.
5. The difference between the spiritual and the worldly need not necessarily deepen the divide between politics and church, but can help to build true bridges. Thus, appropriate preconditions should not be minimized.
   (a) The church can not transfer spiritual reconciliation directly into politics; rather, the relative autonomy of the state is to be respected, which includes the making of legal decisions regarding punishment.
   (b) Politics may not hinder "preparing the way" for the Gospel by a pri-

ori excluding the spiritual dimension of reconciliation in the mere legal working out of guilt.

4. The church has decided to determine the boundary for the relative autonomy of the political, through which the worth of people is determined. Accordingly, the death penalty is to be categorically rejected because it imposes a final judgment over the person and forever excludes the possibility of reconciliation.

Notes

Notes to the Introduction

1. Dialogue abbreviated (without designating omissions). Full transcript available at http://www.truth.org/za/hrvtrans/Wineland/maxam.htm.

2. Citations are taken from the proceedings of the Investigative Commission; compare EK VIII, 66f.

3. The areas of cult, justice, and society are the defining areas of the theological concept of reconciliation: "In cult God creates the possibility to come before him and to come to him." "In the sphere of justice, relationships between persons are aligned. In the social dimension we see people living together as regulated not only by rules of conflict and in the readiness to reduce coexistence, but also in the purification of guilt and its consequences." *The Art of Reconciliation,* in: EKL 3, A. Volume IV, 1166.

4. "Univocal" is the term used according to Aristotle's definition (Cat. 1a 6f), in which the word denoting the subject it describes is the descriptor or the name, and also the essential concept communicated by the term is the same.

5. Compare G. Sauter et al. 1986, 155. Following citation Ibid.

6. M. Kähler, *Doctrine of Reconciliation,* 42.

7. G. Sauter 1997, 47.

8. Compare entries in Dictionary of Synonyms, 1989.

9. Compare F. Kluge, *Etymological Dictionary* (Berlin-New York, 1989), 22.A. "Reconciliation" stems from a Middle High German word for reconciliation that is related to "sin."

10. It is noteworthy that in pertinent, dominant political science publications the preference is for language pertaining to folk-understanding rather than folk-reconciliation, to German-American "relations," "partnership," or "diplomatic history," rather than to reconciliation between Americans and Germans (compare C. B. Riess/ H. Bortfeld 1994; D. Gutzen et al. 1992; M. Jonas 1984). Meanwhile, regarding the relationship between Germany and Poland, the talk of "German-Polish reconciliation" is accept-

able (compare H. Pfister 1972; R. Dohrmann 1968). The sense for language appears to follow the language of morality: where there is a connotation of guilt then "reconciliation" is used, but where it has to do with a bilateral process, then "understanding" is used.

11. Christian Frey 1993, 19.

12. G. Kraus 1990, 190.

13. D. Ritschl, *The Logic of Theology* (Philadelphia: Fortress, 1987), 223.

14. Chr. Gestrich 1989.

15. R. F. Capon 2000.

16. J. Zehner 1998.

17. Regulative statements are what I term in this study something akin to D. Ritschl's "the implicit axiom, with which a person or a group (with the same story) is equipped. They are concerned about examined thinking, speaking, and ordered activity. They are not formulated unconditionally and forever" (D. Ritschl, *The Logic of Theology*, p. 21). More on the theological concepts of analysis of this research is in Part I.B.3.

18. W. Huber 1996a, 9.

19. In Biblical tradition, in which the concept of reconciliation does not occur broadly (compare already M. Kähler, *Doctrine of Reconciliation,* 1ff.; 63ff.), there are large hurdles standing in the way of reciprocal transferability. It is first apparent in the framework of the Introduction that in Paul reconciliation is uniquely soteriologically qualified, since it is a concept that is connected with the death of Jesus. Outside of the Biblical concept of forgiveness, which in the Synoptic tradition is also mentioned without any connection to the Cross, the political dimension of forgiveness between God and man can be made. This connection will be developed theologically in Part I.B.3.

20. Compare results at the end of Part III.A.II.3.a and b as well as A.III.3.a.

Notes to Part I.A

1. W. Huber 1991 (in first edition, 1973).

2. J. Zehner 1998.

3. J. Kreuter 1997.

4. J. de Gruchy 1995.

5. D. Shriver 1995, 73-118.

6. W. Huber 1991, 380f. treated the German-Polish understanding in the context of case studies and uses the EKD-Memoir of 1965 as a basis.

7. J. Zehner 1998, 117-33.

8. D. Shriver 1995, for example, processes his three case studies during an examination period of a total of 120 years and bases his conclusions accordingly: "The argument for a certain thoroughness of the case study in these matters, as opposed to a survey, is strong here. . . . Better to wrestle with a limited number of large, central, tough histories than to presume to speak to or for a great number of them" (p. 72).

9. Compare J. Zehner 1998, 119, 127f., 137 and the talk of "path of reconciliation," 280-305.

10. Compare D. Ritschl *(Logic),* 68f.

11. J. Zehner 1998, 114.

12. J. Zehner 1998, 135f.

13. W. J. Patzelt 1997, 23.

14. W. J. Patzelt 1997, 24.

15. Compare W. J. Patzelt 1997, 33f.

16. W. J. Patzelt 1997, 34.

17. An unavoidable tension in the interview method exists for the social scientist. On the one hand, the social scientist must take a thoroughly neutral position in order to avoid suggestive questions and on the other hand he/she has to deal with personal requests and individual accounts in order to break through the potentially affected homogeneous positions of the dialogue partners to better determine the basic intentions and experiences of the actors.

18. Petra Bock, in: P. Bock et al. 1999, 98. In her article, the politician gives clues to the history of research on the concept of "past politics" in political science (99, comment 3).

19. Petra Bock and Edgar Wolfrum, in: P. Bock et al. 1999, 8.

20. W.-D. Narr, "Logic of Political Science," in: G. Kress et al. 1969, 22.

21. In: P. Bock et al. 1999, 8.

22. E. Wolfrum 1996, 376.

23. Ibid.

24. Wolfrum offers clues to the state of the research in various publications. Compare the short piece titled "What is history of politics?" in: P. Bock et al. 1999, 56-60 (and comments). In his accreditation piece, he works with the history of politics as a category of analysis for a historical account of West German post-war history. Compare E. Wolfrum's history of politics in the German Republic in "The Path to Memories of the United German Republic 1948-1990." Darmstadt, 1999.

25. P. Bock et al. 1999, 9.

26. E. Wolfrum 1996, 381.

27. Edgar Wolfrum, in: P. Bock et al. 1999, 58.

28. P. Steinbach 1999, 3.

29. In: P. Bock et al. 1999, 83.

30. Compare the function of comparison in historical science (G. Haupt/J. Kocka 1996) to the comparative statement in political science ("comparative politics") in initiatives like D. Berg-Schlosser et al. 1995, 220-71; also H. Munkler, in political science. As for history and situation, see: I. Fetscher et al. 1985, 22f. According to Munkler the comparison serves as "a substitute for what in politics is the lack of the possibility of scientifically controlled experiments" (art. cit., 22).

31. Compare J. de Gruchy 1997, 616: "without the fall of the wall in Berlin in 1989 it would have been impossible for the changes in South Africa to have happened at that point in time." See also W. Huber 1990, 1.

32. Compare Hansard 1990: "The dynamic developments in international politics have created new opportunities for South Africa as well. . . . Southern Africa now has a historical opportunity to set aside its conflicts, and ideological differences and draw upon joint programme and reconstruction."

33. D. Tutu 1994, 192.

Notes to Part I.B

1. On the difference between (Buddhist) religion of salvation and (African) religion of reconciliation see T. Sundermeier 1993, 126f., 129f.

2. Significant citations from his seminar lectures on "Dietrich Bonhoeffer and South Africa," University of Cape Town, 9 Feb. 2000 (citations from taped notes).

3. Compare to the judgment of Desmond Tutu also the contribution of Janet Hodgson: "Tutu: Anglican and African" and John de Gruchy, "The Transformation of Politics" in *Archbishop Tutu — Prophetic Witness in South Africa* (Cape Town, 1996), 106ff., 49ff.

4. The concept should be even more illuminating than that of "confessional theology." Theology also exists in an overlapping confessional horizon that is influenced by the culture. Compare D. Ritschl *(Logic)* on the problem, 147f. For the South African context see: J. de Gruchy and C. Villa-Vicencio, *Doing Theology in Context: South African Perspectives* (Cape Town/New York, 1994).

5. Compare to the hierarchy of D. Ritschl *(Logic)*, 143f.: D. Ritschl 1994b, 393f.

6. Compare the nature of Anglo-Saxon theology of incarnation with that of U. Link-Wieczorek 1998 (see here ideas and literature that provide relevant avenues of theological Christological inquiry for the purposes of our problem). Here the theme is that the direction indicated by the question is decisive: if one asks from the point of view of God how He stands in relation to Jesus, then the incarnation is a meaningful way of responding; however, if one asks from the point of view of man how it is that Jesus stands in relation to God, then inspiration offers potentially meaningful answers. For the Anglican incarnation, Christology as "the history of God in the man Jesus is determinative for the experience of learning about God, and is one by which his relationship to the world remains defined" (360).

7. DBW 6, 143. In contrast to Karl Barth, Bonhoeffer is less interested in the opposition of extent of "justification and justice." In his work *Karl Barth in the Theology of Dietrich Bonhoeffer* (Berlin, 1989) Andreas Pangritz says: "Bonhoeffer also speaks of a 'total break' of the penultimate by the ultimate. His primary interest is however the 'relationship' between the penultimate and the ultimate, the 'preparation' for the ultimate by the penultimate" (73).

8. When a concept like correspondence is transferred constructively from a theory of truth in theological ethics and teaching to one of knowledge and recognition, changes occur that need to be considered over against the background of other ontological assumptions. In a philosophical discussion of truth, the expression "theory of correspondence" describes a class of prominent conceptions of truth according to which truth exists in a particular relation of agreement between language and the world. Thomas Aquinas (and also Albertus Magnus) offered a classical definition for the essential connection between truth and nature: as the agreement between the mature understanding judgment *(intellectus)* and the reality *(res)*, as *adaequatio intellectus et rei* (*De veritate*, q.1.a.1) — in the sense of *adaequatio intellectus (humani) ad rem*. In philosophical discussions it is emphasized whether these characteristics of the correspondence theory refer to a correlation between "truer" or "more false" language, and to that of Being (esp. not-Being) that Aristotle refers to, in so far as his definition ("To say namely, that Being is not or that Not-

Being is, is false, and on the other hand to say that Being is or that Not-Being is not, is true." Metz, 1011b, citing Aristotle (*Philosophical Writings of Darmstadt* 1995, 85) contains no explicit relational conception of truth according to which a "more true" laden truth is discernable as it stands in a specific relationship of correspondence to certain facts or events of the world. (Compare the current discussion in the overview with E. Brendel, "Correspondence," in: *Encyclopedia of Philosophy* I [Hamburg, 1999], 728-31, as well as R. L. Kirkham, "Truth, Correspondence Theory of," in: *Routledge Encyclopedia of Philosophy* IX, 472-75.) In contrast to the characteristics of the theory of correspondence as correlation, the main representative in the newer English philosophy of J. L. Austin (compare "truth" in: *Word and Meaning,* Munich 1975) establishes the theoretical version of truth as congruence between true opinions and facts. For B. Russell, who measurably influenced this definition, an opinion is true when it gives a structural congruence between a fact of the world and that of the perceived asserted relationship between the objects (compare *Problems of Philosophy,* Frankfurt/M. 1967). As a basic problem of the correspondence model we cite in the philosophical discussion: (1) the explanation of the ontological status of the facts; (2) the explanation of appropriate criterion for the identification of facts. The second problem has already been worked out in terms of political forms of appearance of reconciliation, in so far as the inter-disciplinary guiding questions for the case studies yield criteria for the "identification of the facts" of political reconciliation. The first problem is primarily discernable in connection to the criticism of a (naïve) realistic concept of truth. (Although Kant's description of truth as "the agreement of knowledge with its occasion" [*Critique of Pure Reason* A 58, cited after Kant-Study Version II, 102] recollects the correspondence theory, with the assertion of the *adaequatio rei et intellectus* a mistaken ontological presupposition of the metaphysic of substance is achieved. "The asserted identity between the knowledge as such and its objective content is relinquished." E. Cassirer, *Philosophy of Symbolic Forms* III, 6.) For our position this problem means that if a stipulating definition is to be achieved, as may occur when the theological correspondence question is placed in the horizon of another such as the ontological Being, namely One in whom individual truth is normative, and against the background of the Thomist concept of truth, it must appear to be the opposite of truth and through the claim of the Gospel always have more to say than what is real, and thus no longer agrees with reality. In this difference we view the constructive core of what a Christian dogmatics may contribute to solving the problem: our case studies (in Part II) are presented with the claim that they are true in the forum of reality and the *res*. The theological interpretation (in Part III) testifies to a "more" and a "different" way; to a reality *changed* by the Gospel, so that truth now appears as *adaequatio intellectus ad rem mutatam.*

9. D. Ritschl, *Logic,* 21: 295f. The "Questions of Correspondence" is the "seminal question of what is currently 'pressing' of 'lasting importance' or that of an individual story to a higher story; of my life in God's promise and the life of Jesus." Frankfurt/M. 1967.

10. As in connection to the metaphorical structure of religious language. Thetically it means: "The agreement of the discovery with the discovered in the sense of the *adaequatio intellectus ad rem* is ontologically only possible on the basis of the connection between the discovered and what is already discovered and on the basis of the contrast be-

tween the discovered and the discovery; on the basis of experience, in which the being allows itself to be discovered" (from: P. Ricoeur et al. 1974, 121).

11. Compare overview of correspondence and feeling of affinity with M. Weber, C. Baudelaire and M. Lowy, in: M. Lowy, *Solution and Utopia: Messianic Judaism and Libertarian Thought* (Berlin, 1997), 20f.

12. D. Ritschl 1981, 493f. In connection to medical ethics.

13. On the abundance of the literature I would like to refer to the concepts and currents in the political theology in the article "Political Theology" in: *Handbook of 20th Century Theology*, R. Gibellini, 1995, 290-311.

14. In uncritical connection to K. Barth, "The Christian Congregation and Civil Society" indicates that there are direct correlations to the Gospel found in politics. At the very least it should be asked, whether Barth, (on his part), gave credence to the critical. H. Thielicke (*Theological Ethics* II, 2, 714) criticizes that the customary method of analogy used in political reality is not adequate because it misinterprets the problem of relative autonomy in the political arena. Thus, Barth says for example, "The just state must have its model in the just church" (*Christian Congregations and Civil Societies,* Stuttgart 1946, 51). Compare the order of the tract, among others, with the analysis of W. Huber 1991, 459ff.

15. Compare D. Ritschl 1994b, 390.

16. Compare P. Tillich, *Systematic Theology* I, 65ff.

17. For example, the numerous non-church initiatives and circles of offender-victim-dialogue claim their own weight with regard to a theological perspective, but without final substantiation.

18. In the principal areas of concern driving the discussion between theology and the church (functionally also described as the "watch bureau"), there are certainly points to be made along with K. Barth, who describes it as primarily a problem of the separation of the two kingdoms: the kingdom of the world attempts to elevate itself to a form of the kingdom of God and to make itself absolute.

19. Let us recall Bonhoeffer's formulation: "The penultimate must be protected for the sake of the ultimate" (DBW 6, 152).

20. Compare the main current in the article on Political Theology, in: *Handbook,* op. cit., 302f. Following citation ibid.

21. Compare article on Political Theology in: op. cit., 295f.: 303. D. Sollë's research plan is sketched out in the introduction.

22. Compare to these trends the article on Political Theology, in: *Handbook,* op. cit., 303.

23. In recent publications D. Ritschl has already (in an expansion on the application in the "Logic," 23) deepened the concept of "recognition" as a concept of analysis. Compare also D. Ritschl 1988, 60f.: ibid. 1994a, 144ff.; ibid. 199, 169f. Accordingly, the "phenomenology of recognition" means that "one (encounters) the basic element of revelation; namely the re-encounter with the remembered content of the presence of God in the process of recognition. This is initiated through 'occasions' (to use a term from A. N. Whitehead). They can take place in and outside of worship, in ordinary daily life or in larger political and social interactions — an acceptance of the presence of God in listening or in the rekindled remembrance of heard texts, words, and moments of recognition"

(D. Ritschl 1999, 169). As with the men on the road to Emmaus (Luke 24:13f.) for example, it was at the breaking of bread that recognition was initiated (compare here D. Ritschl 1994a, 144ff.). Certain "stories, situations and pictures" are recognized again because they provide the "occasion." "I recall anew what it means that Jesus hung on the cross, that Abraham trusted in God, that the father took back the prodigal son. But certainly, I see everything in a certain perspective. My acceptance is not secondary to the perspective of this story from the Bible, but it is simultaneously impressed with perspective" (D. Ritschl 1988, 60f.). The difference from Platonic ontology, which is conceptualized in Ritschl, is to be underscored by this research. With the use of the concept "recognition" in theological analysis, the primacy of the content recognized by faith is decisive in past political events: political reality does not emerge as a new revelatory source of reconciliation; a recognition of a reconciliation-theological nature completes itself a posteriori and is normatively examined using seminal ideas about the Christian concept of reconciliation.

24. "Corresponding," in: *Philosophical Dictionary,* ed. M. Stockhammer, Cologne 1967, 197.

25. E. Cassirer, *Philosophy of Symbolic Forms* III, 6.

26. Compare scheme of reciprocal non-transferability in the introduction to the emergence of the cosmic, legal, humanistic, and historical-process models of reconciliation (Part III.A.I.3.a-d).

27. Emergence of the cosmic, legal, humanistic, and historical-process models of reconciliation (Part III.A.I.3.a-d).

28. Systematic development in connection with the central categorical difference of "ultimate" and "penultimate" (Part III.A.II.2.a).

29. Systematic development in connection with the category main difference of "ultimate" and "penultimate" (Part III.A.II.2.b).

30. We accept constructively with J. Zehner the systematic development train of thought to the meaning of Baptism and Last Supper for the inter-personal forgiveness of sins and reconciliation; J. Zehner 1998, 251ff. and 347ff.; compare Part III.A.II.3.a and b.

31. A significant concept of analysis with K. Barth in KD III, which was introduced in the framework of the doctrine of creation; compare esp. KD III, 1, 218f.; there in explicit reference to D. Bonhoeffer (DBW 3, 60f.). From the secondary literature is emphasized in the section on *analogia relationis:* W. Härle 1995, 205-26 as well as the research into K. Barth's understanding of analogy: E. Jüngel 1962, 535-57. Compare to the placement of the *analogia relationis* in the teaching on analogy: The Art of Analogy, TRE 2 (1978) 625-50, 641f. (further literature 648-50).

32. According to K. Barth the choice of the man Jesus by the Triune God describes a relationship. That it results in an *analogia relationis* is clear according to the Barthian thesis. This is love, the essence of the inner Trinitarian "being-in-relation" (compare KD II, 2, 130). W. Härle 1975, 208 says: "Because God chooses the man Jesus with the same love that he himself is, the relationship between the choosing God and the chosen man Jesus is analogous to the relationship to the Being of God. A similarity of relation for Barth thus does not come into question, because the partners in this relation (former: God-God; later: God-Jesus) are not similar."

33. W. Härle 1975, 209.

34. Compare KD III, 2, 391. "God is in relationship; in relationship also to man whom he created."

35. KD III, 1, 219.

36. In as far as our pole for the question of correspondence is concerned (which describes [1] the activity of creation and [2] activity of God) it is appropriate to ask whether the *analogia relationis* would more precisely be classified as an *analogia operationis*. Accordingly, an account of the theological situation would be decisive where the inequality between God and man has its basis in the different character of activity. While God's activity has the character of pure creation, the activity of man is "effected," that is, created. The similarity exists between the activity of God and of man in the sense of the *analogia operationis;* in that God's activity in man and the activity of man himself is an activity of already having been effected — namely, it is the change of an already active operation. The question remains, however, whether this creative theological difference contributes much to the development of our problem, especially as this analogous relation of the *analogia relationis* is not general and independent from God's revelatory activity, but is, above all, recognized through the revelation. And this is decisive for the analysis category in which our question of correspondence is situated.

37. Citation W. Härle 1975, 210.

38. Art of Analogy, TRE 2 (1978), 641.

39. The difference in the *analogia entis* also appears gradually, since "it only had to do with a possibility, which first has to be realized and which factually, in the banishment of sin — in the impossible possibility — is not yet realized" (art. cit., ibid.).

40. W. Härle 1975, 212; compare also E. Jüngel 1962, 548, which characterizes the *analogia relationis* as "the correspondence of relationship constituted by 'yes.'"

41. Citation: W. Härle 1975, 212.

42. Citation: E. Jüngel 1962, 546.

43. W. Härle 1975, 213.

44. W. Härle 1975, 212-13.

45. Compare this to the Christological conditions as well as to the difference between structural possibility and analogous being which was shown in the previous text.

46. O. Weber 1966, 271.

47. Art of Analogy, TRE 2 (1978), 648.

48. C. Breytenbach 1993, 78f.

49. Paul is the legate empowered by God who in the tradition of ancient diplomacy was entrusted with a message of peace, namely, "that God had already reconciled man to himself." According to C. Breytenbach 1989, 135, can one speak "in a qualified sense . . . of an invitation to reconciliation." It is however "important to see, that God and man according to Paul are in no way equal partners, who would be able to arrive at some kind of peace contract with each other. Humanity finds itself in a dilemma (Romans 1–3) and God takes the initiative, by transforming the relationship of animosity into one of a relationship of friendship." Compare on reconciliation and the Apostle Paul the entire chapter 7 of Breytenbach, op. cit. 107ff.

50. C. Breytenbach 1989, 180.

51. 1 Cor. 7:11 is an exception, wherein, however, again the aspect of relation in thought concerning reconciliation appears decisive.

52. In this regard, the reception of the Pauline concept of reconciliation in the New Testament is interesting. C. Breytenbach underscores in reference to a research study, the indirect influence on the South African Kairos document of 1985, the constructive elements that are already there for Paul for a reconstruction of reconciliation theology within the political. Thus, Breytenbach enlightens the inner–New Testamental reception of the Pauline thinking on reconciliation in the letters to the Ephesians and the Colossians and demonstrates how with Paul the applied connection between the reconciliation of God with man and of individual men is achieved in the Deutero-Pauline letters, be it as salvation history reconciliation between Jews and heathen (Eph. 2:14-18) or be it as cosmic reconciliation (Col. 1:20-22). Correspondingly, he titles his chapter "The Reconciliation of Cultures in Ephesians" as well as "The reconciliation of the universe in Colossians" (compare C. Breytenbach, "Reconciliation-Shifts in Christian Soteriology," in: *Reconciliation and Reconstruction: Creative Options for a Rapidly Changing South Africa*, ed. W. S. Vorster, Pretoria 1986, 1-2, esp. 4f. and 19f.). For our problem, it is important that from the Biblical perspective a multiplicity in the derivations of the Pauline idea of reconciliation need to be factored in. Our large reconciliation model from the theological historical perspective reflects this content and represents certain systematic-theological versions of Biblical basic motives of reconciliation.

53. As a basic line of Pauline statements on reconciliation in Romans 11:15; II Cor. 5:17-21 and Romans 5:1, 6-11, C. Breytenbach says 1989, 183 that: "Reconciliation with the world means that all people may take part in the event of reconciliation."

54. In this connection it is noteworthy that in the current discussions in connection to the cited considerations, it can be asked whether Paul's implied theological axiom was expressed in such a way that reconciliation can be considered a metaphor in the sense of P. Ricoeur; compare the contributions of C. Villa-Vicencio ("Reconciliation as Metaphor") and of C. Breytenbach ("Using Exegesis") in: L. Holness and R. Wüstenberg (eds.), *Theology in Dialogue: The Impact of the Arts, Humanities, and Sciences on Contemporary Religious Discourse* (Grand Rapids/Cambridge, 2002), 224ff. and 245f. In connection to this turn to the discussion in the Systematic Reconstruction in Part III.A.III as to whether we accordingly are dealing with *more* than the recognition of a symbolic reproduction of reconciliation in political reality and whether this has more of a reality-illuminating or reality-establishing function in theological terms.

Notes to Part II.A

1. In the transitional process in Latin America (Argentina, Uruguay, and Chile), different experiences were connected with a "Truth Commission." Since the process of change in Eastern Europe was of "pressing necessity," according to the Cape Town political scientist André du Toit, the experiences were broadened and globally interconnected. "The new and complex problems of 'justice in transition' became the topic for a series of international workshops and conferences building a specialist and wide-flung network of human rights lawyers and activists, philosophers, church leaders, politicians" (A. du Toit 1994, 66). Conferences from the project "Justice in the Time of Transition," which is found in Charter 77 of the New York archives, took place, among other places, in Salzburg

(1992), San Salvador (1993) and Cape Town (1994). In the last conference, the foundations for the TRC were discussed. Compare: Justice in Transition Document 1995. A. du Toit comments on the work of the project: "These intensive and ongoing discussions . . . have produced a sophisticated understanding of the complex issues at stake in dealing with the problem of truth and justice in transition" (art. cit. 67).

2. From the abundance of literature these are foundational: S. P. Huntington 1991; N. Kritz 1995. Particularly on the transition process in South Africa, compare A. S. Minty 1993; T. D. Sisk 1995; M. Szeftel 1994; S. v. Zyl 1992; G. Werle 1998.

3. Foundational: P. B. Hayner 1994; A. du Toit 1994.

4. Compare above all the Institute for Democracy Document 1994; Justice in Transition Document 1995. From the legal standpoint: J. Sarkin 1996; T. Wong 1996; G. Werle 1996. From the philosophical perspective: A. du Toit 1995 and 1996a. From the psychological perspective: B. Hamber 1996. (The literature on the theological perspective of the TRC is primarily referred to in Part III where monographs of the TRC Commission members are included which were published at the end of the TRC; for example D. Tutu 1999; C. Villa-Vicencio et al. 2000.)

5. J. Friedrichs et al. 1971, 19.

6. On the Internet homepage of the TRC (www.truth.org.za).

7. I was able to take part in the Fall 1996 hearings of the TRC in Paarl and Cape Town in which more than thirty victims' statements were heard.

8. Final Report V, 7, §51 (p. 273).

9. H. Adam 1998. Other essential literature on the TRC also includes participant observations, even if they are not reflected in the method. Compare A. Krog 1998a.

10. Compare for the practical structure of the interviews P. Atteslander, *Methods of Empirical Social Science Research* (Berlin/New York, 1993), 156ff., 171. The notes on the interviews are contained in the Appendices.

11. In addition to the president of the Commission, Desmond Tutu, I was able to speak with commissioners from many of the committees: Marry Burton (Committee on Human Rights), Glenda Wildschut (Committee on Reparations) and Dumisa Ntsebeza (Amnesty Committee). From the research department of the TRC, I interviewed the Director, Charles Villa-Vicencio and his representative Wilhelm Verwoerd. In the area of administration I was able to speak with the Executive Secretary Ruben Richards and the Coordinator of the Regional Office of the TRC in Cape Town, Louis du Plooy. (In the following are cited: D. Tutu 1996a; G. Wildschut 1999; D. Ntsebeza 1999; C. Villa-Vicencio 1996b, esp. 1999a; W. Verwoerd 1999; L. du Plooy 1996.)

12. Michael Lapsley, Trauma Center, Cape Town; Brandon Hamber, Center for the Study of Violence and Reconciliation, Johannesburg; in addition I was able to speak with the representatives of the Religious Response to the TRC and of the Center for Conflict Resolution, both in Cape Town (in the following are cited: M. Lapsley 1996; B. Hamber 1996, esp. 1999a; Religious Response Documents 1994-1995; Track Two 1997).

13. Beyers Naudé, Wolfram Kistner, Stiaan von der Merwe, all of the Ecumenical Advice Bureau, Johannesburg; John de Gruchy, University of Cape Town; Desmond van der Water, Theological College, Turffontain; Denise Ackermann, Dirkie Smit, both of the University of the Western Cape; Fani du Toit, University of Stellenbosch (in the following are cited: B. Naudé and W. Kistner 1996; W. Kistner and B. Naudé 1999; S. van der Merwe

1996b, esp. 1999; J. de Gruchy 1996c, esp. 1999; D. Ackermann 1999a; D. Smit 1999; F. du Toit 1999).

14. André du Toit, University of Cape Town; Kenneth Christie, University of Stellenbosch; Gunnar Theissen, first cited University Western Cape (named first in the following citation: A. du Toit 1996a; F. du Toit 1999).

15. A very important dialogue partner was Heribert Adam, University of Cape Town (in following cited: H. Adam 1999).

16. A very important dialogue partner among the philosophers was Wilhelm Verwoerd, University of Stellenbosch (cited W. Verwoerd 1999).

17. Very important dialogue partners were Chirevo Kwenda and Malinge Njeza, both of the University of Cape Town. (With them I could discuss the TRC hearing transcripts on the basis of traditional African thought.)

18. A very important dialogue partner among Islamic scholars was Ibraim Mousa, University of Cape Town (in the following cited I. Mousa, 1996).

19. Final Report 1998. Cited in the following according to volume (= I), Chapter (= 1) and Paragraph (= §). In German until the end of the manuscript where two summaries of the Final Report appear.

20. Even the methodological reflections of the TRC end with the view: "The Act demands methodological pluralism." Final Report I, 6, Appendix 1, 12 (p. 162).

21. A. Sparks 1995.

22. Compare to the international discussion L. Kritz 1995; S. P. Huntington 1991.

23. J. Sarkin 1996, 618.

24. A. Boraine 1995, 1.

25. Cited by A. Sparks 1995.

26. The argument stemmed from the international literature on transition research; compare above all N. Kritz 1995; S. P. Huntington 1991; Institute for Democracy Document 1994; Justice in Transition Document 1995.

27. Final Report 1998, I, 1, §21c.

28. K. Asmal et al. 1996, 18.

29. In South Africa one is of the opinion: "To heal the nation implies that the nation as a whole is affected." In: H. Botman et al. 1996, 121.

30. "It is well known that vital documentation has been destroyed or tampered with, while other cases may concern events of many years ago" (A. du Toit 1996b, 13). A report of the Goldstone Commission indicates that around 135,000 acts of the Security Police before 1994 were annulled.

31. A. du Toit 1996b, 13.

32. G. Werle 1995, 8. What was legal in the apartheid state, in the sense of the basic sentence *nulla poena sine lege*, was declared not legal in the aftermath. The so-called "Broken Bicycle Formula" found no application in South Africa. The most severe human rights violations, like torture, kidnapping, or the hiring of hit squads, were also illegal in apartheid law (compare TRC Document 1994b, 4).

33. B. Naudé and W. Kistner 1996.

34. R. Goldstone 1994, 2.

35. Ibid., 16.

36. S. van der Merwe 1996b, 1.

37. Compare to both points in the HRW Document 1992, 19.22.

38. Self-description of the white South Africans of Dutch descent.

39. N. Mandela 1995, 692.

40. N. Mandela 1995, 737.

41. At his first press conference after being released, he said: "I knew that people expected me to harbor anger towards whites. But I had none" (N. Mandela 1995, 680).

42. Op. cit. 1995, 680.

43. Resolution Nr. 556, § 1, passed by the Security Office of the United Nations on 13.12. 1984. Already in 1976, after the bloody massacre of the student uprising in Soweto, the Security Office stated that: "apartheid is a crime against the conscience and dignity of mankind." Compare the arrangement of the international decisions on apartheid in: Final Report 1998, I, 4, Appendix 1-35 (pp. 94f). An analysis of the problem has been produced by the Ecumenical Advice Bureau, Johannesburg; compare S. van der Merwe 1996a.

44. K. Asmal et al. 1996, 7.

45. Ibid., 51.

46. S. van der Merwe 1996b, 1.

47. Ibid., 46f.

48. S. van der Merwe 1996a, 3.

49. F. de Klerk 1995. Here the concept of reconciliation of the apartheid era appears again, which assumes the non-reconcilability of the races. Reconciliation meant: separate development!

50. The arguments stem again from the international literature on transition research.

51. Compare the development of power in South Africa. G. Porzgen, in: M. Behrens et al. 1994, 109-20.

52. HRW Document 1992, 1. In the letter, the Human Rights Watch Africa ties the question of amnesty to the remembrance of the past. Past human rights violations should not be forgotten; it assumed it could reach a compromise, "a balance between retribution and forgetfulness in the interest of national reconciliation" (20). However, the Further Indemnity Act did not assume a compromise: "it is impossible to expect 'reconciliation' if part of the population refuses to accept that anything was ever wrong, and the other part has never received any acknowledgement of the suffering it has undergone" (ibid.).

53. K. Asmal et al. 1996, 23.

54. In: TRC Document 1994b, 4. Albie Sachs says upon looking back: "The insistence on an amnesty was so strong that the election would not have taken place if their concern in this matter was not taken account of."

55. Ibid. The result would be, says Sachs: "The government could encounter tremendous opposition if an amnesty would be granted without the people concerned disclosing what had actually happened."

56. In: TRC Document 1994b, 4. Sachs suggested that the hearing committee name this section the "Postamble" because this final part presumed the whole.

57. Xhosa word "humanity."

58. Act No. 200 (1993), Final Clause.

59. The lawyer Jeremy Sarkin observed critically, "the drafters of the interim constitution recognized the primacy of reconciliation and reconstruction to the pursuit of na-

tional unity and peace and they accepted the principle of amnesty as a necessary tool for this purpose" (J. Sarkin 1996, 620).

60. Compare J. Sarkin 1996, 618 note 5.

61. B. Hamber 1996, 2.

62. J. Sarkin 1996, 619.

63. Compare to this among others C. Villa-Vicencio 1999c, 4.

64. K. Asmal et al. 1996, 10f.

65. R. Gerloff 1998a, 18. See there the literature on *ubuntu*, especially 49.

66. D. Tutu 1996, 1.

67. B. Naudé, in: B. Naudé and W. Kistner 1996.

68. C. Villa-Vicencio 1996b.

69. R. Goldstone 1994, 4.

70. I. Mousa 1996, 1.

71. A. Boraine 1994b, 1.

72. A. Boraine 1994b, 4.

73. Victims have, for example, according to Article 14 of the "Torture Convention" the right to a "just and appropriate compensation"; compare "Agreement against torture and other cruel, inhuman or humiliating treatment or punishment" of December 10, 1984. BGB1. II, 246ff.

74. B. Naudé, in: B. Naudé and W. Kistner 1996.

75. Thus arises a particular problem in relationship to the question of giving back land, which in the framework of a case study can only be recorded on tape. Forced re-settlements were allowable. So a law had to be passed that regulated restitution claims. The so-called Land Rights Act came into play in 1994 before the Land Claims Court cases could be brought up for negotiation. Until June 1998 over 27,000 restitution claims were lodged. Of those, 18,000 cases were agreeably settled in which a total of 30,000 hectares of land were involved. The remaining cases, as in the instance of the case study, are still pending. (Compare Press briefing pack on progress with the Restitution of Land Rights, September 13, 1998, 2.)

76. SACC Theological Consultation Document 1996, 1.

77. The so-called Goldstone Commission was convened as a result of a bi-partisan peace conference whose goal it was to curb power in South Africa at the beginning of the 1990s. The legal basis for the Goldstone Commission was provided by the Prevention of Public Violence and Intimidation Act (Act No. 139, 1991). Its mandate stretched from the investigation of public power and intimidation in South Africa from July, 1991 on. Compared to previous governmental investigation committees (such as the one in February 1990 founded by de Klerk, the so-called Harms Commission for the Exposure of Deed by Killer Commandos), the Goldstone Commission had broad reaching powers: it could call witnesses and demand the surrender of evidence. Hearings of this commission took place regularly.

78. R. Goldstone 1994, 3.

79. Ibid., 4.

80. A. du Toit 1996a, 4. Following citation ibid.

81. Thus the later Coordinator of the TRC Office in Cape Town: L. du Plooy 1996, 1.

82. R. Goldstone, in: K. Asmal et al. 1996, 13.

347

83. Thus L. du Plooy 1996, 2.

84. Cited from: AWEPA Documents 1992, 13.

85. G. Werle 1995, 9. Continuity is the overall guiding motif of the Interim Constitution of 1993. Act No. 200 (1993) deals with legal continuity (Article 229), continuity of public office, including the police and military (article 235 and 256), and continuity of the courts (Article 241).

86. The theological-normative test of the following statements follows in Part III.A.II.3.a.

87. D. Ritschl, *Logic*, 142.

88. Op cit., 139.

89. To demonstrate how regulative nation building has been, W. Kistner notes concerning those present at a round table discussion organized by the IDASA concerning the planned TRC on September 1, 1994 in the neighborhood of Pretoria: "Only by reflection on the past of individual persons who were present at this meeting one could explore in depth for the struggle for reconciliation and for finding a common ground for a new South Africa that was taking place: Albie Sachs with his truncated arm (a victim of a car bomb explosion by the apartheid regime); Carl Niehaus, an ANC member who at one time had planned an attack on the gas station in Johannesburg and had spent eight years in prison; General Viljoen who has been responsible for the military operations in Angola; who had planned a war prior to the election and then by reaching a compromise contributed to the peaceful process of the election; Abraham Viljoen, once a Professor of theology, differing widely from the political outlook of his brother who had established contact between Mr. Mandela and his brother and paved the way for negotiations . . . ; representatives of the South African Police who had prominent positions in the security service of the apartheid regime" (cited from: TRC Document 1994B, 9).

90. J. de Gruchy 1996.

91. In Ritschl's (*Logic,* 139) assumed "hierarchical arrangement" of regulative statements, this would be placed at the top: the "group" which is referred to in this statement is the greater part of the "South African nation."

92. Act No. 34 (1995).

93. On December 13, 1996 Mandela first set a cut-off date of May 10, 1994. Not to set a legal cut-off date would have been to accommodate the Freedom Front (FF) on the one hand and the Inkatha Freedom Party (IFP) on the other. Both parties were involved in human rights violations after the coming to power of the Transitional Constitution. Compare to the basic problem of placing the human rights violations of the Apartheid Era (until 1990) in relationship with those after 1990. A. Sachs 1994, 1.

94. The process of nominations took place from September to November 1995. From a short list of 25 applicants, the President chose seventeen members of the Commission on November 29, 1995.

95. Act No. 34 (1995), Ch. 2 Sec. 3 (3) (a) and Ch. 3.

96. The Apartheid injustices thus remain unexplained. J. Sarkin 1996, 623 illustrates the dimensions: "More general injustice, such as the detention without trial of at least 78,000 people over the 30-year period under examination, the jailing of 18 million for past law offences, and the forcible removal of millions of people, do not fall within the brief of the Commission."

97. Act No. 34 (1995), Ch. 2 Sec 3 (3) (b) and Ch. 4.

98. Act No. 34 (1995), Ch. 2 Sec. 3 (3) (c) and Ch. 5.

99. The Amnesty Commission is separate from the others first installed on January 24, 1996. Its work is not limited, but ends when the decisions about the pending amnesty claims are decided.

100. Compare Act No. 34 (1995), Ch. 2 Sec. 3 (1) (b): "full disclosure of all the relevant facts relating to acts associated with a political objective."

101. Cited from B. Naudé and W. Kistner 1996.

102. L. du Plooy 1996, 2.

103. C. Villa-Vicencio 1998, 5.

104. During the hearings of the Committee for Human Rights Violations distinctions were made between Victim Hearings (hearings of individual victims), Event Hearings (for example in the student uprising of Soweto 1976), Special Hearings (for example the role of women in apartheid), Institutional Hearings (for example of faith communities), and Political Party Hearings (also the parties); compare to this the categories of the Final Report I, 6, §§33-41 (pp. 146-49).

105. The sculpture consists of three interconnected pillars and a more than 50-meter-high tower. Each of the four elements recollects a different group of people, who to the origin of the language have contributed: Khosian and Xhosa for the African part, the slaves from the Mallai-Indonesian islands and — represented by the highest column — the first European settlers.

106. Throughout the entire country during the debates of the TRC so-called "letters" were circulated to which people could turn who wanted to make statements about their experiences with human rights violations. The "letters" help to complete the 23 pages of comprehensive questions (compare TRC Document 1996b) containing "statements" that accompany the victims before and after the hearings. During the functioning time of the TRC over 21,000 statements were registered. If enough "statements" were gathered in a particular region, the TRC would decide to conduct hearings in that area.

107. Compare the Final Report I, 6 §33 (p. 146). A group of victims was chosen whose experiences represented different forms of human rights violations than were typical for the region (compare the Final Report III of Paarl, 5, pp. 399f.). Additionally, victims were chosen that represented the different sides of the conflict. Finally, there had to be representation by gender, age, and skin color. Victims were allowed to give testimony in the language of their choice.

108. Citations from the hearings of the transcript: http://www.truth.org.za/hrvtrans/index.htm.

109. Township in the area of Paarl.

110. Approximately 3,000 German Marks.

111. In the sense of the participating observer, several observations made in succession are noted in connection to the hearings documents; they will subsequently be systematically arranged in section 3. The observations are taken from discussions recorded in documented transcripts of Africans Chirevo Kwenda and Malinge Njeza, both from the University of Cape Town.

112. In this connection Kwenda criticized that the TRC accepted too little of the Afri-

can tradition. It should have made possible more meetings on the level of offender-victim.

113. The TRC distinguished different "reconciliation levels": the personal level ("coming to terms with painful past"), that of between offender and victim ("Reconciliation between victims and perpetrators"), the social on the level of community ("reconciliation at a community level") and on the national level ("promoting national unity and reconciliation"). Compare Final Report I, 5, §§14-23 (pp. 107f.).

114. Final Report 1, 5, §14 (p. 107).

115. In the dialogue, Njeza elaborates that normally the "elder" in the family is the first to pronounce the ritual: what has happened, why is a ritual pronounced? The experience of the TRC is that healing is only possible through the re-telling; re-experiencing has many parallels with the African idea of ritual.

116. Final Report I, 5, §26 (p. 110).

117. What follows is the English version of the drastically shortened dialogue. (Redundancy is necessary for the on-going development of the theme.)

118. A plan of the ANC for political liberation.

119. See note 111 above.

120. Njeza elaborates the observation.

121. Njeza remarks that in this choice of concept the African and Christian traditions intersect for Maxan. Christian concepts are "borrowed" in order to connect them with the African conceptual world. It is also conceivable that he is a practicing Christian, who is, however, completely at home in African thought.

122. Final Report I, 5, 16 (p. 107).

123. Ibid.

124. This provides, as presented, far-reaching legal jurisdiction. The number of members of the Commission increased a total of 19 (compare Act No. 18 of 1997 and Act No. 84 of 1997 [Amendments to Act No. 34 of 1995]). In this way one wanted to do justice to the flood of applications that came in after the application process was extended to September 30, 1997. The Committee had to deal with 7,127 amnesty applications of which the greater number had to be heard publicly. Of that number: 4,443 applications had been heard by June 30, 1998, shortly before the end of the TRC. In only 122 cases was amnesty conferred. The greater part of the rejections — in total 2,629 — were a result of the lack of political motive on the part of the deed (compare Final Report I, 10 [0.276]). The members of the Commission comprised members of the legal community. "The full committee includes six High Court judges, eight advocates and five attorneys." The Chairperson is the judge Hassen Mall, the Vice Chairperson Richter Andrew Wilson. The following transcript cites: http://www.truth.org/za/amntrans/ct#/maxam.htm.

125. Co-applicant to the Amnesty Committee.

126. I am grateful to the Executive Secretary of the TRC, Ruben Richards, of Johannesburg for the clues of this case. Following transcript cited from: http://www.truth.org.za/amntrans/ct3/benzien.htm.

127. A. Krog 1998a, 73.

128. A former victim of torture is now Director of the Police in Cape Town.

129. Of the body language of the victims, says A. Krog 1998a, 73: "Initially, the body language of the tortured was clear: no one else counts, not the Amnesty Committee, not

the lawyers, not the audience — what counts today is you and me. And we sit opposite each other, just like ten years ago. Except that I am not at your mercy — you are at mine. And I will ask you the questions."

130. Notorious torture methods of Benzien, which he explained on the demand of one of his victims: "It was a cloth bag that would be submerged in water to get completely wet. And then the way I applied it was I get the person to lie down on the ground, on his stomach normally on a mat or something similar with that person's hands handcuffed behind his back. Then I would take up a position in the small of the person's back, put my feet through between his arms to maintain my balance and then pull the bag over the person's head and twist it closed around the neck in the way, cutting off the air supply to the person."

131. Military branch of the ANC.

132. Several observations have been discussed by the psychologist Brandon Hamber, Center for the Study of Violence and Reconciliation, Johannesburg.

133. T. Winslow, in: Track Two 1997, 24.

134. D. Ntsebeza 1999, 1.

135. As per B. Bozzoli 1998; A. Krog 1998a; W. Everett 1998a; B. Hamber 1999a; F. Ross, in: Track Two 1997, TRC Public Debate 1998.

136. Above all Malinge Njeza and Chirevo V. Kwenda. I asked specific questions about the symbolic forms of all of the interview partners. Compare guiding interview questions 1999, Questions 2 and 3 in Appendix.

137. T. Sundermeier 1997, 51. Following citation ibid.

138. W. Everett 1998a, 76.

139. M. Guma, in: TRC Public Debate 1998, 8.

140. R. Smith, in: TRC Public Debate 1998, 13.

141. J. Cochrane 1999, 1. The Final Report reported of "Mini-TRC's"; compare Final Report V, 9, §13f. (pp. 431f.).

142. W. Kistner and B. Naudé 1999, 5.

143. C. Villa-Vicencio 1999a, 2.

144. J. Zehner 1998, 243.

145. G. Wildschut, in: Contributions to Multi Event 1999, 1.

146. Proof of this can be submitted in that the Final Report had to come to a special vote, because the TRC commissioners could not agree on a single text; compare Final Report V, 0. 436ff "Minority Position." The TRC symbolized here a democratic process; namely that one should respect individual opinions and not suppress them. Compare to this also the testimony of the member of the commission, Meiring (P. Meiring 1999).

147. W. Kistner and B. Naudé 1999, 3.

148. A. Boraine 1997, 22.

149. Cited from: TRC Public Debate 1998, 26.

150. B. Hamber 1999a, 19.

151. J. de Gruchy 1999, 1.

152. F. du Toit 1999, 1.

153. Z. Mda 1994, 16.

154. As in B. Bozzoli 1998; A. Krog 1998b.

155. Compare A. Krog 1998b, 10-14. Krog bases the following broad understanding of

ritual on "a highly condensed form of action composed of metaphors and symbols, the essence of which is to focus the intimate attention of an individual or a group" (ibid., 7).

156. Ibid., 10.

157. F. Ross, in: Track Two 1997, 8.

158. A. Krog 1998b, 10f. By the "chosen ones" is meant the selection of small groups of those who were able to tell their stories at the hearings.

159. A. Krog 1998b, 11.

160. Ibid.

161. B. Bozzoli 1998, 187.

162. The African scholar Mthobeli Guma refers to the meaning of the TRC as "ritual of healing": The "African perspective on reconciliation and restitution rests mainly on the notion of purity and pollution" (in: TRC Public Debate 1998, 6).

163. However, in contrast to the written version which was distributed during the hearings, the oral version is longer and much more detailed.

164. Compare B. Bozzoli 1998.

165. A. Krog 1998b, 13 knows also of cases where this event drew blood. At a TRC hearing the commissioner Dumisa Mtsebeza was questioned by a member, as having been seen transporting weapons for the ANC. Ntsebeza's view was first made known when the guilty partner admitted to lying to the commission. "An unwritten TRC assumption is that simple illiterate people tell the truth, well-dressed powerful people do not."

166. A. Krog 1998b, 12f.

167. W. Verwoerd 1999, 1.

168. H. Grunebaum-Ralph, in: TRC Public Debate 1998, 3.

169. B. Bozzoli 1998, 176.

170. Ibid., 173. Only in view of the western understanding of law does the ritual seem opposed to the law. Rituals assume in African tradition also a legal function (compare T. Sundermeier 1997, 69).

171. P. Bourdieu 1992, 18.

172. L. Buur 1998, 37.

173. F. Ross, in: Track Two 1997, 10.

174. I. A. Phiri 1996.

175. In African thinking it is through "the ritual the new status of the person is acknowledged"; it "makes certain that the (not codified) law is made into law" (T. Sundermeier 1997, 69).

176. H. Adam's 1998, 12, critical comment that the hearings did not bring any justice for the victim because the hearings "only" involved a "cleansing ritual," runs into difficulty because these criticisms leave out the African context and argue only from a western point of view. In African thinking, which impacts most of the black victims of apartheid, the ritual is not something marginal, but is essential for the development of symbolically mediated reality. Once again T. Sundermeier 1997, 106: "Symbols invite reflection; rites involve the participant in what it is they are designed to communicate."

177. B. Hamber 1999a, 1.

178. B. Bozzoli 1998, 185. Following citation ibid., 186.

179. B. Harris 1998, 23.

180. Ibid. Thus one may conclude that for a common memory, which takes as the basis for nation building the stories of victims and offenders, it does not have to do with the creation of "totalitarian concepts" and an assault on the plurality of liberalism (thus however H. Adam 1998).

181. D. Ntsebeza 1999, 2. Following citation ibid.

182. Ibid.

183. A. Krog 1998b, 7. Antje Krog suggests in view of the regularity: the TRC appears in the news every evening; in addition there is the decision of the media to have a one hour broadcast "The TRC Special Report" once a week. "Seldom has the question been asked: 'Is this news?'" Of the visual symbols of the TRC Krog mentions, among others, the green logo of the TRC "Truth. The Road to Freedom" which appeared behind the news broadcasters (citation ibid.).

184. D. Tutu, in: The TRC Special Report (SABC 1, 25.5. 1997).

185. Compare A. Krog 1998b, 14f. On the opposite side, one could view it as proof for the broad readership, which was published as a supplement to the final report (excerpted) in the large daily newspapers.

186. H. Adam 1999, 1.

187. D. Smit 1999, 3. The cooperation of the above-named convictions in the context of the TRC becomes vividly clear when it is noted that on the Sunday before the hearings a common worship service was held.

188. W. Kistner and B. Naudé 1999, 4.

189. W. Kistner 1997f, 21.

190. J. de Gruchy 1997, 624.

191. C. Villa-Vicencio 1999a, 2.

192. Final Report V, Minority Position submitted by commissioner Wynand Malan (pp. 436ff.). Following citations ibid., 439f.

193. D. Ntsebeza 1999, 4.

194. D. Smit 1999, 3.

195. J. Cochrane 1999, 3.

196. Both citations: W. Kistner and B. Naudé 1999, 3f.

197. D. Tutu 1997, 14.

198. D. Tutu 1997, 13.

199. In the case of Benzien, the personal and inter-personal dimensions of reconciliation hang together: Ashley Forbes needs the recollections of Benzien in order to get more clarity on his own story; Benzien needs the meeting with the victims in order to put himself into question.

200. W. Kistner and B. Naudé 1999, 8.

201. D. Tutu, in: R. K. Wüstenberg 1998a, 7.

202. J. Wilson 1963, 25f.

203. W. Verwoerd, oral communication.

204. Interim Report 1996. The comparatively small intermediary report (approximately 60 pages) of June 1996 essentially provides facts. There is no reflective chapter.

205. Compare primarily volumes I and V, which contain the definitions for the concepts as well as the political orders for action; an independent chapter on "Reconciliation" provides benchmarks for an evaluation. (The noted volumes are essentially worked on by

W. Verwoerd and C. Villa-Vicencio from the research department of the TRC, who have taken individual sections and repeated them in more depth and have expanded upon the questions.)

206. So for example F. du Toit 1999, 1.

207. Final Report I, 5, §10 (p. 106).

208. D. Tutu, in: C. W. du Toit 1998, 6.

209. Final Report I, 5, § 19 (p. 108).

210. W. Verwoerd 1999, 1. Similarly expresses it B. Hamber 1999b, 19 in a valuation study of the TRC: "The mandate of the TRC is still a subject of debate."

211. G. Wildschut 1999.

212. J. Langa, in: CSVR Document 1998a, 8.

213. C. Villa-Vicencio, in: Notes on a Multi Event 1999, 2.

214. Compare F. du Toit 1998, 8.

215. D. Tutu, in: Truth Talk 1998, 2.

216. N. Mandela, in: Hansard 1999.

217. TRC Public Debate 1998, 1.

218. D. Ntsebeza 1999, 1.

219. N. Mandela warns in the final debates on the final report in Parliament of exaggerated expectations of the TRC. Cited in: Hansard 1999.

220. S. Dwyer 1999, 2.

221. Final Report V, 9, §4 (pp. 350f.). In the documents from the hearings, many of these examples came to the forefront, as in reconciliation on an inter-personal level between the offender and the victim (cases of Maxan-Siebert and Benzien-Forbes), or the reconciliation on the personal level as reconciliation with individual stories (as in the case of Conraad van Rooyen), finally the reconciliation of the individual with his community on the community level (as in the case of Maxan and the community of Mbekweni).

222. Final Report V, 9, §62 (p. 392). Following citation ibid.

223. Final Report I, 5, §19 (p. 108).

224. Final Report V, 4, §192 (p. 169).

225. S. Dwyer 1999, 2.

226. H. van der Merwe 1997, 16.

227. "Things could have gone terribly wrong," said D. Smit and referred to the achievements. "We should be very grateful about what the TRC has achieved" (D. Smit 1999, 4).

228. C. Villa-Vicencio 1999a, 3. The fact that this is a beginning becomes clear by comparison. In the parliamentary debates on the Final Report in February, 1999 expressed a visitor from Nordirland excitedly during the break, "That is fantastic, that everyone can sit together in Parliament and talk. That is reconciliation."

229. Final Report V, 9, §2 (p. 350). C. Villa-Vicencio comments accurately: "Whoever after 300 years of colonialism and over 40 years of apartheid, expects a Commission in two and a half years to reconcile a country, that person lives in la-la-land." (Cited from R. K. Wüstenberg 1999, 31).

230. W. Kistner 1998, 34.

231. Compare T. Mbeki 1998, 68f. Here is to be found his famous parliamentary speech, "South Africa: Two Nations" which he gave on May 29, 1998, a month before the

end of TRC. Mbeki said: "the objective of national reconciliation is not being realized" (72). He answered the question of the successful coming together with an explicit "No!" (74).

232. Compare N. Ndungane 1999, 11. The follower of Tutu said in the office of the archbishop of Cape Town, "just now" (at the point in time of the vote in June 1999) the rebuilding of the nation has been reached.

233. W. Verwoerd, "Individual and/or Social Justice after Apartheid? The South African Truth and Reconciliation Commission," in: *The European Journal of Development Research* 11/2 (1999): 115-40, 116f.

234. W. Kistner 1999, 6.

235. C. Villa-Vicencio 1997a, 1.

236. Compare to the objective criteria in the history of J. Rusen, *Historical Objectivity,* 1975.

237. Cited in: Final Report I, 5, §31 (p. 111).

238. Compare Final Report V, 6 (pp. 196ff.).

239. Final Report V, 6, §101 (pp. 222f.).

240. The Final Report clears a place in the search for truth for "The Commission's shortcomings," which, for example, refers to the main emphasis within the mandated period of investigation in relation to violence. "In particular, the commission has failed to make significant breakthroughs in relation to violence in the 1990s." Final Report V, 6, §53 (p. 206).

241. M. Ignatieff, Articles of faith, in: Index on Censorship 5 (1996), 110-112, 11. The Final Report I, 5, §34 (0.111f) mentions this vote explicitly and gives prominent examples for factual lies: "for example, that the practice of torture by state security forces was not systematic and widespread; that only a few 'bad apples' or 'rotten eggs' committed gross violations of human rights" (ibid.). W. Verwoerd cites in another place the three myths that circulated among the white population: "First they say, they are shocked by the revelations of the TRC; had they only known about the atrocities at the time, they would surely have objected." "The second response from the white community is that, well, we knew what was happening and we did everything in our power to object. This is also a myth." "The third position comes from whites who say, let bygones be bygones, rehashing the past will only perpetuate divisions and inhibit reconciliation." (in: C. W. du Toit 1998, 127f.).

242. Final Report I, 6, §109 (p. 133).

243. Compare Final Report VI, 2 (pp. 26-107).

244. Representative of many others, I would like to cite two experiences. A woman from Soweto says: "I was able to speak and say what is inside me, and express my anger and my frustration." A man from Natal said that testifying before the TRC helped: "it exposes the hurt and can help to redress problems." Cited in: Truth Talk 1996, 3.

245. Compare Final Report II, 6 (pp. 243-54) and V, 9, §30 (pp. 365f.). D. Ntzebesa, who led the inquiry that led to the location of the victims' remains, says of the lack of dignity of the way in which the dead were hastily buried: "Through the country persons were buried in a manner that suggests that there was such a policy in burying people that caused them not to be remembered as heroes" (cited in Press Conference 17th April 1997, compare: www.truth.org.za/audio/trc0417/wav).

246. D. Tutu, in: C. W. du Toit 1998, 5.

247. Final Report I, 5, §14 (p. 107).

248. This recommendation of the Final Report was taken up in the parliamentary debates. The Minister of Justice sees in that a meaningful strategy for the practical working out of the politics of reparations. "The TRC has recommended . . . that a structure be developed in the President's office, with a limited secretariat and a fixed life span whose functions will be to oversee the implementation of reparation and rehabilitation policy proposals and recommendations" (Hansard 1999).

249. D. Ntsebeza 1998.

250. R. Richards 1998, 35.

251. Opening address to Parliament 5.2. 1999, 7.

252. P. Meiring 1999, 375.

253. Cited in Cape Argu 4.3.1999. Following citation ibid.

254. Speaking in the parliamentary debates, Dumisa Ntsebeza said in 1999, 1: "Everything that went wrong was blamed on the TRC. It has become the scapegoat for the nation." One may ask: could it have been otherwise? Where the various expectations came from was already clearly noticeable from the reactions of political camps well before the report was presented to the president. Both the ANC and the NP wanted to stop the appearance of the Final Report by use of legal means. The expectations are easy to discern: the TRC was supposed to justify both camps — the ANC was to appear as a legitimate resistance movement and the old apartheid regime was to disappear from history as quietly as possible. At the same time, however, the TRC was to investigate the truth. The reactions prove that such an undertaking is impossible. It also shows that the TRC had to maintain a balancing act of political objectivity, which otherwise politics had long ago given up. (The government of national unity with the double pinnacle of Mandela and de Klerk was, as is known, a failure two years after the vote.) The Human Rights Watch organization was outraged by the legal proceedings of the TRC. It rejected the viewpoint of the ANC at the time of the appearance of the Report, stating that it was only able to claim a small number of human rights violations, because it had engaged in a just war (compare Sunday Argus, Oct. 31–Nov. 1, 1998).

255. Hansard 1999.

256. D. Ntsebeza 1999, 2. Following citation ibid.

257. Hansard 1999.

258. Hansard 1999. Following citation ibid.

259. Hansard 1999. Following citation ibid.

260. The most prominent criterion is on the order of international law as "apartheid as a crime against humanity" (compare for example the Resolution Nr. 2189 or 2202 of the United Nations). It has been discussed — also among the members of the commission (compare minority position of Wynand Malan) — whether the TRC overstepped its mandate by naming apartheid a crime against humanity. The fact that the TRC states its accomplishments in the Appendix (Final Report I, 4, Appendix, pp. 94-102) documents its clear intent. This criterion is presented as a historical development, but was not prescribed.

261. Final Report I, 4, §61 (p. 65).

262. Comprehensively discussed in view of the TRC, in: TRC Just War Debate 1997.

263. Final Report I, 4, §69 (p. 67).

264. Final Report I, 4, §70 (p. 67).

265. Compare Final Report I, 4, §74 (p. 69).

266. Main examples of illegal, morally unacceptable deeds of the Freedom Movement, above all of the ANC, are to be found in the actual corpus of the Final Report; compare Final Report II, 4 (pp. 325-99). In the Findings, regarding the human rights violations that were incurred by the ANC in its exile camps, it was explicitly stated: "The Commission camps, were guilty of gross human rights violations." Final Report V, 6, §137 (p. 242); compare the deliberations in: Final Report II, 4, §98ff. (pp. 347ff.).

267. P. Meiring 1999, 376.

268. D. Ntsebeza 1999, 1.

269. Cited in CSVR Document 1998a, 4.

270. Survivors' Perceptions 1998, 4.

271. Truth Talk 1998, 5.

272. Cited in *The Sunday Independent,* Dec. 6, 1998.

273. W. Malan in TRC Public Debate 1998, 8.

274. C. Niehaus 1999, 1: "I think one can go as far as to say it is unchristian."

275. The Final Report I, 5, §46 (p. 115) criticized: "It was frequently suggested that the Commission's quest for more truth and less falsehood would result in deepened divisions rather than in the promotion of national unity and reconciliation. This concern must be taken seriously, although some of the mistaken assumptions underlying (much of) this criticism must be noted." The basic mistake may be found in that the TRC was burdened with something that exceeded its mandate. The task of the TRC consisted not in achieving reconciliation, but in promoting it. From the example of the expressed criticism of Mamdani we saw: the criticism lacks the differentiation between the task of the TRC and what the country needs. On the other hand, the representatives of the TRC admitted that the broad-reaching expressions of the initial euphoria itself had invited — judging by actual achievements — exaggerated expectations.

276. Cited in Truth Talk 1996, 3.

277. W. Kistner 1997f, 20 points in this connection to the fact "that in the English language a conceptual difference between justice and law is more laborious than in the German."

278. The concept is used in the sense of philosophical analysis; compare to the "model case" in J. Wilson 1963, 28f.

279. Thus observes Wolfram Kistner sharply, in W. Kistner and B. Naudé 1999, 6.

280. C. Villa-Vicencio 1999a, 1. Following citation ibid.

281. Final Report V, 9, §159 (p. 435). Compare the deliberations in V, 9, §§94-97 (pp. 400f.).

282. In the final report on the "policy of elimination" there is a list with concepts in Afrikaans, primarily verbs, which were used to veil the apartheid atrocities. For example, "kidnapping" in apartheid jargon is "verwyder" = remove/cause to disappear (compare Final Report V, 6, §89 [p. 215]). Other concepts were used in order to criminalize opponents of apartheid. The Final Report claims the descriptions were used in an official document of the police, and with them the designations given to former anti-apartheid activ-

ists: "arsonists," "looters," "murderers," "muggers," "hooligans," "vandals," "thugs." Compare Final Report VI, 9, §20 (p. 357).

283. Final Report V, 7, §124 (p. 294).

284. Final Report V, 7, §93 (p. 285). Foster opposes the popular opinion, according to which all torturers are sadistic or that it lies in human nature to give in to authority: "only about 5 percent of all types of perpetrators may be classed as sadists" (ibid., p. 284).

285. Final Report V, 7, §100 (p. 287).

286. The TRC Report cites the known expression of the historian C. Browning: "Explaining is not excusing, understanding is not forgiving." Final Report V, 7, §45 (p. 271).

287. Final Report V, 7, §54 (p. 274).

288. Final Report V, 7, §55 (p. 274).

289. Final Report V, 9, §33 (p. 366).

290. Nevertheless T. Yengeni, an earlier victim of Benzien's torture and critic of his amnesty, said during the TRC debates in parliament: "Reconciliation requires that we break out of the ghettos of the past and try to understand each other, although we may not agree" (Hansard 1999).

291. Cited in *The Sunday Independent,* Dec. 6, 1998.

292. Final Report I, 5, §20 (p. 108).

293. A. Boraine, in CSVR Document 1998a, 4.

294. P. Meiring 1999, 376.

295. Compare H. van der Merwe 1997, 9. "The programme aims to provide forums in which victims and offenders can enter a safe dialogue to address the legacy of past abuses."

296. S. Laufer, in *Business Day* 3.3. 1999. For Laufer, the talk of reconciliation in South Africa has not led to social equality. This much the concept itself has accomplished. It must be replaced by "national consensus." (This statistical, results-oriented concept of reconciliation lacks any political anchor. Apart from social equality there is social peace. Finally, Laufer's criticism is hostage to the scheme of projecting onto the past the disappointments of the TRC process.)

297. M. Mamdani 1997, 22. Mamdani places this concept of reconciliation against that of Kader Asmal et al. 1996.

298. J. de Gruchy 1999, 1.

299. Compare to the following W. Kistner 1999, 3, and 1992b; to the total problem O. H. Kaiser 1996.

300. Compare to the problem of the appropriate publication of J. de Gruchy from the 1980s, in which reference again is made to the struggle of the German church.

301. Compare to the concept of reconciliation in the 1980s the distinguished research of O. H. Kaiser 1996, especially pp. 63ff. Compare these documents with the relevant publications of the South African Church (SACC) and of the Institute for Contextual Theology (ICT). (For example, the SACC Document 1986; Idecesa Document 1989.)

302. W. Kistner 1999, 4.

303. S. Dwyer 1999, 8, raises the correct question, without however following it up in the course of the article.

304. H. van der Merwe 1997, 11. Following citation ibid.

305. Compare also Survivors' Perceptions 1998, 5.

306. Final Report V, 9, §130 (423ff.). Given that the study appears under this title, the TRC signals two things: it shows that it was not its mandate to advance reconciliation between and within the communities. On the other hand, it underscores the significance that these reconciliation hearings have the goal of reaching national reconciliation.

307. Both questions cited in: TRC Public Debate 1998, 1.

308. Compare regulative sentences under section I.6.

309. F. du Toit 1998, 8. Also here the truth must change. "The mere showing of political power," says Brandon Hamber correctly, "is not sufficient to change the attitude of people . . . and to confront the persistent power" (in: South Africa 1998, 15).

310. The theologically normative examination of the subsequent statements follows in Part III.A.II.3.b (partially under 3.a).

311. This goal is directed by the following axioms: (1) I can forgive when I know what has happened; (2) to speak the truth is to heal; (3) to hear the truth hurts; (4) reconciliation involves change.

312. These goals are, among others, directed by such axioms: (1) reconciliation is important and costly; and has something to do with justice; (2) reconciliation is meaningful; we want to have a common future; (3) reconciliation is something other than forgiveness in the national arena: there can be reconciliation without forgiveness.

313. The goals are regulated by statements such as these: I can forgive when I see the person; I can take responsibility when I see what I have done.

314. Such "regulative statements" are effective behind the statements, like: "In this world of ours we are dealing with processes" (C. Niehaus 1999, 1).

315. The Commissioner of the TRC and lawyer Wynand Malan says, for example, "Reconciliation is an approach, not an event. It should be understood in the context of national unity, which is the charge of the TRC" (in: Truth Talk 1997, 6).

316. In this context, one could ask whether the TRC has become a surrogate for religion. In view of the initial process of secularization in South Africa, has a neutral religious potential, without confessional orientation, been connected with the TRC process?

Notes to Part II.B

1. T. G. Ash 1997, 44. On the legitimacy of a comparison of two types of overcoming the past see E. Jesse in "Handbook on German Unity." "Independent from whether or not one shares this thesis, the crimes of the National Socialists were unique . . . it must be considered legitimate to be able to compare the Third Reich and the injustices incurred by the DDR" (in: Weidenfeld et al. 1999, 719).

2. P. Steinbach 1996, 399.

3. W. Thierse 1999, 642.

4. The use of the totalitarian theory in the DDR is contested, so that the comparison of dictatorships in historical and political-science research exhibits various characteristics. They extend from the 1950s use of the term classic totalitarianism (Hannah Arendt) which employs an analytical comparison of the concepts of nationalism and communist dictatorships, to more recent interpretations which, since the 1960s, speak in terms of the DDR as an "authoritarian government" rather than a "totalitarian dictatorship" (Eckhard

Jesse), as well as to some extremely differentiated versions, which only suggest a partial comparison which includes various frameworks and the role of partially autonomous institutions such as the church (Günther Heydemann). Compare the historical survey of A. Bauerkämper 1999b, 170f. (there is also literature on research into totalitarianism). In this case study, E. Jesse's position is favored, as it was developed in dialogue with research on totalitarianism (compare E. Jesse, 1998, 16f.).

5. R. Reißig 1998, 305.

6. Research on transitions requires more than a look at system theory. The uniqueness of a social collapse with its empirical-sociological implications is determinative. "For an actual analysis and clarification of (social) transitions, a foundation limited to system theory is too abstract and one-sided" (R. Reißig 1995, 150). I include here the research on global transition processes as well as that of East German transitions (compare to the literature of R. Reißig 1998, 324-28).

7. P. Hayner 1997, 3.

8. In Germany, a historical view in the sense of international transition processes is not possible without including a comparison of national dictatorships. Contrary to Latin American countries or even South Africa, there can be no post-1989 "unbiased" historical account in the sense that there has been no attempt to overcome the history of dictatorship. U. Poppe 1998, 2, writes: "It has been prophesied by many that through the conflict with the second German dictatorship an end to national socialism has finally been reached." However, the opposite was the case. Again and again each side referred to the "Third Reich" in their debates about how to deal with the post-war period. Poppe emphasized the powerful influence of the NS past in unified Germany. E. Jesse 1992, 27f. points to the previous other "dimensions of overcoming the past in Germany," with which the present discussion agrees: that of the NS past of the (old) German Republic; the NS past of the DDR; and the NS past of Communism in the DDR. These three discussion trajectories overshadow the entire German debate concerning rebuilding after the NS past and after Communism. For partial treatment of the problem of the relationship between research on the "old" DDR and that of current DDR research in the German Republic, see H. Weber 1994. Compare also the discussion in its entirety in the article by K. Sühl, 1998.

9. R. Reißig 1998, 324. Also Peter Steinbach sees that "the collapse of dictatorships . . . in Latin America . . . (opens) a broad and heretofore untouched area for comparative research" (P. Steinbach 1993, 8). The results of international and national research, however, are not connected. Therefore, a challenge is: "Embedding the (East) German case of transition into comparative research on transitions" (R. Reißig 1995, 151).

10. Compare K. Jaspers 1978.

11. Joachim Gauck has noted that in contrast to South Africa, the German state is "too modern and too multi-faceted for everything to find its place" (cited from R. K. Wüstenberg 1998a, 117): here the Investigative Commission, which was convened by Parliament under the chairmanship of a pastor in 1992 to investigate the "political" dimension of SED injustices. These are laws that have to do with the criminal acts of the DDR government. And the important "moral dimension of guilt"? Was it overtaken by the media? It is the "dead social token of the new Germany," says at least on "IM" at the beginning of the 1990s (cited by T. G. Ash 1997a, 44).

12. The Commission has already in its title the concept "SED Dictatorship," which is

supposed to reflect an anti-totalitarian consensus and presumes, within the theory on totalitarianism, a comparison of both dictatorships in the sense of a proffered "middle position" (see note 4).

13. Compare P. Hayner 1994, 626f.

14. On the specific problem that the Investigative Commission, in contrast to the
TRC, did not develop any comparable social influence is treated later on with the resulting question as to why there is a shortage of "institutional overcoming of the past."

15. An important opposing criterion is offered regarding the renovation of the penal
system in connection to DDR injustices, as substantiated by the Institute for Criminology
at the HU in Berlin and the evidence accumulated by the attorney general's office II in
Berlin. Compare K. Marxen and G. Werle 1999.

16. Citation from the speech that D. Ntsebeza ostensibly gave at the occasion of a
school dedication on November 21, 1998, in South Africa (Manuscript).

17. H. Wollmann 1998, 3J.

18. Sarkin 1996, 618.

19. There is in the literature and in public discussion the repeated phrase "the
uniqueness of this revolution," in that it "was conducted peacefully and without bloodshed." (Citation from Wolfgang Schäuble in *German Unity* V, 14.) A typical "overthrow"
of government is generally connected with bloodshed. Compare this to the issue of
"peaceful revolution"; D. Grosser et al. 1991, 68f.

20. Since the enthusiastic reception of Helmut Kohl in Dresden on December 19,
1989, it is clear to foreign observers that "the prospect of an orderly unification process after the implosion of the East German state over the course of several years would be pre-
mature" (R. Hutchings 1999, 154). On the banners were written "We are one people"; cho-
ruses of people sang "Germany, our united fatherland." A process of becoming a
democracy within the DDR which would be able to lead to "federal structures serving
both German states" (like Kohl's "10 point program"; compare *German Unity* I, 78) was
unlikely. A "politics of small steps" (Helmut Kohl, compare *German Unity* I, 73) was in
view of the realities (2,000 refugees daily, even in January!) not maintainable (compare
H. Teltschik 1991, 95f.). Already, the prospects for business made the continued existence
of the DDR impossible without external assistance. The country was bankrupt. In a communication to Gorbachev in October 1989, Egon Krenz anticipated the level of national
debt to grow to 3.5 million in 1990, for a total of 30 billion US dollars (compare DDR historical documents, 161). The country needed immediate help (compare debates in parliament in *German Unity* I, 487ff.). Without the monetary union which existed up until July
1, 1990, the businesses could not have paid their employees that August (so L. de Maizière
1998, 348). R. Hutchings 1999, 154, sees correctly that there were no alternatives to an "independent, democratic DDR."

21. W. Thierse, cited in: *German Unity* V, 173.

22. Compare to the arguments from the international debates on transitions, which
are briefly indicated on pages 40-41.

23. The peacefulness of the revolution finds expression in the slogans on banners.
With intelligence and humor the slogans point in the direction of a just state. "Justice is
the best security"; "A constitution is not up for grabs"; or "Wait time: cars 15 years; telephone 20 years; democracy 40 years." Cited in DDR in Documents 332f. One can also see

that the "happy rebuilding" was underway in the portrayal of the DDR power elite "in the form of cartoons or satire" in DDR newspapers (S. Wolle 1999, 22).

24. J. Isensee 1992, 103.

25. Compare B. Schlink 1994, 436: "The revolution knows no constitutional restrictions or limitations. It clears them away. . . . The revolution is the zero hour of constitutional law as well as of the constitutional state."

26. J. Isensee 1992, 103.

27. Cited by I. von Munich, 1994, 164.

28. Enumeration by F. Werkentin 1998, 71.

29. Deprivation of freedom can result in a perversion of justice and in many cases also interference with life and limb (compare K. Marxen and G. Werle 1999, 37ff.; 226ff. as well as the observations of C. Schaefgen, in: R. K. Wüstenberg 1998a, 57). This is also true of the criminal acts of the Ministry of State Security (MfS) and the group responsible for "mistreatment of prisoners."

30. The counter arguments to the treatment in the criminal code of the DDR injustices perpetrated by Klaus Marxen and Gerhard Werle provide an overview of the forms of injustice and are referenced to help focus the discussion on Option 1. According to tort law, K. Marxen and G. Werle 1999, 7ff., are cited for various offenses as "acts of violence on the East-West German border," "electoral fraud," "breaking the law," "denunciation," "MfS criminal acts," "drugging," "misuse of office and corruption," "bribery," and "spying."

31. BGH, Judgment v. 3.11.1992 — Az 5 StR 370/92, BGHSt 39, 1-36.

32. These and the following citations in: BGHSt 39, 1-2.

33. §27 Abs, 2 Sentence 1 Border law of 25 March 1982 (GBi DDR I 197).

34. BGHSt 39, 2f.

35. According to §213 StGB-DDR. Compare at length to external travel law, K. Marxen and G. Werle 1999, 8.

36. BGHSt 39, 3.K.

37. K. Marxen and G. Werle 1999, 250.

38. "Much of what has happened is morally and politically reprehensible. Much, however, was done well *below* the line of the criminally elusive" (K. Kinkel 1992, 485). An example: "No worker of the MfS was pursued as a criminal for the simple fact that he worked there" (R. Wassermann 1994, 2668).

39. G. Jakobs 1992, 63.

40. K. Lüderssen 1992, 17, observes of the order to shoot at the wall: "Whoever is entrusted with the problem of punishing criminals has little room for argument. The non-specialists, however, namely the majority of the public — What do they say? It's contradictory — for one it is too little, for the other it is too much. Above all, however, the victims are made to feel uncomfortably scared."

41. Thus, in view of the DDR is G. Jakobs 1992, 58; also Richard Schröder, in: M. Dönhoff et al. 1993, 26.

42. For example, could the German way serve as a deterrent for the violence between North and South Korea?

43. R. Wassermann 1992, 209.

44. G. Werle 1999, 246.

45. G. Jakobs 1992, 63.
46. Compare G. Werle 1997, 822.
47. H. Quaritsch 1992, 402.
48. List of arguments for Option 2 on page 44.
49. R. Wassermann 1992, 206. Thus, Peter Bender, in: M. Döhnhoff et al. 1993, 27. Similar to Uwe Wesel, in: op. cit. 102.
50. Thus, Peter Bender, in: M. Döhnhoff et al. 1993, 27. Similar to Uwe Wesel, in: op. cit. 102.
51. H. Quaritsch 1992, 406. Following citation ibid., 418.
52. H. Quaritsch 1992, 393.
53. Cited in: *German Unity* V, 45f.
54. Cited in: *German Unity* V, 133.
55. Compare at length to spying as a form of DDR injustice; K. Marxen and G. Werle 1999, 128-31.
56. Compare regarding the spying activities of the head office the explanation from a legal perspective: K. Marxen and G. Werle 1999, 129f.
57. On January 1, 1990, the Security Working Group for the then existing Central Round Table was formed, which was also concerned with the job of dissolving foreign spying by the MfS (the HVA). Among the group, the pervasive idea was that "the (foreign) clientele of the former DDR" must be protected; as, for instance, the threat of capital punishment in the USA. On this basis, the Working Group agreed on February 20, 1990, to allow the self-dissolution of the HVA at a particular point in time. On June 30, 1990, the self-dissolution was completed and with it almost all of the documents destroyed (legal evidence in K. Marxen and G. Werle 1999, 132f.; compare to the political classification in D. Gill and U. Schröter 1991, 79ff., 218f.).
58. An exception is made in the attempt for "celebratory amnesty," which comes very close to the notion of general amnesty. Another example is that of the demand for amnesty for youth. T. Hillenkamp 1996, 185 says: "In appeal to the idea of amnesty for youth and the precedent of the law of exemption from punishment of 1954 . . . an amnesty (is conferred) for deeds perpetrated by children and youth ages 28 and younger." Would such an amnesty also procure exemption from punishment for youth who enacted the order to shoot at the wall?
59. The following suggestions have not prevailed in the German discussion: (1) Amnesty with respect to leaving in peace of minor offenses on the grounds of morality ("We couldn't have done anything else"). (2) Amnesty for spies who did not incur any serious human rights violations on the basis of pragmatism ("Spying is spying"). (3) Likewise in connection to spying: any exemption from punishment can only be waived on constitutional grounds ("Or else the law determines the politics"). (4) A "general amnesty 2000" on the grounds of public symbolism (since applications for amnesty were meaningless in 2000 due to the statute of limitations on medium offenses of October 30, 2000). C. Schaefgen talks of a "general amnesty" in: the *Tagesspiegel (Daily Mirror)*, November 9, 1999, 3.
60. J. G. Schätzler 1995, 59.
61. K. Tanner 1995, 172.
62. K. Marxen and G. Werle 1999, 256.

63. DDR People's Parliament, Protocol of the 32nd Session, August 24, 1990, 1452.

64. Cited from: R. K. Wüstenberg 1998a, 131.

65. Peter Bender, in: M. Dönhoff et al. 1993, 47.

66. K. Kinkel 1992, 488.

67. E. Neubert, proceedings of the "Gauck Administration" in social context, in: R. K. Wüstenberg 1998a, 65-86, citation 67. The named principles describe "goal and implementation area" of the law; compare §1, 1 (1-4) State Security Service Document Law. §3 is a detailed account of the right to view files. §§23 and 24 of the State Security Service Document Law regulate the possibilities for criminal punishment, also §§15, 1 (1); 19, 5 (10 and 21, 1 of the rehabilitation [regulations]).

68. Compare §§15 and 21, 3 (3) State Security Service Document Law.

69. § 1, 1 (1) State Security Service Document Law.

70. Compare §3 State Security Service Document Law. According to the law concerning records, former assistants of the Stasi had the right to review the administrative records; but they didn't have permission to view their own records (compare § 16 St UG). Here it has to do with a "sizeable appropriation" (§ 16, 4). Obversely, the workings of the "Gauck Administration" were adopted as a necessary supplement of the Truth Commission in South Africa; compare G. Simpson 1994, 16: "It seems clear that, in the interests of a fledgling democracy in South Africa, there is a vital need to address the absence of any legislated rights of access to information."

71. In contrast, the workings of the "Gauck Administration" were adopted as a necessary supplement of the Truth Commission in South Africa; compare G. Simpson 1994, 16: "It seems clear that, in the interests of a fledgling democracy in South Africa, there is a vital need to address the absence of any legislated rights of access to information."

72. Compare arguments for Option 3, such as: "Large portions of the population were completely unaware of the enormity of the incurred injustices. Public exposure is therefore necessary. . . ." Or: "Comprehensive exposure can help to induce the assumption of responsibility within broader society."

73. Volker Rühe, in: *Hamburg Morning Post,* February 12, 1992.

74. G. Jakobs 1992, 38.

75. P. Bock 1995, 1171.

76. Investigative Commission I, 188.

77. Investigative Commission I, 188. Following citation, ibid.

78. In a comparison with South Africa the question arises: how great will the public interest still be in an Investigative Commission after the files are made accessible? The making accessible of the Stasi files determines yet another offshoot, which was decisive for the public acceptance of a Truth Commission. Six months before the Investigative Commission began its work in the summer of 1992, the Stasi Archives were opened up as a consequence of the State Security Service Document Law framework of legal regulations. One can, in my opinion, make a connection: the general interest in the development of the DDR injustices through the statements of injured parties under the auspices of an established Commission had the potential of being underestimated. *The Stasi disclosures presented a picture of East Germany.* Spectacular accounts of past injustices, which through the statements of injured parties were evident in the first sessions of the South African TRC, were not to be expected in an institutionalized form of dealing with the

DDR past. Compare decisions of the Cabinet Ministry 4/6/89 of December 7, 1989 and 6/18c/89 of January 4, 1990.

79. Compare decisions of the Cabinet Ministry 4/6/89 of December 7, 1989 and 6/18c/89 of January 4, 1990.

80. Compare outline of the Rehabilitation Law of July 4 and 18, 1990: BArch 1 I/3-3009 and I/3-3027.

81. Compare Documents on the Politics of Germany, 220.

82. The First Law Rectifying SED Injustices, October 20, 1992, BGB1. I, 1814 and Second Law Rectifying SED Injustices, June 23, 1994, BGB1. I, 1311. The Investigative Commission had stated in Article 17: "that immediately a legal regulation is created that allows for the rehabilitation of all persons who were the victims of politically motivated criminal prosecution." The agreement in the appendix between the German Democratic Republic and the former East German Republic in Chapter III of the Investigative Commission (area of responsibility of the Minister of Justice) further delineates the question of rehabilitation.

83. R. Wassermann 1993, 11. Following citation ibid.

84. J. von Bismarck 1999, 226.

85. R. Wassermann 1993, 11. Following citation ibid.

86. J. von Bismarck 1999, 257.

87. J. von Bismarck 1999, 258. "According to the understanding of the DDR regime, the people of the former DDR wanted to keep the results of the 'grassroots democratic reforms.' At least that was the impression given to the German government."

88. Wolfgang Schäuble in the debates of the Unification Agreement of September 5, 1990, cited in: *German Unity* V, 19. Following citation op. cit. 18.

89. Material reparations are important for two reasons: victims were "prevented from working during their imprisonment . . . ; at the same time their internment and its 'social consequences' included being barred from the possibility of making any progress in their profession" (H. Kaschkate et al. 1991, 243). In addition to material reparations, continuing psychological care was necessary. Christian Pross, who directs the trauma center in Berlin — one of the few institutions that dealt with long-term therapy for former SED victims — had to acknowledge in an open forum on the theme "The Consequences of (SED) Pursuit": "Our capacity in the Berlin treatment center for treating the victims of torture is very limited. We are overwhelmed with patients. In our area, we also handle refugees from other countries who have fled from dictatorships or situations of civil war. For this reason we have a long waiting list." Cited in: The Federal Commission 1995, 31.

90. Citation from: Reinhard Dobrinski, in: *The Barbed Wire* (newspaper of the Federation of Victims of Stalinism BSV) 5/1999, 3.

91. Cited in the Federal Commission 1995, 52.

92. Compare, for example, the Green Party's bill to improve the legal standing of victims of the SED dictatorship of November 21, 1995 (BT-Publication 13/3038).

93. U. Poppe 1998, 9.

94. We have repeatedly referred to the organization of the Gauck Administration of October 27, 1994 in "The Consequences of (SED) Pursuit." The director of the Berlin Trauma Center, Christian Pross, who took part in the organization, said in the discussion: "I think that such organizations as this are very important today; organizations where

victims can openly relate their experiences. Even that can unburden them. And that the public listens and acknowledges their experiences is likewise necessary" (cited in: The Federal Commission 1995, 34).

95. U. Poppe 1998, 9f.

96. P. Bock 1999, 95.

97. Cited in H. Teltschik 1991, 198.

98. Also in view of Option 5 are the proceedings after 1989 to be understood against the background of a learning curve in dealing with the consequences of the NS dictatorship. Phrases such as "a de-Stasification" in the style of the clean-up after 1945 is in any case to be avoided (A. Weinke 1998, 181).

99. Thus, P. Bock 1999, 96.

100. Thus, U. Battis 1992, 80. Battis makes reference in this attempt to sources of government as well as the circle of Maizière and of Kohl.

101. U. Battis 1992, 81.

102. E. Bahr 1991, 168.

103. Investigative Commission (IC) Report, Chapter 1, XIX Subject Area A, Paragraph III, Nr. 1, line 4.

104. Investigative Commission (IC) Report, Chapter 1, XIX Subject Area A, Paragraph III, Nr. 1, line 5.

105. Annotation to the Commentary: "Unification Agreement and Voting Accord Volume II, Accords and Legal Acts of German Unity," edited by K. Stern et al. Munich 1990, 715.

106. The theologically normative examination of the following statements appears in Part III.A.II.3.a.

107. Compare to the hierarchy of regulative statements those of D. Ritschl, *Logic,* 139.

108. R. Eppelmann, in: The Parliament, 1998, 2.

109. Investigative Commission (IC) I, 30.

110. IC, I, 32.

111. D. Hansen 1995, 73. Preceding citation ibid., 72.

112. IC, I, 188.

113. D. Hansen, in: The Parliament 1998, 4.

114. I.-S. Kowalczuk, in: The Parliament 1998, 5.

115. IC, I, 188.

116. W. Kusior 1999, 89. Following citation, ibid.

117. W. Kusior 1999, 90.

118. R. Eppelmann, in: The Parliament 1998, 2.

119. "During the second Investigative Commission, I at least succeeded in promoting the area of the everyday as a similarly complex theme for the work of the Committee: thus, the normal, everyday life of the DDR citizen." (Narrative interview with R. Eppelmann, December 9, 1999. Cited in a taped interview: appears in abridged version in the *Rheinland Mercury* of September 15, 2000, 27.) Compare also the public hearings titled "Everyday life in the DDR between self-determination and adaption: experiences and strategies for overcoming in a deficient society," in the City of Eisenhüt, April 27-29, 1997. After the first day of hearings, the presiding official said: "This is a piece of the history of

Germany and has an impact on our lives now. It is once again made very clear to me as I listen to the accounts how important our work here is" (cited from: IC, 2, V, 124).

120. "If it were up to me, not only hundreds, but thousands of former DDR citizens would have had the chance to tell their stories. The idea of atonement was totally unthinkable in the power structures of the German Parliament. The idea was "such things didn't happen." And as we began our accounting, we knew that dealing with this would cost money. We would have to hire additional people. I was nevertheless a bit sad that such a wealthy country as Germany had not at least utilized this opportunity (before now). And each of these 16 million people is not in a position to write a book." (Narrative interview with R. Eppelmann, December 9, 1999. Cited in taped interview: appeared in abridged version in *Rheinland Mercury* of September 15, 2000, 27.)

121. A. Bauerkämper 1999b, 183.

122. B. Lutz 1996, 5.

123. M. Wilke 1997, 607. Wilke develops in the following the historical political intention of the Parliament with respect to the debates on appointments from whose introduction we have cited.

124. J. Zehner 1998, 243.

125. U. Poppe 1998, 12.

126. In January 1992 a parliamentary investigative board was assembled. Ingrid Köppe, Parliament 90/Green Party stated in a press conference of January 26, 1992 that the parliamentary rebuilding "would quickly lack teeth" if it did not concede the right "to subpoena former tormentors for their statements."

127. H. M. Kloth 1998, 861.

128. Martin-Michael Passauer, in: IC, II, I, 191. Passauer's motto from the days of the fall of the wall was: "Everything on the table — offenders and victims!"

129. T. Ammer in: The Parliament 1998, 6.

130. P. Bock 1995, 1171.

131. C. Klessmann, in: The Parliament 1998, 1.

132. An exception is in the dialogue excerpts quoted in the Introduction between Lothar Tautz and Michael Altwein (from: IC, VIII, 66ff.). This case is according to member of the commission unique among the proceedings of the IC; thus commission member D. Hansen (written information).

133. Berlin Newspaper of November 28/29, 1992 (local section). Commission member Markus Meckel maintains during the hearings: "The information from the current meeting was damaging to catastrophic. This also concerns . . . public information" (IC, II, 1, 212).

134. The hearing is documented verbatim in the volumes of the IC; compare IC, II, 1, 111-276 (= 20th and 21st sitting of the IC's "Reconstruction of the history and consequences of the SED Dictatorship in Germany").

135. Documents of subsequent stories according to the IC, II, 1, 154f. (Wendel); 156f. (Rührdanz).

136. Many other biographical accounts were related on this and subsequent days which due to lack of space are not documented, but are worthy of reading. For example, the report of the day care centers (IC, II, I, 163ff. and 179f.). "We do not want to forget

what happened to the children and to the youth in order to make them ready and willing to accept the ideology of the socialist state" (IC, II, 1, 180).

137. Although the observing participant has no culturally anthropological function in the development of the symbolic forms of expression in the German reconstruction process, additional specific and foreign observations enter into the text analysis. Based on the hearings of the IC, at which I was present, transfers were made. The "Situation of Women in divided and united Germany" was looked at on October 20, 1997 in Berlin (= 41st session). The session protocol even recorded reactions (crying, applause). During the parliamentary hearings I asked Commission members Maser, Hanse, Passauer and Kowalzcuk, among others, the following question: Outside of the hearings at the Reichstag (20th and 21st sessions) are there other hearings in which persons who had experienced repression under the DDR were allowed to tell their stories in brief? Why was the Parliament (Reichstag) chosen as the place for this? What were the criteria by which victims were selected to tell their stories? Were the victims relieved after they were able to tell what happened to them? Were the listeners attentive? The answers are primarily found in section 5, "Interpretation of Symbolic Forms and Rituals."

138. Ch. Dieckmann, in: *The Times (Die Zeit)* v. December 3, 1992.

139. Cited from IC, I, 1, 813. Regarding the effective history of the recited apologies it should be noted that Keller's statements unleashed a controversy over the values of the SED within the PDC (compare the complete documentation of writings: "In-between the chairs. Pro and contra SED," ed. by Dietmar Keller et al., Berlin 1993). Keller himself appeared only as a research assistant in the subsequent commission.

140. "Artists in the Stasi-system: Now the truth must come out. A disagreement between the writer Erich Loest and the PDS official Dietmar Keller" in: Frankfurter Rundschau Nr. 9 (11.1. 1992), 607. The following citation and the entire record of documentation refers to this article.

141. IC, I, 1, 188. Rainer Eppelmann refers additionally to the fact that "forgiveness" and its attending "working out," even on political grounds, was directed. In contrast to Latin American countries and also in South Africa, the "impression of social conciliation" was not as great in the German transition process as a result of the genuine initial conditions of 1989/1990. One wanted to "fearlessly" take on a thorough "working out" because there was a threat of a civil uprising. (Narrative interviews with R. Eppelmann, December 9, 1999. Cited in taped interviews; appearing in abridged version in the *Rheinland Mercury* of September 15, 2000, 27.)

142. IC, I, 1, 742.

143. IC, I, 1, 742.

144. IC, I, 1, 743.

145. Ibid.

146. I am aware of the methodological danger that use of the criteria used in the South African case studies may serve to predispose toward particular answers. On the other hand, the criteria are not only generally valid as a guide for the German discussion, but without their help questions would not have been posed during the German rebuilding process that illuminated the internal perspective (such as a comparison of dictatorships).

147. The eleven external members of the parliament were chosen according to their

research areas. Most of the participants were academics in the areas of history, political science, (East German) state law, and theology.

148. Of the sixteen parliamentary members, approximately two-thirds came from East Germany.

149. Narrative interview with F. Schorlemmer, September 19, 1999 (cited from taped interviews).

150. Against this background, it is appropriate to ask if commission member Dirk Hansen is speaking about the IC as a "*Fundus* (sic!) for democracy" (in: The Parliament 1999, 4.

151. Commission Member Hansen summarized: "In broad sections of the public there is little knowledge of the fact that in the task of the IC there is not just something specific to the DDR at stake, but something that affects all of Germany" (D. Hansen 1995, 77).

152. One could say: the victims were represented. Eppelmann refers in this connection to the problem of the parliamentary practice of invitation. As a rule, victims had to be invited to speak before the IC Forum (exceptions were made in parliamentary hearings). In order to be invited, one had to be a known party, at least by one of the Commission members. Many stories of "nameless" victims could thus not be heard (contrary to South Africa where victims decided themselves to appear before the TRC). (Narrative interviews with R. Eppelmann, December 9, 1999. Cited in taped interviews; appearing in abridged version in the *Rheinland Mercury* of September 15, 2000, 27.)

153. Compare J. Gauck 1991, 11ff.

154. Literature is not available for this line of questioning, so that I include the following from my own observations and in the style used in South Africa.

155. Compare above, note 137.

156. Peter Maser, written report of December 16, 2000.

157. Peter Maser, written report of December 16, 2000.

158. Compare *Die Zeit*, December 3, 1992; *Welt am Sonntag*, December 6, 1992; *Tagesspiegel*, December 1, 1992; *Berliner Morgenpost*, December 1, 1992; *Berliner Zeitung*, November 30, 1992, and December 2, 1992; *Das Parlament*, December 11, 1992; *Mitteldeutsche Zeitung*, December 2, 1992; *Sächsische Zeitung*, December 1, 1992; and *Neue Zeit*, December 1, 1992.

159. The naming of names and telling of stories can in themselves be seen as rehabilitation.

160. *Der Tagesspiegel*, December 1, 1992, 3.

161. Cited from: *Presseerklärung* Hansen/Schmieder: The past writes the future, FDP Parliamentary Faction on December 1, 1992. Following citation ibid. Dirk Hansen was more clear in another place: "For myself, I can say with certainty that the so-called victim hearings in the Parliament were the most horrifying that I've ever heard. The specific task of the IC proves itself in the hearings, not in expertise" (written report of February 3, 2000).

162. T. G. Ash 1997b, 21.

163. Cited in: Parliamentary Commission 1999, 13.

164. The survey of the "Gauck Administration" is contained under the title "Inspection of Files as an Individual Form of Concern with the Past": "33% consider the knowl-

edge gained from inspection of their files as shocking, horrifying, or surprising: 'It was shocking! I was completely beside myself for a long time!'; 'the insidious German thoroughness! The level of detail was something that I would have thought impossible'" (Parliamentary Commission 1999, 13).

165. This concept was not used in view of the inspection of files. When I suggested the talk of ritual against the background of the ritualized proceedings of the TRC, it met with positive response.

166. The Parliamentary Commission 1999, 15.

167. A survey of the "Gauck Administration" reported that 14% of those surveyed valued the files "in family circles, among relatives and friends: 'Above all to be able to read carefully in peace what all the excitement was about in the first lectures. It was worth it! Then copies were handed out to all concerned friends and shared'" (Parliamentary Commission 1999, 14).

167. Note the symbolism of the date: D. Hansen 1995, 77.

168. Note the symbolism of the date: D. Hansen 1995, 77.

169. Frankfurter Rundschau Nr. 24 (January 28, 1995), 10.

170. In this statement a contemporary witness summarizes the many years of internment in the Stasi jail (he now leads tours of the Berlin Hohenschönhausen facility) for a session of the Evangelical Academy of Berlin-Brandenburg and portrays the personal stories as the grout between the bricks of fate of the nation. The session is under the title "Recalling the wounds. A social reception of the stories of victims," September 25-27, 1998.

171. A. Weinke 1998, 173.

172. As for the problem of "historical truth" in connection with the debates on the DDR past, compare C. Klessmann, in: The Parliament 1998, 1.

173. National reconciliation means not only the overcoming of mental differences, but the discovery of common democratic roots that reach back before the onset of National Socialism.

174. More will be said in detail about the concept of nation.

175. Cited in: L. von Törne 1996, 77. It is of note that the Parliament speaks of "change." It appears that the idea is basic that reconciliation has something to do with change: here in view of the national level of reconciliation (East and West).

176. D. Hansen 1995, 76. Following citation ibid.

177. Ibid. Only "a small number of newspapers of outlying regions saw it as their responsibility to report on the continuing activities of the IC." Exactly opposite of the number in South Africa: the South African Press Association (SAPA) published daily approximately five articles on the TRC.

178. Narrative interviews with R. Eppelmann, December 9, 1999. (Cited in taped interviews; appearing in abridged version in the *Rheinland Mercury,* December 1, 2000, 27.)

179. Written information of December 20, 2000.

180. The theologically normative examination of the following statements follows in Part III.A.II.3.b and III.3.

181. T. Mb, Investigative Commission, 1998, 72f.

182. Dae-jung Kim, President of the Republic of Korea, expressed in a speech on March 6, 2000, at the Free University of Berlin: "If we think that Germany, despite her ad-

vantages, had to face difficulties, then we must think very carefully about unification in Korea." In his speech under the title of "Lessons on unification and questions for the Korean peninsula," President Kim gives two reasons for caution: "First, because of the high cost of unification. . . . Second, because the psychological conflicts between West Germany and East Germany still cause problems." (Cited from prepared manuscript, p. 7.)

183. Parliamentary publication 13/8450.

184. This goal was also quickly the goal of political actors in East Germany. Richard Schröder, the then leader of the faction of the SPD (East), recalls: "One point however became quickly an issue of broad consensus: we wanted German unity" (in: H.-J. Vogel 1994, 37). Ehrhart Neubert factors in that formed a "synergy . . . between the pressure of the opposition and the demonstrators in the East on the one side, and the federal government on the other" (*Rheinland Mercury* Nr. 11 [March 17, 2000]: 3).

185. Speeches and Addresses, 140.

186. H. Kohl 1996, 213.

187. Compare Speeches and Addresses, 141.

188. H. Kohl 1996, 217. For this case the Chancellor planned to sing "Now thank we all our God."

189. R. Reißig 1999, 138.

190. B. Faulenbach, in: C. Kleßmann et al. 1999, 27.

191. R. Reißig 1999, 135.

192. Not only that the goal of creating equal living conditions cannot be reached and still hasn't been reached; it shows at the close of the state (proceedings) that over the long-term the goal came up short for East Germany. "Comparability can not be the goal of a mature person," says Lothar de Maizière critically (source: Narratives Interview November 25, 1999). The continual talk of "inner unity" since 1990 contradicts markedly the acceptance of the time after the fall of the wall, which is already "of one mind" in terms of currency and full material comparability of the nation. Now the problem is one that had not been a problem previously: "nation building" is suddenly a theme. The enthusiasm of Dresden over becoming a nation did not guarantee continuity.

193. Clearly, the external and internal political aspects of the unification process were not connected before the establishment of state unity. If the political and military integration of the West *before* national unity was a defined and achievable goal, then the process of inner unity of Germany remains connected to the larger European process of unification. Rudolf Seiters formulates in 1999: "The most important job of the future that lies ahead of us is the establishment of the inner unity of Germany and secondly, the consequential furthering of European unity" (R. Seiters 2000, 18).

194. With regard to these five aspects of the unification process, the Handbook on German Unity 1999 (pp. 13f.) categorizes the central political fields. For our line of questioning, we gain from this primarily a delineation of the "inner aspects of unity."

195. *Handbook on German Unity* 1999, 454.

196. R. Süßmuth 1997, 13.

197. Televised discussion on the 10th anniversary of the fall of the wall, November 9, 1999, cited in: www.bundespraesident_de/reden/rau/de/991109.html.

198. L. Probst 1998, 3.

199. Compare for example the use of the phrase "process" in the title of the IC

"Overcoming of the consequences of the SED dictatorship in the process of German unity."

200. H.-J. Veen 1997, 20.

201. H.-J. Veen 1997, 20. There is also evidence for the positions.

202. L. Niethammer, in: C. Kleßmann et al. 1999, 320.

203. These ideas were expressed by the Munich historian Christian Meye in the course of his lectures on the theme "European Historical Consciousness, a Utopia" in: International Conference "Revolution, Transformation, Integration: The Course of Young Democracies in Europe," Berlin, Red Courthouse, March 16-19, 2000.

204. E. Schulz 1995, 338.

205. E. Schulz 1995, 337.

206. R. Wildemann 1991, 7.

207. T. G. Ash 1990, 19. An impressive affirmation of the thesis is recognizable in the situation, in that the South African constitutional (federal) court was conceived after the model of the German constitutional (federal) court.

208. G. Rüther 1995, 694.

209. Compare J. Kocka 1995, 17.

210. Compare J. Kocka 1995, 5.

211. In: C. Kleßmann 1999, 53.

212. G. Rüther 1995, 694.

213. *Handbook on German Unity* 1999, 315.

214. Such exaggerations are also symbolized in the language used. The talk of "our dear brothers and sisters in the East" became "tiresome," according to a news commentary: "Mythical Thinking: From national unity to affection?" in: *The Daily Mirror (Tagesspiegel)*, October 4, 1999.

215. Speech by Gerhard Schröder, October 3, 1999, cited in: www.bundeskanzler.de

216. L. Probst 1998, 8.

217. *Handbook on German Unity* 1999, 438.

218. L. Probst 1998, 8.

219. H.-J. Veen 1997, 21.

220. Art. Cit., 26.

221. S. Hilsberg 1996, 607,608.

222. Art. Cit., 28.

223. *Handbook on German Unity* 1999, 334.

224. Ilko Sascha Kowalczuk, in: The Parliament 1998, 5.

225. IC2, I, 154.

226. These can be monitored in the "critical questions" — 2.a, b.

227. Compare IC2, I, 697.f.

228. IC2, I, 528.

229. Compare protocol of 42nd Session: IC2, V, 426ff.

230. Narrative interview with Peter Maser, November 6, 1999 (cited from taped interviews).

231. IC2, I, 528.

232. R. Schröder, in: IC2, VII, 897f.

233. R. Seiters 2000, 16.

234. In the South African process, as documented, the chain of command was not evidenced in the political leadership, nor was it allowed to make decisions. The truth about whether or not de Klerk carried the responsibility for the death squads having been struck from the record is also not an official finding of the South African Truth Commission.

235. IC2, I, 249.

236. I refer again to the survey and to the discussion circulated by the "Gauck Administration" during its term (cited in: The German Parliamentary Report/Commissary 1999) that I was able to engage with assistance of the administration.

237. Compare The German Parliamentary Report/Commissary 1999, 15.

238. R. Schröder, in: IC2, VII, 898.

239. Both citations in: The German Parliamentary Report/Commissary 1999, 16.

240. Physician Christian Pross, who works in the Trauma Center of Berlin-Spandau with victims of the DDR dictatorship, cited in: The German Parliamentary Report/Commissary 1995, 33.

241. Compare The German Parliamentary Report/Commissary 1999, 11.

242. L. von Törne 1996, 83.

243. Narrative interview with W. Ullmann, July 12, 1999 (cited in taped interviews).

244. K. Söll 1997, 145.

245. K. Söll 1997, 157.

246. *Handbook on German Unity* 1999, 334.

247. Marlies Jansen, in: *Handbook on German Unity* 1999, 334.

248. Narrative interview with W. Ullmann, July 12, 1999 (cited in taped interviews).

249. Narrative interview with R. Eppelmann, December 9, 1999 (cited in taped interviews, appearing in abridged version in the *Rheinland Mercury,* November 15, 2000, 27).

250. Compare the numerous surveys in *Handbook on German Unity* 1999.

251. Compare IC2 I, 616ff.

252. Thomas Hoppe, "Between the Thrill of Pursuit and the Mentality of the Bottom Line," in: FAZ, March 7, 2000, 14.

253. IC2, I, 153.

254. Compare W. Ullmann 1998, 25.

255. F. Schorlemmer 1999, 7.

256. Cited in: R. von Weizsäcker 1999, 410.

257. E. Krenz, in: *Handbook for the German Nation* 4, 123.

258. The Commission should "contribute to reconciliation in society, based on the desire for openness; and to historical truth and mutual understanding" (IC2, I, 154).

259. Gerd Poppe, in: IC2, I, 33f.

260. Narrative interview with R. Eppelmann, December 9, 1999 (cited in taped interviews; appearing in abridged version in the *Rheinland Mercury,* November 15, 2000, 27).

261. Compare G. Rüther 1995, 689.

262. E. Neubert, in: R. K. Wüstenberg 1998a, 72.

263. Art. Cit., 73.

264. Ibid. Neubert suggests to Schorlemmer, for example, the misassignment of "eschatological theological categories" in this world.

265. F. Schorlemmer 1999b, 9. Following citation ibid.

266. Thus the minister of Sachsen-Anhalt Reinhard Höppner, in: *German General Sunday News (Deutsches Allgemeines Sonntagsblatt/German Sunday Times)*, December 3, 1999, 38.

267. So Friedrich Schorlemmer, in: *Deutsches Allgemeines Sonntagsblatt/German Sunday Times*, December 3, 1999, 38.

268. Reinhard Höppner, in: *Deutsches Allgemeines Sonntagsblatt/German Sunday Times*, December 3, 1999, 38.

269. With a tribunal, no one needs to go to jail.

270. Narrative interview with R. Eppelmann, December 9, 1999. (Cited in taped interviews; appearing in abridged version in the *Rheinland Mercury*, November 15, 2000, 27.)

271. Cited in: www.budeskanzler.de/01/0101/51/index.html.

272. The German Parliamentary Report/Commissary 1999, 18.

273. Narrative interview with U. Poppe, March 6, 2000 (cited from taped interviews).

274. Narrative interview with M. Meckel, March 5, 2000.

275. Compare the German Parliamentary Report/Commissary 1999, 14.

276. Ibid., 19.

277. R. Wassermann 1994, 2668.

278. Narrative interview with M. Meckel, March 5, 2000 (cited from handwritten notes).

279. IC2, I, 249.

280. Compare the achievements of R. Schröder, in: IC2, VII, 902.

281. Narrative interview with P. Maser; November 9, 1999.

282. Ulrike Poppe directed my attention to this connection (See: Narrative interview).

283. From narrative interviews with R. Eppelmann, December 9, 1999; M. Meckel, March 5, 2000; and P. Maser, November 6, 1999 (cited from taped interviews as well as from handwritten notes).

284. R. Schröder 1999, 138.

285. R. Schröder 1999, 104.

286. L. Fritze 1998c, 117.

287. H.-J. Misselwitz 1999, 27.

288. R. Schröder 1999, 143.

289. W. Thierse 1999, 637.

290. R. Schröder 1999, 144.

291. Cited in: Parliamentary Viewpoint, November (10/1999), 7.

292. In: W. Huber 1996a, 35.

293. Oral information from P. Maser.

294. R. von Weizsäcker 1991, 89.

295. Compare above I.1.

296. K. Lüderssen 1992, 68.

297. G. Jakobs 1992, 59.

298. IC2, I, 218.

299. At the basis are the considerations in I. 4 (reparations). We limit ourselves in the following to a basic problem of legal reparations.

300. Edited by Hans-Hermann Lochen. Leipzig 1994, V.

301. In the following reference is made to the narrative interview with C. Schaefgen on April 5, 2000 (Cited from taped interviews).

302. Ulrike Poppe. Theses on amnesty/financial debates, February 21, 1995 (Ms., 1).

303. G. Werle 1997, 822.

304. IC2, I, 193.

305. IC2, I, 192.

306. Compare IC2, I, 188.

307. IC2, I, 194.

308. IC I, 30.

309. IC2, I, 154.

310. Narrative interview with M.-M. Passauer of October 11, 1999 (cited from taped interviews).

311. Written information, Peter Maser, January 26, 2000.

312. Press release of Markus Meckel, December 2, 1992: "The adverse effects and oppression of the DDR period should not be allowed to happen again."

313. Compare the following IC2, I, 617.

314. IC2, I, 617.

315. Let us recall the sense and aim of punishment in both of the major theories on punishment. According to the so-called "absolute theory of punishment," whose main representative was Kant, the basis for punishment lies only in the punishable deed, which should be equal (to the punishment). Punishment is a balance to guilt, repayment, and atonement. In the sense of the so-called "relative theory of punishment," whose main representatives were Paul Johann Anselm von Feuerbach and Franz von Liszt, punishment serves the goal of preventing a recurrence of the punishable deed. It should be achieved through having an effect on the offender (special prevention), through an effect on the offender and the victim with the goal of equalization (offender-victim equalization) or through an effect on the public good (general prevention). General prevention follows the goal of scaring other people from similar misdeeds; it should have a positive effect on the sense of justice of the general public. Special prevention has the goal of scaring an individual offender from repeating the offence, especially with respect to safeguarding society (internment). Additionally, it should have a positive influence on the offender of preventing him from repeating the offence (re-socialization). We return to this problem in the legal ethical discussion to parallel theological arguments in Part III.A.II.3.a; also in the literature.

316. H. Ostendorf 1999, 16.

317. Investigative Commission 2, I, 245f.

318. Compare to the discussion above, I.1.

319. Investigative Commission 2, I, 246f.

320. Compare to this and the following numbers in the table of K. Marxen and G. Werle 1999, 212.

321. On November 8, 1999, the BGH confirmed the decision of the Berlin Regional Court of August 25, 1997 (Az. 5, StR 632/98). Krenz received a jail term of six and a half years, Kleiber and Schabowski of about three years. (Kleiber and Schabowski were released on October 3, 2000.)

322. E. Krenz 1999, 374.

323. Ibid., 375.

324. Ibid., 387.

325. Ibid., 375. Following citation ibid.

326. *Frankfurter Allgemeine* newspaper, November 9, 1999, Commentary S. 1.

327. P. J. Winters 1997, 693.

328. Cited in: *Der Tagesspiegel/Daily Mirror,* November 9, 1999, p. 2.

329. Cited in: *Der Tagesspiegel/Daily Mirror,* November 9, 1999, p. 2.

330. This and the following assessment cited in: *Der Tagesspiegel/Daily Mirror,* November 9, 1999, p. 1.

331. IC2, I, 248.

332. R. v. Weizsäcker 1999, 406.

333. Richard Schröder, in: IC2, VII, 901.

334. Ibid.

335. Erhart Neubert, in: R. K. Wüstenberg 1998a, 84.

336. Richard Schröder, in: Investigative Commission 2, VII, 901.

337. Investigative Commission, 2, I, 215.

338. Cited in: *Der Tagesspiegel/Daily Mirror,* November 13, 1998, 5.

339. F. Schorlemmer 1999b, 119.

340. Compare R. Ellmenreich, *Remembering the Victims,* in: R. K. Wüstenberg, 1998a, 87ff.

341. G. Rüther 1995, 689f.

342. G. Rüther 1995, 689.

343. F. Schorlemmer 1999b, 9.

344. "Further dealings with DDR injustices." Parliamentary proposal by the Green Party 90 (March 17, 1995).

345. Narrative interview with C. Schaefgen, March 5, 2000 (cited in taped interviews).

346. Thus approximately 40 percent of the East German legal employees come from the legal system of the DDR (compare Investigative Commission 2, I, 207f.). Ulrike Poppe comments on the number: "Actually, the clearing out of the public offices has not been particularly successful. Unjust decisions still remain" (U. Poppe 1998, 4).

347. Investigative Commission, I, 743. We have gone into detail with regard to the concept of reconciliation of the Investigative Commission in the case study.

348. A just state would have had to bring new, more thorough considerations into the discussion with respect to the special case of transition. Such a promotion, which would have entailed broad public debates on the question of dealing with the past was — contrary to South Africa — not undertaken.

349. Hopeful attempts were offered, in addition to the offender-victim discussions and television programming to which both offenders and their victims were invited, in the form of open forums in churches, for example. Compare the Leipzig Church Assembly of 1997, where an especially intense discussion ensued on "Is reconciliation possible?"

350. Investigative Commission 2, I, 249.

351. Investigative Commission 2, VII, 902.

352. The theologically normative examination of statements follows in Part III.A.II.3.a and b.

353. Note the contrast of the German proceedings on the level of "national reconciliation" with those of South Africa where reconciliation was possible on this level without "forgiveness"; that is, without acknowledging a connection to guilt. From an analytical standpoint, the following question emerges from the comparison: is the German process potentially theologically more powerful as a statement, because less mention is made of "reconciliation" in a religious sense than in the South African context?

Notes to Part III.A

1. The question of acceptance with regard to concepts has an interesting history in the theory of philosophy, especially with respect to English empiricism to the American pragmatism and the phenomenology of the twentieth century. Compare W. Härle's overview of the problem in *Systematic Theology* (Munich, 1982), 130-87, esp. pp. 149ff. See also E. Husserl, *Logical Investigations,* Vol. 2: *Investigations in Phenomenology and the Theory of Knowledge,* 1901 (*Husserliana* XIX/1-2, ed. U. Panzer). H. O. Jones discusses the "experience as if," the "interpretation as if" and "aspect as if" with regard to the theology of phenomena in his book: *Logic in Theology: A Linguistic Investigation* (Göttingen, 1985).

2. D. Ritschl, *The Logic of Theology* (Philadelphia: Fortress Press, 1987), 59. Ritschl calls this broadening of acceptance in connection to W. James the "court" or the "halo," "halo" in the sense of what we see when a halo surrounds the moon. "When we see a coin on the table, we do not see just a colored piece of paper, but we 'see as if'; we see money as something to earn or to spend" (ibid.).

3. Compare Part I.A.IV.

4. C. Schwöbel, in: M. Marquardt 1997, 40.

5. The analyzed regulative statements reveal the many levels involved in the foundation of reconciliation. Norms, but also ideologies, play a part wherever reconciliation is encountered in the political arena.

6. With Bonhoeffer, one could say that the "penultimate" points only to the "ultimate" for those who think retrospectively.

7. Compare P. Abelard, *Commentary on Romans.* Reconciliation here means God's love and the love of God.

8. M. Kähler, *Current Dogmatic Questions,* complicates the problem of exhibiting reconciliation in Anselm and Abelard. "The teaching of reparations only knows of the effect of the event on God and separates the effect from the sinner in the main and middle sections of the economy of salvation. The other doctrine only deals with the effect of the individual minds, without being able to show that the main and middle sections are at work on it" (384). Kähler himself solves the problem of presenting reconciliation with the phrase the "illuminating word." It "effects actually only the news of God's disposition to love" (ibid.). Compare to Kähler: G. Wenz II, 132ff.; J. Wirsching 1963, from an earlier time: H.-P. Göll 1991.

9. M. Kähler, *Current Dogmatic Questions,* 419.

10. Ibid., 402.

11. M. Luther in the discussion with the theologian Johannes Latomus of Löwen; compare especially WA 8, 36-128. Compare to Luther's concept of reconciliation, also to his transfer from the Greek: G. Ebeling 1990, 9. 20ff.

12. Compare M. Luther in his writings on freedom, WA 7, 20-38.

13. WA 7, 25f. J. Calvin, *Institutes* II.16.3, argues in this regard that "reconciliation in Christ dispels evil in us so that we appear before Him as righteous and justified."

14. M. Kähler, *Current Dogmatic Questions*, 394.

15. D. F. Schleiermacher, *The Christian Faith* II, § 101 principle, p. 431.

16. A. Ritschl, *The Christian Doctrine of Justification and Reconciliation* (Edinburgh, 1902), III, 519.

17. Ibid., 532.

18. In his ethics he maintains that "the decisive moment of confession is not the act of confession, but the disposition of deep, internal remorse." It depends on the direction of the "intent." Compare A. M. Schmidt 1988, 575.

19. G. Aulén, *The Christian Idea of Atonement* (Stockholm, 1930), 529.

20. A. Ritschl, *Justification and Reconciliation*, III, 556.

21. G. W. F. Hegel, *Lectures.* Selected papers and manuscripts. Vol. III: *Lectures on the Philosophy of Religion, Part I: The Concept of Religion.* Edited by Walter Jaeschke. Hamburg 1983, 22. For Hegel, reconciliation as the epitome of the philosophy of religion precedes the "division" of God. In Anselm's program of *fides quaerens intellectum* one feels reminded, as Hegel says, that "philosophy is to this extent theology. It presents the reconciliation of God with himself and with nature, showing that nature, otherness, is implicitly divine, and that the raising of itself to reconciliation is on the one hand what finite spirit implicitly is, while on the other hand it arrives at this reconciliation, or brings it forth, in world history. This reconciliation is the peace of God, which does not "surpass all reason," but is rather "the peace that through reason is first known and thought and is recognized as what is true" (*Lectures.* Selections from papers and manuscripts. Vol. III: *Lectures on the Philosophy of Religion,* Part 3: *The Consummate Religion.* Ed. Peter Hodgson. Berkeley: U. of California Press, 1985, p. 347). The overcoming of the gap between *sola ratione* and *sola fide* is found in the dialectic of spirit. Compare criticism of Hegel's theology: P. Cornehl 1971, esp. 106ff., 115, 335, on the problem of method; from the left Hegelian point of view: W.-D. Marsch 1965; on Hegel's ontological concept of reconciliation: B. Seiger 1996, 85-99.

22. KD IV/I § (principle), 83.

23. W. Pannenberg, *Systematic Theology* II, 441ff.

24. "The idea of reconciliation does not have a cultic attraction, but is connected with diplomatic processes for crafting peace agreements between opponents." Op. cit., 474.

25. G. Aulén 1930, 531.

26. O. Weber 1966, 263 in connection to his deliberations on Anselm and Abelard.

27. Chr. Frey 1993, 26, sees a paradigm shift in the teaching on (doctrine of) reconciliation. While he illustrates the paradigm of redemption in Schleiermacher, he illustrates that of reconciliation in Barth. Frey says: "Redemption means the becoming real of reconciliation in a world that has not yet experienced the results of reconciliation" (ibid., 27).

28. M. Welker asks the question (1993, 51): "How do we reconcile the idea that the

spirit of God is in everything and effects everything with the idea that the spirit actively creates?"

29. B. Seiger 1996, 159.

30. *The Christian Idea of Atonement* (Stockholm/Lund, 1930); English: *Christus Victor: An Historical Study of the Three Main Types of the Idea of Atonement* (1931; London, 1970). Citations in this paragraph refer to the German summary of research in the ZSTh (G. Aulén 1930).

31. Compare B. Seiger 1996, 155ff., esp. 162f.

32. Compare D. Wheeler 1990, 165ff.

33. Thus G. Aulén's Latin type returns formally under the "legal model" (b), the idealistic with respect to the subjective type of reconciliation is broadened under the "humanistic model" (c) and from the more current research the comprehensive historical process type as "historical process model" (d).

34. Aulén (art. cit.) limits himself in the handling of the ancient church to evidence of the "classical motif of reconciliation." This is found mainly in Irenaeus. The work of Christ is centered on "setting free from the adversarial powers" (512).

35. The title signals something more closed, as is seen in the following presentation. A cosmic model should indeed be modeled on Origen, but the following is more similar to the punctuating of a type as if one can demonstrate such a model with relative consistency. Thus, the question is less for these preliminary remarks whether or not cosmic strains are already contained in the classical type. Rather, a particular openness should be underscored in Origen's model, especially in the context of the problem of the relationship between ontology and the Christological idea of reconciliation. In general, reference is made in the literature to the people and works in the reference books (DThC, LThK, PW, RE, RGG) as well as on the Bibliography of Patristics (ed. W. Schneemelcher); main works of Origen in MPG 11-17; GCS 1-12; SC *passim*. Compare to the state of research from 1973 to 1980 on the literary references of the parallel language volume by Origen *(On principles)*, 51-59: H. Crouzel, bibliography criticism on Origen, La Haye-Steenbrugge 1971, Supplement 1982; new and recent literature on the Apokatastasis in the monograph H. Rosenau 1993, 524ff., and J. C. Janowski 2000, I, 17; Notes 69; ii, 627ff.

36. U. Swarat, in: *Evangelical Lexicon for Theology and the Church*, 3 (1994), 2090.

37. Irenaeus understands reconciliation from the point of view of his teaching on recapitulation and for the first time, provides an answer to the question why the Word became man and suffered. He develops the following line of thinking (*Adv. Haer.* V.16.2): in the first Adam we insulted God and became indebted to him; in the second Adam we became obedient unto death and thus reconciled with God.

38. Compare the line of thinking and theme of *De Principiis* in the introduction to Origen *(De Princ.)*, 10f., to the *thetic* arrangement of the thought world of Origen's in the historical dogmatic questions of his time. A. M. Ritter 1988, 122-23. Origen's discussions are taken up in the more current systematic theological discussion by H. Rosenau 1993, 113-50.

39. According to Origen, punishment is not an emotional reaction on the part of God. The "wrath of God" does not occur without the intention of healing. God punishes with a pedagogy; He is not himself angry, but is concerned with the powers of evil. Compare here H. Chadwick 1972, 118f.

40. When hope is spoken of as the reconciler of all, this is already a constructive interpretation. In the Origen research it is not decisive whether in the context of the distinction between *securitas* and *certitudo* the reconciliation of all in the *De principiis* is actually taught, or whether it is the basis for hope. For this question I refer fundamentally to the understanding that in "the *apokatastasis* it is indeed hoped for, but it is not taught with certainty" (W. Härle, *Dogmatics*, 626).

41. H. Chadwick 1972, 120.

42. All of creation takes part in God's "benefits" *(beneficia)* (compare *De Princ.* IV.4.9). With this the formula again returns, "that everything that was created by God and nothing that was not created exists apart from the essence of the Father, the Son, and the Holy Spirit" (*De Princ.* I.3.3; I.7.1; IV.4.8). The "by nature benevolent God" created "creatures according to his standards" "because he wanted to have beings to whom he could be good and who would rejoice in receiving his benefits" (*De Princ.* IV.4.8).

43. Compare *De Princ.* III.6.6. According to Origen, one should not view the *apokatastasis* as a "sudden occurrence, but as a gradual, stepwise process completed in the course of countless and eternally long periods of time" (ibid.). The six periods of the world, which Origen factors into the *apokatastasis,* each comprise an entirely new formation of the cosmos, as well as a judgment of the world and a period of purification by fire.

44. Thus, in the sense of a nondualistic eschatology, J. C. Janowski 2000. Also H. Rosenau 1993, 147: "In Origen's thought there is no eschatology."

45. Compare *Num. hom.* 27. Also, the idea of the anticipation of *apocatastasis* in prayer, where the aesthetic God is similar *(homoios),* leaves the body behind, slips off the physical, in order to be overcome by God's splendor.

46. H. Chadwick 1972, 117.

47. In the introduction to his basic writings, Origen rejects the assumption of the predetermined influence of the stars: every soul has the freedom to choose and a will. "Thus, there is the resulting view that we are not subject to a necessity" (*De Princ.* I.5). In the interpretation of Matthew 5:13 it says (*C. Cels.* 8.70) decidedly: "The people of God are the 'salt' of the world who concern themselves for the state of earthly things; whatever is of the earth has the task, like 'salt,' not to 'lose its saltiness.'"

48. Origen does not agree with Celsus's understanding that "God" is only another term for an impersonal cosmic process. For Origen, the idea of freedom is a characteristic of a Christian philosophy that involves "the possibility of change under moral turning, the spontaneity and creative power and finally the critical distance from generally accepted conventions and traditions" (H. Chadwick 1972, 125).

49. A. M. Ritter 1988, 124. Following citations ibid.

50. Named are the preexistence of the soul, the complete similarity of the original state with the end state, and later, the acceptance of the *liberum arbitrium*. Compare to the ancient church's anathema of preexistence and the similarity of original and end state in the critical analysis of J. C. Janowski 2000 I, 102f. and 108f. Compare the reformed heretical claim of *apocatastasis* in CA XVII in the critical discussion of J. C. Janowski (op. cit., 36f.).

51. The fact that this model is exemplified in Anselm, appears in key points of G. Aulén's typology (compare to the "Latin reconciliation type," G. Aulén 1930, 513ff.). In any case, the key points are, as will be seen, of a formal type. Both attempts at assigning

type proceed from the *Cur deus homo*. In terms of content, the subsequent Anselm representation has little in common with G. Aulén and becomes a contrary judgment re: the question of the classification of the Anselm type. (Compare the criticism of B. Seiger 1996, 157f.; G. Plasger 1993, 9-12, to G. Aulén's classification of Anselm.) The "legal model" is mentioned in so far as the connection of the law is a decisive viewpoint in the reconciliation model. Thus, the concept of justice should not be hastily devalued theologically. In the history of criticism, Anselm is understood against the background of the teaching on confession of the middle ages, and in part, is seen as its representative. The current Anselm research mainly shows how abbreviations and misconstructions of the *Cur deus homo* have been admitted into the history of theology (compare G. Gäde 1989, 13ff.; G. Plasger 1993, 39f.). The new interpretation of Anselm by G. Gäde and G. Plasger contrasts with the weighty interpretations in the history of ideas from F. C. Baur through A. Ritschl to A. von Harnack. The "Anselm Renaissance" (Gombocz) had shed new light on the disputed key concept of "God's honor," "mercy and justice," "satisfaction and punishment" (compare the systematic summary of the literature on Anselm in G. Plasger 1993, 39f.) Whoever studies Anselm today cannot avoid the current state of the research. (Compare to the newer literature the bibliography in G. Gäde 1989, 302-322; G. Plasger 1993, IX-XX.)

52. O. Kirn says this in his overview article on "reconciliation" in the RE 3.A. Vol. 20, 560.

53. Compare to the dialogical character G. Plasger 1993, 71f. According to Plasger, the dialogue clearly belongs to the program of *sola ratione:* "Only the person who goes down the path of Anselm's understanding can reach the same goal" (ibid., 74).

54. Compare to "ratio" in the thinking of Anselm basically E. Mühlenberg 1988, 554ff., especially 565. For Anselm there is a difference between his methodological approach *(remoto Christo)* and the factual presuppositions of faith. K. Barth points out in his book on Anselm that the entry point for Anselm is always faith, not the intellect. His goal is not to argue God's becoming man, but to "reflect on what is said in the Creed" (K. Barth, *Fides quaerens intellectum. Anselm's proof for the existence of God in connection to his Theological Program,* 1931). Ed. E. Jüngel et al., Zürich 2.A. 1986, 40). Anselm identifies *a posteriori*: faith is not the goal of the answer to the question of *Cur deus homo,* but its assumption. The certainty that faith exists is sought by understanding: "*Si possum intellegere quod non dubito*" (II, 18). Compare the relationship between *fides* and *ratio* in G. Plasger 1993, 57-64; J. Wirsching 1993, 75f.; F. S. Schmitt says with Anselm "*intellectus fidei,* which has the middle ground between faith and sight" (RGG 3.A. Vol. I, 398).

55. *Si angelus et homo semper redderet deo quod debet, numquam peccaret* (I, 11). Translation: If an angel or (and) a man would always render to God what he ought (to render), he (the angel or man) would never sin.

56. *Omnis voluntas rationalis creaturae subjecta debet esse voluntati dei* (I, 11). Translation: Every will of the rational creature ought to be subject to the will of God.

57. *Deum impossibile est honorem suum perdere* (I, 14). Translation: It is impossible for God to lose (destroy) His honor. See an explanation of "God's honor" in Baur, A. Ritschl and Harnack; compare G. Plasger 1993, 88f.; G. Wenz I, 45f.

58. I, we (didn't he take from God everything that God wanted to have to do with human nature?).

59. The different legal understandings, which in the Anselm research have been represented, are in the lectures of G. Wenz I, 42-55, especially 45f.

60. For Augustine, similar to Origen, as we have seen, the devil is the implementing agent of God's justice. The right of punishment has been transferred to him, but in order to annul it again, God allows the innocent man Jesus to deliver it. To the degree that He places himself under His own loaned justice, He places Himself in the position of the unjust and thereby brings about His justice.

61. "Cheap grace" according to Anselm contradicts the essence of God that each attribute of God has to be identical with God himself. Compare *Monol.* XVII; *Prosl.* XII.

62. "The punishment," so interprets G. Gäde 1989, 94, "consists in the loss of eternal blessedness."

63. *Tene igitur certissime quia sine satisfactione, id est sine debiti solutione spontanea* (I, 19). Translation: So, understand this most assuredly, because without satisfaction, that is, without the spontaneous payment of debt . . .

64. *Quomodo mors eius praevaleat numero et magnitudo peccatorum omnium* (II, 14). Translation: In what manner his death may prevail over the number and magnitude of all sins.

65. Anselm writes in another place: "It is not necessary for God to take such trouble, but it is necessary for man in order to be reconciled again." *Med. Red.* (III, 86, 65f.).

66. *Credere:* I, 20, 2; *fiducia:* II, 19.

67. Compare the systematic combined look at the difficulties and meaning of the doctrine of reconciliation in W. Härle, *Dogmatics,* 321f.; 324f.

68. H. Ott, "Anselm's doctrine of reconciliation," in: *ThZ* 13 (1957), 190. (The citation also indicated that the Protestant concept of "justice" does not necessarily need to be separated from the chain of association of "Catholic teaching on confession," "synergism," etc.)

69. G. Plasger 1993, 171 (in explicit reference to Bonhoeffer's "succession"; compare DBW 4, 30ff.)

70. Thus translates G. Plasger 1993, 122, the Anselm phrase *"aut satisfactio aut poena."*

71. Even where hypothetical punishment is included in the consideration, it doesn't describe the activity of God (in the sense of legal option for action), but rather an "idleness."

72. G. Wenz I, 49.

73. The humanistic model of reconciliation correlates formally to the third main type of reconciliation in G. Aulén 1930, 526ff. The "idealistic type" is, however, broadened and deepened in content in the historical development. The line is traced back to Abelard; moreover, the evidence can not be missed that since the writing of Aulén's typology, especially in view of the third type, "serious changes" have resulted: "If with Aulén there was the difficulty of the motif of change in consciousness in the sense that in individual people an attitude of reconciliation occurs and thus another moral behavior is possible, so in relation to the ethical program of reconciliation increasingly the social-political moment is placed in the middle" (B. Seiger 1996, 161f.). The classification of the "humanistic model" appears adequate in consideration of the fact that theological history extends further than talk of an "idealistic type"; moreover, it may be less loaded with a linguistic polemic than the talk of "subjective" with respect to the "idealistic type." It is clearly evident,

as will be shown, that the core theological decision of the "humanistic concept of God and the relativized concept of sin" (G. Aulén 1930, 527, 529 etc.) is preserved in the concept of reconciliation.

74. To what extent Abelard's concept of love has to reckon with that of Augustine is viewed ambivalently in the literature. F. H. Kettler describes an "abbreviation" of Augustine's concept of love in Abelard's (in: "Reconciliation, A Dogmatic History," RGG 3.A. Vol. 6, 1374).

75. Compare in this regard G. Plasger 1993, 68.

76. Especially impressive are the observations on Romans 3:22ff., in: *Petri Abaelardi Opera* (ed. Cousin), Paris 1959, 204ff. I cited in the following from the German translation in: G. Sauter 1997, 62-69. For a historical theological account of the commentaries on Romans, compare A. Ritschl, *Justification and Reconciliation*, I, 48-52.

77. Unique agreements between Anselm and Abelard can be seen in their unreserved denial of the devil's claim on man.

78. In his interpretation of Romans 3:25, Abelard asks the rhetorical question: "How, say I, was it necessary that on our account God's only Son, after he had taken the form of flesh, had to endure so many fasts, abuse, lashings, and was spit on, and finally had to endure the most painful and humiliating death?"

79. ". . . for it concerns only this in reconciliation: that it is believed and expected." Abelard also does not espouse the "reconciliation of all." Reconciliation is an exclusive event limited to believers.

80. Compare to the various lines of development of the doctrine of reconciliation in the nineteenth and twentieth centuries the overview in "Reconciliation, A Dogmatic History," in: RGG 3A. Vol. 6, 1373-1378, 1376f. (here there is information in brief on the relevant concepts of reconciliation of the nineteenth and twentieth centuries); clearly unfolded are the ideas of G. Wenz I, 277ff. (idealism), 343ff. (F. Schleiermacher); II, 63ff. (A. Ritschl), 133ff. (M. Kähler), 193ff. (dialectical theology). Compare to the early enlightenment also the presentation by G. Wenz I, 87ff.; on the enlightenment's criticism of the doctrine of reconciliation J. A. Steiger 1994, 125ff.

81. G. Wenz I, 54.

82. J. A. Steiger 1994, 125.

83. Ibid.

84. G. Wenz I, 54.

85. G. Wenz I, 125.

86. K. Heim 1938, 311.

87. G. Wenz I, 127.

88. Op. cit., 114.

89. A new shift in accent of the subjective type is seen (after the rediscovery and new interpretation of Anselm by Hugo Grotius) in pietism and neology. Compare here the informative section in G. Wenz I, 149ff. J. A. Steiger 1994, 129, draws a direct line from enlightenment neology (A. H. Niemeyer) with the legal-ethical call "to apply oneself in one's profession and job as Jesus did in his roles as martyr," to the professional ethics of Albrecht Ritschl.

90. K. Heim 1938, 305. In contrast to K. Heim, G. Aulén 1930, 529, sees F. Schleiermacher in the subject reconciliation camp. That Schleiermacher is seen as the "reviver of

the Abelard teaching with respect to modern subjective reconciliation" is "correct to the extent" (according to G. Wenz) "that Schleiermacher shares with Abelard a basic antipathy toward Anselm in particular, and against the judicial formulation of the teaching on reconciliation in general" (G. Wenz I, 372). According to Schleiermacher, reconciliation only occurs where the believer does not see the evil in their life as punishment for sin; the acceptance of God's grace leads to the overcoming of a consciousness of sin; compare F. Schleiermacher *(The Christian Faith)* §§100f., esp. §104. Compare Schleiermacher's concept of reconciliation in the framework of history of the Christian teaching on reconciliation in G. Wenz I, §11 366ff. O. Kirn, in: RE 3.A. Vol. 20, 569 takes a different position on Schleiermacher's concept of reconciliation, where he on the one hand criticizes "that it places reconciliation prior to redemption, relates it to the evil of the world and accordingly misjudges the decisive weight of the forgiveness of sins." On the other hand, he cites as "valuable" the "strict uniformity" "with which Christ the person is connected with his work. Thus, Schleiermacher has overcome the isolating view of the individual side of the work of salvation . . . and has provided the impetus for a foundation of reconciliation on the basis of inner experience and historical conception."

91. A. Ritschl, *Justification and Reconciliation*, I, 2.

92. G. Wenz I, 23. Compare to A. Ritschl's "Concept of Reconciliation in the History of Christian Doctrine of Reconciliation" in G. Wenz II, §14, 63ff.

93. Compare A. Ritschl, *Justification and Reconciliation*, I, 31f.

94. Compare E. Günther, *The Development of the Doctrine of the Person of Christ in the Nineteenth Century* (Tübingen, 1911), 312.

95. A. Ritschl, *Justification and Reconciliation*, III, 577.

96. Compare B. Seiger 1996.

97. B. Seiger 1996, 162.

98. Let us recall, for example, the concept of D. Sölle.

99. Interpretation of Romans 3:25. Cited from the German translation in: G. Sauter 1997, 64.

100. G. Aulén 1930, 529.

101. B. Seiger 1996, 162.

102. B. Seiger has, in reference to Aulén, introduced this new conception of reconciliation into the German discussion from the British debate on atonement. He lectured on the section of British research (D. L. Wheeler 1990, 165ff.) which develops the "internal type of atonement" as a conscious extension of Aulén's classification. B. Seiger 1996, 165 describes this type as applicable to the German "historical procedural," a "procedural" because in this understanding of it reconciliation does not — in the course of history — primarily refer to an activity devoted to salvation, but is described as taking place over a long period of time, and by it something emerges that is akin to progress over against early stages of development. His brief lecture gives a first impression of the outlines of the "historical procedural model"; the concept does not replace individual attempts because they do not refer to D. L. Wheeler, above all those of the basic Christological decisions of process theology. (B. Seiger remains in agreement with D. L. Wheeler's conclusions that a "historical procedural type" is not correctly developed, and appears too early — in my opinion, too early — in a criticism of process theology.)

103. In this regard, see J. Dantine 1978 in his critical analysis of Aulén's typology, 18f., without, however, suggesting a "historical procedural type."

104. B. Seiger 1996, 162.

105. Compare the theological interpretation of this connection for the continental European discussion in the monographs of M. Welker 1981. For our question, which is in addition to the differentiated analysis of Whitehead (op. cit., 35ff.), is the constructive presentation and theological criticism of the diverse trajectories within process theology (op. cit., 138ff.) For more literature on Whitehead and process theology see M. Welker 1981, 236, appearing in "Process Theology/Process Philosophy," in: TRE 27 (1997), 602-4.

106. Compare the concept in M. Welker 1981, 13f., especially 18.

107. W. D. Beck, "Process Theology," in: *A New Dictionary of Theology*, ed. S. B. Ferguson et al. (London, 1988), 534-36, 534. The subsequent pagination refers to this article.

108. D. L. Wheeler's account of Origen is closely connected to ours. Wheeler cites similar viewpoints with regard to the cosmic aspect of the idea of reconciliation.

109. D. L. Wheeler 1990, 173.

110. Subsequent pagination refers to D. L. Wheeler 1990.

111. Wheeler, as already stated, prefers a path along the edge of process theology in general and along that of Cobb's in particular (D. L. Wheeler 1990, 182-83).

112. D. L. Wheeler 1990, 183, maintains a difference: "Christ's redemptive function in a process model is thus basically exemplary, as in the subjective-internal tradition, but his exemplification is not a mere 'showing,' but the constitution of a sphere of influence; a 'force field' impacting all subsequent human and cosmic history."

113. For D. L. Wheeler 1990, 131ff., Karl Barth is the main representative of the "external type of atonement," which is called the "classical type" in G. Aulén. In his account of the "internal type" (i.e., the historical procedural model), he contrasts Barth with process theology: "Barth . . . has spoken eloquently of God's preparation of a place for himself within human history. . . . The internal type of atonement meets this question head on and affirms unequivocally that real atonement is a true emergent from history" (D. L. Wheeler 1990, 175).

114. For the idea of the kingdom of God, says Wheeler: "And thus the kingdom of God does not so much invade as emerge from and consummate the terrestrial cosmic process" (D. L. Wheeler 1990, 179).

115. Subsequent representation of J. Cobb according to M. Welker 1981. (I was made aware of the concept of "creative change" in a critical analysis of Cobb in M. Welker 1981, 175-202.)

116. M. Welker 1981, 192f. Subsequent pagination ibid.

117. J. Cobb 1970, 166, maintains: "We only love, because we have been loved. Thus, and only thus, can the spiritual person live truly and purely."

118. Compare to M. Welker 1981, 187.

119. D. L. Wheeler 1990, 183.

120. Cited in: M. Welker 1981, 180.

121. Cited in: D. L. Wheeler 1990, 182.

122. J. Dantine 1978, 16.

123. G. Aulén 1930, 502.

124. Compare B. Seiger 1996; D. L. Wheeler 1990.

125. D. L. Wheeler 1990, 185.

126. How is it to be understood under the political challenges to reconstruction in which the assumptions of the history of ideas of the twentieth century play a part?

127. J. C. Janowski 2000, I, 13. The depreciation of the concept of reconciliation with the offhand observation that "the talk of God's reconciliation through reading reconciliation through the lens of God's wrath (op. cit. 15) is a loaded view and does not hold up in view of our observations on the legal model.

128. W. Härle *(Dogmatics)*, 626. In the sense of a counter argument it can be said that no common category with Part II would result in a "double outcome" of the concept of eschatology. Wherever in theology the regulative idea reigns that reconciliation only has to do with a small, select circle, then the love of God is "limited," "in its power and scope" (op. cit., 618; on the complex problem "double outcome" 611-20).

129. W. Härle, *Dogmatics*, 626.

130. C. Schneider, *History of Ideas of Ancient Christianity* (Munich, 1978), 122.

131. H. Rosenau 1993, 150.

132. The hearings of Conraad van Rooyen; see Part II.A.II.2.

133. In view of the concept of restorative justice, it is appropriate to recall that justice is viewed as a social concept. In a mutual process of change, offenders and victims are given the opportunity to win back their humanity and dignity. The condition for this reconciliation is insight on the part of the offender and the readiness to forgive on the part of the victim. It belongs to the principle of justice to identify the individuals responsible and to place persons at the center of the issue. Compare to the *Principles:* C. Villa-Vicencio et al. 2000, 69.

134. G. Plasger 1993, 124.

135. G. Gäde 1989, 293. Gäde interprets *Cur deus homo* in terms of the epistemological basis of Anselm's *Proslogion.*

136. There appears here a structural similarity to the question of correspondence in the framework of the humanistic model.

137. It cannot be forever broadened. Otherwise offenders must endure permanent guilt and victims can not get closure on their fate (i.e., arrive at forgiveness). The question must be considered as to how the psychological concept of closure relates to the theological idea of a change of perspective as a result of reconciliation (compare considerations in Section III.3.b).

138. Regulative statements from the South African case studies; compare Part II.A.II.4.

139. Citations from T. Sundermeier 1993, 132.

140. H. Hofmeister, *Philosophical Reflections* (Göttingen, 1991), 172 and 173; compare also "Logic," TRE 21, 1991, 423-32, esp. 423-25, as well as the authoritative study by J. M. Bochénski, *The Logic of Religion*, 2.A. (Paderborn, 1981).

141. Following citations DBW 6, 151.

142. DBW 6, 143. Following citations ibid.

143. Bonhoeffer asks, for example, why in view of a person's death he decided for a penultimate stance, namely, for "human solidarity" instead of "Biblical comfort." It is possible that, upon reflection, he felt that there is not always a "spiritual rule over the situ-

ation" and that a hint of the ultimate is also to be seen in a known remnant of the penultimate. (Compare DBW 6, 143.)

144. W. Härle, *Dogmatics,* 602. Following citations ibid.

145. W. Härle, *Dogmatics,* 520.

146. M. Welker 1992, 509.

147. J. Cobb et al. 1976, 12.

148. Ibid., 13.

149. M. Welker, in: TRE 27 (1997), 598.

150. Citation D. Ritschl, 1994a, 149.

151. G. von Rad, I, 225, note 79.

152. M. Welker 1981, 221f.

153. M. Welker 1981, 214. In contrast to the idea of continuity in the humanistic model it is clear that in order for something new to happen the old must pass away; the ultimate means breaking with the penultimate. Thus, the critical sentence in the context of process theology should be underscored "that the world, namely heaven and earth, will not be able to maintain their identity" (op. cit. 216).

154. J. Cobb et al. 1979, 100.

155. This and following citations in M. Welker 1997, 73.

156. R. Bernhardt 1999, 446.

157. M. Welker 1993, 33. Reconciliation is — in the context of the reality of the spirit — strictly to be divided from a misunderstanding of "seeking harmony."

158. R. Bernhardt 1999, 447.

159. M. Welker 1992, 508.

160. D. Shriver, in: W. Huber 1996a, 27, includes in the "components of forgiveness" the "rejection of (eye for an eye) revenge" among other things.

161. G. Sauter 1997, 17.

162. F. Lobinger 1990, 381.

163. J. Rogge et al. 1980, 33.

164. W. Huber 1991, 452.

165. Compare the newer discussion in the collected volumes of M. Welker and D. Willis, *Toward the Future of Reformed Theology* (Grand Rapids/Cambridge 1999).

166. J. de Gruchy, 1996b, 6. De Gruchy sees the task of the church in the new South Africa at the same time as a voice of warning for the absolutizing of the political. "Critical theological reflection on the state and the challenge of democratic transformation must . . . continually return to the prophetic source of Christian faith and its witness to the reign of God. Indeed, this provides the basis upon which Christianity must reject all absolutist political claims as idolatrous, and therefore keep the political process open-ended" (ibid., 7).

167. M. Welker 1999, 36. The connection to the above-analyzed concept of process consists in the fact that "at the same time" does not mean "simultaneously."

168. Compare to the overview of the concept of justice in the more recent systematic theology of H. R. Reuter 1996, 93ff.

169. Ernst Troeltsch has interpreted the Doctrine of the Two Kingdoms in the sense of such autonomy, "The Social Doctrine of the Christian Church and Groups," *Collected*

Works, Vol. I, 3.A. (Tübingen, 1923), 500ff., and in terms of the Lutheran "double moral-ity."

170. W. Huber 1991, 45of. (in connection to Luther's interpretation of the *Magnifi-cat*).

171. The "Lutheran type" tends to legal positivism, and the other to natural law. Compare W. Huber 1996b, 113f. and 119f.

172. Legal ethics from the theological perspective accounts for the relative autonomy of law over against religion. Under the conditions of a pluralistic political culture the sys-tematic application of the law can not be made dependent upon theological finalities. Rather, the "law presents a relatively autonomous sphere of reciprocally recognized rela-tionships," against which "some are recognizable from the sphere of Christian ethics and have clearly profiled contributions to make in the area of communication, education, and legal regulations of society"; thus: *Legal Ethics from the Theological Perspective* (Citation from: H. R. Reuter 1996, 20.19). Representatives of legal ethics from the theological per-spective are Hans Richard Reuter as well as W. Huber 1996b, J. Kreuter 1997, W. Liene-mann 1995.

173. A distinction should be made between Christological legal arguments that refer to the theme of justice in Christology in order to achieve a deducible basis for an analogy between justification and justice, and those of the legitimate justice of civil religion, which allocate to theology the task of reconstructing a culturally legitimate basis for a so-cial institution of law. A classical representative of a Christological legal argument is K. Barth's "Justification and Justice" (1938). (Regarding the stages of the concept of justice in K. Barth, compare H.-R. Reuter 1996, 106ff.; DERS. 1991, v.a. 122f.) In the more recent debates a Christological legal argument is, among others, represented by K. Gäfgen, *Jus-tice in Correlation to Dogma and Ethics* (= TBT 52) (Berlin/New York, 1991; J. Zehner, 1998); on the legitimate justice of civil religion see W. Vögele, *Civil Religion in the Federal Republic of Germany* (= Public Theology 5) (Gütersloh, 1994). An overview of the discus-sion is given in H.-R. Reuter 1996, 13-22, esp. 19.

174. Compare J. Kreuter 1997, 108: Punishment is necessary as "human structure" "in order when the need arises to make this sinful world possible for human life together, in as much as it is also the goal to limit force as much as possible."

175. W. Huber 1996b, 325.

176. Ibid.

177. T. Rendtorff, in: U. Duchow 1977, 53ff. (citation 60).

178. W. Huber 1996b, 341. Compare T. R. Snyder on the theme, *The Protestant Ethic and the Spirit of Punishment* (Grand Rapids/Cambridge, 2001), esp. 74ff.

179. W. Huber 1996b, 266.

180. Ibid., 267. Huber adheres to a model of correspondence and difference as a pro-ductive contribution to the theological interpretation of human rights, which at the same time is conscious of its basic openness.

181. E. Seidler 1995, 19.

182. Chr. Frey 1990, 31.

183. Compare DBW 6, 134f.

184. The statement from the *Treaty of Westphalia* of 1648 at the end of the Thirty Years' War can be seen as exemplary: "There shall be on one side and the other a perpetual

Oblivion, Amnesty, of Pardon . . . of all that has been committed since the beginning of these troubles" (Article 2).

185. DBW 6, 134. In the distinction between cicatrisation and forgiveness, Bonhoeffer does not arrive to a duality. For him, there is also "in the historical external and internal political disagreements between people a kind of forgiveness that is only a weak shadow of the forgiveness that Jesus Christ gives in faith" (ibid.).

186. Inner historical forgiveness/forgiveness that is given as a gift; political amnesty/spiritual reconciliation; worldly healing (as a process of cicatrisation)/spiritual healing (as its interruption) — these three pairs of concepts can be effortlessly arranged according to the Doctrine of the Two Kingdoms.

187. Compare the above discussion on the interim constitution. In the theological rendering of the question of amnesty Bonhoeffer's manuscript on ethics plays a decisive role. Compare W. Kistner, "Guilt and Reconciliation in South Africa," in: W. Huber 1996a, 55ff., esp. 71f., or D. Smit 1995, 8f. I have taken up this discussion in other places and elaborated on it; compare R. K. Wüstenberg, "Basic Philosophical and Theological Problems in Understanding the Reconciliation Process in South Africa," in: *Religion and Theology* 7,2 (2000), 169ff., esp. 182f.

188. DBW 6, 135f.

189. O. Meyer 1996, 277.

190. D. Shriver 1999, 1169f., runs into the danger of being misunderstood where he speaks of a "relationship" between forgiveness and amnesty. Additionally, his discussion of "regret in politics" can provide a focus for mistakes in assigning categories, because it is not entirely clear whether "politics" means personal processes in political reality (which would be open to theological interpretation), or whether politics is meant to be an a-personal subject that would be capable of remorse. In a similar way, Shriver's formulation can be misunderstood where it indicates that nations can show remorse, especially with respect to forgiveness (compare D. Shriver 1995, 71ff.). What is intended is clearly a central idea for our research; namely, that individual persons, mainly political leaders, perform symbolic acts that can be seen as representative for a nation (see impressively D. Shriver, in: W. Huber 1996a, 21ff.).

191. W. Huber 1996b, 361.

192. Ibid.

193. D. Kraus, art. cit., 411.

194. D. Kraus, art. cit., 427.

195. J. Kreuter 1997, 358 convincingly qualifies the popular talk of moral guilt: "social ethical guilt" is incurred "whenever someone receives treatment that is against ethical laws." Along different lines, M. Sievernich speaks of social sin ("Social Sins and Their Acknowledgment," in: *Concilium* 23 [1987], 124-31, esp. 128f.).

196. The statements of the offenders can be cross-examined. Victims have the right to substantiate the veracity of the offender's statements or to call them into question.

197. W. Härle 1990, 64.

198. J. Kreuter 1997, 380.

199. R. Wassermann 1993, 11.

200. W. Hüber 1996b, 170.

201. G. Müller-Fahrenholz 1996, 31.

202. Compare W. Härle 1997, 309.

203. In this regard: the "basic claim for justice in the law" "can stop the destructive consequences of disturbed relationships" (W. Härle 1997, 310).

204. Let us recall the core idea of the concept of justice: "The aim of restorative justice is . . . 'to make things right' between adversaries" (C. Villa-Vicencio et al. 1999, 73). The "between" indicates a moral level. "Relationships" are to be restored; even those of offenders and victims with society, as well as those between offenders and victims. Under the option for action "reparation" we first see the relationship of victim to society. "In the restorative justice approach, victims become key participants and are placed at the centre of the justice process" (W. Verwoerd 1999,125). The "fundamental principles" of the concept of justice are to be found in: www.fresno.edu/dept/pacs/rjprinc.html.

205. M. Welker 1994, 26. Following citation art. cit., 24.

206. E. Neubert, in: R. K. Wüstenberg 1998a, 84.

207. The connection between John 8:32 and 14:6 will be taken up more comprehensively in the final section: truth frees where Christ is the subject of the action of freedom.

208. The schema above does not require a didactic breakdown; also the following overview is a simplification and not capable of presenting the many-faceted development of the prior discussions. The overview above is more like a representation. It represents verbally what is really something much more dynamic. The fact that amnesty (Option 2) is not theologically "transferable" to truth (Option 3) evades schematic representation.

209. C. Breytenbach 1989, 223f.

210. J. Zehner 1998, 280f. For his results, Zehner refers in a later place (op. cit. 340-344) to the Joseph story (Gen. 37–50).

211. D. Shriver 1995, 22f. In addition to the Joseph story (Gen. 37–50), Shriver refers to the Biblical findings in Matthew 6:12 as well as Psalm 130:4 in connection with Mark 2:7 for his analysis.

212. In order to cite only one title: the story of Zacchaeus (Luke 19:1-10) is interpreted in the context of South Africa by Robin Peterson, "The Politics of Grace and the Truth and Reconciliation Commission," in: H. Botman et al., *To Remember and to Heal* (Cape Town, 1996), 57ff., esp. 62f. On the German and South African transition process see Gerd Decke's "Biblical Dimensions of Reconciliation: The Prodigal Son and Zaccheus," in: R. K. Wüstenberg 1998a, 101ff. Passages on reconciliation (as in Genesis 18–19; Genesis 25–33; Heb. 9:22; Luke 7:36-50; 23:34; 15:11-21) are helpful for our theme: G. Müller-Fahrenhols 1996a, 87-171. Biblical dimensions of reconciliation, in view of Luke 15:11-32, are also worked out by W. Huber et al. 1991, 226f. Compare the similarity of the prodigal son in M. Volf 1996, 156-65. A catalogue of conditions that help make reconciliation possible are collected in the "Paper of the Reconciliation Project Group of the German Commission *Justitia et Pax*." These elements include "analysis of the conflict, readiness to communicate, empathy, seriousness, remembering, patience, acceptance of sadness and truthfulness," which "can lead to reconciliation and release" (reconciliation — gift of God and source of new life [1997, 11f.]). However, it still remains unclear whether the basis for the elements of reconciliation is Biblical-theological or rational-political. The elements of reconciliation are used unilaterally, as is the concept of reconciliation itself.

213. C. Breytenbach 1989, 223.

214. J. Zehner 1998, 340. Zehner refers here to the Joseph story.

215. J. Zehner 1998, 306.

216. J. Zehner 1998, 294.

217. Fundamentally: D. Shriver 1995; a summary in German is given in his article in W. Huber 1996a, 21-41. Compare the more recent D. Shriver 1999.

218. D. Shriver, in: W. Huber 1996a, 27.

219. Ibid.

220. He writes (ibid.): "Reconciliation, as it is used in the New Testament, includes elements of the future and remains eschatologically connected to mention of the 'kingdom of God' in the Lord's Prayer. However, the request for forgiveness in this prayer is not connected to the future."

221. Joseph clearly speaks of guilt; it is named. "I am Joseph, your brother, whom you sold into slavery in Egypt" (Gen. 45:4). The consciousness of justice is not removed.

222. C. Gestrich 1989, 366.

223. C. Gestrich 1996, 366.

224. Compare R. F. Capon 2000.

225. Citation from F. Lobinger 1993, 281.

226. I will return to the submitted ecumenical request to discuss "confession" by D. Sattler 1992, 371ff. in the discussion of reparation/*satisfactio*.

227. CA XII (BSLK 66,3.f).

228. Compare G. Wenz on Luther's position to the Augsburg Confession in *Theology of the Confessional Writings of the Evangelical Lutheran Church: A Historical and Systematic Introduction into the Book of Concord*, Vol. 1 (Berlin/New York, 1996), 499ff., esp. 506.

229. Compare Thesis 36 in which Luther states that already through true remorse one's sins are forgiven by God.

230. Compare the famous Thesis I: "If our lord and master Jesus Christ says: Repent!, then he meant for the entire life of the believer to be one of repentance."

231. WA 1, 319-24.

232. Luther finds solace in the word of mercy of the "power of the keys" (Matthew 18:18f.). It is a word "against all horror of the conscience" and "for the contrition and blessedness of the soul" (Sermon on the Sacrament of Penance 1519, WA 2, 713-24, citation 715, 19f.)

233. Declared at the Council of Florence; compare the Bull *Exultate deo,* Nov. 22, 1439 (D. 1323).

234. In the "Babylonian Captivity," Luther states that remorse is no longer a condition for the obtainment of mercy, but the fruit of the spirit of faith in God's promises (Compare esp. WA 6, 545).

235. Melanchthon explicitly places "remorse" and "law" parallel to each other in the Apology: in other words, remorse is a work of the law. Compare *Apology* XII (BSLK 257, 29, d.T.).

236. Compare the *Schmalkald Articles* III, 3f. (BSLK 437).

237. DBW 6, 157: "Repentance prepares the way (Matthew 3:1ff.)." In Matthew 3:1-3, Isaiah 40:3 ("Prepare the way of the Lord") is referred to in the confessional prayer of John the Baptist.

238. According to the teaching of the Scholastics, remorse is close to the granting of forgiveness of sins in the sacrament of penance, which must awaken the person to the

love of God and to works of reparation, which are dependent upon a thorough confession of sin. Compare CA XI; BSLK 66,1: *in confessione non sit necessaria omnium delictorum enumeratio* (complete version CA XV). The Council of Trent limits the "complete understanding" of the confession of sin (from the definition of the Fourth Lateran Synod, 1215; D 812-14): what is remembered should be made known (compare Session XIV, Cap. 5 "De confessione" D. 1679f., esp. 1680).

239. CA 11 (BSLK 66, 1) speaks of the "absolutio privata in ecclesiis." Luther knew this as part of the four forms of confession: "1. The confession of the heart *(confessio fidei)* before God alone; 2. public confession on the basis of church discipline; 3. apology to the neighbor *(confessio caritatis);* and 4. individual confession before the congregation or the clergy" (R. Müller, "Reflections on Confession," in: E. Henze, ed., *The Confession* [Göttingen, 1991], 33-44, citation on 39).

240. KD IV, 2, 633. Clearly, Barth does not overlook the fact that the substance of the picture "springs forth." Upon awakening to *contritio* it has to do with "an awakening from the sleep of death: a sleep from which — be it of the power of a secret and the awe of God — there is no waking" (ibid., 628).

241. This, the philosopher L. Fritze 1998d, 865, explains, is the function of the naming of guilt.

242. M. Volf 1996, 120.

243. M. Volf 1996, 120 n. 13: "I am not suggesting that there is a necessary temporal sequence between repentance and forgiveness such that, say, one first repents and then offers or receives forgiveness." As in our analysis, for Volf it is "to indicate various elements of this circle."

244. D. Shriver 1999, 7.

245. G. Müller-Fahrenholz 1996, 111 (in a work on Genesis 18–19).

246. Cited from the *Rheinland Mercury,* September 15, 2000, p. 26.

247. G. Sauter 1997, 24f.

248. Compare CA XII, BSLK 66, 2.

249. "The only sin we know is sin that has already been forgiven" (D. Smit 1995, 7). CA XII, BSLK 67,4 formulates ahead of time: "... *agnito peccato.*" The knowledge of sin precedes faith (elsewhere in Rom. 7:17f.).

250. Luther fought against forcing confession and also against the so-called *reservatio,* in which in certain cases the forgiving of sins was reserved for the Pope. (Compare WA 6, 546-47.)

251. Compare *Religion within the Limits of Pure Reason,* B 171 (Companion to Kant IV, 779): "It is not conceivable that a rational person who knows himself to be worthy of punishment could seriously believe that it is only necessary to believe that reparations are meant for him." Thus, the victims have alone the singular right to forgive, because forgiveness is connected to the waiving of rights. Renunciation is meant here in terms of reparation. The one forgiven must bring a "sacrifice." This waiving of rights may not be forced on the state where it concerns the dealings of citizens.

252. W. Härle, in: M. Marquardt 1997, 74.

253. C. Villa-Vicencio et al. 2000, 74.

254. J. Llewellyn et al. 1998, 50.

255. Tony Marshall, in: J. Llewellyn et al., 19.

256. W. Huber et al. 1990, 227.

257. E. Jüngel 2000, 22.

258. M. Volk 1996, 272f.

259. Following citations C. Breytenbach 1989, 223.

260. Accordingly, there is no passivity with respect to responsibility in the church; in Paul there is evidence of the unfinished process of reconciliation in an appeal for the particular responsibility of the congregation as the medium for the word of reconciliation (s. Section — B. Ecclesiastical Conclusions).

261. See Overview.

262. D. Sattler 1992.

263. CA XII, 6: BSLK 67, 9f.

264. In the history of dogma, the interpretation of the CA by Melanchthon begins with a development of the teaching on the *tertius usus legis.* One could simplify it by saying: what is not distinguished in Luther, is first highlighted in Melanchthon and then in a particular way in the Reformed tradition. Whereas Luther believed that when a person is free and lives by faith he does good as a matter of course, Melanchthon is interested in identifying the righteous not only on the basis of faith. They also need God's instruction — namely, the third use of the law — for those who are born again who no longer misunderstand the law as a means of salvation, but at the same time want to be led by God's instruction in life.

265. Compare for example the metaphor in WA 57 on Galatians, 105, 24-47: "Sic tria et septem non debent esse decem, sed sunt decem . . . Ita iustus non debet bene vivere et bene facere, sed bene vivit et bene facit." Translation: Thus, three and seven ought not to make ten, they are ten. So the righteous ought not to live and do well, he does live and do well.

266. Compare the Commentary on Galatians WA 40, 1, 417, 12ff. and 427, 11ff.

267. J. Zehner 1998, 394.

268. E. Seidler 1995, 11.

269. Citation: D. Sattler 1992, 379. However, Sattler speaks of a "symbol for the sake of human conversion" (ibid.).

270. D. Sattler 1992, 375. Similar observations are also made from the Evangelical side. Compare U. Kühn, "Celebrating Reconciliation: (Evangelical) Notations to the (Catholic) Sacrament of Penance," in: *ThLZ* 108 (1983), 2-16, esp. 13: A. Peters, "Penance-Confession-Forgiveness of Guilt in Evangelical Theology and Practice," in: *KuD* 28 (1982), 42-72, esp. 65.

271. Following citation D. Sattler 1992, 377.

272. T. S. Maluleke writes 1997, 76: "The idea of the TRC is . . . borrowed from the Roman Catholic model of penance, confession, and absolution." This is no wonder, says Maluleke, because ultimately the TRC Commission took as its model the Latin American Truth Commission.

273. Where regret or excuses were mentioned in political forums, common categories cannot be confirmed in every case, especially with regard to the theological category of remorse. However, there are a few examples of it.

274. G. Sauter 1997, 18, expounds further on this position.

275. Compare Matthew 5:24.

276. J. Dantine 1996, 434.

277. G. Kraus 1990, 195, develops this "energetic model" as a synthesis of monergism and synergism.

278. K. Barth, KD IV, I, 99f.

279. G. Müller-Fahrenholz 1996, 83: "We should always count on a third power that is active in both and which has the ability to loosen the entrenched fronts."

280. M. Beintker et al., eds., *Justification and Experience*, FS Sauter (Gütersloh, 1995), 150.

281. DBW 3, 60.

282. Compare the above theoretical foundation to Part I.B.III.3.

283. DBW 3, 61.

284. Current summary of the state of the research in M. Buntfuss 1997, 1-7; U. Link-Wieczorek 1998, 341-47; R. Bernhardt et al. 1999, 9-19. Further accounts of the literature concerning a theological discussion of the problem in G. Ebeling 1991, 16 n. 34. An overview of the discipline addressing the fundamental problems of the theme in J.-P. van Noppen, ed., *Remember in Order to Say Something New: The Meaning of Metaphor for Religious Language* (Frankfurt/M., 1988), 7-51.

285. P. Ricoeur et al. 1974, 49.

286. M. Buntfuss 1997, 5. Metaphors that illuminate reality are divided into substitutive and comparative metaphors. In the classical metaphor "Achilles is a lion," Buntfuss (op. cit., 8) explains that a substitutive metaphor would translate it as "Achilles is brave," whereas a comparative metaphor would translate it as "Achilles is like a lion." Common to both theories of metaphor is that "both the analogous and substitutive metaphor can be replaced by either actual or linguistic formations and do not represent an actual or irreducible statement."

287. E. Jüngel, in: P. Ricoeur et al. 1974, 86 (previously in R.W.)

288. M. Buntfuss 1997, 8.

289. P. Ricoeur et al. 1974, 70.

290. P. Ricoeur et al. 1974, 65.

291. R. Volp, article in Bild VII, TRE 6 (1980), 559.

292. D. Ritschl (Logic), 22.

293. D. Ritschl 1999, 168.

294. M. Buntfuss 1997, 224.

295. Citation: P. Biehl, learning about symbols. Neukirchen-Vluyn. 2. A. 1991, 53. Compare the classification of Biehl in the symbol construction of H. Schmidt, *Symbols: Basic Building Blocks of Religious and Moral Education,* in: R. Bernhardt et al. 1999, 221-39, esp. pp. 225f.

296. H. Schmidt, *Symbols: Basic Building Blocks of Religious and Moral Education,* in: R. Bernhardt et al. 1999, 221-39, 235.

297. Signs of transcendence are not a means of grace; they are not sacraments, which "transfer on the basis of divine intervention" or, as Melanchthon says in the previously quoted statement, immediately are "deployed by Christ in the Gospel" (Loci 8.22). Signs of transcendence do not belong to "solid evidence of God's will" (8.5); they are not "a witness and seal of God's will" (8.13). In contrast to sacramental signs, they are not "the clearly expressed power of the sacrament" (8.19).

298. J. B. Metz 1973, 138.

299. The following categorization of the theology of Metz is taken from "Political Theology, 3. The Categories of Political Theology," in: *Handbook of Twentieth Century Theology* (Regensburg, 1995), 291-311, 305f.

300. The following categories from the theology of Metz are based in "Political Theology, 3. The Categories of Political Theology," 305f.; individual documents of Metz's are contained here.

301. J. B. Metz, *Faith in History and Society: Studies in Fundamental Practical Theology*, 3.A. (Mainz, 1980), 176.

302. J. B. Metz, "For an Anamnetic Culture," in: H. Lowey, ed., *Holocaust: The Limits of Understanding* (Reinbeck, 1992), 39.

303. M. Volf 1996, 235.

304. M. Volf 1996, 235.

305. O. Meyer 1996, 10. In the previous analysis of the concept of process we have already discussed the Deuteronomical "theology of remembrance" that contains the recollection of slavery in Egypt and God's liberating intervention.

306. E. Jüngel, *Death* (Stuttgart/Berlin, 1971), 153.

307. O. Meyer 1996, 281.

308. This appears finally also in the actual European conflict: remember Nordirland!

309. O. Meyer 1996, 282.

310. M. Volf 1996, 140.

311. The representation of "story" as a category of political theology in Metz appears again in historical research under "Political Theology, 3. The Categories of Political Theology," 306f.

312. In terms of the history of the concept, J. B. Metz and H. Weinrich have introduced the term "narrative theology" into the German discussion in a programmatic work of 1973. Compare J. B. Metz, "A Small Apology for Narrative," in: *Conc* (d) 9 (1973), 334-41, and H. Weinrich, "Narrative Theology," in: *Conc* (d) 9 (1973), 329-34.

313. J. B. Metz 1973, 139.

314. "Political Theology, 3. The Categories of Political Theology," 307.

315. A bibliography on the topic of "narrative theology" can be found in: R. Zerfaß, ed., *Narrated Faith — Narrating Church* (1988), 198-203 (in following cited as R. Zerfaß 1988). Important leads on the newest literature are contained in the volume *Revelation and History*, ed. G. Sauter and J. Barton 2000. The volume of essays (in the following cited as J. Barton and G. Sauter 2000) is the documented results of a German-English research project on the theme.

316. Compare R. Zerfaß 1988; J. Barton and G. Sauter 2000.

317. Compare E. Arens, "'Who Can Utter the Mighty Acts of the Lord?' (Ps 106,2) — The Narrative Structure of Christian Faith from the Perspective of Systematics," in: R. Zerfaß 1988, 13-27, esp. pp. 25ff.

318. D. Ritschl, *Logic*, 45.

319. B. Wacker, "Ten Years of 'Narrative Theology' — An Attempt at a Counterweight," in: W. Sanders et al., *Stories for Children — Stories of God* (Stuttgart, 1983), 13-32, 25.

320. Based on this perspective, the artist and narrative theoretician U. Eco decided to write his 1980 novel: *The Name of the Rose* (Munich, 1982).

321. Following citations from: R. Zerfaß 1988, 23ff.

322. The title of the volume J. Barton and G. Sauter 2000. The English word "story" is used; it should be a "process of story telling" (less on the much debated problem of story and revelation); compare J. Barton and G. Sauter 2000, 14ff.

323. Compare as the basis sola scriptura in connection with "Revelation and Story," G. Sauter: "Being 'true to the text' is not a 'textual principle'" (J. Barton and G. Sauter 2000, 21ff.).

324. J. Barton and G. Sauter 2000, 13.

325. Following citations J. Barton and G. Sauter 2000, 12.

326. "What would be 'revealed' by divine intervention are the hidden circumstances that are trapped and veiled" (J. Barton and G. Sauter 2000, 12).

327. In: J. Barton and G. Sauter 2000, 82.

328. Previous and following citations in: J. Barton and G. Sauter 2000, 84ff.

329. W. Jetter 1986, 49.

330. J. Barton and G. Sauter 2000, 86.

331. This "similarity" will be again examined in terms of systematic theology in the sense of *analogia relationis.*

332. H. P. Siller, "The Gospel in the Individual Experience of Telling and in the Experience of Hearing," in: R. Zerfaß 1988, 159-70, 161.

333. *Faith in History and Society,* 205. Compare such solidarity to the "mystical political": J. B. Metz, *The Time of Fraternities? Mysticism and the Politics of Succession.* Solidarity has a mystical structure, because it proceeds from a faith as remembrance and story telling; it has a political structure because it is "practiced" in history and society; the task of each person as a person.

334. A brief summary of the history of ideas on the theme of suffering in philosophy and theology of the twentieth century from W. Benjamin to J. Moltmann, who placed the theme within the context of a theology of the cross, is available in "Political Theology, 3. The Categories of Political Theology," 308-9.

335. J. B. Metz 1973, 133. In this context Metz also asserts that "middle class religion" has its place in conversion; in contrast the "messianic religions" are an expression of a "Christianity of apostolic succession"; compare *Beyond Civil Religion* (Main, 1980).

336. J. Moltmann, *Political Theology — Political Ethics* (Munich, 1984), 10.

337. Op. cit., 163f.

338. J. B. Metz 1973, 132. Thus, "Christianity in its message of salvation has not exhausted its meaning for the unatoned for sufferings of the past; it is rather a very particular story of freedom: the freedom through God's deliverance in the Cross of Jesus" (ibid.).

339. J. B. Metz 1973, 133.

340. Compare WEN 413ff. The following remarks are assembled summaries from my analysis of the "Outline for a Book" from "Resistance and Submission"; compare R. K. Wüstenberg, 1998.

341. Citation WEN 414 (prior and following).

342. H. Dembowski, *Basic Christological Questions* 3.A. 1993, 244f.

343. WEN 414.

344. Messianic history as the history of suffering, in: J. B. Metz and J. Moltmann, *History of Suffering* (Freiburg, 1974), 44.

345. Following citations from: "The Suffering of the Son of Man and the Call to Follow," in: J. B. Metz and J. Moltmann, *History of Suffering* (Freiburg, 1974), 28f.

346. Ibid., 29.

347. In the example of the two-word metaphor "blushing red" E. Cassirer illuminates: "Blushing is not just a combination of redness and shame. . . . The whole displays itself as an internal structure; it is an articulated (expressed) whole and only becomes what it really is through this articulation (expression)" (in "Logic of the Concept of Symbol," in: E. Cassirer 1956, 223).

348. Compare E. Cassirer, *Philosophy of Symbolic Forms* III, 3.

349. D. Smit 1995, 15.

350. The silence is broken. *The Truth and Reconciliation Commission in South Africa* ("Out of the Shadows," in German) (Frankfurt/Vienna, 2000), 364.

351. Compare here W. Jetter 1986, 87-122; K.-H. Bieritz, in: *Liturgical Handbook* (Göttingen, 1995), esp. 119-25; R. T. Volp, Liturgy Volume I, Gütersloh 1992, 109ff., 226ff.; Volume II, 1994, 969ff.; K-F. Daiber 1978, 16f.; further literature on symbol and ritual in worship in R. Volp, *Liturgy* Volume I, 111ff.

352. On the concept see W. Jetter 1986, 119. Jetter sees in the "symbolic added value," the ritual carries an actual communicative task that also corresponds to the "communication of the Gospel" in ritual processes; compare op. cit., esp. 87f.

353. W. Jetter 1986, 108.

354. Compare W. Jetter 1986, 93-108.

355. W. Jetter 1986, 94.

356. The nine characteristics, which W. Jetter 1986, 94ff., mentions in order, are arranged in the following based on their orientation to the problem. (The following citations refer to W. Jetter 1986). An overview of the research yields a typical representation of selected theories of ritual by S. Freud ("Ritual as a Neurotic Phenomenon") to E. E. Erikson ("Ritualization as Ontogenetic Condition of Social Institutions") and G. H. Mead ("Identity Awareness through the Ritual of Interaction") through E. Durkheim ("Ritual between Stable and Transformative Functions") in the fundamentally anthropological work of K.-H. Beiritz, in: *Liturgical Handbook* (Göttingen, 1995), 119f.

357. Listing of literature on the theme above in the first reference to "Worship as Ritual."

358. K.-F. Daiber 1978, 22.

359. W. Jetter 1986, 109ff., states why "ritual manners," although they are "still thus founded and useful," may not "be understood as necessary for salvation": "because in worship one must especially guard against the tendency to make the endorsed rules of ritual a determining factor."

360. The thesis of W. Jetter 1986, 112, that rituals are "indispensable and dangerous," finds entrance into handbooks of modern practical theology literature, among other things. Compare K.-H. Bieritz, "Rituals."

361. K.-H. Bieritz, in: *Liturgical Handbook* (Göttingen, 1995), 121.

362. W. Jetter 1986, 104.

363. Citation: W. Jetter 1986, 112.

364. W. Jetter 1986, 121.

365. K.-H. Bieritz, in: *Liturgical Handbook* (Göttingen, 1995), 122.

366. K.-F. Daiber 1978, 18 (before and after).

367. Citation: W. Jetter 1986, 118.

368. Citation: W. Jetter 1986, 120.

369. W. Jetter 1986, 110.

370. R. Volp, *Liturgy* Volume II (Gütersloh, 1994), 974.

371. W. Jetter 1986, 120. Following citation in connection to P. Ricoeur. Ibid.

372. K.-H. Bieritz, *The Church Year: Festivals, Memorials, and Celebrations of the Past and Present* (Munich, 1987), 57.

373. Ibid.

374. K.-F. Daiber 1978, 19 (compare on the same page the picture of the "Structure of Worship as Symbolic Representation of the Coming of God").

375. E. Hauschild, "What Is a Ritual? Attempt at a Definition and Typology in Connection to a Theory of Everyday Life," in: *WzM* 45 (1993), 24-35, 30.

376. Compare E. Hauschild, art. cit., 33.

377. In: H. Botman et al. 1996, 114.

378. K.-F. Daiber 1978, 21.

379. Illustration VII, in: TRE 6 (1980), 561.

380. K.-F. Daiber 1978, 17.

381. K.-F. Daiber 1978, 16.

382. K.-F. Daiber 1978, 20.

383. K.-H. Bieritz, in: *Liturgical Handbook* (Göttingen, 1995), 123.

384. Ibid.

385. K.-F. Daiber 1978, 20.

386. D. Smit, "Confession-Guilt-Truth-and-Forgiveness in the Christian Tradition," in: H. Botman 1996, 97.

387. Regarding the leading normative theological difference between the "pure teaching of the Gospel" (CA 7) and the narrative history of the Truth Commission, a question of homiletics arises with regard to what extent the stories of victims from the area of political reality can be employed in sermons to underscore the Christological content (of the sermon) in the proclamation of the Gospel.

388. D. Smit, "Confession-Guilt-Truth-and-Forgiveness in the Christian Tradition," in: H. Botman 1996, 97.

389. Revised agenda. Preliminary draft. Bielefeld 1990, 25.

390. "The applicants arrive agitated and leave relieved," as we cited an observer saying above on the effect of the ritualized process of the Gauck Administration.

391. C. Villa-Vicencio 1999a, 2.

392. K.-F. Daiber 1978, 20, says: "God encounters us as the Coming, Answering, and finally as the Giver. People encounter God as the One who calls, as the One who draws us to Himself, and finally as the One who receives us."

393. Compare to this translation what is already outlined regarding the case studies, esp. R. Ellmenreich, "Reflections on Victims," in: R. K. Wüstenberg 1998a, 87ff.

394. E. Neubert, "Victims of Non-physical Arrest," in: U. Baumann et al., eds., *Politically Motivated Pursuit: Victims of SED Injustice*, Criminology Research Reports from the Max Planck Institute for Foreign and International Criminal Law 84 (Freiburg, 1998), 277-302, 298. Following citation ibid.

395. G. Müller-Fahrenholz 1996a, 162.

396. W. Huber et al. 1990, 231.

397. W. Huber et al. 1990, 231.

398. G. Müller-Fahrenholz 1996a, 162.

399. C. Gestrich 1997, 504f. Following citation, ibid.

400. S. McFaue, "Metamorphic Theology," in: J.-P. van Noppen, *Remembering in Order to Say Something New: The Meaning of the Metaphor for Religious Language* (Frankfurt/M., 1988), 176f., citation 195.

401. H. Beintker, "Victims, Dogmatics of Ethics," in: RGG 3.A., 1656f., citation 1657.

402. Compare to the anthropological hallmarks of symbolic communication in W. Jetter 1986, 48f.

403. The meaning of the proceedings is repeated in the philosophical literature on transitional processes. Compare J. Harvey 1995, 57: "Victims of institutional wrongs . . . lack an appropriate level of power."

404. C. Gestrich 1993, 502.

405. Compare W. Jetter 1986, 48f. to the following.

406. C. Franz 1997, 61.

407. J. Gauck in a narrative interview of July 19, 2000.

408. D. Shriver 1999, 10.

409. Compare to M. Luther's theological insight on the meaning of metaphorical speech for life in the happy Exchange and struggle of Christ, esp. "On the Freedom of the Christian" (12th par.) WA 7, 20-38, esp. 25f.

410. G. Sauter 1997, 26.

411. Compare to the following meaning the entries in: TBLNT, Volume ii/2, 130f.; *Exegetical Dictionary to the New Testament,* Volume II, 644f., esp. 645; *A Greek English Lexicon* (Oxford, 1961), 899.

412. H.-G. Link. "καταλλαγή," in: TBLNT, Volume II/2, 1308.

413. H.-R. Reuter 1996, 176.

414. Ibid.

415. So that the victims are not forgotten, but are able to tell their stories, their burden is lifted without new victims (through revenge) being created.

416. Following citations from: *On the Freedom of the Christian* (12th par.), WA 7, 25f.

417. C. Franz 1997, 40, defines in the framework of the analysis on narrative in the TRC proceedings: "Closure occurs in narrative when meaning is shifted from one social space to another."

418. We cite, for example, A. Forbes above: "Now I can carry on with the rest of my life."

419. C. Franz 1997, 64.

420. Compare as the basis for both of the above assumptions in the Theoretical Foundations the section "Question of Correspondence in the Category of *analogia relationis,*" Part I.B.III.3f.

421. The symbolic quality of the aftermath is clear where W. Härle 1975, 212, says: God corresponds "in a relationship," namely person to person, "in which He does not appear as an element."

422. G. Sauter 1997, 16.

Bibliography of Sources

Primary Literature

1. Theology: Doctrine of Reconciliation

Abelard, P. Commentary on Romans. *Petri Abaelardi opera theologica. I. Commentaria in Epistolam Pauli ad Romanos,* ed. Eligius Buytaert. Brepols, 1969 = CCMXI, 41-340.

Anselm of Canterbury. *Cur deus homo.* (Why God became man.) Translated with an introductory analysis and notes by Joseph M. Colleran. Albany, NY: Magi Books, Inc.

Barth, K. *Church Dogmatics,* IV, 1-3. Edinburgh: T. & T. Clark; New York: Scribner, 1936-1969.

Kähler, M. *Christliche Versöhnungslehre. Eine systematisch-historische Studie.* Leipzig, 1916.

Mandel, H. *Christliche Versöhnungslehre: Eine systematisch-historiche Studie.* Leipzig: A. Deichert, 1914.

Origen. *De principiis.* On first principles, Koetschau's text of the *De principiis,* translated into English, together with an intro. and notes by G. W. Butterworth, intro. to the Torchbook ed. by Henri de Lubac. New York: Harper & Row, 1966.

Origen. *Commentary on the Epistle to the Romans.* The Fathers of the Church, vol. 103. Washington, DC: Catholic University of America Press, 2001.

Ritschl, A. *The Christian Doctrine of Justification and Reconciliation.* Volumes I-III. Edinburgh: T.& T. Clark, 1902.

2. Dogmatics, Dogma, and History of Theology

Calvin, J. 1989. *Calvin's Institutes,* edited by Hugh T. Kerr. Louisville: Westminster/ John Knox Press.

Harnack, A. von. 1976. *History of Dogma,* translated from the third German edition by Neil Buchanan. Gloucester, MA: P. Smith.

Kähler, M. 1898. *Dogmatische Zeitfragen: Alte und neue Ausführungen zur Wissenschaft der christlichen Lehre.* Leipzig: A. Deichert.

Melanchthon, P. 1965. *Melanchthon on Christian Doctrine: Loci communes, 1555.* Translated and edited by Clyde L. Manschreck. Intro. by Hans Engelland. New York: Oxford University Press.

Pannenberg, W. 1991-1998. *Systematic Theology,* translated by Geoffrey W. Bromiley. Grand Rapids: Eerdmans.

Ritschl, D. 1987. *The Logic of Theology.* Philadelphia: Fortress Press.

Schleiermacher, F. 1850. *The Christian Faith.* Edinburgh: Clark.

Tillich, P. 1951-1963. *Systematic Theology.* Volumes I-II. Chicago: University of Chicago Press.

Wenz, G. *Geschichte der Versöhnungslehre in der Evangelischen Theologie der Neuzeit.* Volumes I-II. Munich, 1984-1986.

Other Primary Sources

1. Documents for the South African Case Studies

Laws

Act 35: Indemnity Act of 1990.

Act 139: Prevention of Public Violence and Intimidation Act of 1991.

Act 151: Further Indemnity Act of 1992.

Act 200: Constitution of the Republic of South Africa of 1993.

Act 34: Promotion of National Unity and Reconciliation Act of 1995.

Documents

ABC: Applied Broadcasting Centre (ABC). Reporting the Truth Commission Conference Proceedings. Johannesburg, March 1-2, 1996.

ANC: Report of the Commission on inquiry into complaints by former African National Congress prisoners and detainees. August 1992.

ANC: African National Congress National Executive Committee's Report to the Montsuenyane Commissions' Report. August 12, 1993.

ANC: ANC Research Department Briefing No. 1 Truth Commission. October 13, 1993.

AWEPA: Conference Report. Reconciliation and Democratization. Windhoek, Namibia, October 28-31, 1992 (Archiv Kistner No. 2593A).

BMW: South Africa 1996. Truth and Reconciliation. Berlin Mission Work (BMW).

BMW: South Africa 1997. Truth, Justice and Reconciliation. Berlin Mission Work (BMW).

CSVR: Annual Report 1995, Center for the Study of Violence and Reconciliation (CSVR), Johannesburg.

CSVR: Minutes of the "From Truth to Transformation" Conference on the Truth and Reconciliation Commission. Conference convened by The Center for the Study of Violence and Reconciliation (CSVR), April 21-22, 1998, Johannesburg.

CSVR: The TRC status as of February 4, 1998. Center for the Study of Violence and Reconciliation (CSVR), Johannesburg.

EAB: Report and analysis on matters of concern to the Ecumenical Advice Bureau (EAB). February-March 1996, Johannesburg.

EAB: A brief analysis on matters of concern to the Ecumenical Advice Bureau (EAB). July-August 1996, Johannesburg.

Final Report (I-V). Truth and Reconciliation Commission of South Africa Report (five volumes), presented to President Mandela on October 29, 1998. Cape Town.

Groote Schnuur minutes, Cape Town, May 4, 1990, in F. Meer, ed., *The CODESA File: Negotiating a Non-racial Democracy in South Africa 1989–March 1993.* Durban, pp. 273-75.

Hansard 1990: Debates of Parliament (Hansard); Friday, February 2, 1990 (Joint Sitting), 1-18.

Hansard 1995: Debates of the National Assembly (Hansard), May 17, 1995 (Second reading debate: Promotion of National Unity and Reconciliation Bill), 1339-1441.

Hansard 1999: Debates of Parliament (Hansard), Thursday, February 25, 1999 (Joint sittings of both Houses of Parliament February 5–March 26, 1999), 34-182.

HRC Document. 1994. Human Rights Committee (HRC) of South Africa. Summary Report for the Month of June 1994 and Half-Year Review, Braamfontein, 1994.

HRC Document. 1995. Human Rights Committee (HRC) of South Africa. Summary Report. Main events and trends in June 1995, Braamfontein, 1995.

HRW Document. 1992. South Africa. Accounting for the Past. Human Rights Watch/Africa (HRW). October 23, 1992.

ICT Document. Message from the Institute for Contextual Theology (ICT) to the National Churches Conference, Johannesburg (Archiv Kistner No. 1726 A).

IDECESA Document. Kairos in Africa. Ecumenical Documentation and Information for Eastern and Southern Africa (EDICESA). September 19-21, 1989, Harare.

Institute for Democracy Document. *Dealing with the Past. Truth and Reconciliation in South Africa.* Edited by A. Boraine et al. Cape Town, 1994.

Justice in Transition Document. 1994. *Truth and Reconciliation Commission.* Pamphlet, published by Justice in Transition on behalf of the Ministry of Justice. Rondebosch, 1994.

Justice in Transition Document. 1995. *The Healing of a Nation?* Edited by A. Boraine et al. Cape Town, 1995.

Pretoria Minute. Pretoria, August 6, 1990, in F. Meer, ed., *The CODESA File: Negotiating a Non-racial Democracy in South Africa 1989–March 1993.* Durban, 1990, pp. 280-83.

Religious Response Document. *The Religious Response to the TRC,* Newsletter to the TRC Campaign, 1/1 (July 1995)–2/6 (June/July 1996), Cape Town.

SACBC Document. Comments of the South African Catholic Bishops Conference (SACBC) on Amnesty and Indemnity by the Minister of Justice Mr. Dullah Omar MP (Archiv Kistner No. 3324 A).

SACC Document. 1986. *Hope in Crisis: Report of the Eighteenth Annual National Conference of the SACC, Johannesburg, June 23-27, 1986.* Edited by S. Jacob.

SACC Document. 1991. *South African Council of Churches (SACC): National Conference 1991* (Archiv Kistner No. 1577 A).

SACC Document. 1994a. *South African Council of Churches (SACC): Consultation on the Truth Commission.* Khotso House, August 12, 1994.

SACC Document. 1994b. *South African Council of Churches (SACC): The Truth Will Set You Free* (booklet), December 1994.

SACC Document. 1994c. *Report of the SACC Review Task Group to National Conference: The SA Council of Churches: Towards a New SACC,* June 9, 1994.

SACC Document. 1996. *South African Council of Churches (SACC): Great Start to Truth Commission,* SACC Communications (clarification of the TRC), April 16, 1996.

TRC Document. 1994a. Working document. Draft legislature framework for proposed Bill to set up a Truth and Reconciliation Commission (TRC). Cape Town, July 1994 (Archive of the TRC No. 111).

TRC Document. 1994b. Notes on Institute for Democracy meeting on proposed Truth and Reconciliation Commission (TRC). Pretoria, September 1994 (Archiv Kistner No. 3376 A).

TRC Document. 1996a. Interim Report. Truth and Reconciliation Commission (TRC). Cape Town, June 1996.

TRC Document. 1996b. Truth and Reconciliation Commission (TRC). Statement Victim (official document of victims' statements). October 1996.

TRC Document. 1997a. UIR and Final Reparation. Truth and Reconciliation Commission (TRC). National Consultation, February 1997.

TRC Document. 1997b. Draft. Reparation and Rehabilitation Policy Discussion Document. July 7, 1997.

TRC Just War Debate. Public Discussion on the Just War Debate and Reconciliation, Cape Town, May 6, 1997 (see: www.truth.org.za).

TRC Public Debate. Truth and Reconciliation Commission. Public Discussion. "Transforming Society through Reconciliation: Myth or Reality?" Cape Town, March 12, 1998 (see: www.truth.org.za).

UNISA Document. Christians and Their Confessions in Post-Apartheid South-Africa Conference UNISA, March 23-24, 1998.

WCC/SACC Document. An Ecumenical Consultation of Member Church Representatives of the WCC and the SACC and Other Christian Bodies. "Towards an Ecumenical Agenda for a Changing South Africa." A Cape Town Statement and Plan of Action Proposals, March 21-24, 1991, Cape Town.

WCRP-SA Document. Introduction to a Religious Consultation on the Truth and Reconciliation Commission. World Conference on Religion and Peace — South African Chapter (WCRP SA). Johannesburg, September, 1994.

WPCC Document. Western Province Council of Churches (WPCC). Statement on Amnesty (Archiv Kistner No. 2127 A).

2. Documents for the German Case Studies

Laws

BGBl, II, 885, 1246. Gesetz zu dem Vertrag vom 31. August 1990 zwischen der Bundesrepublik Deutschland und der Deutschen Demokratischen Republik über die Herstellung der Einheit Deutschlands — Einigungsvertragsgesetz — und der Vereinbarung vom 18. September 1990.

BGBl, I, 2272. Gesetz über die Unterlagen des Staatssicherheitsdienstes der ehemaligen Deutschen Demokratischen Republik (Stasi Unterlagen Gesetz, StUG, December 20, 1991).

BGBl, I, 1257. Zweites Vermögensrechtsänderungsgesetz, June 14, 1992.

BGBl, I, 1814. Erstes Gesetz zur Bereinigung von SED Unrecht, October 20, 1992.

BGBl, I, 1311. Zweites Gesetz zur Bereinigung von SED Unrecht, June 23, 1994.

BGBl, II, 889. Gesetz zur Regelung offener Vermögensfragen, December 2, 1994.

BGBl, I, 980. Gesetz über Verkauf von Mauer und Grenzgrundstücken an die früheren Eigentümer, July 15, 1996.

BGBl, I, 1609. Gesetz zur Verbesserung rehabilitationsrechtliches Vorschriften für Opfer der politischen Verfolgung in der ehemaligen DDR, July 1, 1997.

EV. Vertrag zwischen der Bundesrepublik Deutschland und der Deutschen

Demokratischen Republik über die Herstellung der Einheit Deutschlands-Einigungsvertrag, August 31, 1990.

Other

Datenreport 1997. Zahlen und Fakten über die Bundesrepublik Deutschland, herausgegeben vom Statistischen Bundesamt (Bundeszentrale für politische Bildung. Schriftenreihe 340). Bonn, 1998.

Der Bundesbeauftragte 1995. Verfolgung und die Folgen. Über den Umgang mit den Opfern. Analysen und Berichte. Aus der Veranstaltungsreihe des Bundesbeauftragten für die Unterlagen des Staatssicherheitsdienstes der ehemaligen DDR (October 27, 1994). Abteilung Bildung und Forschung. Reihe B, Nr 2/1995.

Der Bundesbeauftragte 1999. Vierte Tätigkeitsbericht des Bundesbeauftragten für die Unterlagen des Staatssicherheitsdienstes der ehemaligen DDR, 1999.

DDR Geschichte in Dokumenten. Beschlüsse, Berichte, interne Materialien und Alltagszeugnisse, herausgegeben von M. Judt (Bundeszentrale für politische Bildung. Schriftenreihe 350). Bonn, 1998.

Deutsche Einheit I-V. Zur Sache. Themen parlamentarischer Beratung: Auf dem Weg zur deutschen Einheit. Deutschlandpolitische Debatten im Deutschen Bundestag und der Volkskammer in fünf Bänden. Ed. Deutscher Bundestag. Referat Offentlichkeitsarbeit. Bonn.

Dokument Bürgerkomitee. Gesetzentwurf über die Sicherung und Nutzung der Daten und Unterlagen des Ministeriums für Staatssicherheit der Deutschen Demokratischen Republik. Teil A: Gesetzetext; Teil B: Gesetzesbegründung. Erarbeitet und beschlossen von den Bürgerkomittes zur Auflösung des MfS/AfNS, February 10, 1991 (manuscript).

Dokumente zur Deutschlandpolitik. Deutsche Einheit. Sonderedition aus den Akten des Bundeskanzleramtes 1989/90. Bearbeitet von H. J. Küsters/d. Hofmann. Munich, 1998.

EK I-IX. Materilien der Enquete-Kommission "Aufarbeitung von Geschichte und Folgen der SED Diktatur in Deutschland" (12. Wahlperiode des Deutschen Bundestages), neun Bände in 19 Teilbänden (I-IX), herausgegeben vom Deutschen Bundestag. Baden-Baden, 1996.

EK 2 I-VIII. Materilien der Enquete-Kommission "Überwindung der Folgen der SED Diktatur im Prozeß der deutschen Einheit" (13. Wahlperiode des Deutschen Bundestages), acht Bände in 14 Teilbänden (I-VIII), herausgegeben vom Deutschen Bundestag. Baden-Baden, 1999.

Handbuch zur deutschen Einheit. Handbuch zur deutschen Einheit. Edited by W. Weidenfeld et al. Frankfurt am Main, 1996.

Handbuch zur deutschen Einheit. Handbuch zur deutschen Einheit 1949-1989-

1999. Edited by W. Weidenfeld and K. R. Korte (Bundeszentrale für politische Bildung. Schriftenreihe 363). Bonn, 1999.

Handbuch zur Deutschen Nation 1. Handbuch zur Deutschen Nation Bd. 1: Geistiger Bestand und politische Lage. Edited by B. Willms. Tübingen/Zürich/Paris, 1986.

Handbuch zur Deutschen Nation 2. Handbuch zur Deutschen Nation Bd. 2: Nationale Verantwortung und liberale Gesellschaft. Edited by B. Willms. Tübingen/Zürich/Paris, 1987.

Handbuch zur Deutschen Nation 4. Handbuch zur Deutschen Nation Bd. 4: Deutschlands Einigung und Europas Zukunft. Edited by B. Willms. Tübingen/Zürich/Paris, 1992.

Handwörterbuch zur Gesellschaft Deutschlands. Edited by B. Schäfers and W. Zapf (Bundeszentrale für politische Bildung). Bonn, 1998.

KSPW 3. Berichte der Kommission für die Erforschung des socialen und politischen Wandels in den neuen Bundesländern e.V. (KSPW). Bericht 3: Max Kaase, Politisches System. Opladen, 1996.

Das Parlament. Das Parlament 48. Jahrgang, No. 46-47 (November 6/13, 1998). Thema: Enquete Kommission "Folgen der SED Diktatur."

Das Parlament. Das Parlament 49. Jahrgang, No. 43-44 (October 22/29, 1999). Thema: Fall der Mauer.

Probleme der Einheit 5. Probleme der Einheit Bd. 5: Institutionelle Reorganisation in den neuen Ländern. Selbstverwaltung zwischen Markt und Zentralstaat (Die ökonomische und institutionelle Integration der neuen Länder 2). Marburg, 1992.

Probleme der Einheit 6. Probleme der Einheit Bd. 6: Konsolidierung des Binnenmarktes. Strukturpolitik und westeuropäische Integration (Die ökonomische und institutionelle Integration der neuen Länder 2). Marburg, 1992.

Report. "Und diese verdammte Ohnmacht." Report of an independent investigative committee on the events of October 7-8, 1989, in Berlin. Berlin, 1991.

Speeches and remarks: Helmut Kohl and remarks on the German Republic. (Reihe Berichte und Dokumentationen. Presse — und Informationsamt der Bundesregierung.) Bonn, 1990.

Secondary Sources, Including Seminal Interviews of the South African Case Studies

Ackermann, D. 1999a. Interview with Denise Ackerman, Cape Town, March 15, 1999.

Ackermann, D. 1999b. "Faith Communities Face the Truth," *JTSA* 103 (1999), 88-93.

Adam, H. 1997. *Comrades in Business: Post-Liberation Politics in South Africa.* Cape Town.

Adam, H. 1998. "Trading for Justice," *The World Today* (January), 11-13.

Adam, H. 1999. Interview with Heribert Adam, Cape Town, March 15.

Ahbe, T. 1997. "Ostalgie als Selbstermächtigung. Zur produktiven Stabilisierung ostdeutscher Identität," *Deutschland Archiv* 30/2:614-19.

Ahbe, T. 1999. "Zwiespältige Bilanz. Über Ostalgie und ihre Gründe," Universitas. Zeitschrift für interdisziplinäre Wissenschaft 54/634, 339-51.

Albrecht, P.-A., et al. 1992. "Zur strafrechtlichen Verfolgung von DDR-Aussenspionage. Völker und verfassungsrechtliche Fragen," *Neue Justiz* 4/46, 137-47.

Allen, J. 1999. "Balancing Justice and Social Unity: Political Theory and the Idea of a Truth and Reconciliation Commission." Unpublished paper, Department of Politics, Princeton University.

Alpers, H. 1964. *Reconciliation through Christ: A Typology of the Lund School.* Göttingen: Vandenhoeck & Ruprecht.

Amano, Y. 1994. "Karl Barth's Ethik der Versöhnungslehre. Ihre theologische Rezeption," in *Japan and ihre Bedeutung für die kirchlich-gesellschaftliche Situation in Japan.* Frankfurt am Main.

Ash, T. G. 1990. "Après le deluge, nous," *European Review* 1.

Ash, T. G. 1997. "Vier Wege zur Wahrheit," *Die Zeit* 41 (October 3), 44.

Ash, T. G. 1997. "Bad Memories," *Prospect* (August/September), 20-23.

Ash, T. G. 1998. "The Truth about Dictatorship," *The New York Review of Books* 45/3 (February 19), 35-40.

Asmal, K. 1993. "After Motsuenyane," *Mayibuye* 10:14-15.

Asmal, K., et al. 1996. *Reconciliation through Truth: A Reckoning of Apartheid's Criminal Governance.* Cape Town.

Aster, R., et al. 1989. *Teilnehmende Beobachtung: Werkstattberichte und Methodische Reflexionen.* Frankfurt and New York.

Auerbach, F. 1996. "Reconciliation as Seen by the Major Religions of South Africa. TRC Sub-Committee Report." Unpublished manuscript, Johannesburg, December 16.

Aulén, Gustaf. 1961. *Christus Victor: An Historical Study of the Three Main Types of the Idea of Atonement.* New York: Macmillan.

Bahr, E. 1991. *Sicherheit für und vor Deutschland. Vom Wandel durch Annäherung zur Europäischen Sicherheitsgemeinschaft.* Munich and Vienna.

Baillie, D. M. 1948. *God Was in Christ: An Essay on Incarnation and Atonement.* New York: Charles Scribner.

Barton, J., and G. Sauter, eds. 2000. *Revelation and Story: Narrative Theology and the Centrality of Story.* Aldershot, Hants, England; Burlington, Vt.: Ashgate.

Battis, U. 1992. "Aufbau des öffentlichen Dienstes in den neuen Bundesländern — Recht und Realität," in U. Battis et al., *Vergangenheitsbewältigung durch Recht.*

Drei Abhandlungen zu einem deutschen Problem, Wissenschaftliche Abhandlungen und Reden zur Philosophie, Politik und Geistegeschichte 16. Berlin, pp. 65-89.

Bauerkämper, A. 1996. "'Gute Absichten,' 'Verblichene Errungenschaften,' 'Verlorene Siege?' DDR-Geschichte und politische Kultur im vereinten Deutschland," *Deutschland Archiv* 9/1:128-32.

Bauerkämper, A. 1999. "DDR — Vergangenheit zwischen Theologie, Strafjustiz und Geschichtswissenschaft. Umgang mit Schuld und Verantwortung im vereinten Deutschland," in W. Vögele, ed., *Verantwortung — Schuld — Vergebung,* Loccom Protocol 54/98. Rehburg-Locucum, pp. 146-62.

Bauerkämper, A. 1999. "Das Erbe des Kommunismus im vereinten Deutschland. Die Zeitgeschichtsschreibung und die DDR," *Revue d'Allemagne* 31/1:169-94.

Behrens, M., et al. 1994. *Südafrika nach der Apartheid.* Baden-Baden.

Berger, P. L. 1969. *Auf den Spuren der Engel. Die moderne Gesellschaft und die Wiederentdeckung der Transzendenz.* Frankfurt.

Berger, P. L. 1994. "Rückkehr der Engel," *Investigative Commission* 27/1:93-96.

Berg-Schlosser, D., et al. 1995. *Einführung in die Politikwissenschaft.* 6th edition. Munich.

Bernhardt, R., et al. 1999. *Metapher und Wirklichkeit. Die Logik der Bildhaftigkeit im Reden von Gott, Mensch und Natur.* Göttingen.

Besier, G., and S. Wolf. 1992. "Pfarrer, Christen und Katholiken." *Das Ministerium für Staatssicherheit der ehemaligen DDR und die Kirchen.* 2nd edition, Neukirchen-Vluyn.

Best, E. 1957. "Die Aufgabe des Versöhnungsbundes in der Zukunft," *Versöhnung und Friede,* 2:1-3.

Beyme, K. von. 1999. "Kohl hat es einfach gemacht," *Deutsches Allgemeines Sonntagsblatt* 48 (November 26), 10.

Bismarck, J. von. 1999. *Wiedergutmachung von Enteignungsunrecht: Landrestitution nach einem Systemwechsel. Das südafrikanische Gesetz zur Restitution von Landrechten von 1994 unter vergleichender Berücksichtigung des deutschen Rechts der offenen Vermögensfragen.* Aachen.

Bock, P. 1995. "Von der Tribunal-Idee zur Enquete Kommission," *Deutschland Archiv* 11:1171-83.

Bock, P. 1998. "Vergangenheitspolitik im Systemwechsel. Die Politik der Aufklärung, Strafverfolgung, Disqualifizierung und Wiedergutmachung im letzten Jahr der DDR." Diss. FU. Berlin.

Bock, P., et al. 1999. *Umkämpfte Vergangenheit. Geschichtsbilder, Erinnerung und Vergangenheitspolitik im internationalen Vergleich.* Göttingen.

Bollig, A. 1995. "Der südafrikanische 'Wahrheitsausschuss.' Ein Versuch der Vergangenheitsbewältigung," *Konrad-Adenauer-Stiftung Auslandsinformationen* 11:53-75.

Boraine, A. 1994a. "Truth Sets a Nation Free," *Democracy in Action. Journal of the Institute for Democracy in South Africa* 8/1:12f.

Boraine, A. 1994b. "Truth and Reconciliation Commission: What about Justice?" Unpublished lectures.

Boraine, A. 1995. "Truth and Reconciliation in South Africa." Paper presented at a conference August 7-9, 1995, Guatemala City.

Boraine, A. 1996. "Alternatives and Adjuncts to Criminal Prosecutions." Unpublished lectures, Brussels, July 20.

Boraine, A. 1996. Statement by Dr. Alex Boraine, Vice-Chairperson of the Truth and Reconciliation Commission, October 3 (press release).

Boraine, A. 1997. "TRC to Discuss Internal Tensions," *Sowetan* (January 22).

Boraine, A. 1998. "Can Truth Telling Promote Reconciliation?" TRC speech, March 3 (manuscript).

Bosch, D. 1991. "The Role of the Church in a New South Africa." Manuscript (Archiv Kistner, no. 184 A).

Botman, H., et al. 1996. *To Remember and to Heal: Theological and Psychological Reflections on Truth and Reconciliation.* Cape Town, Pretoria, and Johannesburg.

Bourdieu, P. 1992. *The Logic of Practice.* N.p.

Bozzoli, B. 1998. "Public Ritual and Private Transition: The Truth Commission in Alexandra Township. South Africa 1996," *African Studies* 57/2:173-201.

Brande, C. 1997. "Yutar and the 'Holy Disbelieve,'" in *Mail & Guardian* (April 3), 22.

Brandt, W. 1993. "Was zusammengehört. . . ." In *Über Deutschland.* Bonn.

Braun, D. 1989. "Luther über die Grenzen des Staates 1523," *JBBKG* 57:27-64.

Breytenbach, C. 1989. *Versöhnung. Eine Studie zur paulinischen Soteriologie* (WMANT 60), Neukirchen.

Breytenbach, C. 1993. "Versöhnung, Stellvertretung und Sühne. Semantische und Traditionsgeschichtliche Bemerkungen am Beispiel der paulinischen Briefe," *NTS* 39:59-79.

Bryson, L., ed. 1948. *Communication of Ideas.* New York.

Buntfuss, M. 1997. *Tradition und Innovation. Die Funktion der Metapher in der theologischen Theoriesprache,* TBT 84. Berlin/New York.

Burckhardt, H. 1993. *Politische Ökonomie des Teilens. Wirtschaftliche und soziale Probleme in der deutsch-deutschen Vereinigung,* Forschung 22. Berlin.

Buruma, I. 1993. *Erbschaft der Schuld. Vergangenheitsbewältigung in Deutschland und Japan.* Munich.

Buthelezi, M. 1994. "The Role of the Church in the Post-Apartheid Era in South Africa: Some Thoughts." EKD Consultation with Lutheran Churches in South Africa, June 13-17, 1994, Berlin.

Buur, L. 1998. "'As Christians We Forgive Them.' An Analysis of the St. James Amnesty Hearing and How 'Victims' Responded to the Ritualized Hearing

Form." Unpublished paper presented to the Danish Foreign Political Institute, April 1998.

Capon, R. F. 2000. *The Fingerprints of God: Tracking the Divine Suspect through a History of Images.* Grand Rapids.

Cassirer, E. 1956. *Cause and Effect of the Concept of Symbol* (in German). Darmstadt.

Chadwick, H. 1972. *Die Kirche der alten Welt.* Berlin and New York: De Gruyter. (English ed.: *The Early Church.* Harmondsworth: Penguin, 1967.)

Christie, K. 1999. "The South African Truth Commission: Human Rights, Nation-Building and Reconciliation." Unpublished paper.

Cobb, J. B. 1967. *The Structure of Christian Existence.* Philadelphia: Westminster Press.

Cobb, J. B. 1970. *Die christliche Existenz. Eine Vergleichende Studie der Existenzstrukturen in verscheidenen Religionen.* Munich: Christian Kaiser.

Cobb, J. B. 1976. *Process Theology: An Introductory Exposition.* John B. Cobb Jr. and David Ray Griffin. Philadelphia: Westminster Press.

Cochrane, J. 1999. Interview with Jim Cochrane. University of Cape Town, March 13.

Conference Paper: Multi-Event. 1999. Papers from the Conference: "Multi Event 1999." Forum on the results of the TRC, February 16, 1999, Cape Town (cited from transcribed tapes).

Cornehl, P. 1971. *Die Zukunft der Versöhnung. Eschatologie und Emanzipation in der Aufklärung, bei Hegel und in der Hegelschen Schule.* Göttingen.

Daiber, K.-F. 1978. "Der Gottesdienst als Ritual und Sprechhandlung," in *Gemeinde erleben ihre Gottesdienste. Erfahrungsberichte.* Gütersloh, pp. 16-23.

Dantine, J. 1978. *Versöhnung. Ein Grundmotiv christlichen Glaubens und Handelns.* Gütersloh.

Dantine, J. 1996. "'Versöhnung' und die Grazer Versammlung," *ÖR* 45/2:431-43.

Decke, G. 1995. "Partner-Konsultation über Versöhnung und Gerechtigkeit." Unpublished document, October 28, Berlin.

Decke, G. 1996. "Den Opfern ihre Würder zurückgeben," *JK* 12:682-86.

Decke, G. 1997. "Report of the Mission Trip to South Africa of September 13–October 17, 1997." Manuscript (in German), Berlin Mission Society, Berlin, November 19.

Dodd, C. H. 1952. *Christianity and the Reconciliation of the Nations.* London: SCM Press.

Dönhoff, U. 1993. *Ein Manifest II. Weil das Land Versöhnung braucht.* Reinbek.

Dohrmann, R. 1968. *Versöhnung hat politische Gestalt. Stimmen zur Begegnung mit Polen,* EZS 39. Hamburg.

Doyé, K., and H. Haberlandt. 1992. "Personal für ein demokratisches Bildungswesen — Vergangenheitsaufarbeitung im Ministerium," in *Erinnerung für die*

Zukunft. Zur Geschichte der Volksbildung der DDR. Ein Kongressbericht. Ludwigsfelde, pp. 25-33.

Duchrow, U., ed. 1977. *Zwei Reiche und Regimente. Ideologie oder evangelische Orientierung? Internationale Fall- und Hintergrundstudien zur Theologie und Praxis lutherischer Kirchen im 20. Jahrhundert (SEE 13).* Gütersloh.

Duchrow, U. 1983. *Christenheit und Weltverantwortung. Traditionsgeschichte und systematische Struktur der Zwei-Reiche-Lehre,* FBESG 25. 2nd edition. Stuttgart.

Dudek, P. 1992. "'Vergangenheitsbewältigung.' Zur Problematik eines umstrittenen Begriffs," *Aus Politik und Zeitgeschichte. Beilage zur Wochenzeitung Das Parlament* 1-2 (1992), 44-53.

Dwyer, S. 1999. "Reconciliation for Realists." *Ethics and International Affairs* 13 (1999): 81-98.

Ebeling, G. 1990. "Der Sühnetod Christi als Glaubensaussage. Eine hermeneutische Rechenschaft," *ZThKB* 8:3-28.

Eggensperger, T., et al., eds. 1991. *Versöhnung. Versuche zu ihrer Geschichte und Zukunft (FS Paulus OP),* WSAMA. P 8. Mainz.

Everett, W. J. 1998a. "Seals and Springboks: Theological Reflections on Constitutionalism and South African Culture," *JTSA* 101 (July), 71-80.

Everett, W. J. 1998b. "Reconciliation's Public Face," *New Routes* 4:29-33.

Fehr, H. "Offentlicher Sprachwandel und Eliten Konkurrenz. Zur Rolle politischer Semantik in den Dekommunisierungskampagnen post-kommunistischer Gesellschaften," in *Eliten, politische Kultur und Privatisierung in Ostdeutschland, Tschechien und Mittelosteuropa.* Edited by I. Srubra. Kontanz, pp. 65-96.

Fetscher, I., et al. 1985. *Politikwissenschaft. Begriff-Analysen-Theorien. Ein Grundkurs.* Reinbek.

Feydt, S., et al. 1994. "Die Leipziger Friedensgebete," in *Leipzig im Oktober. Kirchen und alternative Gruppen im Umbruch der DDR. Analysen zur Wende.* Edited by W.-J. Grabner et al. Berlin, pp. 123-35.

Franz, C. 1997. "South African's TRC: An Enquiry into the Nature of the 'Truth' Produced at the Hearing on the Committee of Human Rights Violations." Honors Dissertation. Ms. 68,S.

Frey, Chr. 1993. "Versöhnung als Neubestimmung der Zukunft," *GILern* 8:19-34.

Fricke, K. W. 1995. "Merkwürdige Schlussstrich-Diskussion," *Deutschland Archiv* 28/1:113-15.

Friedrichs, J. 1980. *Methoden empirischer Sozialforschung.* Opladen.

Friedrichs, J., et al. 1971. *Teilnehmende Beobachtung. Zur Grundlegung einer sozialwissenschaftlichen-Methode empirischer Feldforschung.* Weinheim et al.

Fritze, L. 1995a. "Irritationen im deutsch-deutschen Vereinigungsprozess," *Aus Politik und Zeitgeschichte. Beilage zur Wochenzeitung Das Parlament* 27/95 (June 30, 1995), 3-9.

Fritze, L. 1995b. "Identifikation mit dem gelebten Legen. Gibt es DDR Nostalgie in den neuen Bundesländern?" In *Das wiedervereinigte Deutschland. Zwischen-bilanzen und Perspektiven*, Bayrische Landezentrale für politische Bildung. Munich, pp. 275-92.

Fritze, L. 1995c. "Gewinne und Verluste im Vereinigungsprozess," *Deutschland Archiv* 28/4:411-20.

Fritze, L. 1996. "Vergangenheitsbewältigung als Interpretationsgeschäft," *Leviathan. Zeitschrift für Sozialwissenschaft* 24/1:109-23.

Fritze, L. 1998a. "Noch einmal: 'Vergleichen' gleich 'Gleichsetzen?' Ein Vorschlag zur Güte," *Zeitschrift für Politik* 45/4:427-31.

Fritze, L. 1998b. "Herrschaft und Konsensus — Über Stabilitätsbedingungen von Weltanschauungsdiktaturen," in *Diktaturenvergleich als Herausforderung. Theorie and Praxis*. Edited by G. L. Heydemann and E. Jesse. Berlin, pp. 95-119.

Gablentz, H. von der. 1965. *Einführung in die Politische Wissenschaft*, Die Wissenschaft von der Politik, 13. Opladen.

Gäde, G. 1989. *Eine andere Barmherzigkeit. Zum Verständnis der Erlösungslehre Anselms von Canterbury*. Würzburg.

Gardner-Feldmann, L. 1984. *The Special Relationship between West Germany and Israel*. Boston.

Gauck, J. 1991. *Die Stasi Akten. Das unheimliche Erbe der DDR*. Reinbek.

Gauck, J. 1993. Interview with Joachim Gauck, *Deutschland Archiv* 26:491-95.

Gauck, J. 1994. *Wahrnehmen-Aushalten-Widerstehen. Zivilcourage: Erwägung zu einem schwierigen Begriff in einem schwierigen Jahrhundert*, Tübingen Universitätsreden N.F. 15. Tübingen.

Gerloff, R. 1998a. "Menschliche Begegnungen in Südafrika," *RKZ* 1:17-23.

Gerloff, R. 1998b. "Truth, a New Society and Reconciliation: The Truth and Reconciliation Commission in South Africa from a German Perspective," *Missionalia* 26/1 (April), 17-53.

Gestrich, Chr. 1989. *Die Wiederkehr des Glanzes in der Welt. Die christliche Lehre von der Sünde und ihre Vergebung*. Tübingen.

Gestrich, C. 1997. "Die Sprache der Versöhnung," *ZThK* 94:488-510.

Gibas, M. 1999. "'Hammer und Zirkel im Ahrenkranz.' Anmerkungen zur Symbol und Repräsentationskultur der DDR," *Deutschland Archiv* 32/4:552-63.

Gill, D., and U. Schröter. 1991. *Das Ministerium für Staatssicherheit. Anatomie des Mielke-Imperiums*. Reinbek.

Glaessner, G.-J., ed. 1993. *Der lange Weg zur Einheit. Studien zum Transformationsprozess in Ostdeutschland*. Berlin.

Göll, H.-P. 1991. *Versöhnung und Rechfertigung. Die Rechfertigungslehre Martin Kählers*. Giessen.

Goldstone, R. 1994. Address by the honourable Mr. Justice R. J. Goldstone at the graduation ceremony at the University of Natal, Durban, April 13, 1994 (manuscript).

Goldstone, R. 1996. "The Legacies of Nuremberg," *University of Cape Town Monday Paper* 15/33 (Nov. 4-11), 4.

Gollwitzer, H. 1983. "Von Glauben und Unglauben bei Luther," *EvTh* 44:360-79.

Gornig, G. 1992. "Die Verantwortlichkeit politischer Funktionsträger nach völkerrechtlichen Strafrecht," *Neue Justiz* 1 (1992), 4-14.

Grande, D., et al. 1998. *Kirche im Visier. SED, Staatssicherheit und katholische Kirche in der DDR. 2 A.* Leipzig.

Grimm, Jakob and Wilhelm. 1965ff. *Deutsches Wörterbuch von Jakob und Wilhelm Grimm.* Edited by Deutsche Akademie der Wissenschaften. Neubearbeitung, Leipzig.

Gropengiesser, H. 1996. "Amnestietagung des Einsteinforums," *Deutsch-deutsche Rechts-Zeitschrift* 12:372.

Grosser, D., S. Bierling, and F. Kurz. 1991. *Die Sieben Mythen der Wiedervereinigung. Fakten und Analysen zu einem Prozes ohne Alternative.* Munich: Ehrenwirth.

Gruchy, J. W. de. 1993. "Theologie im Übergang zu einem neuen Südafrika," *EvTh* 53:75-85.

Gruchy, J. W. de. 1994. "Forgetting or Exorcising the Past?" Manuscript (Archives of the TRC No. 2).

Gruchy, J. W. de. 1995. *Christianity and Democracy: A Theology for a Just World Order.* Cambridge: Cambridge University Press.

Gruchy, J. W. de. 1996a. "Koinonia and the Ecumenical Church. Perspectives from South Africa." Working paper WCC, Geneva.

Gruchy, J. W. de. 1996b. "Christian Witness in a Secular State: Rethinking Church-State Relations in the New South Africa." A draft paper. Theological Consultation SACC, October 9-11, 1996, Johannesburg.

Gruchy, J. W. de. 1996c. Interview with Prof. John de Gruchy, Theological Faculty, University of Cape Town, November 1996. Appeared in (German): *The Church* 25 (June 15, 1997), 4.

Gruchy, J. W. de. 1997. "Healing of the Past for the Sake of the Future. The Power of Truth, Forgiveness, and Hope in the Search for Justice and Reconciliation in South Africa" (in German), in German Evangelical Church Conference document, Leipzig. Gütersloh, pp. 616-29.

Gruchy, J. W. de. 1999. Interview with John de Gruchy, Cape Town, March 12.

Gruchy, J. W. de. 2002. *Reconciliation: Restoring Justice.* Philadelphia: Fortress Press.

Gründel, J. 1985. *Schuld und Versöhnung.* Mainz.

Gründel, J. 1990. "Schuld-Strafe-Versöhnung. Aus theologischer Sicht," in A. Köpke-Duttler, ed., *Schuld, Strafe, Versöhnung. Ein interdiziplinäres Gespräch.* Mainz, pp. 93-116.

Gutzen, D., et al. 1992. *Transatlantische Partnerschaft. Kulturelle Aspekte der deutsch-amerikanischen Beziehungen.* Bonn and Berlin.

Haack, D. 1992. "Vergangenheitsbewältigung in Deutschland nach 40 jähriger Teilung. Referat bei der Tagung Gemeinsinn in Eisenach," March 21, 1992 (manuscript).

Haberlandt, H. 1993. "Gedanken zur Vergangenheitsaufarbeitung im Bildungswesen des Landes Brandenburg. Personelle Überprüfung und Erneuerung," *Schulverwaltung* 5:109-15.

Hamber, B. 1996. Interview with Brandon Hamber, Center for the Study of Violence and Reconciliation, October 14, Johannesburg.

Hamber, B. 1999a. "Symbolic Closure through memory, reparation and revenge in post-conflict societies" (published as documentation of the Center for the Study of Violence and Reconciliation). Johannesburg.

Hamber, B. 1999b. "From Truth to Transformation. The Truth and Reconciliation Commission in South Africa." CIIR Report. London. 1999.

Hamberger, E. 1996. *Was heist "moralisch" und welchen Platz hat Moral in der Politik?* Schriften der Johannes Kepler University, Linz 12. Linz.

Hampton, J. 1988. "The Retributive Idea," in J. G. Murphy and J. Hampton, *Forgiveness and Mercy*. Cambridge, pp. 111ff.

Hansen, D. 1995. "Befreiung durch Erinnerung," *German Studies* 125:718f.

Hansen, D. 1998. "Zur Arbeit der Enquetekommission des Deutschen Bundestages 'Überwindung des Folgen der SED-Diktatur im Prozess der deutschen Einheit,'" *Deutsche Studien* 139-40 (1998), 380-402.

Härle, W. 1975. *Sein und Gnade*, TBT 27. Berlin and New York.

Härle, W. 1990. "Die Rede von der Liebe und vom Zorn Gottes," *ZThKB* 8:5-69.

Härle, W. 1992. "Kritik an der Macht ist gefordert. Sinn und Bedeutung von Luthers Zwei-reiche-Lehre," *LM* 8:363-64.

Härle, W. 1997. "'Suum cuique.' Gerechtigkeit als sozialethischer und theologischer Begriff," *ZEE* 41:303-12.

Hartmann, B., et al. 1998. "Erhoffte Versöhnung. Die Wahrheitskommission in Südafrika," *Freibeuter* 76:37-48.

Harvey, J. 1995. "The Emerging Practice of Institutional Apologies," *The International Journal of Applied Ethics* 9/2:57-65.

Haupt, H.-G., and J. Kocka. 1996. *Geschichte und Vergleich. Ansätze und Ergebnisse vergleichender Geschichtsschreibung*. Frankfurt am Main.

Hayner, P. 1994. "Fifteen Truth Commissions 1974-1994: A Comparative Study," *Human Rights Quarterly* 16:597-655.

Hayner, P. 1997. Interview with Priscilla Hayner, August, Berlin. The discussion was led by Hans Michael Kloth (manuscript of 7 pages).

Hegel, G. W. F. 1968. *Lectures on the Philosophy of Religion*. London: Routledge & Kegan Paul.

Heim, K. 1938. "Die Haupttypen der Versöhnungslehre," *ZThK* NS 19:304-19.

Herrmann, A. 1998. "Menschenrechte in der internationalen Politik," in *Menschenrechte,* Informationen zur politischen Bildung 210, pp. 32-35.

Hillenkamp, T. 1996. "Offene oder verdeckte Amnestie — über Wege strafrecht-
licher Vergangenheitsbewältigung," *Juristenzeitung*, pp. 179ff.

Hilsberg, S. 1996. "Die innere Einheit Deutschlands — eine brauchbare Vision?"
Deutschland Archiv 29/4:607-12.

Hofius, O. 1980. "Erwägungen zur Gestalt und Herkunt des paulinischen Ver-
söhnungsgedankens," *ZThK*, 186-99.

Hogebrink, L. 1993. "How to Deal with the Past? A Joint Responsibility of the
Churches in the East and West After the End of the Cold War." Manuscript,
Nederlandse Hervormde Kerk, September (Archiv Kistner No. 3343 A).

Huber, W. 1990. "The Role of the Church in Situations of Transition." Manuscript
(Archiv Kistner No. 2133 A).

Huber, W. 1991. "Kirche und Offentlichkeit," in FBESG 28, 2.A. Munich.

Huber, W., ed. 1996a. *Schuld und Versöhnung in politischer Perspektive*, IBF 10.
Gütersloh.

Huber, W. 1996b. *Gerechtigkeit und Recht. Grundlinien christlicher Rechtsethik*.
Gütersloh.

Huber, W., and E. Tödt. 1988. *Menschenrechte. Perspektiven einer menschlichen
Welt*. 3rd edition. Munich.

Huber, W., et al. 1990. *Friedensethik*. Stuttgart, Berlin, and Cologne.

Hübner, H. 1983. "Sühne und Versöhnung. Anmerkungen zu einem umstrittenen
Kapitel Biblischer Theologie," *KuD* 29:284-305.

Hummel, G. 1993. *Sehnsucht der unversöhnten Welt. Zu einer Theologie der
universalen Versöhnung*. Darmstadt.

Huntington, S. P. 1991. *The Third Wave: Democratization in the Late Twentieth Century*. Oklahoma City.

Hutchings, R. L. 1992. *Als der kalte Krieg zu Ende war. Ein Bericht aus dem Innern
der Macht*. Berlin.

Isensee, J. 1992. "Der deutsche Rechtsstaat vor seinem unrechtsstaatlichen Erbe," in
U. Battis et al., *Vergangenheitsbewältigung durch Recht. Drei Abhandlungen zu
einem deutschen Problem*, Wissenschaftliche Abhandlungen und Reden zur
Philosophie, Politik, und Geistesgeschichte, 16. Berlin, pp. 91-111.

Iwand, H. J. 1959. *Um den rechten Glauben. Gesammelte Aufsätze*, TB 9. Munich.

Jacobi, K. 1991. "Versöhnung. Wo sie not tut — und wo nicht," in T. Eggensperger
et al., *Versöhnung. Versuche zu ihrer Geschichte und Zukunft (FS Paulus OP)*,
WSAMA. P 8. Mainz, pp. 9-16.

Jakobs, G. 1992. "Vergangenheitsbewältigung durch Strafrecht? Zur leistungs-
fähigkeit des Strafrechts nach einem politischen Umbruch," in U. Battis et al.,
*Vergangenheitsbewältigung durch Recht. Drei Abhandlungen zu einem
deutschen Problem*, Wissenschaftliche Abhandlungen und Reden zur Philosophie, Politik, und Geistesgeschichte, 16. Berlin, pp. 37-64.

Jakobs, G. 1994. "Untaten des Staates — Unrecht im Staat. Strafe für die Tötungen
an der Grenze der ehemaligen DDR?" *Goltdammer's Archiv für Strafrecht*, 1-19.

Janowski, J. C. 2000. *Allerlösung. Annäherung an eine entdualisierte Eschatologie,* NBST 23/1.2. Neukirchen.

Jaspers, K. 1978. *The Question of German Guilt.* Westport, CT: Greenwood Press.

Jesse, E. 1992. "'Entnazifizierung' und 'Entstasifizierung' als politisches Problem. Die doppelte Vergangenheitsbewältigung," in U. Battis et al., *Vergangenheitsbewältigung durch Recht. Drei Abhandlungen zu einem deutschen Problem,* Wissenschaftliche Abhandlungen und Reden zur Philosophie, Politik, und Geistesgeschichte, 16. Berlin, pp. 9-36.

Jesse, E., ed. 1996. *Totalitarianismus im 20. Jahrhundert. Eine Bilanz der internationalen Forschung.* Baden-Baden.

Jesse, E. 1998. "Die Totalitarismus Forschung und ihre Repräsentanten," in *Aus Politik und Zeitgeschichte. Beilage zur Wochenzeitung Das Parlament* 20:3-18.

Jetter, W. 1986. *Symbol und Ritual. Anthropologische Elemente im Gottesdienst.* 2nd edition. Göttingen.

Johnston, D., et al., eds. 1994. *Religion, the Missing Dimension of Statecraft.* New York.

Jonas, M. 1984. *The United States and Germany: A Diplomatic History.* Ithaca and London.

Jones, L. G. 1995. *Embodying Forgiveness: A Theological Analysis.* Grand Rapids.

Jordaan, W. 1994. "Towards a Psycho-theology of Reconciliation." Manuscript (Archiv Kistner No. 3359 A).

Jüngel, E. 1962. "Die Möglichkeit theologischer Anthropologie auf dem Grunde der Analogie. Eine Untersuchung zum Analogieverständnis Karl Barths," *EvTh* 22:535-57.

Jüngel, E. 2000. "Nur Wahrheit befreit," *German Daily News* 37, September 15, 2000, pp. 20-22.

Kaase, M., et al. 1998. "Deutsche Vereinigung und innere Einheit 1990-1997," in *Werte und nationale Identität im vereinten Deutschland: Erklärungsansätze der Umfrageforschung.* Edited by H. Meulemann. Opladen, pp. 251-67.

Kaiser, G., et al. 1996. *Christen, Staat, und Gesellschaft in der DDR.* Frankfurt am Main.

Kaiser, Th. O. H. 1996. *Versöhnung in Gerechtigkeit. Das Konzept der Versöhnung und seine Kritik im Kontext Südafrika,* Neukirchener theological dissertation and habilitation series 2. Neukirchen-Vluyn.

Kallschauer, O. 1997. "Nation mit Erbsünde. Auf der Suche nach der Seele Südafrikas," *Frankfurter Allgemeine Zeitung* (July 22).

Kaschkat, H., et al. 1991. "Zur Entschädigung der Opfer des SED Unrechtsregimes. Rehabilitierungsgesetz, Kassation und Häftlingsgesetz," *Deutschland Archiv* 41/1:238-46.

Keightley, R. 1993. "Political Offences and Indemnity in South Africa," *South African Journal on Human Rights* 9/3:334-57.

Keller, D., et al. 1998. "Wir wollten die DDR nicht wiederhaben. Wir lassen sie uns auch nicht nehmen. Ergebnisse der Arbeit der Enquete Kommission 'Überwindung der Folgen der DDR Diktatur im Prozess der deutschen Einheit': Versuch einer Bilanz," in *Ansichten zur Geschichte der DDR IX/X*. Bonn and Berlin, pp. 8-31.

Kinkel, K. 1992. "Wiedervereinigung und Strafrecht," *Juristen Zeitung*, 47/10:485-89.

Kistner, W. 1992a. "The Role of Theology in the Transformation of South Africa." Lecture delivered at the Annual Meeting of the Theological Society of Southern Africa, August 26, 1992 (Archiv Kistner No. 2534 A).

Kistner, W. 1992b. "Reconciliation and Democratization in South Africa from a Christian Perspective." Address delivered at a conference organized by CCN and AWEPAA, Windhoek, October 28-31, 1992 (manuscript).

Kistner, W. 1994. "Jeremiah 1:10-17." Sermon delivered in Berlin-Zehlendorf, June 15, 1994 (manuscript).

Kistner, W. 1995a. Schuld und Versöhnung in Südafrika. Unpublished paper, February (Archiv Kistner No. 3557).

Kistner, W. 1995b. "The Churches' Contribution to Reconciliation and Reconstruction in Mozambique." Draft. June 1995 (Archiv Kistner No. 3575 A).

Kistner, W. 1996a. "Creator Spirit suffering with creation. The struggle for the new South Africa." Unpublished article in consultation with the SACC on October 9-11, 1996, Johannesburg.

Kistner, W. 1996b. "Koinonia." Draft of an unpublished paper of the Consultation of the SACC of October 9-11, 1996, Johannesburg.

Kistner, W. 1996c. "Notes on the Ecumenical Movement in South Africa," December 1996 (unpublished).

Kistner, W. 1997a. "Notes on Dutch Reformed Church Publication on 'The Journey with Apartheid,'" August 12, 1997 (unpublished).

Kistner, W. 1997b. "Remembering an Old Message to the People in the New South Africa." Unpublished lecture, August 1997.

Kistner, W. 1997c. "My Experience with the Christian Anti-Apartheid Solidarity Movement in the Two German States and Its Interaction with the Liberation Struggle in South Africa." Unpublished paper, September 4, 1997.

Kistner, W. 1997d. "The South African Truth and Reconciliation Commission. How Far Can They Reach the Goal of National Reconciliation?" (German). Unpublished manuscript, September 10, 1997.

Kistner, W. 1997e. "Das Ringen um Versöhnung im neuen Südafrika." Unpublished lecture, University of Bern, October 4, 1997.

Kistner, W. 1997f. "Noch ein langer Weg," *epd-Entwicklungspolitik* 18:17-21.

Kistner, W. 1998. "Versöhnung ist kein Kompromiss, sondern ein Heilungsprozess," *epd-Entwicklungspolitik* 2:34-35.

Kistner, W. 1999. "Preparatory Material for Contributions on the Topic Reconciliation." Unpublished manuscript (Archiv Kistner No. 4472A).

Kistner, W., and B. Naudé. 1994. Newsletter on the Fortnight April 25 to May 8, 1994, Johannesburg; May 9.

Kistner, W., and B. Naudé. 1999. Interview with Wilfram Kistner and Beyers Naudé, Johannesburg, April 20.

Klappert, B. 1989. "Versöhnung, Reich Gottes und Gesellschaft. H. J. Iwans teologische Existenz im Dienst der einen Menschheit," *EvTh* 49:341-69.

Klappert, B. 1994. *Versöhnung und Befreiung. Versuche, Karl Barth kontextuell zu verstehen*, NBST 14. Neukirchen-Vluyn.

Klerk, F. W. de. 1992. "Statement by the State President Mr. F. W. de Klerk, October 1, 1992." Issued by the Office of the State President (press release).

Klerk, F. W. de. 1995. In *Cape Times*, October 2, 1995.

Klerk, F. W. de. 1997. "'Mein Gewissen ist rein.' Discussion with Frederik de Klerk," *Die Zeit* 43 (October 17), 11.

Klerk, F. W. de. 1998. *The Last Trek — A New Beginning. The Autobiography.* London.

Klessmann, C., et al. 1999. *Deutsche Vergangenheiten — eine gemeinsame Herausforderung. Der schwierige Weg mit der doppelten Nachkriegsgeschichte.* Berlin.

Kloth, H. M. 1998. "'Versorgungsfall' Vergangenheit? Stiftung zur Aufarbeitung der SED Vergangenheit gegründet," *Deutschland Archiv* 31/5:861-65.

Kobylinska, E., et al. 1995. *Deutsche und Pole.* Munich/Zurich.

Koch, E., et al. 1995. "Firing Up the Truth Machine. The Truth and Reconciliation Commission: South Africa Can Learn Important Lessons," *Mail & Guardian* (July 28–August 3).

Kocka, J. 1995. *Vereinigungskrise. Zur Geschichte der Gegenwart.* Göttingen.

Kocka, J. 1998. "Geteilte Erinnerungen. Zweierlei Geschichtsbewusstsein im vereinten Deutschland," *Blätter für deutsche und internationale Politik* 43.

Kohl, H. 1996. *Ich wollte Deutschlands Einheit,* Berlin.

Kollmorgen, R., et al., eds. 1996. *Sozialer Wandel und Akteure in Ostdeutschland,* KSPW 8. Opladen.

König, R. 1974. *Das Interview; Formen, Technik, Auswertung.* Edited by R. König, Praktische Sozialforschung 1. Cologne.

Koyama, K. 1996. "Vergebung und Politik. Eine japanische Sicht," in W. Huber, *Schuld und Versöhnung in politischer Perspektive,* IBF 10. Gütersloh, pp. 42-54.

Kraus, G. 1990. "Gott versöhnt den Menschen mit sich. Versöhnung in gnadentheologischer Sicht," in E. Garhammer et al., eds., . . . *und führe uns in Versöhnung. Zur Theologie und Praxis einer Christlichen Grunddimension.* Munich, pp. 188-96.

Krenz, E. 1999. *Herbst 1989.* Berlin.

Kress, G., et al. 1969. *Politikwissenschaft. Eine Einführung in ihre Probleme,* Kritische Studien zur Politikwissenschaft. Opladen.

Kreuter, J. 1997. *Staatskriminalität und die Grenzen des Strafrechts. Reaktionen auf*

Verbrechen aus Gehorsam aus rechtsethischer Perspektive, Offentliche Theologie 9. Gütersloh.

Kritz, N. 1995. *Transitional Justice. How Emerging Democracies Reckon with Former Regimes.* Volume I: *General Considerations.* Washington, DC.

Krog, A. 1998a. *Country of My Skull.* Johannesburg.

Krog, A. 1998b. "The Truth and Reconciliation Commission — A National Ritual?" *Missionalia* 26/1:5-16.

Kusior, W. 1999. "Die Aufarbeitung der SED Diktatur ist gesellschaftliche Aufgabe," *Deutschland Archiv* 4:87-91.

Lapsley, M. 1995. "A Theological Reflection on Truth and Reconciliation," *Parish Profile. A Publication by St. John's Parish Wynberg* 14/2:7 (Archives of the TRC No. 171).

Lapsley, M. 1996. Interview with Michael Lapsley (Trauma Center, Cape Town, November 12, 1996, unpublished manuscript).

Lapsley, M. 1997. "From Freedom to Healer," *Odyssey* (October 1997 to January 1998), 8-10.

Lienemann, W. 1995. *Gerechtigkeit. Ökumenische Studienhefte 3,* BenshH 75. Göttingen.

Lindner, B. 1998. *Die demokratische Revolution in der DDR 1989/90,* Bundeszentrale für politische Bildung. Bonn.

Link-Wieczorek, U. 1998. *Inkarnation oder Inspiration?* FSOTh 84. Göttingen.

Llewellyn, J., et al. 1998. "Restorative Justice — A Conceptual Framework." Prepared for the Law Commission of Canada (Ms. 108 S).

Lobinger, F. 1993. "Versöhnung oder Befreiung? Politisches und theologisches Ringen in Südafrika," in *"Führe uns in Versöhnung." Zur Theologie und Praxis einer christlichen Grunddimension.* Edited by E. Garhammer et al. Munich, pp. 373-84.

Lochman, J. M. 1977. *Absage an ein eindimensionales Heilsverständnis.* Gütersloh.

Lucas, J. R. 1993. *Responsibility.* Oxford.

Lüderssen, K. 1991. "Zu den Folgen des 'Beitritts' für die Strafjustiz der Bunderepublik Deutschland," *Der Strafverteidiger* 10:482-87.

Lüderssen, K. 1992. *Der Staat geht unter — das Unrecht bleibt? Regierungskriminalität in der ehemaligen DDR.* Frankfurt am Main.

Lutz, B. 1996. "Einleitung," in *Arbeit, Arbeitsmarkt und Betriebe.* Berlin, pp. 1-16.

Maaz, H. J. 1990. *Der Gefühlsstau. Ein Psychogramm der DDR.* Berlin.

Maaz, H. J. 1991. *Das gestürzte Volk. Die verunglückte Einheit.* Berlin.

Maaz, H. J. 1992. *Die Entrüstung. Deutschland, Stasi, Schuld und Sündenbock.* Berlin.

Maizière, L. de. 1999. "Nichts fürchtet die Diktatur mehr als die Offentlichkeit," in F. Schorlemmer, ed., *Life Paths.* Halle, pp. 333-54.

Maluleke, Z. S. 1997. "'Dealing Lightly with the Wound of My People'? The TRC Process in Theological Perspective," *Missionalia* 25/3:324-43.

Mamdani, M. 1997. "Reconciliation without Justice," *Southern Review* 10/6:22-25.

Mandela, N. 1995. *Long Walk to Freedom: The Autobiography of Nelson Mandela.* London.

Marquardt, M., ed. 1997. *Theologie in skeptischer Zeit,* TSB 8. Stuttgart.

Marsch, W.-D. 1965. *Gegenwart Christi in der Gesellschaft. Eine Studie zu Hegels Dialektik,* FGLP 31. Munich.

Marx, L. 1998. "Slouching towards Bethlehem: Ubu and the Truth Commission," *African Studies* 57/2:212f.

Marxen, K. 1999. *Die strafrechtliche Aufarbeitung von DDR Unrecht. Eine Bilanz.* Berlin/New York.

Mbeki, T. 1998. *Africa, the Time Has Come: Selected Speeches.* Cape Town.

Mda, Z. 1994. "The Role of Culture in the Process of Reconciliation in South Africa." Published as a document of the Center for the Study of Violence and Reconciliation. Johannesburg.

Meiring, P. 1999. *Chronicle of the Truth Commission. A Journey through the Past and Present — into the Future of South Africa.* Vanderbijlpark.

Merkel, A. 1992. "Geschichte aufarbeiten: Erfahrungen in den Ländern des ehemaligen Ostblocks. Statement zur Eröffnung des Fachgespräch, June 10, 1992, Bonn" (manuscript).

Merwe, H. van der. 1997. "Reconciliation: What Role for Victims and Perpetrators," *Cantilevers* 3:7-9.

Merwe, H. van der. 1999. "The South African Truth and Reconciliation Commission and Community Reconciliation." Published as a document of the Center for the Study of Violence and Reconciliation, Johannesburg.

Merwe, S. van der. 1996a. "Analysis of Issues of Concern to the Ecumenical Advice Bureau." Paper EAB Johannesburg, September.

Merwe, S. van der. 1996b. Interview with Stiaan van der Merwe, Ecumenical Advice Bureau, October 14, Cape Town.

Merwe, S. van der. 1999. Interview with Stiaan van der Merwe, February 16, Cape Town.

Metz, J. B. 1973. "Erlösung und Emanzipation," in *Erlösung und Emanzipation.* Edited by L. Scheffczyk (QD 61). Freiburg and Basel and Vienna, pp. 120-40.

Metz, J. B. 1977. *Glaube in Geschichte und Gesellschaft. Studien zu einer praktischen Fundamentaltheologie.* Mainz.

Meyer, O. 1996. *Vom Leiden und Hoffen der Städte,* Urbane Theologie 1. Hamburg.

Meyer-Blank, M. 1997. "Der Ertrag semiotischer Theorien für die Praktische Theologie," *BThZ* 14/2:190-219.

Mills, G. 1995. "Africa's Nuremberg Trials?" *Africa Institute Bulletin* 35/3:1-3.

Minty, A. 1993. "South Africa: From Apartheid to Democracy," *Security Dialogue* 24/4:313-22.

Misselwitz, H. J. 1999. "Annäherung durch Wandel. Für eine neue Sicht auf die 'innere Einheit' und die Rolle der politischen Bildung," *Politik und Zeit-*

geschichte. Beilage zur Wochenzeitung Das Parlament 7-8/99 (February 12), 24-30.

Moellendorf, D. 1997. "Amnesty, Truth and Justice: AZAPO," *South African Journal on Human Rights,* 283-91.

Moltmann, J. 1970. "Gott versöhnt und macht frei," EK 3:515-20.

Moltmann, J. 1985. *Theologie der Hoffnung. Untersuchungen zur Begründung und zu den Konsequenzen einer christlichen Eschatologie.* 12th edition. Munich.

Moltmann, J., ed. 1989. *Versöhnung mit der Natur?* KT 92. Munich.

Moltmann, J. 1990. *The Way of Jesus Christ: Christology in Messianic Dimensions.* San Francisco: Harper & Row.

Moltmann, J. 1996. *The Coming of God: Christian Eschatology.* Minneapolis: Fortress Press.

Moore, K. D. 1989. *Pardons, Justice, Mercy, and the Public Interest.* Oxford.

Mousa, I. 1996. Interview with the Islam scholar Ibriahim Mousa, University of Cape Town, October.

Mühlenberg, E. 1988. "Die 'ratio' im Denken Anselms von Canterbury," *HDThG* I, 555-66.

Müller-Fahrenholz, G. 1996a. *Vergebung.* Frankfurt am Main.

Müller-Fahrenholz, G. 1996b. "Ausbruch aus dem Teufelskreis der Gewalt. Die Aufrichtung der Opfer schafft mehr Gerechtigkeit als die Bestrafung der Täter," *Publik Forum* 23 (December 6), 50-52.

Münch, I. von. 1994. "Rechtsstaat versus Gerechtigkeit," *Der Staat* 33:165-84.

Nachlese. 1993. Nachlese: Die Kirchen und der Kommujnismus. Seminar zur Aufarbeitung der jüngsten Vergangenheit in den Kirchen Ost und Westeuropas. Ed. Rat für Kirche und Gesellschaft der Nederlandse Hervormde Kerk und der Evangelischen Akademie Berlin-Brandenburg. Berlin.

Naudé, B. 1991. "The Challenge to the Church in a Changing South Africa." Address delivered at the Theological Faculty of the University of the Western Cape, February 1991 (Archiv Kistner No. 1658 A).

Naudé, B. 1995a. "Eine Gabe Gottes," *Reformierte Kirchenzeitung* 7:310-313.

Naudé, B. 1995b. "'Wie baut man Versöhnung in solch einer Township'? Über die neue Rolle und Verantwortung der südafrikanischen Kirche," *Frankfurter Rundschau* 108 (May 10), 12.

Naudé, B. 1995c. "My Seven Lean Years." Address delivered on the occasion of the presentation to Naudé of the Festschrift entitled *Resistance and Hope* at the University of Cape Town, May 8, 1995.

Naudé, B. 1996. "The Task and Role of the Church in the New South Africa." Manuscript, February 5, 1996 (Archiv Kistner No. 3855 A).

Naudé, B., and W. Kistner. 1994. "100 Days in the New South Africa." Manuscript, September 5, 1994.

Naudé, B., and W. Kistner. 1996. Interview with Beyers Naudé and Wolfram

Kistner, Johannesburg, October 1996. Appeared *Frankfurter Rundschau* 40 (February 17, 1997), 10.

Naude, P. J. 1997. "Ecumenical Reception as Theological Process." Unpublished lecture at the University of Heidelberg, January 31.

Ndungane, N. 1999. "'Jetzt muss die zweite Phase folgen.' Der Nachfolger von Bischof Desmond Tutu sieht Südafrika versöhnt und hofft auf die neue Elite," *Deutsches Allgemeines Sonntagsblatt* 22 (May 28), 11.

Neubert, E. 1992. "Zur Aufarbeitung des Stasiproblems in den Kirchen," *Aus Politik und Zeitgeschichte. Beilage zur Wochenzeitung Das Parlament* 21:11-22.

Neubert, E. 1997. *Geschichte der Opposition in der DDR 1949-1989, Forschungen zur DDR Gesellschaft. Berlin.*

Niehaus, C. 1999. Interview with Carl Niehaus, Cape Town, February 15, 1999.

Ntsebeza, D. 1998. Macht Wahrheit frei? Unveröffentlichter Vortrag auf der Tagung der Evangelischen Akademie Berlin-Brandenburg. "Auf dem Weg zur Regenbogennation. Südafrika und die Wahrheits- und Versöhnungskommission" of November 13-15, 1998, Berlin.

Ntsebeza, D. 1999. Interview with Dumisa Ntsebeza, High Court, Cape Town, March 19.

Nuttall, S., et al. 1998. *Negotiating the Past: The Making of Memory in South Africa.* Edited by Sarah Nuttall and Carli Coetzee. Oxford.

Ostendorf, H. 1999. "Vom Sinn und Zweck des Strafens," in *Kriminalität und Strafrecht*, Informationen zur politischen Bildung 248, pp. 14-17.

Paech, N. 1994. "Eine Verfassung, die den Schild der Apartheid zerbricht. Eine Analyse," *Blätter für deutsche und internationale Politik* 1.

Patzelt, W. J. 1997. *Einführung in die Politikwissenschaft. Grundriss des Fachs und studiumsbegleitende Orientierung. Passau.*

Pesch, O. H. 1991. "Versöhnung in der Kirche. Eine theologiegeschichtliche Hypothese — und einige Fausregeln des Verhaltens," in T. Eggensperger et al., eds., *Versöhnung. Versuche zu ihrer Geschichte und Zukunft (FS Paulus OP),* WSAMA. P 8. Mainz, pp. 189-213.

Pfeiler, W. 1998. "Wann wächst zusammen, was zusammengehört? Deutschland auf dem Weg zur inneren Einheit," *Deutschland Archiv* 31/1:278-82.

Pfister, H. 1972. *Polen und Deutsche. Der lange Weg zu Frieden und Versöhnung.* Waldkirch.

Phiri, I. A. 1996. "African Religion: The Misunderstood Religion," in *Cultural Synergy in South Africa: Weaving Strands of Africa and Europe,* ed. M. E. Steyn and K. B. Motshabit, chapter 5.

Planer-Friedrich, G. 1989. "Die Moral der Politik. Versöhnung als Voraussetzung für politische Verständigung zwischen Gegnern," *EK* 5:5-8.

Plasger, G. 1993. *Die Not-Wendigkeit der Gerechtigkeit. Eine Interpretation zu "Cur Deus homo" von Anselm von Canterbury,* BGPhMA. Münster.

Plooy, L. du. 1996. Interview with the Coordinator of the TRC Office in Cape Town, October 1996, Cape Town.

Pollack, D. 2000. *Politischer Protest. Politisch alternative Gruppen in der DDR.* Opladen.

Poppe, U. 1997. "Das weidervereinigte Deutschland und die DDR Vergangenheit. Der Weg zum Stasiunterlagengesetz." Unpublished lecture, Berlin.

Poppe, U. 1998. "Suche nach Wahrheit und Umgang mit Schuld — ein gesamtdeutscher Lernprozess. Konferenzbeitrag für 'Burying the Past?' Oxford, September 14-16, 1998" (manuscript).

Prechtl, C. 1996. *Innere Einheit Deutschlands. Gegenstand der schulischen und ausserschulischen politischen Bildungsarbeit. Eine empirische Untersuchung der Angebots- und Inhaltsstrukturen von Bildungsmassnahmen,* Studien zu Politik und Wissenschaft 4. Schwalbach/Ts.

Press release. 1997. Reflections on the Truth and Reconciliation Commission among members of the general public. June/July.

Probst, L. 1994. "Das Dilemma der Intellektuellen mit der Nation. Ein Plädoyer gegen die Kontinuitätslogik," *Deutschland Archiv* (Dec. 27), 1287-91.

Probst, L. 1998. "Ost-West Differenzen und das republikanische Defizit der deutschen Einheit," *Aus Politik und Zeitgeschichte. Beilage zur Wochenzeitung Das Parlament* 41-42/98 (October 2), 3-8.

Prozesky, M. 1995. "Religious Justice at Last? Believers and the New Constitution in South Africa," *JTSA* 92:11-21.

Quaritsch, H. 1992. "Über Bürgerkriegs und Feind-Amnestien," *Der Staat. Zeitschrift für Staatslehre, öffentliches Recht und Verfassungsgeschichte* 31:389-418.

Rad, G. von. 2001. *Old Testament Theology.* Translated by D. G. M. Stalker. Louisville, KY: Westminster John Knox Press.

Raiser, K. 1991. "Schuld und Versöhnung. Erinnerung an eine bleibende Aufgabe der deutschen Kirchen," *KZG* 4/2:512-22.

Reissig, R., ed. 1993. *Rückweg in die Zukunft. Über den schwierigen Transformationsprozess in Ostdeutschland.* Frankfurt am Main and New York.

Reissig, R. 1995. "Transformationsforschung zum (ost) deutschen Sonderfall — Blockaden und Chancen theoretischer Innovation," *Soziologische Revue* 18 (1995), 147-53.

Reissig, R. 1998. "Transformationsforschung: Gewinne, Desiderate und Perspektiven," *Politische Viertejahreszeitschrift* 39/2:301-28.

Reissig, R. 1999. "Spezifika und Eignarten des (ost)deutschen Transformationsfalles," *BISS Public* 27/9:133-46.

Renzikowski, J. 1992. "Vergangenheitsbewältigung durch Vergeltung?" *Juristische Rundschau* 7 (1992), 270-74.

Reuter, H. R. 1996. *Rechtethik in theologischer Perspektive. Studien zur Grundlegung und Konkretion,* Öffentliche Theologie 8. Gütersloh.

Reuter, L. 1992. "DDR Strafrecht zwischen friedlicher Revolution und deutscher Einheit," *Neue Justiz* 1:15-18.

Richards, R. 1998. "'Heilende Wahrheit,' Das Selbstverständnis der südafrikanischen 'Wahrheits und Versöhnungskommission,'" in R. K. Wüstenberg, ed., *Wahrheit, Recht und Versöhnung. Auseinandersetzung mit der Vergangenheit nach den politischen Umbrüchen in Südafrika und Deutschland,* Kontexte 24. Frankfurt am Main et al., pp. 33-47.

Ricoeur, P., et al. 1974. *Metapher. Zur Hermeneutik religiöser Sprache,* Sonderheft EvTh. Munich.

Riecke, Chr. 1997. "Rosen für die Gemeinschaft. Erfahrungen mit Kirche im neuen Südafrika," *In die Welt für die Welt. Magazin für Mission und Partnerschaft* 1:9-10.

Riedel, J. 1992. "'Schiessbefehl' und 'Verjährung': Zum Problem der Strafverfolgungsverjährung bei Schusswaffengebrauch an der ehemaligen DDR Grenze," *DtZ* 6:162-69.

Riess, C. B., and H. Bortfeld. 1994. *Die deutsch-amerikanishcen Beziehungen der Nachkriegszeit 1945-1993,* Deutschland Report 21. Melle.

Ritschl, D. 1981. "Die Herausforderung von Kirche und Gesellschaft durch medizinisch-ethische Probleme," *EvTh* 6:483-507.

Ritschl, D. 1988. "Gedächtnis und Antizipation. Psychologische und theologische Bemerkungen," in *Kultur und Gedächtnis.* Edited by J. Assmann et al. Frankfurt am Main, pp. 50-64.

Ritschl, D. 1994a. "Gotteserkenntnis durch Wiedererkennen," in *Einfach von Gott reden: ein theologischer Diskurs (FS F. Mildenberger).* Stuttgart, Berlin, and Cologne, pp. 144-52.

Ritschl, D. 1994b. "Welchen Sinn hat die Suche nach Strukturen hinter den Texten?" in *Language, Theology, and the Bible: Essays in Honour of James Barr.* Edited by S. E. Balentine et al. Oxford, pp. 385-97.

Ritschl, D. 1999. "Vorsprachliches, Räumliches, Zeitliches. Zur Phänomenologie des Glaubens," *ThZ* 55/2-3:155-75.

Ritter, A. M. 1988. "Dogma und Lehre in der alten Kirche." In *Handbuch der Dogmen- und Theologiegeschichte,* vol. 1. Göttingen: Vandenhoeck & Ruprecht, pp. 99-283.

Rode, C. 1996. *Kriminologie in der DDR. Kriminalitätsforschung zwischen Empire und Ideologie,* Kriminologische Forschungsberichte aus dem Max Planck Institut für ausländisches und internationals Strafrecht 73. Freiburg.

Roenne, H. von. 1997. *"Politisch untragbar . . . ?" Die Überprüfung von Richtern und Staatsanwälten der DDR im Zuge der Vereinigung Deutschlands,* Grundlagen des Rechts 7. Berlin and Baden-Baden, 1997.

Roesler, J. 1999. "Der Beitritt der DDR zur Bundesrepublik," *Deutschland Archiv* 32/3:431-40.

Rogge, J., et al., eds. 1980. *Kirchengemeinschaft und politische Ethik. Ergebnis eines theologischen Gesprächs zum Verhältnis von Zwei-Reiche-Lehre und Lehre von der Königsherrschaft Christi*. Berlin.

Rosenau, H. 1993. *Allversöhnung. Ein tranzendentaltheologischer Grundlegungsversuch*. Berlin and New York.

Roth, E., and K. Heidenreich. *Sozialwissenschaftliche Methoden*. Opladen.

Rüther, G. 1995. "Politische Bildung, politische Kultur und innere Einheit," *Deutschland Archiv*, 28/7:684ff.

Sachs, A. 1994. "Comment on a First Perusal of the Bill Setting Up the Truth and Reconciliation Commission." Working paper (Archive of the TRC No. 113).

Sarkin, J. 1996. "The Trials and Tribulations of South Africa's Truth and Reconciliation Commission," *South African Journal on Human Rights* 12:618ff.

Sattler, D. 1992. *Gelebte Busse. Das menschliche Busswerk* (satisfactio) *im ökumenischen Gespräch*. Mainz.

Sauter, G., ed. 1973. *Zur Zwei Reiche Lehre Luthers*, TB 49. Gütersloh.

Sauter, G., ed. 1997. *"Versöhnung" als Thema der Theologie*, TB 92. Gütersloh.

Sauter, G., et al. 1986. *Arbeitsweisen systematischer Theologie. Eine Anleitung*. 2nd edition. Munich.

Schätzler, J. G. 1995. "Die versäumte Amnestie. Vorwärts gelebt, rückwärts nicht verstanden," *Neue Justiz* 49/2:57-62.

Schätzler, J. G. 1997. "Staatenfusion und Abrechnungsmentalität," *Deutschland Archiv* 30/1:105-17.

Schäuble, W. 1991. *Der Vertrag*. Berlin.

Schäuble, W. 1992. "Der Einigungsvertrag in seiner praktischen Bewährung," *Deutschland Archiv* 25/1:233-42.

Schleiermacher, Friedrich. 1948. *The Christian Faith*. Edited by H. R. Mackintosh and J. S. Stewart. Edinburgh: T & T Clark.

Schlink, B. 1994. "Rechtsstaat und revolutionäre Gerechtigkeit," *Neue Justiz* 19:433-37.

Schmidt, A. M. 1988. "Peter Abaelard und seine Schule," *HDThG* 1:570-75.

Schneider, R. 1992. *Volk ohne Trauer. Notizen nach dem Untergang der DDR*. Göttingen.

Schönherr, A. 1992. *Ein Volk am Pranger? Die Deutschen auf der Suche nach einer neuen politischen Kultur*. Berlin.

Schorlemmer, F. 1992. *Versöhnung in der Wahrheit. Nachschläge und Vorschläge eines Ostdeutschen*. Munich.

Schorlemmer, F. 1999a. *Lebenswege*, volume 2, Landeszentrale für politische Bildung. Halle.

Schorlemmer, F. 1999b. *Zeitansagen*. Munich.

Schröder, R. 1999. "Wann ist die Einheit vollendet?" in *Das wiedervereinigte Deutschland — eine erweiterte oder eine neue Bundesrepublik?* Edited by K. Eckart and E. Jesse. Berlin, pp. 135-45.

Schwabe, U. 1998. "'Symbol der Befreiung.' Die Friedensgebete in Leipzig," *Horch und Guck. Historisch-literarische Zeitschrift des Bürgerkomitees* 23/2 (Jan. 15), 1-22.

Schwan, G. 1997. *Politik und Schuld. Die zerstörerische Macht des Schweigens.* Frankfurt am Main.

Seidler, E. 1995. "Versöhnung. Prolegomena einer künftigen Soteriologie," *FZPhTh* 42/1:5-48.

Seiger, B. 1996. *Versöhnung — Gabe und Aufgabe. Eine Untersuchung zur neueren Bedeutungsentwicklung eines theologischen Begriffs,* EHS.T 563. Frankfurt am Main.

Seiters, R. 2000. *Zehn Jahre nach dem Fall der Mauer. Erinnerungen und Gedanken. Vortrag am 2. November 1999,* Veröffentlichungen der Kester-Haeuser-Stiftung 20. Fürstenfedlbruck.

Shriver, D. 1995. *An Ethic for Enemies: Forgiveness in Politics.* New York and Oxford.

Shriver, D. 1999. "Brücken über den Abgrund der Rache. Reue und Vergebung können zur Heilung von Gesellchaften beitragen," *Der Überblick. Zeitschrift für ökoumenische Begegnung und internationale Zusammenarbeit* 35/3:6-11.

Shriver, D. 2005. *Honest Patriots: Loving a Country Enough to Remember Its Misdeeds.* Oxford.

Simon, H. 1998. "Wie halten wir's mit Recht und Gerechtigkeit — die Gretchenfrage in unserer Zeit?" *Neue Justiz* 51/1:2-6.

Simson, G. 1994. *"Truth Recovery of McCarthism Revisited." An Evaluation of the Stasi Records Act with Reference to the South African Experience.* Publication of the Centre for the Study of Violence and Reconciliation. Johannesburg.

Sisk, T. D. 1995. "Perspectives on South Africa's Transition: Implications for Democratic Consolidation," *Politikon* 21 (1995).

Siyaya. 1998. *Siyaya! An Idasa Publication* 3 (Spring 1998): Truth and Reconciliation Commission.

Smit, D. 1995. "The Truth and Reconciliation Commission — Tentative Religious and Theological Perspectives," *JTSA* 90:3-15.

Smit. D. 1999. Interview with Dirkie Smit, University of the Western Cape, April 13, 1999.

Söll, K. 1997. *Institutionalisierte Vergangenheitsbewältigung. Die Enquete Kommission "Aufarbeitung von Geschichte und Vergangenheit der SED Diktatur in Deutschland," im Vergleich mit der "Truth and Reconciliation Commission" in Südafrika,* Schriftliche Hausarbeit im Rahmen der ersten Staatsprüfung für das Lehramt für die Sekundarstufe II. Bonn.

Sölle, D. 1982. *Stellvertretung. Ein Kapitel Theologie nach dem "Tode Gottes."* 2nd edition. Stuttgart.

Sold, A. du. 1993. *Restitution vor Entschädigung. Wiedervereinigung zu welchem Preis? Analyse und Wertung nach rechtlichen, wirtschaftlichen und politischen Gesichtspunkten,* Archiv der deutschen Hochschulwissenschaften III/I. Baden-Baden.

South Africa. 1998. Newspaper. No. 6 (November/December). "South Africa: Truth and Reconciliation."

Sparks, A. 1995. "'Als der Chef des Geheimdienstes am Häftling die Schuhe schürte.' Nelson Mandelas Begegnungen mit den Staatschefs Botha und de Klerk," *Frankfurter Rundschau* 60 (March 11), 18.

Steiger, J. A. 1994. "Aufklärungskritische Versöhnungslehre. Zorn Gottes, Opfer Christ und Versöhnung in der Theologie Justus Christoph Kraffts, Friedrich Gottlieb Klopstocks und Christian Friedrich Daniel Schubarts," *PuN* 20:125-72.

Steinbach, P. 1993. *Vergangenheitsbewältigung in vergleichender Perspektive*, Historische Kommission Berlin 18. Berlin.

Steinbach, P. 1996. "Neue Arbeitsstelle 'Diktatur und Demokratie' zur vergleichenden Diktaturforschung am Fachbereich Politische Wissenschaft der FU Berlin gegründet," *KZG* 9/2:397-403.

Steinbach, P. 1999. "Der 9. November in der deutschen Geschichtes des 20. Jahrhunderts und in der Erinnerung," *Aus Politik und Zeitgeschichte* 43-44/99 (October 22), 3-11.

Steindl, H. 1989. *Genugtuung. Biblisches Versöhnungsdenken — Eine Quelle für Anselms Satisfaktionstheorie?* SFN.F 71. Freiburg.

Sühl, K. 1998. *Vergangenheitsbewältigung 1945 und 1989. Ein unmögliocher Vergleich?* Edited by K. Sühl. Berlin.

Süssmuth, R., ed. 1997. *Eine deutsche Zwischenbilanz. Standpunkte zum Umgang mit unserer Vergangenheit.* Landsberg am Lech.

Sundermeier, T. 1993. "Erlösung oder Versöhnung? Religionsgeschichtliche Anstöße," *EvTh* 53/2:124-46.

Sundermeier, T. 1997. *Nur gemeinsam können wir leben: Das Menschenbild schwarafrikanischer Religionen*, Historische Studien 8. 3rd edition. Hamburg.

"Survivors' Perceptions of the Truth and Reconciliation Commission and Suggestions for the Final Report." 1998. Published document of the Centre for the Study of Violence and Reconciliation, Johannesburg.

Synonyme-Lexikon. 1989. *Lexikon der deutschen Synonyme.* Eltville.

Szeftel, M. 1994. "Ethnicity and Democratisation in South Africa," *Review of African Political Economy* 21/60:185-99.

Tanner, K. 1995. "Amnestie Fragezeichen," *ZEE* 39:170-73.

Teltschik, H. 1991. *329 Tage: Innenansichten der Einigung.* Berlin.

Theis, R. 1989. *Wiedergutmachung zwischen Moral and Interesse. Eine kritische Bestandsaufnahme der deutsch-israelischen Regierungsverhandlung.* Frankfurt am Main.

Theissen, G. 1996. *Vergangenheitsbewältigung in Südafrika. Die südafrikanische Wahrheits und Versöhnungskommission. Politikwissenschaft, Dipl.* Berlin.

Thierse, W. 1999. "Eröffnungsvortrag auf dem Berliner Geschichtsforum," *Deutschland Archiv* 32/4:633-44.

Tiililä, O. 1941. *Das Strafleiden Christi. Beitrag zur Diskussion über die Typeneinteilung der Versöhnungsmotive*, AASF 47. Helsinki.

Tillich, P. 1966. *Symbol und Wirklichkeit*. 2nd edition. Göttingen.

Toit, A. du. 1994. "Laying the Past to Rest," *Indicator SA* 11/4:63-69.

Toit, A. du. 1995. "Learning How to Settle Accounts with the Past: Background to the Truth Commission." Working paper (Archive of the TRC No. 121).

Toit, A. du. 1996a. Interview with André du Toit, Faculty of Political Science, University of Cape Town, November 1996.

Toit, A. du. 1996b. "Philosophical Perspectives on the Truth Commission: Some Preliminary Notes and Fragments." Paper presented to the annual congress of the Philosophical Society of Southern Africa, Stellenbosch, January 1996. Appeared in *Comment* 20:2-14.

Toit, C. W. du. 1998. *Confession and Reconciliation: A Challenge to the Churches in South Africa*. Pretoria.

Toit, F. du. 1998. "A Theological Appreciation of the South African Truth and Reconciliation Commission." Unpublished paper, 1998.

Toit, F. du. 1999. Interview with Fani du Toit, Cape Town, February 27, 1999.

Törne, L. von. 1996. Die politische Aufarbeitung von DDR-Geschichte am Beispiel der Enquete-Kommission des Bundestages 'Aufarbeitung von Geschichte und Folgen der SED-Diktatur in Deutschland' (= Dip.-Arbeit FU Berlin).

Track Two. 1997. *Track Two: Constructive Approaches to Community and Political Conflicts. A Quarterly Publication of the Centre for Conflict Resolution* 6/3-4 (December).

Track, J. 1991. "Sühne und Versöhnung. Zum Umgang mit Schuld und Strafe," EK 1:28-30.

Truth Talk. 1996. *Truth Talk: The Official Newsletter of the TRC* 1/1 (November).

Truth Talk. 1997. *Truth Talk: The Official Newsletter of the TRC* 2/1 (March).

Truth Talk. 1998. *Truth Talk: The Official Newsletter of the TRC* 4/1 (July).

Tutu, D. 1982. *Crying in the Wilderness: The Struggle for Justice in South Africa*. Grand Rapids: Eerdmans.

Tutu, D. 1993. "'Ihr habt der Bestie ins Angesicht gesehen.' Erzbischof Tutu über die Deutschen und den Rassismus," *Mission* 4:16-20.

Tutu, D. 1994. *The Rainbow People of God*. London.

Tutu, D. 1995. "Wer die Vergangenheit vergißt, wiederholt sie," *INDABA* 9:3-7.

Tutu, D. 1996a. Interview with Archbishop Desmond Tutu, Cape Town, November.

Tutu, D. 1996b. Statement by Archbishop Desmond Tutu, Chairperson of the TRC, November 22, 1996 (press release).

Tutu, D. 1997. "Forgiving the Unforgivable: An Interview with Archbishop Desmond Tutu," *Commonweal* (November 12), 13-18.

Tutu, D. 1999. *No Future without Forgiveness*. London.

Tutu, D., and J. Gauck. 1997. "'Gott ist nicht neutral.' Desmond Tutu und Joachim Gauck im Gespräch," *Süddeutsche Zeitung Magazin* (February 7), 16-21.

Ultmann, W. 1998. "Tribunale zur politisch-moralischen Beurteilung von SED Staatskriminalität. Podiumsdiskussion, March 22, 1998." Taped protocol (Selbstverlag FORUM zur Aufklärung und Erneuerung e.V.). Berlin.

Veen, H. J. 1997. "Innere Einheit — aber wo liegt sie? Eine Bestandsaufnahme im siebten Jahr nach der Wiedervereinigung Deutschlands," *Aus Politik und Zeitgeschichte. Beilage zur Wochenzeitung Das Parlament* 40-41:19-28.

Versöhnung und Friede. 1964. "Versöhnung und Friede." Published in Auftrag des deutschen Versöhnungsbundes von H. Gressel und H. Kloppenburg — 50 Jahr Internationaler Versöhnungsbund (August 3, 1964).

Verwoerd, W. 1997. "Justice after Apartheid? Reflections on the South African Truth and Reconciliation Commission." Unpublished paper delivered at the Fifth International Conference on Ethics and Development, Madras, India, January 2-9, 1997.

Verwoerd, W. 1999. Interview with Wilhelm Verwoerd, University of Stellenbosch, March 11, 1999.

Villa-Vicencio, C. 1990. "A Voice from South Africa." Interview published in *Woodstock Report* 23 (October), 3-5.

Villa-Vicencio, C. 1995. "The Truth and Reconciliation Commission: Its Theological Challenge." Manuscript (Archive of the TRC No. 39).

Villa-Vicencio, C. 1996a. "The Burden of Moral Guilt: Its Theological and Political Implications." Manuscript (August 28).

Villa-Vicencio, C. 1996b. "Wunden der Apartheid." Interview by the author with Charles Villa-Vicencio, published *Rheinischer Merkur* 20 (May 16), 25.

Villa-Vicencio, C. 1997a. "Don't Blame Me, I Just Live Here: Political Accountability, Moral Responsibility, and Reconciliation." Manuscript (October).

Villa-Vicencio, C. 1997b. "A Different Kind of Justice: The South African Truth and Reconciliation Commission." Manuscript.

Villa-Vicencio, C. 1998. "From Coexistence to Reconciliation: The TRC; A Step along the Way." Lecture, Yale University, February 8, 1998.

Villa-Vicencio, C. 1999a. Interview with Charles Villa-Vicencio, Cape Town, February 25, 1999.

Villa-Vicencio, C. 1999b. "Restorative Justice: Dealing with the Past Differently." Unpublished paper.

Villa-Vicencio, C. 1999c. "Getting On with Life: A Move towards Reconciliation." Unpublished paper.

Villa-Vicencio, C., et al., eds. 2000. *Looking Back, Reaching Forward: Reflections on the Truth and Reconciliation Commission of South Africa.* Cape Town and London.

Villa-Vicencio, C. No date. "Truth and Reconciliation: In Tension and Reconciliation." Manuscript.

Vogel, H. J., ed. 1994. *Gegen Vergessen — für Demokratie.* Munich.

Volf, J. 1996. *Exclusion and Embrace: A Theological Exploration of Identity, Otherness, and Reconciliation.* Nashville.

Vollnhals, C., ed. 1996. *Die Kirchenpolitik von SED und Staatssicherheit: Eine Zwischenbilanz,* Wissenschaftliche Reihe des BStU. Berlin.

Walz, D., et al. 1997. "Das Sein bestimmt das Bewußtsein. Oder: Warum sich die Ostdeutschen als Bürger 2. Klasse fühlen," *Aus Politik und Zeitgeschichte* 51:13-19.

Wassermann, R. 1992. "Die strafrechtliche Aufarbeitung der DDR Vergangenheit," *Recht und Politik* 28:204ff.

Wassermann, R. 1993. "Zur Aufarbeitung des SED Unrechts," *Aus Politik und Zeitgeschichte. Beilage zur Wochenzeitung Das Parlament* 4:3-12.

Wassermann, R. 1994. "Schlußstrich unter die SED Verbrechen? Zur Debatte um eine Amnestie für SED Funktionärs und DDR Regierungskriminalität," *Neue Juristische Wochenschrift* 41:2666-68.

Weber, H. 1994. "Zur Einschätzung der DDR Forschung. Heutige Rundumschläge und Instrumentalisierungen gehen an den Problemen vorbei," *Deutschland Archiv* 27/2:1186-90.

Weber, O. 1966. "Das dogmatische Problem der Versöhnungslehre," *EvTh* 26:258-72.

Weinke, A. 1997. "Die DDR Justiz im Jahr der 'Wende,'" *Deutschland Archiv* 30/1:41-62.

Weinke, A. 1998. "Der Umgang mit der Stasi und ihren Mitarbeitern," in *Vergangenheitsbewältigung am Ende des zwanzigsten Jahrhunderts,* edited by H. König et al. Leviathan Zeitschrift für Sozialwissenschaften, special issue 18, pp. 176-93.

Weizsäcker, R. von. 1991. *Von Deutschland nach Europa. Die bewegende Kraft der Geschichte.* Berlin.

Weizsäcker, R. von. 1999. *Vier Zeiten. Erinnerungen.* Berlin.

Welker, M. 1981. *Universalität Gottes und Relativität der Welt. Theologische Kosmologie im Dialog mit dem amerikanischen Prozeßdenken nach Whitehead,* NBST 1. Neukirchen.

Welker, M. 1992. "Das Reich Gottes," *EvTh* 52/6:497-512.

Welker, M. 1993. *Gottes Geist. Theologie des Heiligen Geistes.* 2nd edition. Neukirchen.

Welker, M. 1994. "Gewaltverzicht und Feindesliebe," in *Einfach von Gott reden. ein theologischer Diskurs (FS F. Mildenberger).* Stuttgart, Berlin, and Cologne, pp. 243-47.

Welker, M. 1997. "Die evangelische Freiheit," *EvTh* 57/1:68-73.

Welker, M. 1999. "Elend und Auftrag der nach Gottes Wort reformierten Theologie am Anfang des dritten Jahrtausends," *RKZ* 1:27-36.

Werkentin, F. 1998. *Recht und Justiz im SED Staat,* Bundeszentrale für politische Bildung. Bonn.

Werle, G. 1995. *Ohne Wahrheit keine Versöhnung! Der südafrikanische Rechtsstaat und die Apartheidvergangenheit,* Open Lectures of the Humboldt University 60. Berlin.

Werle, G., ed. 1996. *Confronting Past Injustices: Approaches to Amnesty, Punishment, Reparation and Restitution in South Africa and Germany.* Durban.

Werle, G. 1997. "Menschenrechtsschutz durch Völkerstrafrecht," *Zeitschrift für die gesamte Strafrechtswissenschaft* 109/4:808-29.

Werle, G. 1998. "'Wahrheits — und Versöhnungskommission' als Modell — Wird dem Recht Genüge getan?" Unveröffentlichter Vortrag auf der Tagung der Evangelischen Akademie Berlin-Brandenburg "Auf dem Weg zur Regenbogennation. Südafrika und die Wahrheits-und Versöhnungskommission" vom November 13-15, 1998, Berlin.

Weschler, L. 1993. "Getting Over," *The New Yorker* (April 5).

Wesel, U. 1994. *Der Honecker-Prozeß. Ein Staat vor Gericht.* Frankfurt am Main, 1994.

Wheeler, D. L. 1990. *A Relational View of the Atonement: Prolegomenon to a Reconstruction of the Doctrine,* Series VII, Theology and Religion 54. New York, Bern, and Frankfurt am Main: Peter Lang.

Widmaier, G. 1991. "Verfassungswidrige Strafverfolgung der DDR Spionage: Verstoß gegen das Rückwirkungsverbot des Art. 103 II GG," *Neue Juristische Wochenschrift* 39:2460-66.

Wiesenthal, H. 1996. "Die neuen Bundesländer als Sonderfall der Transformation in den Ländern Ostmitteleuropas," *Aus Politik und Zeitgeschichte. Beilage zur Wochenzeitung Das Parlament* 49:46-54.

Wiesnet, E. 1990. *Die verratene Versöhnung. Zum Verhältnis von Christentum und Strafe.* Düsseldorf, 1990.

Wildenmann, R. 1991. *Nation und Demokratie. Politisch strukturelle Gestaltungsprobleme im neuen Deutschland.* Baden-Baden.

Wildschut, G. 1999. Interview with Glenda Wildschut. Cape Town, February 16.

Wilke, M. 1997. "Die deutsche Einheit und die Geschichtspolitik des Bundestages," *Deutschland Archiv* 30/3:607-13.

Wilson, J. 1963. *Thinking with Concepts.* Cambridge.

Wirsching, J. 1963. *Gott in der Geschichte. Studien zur theologiegeschichtlichen Stellung und systematischen Grundlegung der Theologie Martin Kählers,* FGLP 26. Munich.

Wirsching, J. 1988. "Zum dogmatischen Ort der Christologie," in *Glaube im Widerstreit. Ausgewählte Aufsätze und Vorträge,* Kontexte 4. Frankfurt am Main et al., pp. 27-71.

Wirsching, J. 1993. "Gottes Heilstat und menschliche Freiheit. Grundmotive in der Inkarnationslehre Anselms von Canterbury," in *Glaube im Widerstreit. Ausgewählte Aufsätze und Vorträge II,* Kontexte 12. Frankfurt am Main et al., pp. 75-84.

Winkler, H. A., et al. 1993. *Nationalismus-Nationalitäten-Supranationalität,* Industrielle Welt 53. Stuttgart.

Winters, P. 1997. "Das Urteil gegen Krenz und andere," *Deutschland Archiv* 30/ 5:693-969.

Wolfrum, E. 1996. "Internationale Forschungen zum 19th und 20th Jahrhundert," *Neue Politische Literatur* 41:376-96.

Wolle, S. 1999. *Die heile Welt der Diktatur. Alltag und Herrschaft in der DDR 1971-1989,* Bundeszentrale für politische Bildung, Schriftenreihe 349. Bonn.

Wollmann, H. 1998. "Der Systemwechsel in Ostdeutschland, Ungarn, Polen, und Rußland. Phasen und Varianten der politisch-administrativen Dezentralisierung," *Auf Politik und Zeitgeschichte. Beilage zur Wochenzeitung "Das Parlament"* 5 (January 23), 3-17.

Wong, T. 1996. *The Truth and Reconciliation Commission — A Brief Analysis.* Legal Resources Centre. Durban.

Wüstenberg, R. K. 1997. "Wir müssen Wunden öffnen, damit sie sich wieder schließen können" (D. Tutu), in *Südafrika 1997,* ed. Berliner Missionswerk, pp. 5-7.

Wüstenberg, R. K., ed. 1998a. *Wahrheit, Recht und Versöhnung. Auseinandersetzung mit der Vergangenheit nach den politischen Umbrüchen in Südafrika und Deutschland,* Kontexte 24. Frankfurt am Main et al.

Wüstenberg, R. K. 1998b. "Befreiende Wirkung," *Rheinischer Merkur* 39 (September 25), 29.

Wüstenberg, R. K. 1998c. *A Theology of Life: Dietrich Bonhoeffer's Religionless Christianity.* Grand Rapids: Eerdmans. [German edition, 1996.]

Wüstenberg, R. K. 1999. "'Wir müssen teilen.' Wie die Kirche sich für gesellschaftliche Aussöhnung einsetzt," *Rheinischer Merkur* 21 (May 21), 31.

Zapf, W. 1994. *Modernisierung, Wohlfahrtsentwicklung und Transformation. Soziologische Aufsätze 1987-1994.* Berlin.

Zehner, J. 1998. *Das Forum der Vergebung in der Kirche. Studien zum Verhältnis von Sündenvergebung und Recht,* Öffentliche Theologie 19. Gütersloh.

Zerfaß, R., ed. 1988. *Erzählender Glaube — erzählende Kirche,* QD 116. Freiburg, Basel, and Wien.

Zimmermann, B. 1994. "Wiedergutmachung zwischen materieller Gerechtigkeit und politischen Kompromiß. Das Entschädigungs- und Ausgleichsleistungsgesetz," *DtZ* 11:359-62.

Zimmermann, H. 1995. *Die Auslegung und Anwendung des Art. 34 GG im Falle legislativen Unrechts unter Berücksichtigung des gemeinschaftsrechtlichen Staatshaftungsanspruchs und einschlägiger Regelungen der Europäischen Menschenrechtskonvention* (Diss. Jur.). Münster.

Zimmermann-Wolf, D. 1991. *Einander beistehen. Dietrich Bonhoeffers lebensbezogene Theologie für gegenwärtige Klinikseelsorge,* STPS 6. Würzburg.

Zweite Europäische Ökumenische Versammlung. Konferenz Europäischer

Kirchen, Rat der Europäischen Bischofskonferenzen: Versöhnung; Gabe Gottes und Quelle neuen Lebens. Eine Arbeitshilfe für die Vorbereitung der Zweiten Europäischen Ökumenischen Versammlung 1997. Geneva and St. Gallen, 1995.

Zyl, S. van. 1992. *The Quest for Democracy: South Africa in Transition.* London.

List of Persons Interviewed in the German Case Studies

Barbe, Angelika. Member of the EK. Interview of March 27, 2000.

Birthler, Marianne. Former Minister of Education in Brandenburg, now BStU. Interview of December 8, 1999.

Dorfstecher, Ilse-Maria. Founding member of an investigative commission on police excesses in East Berlin in October 1989. Interview of October 15, 1999.

Eppelmann, Rainer. MdB; Chairman of the EK. Interview of December 9, 1999.

Gauck, Joachim. Former BStU. Interview of July 19, 2000.

Hilsberg, Stephan. MdB; member of the EK. Interview of March 16, 2000.

Keller, Dietmar. Member of the EK. Interview of December 16, 1999.

Lowalczuk, Ilko-Sascha. Researcher for the EK. Interview of January 11, 2000.

Maizière, Lothar de. Last cabinet president of the DDR. Interview of September 25, 1999.

Maser, Peter. Researcher for the EK. Interview of September 6, 1999.

Meckel, Markus. MdB; member of the EK. Interview of April 5, 2000.

Passauer, Martin-Michael. Member of the EK. Interview of October 11, 1999.

Poppe, Ulrike. Civil judge; former advisor of the BStU. Interview of April 6, 2000.

Schaefgen, Christoph. Former General Counsel of Berlin. Interview of April 5, 2000.

Schorlemmer, Friedrich. Civil judge; co-initiator of the idea of the tribunal in dealing with SED injustice. Interview of September 19, 1999.